RULES OF EVIDENCE IN INTERNATIONAL ARBITRATION

LLOYD'S ARBITRATION LAW LIBRARY
Series editor: Renato Nazzini

LLOYD'S ARBITRATION LAW LIBRARY

RULES OF EVIDENCE IN INTERNATIONAL ARBITRATION

AN ANNOTATED GUIDE

NATHAN D. O'MALLEY

SECOND EDITION

informa law
from Routledge

First published 2019
by Informa Law from Routledge
2 Park Square, Milton Park, Abingdon, Oxon OX14 4RN

and by Informa Law from Routledge
52 Vanderbilt Avenue, New York, NY 10017

Informa Law from Routledge is an imprint of the Taylor & Francis Group, an informa business

First edition published 2012 by Informa Law

British Library Cataloguing-in-Publication Data
A catalogue record for this book is available from the British Library

Library of Congress Cataloging-in-Publication Data
Names: O'Malley, Nathan D., author.
Title: Rules of evidence in international arbitration : an annotated guide /
    by Nathan D. O'Malley.
Description: Second edition. | Abingdon, Oxon [UK] ; New York, NY :
    Routledge, 2019. | Series: Lloyd's arbitration law library
Identifiers: LCCN 2018036005| ISBN 9781138674738 (hbk) |
    ISBN 9781315561127 (ebk)
Subjects: LCSH: Conflict of laws—Arbitration and award. | International
    commercial arbitration. | Evidence (Law)
Classification: LCC K2400 .O46 2019 | DDC 347/.09—dc23
LC record available at https://lccn.loc.gov/2018036005

ISBN: 978-1-138-67473-8 (hbk)
ISBN: 978-1-315-56112-7 (ebk)

Typeset in Times New Roman
by Apex CoVantage, LLC
Printed and bound by CPI Group (UK) Ltd, Croydon CR0 4YY

BRIEF CONTENTS

CONTENTS

ABOUT THE AUTHOR

Nathan D. O'Malley has practiced in the field of international arbitration as counsel and arbitrator for over eighteen years, during which time he has acted in disputes seated in Europe, the Middle East, Asia and in Central America. After practicing in Europe for more than a decade, he is presently based in Los Angeles, California where he is a partner with the law firm of Musick, Peeler & Garrett LLP. In addition to counsel and arbitrator work, Nathan serves as an adjunct professor at the University of Southern California - Gould School of Law where he teaches courses on international arbitration.

FOREWORD

TO THE FIRST EDITION
BY HIS HONOUR HUMPHREY LLOYD, QC

I am delighted to have been invited to write a foreword to this work. A proper discussion of evidence in international arbitration is long overdue.

Evidence is sometimes relegated to being a matter only of procedure, as if it were less important than substantive law. It is of course of vital importance since in the majority of cases the facts have first to be established. Indeed, the advent of tiered dispute resolution and the popularity of other means of minimising the possibility of having to resort to arbitration suggests that many more of the arbitrations that take place are about intractable matters, such as fundamental conflicts about the facts. So a study of the rules of evidence is highly topical.

Nathan O'Malley brings to the subject the advantages of being a long-established practitioner in international arbitration, honed by experience in a niche practice which gives him an additional edge. He evidently has great enthusiasm and ferreted into recherché corners. Many instructive awards have been found, some in the form of extracts quoted in decisions of national courts which could have been overlooked. Further insight is provided from numerous commentaries and articles. The results have then been carefully considered and lucidly presented. This work is not only well researched but thoughtful, stimulating and, obviously, provocative.

Evidence used to be (and of course still is) about what the arbitral tribunal needs to know to make its decision but which it does not already know (or which it should have confirmed to it). Arbitrators were often people with either knowledge of the type of subject-matter or lawyers with sufficient experience of the sector concerned. Others who did not have much knowledge of the law needed guidance about evidence and to know when to inform the parties of their own experience—one of the points covered by Mr O'Malley in Chapter 6. Nowadays, as the author observes, arbitrators are mainly jurists. Most are generalists, some with limited knowledge of international arbitration. So they need guidance of a different kind, such as being made aware of differences between national court or arbitral practice and international arbitration practice. This might be exemplified by the use of the tiresome phrase "the strict rules of evidence"—as if some rules are stricter than others, whereas they are all rules. The phrase contrasts practice in courts with practice in arbitration where historically the tribunal because of its knowledge, greater procedural flexibility and less accountability was entitled not to operate as if it were a court.

Mr O'Malley in writing for today's arbitration practitioners and arbitrators has wisely structured the work around the 2010 edition of the International Bar Association's Rules on the Taking of Evidence in International Arbitration. Institutional rules do not normally go into evidence in any detail. The IBA Rules being, in essence, a synthesis of existing practice (or what should be good practice) are an ideal basis for a discussion of the subject. The work is not only a highly informed commentary on the IBA Rules but also thereby in the nature of a general treatise. That can be seen both in the introductory first chapter (which poses and answers the question: are there rules of evidence in international arbitration?) and in the second chapter which tackles three topics that are not covered by the IBA Rules—depositions, interrogatories and "judicial notice". Here the latter is about facts that are well known generally (although one might question one old decision which so classified rates of interest). The former two being, in the main, United States practices, lead to a useful discussion as to how their objectives may be achieved by means of techniques that are part of the repertory of techniques that are established in international arbitration.

Since most cases are decided on the basis of the documents, Chapter 3 is rightly the most substantial. Through an examination of article 3 of the IBA Rules it covers all the key aspects of document production. Normally a party that cannot establish its case from its documents should consider if it has a case worth pursuing. The avenues open to such a party are however examined in detail. For example, the discussion of the seemingly pleonastic wording "relevant to the case and material to its outcome" is especially illuminating, as is the treatment of the potential objections in article 9.2.

If the documents do not establish all the facts then witnesses will be required. They are the subject of Chapter 4. It too has many pertinent observations, e.g. the extent to which a witness's evidence might need corroboration by documents—which might bring us back to square one. However, this ought not to lead to the vice of a witness statement repeating the contents of a document. The advantages of cross-examination or questioning as the means of testing if the contents of a witness statement are really the witness's own evidence, and are reliable, are properly explored. The arbitrator who through inexperience or pusillanimity is inclined to characterise an issue as a matter of law rather than one of fact should read this chapter and the later chapters dealing with assessment of evidence. Events are always recalled differently and at times arbitrators have to be able to decide what happened without the aid of documents.

Chapters 5 and 6 deal with experts, party-appointed and appointed by the tribunal, respectively. These chapters are of considerable practical importance. First, the costs of experts can be disproportionate to their effect on the outcome, so the tribunal and the parties here get instruction on how to control the work of experts. Second, certain arbitrators, through inertia or ignorance, do not grapple with differences between apparently conflicting opinions. Some effectively delegate their functions to an expert, although they have been enjoined to ascertain the facts themselves. They will all benefit from studying these chapters, particularly to see the procedures available whereby points of potential conflict can be identified at an early stage and, if not neutralised by agreement, can be presented for a decision in an intelligible and manageable way.

Chapters 7, 8 and 9 move to the reception and treatment of evidence—how it is assessed, the standards of proof (Chapter 7), the ins and outs of the evidentiary hearing itself (Chapter 8) and other aspects of procedure such as dealing with objections on grounds of confidentiality or certain types of privilege and otherwise (Chapter 9). These chapters are full of useful material. The discussion of burden of proof (Onus Probandi Actori Incumbit) should be particularly valuable to some practitioners who can be much exercised by it (when in most cases all that is required is skilful advocacy).

It is common to say that a book should be "on the shelves of every practitioner in arbitration". That may be too much to hope for, but I warmly commend it as an excellent vade mecum for anybody involved in international arbitration, whether as arbitrator, lawyer or client.

HUMPHREY LLOYD

PREFACE

The first edition of this work was written with the intent of providing guidance on the taking of evidence in international arbitration. Like any commentary on the law, however, the moment of publication also signalled the start of the revision process. The law moves on and so too must that which is written about it. With this second edition, the commentary and notes have been updated to take into account a number of developments in the field of international arbitration.

One important change has come in the form of the publication of ethical guidelines for international arbitration counsel in the Guidelines on Party Representation in International Arbitration by the International Bar Association in 2013. The Guidelines speak to a variety of issues including the taking of evidence and thus the commentary has been updated to take them into account.

When preparing the first edition, locating arbitral rulings on evidentiary issues was a persistent challenge. While decisions in the field of international investor-state arbitration are quite frequently made available, it was far more difficult to obtain commercial arbitration precedents on the issue of evidence. This was unsatisfactory because even though investor-state cases may often grab headlines, commercial disputes constitute the greater share of the international arbitration caseload. Happily, with the passing of time, commercial precedents have become more available. This edition reflects this development with the inclusion of a greater number of commercial arbitration cases from institutions like the LCIA, ICC, SIAC and ICDR.

It is also worth noting that at the time of release of this second edition, a new effort at defining the applicable rules of evidence has come about in the form of the publication of the Rules on the Efficient Conduct of Proceedings in International Arbitration, or as they are commonly known, the "Prague Rules". The approach utilized by the Prague Rules is decidedly that of the *civil law* tradition, or more specifically, evidentiary procedure as practiced in Eastern European and CIS jurisdictions. Although initially proposed as a set of procedures and evidentiary rules for parties from those countries, at the time of their launch in December 2018 the Prague Rules are being suggested a means to complement or substitute the widely accepted IBA Rules on the Taking of Evidence in International Arbitration (2010). As with any effort to innovate, time will tell whether this initiative will be worthy of commentary. If the effort is successful in being adopted either in the region for which it was proposed or globally, I anticipate that the third edition of this work will provide due consideration of the Prague Rules.

Like the first, this second edition came into fruition with the assistance of many different individuals. In that regard I would like to recognize the contributions of Marcio

Vasconcellos, who spent considerable time researching precedent and assisting with the editorial process. His assistance in preparing this volume, as well as that of others, is greatly appreciated. In addition to material support, endeavors of this kind would not be possible without the emotional support of family. For this too I am grateful, and would like to acknowledge the patience and support of my wife Tamela and our children, Hannah, Greta, and Bram.

TABLE OF CASES AND ARBITRATIONS

TABLE OF LEGISLATION, CONVENTIONS AND RULES

(all references are to paragraph number)

ABBREVIATIONS AND ACRONYMNS

AAA	American Arbitration Association
ALI/UNIDROIT Principles	ALI/UNIDROIT Principles of Transnational Civil Procedure (2004)
Arbitration Act 1996	Arbitration Act 1996 (England and Wales)
CAS	Court of Arbitration for Sport
CEPANI	Belgian Centre for Arbitration and Mediation
CIETAC	China International Economic and Trade Arbitration Commission
CLOUT	Case Law on UNCITRAL Texts (UN Docs A/CN.9/ SER.C/ ABSTRACTS/1- (1993–))
CRCICA	Cairo Regional Centre for International Commercial Arbitration
DIAC	Dubai International Arbitration Centre
ECJ	European Court of Justice
European Arbitration Convention	European Convention on International Commercial Arbitration (1961)
EWCA	Court of Appeal, England and Wales [neutral official citation]
EWHC	High Court, England and Wales [neutral official citation]
FIDIC	Fédération Internationale des Ingénieurs-Conseils
US-Mexico General Claims Commission	The General Claims Commission (Mexico and United States) constituted under the terms of the General Claims Convention, signed 8 September 1923, between the United States of America and the United Mexican States.
HKIAC	Hong Kong International Arbitration Centre
Hoge Raad	Hoge Raad der Nederlanden (Supreme Court of the Netherlands)
IBA	International Bar Association
IBA Rules or Rules	The IBA Rules on the Taking of Evidence in International Arbitration (2010)
ICC	International Chamber of Commerce, International Court of Arbitration
ICC Bulletin	The ICC International Court of Arbitration Bulletin
ICC Rules	ICC Arbitration Rules (2012)
ICDR	International Centre for Dispute Resolution
ICJ	(UN) International Court of Justice

ICSID	International Centre for the Settlement of Investment Disputes
ICSID Convention	Convention on the Settlement of Investment Disputes between States and Nationals of other States (1965)
Iran-US Claims Tribunal	Iran-United States Claims Tribunal
JAA	Japanese Arbitration Association
LCIA	London Court of International Arbitration
LCIA Rules	LCIA Arbitration Rules (1998)
LMAA	London Maritime Arbitrators Association
NAFTA	North American Free Trade Agreement
NAI	Netherlands Arbitration Institute
New York Convention	Convention on the Recognition and Enforcement of Foreign Arbitral Awards (1958)
PCA	Permanent Court of Arbitration
PCIJ	Permanent Court of International Justice
RIAA	(UN) Reports of International Arbitral Awards
SCC	Arbitration Institute of the Stockholm Chamber of Commerce
SDNY	Southern District Court of New York
SIAC	Singapore International Arbitration Centre
Society of Maritime Arbitrators	Society of Maritime Arbitrators Inc
Swiss Federal Tribunal	Swiss Federal Supreme Court
Swiss Rules	Swiss Rules of International Arbitration (2004)
UNCITRAL	United Nations Commission on International Trade Law
UNCITRAL Model Law or Model Law	UNCITRAL Model Law on International Commercial Arbitration (2006)
UNCITRAL Rules	UNCITRAL Arbitration Rules (2010)
UNCLOS	United Nations Convention on the Law of the Sea (1982)
UNIDROIT	International Institute for the Unifi cation of Private Law
US Dist. Ct.	United States District Court (generally)

Notes to the reader. (1) Throughout this text various arbitral tribunals are described using an adjective drawn from one of the abbreviations set forth above, for example, an "ICC tribunal" or "LCIA tribunal". This should be understood as reference to the fact that the arbitral tribunal was constituted under that institution's arbitration rules, or a corresponding set of arbitration rules (e.g., an "UNCITRAL tribunal"). (2) A reference below to an "article" or, as per the footnotes, an "art.", should be understood as a reference to an article of the IBA Rules, unless otherwise designated.

CHAPTER 1

The rules of evidence and their application

1.01 The phrase "rules of evidence" poses two conceptual challenges when applied to international arbitration. The first is one of perception. Some who have a passive knowledge of international arbitration may believe that it is, for all intents and purpose, a process free of rules. In this sense, arbitration has been variously called "litigation lite", "binding mediation" and other names, some which are arguably accurate and others that are clearly not. Nonetheless, these terms are intended to convey the concept that it is a process that has few, if any, procedural rules. If arbitration is, therefore, the antithesis of rules-based dispute resolution, how then can one speak of "rules of evidence" in international arbitration?

1.02 The second challenge is one of definition. What are the rules of evidence in international arbitration? An astute observer of the various institutional and *ad hoc* arbitration rules will note that in most instances only cursory guidance is given on how evidence is to be taken and admitted. Those articles which do speak to evidence affirm the wide discretion arbitrators have to decide these matters without setting forth detailed rules.[1] As the experienced arbitration professional knows, however, the paucity of direct references to binding rules of evidence does not mean that international arbitration is free of disputes over evidentiary procedure. Quite the opposite, where procedural disputes do arise it is often over questions of proof. Be that as it may, the question still remains that if there are so few written rules of evidence, how can one refer to, or much less write a book about, the "rules of evidence" in international arbitration?

1.03 The above two questions may be answered sufficiently, as will be further explained below, by establishing that arbitration does lend itself to rules of evidentiary procedure, and that such rules are more than merely the *ad hoc* solutions adopted at the whim of various arbitrators. In fact, what becomes evident from a study of this issue is that many of the principles invoked today are rooted in the jurisprudence of international tribunals stretching back for more than a hundred years.[2] In modern practice, these principles are utilised by arbitrators with a wide variety of legal backgrounds, with the somewhat surprising yet satisfying result that they are applied with general consistency.

---

1 The new provisions of the UNCITRAL Arbitration Rules (2010) provide some innovations in the form of clarifying language (see art. 17 and further). However, even these provisions provide only cursory guidance on experts and general references to document production. The discretion granted to arbitrators on matters of evidence often found in arbitration rules is summarised by the position adopted by the 2012 ICC Rules of Arbitration, art. 25(1): "The arbitral tribunal shall proceed within as short a time as possible to establish the facts of the case by all appropriate means."

2 See, for example, the often referenced study of evidence before international tribunals authored by Durward Sandifer, in which reference is made to a number of tribunals from the early part of the last century, as well as nineteenth-century jurisprudence, in support of a number of rules which are today commonly accepted principles of evidentiary procedure. Durward V. Sandifer, *Evidence Before International Tribunals* (1975), Procedural Aspects of International Law Series, Vol. 13.

1.04 It is the intention of this book to catalogue the rules of evidence in international arbitration and to examine their common application. Thus, one will notice that this text draws heavily from the published and unpublished case law of international tribunals as its primary source material. As a result, the commentary herein is intended to account for the views of the many experienced tribunals who have considered and interpreted these rules in their respective decisions.

1.05 The chapters following this initial introduction are organised around common statements of the rules of evidence as found in various sources. The 2010 IBA Rules on the Taking of Evidence in International Arbitration (2010) is the greatest source of such rules, and thus this book contains a wide consideration of that body of rules save for articles 1 and 2, which are discussed only as they relate to the more substantive portions of the IBA Rules found in articles 3–9. Another source is the UNCITRAL Arbitration Rules (2010) and to some extent also the UNCITRAL Model Law (2006) where appropriate, with further reference made in some instances to the ALI/UNIDROIT Principles of Transnational Civil Procedure and institutional rules.

Are there rules of evidence in international arbitration?

1.06 In recent times, it has become widely known that claims worth hundreds of millions and billions of euros and US dollars are decided by international arbitrators on a regular basis. This fact alone should put paid to the notion that the practice of international arbitration is devoid of any rules of evidence. Who would reasonably subject a claim of such magnitude to a process that does not have any rules concerning proof?

1.07 Beyond the circumstantial evidence for the existence of the rules of evidence, there is direct proof of their presence. Beginning with the jurisprudence of international tribunals, such as mixed claims commissions and early state-to-state tribunals, in the late nineteenth and early twentieth centuries, one finds regular references to principles and rules of evidentiary procedure.[3] The rules are in some cases referred to as "normal" or "fundamental" rules of procedure by various tribunals, indicating their inherent applicability irrespective of their absence in a constitutive document setting forth the tribunal's mandate.[4] Many of these tribunals operated, like arbitrators today, under skeletal procedural outlines which made little to no reference to rules of evidentiary procedure. Yet these arbitrators determined to draw inferences, assigned the burden of proof and conducted hearings in accordance with rules of procedure with the confidence that the principles being applied were both correct and should have been anticipated by the parties.

1.08 From where did their confidence come? In this respect Bin Cheng notes that in some instances it was common sense.[5] Indeed, arbitrators must preside over a procedure

---

3   In addition to Sandifer, another work which has reviewed extensively the jurisprudence relating to evidentiary procedure of these early tribunals is Bin Cheng's *General Principles of Law as Applied by International Courts and Tribunals* (reprint 1987).

4   While denying the applicability of domestic rules of evidence in international arbitration, tribunals often affirm an arbitrator's authority, as a matter of international procedural practice, to draw a negative inference from a party's failure to produce evidence within its control. See also: the reference by the Umpire of the Britain-Venezuela Mixed Claims Commission, to the "ordinary rules of evidence" in noting the duty of a party to provide evidence in support of their burden of proof. *Aroa Mines Case*, Great Britain-Venezuela Mixed Claims Commission, 9 RIAA, p. 442 (1903).

5   Bin Cheng quotes from a decision of the British-Mexican Claims Commission, wherein it was noted in relation to principles governing the assessment of evidence, "International tribunals 'can assuredly also apply

that will allow them to fulfil their mandate successfully. An example of "common sense" comes from the Italy-Venezuela Claims Commission of 1903. Here the tribunal was constituted under procedural rules that required the arbitrators to receive "all" evidence that was submitted.[6] Applying its mandate, the umpire of the tribunal noted in reaction to a question over evidence submitted belatedly, that the tribunal had no ability to impose any restriction on the parties as to when they would submit their evidence, because of its duty to receive "all" evidence. Nevertheless, recognising that time limits of some nature were warranted as a means of maintaining order, the tribunal found that it had the ability to set limits on the time frame for submitting claims which permitted it to close the record to new evidence. Common sense prevailed here as the umpire found that "all things must come to an end".

1.09 Further, early tribunals often recognised that common sense was in effect tantamount to applying many of the basic notions of procedure found in domestic law. Consider, for instance, the following observations of the Mexico-US General Claims Commission: "With respect to matters of evidence they [arbitral tribunals] must give effect to common sense principles underlying rules of evidence in domestic law."[7] Bin Cheng further identifies that the rules of evidence often recognised in arbitration are a "large number of general principles of law recognised by States *in foro domestic*".[8] However, that a tribunal would apply procedural principles found in domestic law should not be understood as an acceptance of the applicability of domestic court practices to international arbitration. Common sense in this context meant an acceptance of general principles of evidentiary procedure underlying domestic practice, which often were modified for particular application to international arbitration.[9]

---

common sense reasoning with respect to the value of what might be called purely documentary evidence'." Bin Cheng, *supra* n. 3. Bin Cheng cautions against attempting to define common sense precisely, but notes further that such appeals to common sense may be applied to evidentiary rules concerning documentary as well as testimonial evidence.

6   "The commissioners shall be bound before reaching a decision, to receive and carefully examine all evidence presented to them by the Government of Venezuela and the Royal Italian Legation at Caracas, as well as oral or written arguments submitted by the agent of the Government or of the Legation." *Protocol of 7 May 1903*, Mixed Claims Commission (Italy-Venezuela), 10 RIAA, p. 482. As a later decision of the umpire to the tribunal confirmed, the duty to receive "all" evidence was correctly understood as not permitting the application of rules of exclusion. *Opinions and Questions of Procedure*, p. 488.

7   *Lillie S. Kling v United Mexican States*, US-Mexico Claims Commission, 4 RIAA, p. 582 (1930).

8   Bin Cheng, *supra* n. 3, p. 303.

9   See: the following comments of a member of the British-Mexico Claims Commission relying upon the *Parker* precedent to find against the application of municipal rules of evidence in the *Cameron* case. "In the course of the argument I drew the attention of the Agents of the British and Mexican Governments to the case of *William A. Parker*, which is reported in the American official reports of the American-Mexican General Claims Commission, 1927 Volume, pages 35 to 40 . . . The substance of the judgment is that an international commission cannot be governed by rules of evidence borrowed from municipal procedure. This view is fully established by the conclusive reasons set out therein. In my judgment the reasons which are there advanced ought to be adopted without qualification both by this and every other international commission. In expressing this opinion, I am not overlooking the fact that the decision of one international tribunal is not binding upon another. It is no less true, however, that the general principles relating to evidence and procedure which should guide them should be the same." *Virgnie Lessard Camerion v United Mexican States* (separate opinion of Artemus Jones) Great Britain-Mexico Claims Commission, 5 RIAA, p. 33. See further: the following considerations of Sandifer who notes the following concerning the reliance by arbitrators upon the developed jurisprudence of early tribunals to decide matters of evidentiary procedure:

> In practice, tribunals will be found turning to rules customarily applied and to general principles of law, subject always to the limitations imposed by the arbitral agreements. This is especially true when it comes to the matter of weighing and evaluating the evidence . . . The consequent tendency of each tribunal to adopt

1.10 Moving forward to present arbitral practice, in international commercial arbitration, investor-state arbitration and state-to-state arbitration, there is continued proof in the case law of these tribunals of the existence of rules of evidentiary procedure.[10] Further, academic writings and compilations of views of leading arbitrators show that there is an identifiable consensus on what the rules of evidence are and, moreover, how they should be generally applied. These sources of jurisprudence and commentary provide sufficient proof of the continued existence of rules of evidence in international arbitration.

What are the rules of evidence in international arbitration?

1.11 As noted above, the leading institutional and *ad hoc* arbitration rules often give little more than cursory guidance concerning evidentiary procedure. That being said, there exists in international arbitration evidentiary rules that are commonly understood and applied despite the paucity of direct references to them in institutional and *ad hoc* arbitration rules.

1.12 Starting with the fundamentals, it may be said that the very basic rules of evidence are those principles providing the definition of due process generally in international arbitration, which include a party's right to equal treatment and an opportunity to be heard. These principles are applied to most cases by virtue of the *lex arbitri*,[11] and have been recognised by various *ad hoc* annulment committees in the ICSID system as fundamental principles of international procedure generally.[12] They also feature in the law governing the enforcement of awards such as the UN Convention on the Recognition and Enforcement of Foreign Arbitral Awards of 1958.[13] These rules have a direct connection to the administration of evidence. It is axiomatic that a party who is not afforded a fair opportunity to present its evidence will not have been afforded due process.

1.13 The application of due process principles to evidentiary procedure presents several challenges. First, the principles of the right to be heard and to equal treatment have to be applied in the context of various evidentiary issues. As an example, fairness must be observed in organising an evidentiary hearing, appointing a tribunal expert or ruling on

---

essential points and rules similar to those used by preceding tribunals has resulted in the development of what virtually amounts to customary rules of law.

Sandifer, *supra* n. 2, p. 44.

10 The manner in which rules of evidence will be applied in a given arbitration, may be affected by the nature of the arbitration and the subject-matter of the dispute. However, it has been recognised that the case law of international tribunals, including state-to-state, investor-state and commercial arbitral tribunals, still establish that there are basic rules of evidentiary procedure which have become widely accepted. Consider, for instance, Pietrowski's conclusion that even though there is divergence in practice at various levels, identifiable rules which are applicable generally may be found: "Nevertheless, there are a number of principles and rules of evidence that are generally applicable to all international arbitrations irrespective of the nature of the parties and the law governing the conduct of the arbitration." Robert Pietrowski, "Evidence in International Arbitration", *Arbitration International*, Vol. 22, No. 3, p. 373 (2006). The rules of evidence, as is explained below with specific reference to the IBA Rules, allow the tribunal wide discretion to conduct the proceedings, and therefore do not impinge upon the flexibility which a tribunal has to organise the procedure appropriately.

11 See UNCITRAL Model Law, art. 18.

12 See, for instance, *Fraport AG Frankfurt Airport Services Worldwide v The Philippines*, ICSID Case No. ARB/03/25, Decision on the Application for Annulment, para. 133 (2010).

13 As an example see: UN Convention on the Recognition and Enforcement of Foreign Arbitral Awards of 1958, art. V(1)(b): "the party against whom the award is invoked was not given proper notice of the appointment of the arbitrator or of the arbitration proceedings or was otherwise unable to present his case". Reference may also be had to art. V(2)(b).

the admissibility of evidence. Second, when considering equality and fairness, a tribunal must also balance the consideration of other legal principles, such as, for example, the observance of attorney-client privilege. A third challenge to the application of fairness and equality to evidentiary procedure is to find modes of application accepted beyond the boundaries of one legal system. Clearly, as international arbitration calls upon the service of arbitrators and counsel from a wide variety of legal systems, and involves parties of similarly wide backgrounds, what is considered a "fair opportunity" to present evidence must appeal to those of multiple jurisdictions.[14]

1.14 It follows from the above text the core rules of evidentiary procedure, fairness and equality, require more particular standards. It is, in the interests of the participants to be afforded some idea of what constitutes procedural fairness.[15] It further follows that the codification of such standards will contain both principles that are cast as recommendations and those that are immutable due process norms. For example, in any set of rules regarding document production, one may find a recommendation that the tribunal set a time for hearing such applications, but, at the same time, an inherent rule that the tribunal afford both parties the same opportunity to make them.

1.15 Beginning in 1983, at the initiative of the International Bar Association, an attempt was made at refining those principles into a body of rules which may be thought of as restatements of the law of evidentiary procedure in international arbitration. After another revision in 1999, the IBA Rules of Evidence were revised again in 2010.[16] Through this process the Rules have become widely accepted as an authoritative body of standards restating the accepted rules of evidence for international arbitration. As noted by one ICSID tribunal:

> The IBA Rules are used widely by international arbitral tribunals as a guide even when not binding upon them. Precedents and informal documents, such as the IBA Rules, reflect the experience of recognized professionals in the field and draw their strength from the intrinsic merit and persuasive value rather than from their binding character.[17]

1.16 Thus, international arbitral tribunals today may look to such principles for guidance as to what is considered a fair and equitable manner of administering evidentiary procedure. These and principles like them are the generally recognised "rules of evidence", but seen in the context of due process, they are simply guidelines for what is considered to be fair.

---

14 This principle was followed in the development of the IBA Rules. Speaking of the background to the 1983 version of the IBA Rules of Evidence, it was noted that the rules were the best compromise that could be struck on the competing approaches to evidentiary procedure represented by the civil and common law traditions. "They provide the best compromise, after extensive discussion, that could be arrived at between two incompatible systems. It is thought that they will be found to be fair and acceptable, when a compromise has to be made, to practitioners of both systems." D.W. Shenton, "An introduction to the IBA Rules of Evidence", *Arbitration International*, Vol. 1, No. 2, p. 123 (1985).

15 Park notes, regarding the desire for predictability, that, "The descriptive and normative perspectives of international lawyers are marked by more relativity of tone than the discourse of many Critical Theorists. Assuming that some adjudicatory processes are more neutral and reliable than others, international business lawyers seek to emphasize the neutrality and predictability of one decision-making mechanism over another." William W. Park, "Neutrality, Predictability and Economic Co-operation", *Journal of International Arbitration*, Vol. 12, No. 4, p. 102 (1995).

16 Adopted on 29 May 2010.

17 *Railroad Development Corp (United States of America) v Republic of Guatemala*, ICSID, Case No. ARB/07/23 (October 2008), Decision on Provisional Measures, para. 15.

Application of the rules of one jurisdiction to evidentiary procedure

1.17 The historical view held by some was that evidentiary procedure should be borrowed from the jurisdiction in which an arbitration is seated.[18] This view posits that the tribunal may rely upon the practices of the courts in one jurisdiction or the other to dispose of questions on the taking of evidence. While it is evident that this opinion has attracted some support in the past, it has been since largely abandoned.

1.18 It has been established at virtually all levels of arbitration that the local rules of evidentiary procedure at the seat of the arbitration, or the domestic practices of the parties to the arbitration, do not apply directly to an international arbitration. This includes affirmation of this point by reviewing courts,[19] international commercial arbitral tribunals[20] and investor-state arbitral tribunals.[21] Naturally, this principle will be modified where the parties have agreed to the direct application of local rules, or where there is a specific principle of local law which the parties have involved their pleadings.[22] If the parties have not expressed a preference for the domestic practices of a jurisdiction, then great

---

18 Noting the view of Lord Mustill in favour of applying the domestic evidentiary practices of a particular jurisdiction, the authors of one influential text on ICC arbitral procedure state the following, "While the learned judge's views are entitled to respect, it has been the author's repeated experience in ICC arbitration involving parties from common-law and civil-law backgrounds in the same case that the proceedings have been conducted in a manner which encompassed some of the attributes of each system [referring to civil law and common law systems]." W. Craig, W. Park, J. Paulsson, *International Chamber of Commerce Arbitration*, p. 423 (2000). Born further notes: "Historically, it was frequently said or assumed that arbitrators were required to apply the domestic procedural rules applicable in national courts in the arbitral seat. For the most part, it is now widely accepted that the domestic procedural rules of local courts are not applicable – mandatorily or otherwise – in international arbitrations seated on local territory." Gary B. Born, *International Commercial Arbitration: Cases and Materials*, p. 715 (2011).

19 See the discussion of several domestic court rulings refusing challenges to awards because an arbitrator had not applied the comments to art. 9.1. See also: *Rintin Corp SA v Domar Ltd*, 374 F.Supp. 2d 1165 (SD Fla. 2005), noting that a party loses its right to discovery under the Federal Rules of Civil Procedure by choosing for international arbitration. See further: *Chantiers de l'Atlantique SA v Gaztransport & Technigaz SAS* [2011] EWHC 3383 (Comm), noting that English court rules on evidentiary procedure should not be imposed on an ICC arbitration.

20 See ICC Case No. 12124 recognising in relation to objections brought over the admissibility of hearsay that it was not under a duty to apply the rules of evidence of the seat. *ICC Bulletin, 2010 Special Supplement: Decisions on ICC Arbitration Procedure*, p. 32, (2010). See also: the discussion to art. 9.1 with regard to ICC Case No. 7626.

21 See the discussion of *Tradex Hellas SA v Republic of Albania* in the comments to art. 9.1. See also, for an historical perspective, the comments of the British-Mexico Claims Commission which recognised its independence from the rules of evidence found in both England and Mexico: "Under the rules governing the procedure of the Commission we are not bound by the laws of evidence prevailing in Mexico or in England or in any other country. But it is our duty to apply general principles of justice and equity and to give to any oral evidence or document produced before us such evidential value was we consider in all circumstances of the case it ought to carry." As quoted in Bin Cheng, *supra* n. 3, p. 308.

22 See, for instance, affirmation by a US district court of an ICC tribunal's decision to apply US federal rules on summary judgment: "Specifically, the panel invoked the doctrine of *lex arbitri* – law where the arbitration is to take place – to decide that Federal Rule of Civil Procedure 56 governed this action. Again, at worst, this is an incorrect interpretation of the law of the place where the arbitration is to take place. The arbitration took place in San Francisco, which is located both in California and the United States. A decision to use federal procedural law when presented with two competing procedural standards is not completely irrational nor does it exhibit a complete disregard of ICC Rules. Indeed, the arbitrators are the best qualified to determine what the ICC Rules require, and they specifically affirmed, in their final opinion, the decision to use this particular summary judgment standard." *LaPine v Kyocera Corp*, 2008 US Dist. LEXIS 41172, 26–27 (ND Cal. 22 May 2008). Where the parties are intent on applying an aspect of local evidentiary procedure, it is often the view of the tribunal that such a decision should be respected. See further: the position taken by an LCIA tribunal: "The lawyers did not choose to fight this battle economically. Discovery was American style and extensive. However, the decision to conduct

dissatisfaction may result where a choice is made to transpose the procedural norms of one court system onto the procedure. As an example, the following anecdote related by a well-experienced arbitrator makes the point:

> In at least one recent international case, an English chairman of great distinction endorsed [the] application of the Civil Procedure Rules to document production on the basis that London had been chosen as the venue for hearings. Counsel for the British side was delighted, and confirmed that this was precisely why his client had agreed to arbitrate in London. The American party, represented by a large Midwest firm, felt profoundly misled and had to insist several times that the CPR was not part of the bargain.[23]

1.19 It may be said that in many instances the choice of international arbitration represents not only an aspiration to have the case judged by arbitrators of a neutral nationality but also to subject the dispute to a neutral procedure, including the rules on evidence which do not favour one side over the other.[24] This position finds support in the fact that modern arbitration laws, which are intended to provide an adequate framework for the conduct of international arbitration, such as the UNCITRAL Model Law, make no reference to the application of the local rules of evidentiary procedure.[25] The far better approach to rules of evidence presumption is that in choosing international arbitration, the parties desired an evidentiary procedure commensurate with international standards, such as those found in the IBA Rules.[26]

---

the arbitration in this manner was shared by both sides. It is not for me to second-guess the decision at this time." LCIA Case No. 5680, Final Award, para. 5.4 (2006).

23 William W. Park, "Two Faces of Progress: Fairness and Flexibility in Arbitral Procedure", *Arbitration International*, Vol. 23, No. 3, p. 500 (2007).

24 Paulsson, speaking of several perceived advantages to using international arbitration, writes the following: ". . . all of these elements of evaluation fade into relative insignificance when contrasted with a criterion that is dominant here although it is, by definition, irrelevant in the national context . . . That unique criterion is neutrality." Jan Paulsson, "International Arbitration is Not Arbitration", *Stockholm International Arbitration Review*, n. 2, p. 1 (2008). This criterion, while referring also to the cultural background of the arbitrators, further implies procedural neutrality. Consider the following early but enduring statement of procedural principles applicable to the taking of evidence in international arbitration: "At the outset it should be noted that a practical solution of all problems involved only seems possible if we do not bind ourselves to a global system, whether accusatorial or inquisitorial. The only workable approach, in practice, seems to be to look for the most efficient way in which in each individual situation a solution can be found. This principle from which we start seems of great importance. In fact it means a complete rupture with the application of a pre-established system. The Rules, applicable in court proceedings, cannot provide a guideline. In international commercial arbitration parties may belong to different legal systems, and the same may apply to the arbitrators, or at least one of them. The place of arbitration, whether chosen by the parties or by the arbitrators cannot be the determining factor either. Neither of the parties should be in a privileged position or have an advantage because of the rules of evidence applied in the arbitration case." Jean Robert, "Administration of Evidence in International Commercial Arbitration" in Pieter Sanders (ed), *Yearbook Commercial Arbitration*, Vol. I, p. 222 (1976).

25 In an interesting decision, which considered the comparative suitability of the seat of an arbitration, the tribunal in the UNCITRAL/NAFTA tribunal in *Ethyl Corp v Government of Canada* considered a number of factors, including the "arbitration laws" of the two proposed places of arbitration, New York City and Ottawa. Notably absent from any consideration of the local laws on arbitration procedure was the rules of evidence. *Ethyl Corp v Government of Canada*, Decision on the Place of Arbitration, UNCITRAL/NAFTA (28 November 1997). Nevertheless, it is accepted that the desire for neutrality may be satisfied in some cases by the application of a neutral jurisdiction's rules on evidence. However, it may also be true that if the parties desired local court procedure, they would have designated it.

26 Park further notes: "In England, the genesis of delocalisation might be traced back almost three decades to the Arbitration Act 1979, which abolished the 'case stated' procedure. Under prior law, the finality of commercial arbitration had been diminished through what some perceived as undue judicial intervention. Similar principles have been adopted in other countries that often host international arbitration, such as France and Switzerland,

The application of the IBA rules of evidence

1.20 In consideration of the application of the IBA Rules four principles may be observed. The first principle is that the Rules in and of themselves do not constitute due process. In fact, the general presumption that they are not binding at all. Take, for example, the following approach to adopting the Rules from an LCIA arbitration:

> The IBA Rules on the Taking of Evidence in International Commercial Arbitration, as adopted by the IBA Council on June 1, 1999 may be taken into account by the Arbitral Tribunal, should it consider them appropriate as mere guidelines for establishing the rules of the arbitral proceedings.[27]

1.21 The quote above more or less represents the common manner of incorporating the Rules into an arbitration, although one also finds situations where the rules are applied as binding principles. In this sense, the IBA Rules often constitute points of reference, but are not necessarily definitive. The reasons for this preference among arbitrators appears to be rooted in a basic desire to maintain procedural flexibility. For various reasons, some aspects of the Rules may not apply, be streamlined in certain instances or are not desirable in the context of a particular dispute. This view is consistent with the published jurisprudence of some jurisdictions holding that a breach of the IBA Rules in and of itself does not constitute an offence warranting annulment,[28] and the recognition by the Rules themselves that they may be applied partially or with amendments to them.[29]

1.22 While it may be that the simple failure to apply the IBA Rules does not result in a successful challenge of an award, a failure to observe the underlying principles of fairness and equality very well might. Thus, before one considers that the IBA Rules may be ignored altogether, one should not overlook their intrinsically authoritative value. The Rules in their most basic form are an expression of the due process principles of fairness and equality as applied to evidentiary procedure and thus they are standards which carry persuasive value: a value which may be considered by tribunals and reviewing courts. As will be noted further in the book, the IBA Rules have been consulted by numerous international tribunals on questions of evidentiary procedure expressly, and one may also note that the principles found therein are often espoused by arbitrators whether direct reference to the IBA Rules is made or not. With respect to courts, even though in most instances considered "non-binding", published cases from the United States, England, Singapore and Canada and other jurisdictions may be found where the IBA Rules have been referred to when determining whether the acts of an arbitrator constituted serious departures from

---

and find themselves enshrined in the UNCITRAL Model Law as well. Particularly in an international arbitration, where the parties come from different legal cultures, an arbitrator's knee-jerk adoption of local rules (even with the best of intentions) often runs counter to at least one side's expectations at the time it initially agreed to arbitrate." Park, *supra* n. 15, p. 499.

27 LCIA, No. UN 5699, Procedural Order No. 1 (unpublished).

28 See: the reported decision of the Swiss Federal Tribunal: "[T]he Court ruled that a violation of the IBA Rules, or of the evidentiary rules of the local (Zurich) Procedural Code, were not grounds for challenging an arbitral award." "*X v A*, Decision of 28 March 2007", *ASA Bulletin*, Vol. 25, No. 3, p. 517 (2007).

29 Preamble, para. 2: "Parties and Arbitral Tribunals may adopt the IBA Rules of Evidence, in whole or in part, to govern arbitration proceedings, or they may vary them or use them as guidelines in developing their own procedures. The Rules are not intended to limit the flexibility that is inherent in, and an advantage of, international arbitration, and Parties and Arbitral Tribunals are free to adapt them to the particular circumstances of each arbitration."

fundamental procedural due process. The conclusion to draw from this is that the IBA Rules are a relevant, if not the pre-eminent, body of evidentiary rules in modern arbitral practice, even if they are often considered "non-binding" in many instances.

1.23 The second principle regarding application of the Rules is that they have as their guiding principle of interpretation procedural good faith. This is made plain by the third paragraph of the opening preamble:

> The taking of evidence shall be conducted on the principles that each Party shall act in good faith and be entitled to know, reasonably in advance of any Evidentiary Hearing or any fact or merits determination, the evidence on which the other Parties rely.

1.24 The principle of good faith means that the tribunal should expect cooperation from the parties in administering the IBA Rules. This will have various applications, however, in the 2010 version of the Rules, article 9.7 was added permitting a tribunal to award costs against a party due to a failure to cooperate in good faith with the taking of evidence. Clearly, good faith is a central tenet of evidentiary procedure, and thus the Rules should be interpreted with this in mind.

1.25 A third principle is that the IBA Rules are supplementary in nature.[30] They are intended to fill the gap left by most arbitration rules that make little or no reference to the canons of evidence.[31] In practice they may also be considered supplementary to the procedural orders of the tribunal. It is not uncommon for a tribunal to provide guidance on questions of evidence in an organisational procedural order, and refer to the IBA Rules, in particular article 9, as the standards by which the manuscripted rules ought to be interpreted, or any disputes arising out of them decided.

1.26 The final and fourth principle is that the IBA Rules are applicable to a broad range of disputes that fall under the description of "international arbitration". Originally entitled the IBA Rules on the Taking of Evidence in International Commercial Arbitration, the word "Commercial" was dropped when the rules were revised in 2010. This amendment to the name reflected the wide adoption of the Rules by tribunals sitting in consideration of investor-state disputes.[32] Their acceptance in this category of dispute resolution indicates that the Rules are suitable for disputes which range beyond what has traditionally been thought of as commercial arbitration. This being said, and as is further discussed below, the nature of a dispute may in some instances impact the interpretation applied to the rules by a tribunal.

---

30 The supplementary nature of the rules was originally contained within the title to the rules in the 1983 version.

31 In this regard, the provision set forth in art. 1.4 of the Rules speak to conflicts between the IBA Rules and the arbitration rules: "In case of conflict between any provisions of the IBA Rules of Evidence and the General Rules, the Arbitral Tribunal shall apply the IBA Rules of Evidence in the manner that it determines best in order to accomplish the purposes of both the General Rules and the IBA Rules of Evidence, unless the Parties agree to the contrary." Thus, while supplementary to the arbitration or "general" rules, the 2010 version of the Rules takes the view that the tribunal should still consider the purpose of the IBA Rules when derogating from them to accommodate the arbitration rules.

32 See, for example, the following ruling by an ICSID tribunal: "The IBA Rules on the Taking of Evidence in International Commercial Arbitration, though not directly applicable in this case and primarily provided for use in the field of commercial arbitrations, can be considered (particularly Articles 3 and 9) as giving indications of what may be relevant criteria for what documents may be requested and ordered to be produced in ICSID procedures between investors and host states." *Noble Ventures Inc v Romania*, ICSID Case No. ARB/01/11, Final Award, p. 31 (12 October 2005).

CHAPTER 2

Depositions, interrogatories and judicial notice

Introduction

2.01 The IBA Rules of Evidence consider those modes of taking evidence that are generally used and accepted in modern practice. Falling outside the standard practices covered by the Rules are other procedures that may be less frequently used, but are still known to have been applied in the context of international arbitration.

2.02 It should be noted at the outset that the inclusion of a chapter in this book covering these procedures in no way implies an endorsement of their use. Indeed, it is arguably for good reason that, for example, the practice of taking of pre-hearing depositions does not enjoy wide acceptance in international arbitration. Nevertheless, it is not unheard of for parties to request the use of evidence taking techniques that fall outside the IBA Rules and for Tribunals to acquiesce. The opening sections of this chapter consider evidentiary procedures derived from common law jurisdictions which have, at times, found application in international arbitration. The first, is the witness deposition, which involves interviews conducted by legal counsel of witnesses prior to trial or hearing, for the purpose of creating a written transcript that is submitted as evidence. The second, is the use of written interrogatories, which are in essence questions posed by one side directly to another side's witnesses. Such questions are often a means of narrowing down factual issues within a case so as to clarify the key matters in dispute.

2.03 The practice of taking judicial notice is also considered in this section, as it relates to the acceptance of facts by a tribunal for which no evidence has been formally introduced into the procedure. While also being a means of establishing facts that is not considered by the IBA Rules, judicial notice may be regarded differently than the other two procedures considered in this chapter. The reason is that there seems to be general acceptance of this practice within international arbitration, as many tribunals have regarded themselves as inherently endowed with the power to take judicial notice of certain known facts.

Depositions

Sample Clause:	**At the request of any party, the arbitral tribunal shall [have the discretion to] order the examination by deposition of any witness to the extent the arbitral tribunal deems such examination appropriate or necessary. Depositions shall be limited to a maximum of [number] per party.**[1]
ICDR Rules 21(10)	**Depositions, interrogatories, and requests to admit as developed for use in US court procedures generally are not appropriate procedures for obtaining information in an arbitration under these Rules**

---

1 Based upon a sample clause provided in Paul D. Friedland, *Arbitration Clauses for International Contracts*, p. 236 (2nd edition, 2007).

2.04 Broadly defined, the word deposition may be understood as simply the "written record of a witness's out-of-court testimony."[2] The general definition notwithstanding, the word deposition has come to be closely identified with pre-trial discovery in the United States. In the American context, deposition generally refers to an oral examination of a witness conducted by the legal counsel to the parties. The testimony is usually recorded in some manner for later use at trial. The IBA Rules do not contemplate the use of pre-hearing depositions.

Most often a deposition will be conducted outside the view of the court, with a judge's subsequent involvement only becoming necessary if a dispute arises over the conduct of the questioning. The transcript of the deposition may be used for the purpose of impeaching a witness, introducing testimony of a witness unable to attend the trial or for other reasons specified under the applicable rules of procedure.[3] It is rare in American practice for litigation to take place without the conduct of depositions, as it is, along with interrogatories and document production, one of the most common aspects of US discovery practice.

2.05 As depositions are often used to prepare for US trial proceedings subject to extensive rules governing the admissibility of witness testimony, their utility in the context of a traditional international arbitration hearing, where such rules do not apply, is questionable.[4] As ICDR Rules article 21(10) confirms, the widely held belief of international arbitrators is that depositions are generally inappropriate for international arbitration proceedings. Nevertheless, it is not unheard of for parties to agree on occasion to their use. Moreover, there is arbitral precedent supporting the view that the organisation of a deposition may be appropriate in the limited circumstance that a key witness is unable to attend an oral hearing. Such a possibility may be raised via a petition under article 4.9 of the IBA Rules. Finally, it has also been the case that where a witness freely wishes to meet with opposing legal counsel, a tribunal will permit a witness interview, which may be loosely similar to a deposition. These issues are further considered below.

---

2   Bryan A. Gardner (ed.), *Black's Law Dictionary* (8th edition, 2004), p. 472.

3   See, for example, the summary of the use of depositions provided in John Fellas, *Transatlantic Commercial Litigation and Arbitration*, pp. 20–243 (2004).

4   See the following redacted procedural order taken from an ICDR proceeding presided over by a well-experienced tribunal: "[Claimant's] application to depose [a witness] is denied. The Tribunal considers that depositions generally are not appropriate procedures to be adopted in international arbitrations such as this, and that the proposed deposition is not called for in this case. As indicated in [claimant's] submission made in support of its application, it is apparent that [claimant] has documents relevant to [the witness'] written testimony which it can use in cross examination of [the witness] to test the completeness and candor of his testimony." ICDR Case No. 01-16-0003-8669 [Case name redacted]. Reed and Sutcliffe note that depositions are rarely used in international arbitration and identify the practice as one of the "worst" attributes of US procedural practice, the use of which should be avoided in arbitration. Lucy Reed and Jonathan Sutcliffe, "The Americanization of International Arbitration?", *Mealey's Intl Arb Rep*, Vol. 16, No. 4, p. 11 (2001). See also, in relation to domestic arbitration proceedings, where it has been recognised that normal pre-trial discovery, available in domestic courts, is not consistent with arbitral proceedings: "The fundamental differences between the fact-finding process of a judicial tribunal and those of a panel of arbitrators demonstrate the need of pre-trial discovery in the one and its superfluity and utter incompatibility in the other." *Commercial Solvents Corp v Louisiana Liquid Fertilizer Co*, 20 FRD 359, 362 (SDNY 1957). See also, the same view specifically with regard to the AAA rules of procedure: "Neither the federal statutes nor the rules of AAA give a party an absolute right to demand discovery. As a general rule, discovery is very limited in arbitration proceedings. Once a district court has stayed judicial proceedings pending arbitration, the parties may not continue discovery in the district court." *United Nuclear Corp v General Atomic Co*, 93 NM 105, 117 (Sup. Ct of New Mexico 1979).

Arbitration agreements permitting depositions in international arbitration generally

2.06 In principle, parties to an arbitration may agree to engage depositions at any stage, though it is more likely that the provision for depositions would be found in an arbitration agreement.[5] The inclusion of a reference to depositions often comes about where one or more parties is based in the United States.

2.07 That being said, the first issue confronting a tribunal when considering a reference to depositions in an arbitration agreement is to identify the intent behind the reference. As noted above, there are many reasons why a tribunal may not wish to import the American practice into an international procedure. Therefore, tribunals may wish to confirm that a reference to a "deposition" is truly intended to reference a US-style procedures.

2.08 In this regard, the experience of one ICC tribunal confronted with an arbitration clause that called for the parties to be permitted to take depositions is instructive.[6] Here, the tribunal, which was comprised of non-American arbitrators of mixed civil and common-law background, advised the parties in an initial communication that, "it does not believe that American style depositions would be a useful exercise."[7] In this instance, the tribunal hoped to avoid engaging in US-style procedures by either disregarding the reference to depositions or by interpreting it as simply referring to the obtaining of witness testimony at the hearing.[8] Nonetheless, following exchanges between the parties and the tribunal it became evident that the clause was incapable of holding any meaning other than a reference to American deposition practice. The tribunal thus acceded to their inclusion in the proceedings.

2.09 Given that "deposition" is a term closely associated with American litigation, in most cases it would seem that an agreement permitting "depositions" should be interpreted taking account of this common usage.[9] This does not mean, however, that American proce-

---

5   See the statement of Craig, Park and Paulsson noting that an agreement to take depositions is rarely achieved in the opening stages of an arbitration: "In the authors' experience, such practice is rare. Counsel from non-common law countries are very reluctant to agree to such a procedure at the early date of the Terms of Reference." William Laurence Craig, William Park and Jan Paulsson, *International Chamber of Commerce Arbitration*, p. 457. See also, as McIlwrath and Savage note, it is not unheard of for such provisions to be found in the arbitration clause: "Parties may want to include in their arbitration agreement specific provisions about the procedure they wish to be followed in their arbitration. These may be directions or aspirations as to the overall duration of the arbitration or as to the timing of specific procedural steps. The parties may also agree on issues of evidence: for instance, they may require the arbitrators to follow the IBA Rules of Evidence, or to use the IBA Rules as guidance; they may prefer to have more extensive discovery, including depositions, than is the norm; or they may agree to exclude all discovery." Michael McIlwrath and John Savage, *International Arbitration and Mediation: A Practical Guide* (Kluwer Law International, 2010), p. 79.

6   ICC Case No. 16249, Procedural Order No. 1 (2010), (unpublished).

7   ICC Case No. 16249, Draft Procedural Order No. 1 (2009), (unpublished).

8   As an example, see the following procedural order from ICC Case No. 13155 wherein the word "depositions" is used with regard to the taking of evidence during an oral hearing: "The Sole Arbitrator shall, at all times, have a complete right of control … over the procedure in relation to the examination of a witness, including the right to limit or refuse the right of a party to examine a witness when it considers that the factual allegations(s) on which the witness is intended to depose is sufficiently proven by exhibits or other witnesses or that the particular witness deposition as such is irrelevant." ICC Case No. 13225, Procedural Order of 8 October 2004, *ICC Bulletin, 2010 Special Supplement: Decisions on ICC Arbitration Procedure*, p. 99.

9   Given the general assumption in international arbitration that the parties will be afforded an opportunity to hold a hearing, which will potentially include witness examinations, a specific mention of "depositions" in an

dural rules must be applied to this process. As is widely accepted, domestic procedures do not have automatic application to international arbitration, and this would also be true in regard to conducting a deposition.[10] Thus a tribunal may determine the manner and procedure to be applied to a deposition conducted under its aegis.

2.10 As the IBA Rules do not contain a direct reference to depositions, rules governing the practice in a truly international setting may be gleaned from the experience of past tribunals. The general practice regarding the conduct of a deposition in the domestic US context and in international arbitration is that counsel for both parties will be permitted to attend, and the final transcript deposited as part of the evidentiary record.[11] The American system presupposes that a witness who is deposed will potentially be called to appear in court to be examined at trial. In international arbitration, however, this may not be necessary. It is conceivable that the tribunal will regard the written transcript as sufficient for its considerations, and determine that hearing the witness again, in its presence, is redundant. Such a procedural determination would be generally consistent with the case management authority which is granted to the tribunal in article 8 of the IBA Rules.[12]

2.11 As for the deposition itself, only witnesses presented in support of a party's case would be made available for deposition although this may depend on the wording of the arbitration agreement. It is possible that by analogy, under IBA Rules article 4.9, a witness who is clearly under the control of a party, such as an employee with knowledge of the particular dispute, but who has not been otherwise listed by that party as a witness in the case, could be requested to attend a deposition.[13] In that instance, the purpose of the deposition would be to permit a party to obtain evidence from a potentially adverse witness who has not been presented by either party.

2.12 Regarding the conduct of the deposition, the method of questioning may be taken, by analogy, from the rules regarding the conduct of an oral hearing generally set forth in article 8 of the IBA Rules. Thus, the order of questioning would begin with the party who has listed the witness in support of its case. If a witness statement has been submitted by the witness, then it would be consistent with the IBA Rules for the party, on whose behalf the witness is offering testimony, to waive a direct examination or restrict their questions to a short opening examination of approximately 10 minutes.[14] The examination by the adverse party may then commence with follow-up questions by counsel for the party presenting the

---

arbitral clause would in most instances be considered redundant if it were taken to merely mean the oral examination of witnesses.

10 See comments to art. 9.1 of the IBA Rules.

11 Referring to the use of deposition transcripts in international arbitration, Craig, Park and Paulsson note: "A stenographic record of their statements is filed in the arbitration and serves as the basis for comments in briefs and memoranda." Craig, Park and Paulsson, *supra* n. 5.

12 See: comments to art. 8.2.

13 See, for example: the order in ICC Case No. 12279, "The Parties will meet and confer concerning any request that a Party make available to give testimony a party controlled witness whose testimony is not being submitted by the other Party. The Parties will endeavour to make such witnesses available to give sworn testimony via a deposition in perpetuation of evidence in advance of the hearing, so that the testimony may be submitted at the time of the filing of written submissions." ICC Case No. 12279, Procedural Order of 31 July 2003, *ICC Bulletin, 2010 Special Supplement: Decisions on ICC Arbitration Procedure*, p. 42.

14 See, for example: the comments to art. 8.3. In the instance where the witness has not offered a witness statement, the parties may deem it necessary to set a different order of questioning.

witness. Permissible objections to questions may be, again by analogy, taken from the list set forth in article 9 of the IBA Rules of Evidence.[15] In some instances, the tribunal may wish to ask the parties to meet and confer with it concerning the rules of the deposition.

2.13 The parties and the tribunal would need to ensure that a faithful record of the witness' testimony is taken.[16] In this respect, it is generally the case that the hearing should be transcribed or recorded by video, with interpreters present if necessary.[17] In some instances, the tribunal may request the deposition to take place before a notary public or other witness, however, this may not be considered a general requirement.[18] As witnesses are often located in diverse locations parties and tribunals may consider organising depositions via video conference.[19]

2.14 A tribunal's role in such an exercise may be minimal. As tribunals are limited in their procedural powers, lacking direct means of compelling a witness to attend or answer questions at a deposition, arbitrators should in most instances not become embroiled in disputes over whether a witness is to be made available for the deposition or should answer a particular question. Nevertheless, in most instances a tribunal will retain the authority to resolve any disputes over objections and questions generally,[20] which may mean that a negative inference is drawn against the party who is withholding cooperation.

The use of depositions to obtain testimony from witnesses unable to attend a hearing

2.15 The principal rule regarding written witness testimony in international arbitration is that save for exceptional circumstances, in order for written testimony to be accepted into a proceeding the witness is generally required to be available to attend the oral hearing to be examined by the adverse party and/or the tribunal.[21] While this rule

---

15 As is discussed in the comments concerning the use of interrogatories in international arbitration, objections available to the party seeking to oppose a question may be taken by analogy from the IBA Rules of Evidence. This would seem appropriate for the case of depositions as well.

16 In ICC Case No. 7170, involving parties of a civil law background, the tribunal ordered that the deposition be conducted in front of a public notary, who was also to authenticate the transcript. Dominique Hascher (ed.), *Collection of Procedural Decisions in ICC Arbitration 1993–1996*, p. 56 (2nd edition, 1998). "An English language transcript of all declarations shall be provided, authenticated by the notary public and by a qualified translator and shall be sent to the parties, the Tribunal and the Secretariat ...."

17 *Ibid.*, "Counsel for defendant may be present and may put questions. In that case simultaneous translation is to be provided into English, provisionally at the expense of the plaintiff."

18 *Ibid.*

19 See the following considerations of an ICDR tribunal regarding the use of video conference depositions: "Respondent and Claimant should take all reasonable steps to make their witnesses available for depositions near to or in proximity to the place of arbitration – if not at a location they can mutually agree upon. The aforementioned notwithstanding, the Sole Arbitrator also believes that video conference depositions should be sufficient to fulfill the requirements of the arbitration agreement, unless a Party can demonstrate conclusively that such an approach will pose a special hardship." [Redacted] ICDR Case No. 01-17-0003-2248.

20 As is stated in art. 8.2 of the IBA Rules, a tribunal is vested with control over the conduct of an evidentiary hearing. By analogy, if not by direct application, this principle would extend to the taking of witness testimony during a deposition.

21 While tribunals may allow for a statement of a witness who was not available to attend a hearing to remain in the record, such a decision is often predicated upon the good faith inability of the witness to attend the hearing for matters that were beyond a party's control. See the following procedural direction taken from ICC Case No. 12949 as an example of the standard rule: "The Arbitral Tribunal may consider the witness statement of a witness who provides a valid reason for failing to appear when summoned to a hearing, having regard to all the surrounding circumstances. The Arbitral Tribunal shall not consider the witness statement of a witness who fails to appear

establishes the widely observed approach to questions of admitting written witness testimony, some arbitrators have permitted the use of depositions as a third way of resolving problems over the non-attendance of witnesses in the hearing. In this instance, a deposition may be organised along the following lines set forth by an UNCITRAL tribunal seated in Zurich, Switzerland:

> Both Parties agree that witnesses who are unable to attend the hearing of the Arbitral Tribunal may give testimony at a time and a place other than that of the hearing and their written testimony may be used in the proceedings, provided Counsel of both Parties are present when the witness is heard and have adequate opportunity to question the witness.[22]

2.16 In the situation described above, far from adding needless complications to the procedure, the use of a deposition may provide an efficient means for facilitating the taking of evidence that would otherwise have been lost to the procedure. As noted in the introduction to this chapter, a tribunal may order such a deposition to take place, or otherwise petition a court for assistance in securing a deposition under the terms of IBA Rules art. 4.9.

2.17 In the event the tribunal does order depositions to take place, it is generally required that both parties be notified, and permitted to attend the deposition. In most instances, a notification to the adverse party within a reasonable period will satisfy this requirement. The tribunal in an ICC arbitration formulated the rule as follows:

> As long as the other side had notice of an opportunity to cross-examine the witness at a deposition in perpetuation of testimony, there is no right to cross-examination at the hearing as to witnesses who have been deposed.[23]

2.18 Thus, failure by counsel for the adverse party to attend the deposition will generally not be considered a reason for excluding the transcript as long as notice was provided of the time and location of the deposition.

Interviewing adverse witnesses prior to the hearing

2.19 It is generally considered that a party has the freedom to interview adverse witnesses who voluntarily agree to meet with them, subject to any ethical rules and restrictions that may apply. That being said, tribunals tend to be wary of attempts to intimidate such witnesses and have been known to require any such meetings to be conducted after notice has been given to opposing counsel and after the freely given consent of the witness is obtained.

2.20 In the ICSID case *Azinian v Mexico*, the tribunal laid down a number of principles concerning the conduct of such interviews that are generally considered as appropriate, and that are discussed further in the comments to article 4 of the IBA Rules.[24]

---

and does not provide a valid reason." ICC Case No. 12949, Procedural Order of 7 October 2004, *ICC Bulletin, 2010 Special Supplement: Decisions on ICC Arbitration Procedure*, p. 86. For a further discussion, see comments to IBA Rules, art. 4.7.

22 Documents in *ASA Bulletin*, Vol. 11, No. 2, p. 316 (1993).

23 ICC Case No. 12279, Procedural Order of 31 July 2003, *ICC Bulletin, 2010 Special Supplement: Decisions on ICC Arbitration Procedure*, p. 43.

24 Commenting on the order discussed above in the *Azinian* case, G. Petrochilos notes the following: "There being no on-point provision in the ICSID Rules, the tribunal made a detailed procedural ruling allowing such

It should be noted, however, that the *Azinian* tribunal, while recognising that a party may legitimately conduct such interviews with adverse witnesses in preparation for the hearing, did not permit a transcript or record of such interviews to be submitted into the proceedings.

Interrogatories

General discussion

2.21 Like depositions, the practice of issuing written interrogatories is a feature of litigation in some common-law jurisdictions, but is rarely applied in international arbitration. The word "interrogatories" (outside of criminal procedure) generally refers to a list of written questions directed to a party representative or witness under the party's control with the intention of eliciting written responses concerning matters in dispute.[25] They have multiple uses in domestic litigation, and can be directed to varying topics, such as the location and nature of evidence, substantive questions concerning liability and/or capacity to pay a money judgment and insurance coverage.[26]

2.22 As noted above, interrogatories are not often used in international arbitration. The direct questioning of witnesses is a matter customarily reserved for the oral hearing, with the consequence that arbitrators may be reluctant to accede to requests for written answers prior to the hearing.[27] Nevertheless, there are reported instances of international tribunals allowing interrogatories to be used, albeit largely in cases involving parties with common-law backgrounds. These precedents provide some basic principles for the use of interrogatories in international arbitration and are reviewed below. Additionally, the level of involvement that a tribunal will take in the process of propounding written interrogatories may vary, but there is precedent to suggest that a procedure actively guided by the tribunal may serve the purpose of obtaining relevant evidence best.

General guidelines for the use of interrogatories in international arbitration

2.23 It is commonly understood that for interrogatories to be used in an international arbitration, a tribunal must first be convinced that they would assist in narrowing or clarifying the issues before it. This was the finding of an UNCITRAL tribunal in the investor-state

---

interviews, with certain restrictions ensuring that the quality of the parties and the integrity of the proceedings, would not be frustrated." Georgios Petrochilos, *Procedural Law in International Arbitration*, p. 216 (2004).

25 Black's defines an interrogatory in US practice as, "A written question (usu. in a set of questions) submitted to an opposing party in a lawsuit as part of discovery." *Black's Law Dictionary, supra* n. 2, p. 838.

26 See: Fellas, *supra* n. 3, p. 238, for an overview of the American practice in using interrogatories. Interrogatories may also be used in English practice, where they are often directed to a party just prior to the start of trial and concern obtaining statements regarding the evidence that is to be offered. English practice also allows for the use of a submission of questions concerning the nature of a claim which is called, "Further and Better Particulars". More general than interrogatories, this procedure generally permits a party to inquire in writing as to aspects of a claim which have not been sufficiently detailed in the pleadings. See also: Jonathan Leslie and John Kingston, *Practical Guide to Litigation* (1998), pp. 57, 131–132.

27 However, where a witness is unable to attend a hearing, a tribunal may regard written interrogatories submitted to the witness, to be an appropriate means of allowing the witness to provide further testimony. See, for instance: ICC Case No. 11904 discussed further in the comments to art. 4.7. Arbitrage CCI No. 11904, *ASA Bulletin*, Vol. 22, No. 3, p. 520 (2004).

arbitration *United Parcel Service of America v Government of Canada*, wherein it was stated in respect to the use of interrogatories that, "the overall purpose, as the parties agree, is to facilitate the process of arbitration by narrowing the issues and giving proper notice to the other party."[28] This principle leads to the general rule that interrogatories should be narrowly tailored and used to elicit specific answers to questions of relevant fact relating to a material allegation, and not open-ended queries intended to seek information that will lead to new or enhanced requests for document disclosure.[29] In this sense, interrogatories may serve a narrower purpose in international arbitration than domestic practice. Consistent with this approach, it has further been held that interrogatories should not ask or require the production of documents.[30]

2.24 Generally, an interrogatory must specify the witness or representative to whom it is directed.[31] This description may simply specify a class of persons who should answer the question, such as an "officer" of the corporation.[32] It is customarily considered that the individual to whom the request may be addressed should answer the question from his or her own knowledge without consulting other witnesses, although it is accepted that consultations with legal counsel may be required.[33] If a witness is required to consult another individual on certain facts in order to answer the interrogatory, the identity of the individual consulted should be disclosed in the answer.[34] In any case, answers should be provided truthfully.

2.25 The objections that are available to the party receiving the interrogatories are regarded to be the same as those that may be had in respect of document requests.[35] Thus, a party may refer to article 9 of the IBA Rules in basing a refusal to provide an answer. In order to avoid possible disputes over the interrogatories, the tribunal may determine that the interrogatories first be approved by it, before they are delivered to the receiving party.[36]

---

28 *United Parcel Service of America v Government of Canada*, NAFTA/UNCITRAL, *Decision of the Tribunal Relating to Document Production and Interrogatories* (21 June 2004), p. 7.

29 *Ibid*. In the above mentioned *UPS* arbitration, *supra* n. 28, the tribunal required that the interrogatories were to be clarified, and directed to matters of fact. See also: *SD Myers v Government of Canada*, UNCITRAL, Procedural Order No. 12, p. 3 (26 November 1999), where the tribunal refused to require answers to be given to certain interrogatories because they sought what the tribunal deemed to be further "discovery" as opposed to the testimony of the witness to whom the questions were directed. In this case the tribunal took the view that the interrogatories were only useful for the purpose of eliciting further testimony from a witness and were not general questions to be answered by a party.

30 *UPS v Canada*, *supra* n. 28, *Decision of the Tribunal Relating to Document Production and Interrogatories*, p. 7.

31 See the direction given by the tribunal in *Merrill & Ring Forestry v Government of Canada*, Procedural Order No. 2, p. 5 (21 January 2008): "The interrogatories shall, in addition to the questions posed, list the persons or class of persons (the 'person') to whom the question(s) are targeted."

32 *Ibid.*

33 *Ibid.*: "The person answering may consult the lawyers representing them in the Arbitration for general advice. The person to whom the interrogatories are posed shall not consult other witnesses of the disputing party. In the event that an answer cannot be made without such consultations, the identity of such consulted persons must be disclosed."

34 *Ibid.*: "In the event that an answer cannot be made without such consultations, the identity of all such consulted persons must be disclosed."

35 *UPS v Canada*, *supra* n. 28, *Decision of the Tribunal Relating to Document Production and Interrogatories*, p. 7; "the procedures relating to the refusals to respond to document production shall apply with respect to interrogatories".

36 *Merrill v Canada*, *supra* n. 31, Procedural Order No. 2, "Interrogatories shall be approved by the Tribunal before delivery."

Like document requests, interrogatories will often follow the customary procedural timing for the delivery of the request to produce, which is to say that they will not be permitted prior to the filing of the initial statement of claim and defence.[37]

Tribunal involvement in drafting and approving interrogatories

2.26 The level of involvement by the tribunal in the process of submitting interrogatories can vary according to the needs of the case and preference of the arbitrators. However, there may be instances where it is appropriate for the tribunal to be actively involved. In the instance of *SD Myers v The Government of Canada*, an UNCITRAL arbitration, the tribunal considered it was useful for written interrogatories to be directed to certain individuals under the employ of the government party.[38] The procedure adopted in that case required the questioning party to submit draft questions to the tribunal, and for the governmental party to submit comments on the questions. The tribunal then undertook to reconcile the questions, and criticisms, and approve the final form of the questions.[39]

2.27 It is instructive to note that through this process, the tribunal was able to identify at the outset the witness to whom the questions would be directed, and, moreover, eliminate questions it deemed to simply ask for "further discovery" or which did not relate to matters of fact.[40] Moreover, the tribunal was able also to append needed instructions to the interrogatories.[41] Thus, while it may be that a tribunal would prefer not to engage itself in the interrogatories process, it can be the case that a measure of involvement will assist the process to proceed more smoothly.

Judicial notice

2.28 The IBA Rules provide little guidance on whether a tribunal may take judicial notice of points of fact in international arbitration. Nevertheless, it has been a longstanding practice of international tribunals to accept that arbitrators have the inherent power to take such notice in appropriate circumstances. In this regard, judicial notice should be understood as the acceptance by an arbitrator of a well-known and indisputable fact without requiring the parties to submit proof of it.[42]

2.29 The most often cited precedent concerning the taking of judicial notice in international arbitration is the *Island of Palmas* case, an arbitration between the Netherlands and

---

37 See: further discussion of this point in the comments to IBA Rules, art. 3.2. See also: as it relates specifically to interrogatories, the observations of the tribunal in *Merrill v Canada*, where the tribunal noted that the filing of interrogatories and document requests should occur after the filing of the statements of claim and defence. *Merrill v Canada, supra* n. 31, *Transcript of Procedural Hearing*, p. 91 (15 November 2007).

38 *SD Myers v Canada*, UNCITRAL, Procedural Order No. 8, p. 1 (31 October 1999).

39 *Ibid.*

40 *SD Myers v Canada*, UNCITRAL, Procedural Order No. 12, p. 3 (26 November 1999).

41 *Ibid.*

42 *Black's Law Dictionary, supra* n. 2, p. 864. With specific reference to international arbitration, Pietrowski notes the following regarding judicial notice: "An arbitral tribunal is not required to base its decision solely on the evidence produced by the parties. It may take judicial notice of facts that are so well known or so easily verified that any kind of formal proof would obviously be superfluous." Robert Pietrowski, *Evidence in International Arbitration: Arbitration International*, Vol. 22, No. 3, p. 384 (2006).

the United States over a disputed territory. In this instance, the United States had raised objections to the invocation by the Netherlands of the Treaty of Utrecht, the text of which had not been submitted into the record. In essence, the American position was that "all evidence was to be annexed to the written memorials, the only pleadings contemplated by the Parties in the arbitration agreement" and as the text of the treaty had not been submitted, the tribunal was not able to consult it during its deliberations.[43] Rejecting this position, the tribunal noted as follows:

> It would seem contrary to the broad principles applied in international arbitration to exclude *a limine*, except under the explicit terms of a conventional rule, every allegation made by a Party as irrelevant, if it is not supported by evidence, and to exclude evidence relating to such allegations from being produced at a later stage of the procedure .... No documents which are not on record have been relied upon, with the exception of the Treaty of Utrecht – invoked however in the Netherlands Counter-Memorandum – the text of which is of public notoriety and accessible to the Parties, and no allegation not supported by evidence is taken as foundation for the award.[44]

2.30 Interestingly, the position adopted by the United States here is similar in formulation to article 3.1 of the IBA Rules and article 20.4 of the UNCITRAL Rules, which calls for the parties to submit their documentary evidence on which they intend to rely in support of their case. It follows from this basic principle that a failure by a party to produce evidence in support of its case results in the rejection of an unsupported allegation, and thus the principle of judicial notice may be seen as an exception to this basic rule of procedure. Under this doctrine, a party may rely upon certain facts of public knowledge for which it has not submitted evidence, but that are of such notoriety that a tribunal may take notice of them without working unfair surprise upon the parties. But in order to apply judicial notice in such a manner as to not offend due process, a tribunal should be circumspect, finding only that the knowledge which may be safely assumed to be known or knowable to all may qualify as a basis for taking judicial notice.

Facts of which judicial notice may be taken

2.31 Of the available precedent, it may be said that international arbitrators have historically followed two fundamental principles in determining which facts may be relied upon without requiring specific proof to be produced. The first, is that the fact must be known or knowable to the parties due to its public notoriety. This standard encompasses common knowledge of scientific, geographic,[45] or historical[46] facts that are established

---

43 The *Island of Palmas* case, P. Hamilton et al. (ed.), *The Permanent Court of Arbitration: Summaries of Awards, Settlement Agreements and Reports*, p. 121 (1999).

44 *Ibid.*

45 One UNCITRAL tribunal took judicial notice of the comparative costs of one seat of arbitration over the other: "We now turn to criterion (d), 'availability and cost of support services needed'. It is clear that all necessary support services for this arbitration are available in all three of the cities that have been proposed. The Tribunal believes it appropriate to take judicial notice of the fact that such services inevitably will be more costly in New York City than in either Ottawa or Toronto." *Ethyl Corp v The Government of Canada*, Decision of 28 November 1997 and Award of 24 June 1998, in Albert Jan van den Berg (ed.), *Yearbook Commercial Arbitration*, Vol. XXIVa (1999).

46 Bin Cheng notes that the German-US Mixed Claims Commission of 1922 found that it was permissible to take judicial notice of historical records, "From the record therein and from historical sources and official reports

in the public record.[47] Falling within this category of the known or knowable is foundational knowledge concerning the operation or function of a relevant economic activity. For instance, tribunals have, in cases in which the ownership of a publicly listed company was a relevant issue, taken judicial notice of the fluid nature of the changing ownership of publicly traded shares and devised a standard from this fact, even though it was not pleaded by the parties.[48] Relevant documents or instruments that are of public record, accessible and have achieved a degree of notoriety, may also be subject of judicial notice.[49] Finally, it may also be said that facts that are self-evident, based upon either the procedural[50] or substantive positions[51] adopted by the parties, may be considered as sufficiently known so that a tribunal may draw judicial notice, even if the particular fact has

---

of which the Commission takes judicial notice it appears . . ." Bin Cheng, *General Principles of Law as Applied by International Courts and Tribunals*, p. 303 (reprinted 1987).

47 Knowledge of certain laws and/or legal principles that are of public record may well be open for a tribunal to take judicial notice of. It has been held by arbitral tribunals sitting in consideration of investor-state disputes, that the publicly available decisions of other tribunals may be the subject of judicial notice. See: The following excerpt from an UNCITRAL rules arbitration: "[T]he Tribunal rejected the Respondent's request for leave [to file new evidence] given the fact that the Claimant's last submission had been sent after the record of the jurisdictional phase had been closed . . . and had consequently been ignored by the Tribunal. The Tribunal noted that it could consider any publicly-available awards rendered after the close of the proceedings on jurisdiction, and that the Tribunal might ask the Parties to comment thereon, but that the Tribunal did not consider any comments from the Parties to be necessary at that time." *ICS Inspection and Control Services v Argentine Republic*, UNCITRAL, Award on Jurisdiction, para. 55 (2012).

48 "With respect to evidence of continuous ownership of stock, it must be recognised that there are changes in the stockholders of a publicly traded corporation each trading day. The Chamber takes judicial notice of the fact that on the New York Stock Exchange, where the stock of Flexi-Van is traded, in 1981 the daily average volume of shares traded was over 46 million shares each trading day. *NY Stock Exchange Annual Report 1981*, p. 2. While Flexi-Van is only one of approximately 1500 corporations whose stock is traded on that exchange, this figure is evidence that stock ownership of publicly traded corporations changes frequently. Therefore, it is necessary to measure ownership on a periodic rather than a daily basis." *Flexi-Van Leasing, General Motors Corp v The Islamic Republic of Iran, The Government of the Islamic Republic of Iran*, Case No. 36, Order of 20 December 1982 in Pieter Sanders (ed.), *Yearbook Commercial Arbitration*, Vol. IX, p. 233 (1984).

49 In the *Island of Palmas* case, the tribunal took notice of the Treaty of Utrecht even though the text had not been submitted into the record. *Island of Palmas, supra* n. 43, p. 121. See also: in contrast, that documents that are not publicly available will not qualify for judicial notice, as was noted by the Iran-US Claims Tribunal: "The Tribunal has given due consideration to that submission and notes that no justification was adduced by Iran for the late submission of that document. The said document is not a public document of which the Tribunal could appropriately take judicial notice." *The United States of America v the Islamic Republic of Iran*, Case No. B36, Award No. 574-B36-2, p. 4 (1996).

50 In a case before the Iran-US Claims Tribunal, judicial notice was taken of a change in pleadings by a party, as a supporting fact for drawing a conclusion on an issue of damages: "Under such conditions the Tribunal must take judicial notice of the fact that the Claimant initially conceded that $964,246.62 should be credited to the Respondents against the claims in this Case, and that six days prior to the Hearing it amended this figure to $1,007,095.21. In the absence of any means to calculate this figure more accurately, the Tribunal finds that the Respondents, in any event, are entitled to a credit of the amount so conceded . . .". *Seismograph Service Corp v National Iranian Oil Co*, Case No. 443, Award No. 420-443-3, p. 18 (1988).

51 Bin Cheng notes with regard to the Portugal-German Arbitration of 1919 that the tribunal adopted a position regarding the claims over the duty of the captor of a prize ship to take the vessel to a port, based upon a self-evident conclusion concerning the inability of a captor to bring the captive ship to port because of the size of the vessels: "As has been maintained by the claimant, the captor of a neutral prize must, in principle, take it to port. If he makes use of the exceptional right to destroy his capture, he must prove that he had acted in the face of such necessity . . . . But this proof, contrary to the Portuguese contention, is unnecessary, if it is obvious that the captor, because of its type was not in a position to escort the seized vessel or to detach a prize crew." Bin Cheng, *supra* n. 46, p. 303.

not been pleaded by the parties. In all instances, if a fact is considered known or knowable, a tribunal should be able to easily identify the source of the relevant information.[52]

2.32 As a second criteria to taking judicial notice, arbitral tribunals often consider whether the fact is uncontroverted and is sufficiently clear so that it may be considered accepted and confidently relied upon. Thus, while a tribunal may be sufficiently satisfied that the information upon which it draws is within the knowledge of the parties, if that information may be open to multiple or varying interpretations or is subject to qualifiers, it may be reluctant to take judicial notice without obtaining first the views of the parties.[53]

---

52 See, for instance, the dissenting opinion of Howard Holtzman in a case of the Iran-US Claims Tribunal: "The majority further finds that this 'contradiction' is significant because 'kilims . . . as the Tribunal observes, are typically among the least expensive carpets.' (*Ibid.*) The majority does not explain the basis on which it takes judicial notice of this alleged fact; there is no evidence as to the value of kilims in the record." *Robert R. Schott v Islamic Republic of Iran*, Case No. 268, Separate Opinion of Howard M. Holtzman regarding Award No. 474-268-1, p. 8 (1990).

53 See the following considerations of an ICSID tribunal with regard to published investment law decisions. While this decision considers judicial notice of legal authorities, the standards may also be applied to points of fact. The Tribunal informed the parties, through the Secretariat, on 20 July 2005 that "it believes it is empowered to take judicial notice of such published decisions. However, in accordance with due process principles, the Tribunal is of the opinion that should it consider necessary for its decision on jurisdiction to specifically rely on points raised and discussed in those decisions, it should give an opportunity first to the parties to comment on those possibly relevant points. The Tribunal would accordingly do so should the situation envisaged occur." Dietmar W. Prager and Joanna E. Davidson, "*Continental Casualty Co v The Argentine Republic*, ICSID Case No. ARB/03/9, 5 September 2008", *A Contribution by the ITA Board of Reporters*. See further: with regard to points of fact, the position of the Iran-US Claims Tribunal regarding an issue concerning the price of oil recorded in a public document. As is memorialised in the Supplemental Opinion of George Aldrich, the Tribunal did not take judicial notice of the price information as it was not established that it was beyond controversy, "Judge Khalilian nevertheless argues that the Tribunal should have taken 'judicial notice' of the report. Yet, the interpretation and relevance of the reserve figure in the report is far from clear . . . Thus, the meaning, reliability and applicability to this Case of the figure in the 1979 report that Judge Khalilian says the Tribunal should have accepted is uncertain, to say the least." *Phillips Petroleum Co Iran v The Islamic Republic of Iran*, Case No. 39, Supplemental Statement of George H. Aldrich regarding Award No. 425-39-2, p. 6 (1989).

CHAPTER 3

Document production in international arbitration

Introduction

3.01 As a general rule, documentary evidence is often afforded the highest level of credibility within international arbitration.[1] The preference for the written word over oral testimony is not something unique to the modern era of international arbitration, but is derived from the practices and procedures of some of the earliest arbitral tribunals and commissions. International tribunals from the nineteenth and early twentieth centuries, including "mixed commissions", often incorporated into their rules a stated preference for evidence to be submitted primarily in written form and, in one particular instance, actually prohibited the introduction of oral testimony save for exceptional circumstances.[2] One of the foremost experts on early arbitral procedure summarised this practice by stating, "probably the most outstanding characteristic of international judicial procedure is the extent to which reliance is placed upon its written word, both in the manner of pleadings, and of evidence, but especially the latter."[3]

3.02 This stands in marked contrast to the traditions followed in common law jurisdictions, which often regard oral witness testimony as indispensable. Documentary evidence in those jurisdictions is often introduced only after a foundation establishing its reliability has been laid using witness testimony. This is not the case in countries that take their legal heritage from the civil law tradition. There, witness testimony is clearly supplemental to documentary evidence, which is given greater weight.

3.03 International arbitration has adopted the civil law's preference for documents, but this is not to say that the common law has not influenced the manner in which

---

1 Jean-François Poudret and Sébastien Besson, *Comparative Law of International Arbitration*, p. 554, para. 649 (2nd edition, 2007). The authors refer to documentary evidence as evidence "par excellence" when it comes to the perception of arbitrators. See also: Jean Robert, "Administration of Evidence in International Commercial Arbitration", in Pieter Sanders (ed.) *Yearbook Commercial Arbitration*, Vol. I, p. 221 (1976): "Due to geographical distance generally separating the parties and the members of the tribunal, the importance of documents must be emphasized, and the arbitrators should not transfer their primary responsibility for interpreting them to the witnesses." *Id.* See also: the following observation of Bin Cheng regarding the practice of early international arbitral tribunals: " 'Testimonial Evidence,' it has been said, 'due to the frailty of human contingencies is most liable to arouse distrust.' On the other hand, documentary evidence stating, recording, or sometimes even incorporating the facts at issue, written or executed either contemporaneously or shortly after the events in question by persons having direct knowledge thereof, and for purposes other than the presentation of a claim or the support of a contention in a suit, is ordinarily free from this distrust and considered of higher probative value." Bin Cheng, *General Principles of Law as Applied by International Courts and Tribunals*, p. 319 (1987).

2 "No oral evidence will be heard by the Commission save in exceptional cases for good cause shown, and upon order first entered by the Commission authorizing its introduction. Should oral evidence be introduced on behalf of one party, the agent or counsel for the opposing party shall have the right of cross-examination." Mixed Claims Commission (United States and Germany), Rules of Procedure, art. V(c). 7 RIAA, p. 470.

3 Durward V. Sandifer, *Evidence Before International Tribunals*, Procedural Aspects of International Law Series, Vol. 13, p. 197 (1975).

documentary evidence is treated. Despite resistance, the practice of adverse document disclosure, which is to say requiring a party to produce evidence it has not voluntarily produced on its own, has become accepted within international arbitration.[4] Such procedures are largely foreign in civil law jurisdictions, whereas those that have common law backgrounds recognise the principle of disclosure as akin to the process of discovery. As will be discussed below, there are some fundamental differences between document disclosure as it is practised in domestic courts and as it is customarily applied in international arbitration.

3.04 When a subcommittee was formed in 2008 by the International Bar Association to review and revise the popular 1999 IBA Rules, particular attention was paid to article 3, the portion of the Rules that primarily pertains to the production of documentary evidence. Often considered the mainstay section of the Rules, article 3 contains the most widely used body of accepted practices governing the introduction and production of documentary evidence in international arbitration today. The following chapter considers article 3 of the Rules, and other principles which are applicable to the taking and production of documentary evidence in international arbitration. It should be noted that objections to the production or admissibility of evidence are dealt with more extensively in Chapter 9.

General considerations regarding production of documentary evidence

Article 3.1 2010 IBA Rules:	**Within the time ordered by the Arbitral Tribunal, each Party shall submit to the Arbitral Tribunal and to the other Parties all Documents available to it on which it relies, including public Documents and those in the public domain, except for any Documents that have already been submitted by another Party.**
Related Rules	
Article 20(4) UNCITRAL Rules:	The statement of claim should, as far as possible, be accompanied by all documents and other evidence relied upon by the claimant, or contain references to them.
Article 21(2) UNCITRAL Rules:	The statement of defence shall reply to the particulars (b) to (e) of the statement of claim (article 20, paragraph 2). The statement of defence should, as far as possible, be accompanied by all documents and other evidence relied upon by the respondent, or contain references to them.

---

4 "Whatever differences there may be between the various legal cultures, it is generally agreed that document production has a place in international arbitration. The issue is therefore not whether there will be document production but rather how much document production will be required." Bernard Hanotiau, "Document Production in International Arbitration: A Tentative Definition of 'Best Practices'", in *ICC Bulletin, 2006 Special Supplement: Document Production in International Arbitration*, p. 113. See also: *United Utilities (Tallinn) B.V. and Aktsiaselts Tallinna Vesi v Republic of Estonia*, ICSID Case No. ARB/14/24, Procedural Order No. 1 (2015), §15.2: "The conduct of document production shall be guided by the International Bar Association Rules on the Taking of Evidence in International Arbitration (2010) (the "IBA Rules")." See further: *David Aven et al. v The Republic of Costa Rica*, Arbitration Proceeding Under Chapter 10 of the Dominican Republic-Central America-United States Free Trade Agreement and the UNCITRAL Arbitration Rules (2010) (UNCT/15/3), Procedural Order No 1 (2015), §20.1: "Articles 3 and 9 of the International Bar Association Rules on the Taking of Evidence in International Arbitration (2010) may guide the Tribunal and the parties regarding document production in this case."

General discussion

3.05 The customary approach in international arbitration is that a party is expected to produce the evidence on which it intends to rely.[5] This is naturally the case since parties must substantiate their allegations with evidence in order to meet their respective burdens of proof.[6] Only if the tribunal has authorised it ahead of time, or the parties have agreed as much, should a party assume that representations of counsel, or summaries of the relevant documents, will be adequate in lieu of producing the documentary evidence on which it relies to support its arguments.[7] Article 3.1 restates this important principle of international

---

5   See: ICC Case No. 9078, Final Award, *ICC Bulletin, 2005 Special Supplement: UNIDROIT Principles: New Developments and Applications*, p. 73, para. 8.5.2: "The Claimant bears the burden to allege in a substantiated way and to prove all the above four elements. Only under certain circumstances does one admit that the burden of proof as to the absence of the causal nexus and/or the responsibility (*Schuld, Vetretenmüssen*) is shifted to the Defendant. The Claimant carries the burden to allege in a specified way and to prove not only the fact that a damage has occurred, but also the actual amount of the damage." See also: ICC Case No. 6896, Final Award, *ICC Bulletin*, Vol. 15, No. 1, p. 6 (2004): "In view of these contradictions and of the fact that the loan agreement concluded with the bank was not produced, nor any bank statements concerning the amount of the debts of the Plaintiff towards the bank, during the period under scrutiny, the Arbitral Tribunal considers that it is impossible to take into account the interests claimed by the Plaintiff, which has not brought the necessary proof although the burden of proof laid on it (art. 8 of the Swiss Code on Civil Rights)." See also: the application of this principle by the Iran-US Claims Tribunal: "the Navy has not produced any evidence in support of its contention that Pomeroy Corporation breached its duties under the Contract by failing to supply qualified personnel or failing to point out defects in the work of other contractors. By failing to establish even a prima facie case or contract breach, the Navy has not met its burden of proof on this defence, and it must be rejected." *RN Pomeroy v The Islamic Republic of Iran*, Iran-USCTR, Vol. 2, p. 382 (1983). See also: *Bear Creek Mining Corporation v Republic of Peru*, ICSID Case No. ARB/14/21, Procedural Order No. 1, §16.1 (2015): "The Memorial and Counter-Memorial shall be accompanied by the documentary evidence relied upon by the Parties, including exhibits and legal authorities. Further documentary evidence relied upon by the Parties may be submitted in rebuttal with the Reply and Rejoinder." See also: *Dunkeld International Investment Ltd v The Government of Belize*, PCA Case No. 2010-21/DUN-BZ II, Order No. 2, §8.1 (2011): "All evidence shall be submitted together with the written submissions . . .". See also: *Mesa Power Group LLC v Government of Canada*, PCA Case No. 2012-17, Procedural Order No. 1, §11.5 (2012): "The Parties shall submit all exhibits together with written submissions expressly referring to them. In exceptional cases, the Tribunal may allow a Party to submit additional exhibit at a later stage of the proceedings if appropriate in view of all the relevant circumstances."

6   As an example in relation to allegations concerning corporate liability, see: ICC Case No. 11209, Final Award, *ICC Bulletin*, Vol. 16, No. 2, p. 102 (2005): "[the] question of whether the corporate veil should be pierced depends on the facts of the relationship adduced in this Arbitration. The Claimants had led no evidence of fraud, deceit, collusion, avoidance of income tax legislation or that the underlying Agreement is a sham by the 2nd Respondent or the 3rd Respondent or that the 2nd Respondent is a 'shell' company. They merely relied on the fact that the 2nd Respondent is a wholly owned subsidiary of the 3rd Respondent. I am of the view that the Claimants have the burden of satisfying the Tribunal that there is some exceptional reason why the Tribunal should not regard each company in a group of companies as a separate legal entity, possessing separate rights and liabilities. There must be appropriate circumstances on the facts of this Arbitration, to indicate the distinction between them and treat them as one. There was no evidence led in this particular instance to indicate that distinction. I have looked at the underlying provisions of the Agreement and the transaction and all the circumstances in this case and I am satisfied that there is no reason whatsoever why the corporate veil should be pierced. There is also no evidence whatsoever before the Tribunal, for the Tribunal to take the exceptional step of disregarding the well recognized rule that companies are separate legal entities despite being in the same economic group."

7   See: *Methanex Corp v United States of America*, NAFTA/UNCITRAL, Procedural Order of 10 October 2003, para. 2 (2003): "As also previously ordered by the Tribunal, each Disputing Party is required by art. 3(1) of the IBA Rules to submit to the Tribunal and the other parties, all documents available to that party on which that party relies, including public documents and those in the public domain (except for any documents that have already been submitted by another party). Whilst the Tribunal accepts the reluctance of Methanex at this stage of the proceedings not to burden the Tribunal unnecessarily with 'voluminous and often highly technical scientific papers and reports on which [Methanex's] expert reports rely . . .' that consideration does not apply to

arbitral procedure by obliging parties to submit those documents into the procedure upon which they rely, with the exception of those documents submitted previously into the procedure by another party.

3.06 In addition to the above, article 3.1 sets out another core principle underlying evidentiary procedure in international arbitration; namely, that control over the evidentiary procedure rests with the tribunal provided it acts within the boundaries of the mandatory law and the parties' agreement to arbitrate.[8] In this context article 3.1 requires a party to submit the evidence on which it intends to rely "within the time" ordered by the tribunal. Past decisions by arbitral tribunals denying the admissibility of evidence tendered by a party because it was submitted after a deadline have been upheld by reviewing courts as consistent with due process principles.[9] Furthermore, as the IBA Rules themselves make clear, a tribunal is under a duty to administer an efficient and economical procedure, which may be understood generally to include holding the parties to filing deadlines (see comments to article 9.2(g)).[10] Failure to maintain timetables may cause

---

the USA currently studying Methanex's expert reports." See also: ICC Case No. 9448, Final Award, *ICC Bulletin*, Vol. 11, No. 2, p. 103 (2000) as an example of a situation where a party provided a summary of evidence but not the evidence itself: "Although the Arbitral Tribunal had specifically asked Claimants to submit evidence of their allegation, Claimants only submitted 'five samples' of invoices, bills of lading and bank statements of account. . . . They otherwise base their claim solely on their 'recapitulatory table' which only lists the invoices allegedly paid in delay, but does not supply any proof for this allegation. The Arbitral Tribunal will therefore only take the 'five samples' submitted as proof into consideration, and must neglect the other claimed invoices as no proof whatsoever has been submitted to uphold the allegation that they have been paid in delay, and, furthermore, as Respondent denies having paid any invoices in delay."

8 ICC Case No. 1512, Final Award, Sigvard Jarvin and Yves Derains (eds), *Collection of ICC Arbitral Awards*, Vol. 1, 1974–1985, p. 3: "an arbitrator possessed a wide freedom and discretion to decide matters of procedure, but this was not unfettered; he was bound by the general fundamental principles of procedure". See also: *Dadras International v The Islamic Republic of Iran et al.*, Award No. 567-213/215-3, Iran-USCTR, Vol. 31, p. 127, para. 60 (1995): "the Tribunal is obliged to provide the framework within which the parties may present their cases, but is by no means obliged to acquiesce in a party's desire for a particular sequence of proceedings or to permit repetitious proceedings."

9 See: *International Military Services Ltd v Ministry of Defence and Support for Armed Forces of Iran*, Hoge Raad 24 April 2009, NJ 2010/171 (Noot H. J. Snijders), where the Netherlands Supreme Court upheld the decision of an ICC tribunal to reject documentary evidence which had been proffered after the passing of a deadline. See also: the decision of the US Court of Appeals for the Third District which took into consideration the fact that a tribunal sitting in Switzerland under the UNCITRAL Rules had ordered "all documentary evidence relied upon by the parties was required to be produced with the parties' first submissions (i.e., Claimant's 21 August 2008 Statement of Claim and Respondent's 31 October 2008 Statement of Defence and Counterclaims) . . . as provided by Procedural Order No. 1, Section F.1 the parties may only produce new documents with their Submission insofar as necessary to respond to an argument or allegation of the other party", when determining that a party's request to the court for additional assistance in gaining discovery was moot, since the arbitral tribunal had made clear that the respective phases for introducing new or rebuttal evidence had passed. See also: *Comisión Ejecutiva Hidroeléctrica del Río Lempa v Nejapa Power Co, LLC*, 341 Fed Appx 821, p. 827 (3d Cir. 2009). See further a reported decision of the Swiss Federal Tribunal in which it was concluded: "An Arbitral Tribunal which strictly adheres to [an] agreed time table and repeatedly refuses to extend time limits or to grant requests to suspend the arbitration only violates the right to be heard if such procedural directions made it impossible for one party, due to unforeseeable circumstances, to safeguard its procedural rights." Summary and translation by Georg von Segesser, "14 December 2004 Swiss Federal Court 1st Chamber", *A Contribution by the ITA Board of Reporters*.

10 See: ICC Commission on Arbitration, *Report on Techniques for Controlling Time and Costs in Arbitration*, Publication No. 843, s. 35 (2007): "The arbitrators and the parties should make all reasonable efforts to comply with the provisional timetable. Extensions and revisions of the timetable should be made only when justified. Any revisions should be promptly communicated to the Court and the parties in accordance with art. 18(4) of the ICC Rules." See also: *Harris International Telecommunications Inc v The Islamic Republic of Iran*

substantial delay. A tribunal that permits evidence to be filed late likely must grant the opposing party time to comment on the new evidence and introduce counter-evidence into the record.[11] An example of factors that a tribunal must weigh when confronted with a late submission is summarised in the following statement by the chairman of an ICC arbitral tribunal:

> The arbitrators have a duty to take into account the fundamental right of each party to present its case properly, but they also have a duty to ensure that the arbitration progresses at a reasonable pace and to avoid unwarranted or deliberate delays. If a party which has had ample opportunity to prepare its case or to submit requests to the arbitral tribunal at an earlier stage of the proceedings, applies to a tribunal, belatedly and without giving legitimate reasons for its tardiness, with requests which are liable to cause substantial delays, it may well be the duty of the arbitrators to continue the arbitration without accepting the request of the tardy party.[12]

3.07 Where an arbitrator finds that the tardy submission of evidence will not cause serious delay to the procedure, or that the late submission would not prejudice the other party's ability to present its case, it may follow the traditionally liberal approach towards arbitral procedure and allow the submission of evidence after a deadline has passed.[13]

---

et al., Partial Award No. 323-409-1 of 2 November 1987, para. 63: "Facts and evidence . . . must be introduced in time, as specified by Orders of the Tribunal, to allow for a response by the other side." In some instances, tribunals have been known to adopt the position that only the occurrence of force majeure events will excuse a failure to observe a time frame agreed in the arbitration. See further: the procedural rule adopted by the tribunal in ICC Case No. 13225 concerning time limits: "In general the extension of time limits shall only be granted exceptionally and provided that a request is submitted immediately after the event preventing the Party from complying with the time limit, but in any event before the expiration of the latter. In particular, a time limit that has been jointly agreed by the parties and the Sole Arbitrator shall be extended only in extraordinary circumstances. Unless a party shows proof that it has been prevented to comply with the time limit by events outside of its control, the Sole Arbitrator may, but is not bound to, disregard a belated notification." ICC Case No. 13225, Procedure Order of 8 October 2004, *ICC Bulletin, 2010 Special Supplement: Decisions on ICC Arbitration Procedure*, p. 94.

11 See the observation of an *ad hoc* tribunal in connection with its decision to permit the late introduction of evidence of a contractual amendment: "We ultimately allowed in the amendment on the clear understanding, and on the basis that if in the course of our deliberations it seemed to us that the respondents were in any way prejudiced by the amendment, then we would give them a full opportunity to deal with the matter." *Continental Transfert Technique Ltd v The Federal Government of Nigeria (Ad hoc)*, Final Award, para. 54 (2008) (unpublished). See also: *United States of America v The Netherlands (The Island of Palmas Case)* (4 April 1928) 2 RIAA 842, whereby the sole arbitrator was compelled to note in the award that both sides had been given an opportunity to provide their views on evidence that was submitted late: "The possibility to make rejoinder to the Explanations furnished at the request of the Arbitrator on points contained in the Memoranda and Counter-Memoranda and the extension of the time-limits for filing a Rejoinder has put both Parties in a position to state – under fair conditions – their point of view in regard to that evidence which came forth only at a subsequent stage of the proceedings."

12 ICC Case No. 6465, 121 JDI Clunet 1088, pp. 1093–1095 (1994).

13 As an example of this approach, the following procedural order was issued in an ICSID arbitration: "The Tribunal is of the view that the sanction of non-acceptance of the Counter-Memorial would be in the circumstances excessive. Moreover, the Tribunal considers that it is not appropriate to exclude documents from consideration in the case solely on the ground that they have been filed no more than 10 days late. The Tribunal has been unable to identify significant, if any, harm suffered by the Claimant by reason of the delay in the filing of the translations." *Metalclad Corp v United Mexican States*, ICSID Case No. ARB(AF)/97/1, Decision by the Tribunal on a Request of the Claimant concerning the Filing of the Respondent's Counter-Memorial and its Annexes (31 March 1998), para. 4. See also: *Hooshang and Catherine Etezadi v The Islamic Republic of Iran*, Case No. 319, Award No. 554-319-1: Dissenting Opinion of Richard M. Mosk, p. 1 (23 March 1994): "I believe that the decision to exclude this evidence was incorrect. There was no showing that the admission of the evidence was prejudicial to Respondent. Indeed, Respondent was able to reply to the evidence. Generally in judicial and arbitral

3.08 Tribunals have also adopted creative solutions to the problem of evidence submitted after a deadline by, for example, receiving such evidence and placing it under seal, unread, until such time as the tribunal decides that there is a reason to consider its admission into the record.[14] Moreover, arbitrators have been receptive to documents belatedly submitted where it is shown that it was not possible to produce them beforehand.[15] Exceptions to deadlines are also made where the opposing party waives its right to object to the new evidence (see comments to article 9.2(g)).[16] These exceptions notwithstanding, as the Swiss Federal Tribunal ruled in regard to a recent challenge to a CAS award, "every party to an arbitration has a duty mirroring its burden of proof to contribute to the fact finding exercise in a timely manner in accordance with the applicable procedural rules."[17]

Customary filing deadlines

3.09 It is presumed in international arbitration that a party will file the bulk of its supporting documentary evidence simultaneously with the submission of the first substantial pleading in the matter. Quite often this first filing is referred to as the statement of claim or the statement of defence. This principle is explicitly stated in articles 20(4) and 21(2) of the UNCITRAL Rules (set forth above), and has in practice been used since the earliest days of international arbitration. Consider the following rule of procedure adopted in 1922 by the United States-German Mixed Claims Commission:

> A claim shall be treated as formally filed with the Commission upon there being presented to the Secretaries a memorial, petition or written statement containing a clear and concise statement of

---

proceedings, otherwise admissible and material evidence is not rejected on the basis of lack of timeliness unless there is such prejudice." See also: *Dunkeld International Investment Ltd v The Government of Belize*, PCA Case No. 2010-21/DUN-BZ II, Order No. 2, §8.3 (2011): "If any new and material evidence comes to the knowledge of a Party after the filing of its last written submission, or any new facts or issues arise since the date of a witness or expert's last signed statement, that Party shall address such evidence, facts or issues in its subsequent written submission. . . . If the Tribunal admits new evidence or additional witness or expert statements into the record, it shall grant the other Party an opportunity to submit the evidence or witness or expert statements in rebuttal." See also: *Glen Rauch Sec., Inc v Weinraub*, 768 N.Y.S. 2d 611, 611 (1st Dept. 2003) (affirming that "[t]he arbitrators properly sanctioned respondent for his failure to comply with their order directing the production of documents by precluding the testimony of a witness and the introduction of evidence to which the undisclosed documents related").

14 *Eastern Sugar BV (Netherlands) v Czech Republic*, UNCITRAL, SCC No 088/2004, Partial Award, WL 5366488, pp. 49–53 (2007): "On September 8, 2006, the Parties presented their Post-hearing briefs. Eastern Sugar attached a new factual document. The Arbitral Tribunal sealed this document unread."

15 *Ibid.*, p. 53. "The Order for Directions . . . had said that new documents may not be submitted after a deadline set well ahead of the hearing. However, a new document may be offered as a novum if that document could not have been reasonably presented earlier."

16 ICC Case No. 13133, Final Award, in Albert Jan van den Berg (ed.), *Yearbook Commercial Arbitration*, Vol. XXXV, pp. 137–138 (2010): "The Tribunal issued Procedural Order No. 10, fixing the hearing date. In view of the preparation of the Hearing, the Tribunal instructed the Parties that 'no new documents nor pleadings shall be accepted any more'. On the following day, Claimant submitted pleadings in the form of a letter and ten new documents (the post-expiry documents). It requested that the Tribunal disregard Respondent's letter addressed by the director general of the State X Entity to Claimant's chairman, submitted together with Respondent's Memorial . . . . With Procedural Order No. 11, the Tribunal rejected the post-expiry documents and declined Claimant's second request . . . . At the Hearing, the admissibility of Claimant's post-expiry documents was discussed as a preliminary issue. Respondent's Counsel declared that he was not opposed to their admission, upon which the Tribunal decided that these documents were admitted."

17 Mattias Scherer (ed.), "Introduction to the Case Law Section", in *ASA Bulletin*, Vol. 29, No. 1 (2011) commenting on Federal Tribunal decision 4A-279/2010 of 25 October 2010.

the facts upon which the claim is based . . . accompanied by copies of all documents and other proofs in support of such a claim then in the possession of the American Agent.[18]

3.10 This approach is helpful to both the tribunal, and the parties, as it allows the procedure to develop in accordance with the needs of the case and permits the arbitrators to identify the relevant issues early, in the context of the primary evidence.

Completion of the document production phase

3.11 The voluntary production of evidence by the parties in support of their respective arguments will in most cases be completed prior to an oral hearing.[19] Because written evidence and pleadings have such a central role in evidentiary procedure, tribunals will in most cases wish to review the relevant documents before presiding over oral witness hearings. This was explained by a panel of experienced arbitrators in the context of an UNCITRAL Rules arbitration:

> We are not, however, yet ready to decide upon the precise form of that evidential hearing. We need first to see the scope and nature of [Claimant's] evidential case; hence our decision above that [Claimant] must file more than a fresh pleading. After we have considered [Claimant]'s fresh pleading and accompanying evidential materials, it is our present intention to decide then how to proceed further. It may be that we can identify one or more threshold or other determinative issues on which limited testimony would be adduced at an early oral hearing.[20]

3.12 Following the initial production of evidence, a tribunal will often allow for further evidence to be introduced by a party in rebuttal to points raised in previous submissions.[21] In most cases, however, the submission of supplemental or rebuttal evidence will accompany the rebuttal and reply pleadings, with the intention that shortly thereafter the "document production" phase will be brought to an end before the hearing.[22] In conformity with

---

18 Sandifer, *supra* n. 3, para 3.01. This principle is set forth in the UNCITRAL Model Law at art. 23(1) See also: *Niko Resources (Bangladesh) Ltd v People's Republic of Bangladesh, Bangladesh Petroleum Exploration & Production Company Ltd and Bangladesh Oil Gas and Mineral Corporation*, ICSID Case Nos. ARB/10/11 and ARB/10/18, Procedural Order No. 4, §§13 and 14 (2014): "As directed by Procedural Order No. 3 all evidence on which a party relies must be submitted with its first submission. Reply submissions, therefore, may be accompanied only by evidence that is intended to respond to or rebut matters raised by the opposing party's immediate prior written submission. The Tribunals may refuse, at their discretion, any evidence that has not been filed with the Written Communication, except with prior express permission from the Tribunals in exceptions circumstances."

19 See: *Bear Creek Mining Corporation v Republic of Peru*, ICSID Case No. ARB/14/21, Procedural Order No. 1, §16.3. (2015): "Neither party shall be permitted to submit additional or responsive documents after the filing of its respective last written submission, save under exceptional circumstances at the discretion of the Tribunal upon a reasoned written request followed by observations from the other party." See also: *Standard Chartered Bank v United Republic of Tanzania*, ICSID Case No. ARB/10/12, Procedural Order Nos. 1, 8, and 10 (2011). See also: *Dunkeld International Investment Ltd v The Government of Belize*, PCA Case No. 2010-13/DUN-BZ, Order No. 7, §6 (2015): "Cut-off for Additional Evidence . . . Hereafter, additional documentary evidence will be admitted in extraordinary circumstances and upon a showing of good cause." See also: *British Caribbean Bank Ltd v The Government of Belize*, PCA Case No. 2010-28/BCB-BZ, Order No. 6 (2014), §6.2: "After [the cut-off date], additional documentary evidence will be admitted only in extraordinary circumstances and upon a showing of good cause."

20 *Methanex Corp v United States of America*, *supra* n. 7, First Partial Award, para. 168 (2002).

21 See: IBA Rules, art. 3.11.

22 *TCW Group Inc and Dominican Energy Holdings LP v The Dominican Republic*, CAFTA/UNCITRAL, Procedural Order No. 2, para. 5.3 (2008): "New Factual allegations or evidence shall not be permitted after the respective dates for the Rebuttal Memorials indicated in the above timetable unless agreed between the Parties or

this principle, tribunals often will impose a strict cut-off deadline prior to the oral hearing;[23] such as was ordered by a panel of ICC arbitrators in a matter seated in Abu Dhabi: "New briefs or documents shall not be admitted at the Main Hearing, save in exceptional circumstances as determined by the Arbitral Tribunal. In such circumstances, the other Party shall be afforded sufficient opportunity to study the document(s) and to make its observations thereon."[24]

Good faith and voluntary document production

3.13 Good faith requirements, such as are listed in paragraph 3 of the preamble to the IBA Rules, dictate that it would be improper for a party to an international arbitration to intentionally withhold evidence in order to gain a procedural advantage over an opponent, such as attempting to limit the amount of time that a party has to study new evidence before a hearing.[25] Where it is clear that a party has deliberately withheld evidence in order to gain a procedural advantage, a tribunal may take such actions into consideration when

---

expressly authorized by the Tribunal." See also: the following rule adopted by an ICDR tribunal: "Documentary evidence from a Party which has not been produced pursuant to a Request to Produce in agreement with [citing procedural orders], may not be submitted absent a showing of reasonable cause for the omission, as determined by the Arbitral Tribunal. No production of new documents shall be allowed or accepted during the Hearing." ICDR Case No. 50T180, Procedural Order No. 2, para. 18 (2002) (unpublished).

23 In *Zeevi Holdings v The Republic of Bulgaria et al.*, UNCITRAL Arbitration Case UNC 39/DK, the Tribunal issued Procedural Order No. 17, which excluded documents appended to Claimant's Post-Hearing Brief. *Inter alia*, the Tribunal stated that: "Procedural Order No. 16 expressly provided that 'no new documents' were admitted at this stage" and "[a]dmitting these new documents would give Claimant an unfair advantage in this procedure which could only be levelled by admitting Respondents to reply to these new documents and also be permitted to submit further documents in rebuttal, to which, in turn, Claimant would then have to be permitted to reply. This would re-open and prolong this already by now extremely long arbitral procedure even further. The Tribunal sees no justification for such a prolongation." *Ibid.*, p. 62, §61.

24 ICC Case No. 16249, Procedural Order No. 1 (unpublished). See also: an ICC arbitration where a party produced new evidence for the first time at the hearing. The tribunal ruled as follows: "For the majority of the arbitrators Claimant should not have waited until the end of the oral hearing, after nearly two years during which the Parties exchanged their Briefs, to present those documents, so that its adversary could not usefully explain itself on their meaning and their scope. Claimant which does not invoke any force majeure justifying that delay; is not entitled to produce the said documents at this stage of the proceedings." Dominique Hascher (ed.), *Collection of Procedural Decisions in ICC Arbitrations 1993–1996*, p. 42 (2nd edition, 1998).

25 One NAI arbitrator ruled in relation to the good faith obligations of the parties: "none of the parties should adjourn the production of evidence until a stage in the proceedings that its/their opponent(s) would not be in a position anymore to provide an adequate reply if necessary." NAI Case No. 3643, Procedural Order No. 2 (November 2010) (unpublished). See also: *Uiterwyk Corp et al. v The Islamic Republic of Iran et al.*, Partial Award No. 375-381-1 of 6 July 1988, para. 28. "Absent any convincing explanation by the Respondents, the Tribunal cannot accept a tactic that unveils previously existing evidence at literally the last movements of the hearing. Without prior notice having been given that the witness would testify, without showing that evidence is presented in rebuttal, and when the documents the witness proffered had not been included with – or even referred to in – the Respondent's various prior submissions. For procedural reasons the documents cannot therefore be accepted." See further: *Harris Telecom v Iran, supra* n. 10, para. 66: "In addition to examining the content of late-filed submissions, the Tribunal examines the reasons given which explain or excuse the late filing of documents . . . Even when no or little prejudice would result, the orderly conduct of the arbitral proceedings requires that deadlines be enforced, absent some explanation for the delay." See also: Amy C. Klasener, "*The Duty of Good Faith in the 2010 IBA Rules on the Taking of Evidence in International Arbitration*", in International Arbitration Law Review, Vol. 13, No. 5, p. 162 (2010): the author lists "failing to produce all documents on which a party relies with the intent to sand-bag or surprise parties or witnesses with documents" as a possible violation of good faith under the IBA rules.

awarding costs or may determine to exclude the evidence if submitted after a deadline. (See comments to article 9.7.)[26]

No duty to voluntarily disclose adverse evidence

3.14 Article 3.1 affirms the commonly held position that a party is only required to voluntarily produce, of its own initiative, those documents on which it relies. Failure to voluntarily (e.g., without an order from the tribunal) disclose evidence adverse to a party's position is not a violation of the IBA Rules, or generally accepted international arbitration procedure.[27] Challenges to a final award brought by parties who have discovered that help-ful evidence in the possession of the adverse party had not been voluntarily disclosed to the arbitrator, have rarely, if ever, succeeded.[28] The following quotation from an English Court reflects this view: "Under some agreed or standard procedures for disclosure (for instance the IBA Rules) disclosure is voluntary unless specific documents are either agreed or ordered to be disclosed."[29]

3.15 In sum, under the IBA Rules, and more generally in international arbitration, a party is only required to voluntarily disclose those documents that it intends to rely on. Such a rule, of course, does not excuse a party from its duty to respond truthfully to a doc-ument request or comply with an order for document disclosure (see comments to article 3.4).

A request for document disclosure

Article 3.2 2010 IBA Rules: **Within the time ordered by the Arbitral Tribunal, any Party may submit to the Arbitral Tribunal and to the other Parties a Request to Produce.**

---

26 See: *X.____ SA v Y.____ SPRL, 4A_16/2012*, a civil appeal from an International Chamber of Commerce (ICC) Award filed before the First Civil law Court of the Swiss Federal Tribunal. The Swiss Federal Tribunal held that although the Arbitral Tribunal allowed Claimant to file "extensive and new computations of damages" only 2 (two) days before the hearing on the merits, because Respondent failed to raise any objections to the little time to adequately analyze the documents, Respondent forfeited the right to raise the argument in the proceedings in front of the Federal Tribunal. The Swiss Federal Tribunal also stated that "a party acts contrary to good faith and in an abusive way in particular when it keeps the alleged violation in reserve only to put it forward if the case does not proceed well and a loss is foreseeable."

27 *L. Brown & Sons Ltd v Crosby Homes (North West) Ltd* [2008] EWHC 817, para. 36(ii). See also: the discussion by Coleman J of the differences between English discovery practice and the approach found in civil law countries, and in international arbitration whereby a party is only expected to produce those documents on which it intends to rely. *HZ & Co Ltd v Metzer*, High Court of England and Wales (QBD), Transcript, p. 9 (10 November 1993) (LexisNexis).

28 Speaking about ss. 1(c) and 16(a) of the Federal Arbitration Act, US District Court for New Jersey ruled in respect of an ICC Award: "under neither section will an arbitration award be vacated when a party's real complaint is the failure of the other side to present evidence favorable to its case . . ." *Biotronik Mess- und Therapie GmbH & Co v Medford Medical Instrument Co*, 415 F.Supp, p. 138 (D. N. J. 1976).

29 *L. Brown & Sons Ltd, supra* n. 27. See also the observations of another English court on the approach to disclosure under the IBA Rules, as compared to English practice: "In particular the rules for disclosure of docu-ments were based on the IBA Rules. There was no duty to disclose relevant documents, akin to CPR Part 31, such as would be the case with London arbitration conducted in accordance with English procedure. In these circum-stances, the court must be careful not to import into its assessment of GTT's conduct and the serious allegations of concealment made by CAT English law concepts of the duty of disclosure." *Chantiers de l'Atlantique SA v Gaztransport & Technigaz SAS* [2011] EWHC 3383 (Comm), para. 213.

General discussion

3.16 The inherent power of an international arbitral tribunal to order a party to disclose documents within its possession is generally accepted.[30] The well-known *Parker* case, an award of the US-Mexico General Claims Commission, affirmed this underlying rule in a decision whereby it was held that a party bore an "obligation to lay before the Commission all evidence within its possession to establish the truth, whatever it may be."[31] This decision provides authority for the rule that a party may be required to submit evidence adverse to its case. In modern times it is relatively uncontroversial that a tribunal is empowered to order the production of evidence, as this principle has been set forth expressly in most arbitral rules.[32] A tribunal may issue an order for the production of evidence on its own motion (see article 3.10), or following a request by one of the parties such as is contemplated by article 3.2.

Timing of a request for disclosure

3.17 As noted above with regard to article 3.1, it is the general practice in international arbitration that the parties will submit the bulk of their evidence in conjunction with their initial pleadings in the case, often called a statement of claim and/or defence. This custom

---

30 See: *Eli Lilly and Company v Government of Canada*, Case No. UNCT/14/2, Procedural Order No. 1, §12.1.a (2014): "Each Disputing Party may serve a request for production of documents on the other Disputing Party. Every request for production of documents shall precisely identify each document, or category of documents, sought and establish its relevance. Such a request shall not be copied to the Arbitral Tribunal or the Tribunal Secretary." See also: *Mesa Power Group LLC v Government of Canada*, PCA Case No. 2012-17, Procedural Order No. 1, §12.1 (2012): "At the request of a Party filed within the time limit specified by the Tribunal for this purpose, the Tribunal may order the other Party to disclose to the requesting Party documents or limited categories of documents within its possession, custody or control. Such a request for production shall identify each document or category of documents sought with a sufficient degree of precision and establish its relevance and materiality to the dispute. The Tribunal will, in its discretion, rule upon the disclosure of the documents or categories of documents having regard to the legitimate interests of the other Party and all of the surrounding circumstances."
31 *William A. Parker (United States of America) v United Mexican States*, (31 March 1926) 4 RIAA, p. 39. See also: ICC Case No. 5542, whereby a tribunal constituted under the 1975 ICC Rules noted that the power to order the disclosure of evidence was inherent to its general power to 'establish the facts of the case': "Now, while the ICC Rules do not contain any provision dealing with 'discovery' properly speaking, it is enough to recall here that according to art. 4, para. 1, 'the arbitrator shall proceed within as short a time as possible' to 'establish the facts of the case' by all appropriate measures. This provision allows the arbitrators to ask the parties to produce the documents in their possession or control, which in their view are relevant to the case." ICC Case No. 5542, Procedure Order, Dominique Hascher (ed.) *Collection of Procedural Decisions in ICC Arbitration 1993–1996*, pp. 64–65 (2nd edition, 1998). See further: the position adopted by the Iran-US Claims Tribunal citing its general power under art. 24.3 of the Tribunal Rules (similar to art. 24(3) of UNCITRAL Rules) to order disclosure: "Noting Respondent National Iranian Oil Company's comments concerning its difficulties in gaining access to certain documents, the Tribunal wishes to point out that it could require either party to produce documents, if it deems this necessary, in accordance with art. 24 para. 3 of the Tribunal Rules." *The Ministry of National Defence of the Islamic Republic of Iran v The Department of Defense of the United States of America*, Order of 18 Nov 1983, Iran-USCTR, Vol. 4, p. 58 (1983-III). See also: *William Ralph Clayton, William Richard Clayton, Douglas Clayton, Daniel Clayton and Bilcon of Delaware Inc v Government of Canada*, Arbitration under Chapter Eleven of the North American Free Trade Agreement and the UNCITRAL Arbitration Rules, Procedural Order No. 3, §3.8 (2009): "Tribunal's competence to request document production. Pursuant to Article 23(3) of the UNCITRAL Rules, the Tribunal remains competent, at all times, to require the Disputing Parties to produce documents, exhibits or other evidence within such a period of time as the Tribunal shall determine."
32 See, for example: art. 25(5), 2017 ICC Rules; art. 27(e), 2010 UNCITRAL Arbitration Rules; art. 20(4), 2014 ICDR International Arbitration Rules; art. 22.1(v), 2014 LCIA Arbitration Rules; art. 31(3), 2017 SCC Arbitration Rules; art. 29(1), 2018 VIAC Rules of Arbitration; art. 7.4.1., 2012 CAM/CCBC Arbitration Rules.

is responsible for another procedural presumption in international arbitration; namely, that a request for document production should be submitted after the filing of these statements, and the submission of the primary evidence.[33] An explanation as to why this approach is preferred over scheduling document production earlier in the procedure (as would be consistent with the procedure before US domestic courts) was given by an ICSID tribunal in the *Noble Ventures Inc v Romania* case:

> [T]he Tribunal finds that at a time when only the short Request for Arbitration Proceedings submitted by Claimant [is on the record] the Tribunal is not in a position to identify, within the many and broad requests submitted by Claimant, which documents must be considered relevant and material for the Tribunal to decide on the relief sought.[34]

3.18 A tribunal must, in most cases, be allowed to understand the relevant issues before it can determine what disclosure requests are to be considered relevant to the case and material to its outcome (see discussion on IBA Rules, article 3.7).[35]

3.19 The customary timing of the disclosure phase may also be adopted as a means of avoiding duplication in the production of evidence. Usually a party is allowed the opportunity to produce those documents on which they intend to rely before they are ordered to disclose evidence. Quite often a party will voluntarily produce a majority of the relevant documents with its first substantive pleading, and thus ordering disclosure ahead of this stage would likely lead to inefficiency and duplicative effort.[36] Thus, as the rule articulated

---

33 This custom has developed as a general rule of international adjudication. In the WTO Panel decision *Argentina – Textiles and Apparel*, the tribunal ruled, "the most important result of the rule of collaboration appears to be that the adversary is obliged to provide the tribunal with relevant documents which are in its sole possession. This obligation does not arise until the claimant has done its best to secure evidence and has actually produced some prima facie evidence in support of its case. It should be stressed, however, that 'discovery' of documents, in its common-law system sense, is not available in international procedures." *Argentina – Measures Affecting Imports of Footwear, Textiles, Apparel and Other Items Report of the Panel*, at WT/DS56/R, p. 92 (24 November 1997). See also the comments of one ICSID tribunal on this issue, which noted in response to an application for document disclosure at the outset of the arbitration: "The Tribunal would have been in a better position to deal with the applications covered by the present Decision had it already been in possession of the formal lines of argument adopted by both Parties. The Tribunal, like any other arbitral tribunal in a similar position, could not allow its process to be used as the cover for a mere fishing expedition launched in the hope of uncovering material to serve as the foundation for an argument (preliminary or substantive) not yet formally advanced before it." *Libananco Holdings Co Ltd v Republic of Turkey*, ICSID Case No. ARB/06/8, Decision on Preliminary Issues, p. 31(23 June 2008). See also: Gary B. Born, *International Commercial Arbitration*, p. 1900 (2009): "Tribunals typically provide for document disclosure at the earliest time following the parties' elaboration of their respective claims and defenses. This often will occur after the filing of the 'statement of claim' and 'statement of defense', which allows disclosure to proceed on the basis of the parties' cases . . ."

34 *Noble Ventures Inc v Romania*, ICSID Case No. ARB/01/11, Final Award, p. 32 (12 October 2005). See also: the ruling in *Ronald S. Lauder v The Czech Republic*, UNCITRAL, Final Award, para. 19 (3 September 2001): "the Arbitral Tribunal issued procedural order no 4 rejecting the Claimant's request for production of further documents on the ground that it first needed to receive Claimant's Memorial and Respondent's Response."

35 See: *Glamis Gold Ltd v United States of America*, NAFTA/UNCITRAL/ICSID, Decision on Objections to Document Production, para. 25 (20 July 2005): "The Tribunal concludes that it is at a minimum premature to ask for post-July 2003 documents until the public record has been reviewed. The Tribunal therefore denies the Claimant's request with leave to renew the request. The Tribunal is also not disposed at present to regard the documents requested as material. In any renewal of this request, the Claimant should articulate as fully as possible the likely materiality of the documents requested." See also the following observation of the tribunal in ICC Case No. 11258, Procedural Order No. 4 (unpublished): "It is self-evident that the need for a document may become apparent only after the other party's principle submission."

36 *Europe Cement Investment & Trade SA v Republic of Turkey*, ICSID Case No. ARB(AF)/07/2, Final Award, para. 19 (13 August 2009): "The Tribunal also placed in abeyance the Respondent's request for the production of documents, pointing out that the question of ownership by the Claimant of an investment or investments in

in article 3.2 is applied in practice, the "time ordered by the Arbitral Tribunal" for the filing of a document production request often occurs after the filing of a statement of claim and statement of defence.[37]

Conducting document disclosure without the tribunal's involvement

3.20 Another practice often adopted in international arbitration is for the tribunal to order the parties to exchange requests for document production and objections directly with each other, without involvement by the arbitrators.[38] Such a practice relies upon the professionalism of counsel to the parties, and exerts natural pressure on the parties to act with reasonableness when working out these issues. Many times, a party will be reluctant to bring a matter to a tribunal unless it is a *bona fide* dispute that cannot be resolved. Only those document production issues that cannot be resolved through compromise between the parties are referred to the tribunal for a decision.

Do parties have a right to limited document disclosure?

3.21 Most arbitration laws will ascribe to the tribunal the power to order the disclosure of evidence either implicitly or directly.[39] Insofar as these provisions refer to a tribunal's right to order document disclosure, they are rules that empower a tribunal but do not impose the requirement that it must order disclosure. The same may be said of arbitration

---

Turkey, which was the subject of the request for the production of documents, was a matter that in the normal course of events would have to be established in the Claimant's Memorial. The Tribunal further noted that the Claimant was aware of the documents that the Respondent expects to see produced and presumably will take account of this in the production of evidence in support of its Memorial."

37 This is not to say that variations on this approach do not occur. As an example, some tribunals order staggered phases of disclosure, whereby the respondent is allowed to submit disclosure requests following claimant's filing of a statement of claim, and vice-versa. In some investor-state arbitrations the document disclosure phase has taken place in a different order from what is described above, in particular as it relates to the jurisdictional phase of the proceedings. This being said, the "narrow and specific" criterion, as will be explained further below, relates primarily to whether a request for document disclosure is sufficiently connected to the relevant subject matter and time lines of the case. Whether a document request meets this standard would be often difficult for a tribunal to assess if a request was submitted at a stage when only skeletal outlines of a case have been pled. As an ICC arbitral tribunal ruled regarding an early request for production, "The Arbitral Tribunal, at the present stage, is not convinced of the relevance of the requested documents for the decisions to be made in the framework of this arbitration." See: Virginia Hamilton, "Document Production in ICC Arbitration", in *ICC Bulletin, 2006 Special Supplement: Document Production in International Arbitration*, p. 70.

38 An example of such a rule may be taken from ICC Case No. 16249, Procedural Order No. 1: "Any request by a party for the production of documents which are in the other party's possession, custody or within its control shall first be addressed to such other Party. Such request must describe with sufficient precision why a document or other information sought is deemed to be relevant by the requesting party." See also: *Biwater Gauff (Tanzania) Ltd v United Republic of Tanzania*, ICSID Case No. ARB/05/22, Procedural Order No. 2 (2006). In *L. Brown v Crosby Homes, supra* n. 27, para. 3.14, concerning the conduct of the document disclosure phase during an LCIA Arbitration the court stated: "Disclosure was left to be on a basis of co-operation and liaison between the parties and the order stated: 'Both parties seek disclosure of documents by the other. For that purpose the parties are to make written application to the other and co-operate with one another.'"

39 As an example, the Netherlands Arbitration Act, art. 1039, para. 4 states simply: "The arbitral tribunal shall have the power to order the production of documents." Emmanuel Gaillard and John Savage (eds), *Fouchard Gaillard Goldman on International Commercial Arbitration*, s. 956 (1999), citing to art. 1460 of the French New Code of Civil Procedure state: "if a party is in possession of an item of evidence, the arbitrator may . . . order that party to produce it. . . . This provision could provide the basis for requests for disclosure of documents modeled on common law discovery procedures."

rules from the prominent arbitral institutions, such as the ICC, SCC, LCIA, and the UNCI-TRAL Rules, amongst others, which often directly empower a tribunal to order disclosure, but impose no requirement that it do so.[40]

3.22 It has been argued in the past that the right to be heard and to equal treatment implies a right to receive adverse document disclosure, in particular, if an opposing party has benefited from such an order.[41] However, with regard to the *lex arbitri* of civil law countries, the right to be heard, or the "right to a contradictory proceeding", generally does not include a guarantee that a party will be afforded adverse document disclosure.[42] This is unsurprising since document discovery is not a significant feature of court procedures in those countries.[43]

3.23 In common law jurisdictions such as the United States, there has developed significant case law recognising that discovery, or document disclosure, need not be granted by arbitrators in order for due process to be observed.[44] This view has prevailed based upon

---

40 For example the LCIA Rules state that an arbitrator shall have the power to: "order any party to produce to the Arbitral Tribunal, and to the other parties for inspection, and to supply copies of, any documents or classes of documents in their possession, custody or power which the Arbitral Tribunal determines to be relevant." LCIA Rules, art. 22(v).

41 See the discussion of equality and document production in the comments to art. 9.2(g). See also: *Victor Pey Casado and Foundation "Presidente Allende" v Republic of Chile*, Decision on the Application for Annulment of the Republic of Chile, ICSID Case No. ARB/92/2 (2012). In *Victor Pey Casado and Foundation "Presidente Allende" v Republic of Chile*, the Committee rejected an Application for Annulment, based, *inter alia*, in the Arbitral Tribunal's denial of all discovery requests made by Chile. *Ibid.*, §320. The Committee agreed with Chile that "there is a departure from the right to be heard, which is a fundamental rule of procedure, when a party is not given a full, fair, or comparatively equal opportunity to state its case, present its defense, or produce evidence regarding every claim and issue at every stage of the arbitral proceeding." *Ibid.*, §184. However, the Committee found that "[w]hile it is true that the Respondent [Chile] had to produce a large number of documents (2630 documents) as opposed to the Claimants who were not asked to produce any, this inequality in numbers does not imply an unequal treatment by the Tribunal. In order to make a determination, one has to look at the way the Tribunal treated the requests." *Ibid.*, §325. In rejecting the Application for Annulment, the Committee held that it "is not convinced that had the [Arbitral] Tribunal proceeded differently it could have reached a result substantially different. First, even if the Tribunal had motivated its decision to deny Chile's request, there is no reason to conclude that it would have granted it. Second, the Committee does not find that the Tribunal used the absence of evidence on the issues dealt with in Chile's denied evidentiary requests to conclude that Mr. Pey Casado was the owner of the CPP shares. . . . . In the circumstances, the Respondent's request based on this ground is denied." *Ibid.*, §§331 and 332.

42 Fouchard, *supra* n. 39, para 3.21 refers to the decision from the Paris Court of Appeal, in which it was offered: "However, the decision of the arbitral tribunal to order discovery is within its procedural discretion and cannot be reviewed by the Courts." Paris, 22 January 2004 court of appeal, 1st Chamber *Nafimco v Foster Wheeler*. For the Swiss approach see: *Ruckersicherung-Gesellschaft X v Versicherungs- Gesellschaft Y* (27 March 2006) 4p. 23/2006 in *ASA Bulletin*, Vol. 25, No. 3, p. 528. In that case the Swiss Federal Tribunal ruled that "arbitral tribunals are not obliged to admit further requests for evidence if they conclude by means of an anticipatory assessment of the evidence that the new evidence is not relevant or not properly offered." See also the decision by the Swiss Federal Tribunal of 20 September 2005, where: "The dismissal or requests for production of documents and the refusal to hear witnesses, even if contrary to an earlier procedural order made by the tribunal, were held not to violate a claimant's right to be heard where the arbitral tribunal had concluded that the parties had already established all the facts necessary for it to make its decision regarding jurisdiction." Summary and translation by Georg von Segesser, "20 September 2005 – Swiss Supreme Court, 1st Chamber", in *A Contribution by the ITA Board of Reporters*.

43 See: "As with most continental systems, discovery and similar forms of disclosure are an unknown phenomenon under Dutch law. Although, it is generally accepted that any form of disclosure can be introduced in NAI Arbitrations . . ." Bommel van der Bend *et al.* (eds) *A Guide to the NAI Rules*, p. 140 (2009).

44 See: *Abu Dhabi Inv. Auth. v Citigroup, Inc* (S.D.N.Y. 4 March 2013), aff'd, 557 F. App'x 66 (2d Cir. 2014). The Court considered objections raised over the level of document disclosure that was permitted but noted: "[t]he parties engaged in substantial discovery prior to the ultimate hearing. Citigroup produced over 550,000 pages of documents from thirty-two custodians, including some of Citi's highest executives, such as

the general recognition that procedures common in US court proceedings are not to be transposed onto international arbitration.[45] Where a tribunal has considered the probative value of a request and decided against the production of evidence, such a decision will rarely be successfully challenged.[46]

3.24 The position of various arbitration laws notwithstanding, it is generally accepted in international arbitration practice that a party is not guaranteed a right to obtain adverse document disclosure. The following quote taken from the decision of an ICSID annulment committee succinctly sums up the status of the law:

> The Committee finds that the fundamental rules of procedure referred to above do not require any particular regime of discovery or disclosure to be applied by a tribunal, and do not confer any particular right on a party to compel the production of evidence by the opposing party. The extent to which the tribunal does call upon one party to produce documents at the request of another party will always be a matter for the tribunal to determine in its discretion.[47]

3.25 With respect to the procedural right to "equal treatment", it has long been accepted that it does not require that each party should receive the same degree of adverse document disclosure, as long as each side receives an equal opportunity to petition for document disclosure and the same standard is applied to all (see comments to article 9.2(g)).[48] However,

---

its then Chief Executive Officer, Chief Financial Officer, and several other officers and directors." *Ibid.*, at §3. Notwithstanding, Abu Dhabi ("ADIA") argued "that the tribunal's denial of two of its almost sixty document requests left it unable to present its case and warrants vacating the award." *Ibid.* The Motion to Vacate was ultimately denied because, *inter alia*, the lack of support for the position that denying an opportunity to obtain wider discovery deprived a party of the chance to be heard. "ADIA cites no federal case – and this Court could find none – where a court vacated an arbitral award because the panel denied one party a document request." *Ibid.*, §9. In a 2008 decision by the state Court of Appeals for Illinois where it was observed that a decision to deny a party US-style discovery was correct because to do otherwise would allow it to gain (albeit circuitously) an unfair advantage over its opponents who were subject to the "strict discovery rulings" on the ICC tribunal. The court noted: "In this case if the circuit court permitted discovery in the declaratory judgment action prior to the resolution of the underlying Action [ICC Arbitration] . . . plaintiffs would be allowed to circumvent the discovery ruling made in the [ICC Arbitration]. This result unfairly would benefit the dual role Reinsurers participating both as plaintiffs in this case and as Underlying Claimants." *Certain Underwriters at Lloyd's London et al. v Boeing Co et al.*, 385 Ill. App. 3d 23, p. 49 (Ill. App. Ct 1st Dist. 2008). See also: *Karaha Bodas Co LLC v Perusahaan Pertambangan Minyak dan Gas Bumi Negara et al.*, 364 F.3d 274, p. 302 (US App. 5th Cir 2004), "The record shows that the Tribunal's refusal to grant a continuance and additional pre-hearing discovery did not 'so affect the rights of Petamina that it may be said that [it] was deprived of a fair hearing'." Here the court (p. 300) relied on the recognised rule, "Every failure of an arbitration to receive relevant evidence does not constitute misconduct . . ." See also: *Iron One Co of Canada v Argonaut Shipping* 1985 US Dist Lexis 15572 (SDNY September 1985).

45 See: *Century Indemnity Co v Certain Underwriters at Lloyd's, London*, 584 F.3d 513, p. 559: "Certainly it is clear that in making evidentiary determinations, an arbitrator need not follow all of the niceties observed in federal courts." In relation to domestic arbitration procedure and discovery, the United States Court of Appeals for the Fourth Circuit opined that, "When contracting parties stipulate that disputes will be submitted to arbitration, they relinquish the right to certain procedural niceties which are normally association with a formal trial. One of those accoutrements is the right to pre-trial discovery. While an arbitration panel may subpoena documents or witnesses, the litigation parties have no comparable privilege." *Barton v Bush*, 614 F.2d, p. 389, 390 (4th Cir. 1980), also discussed in Born, *supra* n. 33, pp. 1906–1907.

46 *Petroleum Transport Ltd v Yacimientos Petroliferos Fiscales*, 419 F.Supp 1233 (SDNY 1976).

47 *Azurix Corp v Argentine Republic*, ICSID Case No. ARB/01/02, Decision on the Application for Annulment of the Argentine Republic, para. 217 (2009).

48 *Ibid.*, para. 233, "the Committee observes that the fact that a request by one party is allowed while a request by another party is denied does not mean that there has been an inequality in the treatment of the parties. Each Request by each party must be considered and determined by the tribunal on its own individual merits. It is only where it can be shown that a tribunal has applied inconsistent standards in the way that it has treated the requests

where a tribunal repeatedly orders disclosure on behalf of one party, but routinely denies it to the other without explanation, questions of bias or unequal treatment may arise.[49]

Standards applicable to a request for document disclosure

Article 3.3 2010 IBA Rules: **A Request to Produce shall contain:**

(a) (i) a description of each requested Document sufficient to identify it, or

(ii) a description in sufficient detail (including subject matter) of a narrow and specific requested category of Documents that are reasonably believed to exist; in the case of Documents maintained in electronic form, the requesting Party may, or the Arbitral Tribunal may order that it shall be required to, identify specific files, search terms, individuals or other means of searching for such Documents in an efficient and economical manner;

(b) a statement as to how the Documents requested are relevant to the case and material to its outcome; and

(c) (i) a statement that the Documents requested are not in the possession, custody or control of the requesting Party or a statement of the reasons why it would be unreasonably burdensome for the requesting Party to produce such Documents, and

(ii) a statement of the reasons why the requesting Party assumes the Documents requested are in the possession, custody or control of another Party.

---

of the different parties that there can be said to be inequality of treatment." See also: the decision of the LCIA Court on a challenge to the arbitrator based on his decision to order document disclosure without first receiving and reviewing the opposing party's position. The disclosure of documents was requested and ultimately ordered pursuant to the IBA Rules. The LCIA Court noted that the arbitrator's failure to consider one side's argument resulted from a mishap in communication. This was not evidence of a failure a treat the parties equally: "However, the question for the Division was whether this procedural mishap justified the removal of the arbitrator under article 10 of the LCIA Rules. The Division stated that it was clear from the facts that (i) the arbitrator would have made the same order if he had in fact previously considered the Respondent's application, and (ii) the arbitrator had confirmed his order after seeing and considering the Respondent's application. It was also clear to the Division that the mishap had caused the Respondent no permanent harm or other irremediable prejudice." "Parties Not Indicated, LCIA Court Decision on Challenge to Arbitrator, LCIA Reference No. 7932, 17 June 2008" in William W. Park (ed), *Arbitration International Special Edition on Arbitrator Challenges*, pp. 433–438 (Kluwer Law International, 2011).

49 *ABB AG v Hochtief Airport GmbH* [2006] EWHC 388 (Comm), para. 87: "Whilst the court will never dictate to arbitrators how their conclusions should be expressed, it must be obvious that the giving of clearly expressed reasons responsive to the issues as they were debated before the arbitrators will reduce the scope for the making of unmeritorious challenges as this ultimately has proved to be. It will be of little comfort to ABB but it may be instructive to know that at the end of my pre-reading in this case I was fairly certain that I would have no alternative but to remit or to set aside the award, notwithstanding the court's general approach to strive to uphold arbitration awards . . . Reasons which were a little less compressed at the essential points might have been more transparent as to their meaning and might even have dissuaded the unsuccessful party from challenging the award or, at any rate, from mounting so wide-ranging a challenge."

Other Statements of the Rule

Article 4.4 1983 IBA Rules: A party may by Notice to Produce a Document request any other party to provide him with any document relevant to the dispute between the parties and not listed, provided such document is identified with reasonable particularity and provided further that it passed to or from such other party from or to a third party who is not a party to the arbitration. If a party refuses to comply with a Notice to Produce a Document he may be ordered to do so by the Arbitrator.

General discussion

3.26 As document disclosure has become more common in international arbitration, there has developed a "formula" or checklist of requirements that a request for production must meet.[50] Article 3.3 refers to those general requirements in a succinct fashion in five subparagraphs, (a)(i) to (c)(ii). In summary, these five conditions require a requesting party to:

(1) sufficiently describe the document;
(2) if a category of documents is requested, then provide a "narrow and specific" description of the category;
(3) provide a reasoned explanation as to why they are "relevant to the case" and "material to its outcome";
(4) confirm that the documents are not in its control; and
(5) explain why the documents are assumed to be in the control of the other party.

3.27 Article 3.3 in the 2010 Rules, expands upon the formula adopted by the 1999 Rules, which was itself a departure from the approach originally set forth in the 1983 version.[51]

---

50 See the procedural rule adopted by a tribunal under the UNCITRAL Rules which reflects general considerations similar to that of art. 3.3: "If any of the parties refuses to produce documents upon a simple request by the other party (which need not be copied to the Arbitral Tribunal), the Arbitral Tribunal shall be entitled, upon specific and precise request of one of the parties, to order the parties to produce document(s) in their possession or under their control", as quoted in: Matthias Scherer, "The Limits of the IBA Rules on the Taking of Evidence in International Arbitration: Document Production based on Contractual or Statutory Rights", *International Arbitration Law Review*, Vol. 13, No. 5, p. 198 (2010). See also a similar recitation of criteria by a tribunal in *Aguas del Tunari SA v Republic of Bolivia*, ICSID Case No. ARB/02/3, Procedural Order No. 1 (2003), as reported in Born, *supra* n. 33, p. 1907: "The Tribunal bears in mind a number of considerations in evaluating whether or not to order the production of evidence. These considerations include: the necessity of the requests made to the point the requesting party wishes to support, the relevance and likely merit of the point the requesting party seeks to support, the cost and burden of the request on the Claimant and the question of how the request may be specified so as to fulfil legitimate requests by a party while not allowing inquiries that are an abuse of process." See also: Bernard Hanotiau, "Document Production in International Arbitration: A Tentative Definition of 'Best Practices' in T. Giovannini and A. Mourre (eds), *Dossier VI: Written Evidence and Discovery in International Arbitration*, p. 358 (2009): "The request must establish the relevance and materiality of each document or specific category of documents sought in such a way that the other party and the arbitral tribunal are able to refer to factual allegations in the submissions filed by the parties to date. This shall not prevent a party from referring to upcoming factual allegations in subsequent memorials, provided such factual allegations are made or at least summarised in the document production request. In other words, the requesting party must make it clear with reasonable particularity what facts or allegations each document or category of documents sought is intended to establish."

51 See: quoted rules at the top of this section.

The new article 3.3 in 2010 is remarkable because it specifically addresses electronic documents and provides an exception to the general rule that a party may not seek a document from another party if the document is within its own custody or control. These two additional issues are discussed later in this section. The standards set forth in article 3.3 are discussed below, with the exception of the materiality and relevance criteria, which is discussed in the comments to article 3.7.

Ethical considerations for counsel

3.28 The IBA Guidelines take the position that a "Party Representative should not make any Request to Produce, or any objection to a Request to Produce, for an improper purpose, such as to harass or cause unnecessary delay."[52] The approach is of course sensible and aligned with the general goals of preserving the integrity of the process while controlling time and costs. The Comments to Guidelines 12–17 further clarify that in addition to requests aimed at harassing or causing unnecessary delay, a Party representative should not make a Request to Produce or object to one "for purposes extraneous to the arbitration."[53]

Disclosure in arbitration versus US-style discovery

3.29 The drafters of the 1999 Rules stated that their intention was not to create an Anglo-American-style system of document production for international arbitration.[54] This disclaimer was necessary because of the legitimate concern that by permitting the production of "categories of documents", the door to Anglo-American-style document discovery would be opened. However, practice has shown that under the standard of article 3.3, categories of documents may be produced without it leading to general discovery.

3.30 The approach in arbitration to disclosure in comparison with Anglo-American practice has been variously described as "conservative", or as a procedure aimed at "filling in the gaps" as opposed to building up the factual record.[55] Perhaps one of the most helpful elucidations of this issue comes from the English case *BNP Paribas v Deloitte Touche LLP*, where the difference between discovery and limited disclosure was discussed in relation to an LCIA arbitration: "there is an important distinction between requiring documents to

---

52 See: IBA Guideline 13: "A Party Representative should not make any Request to Produce, or any objection to a Request to Produce, for an improper purpose, such as to harass or cause unnecessary delay."

53 See: Comments to Guidelines 12–17: "Finally, a Party Representative should not make a Request to Produce, or object to a Request to Produce, when such request or objection is only aimed at harassing, obtaining documents for purposes extraneous to the arbitration, or causing unnecessary delay (Guideline 13)."

54 IBA Working Party, *Commentary on the New IBA Rules of Evidence in International Commercial Arbitration* [2000] BLI 2, p. 20 (2000).

55 See: Poudret and Besson, *supra* n. 1, para. 652, and Fouchard, *supra* n. 39, s. 1907. See also *Merrill & Ring Forestry LP v Canada*, an arbitration under the UNCITRAL Rules, in which the tribunal was confronted with a request by the Claimant to organise a document production phase at the start of the proceedings, prior to the filing of the statement of claim, and defence. After a short deliberation, the tribunal declined Claimant's request during the procedural hearing, and ordered that the disclosure phase take place after the filing of primary evidence by both sides with their respective statements. In its comments to the parties, the tribunal noted that document disclosure should be restricted to relevant evidence "still missing" from the record, which may be deemed necessary. Interestingly, in follow-up comments to the decision, the tribunal further noted that it was assumed by the tribunal that the claimant would have had the primary evidence at hand to substantiate its claim prior to filing the arbitration. *Merrill & Ring Forestry LP v Government of Canada*, NAFTA/UNCITRAL, Transcript of Procedural Meeting of 15 November 2007, pp. 209–213.

be produced as evidence of some fact . . . and asking for disclosure to trawl through documents to see if they support the applicant's case."[56] Disclosure in international arbitration adopts the former approach over the latter.

3.31 As noted under article 3.1 above, the presumption in arbitration is that a party will establish its case based largely (if not entirely) on the documents within its own possession. Thus, a wide-ranging discovery process that allows a party to substantiate a case by "discovering" the primary evidence to support its arguments is not compatible with this threshold concept. Indeed, it is more accurate to view disclosure under article 3.3 as a limited process aimed at filling gaps or providing assistance in covering important, but identifiable issues raised by the factual record, for which sufficient evidence has not been voluntarily supplied by the parties.[57]

The civil law view of disclosure in international arbitration

3.32 While article 3.3 does not contemplate a process like "discovery", as is practised in many common law jurisdictions, it also does not embody the restrictive view of document disclosure held by civil law jurisdictions either. Consider, for example, the following quote from a civil law jurist describing the approach to document production in a civil law context: "The request for production of documents must be specific. It should be directed at the production of *an* individual contract, of *a* particular letter, such as a letter mentioned in another letter already produced to the Court, or the like."[58] This view was reflected in article 4.4 of the 1983 version of the IBA Rules. The 1983

---

56 *BNP Paribas v Deloitte & Touche* [2003] EWHC 2874 (Comm), para. 6. Court of Appeal Commercial Court, Case No. 2003/946. In response to a request for assistance in obtaining discovery by a party to an ICC arbitration governed by the IBA Rules, a US federal district court noted the difference between the American practice of discovery and limited document production permitted by the IBA Rules. In particular, the court considered that broad discovery requests were inconsistent with the approach adopted in international arbitration: "turning to the nature and character of the foreign proceeding, applicants may complain that it has not succeeded in using the Tribunal as means to obtaining the information sought, but this objection bears little weight, as the applicants voluntarily entered into the arbitration, specifically including and agreeing to its limited discovery. As noted earlier, applicants specifically eschewed any desire for 'American-style discovery or productions of documents.' Accordingly, an award of substantial discovery would conflict with agreed-to rules for limited discovery in the proceedings before the Arbitral Tribunal." *Re Application by Rhodianyl SAS*, 2011 US Dist. Lexis 72918 (D. Kan.), p. 52 (25 March, 2011). See further the description of the difference between document production in international arbitration and Anglo-American discovery as articulated by one ICC tribunal seated in Switzerland and comprised of continental arbitrators: "The document requests contemplated . . . by the Terms of Reference are not intended as tools for US-Style discovery, that is, to be used by [a] party to seek documents which may or may not exist, and also may or may not ultimately prove relevant, all in order to weave a claim. The purpose of such document requests, rather is to obtain documents to prove specific factual allegations previously made by a party in its pleadings . . . Consistent with this purpose . . . document requests were to be made by the parties after the submission of their second written briefs, at which point the parties pleadings were to have contained all factual allegations . . . [A]t the point at which a party makes a document production request, it must essentially know which document, or category of documents, it needs." Hamilton, *supra* n. 37, p. 71.

57 The tribunal in the ICSID case *Caratube v Kazakhstan* discussed the balance which must be struck in relation to document production in arbitration: "The Tribunal further recognizes that, on one hand, ordering the production of documents can be helpful for a party to present its case and for the Tribunal to establish the facts relevant for the issues to be decided. But, on the other hand, the process of discovery and disclosure may be time-consuming, excessively burdensome and even oppressive. Unless carefully limited, the burden may even be disproportionate to the value of the result." *Caratube International Oil Co LLP v Republic of Kazakhstan*, ICSID Case No. ARB/08/12, Procedural Order No. 2, para. 1.5 (26 April 2010).

58 As quoted in: Stephen R. Bond, "The 1999 IBA Rules on Evidence in International Commercial Arbitration" in *Arbitral Procedure at the Dawn of the New Millennium*, p. 103 (2005).

Rules restricted document production to a single, identified document, and only to those documents which were shared with third parties (e.g., correspondence). Documents which were "internal" were off limits.

3.33 Article 4.4 of the 1983 Rules was replaced entirely by article 3.3 when the Rules were revised in 1999, indicating strongly that the older, stricter view of document production embodied by the 1983 Rules had been superseded by a broader approach.[59] Arbitral practice concerning disclosure, as affirmed by numerous decisions of well-qualified arbitrators, is more accurately expressed in the current article 3.3. Current practice permits parties to seek the production of whole categories of documents, including internal documents.[60]

3.34 Therefore, as the Anglo-American practice of "wide-ranging" discovery is not generally compatible with evidentiary procedure in international arbitration, neither is the civil law approach which is far more restrictive. Instead, the rule in international arbitration, as reflected by article 3.3, is that a party may seek, and a tribunal may order, the disclosure of multiple, relevant documents (both internal and external documents)[61] provided the request is specific and meets the other criteria of article 3.3.

Categories of documents: the "narrow and specific" standard

3.35 As was noted in the procedural order issued by a tribunal under the Swiss Rules of International Arbitration, "the IBA Rules provide a framework which aims at limiting production requests to what is considered acceptable in today's arbitration practice".[62] This purpose is accomplished by requiring that requests for document production meet the "narrow and specific" standard stated in article 3.3(a)(ii). The "narrow and specific" standard has generally been understood to apply to both the time-frame for a request for production,

---

59 See: *ibid.*, Bond, p. 102: "However, the 1983 Rules, containing the sharp restriction on document production described above, were soon disavowed by practice and experience. They were *too* oriented to the civil law approach and too unsuited to the ever-growing complexity of the cases and issues being submitted into international arbitration."

60 See: ICC Case No. 13133, *supra* n. 16, pp. 137–138, between Indian and Tunisian parties, with the seat of the arbitration in Paris, France where the tribunal ordered certain internal "banking documents" to be disclosed: "After having obtained Claimant's comments, the Tribunal issued Procedural Order No. 6 and ordered Claimant, on the basis of art. 20(5) of the ICC Rules, to submit certain categories of documents." See also: Born, *supra* n. 33, p. 1908, on the wide acceptance of the IBA Rules: "In practice, arbitral tribunals generally exercise their disclosure power consistently with the IBA Rules" and Bond, *supra* n. 58, p. 103: "Thus, it is submitted that the 1999 IBA Rules were not a great leap forward, but rather a highly desirable, generally accurate codification of actual document production practice as it had evolved in international arbitration." See further: Poudret and Besson, *supra* n. 1, s. 652: "It is possible to submit to the arbitrators a statement containing a number of specific requests each referring to standard commercial documents which every company will have (minutes of the board of directors, reports to the council of a foundation, or business plans), with the principle aim of discovering internal information."

61 See the official comments of the 1999 IBA Working Party which were adopted by the 2010 Review Subcommittee: "At the same time, however, it was believed that there is a general consensus, even among practitioners from civil law countries, that some level of document production is appropriate in international arbitration. According to some of the most frequently used general rules, arbitral tribunals are to establish the facts of the case 'by all appropriate means'. This includes the competence of the arbitral tribunal to order one party to introduce certain documents, including internal documents, into the arbitral proceedings upon request of the other party. Even in some civil law countries, a State court is entitled to order the production of internal documents, either upon request of one party or because it sees the need for these documents itself." *Commentary on the revised text of the 2010 IBA Rules on the Taking of Evidence in International Arbitration*, p. 7 (2010) available at www.ibanet.org.

62 Scherer (2010), *supra* n. 17, p. 196.

as well as subject matter, as was explained by an experienced tribunal: "In accordance with article 3.3(a) of the IBA Rules, the categories of documents to be produced shall be 'narrow and specific', which the Tribunal interprets to mean narrowly tailored, i.e., reasonably limited in time and subject matter in view of the nature of the claims and defenses advanced in the case."[63]

3.36 Thus, according to the formula articulated above, a request for production should seek the disclosure of documents that relate to well-defined issues in the arbitration,[64] not a general contention or broad description of a claim.[65] While arbitrators will not generally insist on parties providing the formal or proper name of a document, they may seek a description of the technical or commercial function of the record (e.g., business plan, or meeting minutes) or require the parties to indicate an author and possible recipient of the document. A request should further define the category of documents by providing a time frame that is tied to the relevant chronology of the case. Requests for disclosure which look to obtain "all documents" within a vague time frame, "relating" to a broad topic, will in most cases be judged by tribunals to be too broad or in violation of the "narrow and specific" standard.[66] This will be so even if the subject matter pursuant to which the documents

---

63 *International Thunderbird Gaming Corp (United States of America) v United Mexican States*, NAFTA/UNCITRAL, Procedural Order No. 2, p. 3 (2003). See also the adoption of the specificity standard by the Iran-US Claims Tribunal: "Failing any indication by the Claimant as to which documents precisely it wishes to be produced, and failing any information to the Tribunal as to which steps were taken by the Claimant itself to acquire the necessary materials, cannot, at present, make any Order as requested by the Claimant." *MCA Inc v The Islamic Republic of Iran*, Case No. 768, Chamber 2, Order of 6 October 1983, p. 2.

64 See: *Philip Morris Brand Sarl, Philip Morris Products SA and Abal Hermanos SA v Oriental Republic of Uruguay*, ICSID Case No. ARB/10/7, Procedural Order No. 3, §2.1 (2015): "The Tribunal recalls its invitation in Procedural Order No. 10 that 'the Parties [. . .] limit the requests that they will submit in their Redfern Schedules to those documents that are absolutely necessary for the limited purpose of dealing with the preliminary objections to be addressed at the Hearing on Preliminary Objections in February 2015.'"

65 Poudret and Besson, *supra* n. 1, s. 654. See the procedural order rendered in an ICC case discussing the specificity required under this standard: "The description 'assessing or relating to the assessment of [Company] X's equity' does not elicit the type of automatic understanding of the nature of the responsive document, or category of documents, sought, which a sufficiently detailed document request – indicating narrow parameters such as the authors, recipients, specific contents, and specific characteristics of the documents – would. Virtually any [Company X] document could be interpreted as 'relating' in some way to the assessment of its equity and, therefore, be covered by this document request." Hamilton, *supra* n. 37, p. 72. See also the comments of the ICSID tribunal in *Railroad Development Corp v Guatemala*, wherein it was noted when denying a request, that a party had used vague definitions and failed to place proper time frames in its petition: "The breadth of the Request is particularly compounded by the definition of the terms 'documents', 'communications' and 'relating to' which have also been reproduced. As broken down by the Respondent, the term 'documents' includes sixty types of documents, in most cases without time limits." *Railroad Development Corp v Republic of Guatemala*, ICSID Case No. ARB/07/23, Decision on Provisional Measures, para. 33 (15 October 2008). In the *Azurix v Argentina* case, the tribunal affirmed the basic principle that under the IBA Rules general requests for document disclosure are not adequate, by denying the request for production as follows: "because of its general nature and failure to justify it on the basis of the reasons adduced". As noted in the decision of the *ad hoc* tribunal in *Azurix v Argentina*, *supra* n. 47, para. 197.

66 *Ibid.*, *Railroad Development v Guatemala*: "The Tribunal considers that, in the instant case, it does not need the guidance of the IBA Rules to appreciate that the categories of documents requested and reproduced above are excessively broad and their relevance difficult to assess." See also: *Karaha Bodas v Perusahaan*, *supra* n. 44, where it is recorded that the tribunal sitting in Switzerland, under the UNCITRAL Rules denied several requests by the respondent which sought the disclosure of "all documents relating to . . ." a number of broadly defined claims, referring in some instances to nine-month periods of time, or in others, no time limitations were included in the request at all. See also: *Waste Management Inc v United Mexican States*, where an ICSID tribunal ruled that a request for all invoices issued over a period of two years was "prima facie" too burdensome. ICSID Case No. ARB(AF)/00/3, Final Award, para. 21 (30 April 2004). See also the following procedural direction in ICC Case No. 12279 seated in the United States: "The Parties are to consider a limited number of requests for

are sought is relevant, as the tribunal in the well-known *Biwater Gauff* arbitration held in relation to document production requests before it: "The Arbitral Tribunal considers that the requested documents may be relevant to the issues in dispute but on the other hand, that the request is overly broad, in particular to the extent that it covers all documents relating to the decision to create [the corporation], including reasons for the decision".[67] Therefore, broadly framed document requests that provide very little specification run the risk of being denied as prima facie non-compliant with article 3.3(a)(ii).[68]

3.37 On the other hand, as an example of a document request which was considered by a tribunal to meet the narrow and specific standard, the following quote from an ICSID arbitration is reproduced below:

> The Claimant requested the production of documents related to specific [third party] files related to the License, comprising 18 specifically described documents. The Claimant further requested the production of six further categories of documents related *inter alia* to [third party]. These categories were all defined either by dates or by specific file numbers of the [third party]. Further, the Claimant asked for the production of eleven specific documents identified by date and further description.[69]

3.38 Here, a tribunal positively received the request because dates, and a further description of the document, such as file numbers, functionality (e.g., meeting minutes from a certain date) and other characteristics, were given. A second example of a request which met the "narrow and specific" standard is reproduced below from an LCIA arbitration involving companies from civil law jurisdictions in which, after considerable debate over the issue of disclosure, the following request was deemed to be consistent with arbitral practice:

> Agendas, presentations, submissions, memos, reports and other documents (in particular reports prepared by Mr G, Mr and/or Mr H) which were produced for or circulated to members of V's Supervisory Board and/or Management Board and/or Board of Directors (in particular to any of Messrs M, H, G, de L, Gr or R, to the extent that these persons were members of the above-mentioned Boards) between 24th August and 10 September 2001 concerning: (i) V's position in T resulting from the contemplated conclusion of the TIA; (ii) the intended timing of filing by V for

---

production of documents of the opposing party which are directly relevant to a claim or defense. In considering the need for such document requests, the Parties shall bear in mind the requirements of an efficient and expeditious arbitration, which affords each party the opportunity to present its case. The parties shall have the right to object to improper requests, including requests which are overbroad 'fishing expeditions', or requests for which the burden of production outweighs the probative value of the information." ICC Case No. 12279, Procedural Order of 31 July 2003, *ICC Bulletin, 2010 Special Supplement: Decisions on ICC Arbitration Procedure*, p. 42.

67 *Biwater Gauff v Tanzania, supra* n. 38, Procedural Order No. 2.

68 As was noted by the *ad hoc* committee in the *Azurix* case a tribunal has wide discretion in this regard, but will in most cases give consideration to the precision used by a party to describe the documents which it seeks: "Argentina is correct when it argues that under the ICSID Arbitration Rules, a party is not required to make a request for evidence at any particular time, and is not required to tailor its requests for evidence to the points to which the evidence would be directed, and is not under an obligation to explain why the documents are relevant and material to the outcome of the case. However, matters such as the timing of the request for evidence, and whether the request is sufficiently precise in identifying that requested evidence and the reasons why it is needed, are matters that the tribunal is entitled to, and in practice no doubt normally will take into account in deciding how to exercise its discretion. It is not the case that a party has the right to demand any evidence any time without justification. Even where a request is timely, precise and justified, the tribunal may in its discretion reject the request." *Azurix v Argentina, supra* n. 47, Decision on the Application for Annulment of the Argentine Republic, para. 218.

69 *CME Czech Republic BV v The Czech Republic*, UNCITRAL, Partial Award, pp. 16, 17 (13 September 2001).

Governmental Approval required by the TIA; (iii) the intended timing of performance of V of its obligation to proceed with an IPO of T.[70]

3.39 As can be seen from the above, not only are precise time frames provided, which give guidance to the scope of the requested production, but also the names of individuals possibly associated with the documents, as well as the standard functional description and indication as to content of the document. These examples set forth the characteristics of a document request that will generally be found to be acceptable to international arbitrators, since it provides a means for the tribunal to judge whether the described documents meet the "narrow and specific" criteria. Finally, it should also be said that the volume of documents captured by a request is not necessarily an indication of whether a request does, or does not, meet the "narrow and specific" criteria. It is entirely possible that given the context of the dispute, a well-crafted request for the production of documents will encompass a large mass of documents. Document production of more than 18,000 pages was ordered by Swiss arbitrators in the past, as was over 150,000 pages by ICDR arbitrators sitting in New York.[71] In the setting of a high value dispute, such procedures may be necessary.

Narrow and specific: electronic documents

3.40 In 2010, the Review Subcommittee introduced a change which gave rise to considerable debate and academic treatment; namely, the issue of "electronic discovery" or "disclosure". Whether one accepts the need to give specific consideration to electronic

---

70 *Elektrim SA v Vivendi Universal SA* [2007] EWHC 11 (Comm), para. 32 (19 January 2007). See: International Chamber of Commerce, ICC Dispute Resolution Bulletin, 2016, Issue 1, p. 165. In ICC Case 18033, a Saudi Arabian Claimant entered into a memorandum of understanding with Respondent, a company incorporated by a group of companies X in Kuwait. Since the joint venture was allegedly never established, Claimant initiated arbitration in Switzerland against Respondent to recover the licence fee it had paid. The arbitration was bifurcated to allow the sole arbitrator first to address the jurisdictional and procedural objections raised by Respondent, and in this first phase, several procedural orders were issued dealing with evidence. The Sole Arbitrator "regarded the Terms of Reference, the 1998 ICC Arbitration Rules, the Swiss Private International Law Act (PILA) and the 2010 IBA Rules on the Taking of Evidence in International Arbitration, which he was authorized to use for guidance, but without being bound by them." Under these standards, the Sole Arbitrator in ICC Case 18033 found that: "Claimant's specific document requests for: (a) the Memorandum of Understanding (MoU) between [X Luxembourg] and [company Y] related to the [Respondent] executed on [date]; (b) Shareholders Agreement related to [Respondent] between [X Luxembourg] and [company Y] executed on [date]" were "clearly identified with a reasonable degree of specificity . . . [and] these two documents are referred to in other exhibits lodged by both Parties in these proceedings" and granted the requests. The Sole Arbitrator also granted Claimant's request for a "Copy of [Respondent]'s financial statements for 2008, 2009, 2010 and 2011, including P&L statements," because it found them to be "of some relevance in order to determine the involvement of these companies" and "reasonably identified in their years, which makes their production acceptable. However, Claimant's requests for "(c) Copy of any instruction given to Mr [A] withdrawing his signature powers for [Respondent] prior to the MoU dated [date], [and] (d) Any budgets, financial forecasts and/or financial data issued by [Respondent] in relation with [X Saudi Arabia]," were rejected because "Claimant has provided virtually no evidence that the various internal documents requested exist" and they do "no seem to be relevant to the jurisdictional matter at hand, but rather go[] to the issue of liabilities for breach of contract pertaining to the merits of the case."

71 See: *Mofet Etzion Ltd v General Dynamics Land Systems Inc*, US Dist Ct, Lexis 11362 (SDNY February 2008). It is also reported that during an arbitration seated in Switzerland and involving hundreds of millions of US dollars in claims, the arbitrators issued an order that resulted in 18,000 pages of documents being disclosed to one of the parties. W. Laurence Craig, William W. Park, Jan Paulsson, *International Chamber of Commerce Arbitration*, p. 450, fn. 4 (3rd edition, 2000).

discovery in international arbitration procedural rules or not, the Review Subcommittee deemed it necessary to address this issue in article 3.3. The following discussion considers the general application of the "narrow and specific" rule to electronic disclosure.[72]

3.41 While by no means directly applicable in international arbitration, US jurisprudence on electronic discovery has given rise to a recognised set of five categories of electronic data which are useful to evaluate requests encompassing electronic disclosure. Those categories are:

(1) "active on-line data" (e.g., computer hard drives);
(2) "near-line data", which is readily accessible but is stored off-line;
(3) "off-line storage archives", stored on disks which are not easily and readily accessible;
(4) "back-up tapes" that have not been organised for easy search;
(5) "erased or fragmented data" which is, as one can imagine, a reference to data for which a significant, and targeted search will have to be undertaken, and for which information technology expertise in particular will be required.[73]

3.42 The question as to which of the above categories fall within "limited in time and subject matter" depends again on the nature of the claims involved. For those disputes which arise contemporaneously with or shortly after a project is completed, for example, it would seem in many instances that category (1) ("active on-line data") will encompass the files possessing the most relevant information because, as might be expected, the data has not yet been archived.[74] Nevertheless, to the extent some archiving may have occurred, a search of category (2) ("near-line" data) may be required. Where a centralised database is not maintained, the "active on-line data" category may relate strictly to site office hard drives. However, in a dispute that arises out of a warranty claim or a "design build operate" contract, where significant time has passed and records may have been archived, the tribunal could conceivably need to consider categories (3) ("off-line storage" data) or (4) ("back-up tapes").

3.43 It seems that in most cases records falling under category (5) pose a higher burden on a party who is asked to perform a search because it may require retrieval efforts involving a specialist, although, in some instances it may be reasonable that such a task is undertaken.

---

72 See: Grant Henessian (Ed.), *ICDR Awards and Commentaries*, Juris, 2012, p. 61: "In the United States, rapid and intense technological changes have forever altered the domestic legal landscape and have made ESI one of the principal cost drivers in major litigation. US courts and legislators have moved relatively rapidly to address the escalating costs and burdens associated with producing ESI, focusing primarily on cost allocation and appropriate sanctions for spoliation of documents. In the field of international arbitration, several international-arbitral institutions have promulgated guidelines for the parties and arbitral tribunals to apply in managing the e-discovery process. Certain themes appear to have emerged from these guidelines. According to most arbitral institutions and organizations, requests for ESI, as for paper documents, should be specifically- and narrowly-tailored and should seek data that is relevant and material to the outcome of the arbitration."

73 For a more comprehensive review of these categories, and the subject of "e-disclosure" in general, see: R. Smit and T. Robinson, "E-Disclosure in International Arbitration", *Arbitration International*, vol. 24, p. 105 (2008).

74 In describing a search of electronic records that was performed in response to a request during an LCIA arbitration, the following description was given of the approach undertaken: "[the Law firm] reviewed the e-mail boxes of various Vivendi employees that could be reached. These included the e-mail boxes of Messieurs Gibert, Messier and Hannezo, in so far as they were relevant to Vivendi's Polish telecommunications investment." *Elektrim v Vivendi Universal, supra* n. 70, para. 42.

Where a party fails to maintain its records within the first three categories, tribunals would likely be reluctant to approve a request that requires a comprehensive search of deleted or lost and fragmented digital records unless the probative value was high, or other circumstances warranted it. Ultimately, common sense and familiarity with the usages found within the industry which gives rise to the dispute should guide the parties and tribunal on determining which files may be searched in compliance with the limited nature of document production in international arbitration. (See comments to article 9.2(c).)

3.44 Where a party's claim that the information is not accessible is called into question by the fact that industry practice would normally require such data to be stored in an easily accessible manner, or other known facts, a tribunal, as opposed to ordering a more extensive search, may draw an adverse inference from the failure to produce such records.

Not in possession, custody or control of the requesting party

3.45 One of the key criteria of article 3.3 posits that the requesting party must show that the records sought are not within its "possession, custody or control". The rationale behind this standard as it relates to documents in the public domain was explained by one panel of well-known arbitrators as follows: "Where . . . the documents requested are in the public domain and equally and effectively available to both parties, we believe that there would be no necessity for requiring the other party physically to produce and deliver the documents to the former for inspection and copying."[75]

3.46 This rule embodies the "efficient" approach to evidence gathering in international arbitration, which has been widely accepted in practice. To the extent a party may have the documents within its own possession, or has access to them, document disclosure from its opponent is generally not to be ordered.[76]

Burdensome for requesting party to produce

3.47 The Review Subcommittee for the 2010 Rules has allowed an exception to the general rule that if a requesting party is in possession or able to obtain the requested documents

---

75 *ADF Group Inc v United States of America*, ICSID Case No. ARB(AF)/00/1, Procedural Order No. 3, para. 4 (4 October 2001). See also a case before the Iran-US Claims Tribunal, in which a party was required to show that it was unable to obtain the documents through other means as a pre-requisite for ordering adverse document disclosure: "Having regard to the Respondent's submission and in view of the fact that the record does not demonstrate what specific efforts, if any, the Claimant has made to obtain the documents through other sources, the Tribunal finds the Claimant's request inadmissible." *Vera-Jo Miller Aryeh et al. v The Islamic Republic of Iran*, Case Nos 842, 843, 844. Chamber One, Order of 6 March 1992.

76 As one tribunal constituted under the ICC Rules noted, this standard should be taken seriously; failure to do so raises the risk that document production requests will be denied: "Certain requests, including Request Nos. 1, 2, 3, 4, 5, and 6 disregard Article 3(3)(c) of the IBA Rules which requires that a request to produce contain a statement that the requested documents are not in the possession, custody, or control of the requesting party or of the reasons why it would be unreasonably burdensome for the requesting party to produce the requested documents. This is not mere formality; where the parties have equal access to documents, the IBA Rules place the burden of document retrieval on the party seeking to rely on the documents. To the extent that the Claimant's requests seek documents exchanged by the Parties or in the public domain, the requests are denied, and the Respondent is not compelled to produce any such documents other than those that it has already agreed to produce in its responses (internal citation omitted)." *Landmark Ventures Inc v Insightec, Ltd* (Procedural Order No. 2), ICC Case No. 18807/VRO/ AGF, 25 February 2013, *Arbitrator Intelligence Materials* (Kluwer Law International).

it cannot request production of those documents from the adverse party. The new rule states that where it is shown that it would be "unreasonably burdensome" for the requesting party to produce those requested documents, a tribunal may order the non-disclosing party to disclose them. What "burdensome" means in this context is fact-based. Nevertheless, when considering the complained-of burden, the tribunals may consider the proportionality of the request.

3.48 For further discussion of the proportionality principle and the issue of burden, the reader is referred to the discussion of art. 9.2(c).

Demonstrating possession, custody or control

3.49 A party requesting document production must state the reasons why it is reasonable to assume the requested documents are within the possession, custody or control of the other party.[77] Generally, it will be self-evident whether this criterion is fulfilled. In many instances, the fact that such a document would be authored by a party or addressed to it is why it is relevant in the first place.

3.50 In modern business practice, where the use of subsidiary companies, distributors and agents is common, or within government, where different departments, agencies and local branches are involved, it may be that a party which is technically "different" from the party in the arbitration has possession of the document. Thus the "control" issue can become somewhat complicated. In terms of evidentiary procedure, "control" is not a strict concept that is defined by legal personage. If a document is held outside the files maintained by a party, it does not necessarily mean it does not have "control" over it. Parties to arbitration are expected to attempt to obtain requested documents from related corporate entities or parties with whom they have a relationship, as was explained by a tribunal in the context of an UNCITRAL Rules arbitration: "the Tribunal wishes to clarify that, for a party to claim that documents are not in its control, it must have made 'best efforts' to obtain documents that are in the possession of persons or entities with whom or which the party has a relevant relationship."[78]

3.51 Tribunals may, when assessing representations by the parties on this issue, look to the practicalities and not the strict legal definition of the corporate person to determine whether a record is reasonably within the control of one of the parties. It is not uncommon for tribunals to request a party to search the records of an affiliated entity, its advisers and/or agents for responsive documents.[79] The implication of this rule also impacts the

---

77 See the ruling of the ICC tribunal in Hamilton, *supra* n. 37, p. 75: "Claimants have not even made a basic representation that they have undertaken a search for the requested documents, but failed to locate them. But, even more importantly, in addition to not having demonstrated any reason to believe that the documents they request exist, Claimants also have failed to provide a convincing (or, indeed, any) reason to believe that, were they to exist, they would be exclusively in [Respondent]'s possession. For example, Claimants have not alleged any circumstances indicating that the documents sought were submitted directly, and solely, to [Respondent]."

78 *William Ralph Clayton et al. v Government of Canada*, NAFTA/UNCITRAL, Procedural Order No. 8, p. 1 (2009). When considering this issue, a tribunal may also have regard to the legal right which a party has to obtain the documents. As noted in *In re Ecuador*, (considering an application for assistance in obtaining documents for use in an UNCITRAL arbitration) under US precepts, the concept of control is defined, ". . . not only as possession, but as the legal right to obtain the documents requested upon demand." *In re Republic of Ecuador*, LEXIS 143796, p. 8 (ND Fla. 2010).

79 *CME v The Czech Republic*, Final Award, *supra* n. 79 para. 65 (14 March 2003): "Documents of advisors to Claimant shall be disclosed to the extent that these documents are in the possession of the Claimant and/or

drafting requirements of a request to produce. It may be accepted that a party is not required to master the corporate structure of its opponent in order to identify precisely whether it was a parent or subsidiary company that generated the requested document. If it is reasonably described where and how a document would have been issued, and it is clear that the party should have access to it, then the tribunal may be satisfied this criteria has been met. In all situations, however, a practical approach to the issue of "control" should prevail.

3.52 When a party reacts to a request for document production by stating that the document either does not exist, or is not within its control, the reality is that a tribunal is left with few options. As a tribunal constituted under the rules of the HKIAC noted: "Essentially, if a party says repeatedly that no more documents exist, there is little the arbitral tribunal can do in international arbitration. But if the requesting party can persuade the arbitral tribunal that such documents/information must or ought to exist, continuous non-disclosure may result in an adverse inference being drawn against the non-disclosing party."[80] To determine whether a search has been diligently undertaken by the objecting party, a tribunal may be inclined to require that an overview of the producing party's efforts to locate the document be provided, including a listing of sources it has checked.[81] Further, as noted in the quote above, a tribunal is also able to draw an adverse inference if it is satisfied that the requested document should exist, and its non-production is a result of a party's failure to comply with the disclosure order.[82]

---

its affiliated companies or should have been transmitted by the advisor to the Claimant in the ordinary course of business." See also: *Vito G. Gallo v Canada*, NAFTA/UNCITRAL, Procedural Order No. 2 (Amended), para. 8 (10 February 2009): "The Arbitral Tribunal considers that, in this respect, in addition to entities which may be controlled by a party, there may be entities or persons with whom a party has a relationship which is relevant for the purposes of this arbitral proceeding. The duty of production extends to the entities controlled by each party." See also the following directive by the Iran-US Claims Tribunal ordering the Iranian government to submit materials into the proceedings that may have come into the possession of persons under its control as a result of an order of its domestic courts: "If any of the above materials are in the possession of the Respondent Government of the Islamic Republic of Iran or in the possession of any other person or entity as the result of judicial process of any court of Iran, the Government of the Islamic Republic of Iran shall either make the originals of the materials available at the Tribunal for the purposes of inspection and copying by the Parties from 27 August 1983 to 27 October 1983 or shall file two copies of each item with the Tribunal by 27 June 1983." *Dresser Industries Inc v The Islamic Republic of Iran*, Case No. 103, Order of 27 January 1983. See also a reported decision of an LCIA tribunal to order a party in an arbitration to cause a related entity to cooperate with auditors to be appointed by the opposing party: "no Party is to prevent, delay or obstruct any such auditing company from carrying out the audit of the [the subsidiary] and [subsidiary]. [Party X] is ordered to ensure that this order is fully complied with." As quoted in *X v Y*, Judgment of the Amsterdam Court of Appeals, Case No. 200.079.836/01 KG (12 July 2011).

80 As recorded in *Jung Science Information Technology Co Ltd v ZTE Corp* [2008] 4 HKLRD 776, a decision of the Hong Kong High Court of First Instance, at chronological annex to the judgment. See also: *Cortec Mining Kenya Ltd, Cortec (Pty) Ltd and Stirling Capital Ltd v Republic of Kenya*, ICSID Case No. ARB/15/29, Procedural Order No. 1 (2016), §15.6: "The failure to produce as ordered may result in adverse inferences drawn by the Tribunal as regards the merits of the defaulting Party's case."

81 This approach was taken in *Tidewater Inc et al. v The Bolivarian Republic of Venezuela*, ICSID ARB/10/5, Procedural Order No. 1, p. 9 (29 March 2011). A standard for determining whether a party's representations regarding the existence or availability of evidence should be accepted by the tribunal may be borrowed from the jurisprudence of the British-Mexican Claims Commission which found that in order to excuse a party from non-production, a party "is to create the conviction that he has earnestly tried to place all existing evidence at our disposal." As recalled in Cheng, *supra* n. 1, p. 321. See also: the comments to art. 9.2(g).

82 In ICC Case 15583, Claimant filed a Request for Disclose of Documents/Information requesting "the production of contract documents and all contract relevant information by Respondent, especially date, topics, chargeable amounts, payments received and future payments, duration, concerning all contracts – may they have been concluded directly or non-directly – with [designated customers]." *Ibid.*, p. 140, §262. Respondent opposed the request for the reasons, *inter alia*, that the request was "premature and should be examined once the validity

Investor-state arbitration

3.53 It would seem that the IBA Rules are also a useful tool for investor-state arbitration as is evidenced by their adoption by arbitration tribunals sitting in such disputes.[83] This being said, some tribunals have recognised that investor-state arbitration does presuppose a different approach to evidentiary procedure than one might expect in an international commercial arbitration, with respect to document production:

> With respect to the differences between domestic litigation and international arbitration, the Tribunal recognizes that it is generally understood that one reason parties choose arbitration is to avoid the relatively extensive document production practices of courts generally and United States courts in particular. It feels that this expectation is not generally different in the context of NAFTA Chapter 11 arbitration, although the Tribunal notes that the investment arbitration context in which there may not be a contractual relationship between the parties does distinguish such proceedings from international commercial arbitration, and thus militates in favor of some greater receptiveness on the part of the Tribunal for document production requests.[84]

3.54 The more liberal approach to document production exercised by some tribunals in investor-state arbitrations may be based, as stated in the quote above, on the fact that the parties to the dispute have not agreed as a matter of contract to engage in arbitration. In a contractual setting where the parties have a long-standing commercial relationship, it may be presumed that a large proportion of the relevant documents will be in the hands of both

---

and merit of the underlying claims is established." *Ibid.*, §264. The arbitrator reasoned that it had the power to request for disclosure under Article 20.5 of the ICC Rules, which empowers arbitrators to summon parties to provide additional evidence; under the Procedural Order No. 2 signed by the parties; and, under the IBA Rules on the Taking of Evidence in International Arbitration. *Ibid.*, §§266–268. Given the lack of specificity and clarity in Claimant's request, the arbitrator's order of disclosure limited the duty of disclosure for certain contracts and certain years. *Ibid.*, p. 141, §275. The arbitrator held that "it has been established as a matter of fact that [Y] was a mere instrumentality of Respondent . . . [Y] is a 100% subsidiary of Respondent that had been incorporated for the purpose of conducting Respondent's business in Middle East, and is fully controlled by Respondent." *Ibid.*, p. 143, §289. Citing to Procedural Order No. 1, "[i]f a party, contrary to an order by the Arbitral Tribunal, fails to produce the documents without showing sufficient cause for such failure, the Arbitral Tribunal may draw from such failure any conclusion which it deems reasonable, in particular with respect to the content of such document." *Ibid.*, p. 146, §320. The arbitrator further stated that "the "adverse inference" that needs to be deduced from Respondent's failure to disclose some facts does not oblige the Arbitral Tribunal to hold Claimant's allegations over those facts as "established" or deemed "proven"; it simply means that the Tribunal should take into account Respondent's failure to disclose when appreciating the weight of existing evidence and deciding on the allocation of the burden of proof in cases where the key evidence or information are under the exclusive control of the party refusing to cooperate." *Ibid.*, §319. The arbitrator then concluded that "[g]iven Respondent's failure to disclose contracts indirectly concluded (i.e. through [Y]) with the designated customers and, more generally, Respondent's failure to cooperate in good faith for the establishment of key facts related to such contracts, the Tribunal has no other choice but to decide on Claimant's claims . . . on the basis of the available evidence by taking due account of Respondent's failure to fully disclose relevant information that remained in the exclusive field of control or possession of Respondent." *Ibid.*, p. 147, §321.

83 See, for instance, *Noble Ventures Inc v Romania*, *supra* n. 34, Final Award, p. 31.

84 *Glamis Gold v United States of America*, *supra* n. 35, Decision on Parties' Requests for Production of Documents Withheld on Grounds of Privilege, fn. 1 (17 November 2005). See also the position taken by the tribunal in *William Clayton v Canada* providing the following view on the purpose of document production as it pertains to investor-state arbitration: "The Tribunal notes that the purpose of document production is to provide investors with a reasonable opportunity to obtain relevant and material documents beyond those on the public record. Conversely, respondent governments must have the opportunity to obtain relevant and material documents in the possession of investors that they require for their effective defence." *William Clayton et al. v Canada*, *supra* n. 31, p. 7. The position adopted in *William Clayton et al.* appears to broadly be consistent with the position of the *Glamis Gold* tribunal in that there is a receptiveness to broader lines of disclosure. This being said, it is far from certain that this is a position uniformly adopted by international investment tribunals.

sides. In contrast, in an investor-state dispute, the investor typically will not have access to internal government documents necessary to establish its claim. The prohibition on wide-ranging document production in commercial arbitration may be less rigidly applied in an investor-state arbitral forum as compared to international commercial arbitration.

Produce or object: the duty to provide good faith answers to a request

Article 3.4 2010 IBA Rules: **Within the time ordered by the Arbitral Tribunal, the Party to whom the Request to Produce is addressed shall produce to the other Parties and, if the Arbitral Tribunal so orders, to it, all the Documents requested in its possession, custody or control as to which it makes no objection.**

General discussion

3.55 Article 3.4 of the 2010 version of the IBA Rules contains small, but significant, modifications to the text of the 1999 Rules relating primarily to procedural economy. This article specifies that a party who is requested to produce documents shall transmit them to the arbitral tribunal only if so ordered by the arbitral tribunal. The 1999 Rules presumed that the documents would be produced directly to the tribunal as well as the requesting party; however, this practice was not widely followed.[85] As the following example of a procedural rule adopted by an UNCITRAL arbitral tribunal shows, the predominant approach in international arbitration is for parties to exchange evidence amongst themselves, unless otherwise directed by the tribunal: "In the first instance, requests for documents should not be copied to the Arbitral Tribunal; nor should the responding Party furnish copies of documents to the Arbitral Tribunal. Documents produced pursuant to such requests shall be communicated to the Arbitral Tribunal only if a Party wishes to rely on them".[86]

3.56 Tribunals typically prefer not to see documents produced during the disclosure phase, until such document is formally introduced into the procedure as evidence. This is for good reason; if irrelevant documents are produced through disclosure it is best that such documents be kept out of the official arbitral record so that there is no confusion during a subsequent hearing, or during the drafting of an award, as to whether a document has been relied on and is considered evidence. One of the essential functions that a tribunal exercises over evidentiary procedure is to ensure that the parties are afforded the opportunity to answer the case against them.[87] Confusion over which documents are formally submitted

---

85 See: *Biwater Gauff v Tanzania, supra* n. 38, Procedural Order No. 2, p. 2. See also: *L. Brown & Sons Ltd, supra* n. 27: disclosure was left to be on a basis of co-operation and liaison between the parties and the order stated: "Both parties seek disclosure of documents by the other. For that purpose the parties are to make written application to the other and co-operate with one another."

86 See: *GAMI Investments Inc v United Mexican States*, NAFTA/UNCITRAL, Procedural Order No. 1, p. 5, s. 7.7 (2003).

87 See: *Zermalt Holdings SA v Nu-Life Upholstery Repairs Ltd*, [1985] 2 EGLR 14, 15: "Nevertheless, the rules of natural justice do require, even in an arbitration conducted by an expert that matters which are likely to form the subject of decision, in so far as they are specific matters, should be exposed for the comments and submissions of the parties. If an arbitrator is impressed by a point that has never been raised by either side then it is his duty to put it to them so that they have an opportunity to comment."

as evidence (and thus taken into account in a final award) may undermine the tribunal's ability to fulfil that duty.

Ethical considerations for counsel

3.57 The IBA Guidelines adopts the view that a Party Representative should inform the client of "the need to preserve, so far as reasonably possible, Documents, including electronic Documents that would otherwise be deleted in accordance with a Document retention policy or in the ordinary course of business, which are potentially relevant to the arbitration." The comments to Guidelines 12–17 make clear that any such advise should take into account the potential relevance to the case at hand, since the search and preservation of that evidence will occur prior to the parties being in a position to assess materiality to the dispute.

Multi-parties and document production

3.58 The addition to article 3.4 of the phrase, "to the other parties" (also found in other parts of article 3) in the 2010 IBA Rules was introduced in consideration of multi-party arbitrations. Under the revised article 3.4, the production of evidence must be made to all parties in an arbitration irrespective of which party actually lodged the request. Such a principle brings the 2010 IBA Rules into the guiding principle of arbitration laws that require all parties to be afforded an equal opportunity to present their case before the tribunal. The equal opportunity principle generally encompasses the right to have equal access to all of the evidence produced by a party in a procedure.[88]

Duty to provide good faith answers to a request

3.59 Article 3.4 assumes that a party has two responses to a request for document production available to it, either to: (1) produce the document, or (2) file an objection (see also article 3.5). The obligation to provide good faith answers and objections in international arbitration has been affirmed by numerous tribunals as implicit in a party's general duty of cooperation. This obligation on the parties was summarised by an ICSID panel in the *ADF v United States of America* arbitration, which stated that: "The appropriate assumption in every case is that, both parties having proceeded to international arbitration in good faith, neither would withhold documents for its own benefit and that good faith will render any

---

88 As an example, the following case note concerning the conduct of a commodities arbitration, makes the point that the parties should be aware of the arguments (and the evidence) produced in the arbitration: "The Court found that the German company X had had no opportunity to present its case in the arbitration proceedings since all it did after having been advised by the Portuguese company A of the request for arbitration, was to nominate Mr. R. as arbitrator and to send him its documents on the contract in dispute. It was not informed of the arguments presented by the Portuguese company A in the arbitral proceedings. The Court held: The mere possibility to submit documents on a disputed contract or to give its view without knowing the arguments of the opponent, is not sufficient for due process (possibility to present its claims or defenses)." Landgericht (Court of First Instance) of Bremen (1983), in Albert Jan van den Berg (ed.), *Yearbook Commercial Arbitration*, Vol. XII, p. 186 (1987).

practical problems of document production susceptible of prompt resolution without undue hardship or expense on either party."[89]

3.60 To deliberately conceal the existence of a responsive document and not report it to the tribunal or the opposing party is a violation of this duty of good faith and, depending on the circumstances, possibly also mandatory law.[90] This point was addressed in the context of a challenge to an arbitral award rendered under the rules of the London Metal Exchange before the High Court of Justice, Queen's Bench Division as follows: "Where an important

---

89 *ADF v United States of America, supra* n. 75, Procedural Order No. 3, para. 4. See also: ICC Case No. 7365, where the tribunal affirmed the following general principles of evidentiary procedure: "In international arbitrations both parties have the duty, under the general principle of good faith, to co-operate in the offering of the relevant evidence. Under this principle, the party who may possess the relevant documentation may have a duty to submit that documentation in the first place, even though the burden of proof is on the opponent's side." ICC Case No. 7365, Final Award, para. 15.2 (1997) (unpublished). See also the following actions taken by a respondent in regard to a document request which demonstrated bad faith, and were disapproved of by an ICDR tribunal: "Respondents' refusal to furnish specific objections to Claimant's document requests left Claimant with no way of knowing what documents Respondent's objected to producing and with no way to test whether Respondents had in fact produced all documents relevant to the arbitration. Rather than working on the basis of Claimant's document requests, Respondents' Attorney simply hand-picked and produced some documents which he unilaterally concluded were related to 'dealings with Claimant'. This wholly uncontrolled production did not include numerous categories of relevant, much needed documents which had been encompassed by Claimant's document requests. Despite the fact that all Respondents were involved in matters related to this arbitration, Respondents' Attorney refused to produce documents from the files of any Respondent other than Respondent 2, and 5. Ultimately, Respondents and Respondents' Attorney never did produce any additional documents but, rather, sent a letter stating that the Arbitrator did not have power to direct discovery beyond what Respondents had previously provided and that: 'The Respondents therefore decline to produce any additional documents.'" ICDR Case No. [partially redacted] 251-04, Final Award, WL 6346380 (2005). See also: *Győri ETO v UEFA*, Arbitral Award rendered by the Court of Arbitration for Sport, CAS 2012/A/2702 (2012), in which the Panel found that: "the Appellant did not disclose the information required under the EFA Club Licensing Regulations [all financial information], in particular Article 47 and the excuses given were irrelevant under the EFA regulations and Swiss Law. Also the excuses under domestic Hungarian Law and the EC Directive are irrelevant and cannot sustain the Appellant's reasons for concealing the relevant financial information. The debt to Flora was overdue and the Appellant's attitude is not excusable. To the contrary, the Appellant's attitude ought to be opposed because the Appellant tried to mislead UEFA with the information it provided so as to obtain the license." *Ibid.*, p. 23, §146.

90 ICC Case No. 1434, Sigvard Jarvin & Yves Derains (eds), *Collection of ICC Arbitral Awards*, Vol. I, 1975–1981, p. 263: "Further, the parties to arbitration were specially obliged to collaborate in the administration of evidence." See also: *Chantiers de l'Atlantique SA v Gaztransport & Technigaz SAS*, where an English court considered the issue of good faith answers to a request for document production. In this instance, a party had provided an answer to a request for disclosure stating that the requested document could not be found. Subsequently, it was revealed that an incomplete, prior draft of the document had been located. In the testimony before the court, it was noted that the lawyers for the producing party, had reviewed the document, and determined that it was not responsive to the request because it was incomplete and only a draft version of the final document. In finding that the answer provided to the document request was given in good faith, the reviewing court noted the following: "It may be that, if one were looking at this answer in the context of disclosure obligations under English law, it would be open to criticism, but it is important to have in mind that this arbitration was being conducted in the more narrow confines of a disclosure procedure akin to that under the IBA rules, much closer to the procedure applicable before the French courts. With that point in mind and given that [there was no accusation of dishonesty against the legal counsel involved], it seems impossible to characterise GTT's response to the request for internal document 681, that it could not be found, as a dishonest one." *Chantiers de l'Atlantique SA v Gaztransport & Technigaz SAS, supra* n. 29, para. 350. The connection made by the court between the more narrow approach to document production under the IBA Rules, and the duty to provide answers to document requests in good faith, suggests that a party answering a request is free to construe the request in accordance with the narrow and specific standards of art. 3.3. It should be cautioned, however, that in this particular instance, the court also considered that the document was so "incomplete" that it was hardly of use. If the document had been a more complete version, and possibly more relevant, it would have been appropriate for the responding party to have noted the document's existence in its answer, even if it maintained an objection to its production because it was only a draft.

document which ought to have been disclosed is deliberately withheld and as a result the party withholding it has obtained an award in his favour the court may well consider that he has procured that award in a manner contrary to public policy. After all, such conduct is not far removed from fraud."[91]

3.61 Whether the concealment of a document that would in normal course have been subject to disclosure will lead to the successful challenge of a final award will largely depend on whether the document would have had a serious effect upon the arbitration.[92] Aside from raising potential threats to the finality of an award, it should be also noted that intentionally concealing a responsive document would invariably be seen by a tribunal as an act of procedural bad faith, and could well result in an adverse costs award,[93] or lead the tribunal to draw an adverse inference on a relevant factual point at issue.[94]

---

91 *Per* Moore-Bick J in *Profilati Italia SrL v Painewebber Inc* [2001] 1 Lloyd's Rep 715, p. 720. See also: the decision the Singapore High Court in *Swiss Singapore Overseas Enterprise Pte Ltd v Exim Rajathi Pvt Ltd* [2009] SGHC 231, where it was held that for an arbitral award to be overturned because a party had withheld relevant documentary evidence, it must be shown that the evidence would normally have been discoverable during the arbitration, and would have played a decisive role in the final determinations of the case. See further an UNCITRAL arbitration, in which the failure of a party-witness to reveal key evidence prior to the hearing, even though such information had been subject of disclosure requests, was acknowledged by the tribunal as an act of procedural bad faith subject to possible repercussions as to the award on costs: "His concealment, right up until his cross-examination by Respondent's counsel during the hearing, of his ownership of the companies in question was an element of both substantive and procedural significance, with effect on the conduct of the arbitration. Claimants themselves concede, in their Post-Hearing Memorial, that Mr. Genin's conduct could be considered to have affected the case and that it is thus appropriate for the Tribunal to take this conduct into account when considering the allocation of costs. The Tribunal cannot but concur with both parts of that statement." *International Thunderbird Gaming v United Mexican States, supra* n. 91, Final Award, para. 380 (2001).

92 See also: *Elektrim v Vivendi Universal, supra* n. 70, para. 82: "But an award will only be 'obtained by fraud' if the party which has deliberately concealed the document has, as a consequence of that concealment, obtained an award in its favour."

93 See: International Chamber of Commerce, ICC Dispute Resolution Bulletin, 2016, Issue 1, p. 152. In ICC Case 16695, the insurer of a Chilean Company initiated arbitration in Chile against Respondent, a European equipment manufacturer. The arbitrator considered responsibility for the failure of the equipment in light of the evidence produced and "Respondent's refusal to produce certain documents and the failure of two of the Respondent's witnesses to appear at the hearing." The arbitrator found that the statements of those witnesses who did not appear could not be taken into consideration; and, "that although the documents withheld by Respondent were not essential to deciding the case and therefore could not justify the drawing of adverse inferences, Respondent's lack of cooperation should be sanctioned in the arbitrator's decision on costs." Additionally, regarding the witnesses, "[i]n the Sole Arbitrator's view, these witnesses, although duly summoned, did not appear at the hearing without any valid reason. In this regard, the Sole Arbitrator fails to see any justification for departing from the general rule established in Article 4(8) of the IBA Rules, which are applicable in accordance with Section 17 of the Procedural Order No. 1 . . . [t]herefore, these witness statements are excluded from the record and will not be considered evidence as requested by Claimant." *Ibid.*, p. 153, §304. Because the Sole Arbitrator found that "the evidence produced in this case has been sufficient to determine the facts relevant to the issues in dispute," the Sole Arbitrator denied Claimant's request for adverse inferences. *Ibid.*, pp. 154–55, §§389–390. However, the "Sole Arbitrator considers that this lack of due diligence has unnecessarily affected the way in which these proceedings have been conducted . . . [and] will consider these facts when assessing the costs of the arbitration." *Ibid.*, p. 155, §§398–94.

94 See: ICDR Case No. 526-04, American Arbitration Association (AAA), International Centre for Dispute Resolution (ICDR), in Grant Henessian (ed.), *ICDR Awards and Commentaries*, Juris, 2012, pp. 225–284. In ICDR Case No. 526-04, an arbitration held in King County, Washington, with undisclosed parties, regarding breach of contract, trademark infringement, and wrongful passing-off, the Arbitration Panel "ordered RESPONDENT 1 to produce documents and allow site visits," which was reflected in several Panel Orders. After Respondents failed to comply with the document production orders, the Arbitration Panel held that "Respondents' failures to comply with the orders of this Panel support the inference that the documents and evidence that Respondents failed to produce were adverse to their interests, would have further substantiated CLAIMANT's claims that RESPONDENT 1 committed breaches of the Manufacturing Agreement, that all Respondents participated in such breaches and in violation of CLAIMANT trademark rights and in wrongful passing off of their products

The production of documents under protest

3.62 A party may be tempted to produce documents over which it maintains an objection, while "reserving its rights". The general rule adopted in international arbitration, as is illustrated by an LCIA arbitration, is that once intentionally and voluntarily produced, a party has waived its objections to the use of the evidence in the arbitration.[95] Thus, a party may not both voluntarily produce documentary evidence and at the same time maintain its objection. In a similar fashion, parties have attempted in the past to produce evidence only to the tribunal, without copying the opponent, with the purported aim of asking the tribunal to review the evidence in order to determine the validity of its objection.[96] This procedure should be avoided unless the parties have agreed to it beforehand. To submit evidence to the tribunal without copying an opponent raises the possibility of a serious procedural irregularity.

Ethical considerations for counsel

3.63 The IBA Guidelines direct Party Representatives to explain to their clients: (1) the necessity of producing, and the potential consequences of failing to produce, documents as may be required;[97] (2) the necessity of taking reasonable steps to ensure that (a) a reasonable search for documents is made, and (b) all non-privileged responsive documents are produced;[98] (3) the importance of not suppressing or concealing documents that have been requested by another Party or that the party has undertaken, or been ordered to produce;[99] and (4) the need to further produce documents that should have been produced, but were not produced, at the relevant time.[100] Furthermore, the IBA Guidelines commentary clarifies Party Representatives should advise (and assist) their clients to: (i) put in place a reasonable and proportionate system for collecting and reviewing documents; and (ii) provide the Party Representative with copies of, or access to, all such documents.[101]

---

as CLAIMANT licensed products, and that the transfers to COMPANY 1 and COMPANY 2 were and continue to be fraudulent shams arranged in an attempt to avoid Respondents' legitimate obligations." It should be noted, however, that even though "[t]he failure of the Respondents to comply with discovery orders was virtually total despite reminders from the Panel that failure to comply with discovery orders could lead to the Panel's drawing adverse inferences" the Arbitration Panel in ICDR Case No. 526-04 stated that "the use of adverse inferences must be limited and moderate in order to avoid undue presumptions from missing evidence."

95 *Double K Oil Products 1996 Ltd v Neste Oil OYJ* [2009] EWHC 3380 (Comm), para. 58 (18 December 2009): "As regards the assertion in the correspondence that privilege was not waived, it was not (in my view) open to Double K both to produce the correspondence to the tribunal and to Neste, and at the same time maintain its claim to privilege. Once produced, any claim to privilege was lost."

96 Michael Hwang, "8 May 2008 – Singapore High Court", *A Contribution by the ITA Board of Reporters*. In *Dongwoo Mann+Hummel Co Ltd v Mann+Hummel GmbH*, the High Court of Singapore considered a challenge to a final award based on an alleged breach of due process. The complained of breach arose from the fact that a party communicated documents, which had been the subject of a disclosure request and objection to disclosure, directly to the tribunal without copying the adverse party. See also: the comments to art. 3.4.

97 See: IBA Guideline 14.

98 See: IBA Guideline 15.

99 See: IBA Guideline 16.

100 See: IBA Guideline 17.

101 See: Comments to Guidelines 12–17: "Under Guidelines 12–17, a Party Representative should, under the given circumstances, advise the Party whom he or she represents to, and assist such Party to: (i) put in place a reasonable and proportionate system for collecting and reviewing Documents within the possession of persons within the Party's control in order to identify Documents that are relevant to the arbitration or that have been requested by another Party; and (ii) ensure that the Party Representative is provided with copies of, or access to, all such Documents."

Requests and objections (general) and the "redfern schedule"

Article 3.5 2010 IBA Rules: If the Party to whom the Request to Produce is addressed has an objection to some or all of the Documents requested, it shall state the objection in writing to the Arbitral Tribunal and the other Parties within the time ordered by the Arbitral Tribunal. The reasons for such objection shall be any of those set forth in Article 9.2 or a failure to satisfy any of the requirements of Article 3.3.

General discussion

3.64 Objections to requests for document production are almost as common as the requests themselves.[102] The reasons why a party may resist turning over documents in their possession are manifold and may be based upon the practices of the resisting party's own jurisdiction, where document disclosure is unknown, the rules of evidence of their home courts, or other reasons which are based upon locality and expectations. Parties who choose international arbitration must recognise, however, that adverse document disclosure is a possibility, regardless of what may be customary in their domestic courts. The reasons for resisting such disclosure are generally limited to those grounds listed in article 9 of the IBA Rules.

3.65 While a party who seeks documents is under a duty to provide a "narrow and specific" request, a party who resists production should provide motivated and precise objections.[103] Pursuant to article 3.5, a party may object to the production of documents for (1) any of the reasons set forth in article 9.2, which is a comprehensive list of objections

---

102 See: *Eli Lilly and Company v Government of Canada*, Case No. UNCT/14/2, Procedural Order No. 1 (2014). See also: *Mesa Power Group LLC v Government of Canada*, PCA Case No. 2012-17, Procedural Order No. 1, §12.5 (2012): "Requests for document disclosure shall take the form of a so-called "Redfern Schedule" as attached (Annex A)." See also: *Mesa Power Group LLC v Government of Canada*, PCA Case No. 2012-17, Procedural Order No. 4, §19 (2013): "As mentioned above, the Parties' respective document production requests were submitted on 11 June 2013 in the form of Redfern Schedules." See also: *South American Silver Ltd v The Plurinational State of Bolivia*, PCA Case No. 2013-15, Procedural Order No. 1, §5.2.6. (2014): "Document production requests submitted to the Tribunal for decision, together with objections and responses must be in tabular form pursuant to the model appended to this Procedural Order as Annex 1 (alternative Redfern schedule). The Parties shall use the model format throughout their exchange of requests, objections, and responses." See also: *Windstream Energy LLC v Government of Canada*, Arbitration under Chapter Eleven of the North American Free Trade Agreement and the UNCITRAL Arbitration Rules, Procedural Order No. 1, §7 (2013), on document production. See also: *Philip Morris Asia Ltd v The Commonwealth of Australia*, PCA Case No. 2012-12, Procedural Order No. 11 (2014), §4.1: "The Redfern Schedules submitted by the Parties on 8 September 2014, as amended by the Tribunal, are attached to this Procedural Order as Annexes 1 and 2. The Tribunal's order in respect of each Request to Produce is contained in the last column of each Annex."

103 ICC Case No. 6497 (1994), Final Award, in Albert Jan van den Berg (ed.), *Yearbook Commercial Arbitration*, Vol. XXIVa, pp. 76–77 (1999): "By its Procedural Ordinance No 3, the arbitral tribunal decided in particular: 'Requests (i) and (ii) concern subcontracts entered into in relation with Product Agreements P and Q. Claimant confirmed that some subcontracts had been entered into. However, when their counsel was asked to say whether these subcontracts were made in writing or not, he was not sure. Claimant has not submitted any precise argument which would oppose the production by them of such subcontracts. Indeed, such production would clearly be helpful for the discussion of this case. Consequently, requests (i) and (ii) are accepted. Claimant is ordered to produce copies of all subcontracts entered into by them concerning Product Agreements P and Q and made in writing. For those subcontracts which were made orally, claimant is requested to present a written statement exposing the content of such alleged oral agreements, their scope and the identity of the subcontractor . . ." See also: *Poštová banka, a.s. and ISTROKAPITAL SE v Hellenic Republic*, ICSID Case No. ARB/13/8, Procedural Order No. 3 (2014), §17, where the Tribunal granted the requests for document production that were sufficiently "narrow" and "specific."

commonly accepted in international arbitration, and (2) if the request does not satisfy any of the requirements of article 3.3. The 2010 version of this rule requires a party to address objections in writing to the tribunal and the other parties to the arbitration, whereas article 3.5 of the 1999 Rules required an objecting party to address the objections only to the arbitral tribunal. This revision reflects common practice, as arbitrators will rarely, if ever, accept *ex parte* communications.[104] Where a party does communicate any objection or a document to the tribunal only, and not the other party, the possibility that a breach of the principle of equal treatment has occurred is raised.[105]

3.66 When considering the request for document disclosure, and the objections that have been raised, it has become common practice in international arbitration for tribunals to use what is known as a "Redfern Schedule".[106] This schedule essentially follows the following format:

Description of the document requested for production	Justification for the request by the requesting party	Comments and/or objections by the other party	Decision of the arbitral tribunal

---

104 *TCW v Dominican Republic, supra* n. 22, Procedural Order No. 2, para. 2.2: "The Parties shall not engage in any oral or written communications with any member of the Tribunal *ex parte* in connection with the subject matter of the arbitration."

105 Hwang (2008), *supra* n. 96. However, tribunals have been known to order documents to be produced to them, to review *in camera*, in order to determine their admissibility. See: comments to art. 3.8.

106 Named after the originator of this procedural document, Alan Redfern. See, for example: *TCW v Dominican Republic, supra* n. 22, Procedural Order No. 2, para. 3.7.4. See also, for example: *Europe Cement v Turkey, supra* n. 36, Final Award, para. 48: "The Respondent also called on the Tribunal to rule on the production of the remaining documents in the Redfern Schedule." See: the following description of a Redfern schedule, and an affirmation of its wide-spread use in arbitration, by an English court: "That the procedure concerning disclosure adopted in the arbitration was akin to the IBA Rules is borne out by Procedural Order No. 1 of the tribunal . . . That provided in the first instance for the parties to disclose the documents they relied upon, then provided for document requests to be served. In the event that documents were not produced, a joint schedule was to be prepared with columns setting out each party's requests, with brief summary of the grounds for the request, a summary of the grounds of objection and a blank column for the tribunal's decisions. This is what is known in international arbitration as a 'Redfern schedule'." *Chantiers de l'Atlantique SA v Gaztransport & Technigaz SAS, supra* n. 29, para. 214. See also: *Dunkeld International Investment Ltd v The Government of Belize*, PCA Case No. 2010-13/DUN-BZ, Order No. 1, §9 (2014): "Document production requests submitted to the Tribunal for decision must be in tabular form pursuant to the model included with this Order as Annexure B. The Parties are encouraged to use the model format throughout their exchange of requests, objections, and responses." See also: *Eli Lilly and Company v Government of Canada*, Case No. UNCT/14/2, Procedural Order No. 1 (2014), Annex A. See also: *See Philip Morris Brand Sarl, Philip Morris Products SA and Abal Hermanos SA v Oriental Republic of Uruguay*, ICSID Case No. ARB/10/7, Procedural Order No. 3 (2015), Annex 1.

3.67 The requesting party will fill in summaries of their arguments justifying the document requests and the opposing party will complete their comment or opposition to the request in the third column.[107] Often the tribunal will allow for more extensive arguments to be articulated in accompanying correspondence. After reviewing the various arguments, a tribunal will itemise its rulings by filling in the final column of the schedule with its determination, as well as its reasoning.[108]

Consultations between parties

Article 3.6 2010 IBA Rules: **Upon receipt of any such objection, the Arbitral Tribunal may invite the relevant Parties to consult with each other with a view to resolving the objection.**

General discussion

3.68 Disputes over evidence may at times be resolved outside the view of the arbitral tribunal by the parties themselves. Parties who have objections to requests for disclosure may be able to negotiate compromise positions with the opposing party, clarify misunderstandings and find agreed levels of document production which avoid the imposition of unwarranted burdens and without involving the tribunal. Tribunals themselves will often incorporate specific procedural rules into a matter which require parties to meet and confer over document production before bringing their objections to the tribunal, for example: "By Friday, February 13, 2009, the Parties shall try to agree regarding disclosure of the documents to which objections have been made."[109]

3.69 This approach has been incorporated into the latest version of the 2010 Rules, in article 3.6. Pursuant to article 3.6, an arbitral tribunal that has received an objection to a request may choose to invite the respective parties to consult with each other so as to resolve the objection. Requiring parties to meet and confer regarding disputes over evidence is obvious because it places a certain "onus" on them to act in a reasonable manner. When a tribunal requests cooperation between the parties, it is only the most recalcitrant of participants who flatly refuses to seek a reasonable way of addressing its concerns. Often such a conference is all that is required to resolve disputes over

---

107 See also: *United Utilities (Tallinn) B.V. and Aktsiaselts Tallinna Vesi v Republic of Estonia*, ICSID Case No. ARB/14/24, Procedural Order No. 1 (2015), §15.3: "A request for production addressed to the opposing party(ies) shall identify each document or category of documents sought with precision, using the format of a modified Redfern Schedule, in both word and. pdf format. The requested party(ies) shall either produce the requested documents indicating so in the Redfern Schedule provided by the requesting party(ies) or set out in that same Redfern Schedule its (their) reasoned objections for not producing the responsive documents. The requesting party(ies) shall then reply to the objections using that same Redfern Schedule. A template of the modified Redfern Schedule is attached as Annex A." See also: *David Aven et al. v The Republic of Costa Rica*, Arbitration Proceeding Under Chapter 10 of the Dominican Republic-Central America-United States Free Trade Agreement and the UNCITRAL Arbitration Rules (2010) (UNCT/15/3), Procedural Order No 1 (2015), §20.2: "The request, responses or objections to the request, the reply to the responses or objections to the request, and the Tribunal's decisions referred to in this Section shall be recorded in a joint schedule in the form of a Redfern Schedule."

108 Tribunals may adopt variations on the Redfern Schedule to suit multiparty arbitration or to include other columns of relevant information. Nonetheless, the above example provides a template which most schedules will resemble to one extent or another.

109 *Ibid., TCW v Dominican Republic*, Procedural Order No. 2, para. 3.7.3.

document production, and thus the addition of article 3.6 to the IBA Rules was a welcome innovation.

Relevance and materiality standard

Article 3.7 2010 IBA Rules:	**Either Party may, within the time ordered by the Arbitral Tribunal, request the Arbitral Tribunal to rule on the objection. The Arbitral Tribunal shall then in consultation with the Parties and in timely fashion, consider the Request to Produce and the objection. The Arbitral Tribunal may order the Party to whom such Request is addressed to produce any requested Document in its possession, custody or control as to which the Arbitral Tribunal determines that (i) the issues that the requesting Party wishes to prove are relevant to the case and material to its outcome; (ii) none of the reasons for objection set forth in Article 9.2 applies; and (iii) the requirements of Article 3.3 have been satisfied. Any such Document shall be produced to the other Parties and, if the Arbitral Tribunal so orders, to it.**
Other Statements of the Rule Principle 16.2 UNIDROIT/ ALI Principles:	Upon timely request of a party, the court should order disclosure of relevant, non-privileged, and reasonably identified evidence in the possession or control of another party or, if necessary and on just terms, of a non-party. It is not a basis of objection to such disclosure that the evidence may be adverse to the party or person making the disclosure.

General discussion

3.70 One observes as a general rule that if a party objects to a document request, the tribunal will decide the issue on primarily whether it believes the requested evidence would be useful in drafting an award, or is reasonably necessary for a party to have in order to meet its burden of proof. These are the broad parameters for decision-making; however, under the IBA Rules, a tribunal will consider the following three threshold issues in determining a document request: (1) whether the document is relevant to the case and materiality to its outcome; (2) whether there are any objections accepted by the tribunal; and (3) whether the document request satisfies the formality requirements of article 3.3. Generally, where a Tribunal follows this analysis it will not run afoul of its obligations to treat the parties with equality, even if it rules consistently against one party.[110] Of the three aspects

---

110 In a challenge to the sole arbitrator's appointment pursuant to Article 10.4 of the London Court of International Arbitration (LCIA) Rules 1998, LCIA Reference No. 152906, Decision Rendered on 25 May 2016 (available at: www.lcia.org//challenge-decision-database.aspx), the arbitrator's independence and impartiality were challenged for deciding disputed document production requests under the guidance of the IBA Evidence Rules (sic) on behalf of Claimant. The Sole Arbitrator there "rejected the Respondent's document production requests relating to the ownership of the Claimant and the source of its funds because the documents requested are 'irrelevant and immaterial to the issues that need to be decided in this arbitration' and some of the requests were overly broad and amounted to a 'fishing expedition'." *Ibid.*, p. 9, §49. The Respondent claimed that: "the Sole Arbitrator prejudged the issue of the Respondent's defence because he

of this analysis, (1) and (3) are discussed below, and subparagraph (2) is discussed in detail in Chapter 9.[111]

The "relevance and materiality" standard

3.71 The 2010 Rules introduce a change in wording to what has been historically a vague standard. One well-known arbitrator offered the view that in international arbitration "relevant" and "material" documents should be understood as those "essential" to the resolution of a case.[112] Under the 1999 Rules the standard was formulated as "relevant and material to the outcome of the case", which gave the impression that "relevance" and "materiality" were a statement of the same principle, thus implying some redundancy. With the adoption of the new formula, "relevant to the case, and material to its outcome", both prongs of this standard now clearly stand independently and require separate analyses.

"Relevant to the case"

3.72 A party seeking to obtain document disclosure has the burden of demonstrating the relevance of the requested evidence.[113] In the context of document requests, a tribunal will

---

would not have so decided unless he had already decided to dismiss the Respondent's defence that the Claimant funds used in the [Other Arbitration] and the [High Court Case] were from illegal sources and therefore the Respondent was not required to repay the funds to the Claimant. The [former Vice President] was not convinced." *Ibid.*, p. 9, §50. In rejecting the challenge, the LCIA stated that: "The First Procedural Order in this arbitration provided that the document production requests should be made in the form of the Redfern Schedule in compliance with the IBA Rules on the Taking of Evidence 2010, and that the arbitral tribunal was to decide disputed requests guided by the IBA Evidence Rules. This means that the arbitral tribunal has authority to decide whether the requested documents are relevant and material to the outcome of the case in deciding disputed document production requests. Accordingly, to the extent the Sole Arbitrator disclosed his views on the issues, if any, in accordance with the First Procedural Order, and no more, the Sole Arbitrator should not be regarded as biased because he did not express his views 'in such extreme and unbalanced terms as to throw doubt on his ability to try the issue with an objective judicial mind' (*Locabail (U.K.) Ltd v Bayfield Properties Ltd* [2000] Q.B. 451), as put forward by the Respondent as the threshold in determining prohibited prejudgment under English law. Indeed, the Sole Arbitrator merely decided the disputed document production requests under the guidance of the IBA Evidence Rules and such decision does not justify the Challenges." *Ibid.*, p. 9, §51 (emphasis added).

    111 See: *X._____ v Y._____, 4A_672/2012*, a civil appeal from an International Chamber of Commerce (ICC) Award filed before the First Civil law Court of the Swiss Federal Tribunal. In its Appeal, Claimant submitted that the Arbitral Tribunal violated its right to be heard and treated the parties unequally because it did not take into consideration certain documents and made a "finding contrary to the record." The Swiss Federal Tribunal stated that "the inadvertent failure to take into account a pertinent rule or a relevant factual allegation does not constitute unequal treatment within the meaning of Art. 190(2)(d) PILA." The appeal was rejected under the guise that appellant's "submissions are rather in the nature of inadmissible criticism of the contents of the arbitral award without even alleging that it violated public policy (Art. 190(2)(e) PILA). Available at www.swissarbitrationdecisions.com.

    112 Concurring and Dissenting Opinion of Judge Brower, Procedural Order No. 3, *INA Corp v The Islamic Republic of Iran*, Iran-USCTR, Vol. 37, p. 158 (2003).

    113 An ICSID tribunal formulated the "relevance standard" as follows: "a substantive inquiry into whether the documents requested are relevant to, and in that sense necessary for, the purposes of the proceedings where the documents are expected to be used." By "substantive" the tribunal was considering whether the documents were relevant to a substantive issue in the case. *ADF v United States of America, supra* n. 75, Procedural Order No. 3, para. 3.

generally analyse whether a party has put forward a credible argument as to the likely[114] or prima facie relevance of the requested evidence in support of an important contention in the petitioning party's case.[115] An experienced arbitrator in the context of an ICC arbitration described this standard as follows: "the requesting party actually must demonstrate that it requires the document sought in order to discharge its burden of proof."[116] Arguments as to relevance will generally be made on the basis of facts already known to the tribunal, however, as the tribunal quoted above noted, the representations of counsel, may also be given weight.[117] In sum, the rule in regard to relevance simply calls for the moving party to articulate why it believes that document Y will support contention X.[118]

---

114 The standard of proof required for a party to convince the tribunal of the relevance of the requested document is that the evidence is "likely" to be relevant. See, for example, the formulation set forth in *Tidewater v Venezuela*, *supra* n. 81, Procedural Order No. 1, para. 19, wherein the tribunal formulated the standard as follows: "it considers that the two categories of documents requested by the Claimants are reasonably likely to be both relevant and material in assisting it to determine the proper construction of art. 22." The tribunal's formulation is similar to that advocated by Hanotiau in his article on the issue of document production, wherein he affirms this standard: "relevance is generally considered as 'prima facie relevance' or 'likelihood of relevance'." Hanotiau (2006), *supra* n. 4, p. 117.

115 See: Dissenting Opinion of Judge Brower, *International Ore & Fertilizer Corp v Razi Chemical Co Ltd*, Award No. 351-486-3, Iran-USCTR, Vol. 18, p. 102 (1988), as quoted in Poudret and Besson, *supra* n. 1: "A prima facie case is a case sufficient to call for an answer."

116 ICC Case No. [redacted], Procedural Order No. 3, p. 9 (2007) (unpublished). See also: the adoption of this standard by another ICC tribunal: "In ruling on the request for the production of documents, the Arbitral Tribunal will rule on the prima facie relevance of the requested documents, having regard to the factual allegations made by the Parties in the submissions filed to date. At this stage of the proceedings, the Arbitral Tribunal will not be in a position to make any ruling on the ultimate relevance of the requested documents to the final determination of the Parties' claims and defenses in this arbitration." Hamilton, *supra* n. 37, p. 69. See also: the following decision of the Iran-US Claims Tribunal where the tribunal noted that the documents that were requested were not relevant to the present jurisdictional issues before them, and thus denied the request to produce: "Reference is made to the submission filed . . . in which the Agent of the Government of the Islamic Republic of Iran requested the Tribunal to order the Claimant to produce a copy of the contract . . . The tribunal notes that the above mentioned assignment occurred after . . . and therefore has no bearing on the Claimant's locus standi . . . Consequently the request is denied." See also: *Sarah A [Spain] v Moussa R. [Lebanon]* (26 November 2009), a decision of the Paris court of appeal, regarding a challenge to an ICC award. The challenge was brought by the claimant because of the arbitrator's decision not to order disclosure of certain evidence deemed vital by claimant to her case. The arbitrator had instead, after informing himself of the issues, determined the requested documents were irrelevant and declined to order their production. "[Claimant] also contended that the sole arbitrator violated due process and equal treatment in denying her request for production of certain documents related to her late father's estate – documents she claimed would have allowed her to "reveal the true version of events." With respect to due process and equal treatment, the Court found that the parties had filed submissions and had oral argument on Sarah A.'s request for documents regarding her late father's estate – documents the sole arbitrator considered irrelevant to the issue of whether the 20 June agreement was valid. After having heard all the parties, the sole arbitrator considered the validity of the 20 June agreement before ruling on the production request. The sole arbitrator denied Sarah A.'s request for production. Under these circumstances, the Court of Appeal found the sole arbitrator did not violate equal treatment – because all parties had had an opportunity to be heard – and did not violate due process in considering that the requested document production was neither relevant nor useful." Case summary provided in, D. Bensuade, J. Kirby, "View from Paris, December 2009", 25–3 *Mealey's Int'l Arb Rep* 16 (2010). See also: *International Systems & Controls v National Iranian Gas Co*, Case No. 494, Chamber Three, Order of 24 December 1986, p. 2.

117 *Ibid.*, ICC Case No. [redacted], "the affirmation of counsel, for the objecting party, whose good faith is assumed, that the documents in question are neither directly relevant nor material, while not determinative, has to be accorded weight."

118 Consider the following statement regarding the burden on the proposing party from *Glamis Gold v United States of America*, *supra* n. 35, Decisions on Objections to Document Production, para. 15: "the tribunal has endeavoured to make its decision regarding the Parties Objections in such a manner as to focus on the articulated materiality of a given document or category of documents." While the tribunal referred to 'materiality' in this quote, their use of the phrase best corresponds to the 'relevant to the case' condition as used in the IBA Rules. See

3.73 The quote below, taken from a procedural order issued in an UNCITRAL arbitration, provides a practical example of a tribunal's assessment of a party's request as it related to its burden of proof. When confronted with a request from two parties in a multi-party arbitration to receive information relating to sales made under a licence agreement, the arbitrator provided the following analysis:

> Neither Party can quantify its claim or counterclaim without the details of payments received by the other Party. The type of information/documents requested by Claimant and First Respondent is of the same nature, the aim being mainly to enable them to establish the amounts that they consider due to them on the basis of their cooperation. For Claimant the contractual and financial documents required would enable it to assess the amounts received by First Respondent in relation to the ZZ Contract. For the efficient and expeditious settlement of this dispute, the Parties must be in a position to quantify their claim and counterclaims, preferably prior to any witness hearings, so that such hearings can also address issues of quantum.[119]

3.74 In the above example, the tribunal was clearly able to draw a straight line between the request for documents and the requesting party's burden of establishing the royalties due under the contract and thus granted the request.

3.75 Conversely, where a party files a request that broadly pertains to points relevant to its opponents burden, but not its own, it is often considered that such a request should be denied.[120] This point was noted by a tribunal constituted under the SCC rules, and comprised of well experienced practitioners of both civil and common law backgrounds:

> The Tribunal recognizes that, on the one hand, ordering the production of documents can be helpful for a party to present its case and in the Tribunal's task of establishing the facts of the

---

also: where an ICDR tribunal determined to reject certain document requests because it could not establish a relevant connection between the information sought and the arguments of the parties. "Relatively few of the requests were acceded to by the tribunal. As we basically considered the requests for disclosure of documents relating to other projects to be unnecessary for a fair determination of the issues reflected in the submission of the Parties at that time." ICDR Case No. 50198, Partial Award, para. 45 (2007) (unpublished). Using more general language, the tribunal in *Helnan v Egypt* rejected a request for disclosure because it could not anticipate their relevance to a parties' arguments on jurisdiction: "they are not precisely identified and no precise explanation is given as to their relevancy to the problem of jurisdiction that the Arbitral Tribunal has to solve." Dietmar W. Prager and Joanna E. Davidson, "*Helnan International Hotels A/S v The Arab Republic of Egypt*, ICSID Case No. ARB/05/09, 7 June 2008", A Contribution by the ITA Board of Reporters, para. 22.

119 As reported in Scherer (2010), *supra* n. 17, p. 199. See also: a procedural order rendered in ICC Case No. 5542, where the tribunal noted that a request for disclosure would be granted only insofar as the documents that were sought directly related to an important aspect of the claimant's case. "In the circumstances of the case, the tribunal considers that the amended request for disclosure of documents . . . may furnish a basis for an order in this respect. However, the same is to be restricted by deciding that the documents . . . are those relating or referring to the certificate . . . this certificate being the only one which may be relevant to the issue of expulsion of the contractor . . ." ICC Case No. 5542 *supra* n. 31, p. 65.

120 See, for example: *United Parcel Service of America v Government of Canada*, NAFTA/UNCITRAL, Decisions relating to Document Production and Interrogatories, paras 7, 8 (21 June 2004). In that instance Canada raised a number of complaints concerning the insufficiency of claimant's production of evidence, and sought an order compelling the production of certain documents. Noting, *inter alia*, that it was for the investor to establish a breach of the NAFTA provisions on investor protection, the tribunal declined to order further document production. See also the following comments of an Iran-US Claims Tribunal where it was noted that it did not intend to order disclosure of documents which the claimant would likely have to file to meet its own burden of proof: "The tribunal wishes to point out that the Party who carries the burden of proof determines at its discretion what evidence it wishes to submit in support of its claim. It is not normally up to the Tribunal to give directions to any of the parties regarding the evidence to be submitted by them." *The Offshore Co v National Iranian Oil Co*, Case No. 133, Chamber Two, Order of 26 June 1986. See also: Hanotiau (2006), *supra* n. 4, p. 116: "when a party alleges that its opponent has failed to provide the evidence for a submission it has made and requests that party to produce the relevant evidence, this request should in most cases be dismissed."

case relevant for the issues to be decided. On the other hand, the process of disclosure may be time-consuming, excessively burdensome, and even oppressive. Unless carefully limited, the burden may be disproportionate to the value of the result. Further, the Parties may have a legitimate interest in confidentiality.

Further, the Tribunal notes that, insofar as a Party has the burden of proof, it is sufficient for the other Party to deny what the respective Party has alleged and then respond to and rebut the evidence provided by that respective Party to comply with its burden of proof.[121]

3.76 Relevance, in order to be proven in the context of a document request, is typically demonstrated by establishing that the document may be important for the requesting party to meet its burden of proof.

3.77 While the interpretation of the relevance test discussed above appears most consistent with the wording of article 3.7 of the IBA Rules and general practice, there are those who advocate for a broader view in which relevance is decoupled from the requesting party's burden of proof. Under this interpretation, relevance *could* obtain a much wider meaning and apply to documents that may not have a direct relationship to the requesting party's allegations and defenses.[122] This approach runs the risk of opening the document disclosure procedure to a "fishing expedition" wherein parties attempt to "discover" their case, as opposed to substantiate it. Whichever approach is taken, however, it is important to note that tribunals have flexibility in applying these standards and may adopt varying views on their application as the circumstances may warrant.

"Material to its outcome"

3.78 Under the reworded formula that was introduced in the 2010 IBA Rules, it is clear that "materiality" is now distinguishable from "relevance". This aspect of the standard refers to the tribunal's right to evaluate the requested records in the light of whether such documents will bear upon the final award or as one ICSID tribunal phrased it, "the . . . likely merit of the point the requesting party seeks to support."[123] The situation may well arise in

---

121 *Stati v Republic of Kazakhstan* (Award), SCC Case No. V (116/2010), 19 December 2013, p. 29, *Arbitrator Intelligence Materials* (Kluwer Law International).

122 For the arguments against this approach, see Michael Evan Jaffe, Jeetander Dulani, David Stute, *Burden of Proof as a Prerequisite to Document Production Under the 2010 IBA Rules: An Obituary*, Transnational Dispute Management, April 2016. Proponents of this more permissive approach suggest that limiting the relevance test to the context of one's "burden of proof" (1) lays extra requirements upon the parties which were not intended by article 3.7; (2) may unnecessarily restrict access to evidence; and (3) could expose a final award to due process challenges. These criticisms to varying degrees appear to be exaggerated. The danger inherent to a wide-ranging interpretation of relevance is that it opens the door to a "fishing expedition, and eliminates any means of distinguishing "relevant to the case" from "material to its outcome". Far from adding extra hurdles to document production, as some suggest, it would seem interpreting the relevance test in the context of the requesting party's burden of proof gives a meaning to the standard that is consistent with the concept of limited document production under the IBA Rules. In regard to due process challenges, the paucity of reported cases in which a court has overturned a tribunal's evidentiary rulings on the basis of it failing to order the disclosure of evidence belies any notion that this is a realistic concern. Where tribunals adopt an even-handed approach to administering the document disclosure phase, it is unclear on what basis a party could claim it had not been heard. See: *Abu Dhabi Inv. Auth. v Citigroup, Inc, supra*, n. 44.

123 *Aguas del Tunari v Bolivia, supra* n. 50, Procedural Order No. 1, para. 3.26. See further: the decision of the *Glamis Gold* tribunal whereby it recognised that the documents requested may bear some relevant connection to the respondent's arguments, but that it doubted that they would be material to a final award. "Although the Tribunal had some appreciation that this information could assist Respondent in evaluating Claimant's investment expectations, it was not satisfied that the proposed discovery would be in practice transferable to the evaluation of the Imperial Project. In any renewal of this request, the Tribunal thus indicated that Respondent should articulate as fully as possible the likely materiality of the documents requested, including the methodology by which a

an arbitration that a party who is seeking document disclosure has established a clear line between the document it seeks and a contention it seeks to prove. However, the tribunal may determine that the contention itself would not affect the final award.

3.79 A good illustration of this principle is found in an English case, *ABB v Hochtief*, which considered the standards found in article 3 (and article 9) in an application to set aside an LCIA award. The requesting party complained to the court that it had been unfairly discriminated against when a number of its document requests were denied by the tribunal during the arbitration. It contended that it had clearly shown the arbitral tribunal that the records in question were relevant to one of its arguments. In reviewing the conduct of the tribunal in the light of the standards found in the IBA Rules, the court noted that there did appear to be a relevant connection between the document request and the complaining party's arguments in the case. However, it was still appropriate for the tribunal to deny document production because the arbitral record showed that the arbitrators no longer regarded the argument itself to be material to its award.[124] Thus,

---

comparative analysis [would] be made." *Glamis Gold v United States of America*, *supra* n. 35, Final Award, para. 208(e) (8 June 2009). Domestic courts will often follow this approach as well in determining whether a request to either exclude evidence or a refusal to order disclosure by a tribunal may be regarded as depriving a party of a fair hearing. It is often considered that where a tribunal has made an anticipatory determination of proffered evidence and determined that it would not be helpful to a final award, the evidence may be either excluded or the tribunal may decline to order disclosure. See, for example: the ruling in *Lummus Global Amazonas SA v Aguaytia Energy del Peru* which was a decision regarding a challenge to an ICC award before the US District Court for the Southern District of Texas. Here the tribunal determined to exclude witness testimony which was offered as extrinsic evidence on the interpretation of a contract term. Employing the "four corners" rule of contract analysis often used in common law systems, the tribunal ruled that the meaning of the clause on its face was clear, and that under New York substantive law, no further evidence would be received (or was necessary) regarding its proper construction. This ruling had been made during an earlier part of the proceedings, so that subsequent witness testimony offered on the interpretation of this contract provision was struck from the record for the reason that it was immaterial to the tribunal's findings. The reviewing US Court upheld the decision as in the line with discretion that is allotted to the tribunal. *Lummus Global Amazonas SA v Aguaytia Energy del Peru SR Ltda*, 256 F.Supp 2d 594, p. 618 (SD Tex, 2002). See also: the following decision from a German court noting that the determination of a tribunal seated in Istanbul, Turkey not to admit evidence it considered immaterial was not a violation of due process: "The defendant argued that the arbitrators violated due process because in the second arbitration they only admitted evidence that the defendant had already supplied in the first arbitration. The court reasoned that this behavior could only constitute a violation of due process if the new evidence would have affected the outcome of the arbitration. However, it appeared from the reasons for the Second Award that the arbitral tribunal deemed that the new evidence was inadmissible; it did not appear that the arbitrators would otherwise have accepted the new means of evidence as relevant to the defendant's case. "30 September 1999 – Hanseatisches Oberlandesgericht [Hanseatic Court of Appeal], Bremen" in Albert Jan van den Berg (ed.), *Yearbook Commercial Arbitration*, Vol. XXXI, p. 647 (2006).

124 *ABB v Hochtief Airport*, *supra* n. 49, para. 85. See also: *Euroflon Tekniska Produkter AB v Flexiboys I Motala AB*, Swedish Supreme Court, Case No. Ö 1590-11 given in Stockholm on 10 May 2012, §6: "In order for a document to be considered to be of importance as evidence, it is required that it can be assumed that the document adds something to the existing evidence. The arbitral tribunal, which appears to have rather wide discretion to reach its decision, can deny such a motion if the evidence relates to irrelevant circumstances or if the issue has been sufficiently clarified through the existing evidence. However, the arbitral tribunal is not entitled to deny such a motion in cases where the taking of evidence before a court is called for. [. . .]" See also: ICC Case No. 11490: [30] "Claimant requested the Arbitral Tribunal to order Respondents or the Respondent holding accounting records of the Consortium to produce such records. The Arbitral Tribunal decided not to grant such request in the course of the proceedings, and is still of the opinion that such production is unnecessary, since upon Respondents' refusal to produce such records, the allegation of Respondents, that the Consortium was not and has not, since the beginning of the arbitration proceedings, been paid by Owners is not said by Respondents to amount to Force Majeure or a condition precedent which would exonerate them from the payment of amounts that they acknowledge are owed and payable to Claimant. As the only information to be derived from the production of the Consortium's accounting records would be whether Respondents had shared amongst the profits derived from

the contention pursuant to which disclosure was sought was in fact immaterial to the outcome of the arbitration.

3.80 A tribunal may also reject a request for disclosure because to order it would only delay the procedure, and in particular the rendering of a final award, without yielding additional evidence that would have a likely effect on the outcome.[125] If a tribunal believes that the evidence before it is sufficient to decide a matter, further document requests may be judged to be immaterial to the final award.[126]

Other standards

3.81 It has been argued in the past that some arbitration rules, such as those requiring that a document request be granted only if the evidence sought is necessary to a case, impose a "higher" burden on the requesting party than the relevance and materiality test in the IBA Rules.[127] This point was addressed by the *Tidewater v Venezuela* ICSID tribunal when it opined as follows: "The Tribunal further considers that in deciding whether or not it is necessary to order production for a document, it should be guided by the tests of relevance and materiality in the IBA Rules. The Tribunal finds no underlying conflict between these concepts."[128] Therefore, a tribunal will judge what may be "necessary" for disclosure by determining whether the requested evidence is relevant and material.

---

payments by Owners without satisfying their debt towards Claimant, it would not modify or influence in any way the decision of the Arbitral Tribunal." *National Company (State X) v (1) Company A (State Y), (2) Company B (State X), (3) Company C (State X)*, Final Award, ICC Case No. 11490, in Albert Jan van den Berg (ed), *Yearbook Commercial Arbitration 2012* – Volume XXXVII, Yearbook Commercial Arbitration, Vol. 37, pp. 30–42 (Kluwer Law International, 2012).

125 See the procedural conduct of an arbitral tribunal as reported in *JJ-CC Ltd v Transwestern Pipeline Co*, Lexis 7090, para. 19 (Tex App 12 November 1998): "The panel held a hearing regarding this discovery request in April 1995 to determine if this request would delay proceedings, whether the request was reasonable, and if a compromise could be reached. After lengthy discussions with counsel from both sides, the panel decided to allow appellant part of its requested additional discovery, but not so much that the scheduled hearing date would be postponed." See also the decision of the ICSID tribunal in *El Paso v Argentina* wherein it rejected further document production requests on the following grounds: "The information in possession [was] sufficient to decide the jurisdictional issues raised by Respondent, and that, if the proceedings would reach the merits of the dispute it would be open to Respondent to reiterate the above document production requests." *El Paso Energy International Co v Argentine Republic*, ICSID Case No. ARB/03/15, Decision on Jurisdiction, p. 4 (27 April 2006).

126 *Ruckersicherung-Gesellschaft X v Versicherungs-Gesellschaft Y, supra* n. 42. The decision of the Swiss Federal Tribunal stated that: "arbitral tribunals are not obliged to admit further requests for evidence if they conclude by means of an anticipatory assessment of the evidence that the new evidence is not relevant or properly offered." See also: *BSG Resources Ltd, BSG Resources (Guinea) Ltd and BSG Resources (Guinea) SARL v Republic of Guinea*, ICSID Case No. ARB/14/22, Decision On The Proposal To Disqualify All Members Of The Arbitral Tribunal (2016). Claimant attacked the Tribunal's independence and impartiality and stated that: "by concluding that the production of the Emails and Deliberations (that until a few weeks ago were considered relevant and material) will no longer meaningfully contribute to the resolution of the dispute, the Tribunal has undoubtedly prejudged the fiercely contested issues in this arbitration." *Ibid.*, p. 4, §24. However, the Chairman's decision recalled that the tribunal decided that: "pursuing these issues of document production at this stage of the proceedings [would] make no meaningful contribution to the resolution of the dispute" and offered further opportunities to the Claimants to address these evidentiary matters later in the proceedings. *Ibid.*, §§64–65. The Chairman concluded that: "[w]hile the Claimants may not be satisfied with the Tribunal's Decision, the mere existence of an adverse ruling is insufficient to prove a manifest lack of impartiality, as required by Articles 14 and 57 of the ICSID Convention." *Ibid.*, p. 15, §68.

127 See, for example: ICSID Arbitration Rule 34.

128 *Tidewater v Venezuela, supra* n. 81, Procedural Order No. 1, p. 7.

3.82 The IBA Rules capture the pre-eminent test on this point, to which questions of whether a requested document is "necessary", required or otherwise important to a case, are established by demonstrating the likely relevance and materiality of the evidence.

Failure to meet the requirements of article 3.3

3.83 The third criteria of article 3.7 introduces an express "form objection", which is to say an objection which may be raised where it is found that a request does not meet the formal requirements of article 3.3. The revised article 3.3 itself contains a number of pleading requirements that should be complied with when filing a request. Failure to meet the requirements of article 3.3 means that a request may be simply denied on its face as not compliant with the standards found in the IBA Rules.[129]

3.84 It has been common practice for parties to object to a request as "overly broad" when it does not meet the "narrow and specific" criteria found in article 3.3(a)(ii).[130] However, no express objection of this type is listed in article 9.2. With the additional language found in the 2010 version of in article 3.7 (and also article 3.5), the Rules now expressly contemplate an objection that a request is overly broad.

Using experts to resolve document disputes

Article 3.8 2010 IBA Rules: **In exceptional circumstances, if the propriety of an objection can be determined only by review of the Document, the Arbitral Tribunal may determine that it should not review the Document. In that event, the Arbitral Tribunal may, after consultation with the Parties, appoint an independent and impartial expert, bound to confidentiality, to review any such Document and to report on the objection. To the extent that the objection is upheld by the Arbitral Tribunal, the expert shall not disclose to the Arbitral Tribunal and to the other Parties the contents of the Document reviewed.**

General discussion

3.85 IBA Rules, article 3.8 allows a tribunal to appoint an expert to review sensitive documents for which an objection to production or admissibility has been made.[131] Tribunals

---

129 For example, one arbitrator noted when confronted with a number of broadly worded requests for disclosure, "the tribunal rules that the Request to Produce as formulated in each such item . . . is not in conformity with art. 3 of the IBA Rules, and the Request to Produce is declined." *Grand River Enterprises et al. v United States of America*, NAFTA/UNCITRAL, Procedural Order, paras 3 and 5 (14 May 2007). See also: *CME v The Czech Republic, supra* n. 79, Partial Award, para. 47, where the tribunal ruled that requests for productions of general categories of documents were inappropriate under the IBA Rules.

130 See: *Biwater Gauff v Tanzania, supra* n. 38, Procedural Order No. 2.

131 See: *Eli Lilly and Company v Government of Canada*, Case No. UNCT/14/2, Procedural Order No. 1, §3.81 (2014): "In exceptional circumstances, if the propriety of an objection can be determined only by review of the document, the Arbitral Tribunal may determine that it should not review the document. In that event, the Arbitral Tribunal may, after consultation with the Disputing Parties, appoint an independent and impartial expert ("Confidentiality Advisor"), bound to confidentiality, to review any such document and to report on the objection. To the extent that the objection is upheld by the Arbitral Tribunal, the Confidentiality Advisor shall not disclose

may be faced at various times with the need to determine "threshold" questions concerning the nature of the record in question, such as whether it is covered by a privilege or other legal impediment, in order to rule on admissibility and production. As issues involving sensitive governmental documents have arisen more frequently with the growth of investment arbitration, there also has arisen the need to consider special governmental privileges as well.[132] These issues may at times be difficult for a tribunal to rule on because either the volume of the documents in question is quite large or the issues involve highly fact-sensitive questions that require a review of the document to determine the legitimacy of the objection. It is those types of scenarios that will likely qualify as "exceptional" as per the wording of article 3.8.

Appointing an expert

3.86 If a party claims that a document may not be disclosed due to the existence of a legal impediment or other reason, a tribunal may decide to review the document *in camera*, before ordering its disclosure to the opposing party. There is the risk, however, that such an action would subject the tribunal to accusations of bias or failing to treat the parties equally. In reviewing a challenge to an arbitral award rendered under the SIAC rules, where a party complained that its counterpart had sent documents *ex parte* to the tribunal in order for it to determine an objection to production based on confidentiality, the Singapore High Court provided the following analysis of this issue:

> In applications for production of documents, an arbitral tribunal often has to deal with 'threshold questions' on whether a particular document is in fact not relevant or whether it falls outside the relevant parameters for production or disclosure as alleged. There will be instances where the 'threshold questions' can only be determined by a review of the contents of the document itself. A party, who may well be prepared to disclose the document to the tribunal for its review, may not necessarily want to disclose it to the other party often for reasons of confidentiality. But when the party seeking production insists on inspecting the document so that it can submit on the 'threshold questions' (and perhaps also reassure itself that the other party has in fact acted in good faith in opposing the production), then the procedure to adopt for the determination of the 'threshold questions' can be rather contentious unless the procedure has been pre-agreed or pre-determined by the parties as early as possible . . . This minimizes any possible challenge from any party on the basis that there has been contravention of article 18 of the Model Law, which states, *inter alia*, that the parties shall be treated with equality.[133]

3.87 In its further analysis of this issue, the High Court noted that article 3.8 was a commonly accepted procedural rule in international arbitration that assisted tribunals to avoid offending mandatory law which provides for equal treatment of the parties when dealing

---

to the Arbitral Tribunal or to the other Disputing Party the contents of the Document reviewed. Any such Confidentiality Advisor shall be required to sign an appropriate confidentiality undertaking." See also: *South American Silver Ltd v The Plurinational State of Bolivia*, PCA Case No. 2013-15, Procedural Order No. 2, §33 et seq (2014), where the Arbitral Tribunal considered certain documents to be "highly confidential" and prepared, along with the Parties, a Protective Order for Respondent to appoint an expert to comment on the documents (see Annex A of PCA Case No. 2013-15 for a sample protective order).

132 As an example, see: *Piero Foresti, Laura de Carli v The Republic of South Africa*, ICSID Case No. ARB(AF)/07/1, Award, para. 14 (4 August 2010).

133 Hwang (2008), *supra* n. 96.

with "threshold questions" that may be ruled upon only after reviewing the document in question.[134] In certain instances, tribunals have adopted the alternative procedure discussed by the Singapore High Court, that is, the tribunal has received the documents subject to an objection in order to determine whether the objection may be upheld or whether the document must be produced to the other side.[135] However, of the two procedures, namely the *in camera* review of the document by the tribunal or the appointment of an expert to assist the tribunal, the article 3.8 approach is to be preferred because it minimises any risk of offending due process norms.[136]

The independence and impartiality of an expert

3.88 The only criteria which article 3.8 imposes when selecting an expert is that the candidate is "independent", "impartial" and bound to confidentiality. The term "independent" generally refers to relationships with the parties, to which it may be prudent to request an expert to provide a declaration of his or her independence from the litigants in the matter.[137] Arbitrators have, in the past, felt comfortable appointing the secretary to a tribunal to perform this function, demonstrating that it is not the relationship between the expert and the tribunal that is at issue.[138] Not all tribunals may approve of this approach. In some cases, a tribunal may wish to appoint an uninvolved third party as the expert. This is done for several reasons, including the need to engage an expert with particular linguistic capacities, technical understanding or procedural knowledge. This was the case in the *Guyana v Suriname* boundary delineation arbitration administered by the Permanent Court of Arbitration.[139]

---

134 *Ibid.*, p. 145.

135 See: *Jardine Lloyd Thompson Canada v Western Oil Sands Inc* [2005] AJ No. 943, para. 13, where the court noted the tribunal's directions: "the Panel made the following directions and orders: (a) that the Standstill Agreement be produced by Western to the Panel for inspection, following which the Panel will determine whether it meets the test of relevance and should be produced to the Underwriters." See also the decision taken by a Society of Maritime Arbitrators tribunal to review documents over which privilege had been claimed *in camera*: "Owner, thereafter, requested the production of certain documentation, some of which Charterer contended were protected under the attorney-client privilege and attorney work-product doctrine. The parties submitted extensive briefs addressing their positions and a Privilege Log identifying those documents that Charterer considered were protected. On August 24, 2009, the Panel issued its Majority Interlocutory Ruling granting some of Owner's requests and denying others. It directed Charterer to produce certain documents listed in its Privilege Log for *in camera* review by either the full panel or chairman at Charterer's option." *In the Matter of an Arbitration between Scope Navigation Inc, and Standard Tankers Bahamas Ltd*, SMAAS, Final Award, WL 5490766 (2010).

136 See: *Glamis Gold v United States of America*, supra n. 35, Procedural Order No. 8 (31 January 2006): "Given the numerous complications raised with an in camera review [of documents over which privilege is raised], this possible final step in the procedure was suspended temporarily by the Tribunal . . ."

137 "The expert should in all events be impartial and independent. He should be subject to the same conflict of interest standards as the arbitrators. Before accepting the appointment, he should likewise submit a statement of independence, as an arbitrator does." Hans van Houtte, "The Use of an Expert to Handle Document Production: IBA Rules on the Taking of Evidence (art. 3(7))", in Albert Jan van den Berg (ed.), *ICCA Congress Series No. 13* (Montreal, 2006), pp. 622, 637 (2007).

138 *Dr Horst Reineccius v Bank for International Settlements*, PCA, Procedural Order No. 6, p. 1 (11 June 2002).

139 *Guyana v Suriname*, UNCLOS/PCA, Procedural Order No. 1, para. 4 (18 July 2005).

The role of an expert

3.89 Article 3.8 does not describe the procedure for the appointment of an expert, nor does it give guidelines for that expert to follow in the discharge of his or her mandate. However, tribunals in the past have solicited comments from the parties when selecting the expert,[140] issued defined terms of reference to the expert and sought input on those terms[141] and required that the expert review the submission of each party so that adequate opportunity to be heard is given.[142] The expert is not to make a decision him or herself, but is rather commissioned to provide a "report" under the terms of article 3.8. If the tribunal were to outsource a decision to an expert, it may exceed its mandate by allowing procedural determinations to be made by a non-member of the tribunal who is not empowered by the parties to decide the matter. This obstacle may be overcome if the parties consent to the expert rendering a final decision.[143]

3.90 The content of a final report will generally include recommendations and considerations, without revealing the contents of the documents.[144] After receiving the report, the tribunal may determine that the expert should continue in his or her role with regard to further activities. He or she may be asked to supervise the exchange of information, review redactions that have been made to ensure compliance with the report or other activities that are required to bring the document production phase to a successful conclusion.

---

140 See: ICC Case No. 6497, *supra* n. 103, para. 3.62: "By its Procedural Ordinance No 3, with detailed motivation, the arbitral tribunal decided to order an independent expertise. The arbitral tribunal decided in particular: 'At any point of time, if some particular difficulty appears (in particular, if some debits apparently corresponding to the credits had been transferred to other accounts of the claimant group), the expert will report to the arbitral tribunal. After having heard the parties, the arbitral tribunal will give to the expert the appropriate directions and possibly complete the present mission. Claimant is invited to confirm in writing to the arbitral tribunal whether they accept to co-operate in principle with the expert to be appointed. In the affirmative, the arbitral tribunal will appoint an expert. The parties will have a time-limit of ten days to present possibly their grounds for challenging such expert. In the negative, the arbitral tribunal will renounce to such expertise, taking such attitude of claimant in consideration for its final decision."

141 *Guyana v Suriname*, *supra* n. 139, Procedural Order No. 3, para. 2 (12 October 2005).

142 *Ibid.*, Procedural Order No. 4, para. 3 (12 October 2005).

143 Van Houtte, *supra* n. 137, p. 626. The author notes that, "However, parties who can agree in an arbitration clause that their dispute will be settled by arbitrators and not by the state court, *a fortiori* also can agree that a limited and preliminary aspect of this dispute settlement . . . will be carried out by an expert."

144 *Guyana v Suriname*, *supra* n. 139, Procedural Order No. 5 (16 February 2006). Regarding the report and the communications that may take place between an appointed expert and the tribunal generally, the question may arise whether such information is confidential, or should be exposed to the comments of the parties. A case of the Singapore High Court, *Luzon Hydro Corp (Philippines) v Transfield Philippines Inc* [2004] 4 SLR 705 considered whether the communications of a tribunal-appointed expert, which arose out of an ICC arbitration, were subject to disclosure to the parties. The expert in this matter was appointed originally with the intention that he would provide an expert report on technical matters in a manner consistent with art. 6.1. Nevertheless, it was eventually decided that he would not provide such a report, and instead rendered only administrative assistance to the tribunal. That the work of the expert was merely administrative was one of the determinative factors for the High Court in its decision that the challenge to the Tribunal's decision to maintain confidentiality over the communications should be rejected. One may consider by analogy that the same view should be applied to the expert under art. 3.8. Here it is clear that the expert is not providing evidence for the tribunal to consider in its deliberations, but is rather providing administrative or procedural assistance. In this regard, it would seem that the expert's recommendations or general assistance is a procedural matter which the tribunal may consider *in camera* without invitation to the parties for their comments.

Failure by a party to cooperate with expert

3.91 Failure to cooperate with a tribunal-appointed expert on issues of evidence may constitute grounds for drawing an adverse inference against the non-complying party. This was the case in an ICC arbitration where a party had resisted the disclosure of documents based upon its opinion that they concerned, "business secrets over matters which are not in dispute." The tribunal appointed an expert to review the records in question after consulting the parties. When the resisting party challenged the expert's mandate the tribunal regarded such behaviour as obstructionist and made its position clear in a following procedural order:

> The arbitral tribunal considers therefore that, by their letter claimant now refuses to co-operate with the expertise, as decided in Ordinance No. 3. Consequently, such expertise will not take place. The arbitral tribunal will take account of these circumstances in its final Award.
>
> Claimant should be given a last possibility to accept to co-operate with the expertise as decided in Procedural Ordinance No. 3. Such a decision may be notified to the other party and to the arbitrators latest [within one week]. After such date, refusal of claimant will be deemed to be final.[145]

3.92 In such circumstances where a party has failed to cooperate with an expert by, for example, either criticising an expert's credentials after the opportunity for vetting his or her selection has passed, or by questioning his or her instructions, a tribunal may decide that such obstructionist behaviour warrants the drawing of an adverse inference on the merits or should be considered in regard to the determination of costs.

Court assistance in taking documentary evidence

Article 3.9 2010 IBA Rules:	**If a Party wishes to obtain the production of Documents from a person or organization who is not a Party to the arbitration and from whom the Party cannot obtain the Documents on its own, the Party may, within the time ordered by the Arbitral Tribunal, ask it to take whatever steps are legally available to obtain the requested Documents, or seek leave from the Arbitral Tribunal to take such steps itself. The Party shall submit such request to the Arbitral Tribunal and to the other Parties in writing, and the request shall contain the particulars set forth in Article 3.3, as applicable. The Arbitral Tribunal shall decide on this request and shall take, authorize the requesting Party to take, or order any other Party to take, such steps as the Arbitral Tribunal considers appropriate if, in its discretion, it determines that (i) the Documents would be relevant to the case and material to its outcome, (ii) the requirements of Article 3.3, as applicable, have been satisfied and (iii) none of the reasons for objection set forth in Article 9.2 applies.**
Related Rule Article 27 UNCITRAL Model Law:	The arbitral tribunal or a party with the approval of the arbitral tribunal may request from a competent court of this State assistance in taking evidence. The court may execute the request within its competence and according to its rules on taking evidence.

---

145 ICC Case No. 6497, *supra* n. 103, p. 78.

General discussion

3.93 The taking of evidence in international arbitration is not necessarily confined to the boundaries of the arbitration nor is it restricted only to the parties involved in the dispute before an arbitral tribunal. There are instances where a party may seek to utilise local courts to obtain documents from third parties.[146] To the extent that these documents are prima facie relevant and even necessary to the arbitration proceedings, a tribunal may endorse such actions and/or assist the party seeking to obtain the evidence. In such situations, questions may arise over the appropriateness of a tribunal's involvement in evidence taking outside of the arbitration, and also the control that a tribunal may exercise over such activities.[147]

3.94 Under the provisions of this article, a party may petition a tribunal to assist it in the taking of evidence from a third party if it meets a number of threshold requirements discussed below.[148] As is noted in this section, article 3.9 is the evidentiary rule that compliments *lex arbitri* provisions, such as article 27 of the Model Law, or other national laws that authorise a court to render assistance to arbitrators, or parties in securing documentary evidence. While generally seen as a rule which empowers a tribunal to act, article 3.9 has also been interpreted as having a restrictive function in limiting a party's freedom to approach a court for assistance in obtaining evidence, without first seeking the approval of the tribunal. The current version of this rule replaces the text found in the 1999 IBA Rules that contained less detail.[149] Finally, it should also be noted that article 3.9 is concerned with the taking of evidence from non-parties and thus does not apply to a tribunal's right to petition a court for assistance in taking evidence from a party in the arbitration.

---

146 See: *Mesa Power Group LLC v Government of Canada*, PCA Case No. 2012-17, Procedural Order No. 3, §63 (2013): "The principal submission of the Respondent is that the Tribunal should reject the Section 1782 documents, essentially because they have been procured without the authorization of the Tribunal through US court proceedings in which the Respondent was not involved. The Tribunal has sympathy with some of the Respondent's concerns, but is unable to agree with the position as it has articulated it here." However, "if the Claimant wishes to initiate new proceedings for gathering evidence or to make new requests for further evidence in the existing proceedings, it shall seek the authorization of this Tribunal in advance." *Ibid.*, §68.

147 See: *Euroflon Tekniska Produkter AB v Flexiboys I Motala AB*, *supra*, n. 124.

148 See: *The Lao People's Democratic Republic v Sanum Investments Ltd* [2013] SGHC 186, Singapore High Court (2013), in which subpoenas were issued for third parties in arbitration to testify and to produce documents to the arbitral tribunal. The tribunal stated that "[a]fter the first hearing before me on . . ., I informed counsel that I was minded to grant the orders. I then asked counsel to agree on rewording the subpoenas to reflect the suggested amendments made by me." *Ibid.*, p. 16, §30.

149 Article 3.8, 1999 IBA Rules: "If a Party wishes to obtain the production of documents from a person or organization who is not a Party to the arbitration and from whom the Party cannot obtain the documents on its own, the Party may, within the time ordered by the Arbitral Tribunal, ask it to take whatever steps are legally available to obtain the requested documents. The Party shall identify the documents in sufficient detail and state why such documents are relevant and material to the outcome of the case. The Arbitral Tribunal shall decide on this request and shall take the necessary steps if in its discretion it determines that the documents would be relevant and material." Both the 1999 art. 3.8 and the present 3.9, provide a procedural link between the rules of the arbitration and national laws empowering courts to assist tribunals, and parties, to obtain evidence. In this respect, the rules of the arbitration are to be seen as congruent with such laws. This point was made by an ICDR tribunal in response to a party's complaint that it could not subpoena evidence from a third-party under the arbitral rules. "Respondent also argues that it could not under the Rules get a subpoena for the information on the computer server. But that ignores the statutory basis for subpoenaing that information. Respondent was not sufficiently diligent in pursuing the information it says it needs." ICDR Case No. 50117, Award of Arbitrator, para. 6 (2011) (unpublished).

Threshold issues regarding court involvement

3.95 Historically, international tribunals have been reluctant to involve local courts in the taking of evidence. In this respect, article 3.9 is often seen as a measure of last resort.[150] In line with this general reluctance, article 3.9 requires a party to approach a tribunal only after it has shown that it is unable to secure the evidence itself.[151]

3.96 Therefore one may ask what steps must a party take to secure evidence itself. As will be discussed below, whether a party may approach a court unilaterally without prior approval from the tribunal to secure evidence is controversial. Therefore, where article 3.9 refers to a third party from whom the requesting party "cannot obtain the Documents on its own"; the safest interpretation would be that this language refers to an inability to obtain voluntary production of the evidence from that third party.[152] Thus, a party must first satisfy the tribunal that it indeed cannot obtain voluntary compliance with a request for documents from a non-party before it can succeed on a petition under article 3.9.[153]

3.97 While reasons why a party may not obtain documents from a non-party to the proceedings may come down to the simple unwillingness to get involved, there may also be legal barriers to cooperation. If so, as was noted by a tribunal in an ICC arbitration seated in Geneva, a tribunal will have to determine whether a court is capable of rendering the needed assistance.[154] As will be discussed below, the assistance which courts are permitted to provide to arbitral tribunals varies widely between judicial systems, and in this respect reference to relevant local laws is necessary.

3.98 Once it is shown that a party is unable to obtain the documents of its own efforts, and a court is available to provide the needed assistance, a tribunal must be further convinced that the requested evidence could be a subject of a disclosure order within the arbitration. This is made plain by the 2010 version of this article, where it is stated that the standards in article 3.3 and article 9 apply to a party's request for assistance.[155] Thus, any

---

150 *Methanex Corp v United States of America, supra* n. 7, Final Award, Part II, chapter H. para. 25 (3 August 2005).

151 Moreover, as noted above in regard to art. 3.3, it is generally required that a party obtain documents on their own to the extent that access is reasonably open to them.

152 As will be noted below, however, there is authority to suggest that this language would encompass efforts to gain the documents through legal process. See: *Methanex Corp v United States of America, supra* n. 7.

153 *Ibid., Methanex Corp v United States of America,* Orders on Requests to Gather Additional Evidence and to Reconsider First Partial Award, para. 2 (16 March 2004). The tribunal noted that Methanex had not satisfied the prerequisites for obtaining assistance in petitioning a court under art. 3.9 because it had not shown that it could not obtain the documents on its own. This was so, as it appeared that there was a reasonable chance that the witnesses and documents which Methanex had petitioned for help in securing would be produced by the adverse party during the proceedings.

154 As was noted in regard to Swiss law by the tribunal in ICC Case No. 6401: "It should be mentioned that Swiss law and practice impose a duty of confidentiality to the members of certain profession, that authorize them to refuse to testify. It is generally accepted that the same duty authorizes them to refuse to produce documents." The tribunal would then go on to note that courts in Geneva may have the power to lift such confidentiality. ICC Case No. 6401, Procedural Order, Dominique Hascher (ed.), *Collection of Procedural Decisions in ICC Arbitration 1993–1996,* p. 156 (2nd edition, 1998).

155 English courts have also held that a subpoena issued with the permission of a tribunal for a witness to attend a hearing and produce documents should be narrowly construed, similar to the manner in which document disclosure occurs in arbitration. In considering this issue one court noted in particular that this view was justified given the limited document production procedures in international arbitration: "One should not necessarily expect to find complete symmetry between the documentary procedures that apply in arbitral

request for the disclosure of evidence must meet the criteria of article 3.3 of the IBA Rules, which is to say, *inter alia*, that it is narrow and specific and seeks documents relevant to the case and material to its outcome.[156] Moreover, in addition to this, the petitioning party would also have to demonstrate that the person or corporation to whom the petition would be aimed is in a position to divulge the information (e.g., that it has the documents in their possession, custody, control).

3.99 Given the complications that arise when a petition to a court for assistance is involved, a tribunal may determine to postpone a decision on a request for court assistance until it is certain that the evidence that is sought is sufficiently relevant to a party's case and material to the outcome of the matter.[157]

The scope of article 3.9

3.100 The text of article 3.9 authorises the arbitral tribunal to take "whatever steps are legally available to obtain the requested Documents", or in its place, authorise a party to take such measures itself. The term "legally available" steps is generally seen as a direct reference to utilising national or domestic laws that afford a tribunal the right to issue subpoenas or otherwise petition a local court for assistance in taking evidence. The options may be wider.

3.101 When confronted with the scenario where a non-party who bears a relationship with a party to the arbitration is in possession of the relevant documentary evidence, a tribunal may consider exercising its authority to assist in obtaining disclosure of the documents. A tribunal may, for instance, order a party to the arbitration who is aware of the location or type of documents in possession of a third party to make that information known.[158] Or to the extent that it believes a party to the arbitration is capable of obtaining the documents, a tribunal may issue a procedural order requesting the party to take reasonable steps to obtain and disclose the documents.[159] Furthermore, to the extent that the tribunal believes it would be effective, and would not violate any confidentiality obligations, arbitrators may send an inquiry directly to the third party seeking disclosure of the evidence.[160]

---

proceedings and those that apply to proceedings in court." *Tajik Aluminium Plant v Hydro Aluminium AS* [2005] EWCA Civ 1218, para. 26.

156 In denying the petition before it, the ICC tribunal seated in Switzerland noted, "The Request is not a request for production of documents within the meaning of Swiss law and practice. It aims at allowing the Defendants to make their own search through the files and corporate documents of a certain number of companies belonging to third parties, in order to discover whether they contain evidence to support the Defendants' case." ICC Case No. 6401, *supra* n. 154, p. 159.

157 As an example, an *ad hoc* arbitral tribunal seated in Canada noted that before issuing an order allowing a party to petition a local court for assistance in obtaining discovery, it considered the relevance of the witnesses that were to be summoned, their role in the factual issues before the tribunal, and the necessity of hearing them. *Jardine Lloyd Thompson Canada Inc v SJO Catlin* [2006] AJ No. 32.

158 *Waste Management v Mexico, supra* n. 66, Final Award, para 30: Ordering claimant to obtain documents in possession of a third-party.

159 See for example: the actions taken by an arbitrator under the AAA rules cited to in *Life Receivables Trust v Syndicate 102 at Lloyd's of London*, 549 F.3d, p. 210 (2d Cir. 2008).

160 See: where the tribunal in *Aguas del Tunari v Bolivia* wrote to the Netherlands Ministry of Foreign Affairs to obtain information concerning the interpretation of the relevant treaty. *Supra* n. 50, Final Award. See also: the procedural rule adopted by the tribunal in ICC Case No. 12761 affording itself wide authority to request documents from third-parties: "On its own authority or on the petition of a party, the Arbitral Tribunal may request

3.102 If it is not possible to obtain the documents in question without initiating a legal process, arbitrators may consider national laws that authorise a local court to assist a tribunal in the taking of evidence or allow it to issue subpoenas itself. In this regard, laws like article 27 of the UNCITRAL Model Law countenance court assistance to a tribunal in the taking of evidence.[161] However, the level of assistance available under national laws similar to article 27 will vary according to jurisdiction. Some courts may interpret their domestic legislation, which is similar to article 27, as not permitting court assistance to secure documentary evidence,[162] while others may make provision for only limited assistance, expressly prohibiting pre-hearing disclosure to be ordered on behalf of an arbitral tribunal,[163] whereas others have accepted a more liberal interpretation.[164]

3.103 In the United States, section 7 of the Federal Arbitration Act, the US provision that roughly corresponds in scope to article 27, has received varying interpretations by different Federal Circuits as to the level of evidentiary assistance may be given to an arbitral tribunal. Section 7 provides that a tribunal may issue a subpoena to an individual to appear before them and, "in a proper case to bring with him or them any book, record, document, or paper which may be deemed material as evidence in the case". As to the breadth of possible disclosure or discovery that may be ordered pursuant to this provision, some Federal Circuits adopt the position that this subpoena power includes the ability to request pre-hearing disclosure of documents. Other circuits have denied wide-ranging pre-hearing discovery prior to a hearing.[165]

---

the relevant documents which are in the possession of third parties joined to this arbitral proceeding. However, if the third party recipient of such application does not respond or refuses to cooperate, the Arbitral Tribunal may proceed without said third party or the required documents." ICC Case No. 12761, Procedural Order of 12 March 2004, *ICC Bulletin, 2010 Special Supplement: Decisions on ICC Arbitration Procedure*, p. 73.

161 Article 27, UNCITRAL Model Law.

162 See: the discussion by the tribunal in ICC Case No. 6401 concerning the non-availability of assistance in obtaining document disclosure from a third-party from local courts in Switzerland. ICC Case No. 6401, *supra* n. 154.

163 As an example of the English view, see: *BNP Paribas v Deloitte & Touche, supra* n. 56, p. 236: "This clause [art. 27] is dealing with the taking of evidence and not the disclosure process. The taking of evidence is assisted by the issuing of a subpoena to produce, for introduction into the evidence, particular documents. Thus art. 43 gives effect to this Article. There is nothing in the model law which suggests that the court should assist with the process of disclosure." Hong Kong courts have also adopted this view in the past. See: *Vibroflotation AG v Express Builders Co* [1996] 2(3) MALQR in Albert Jan van den Berg (ed.), *Yearbook Commercial Arbitration*, Vol. XX, p. 287 (1995).

164 In Alberta, Canada, an opposite interpretation of art. 27 was arrived at in *Jardine Lloyd Thompson v Catlin, supra* n. 157, pp. 40–41: "The ordinary and plain meaning of evidence includes evidence gathered by way of discovery. In Alberta such evidence may be read in at the trial or otherwise used in pre-trial applications. If the drafters of art. 27 had intended that assistance would only be given for taking evidence at the hearing, they could have expressly said so. This distinction was not made and in the context of an arbitration proceeding conducted in Alberta, the word 'evidence' must be given its ordinary meaning which includes all evidence whether pre-hearing or at the hearing itself. Article 27 should be interpreted in the light of its objects and purposes. The obvious purpose of art. 27 is to facilitate the tribunal in its search for the truth. I do not conceive that a tribunal has any less desire for, or need for, the truth to reach a fair and proper result than does a court of law."

165 *Life Receivables v Syndicate 102, supra* n. 159, p. 213. See also the following excerpt from Report of The International Commercial Disputes Committee of the Association of the Bar of the City of New York summarising the position of US law on this issue: "Two main issues have confronted courts under § 7. The first issue is whether § 7 authorizes arbitrators to compel pre-hearing document production or testimony from non-parties. There is a conflict regarding this issue among the circuits and between federal and state courts in New York. The Second and Third Circuits have held that § 7 does not authorize arbitrators to order the pre-hearing production of documents or testimony from non-parties; rather, non-parties may be ordered to provide documents and testimony only at a

3.104 As noted in article 3.9, a tribunal may simply authorise a party to pursue court action to obtain documents on their own – which may mean permitting a party to issue a subpoena or apply to a court for assistance. In so doing, a tribunal may issue a written directive recording its acquiescence to such an action. Nevertheless, the extent of a tribunal's actual involvement in subpoenaing documents or otherwise petitioning a court to order disclosure of them may depend on the requirements of the relevant domestic law. In the instance of section 7 of the Federal Arbitration Act, the tribunal must sign the subpoena, whereas a similar provision in the English Arbitration Act, section 43, provides that a party itself, with the acquiescence of the tribunal, may issue the subpoena.[166] Article 27 does not make specific reference to the procedure to be followed by the tribunal, but the practice in some jurisdictions which have enacted the Model Law is that a party, following a procedural order by the tribunal authorising it do so, may pursue the subpoena on its own.[167] For reasons owing to expediency, cost, and need to maintain its neutrality, a tribunal will likely wish to limit its actual involvement in the process to as little as possible.

3.105 Two additional issues regarding the scope of article 3.9 are worth further consideration. First, the language of the rule should not be interpreted as implying a duty upon a tribunal to pursue evidence in the possession of third parties. Both domestic courts and international tribunals have recognised that irrespective of the claimed (or even proven) probity of a piece of evidence, the decision to order, or to authorise, further attempts at disclosure through the courts is within the tribunal's discretion and it may decline to take further measures if it so chooses.[168] Secondly, the question has arisen as to whether article 3.9 would prohibit an attempt to pursue assistance from a court without the consultation or approval of the tribunal. That issue is discussed below.

---

hearing before one or more of the arbitrators. The Fourth Circuit has suggested that a federal court may compel a non-party to comply with an arbitrator's subpoena for prehearing document production or testimony upon a showing of 'special need or hardship'. In New York, the Appellate Division for the First Department, purporting to follow the Fourth Circuit, has held that, under § 7, courts may require pre-hearing document production and testimony from non-parties in cases of 'special need.' The Sixth and Eighth Circuits have concluded that arbitrators are authorized by § 7 to issue orders requiring pre-hearing production of documents from non-parties, but have not addressed the question whether pre-hearing testimony is also permitted." *American Review of International Arbitration*, Vol. 20, No. 2, pp. 422–423.

166 Title 9 section 7 of the US Code, reads in part: "Said summons shall issue in the name of the arbitrator or arbitrators, or a majority of them, and shall be signed by the arbitrators, or a majority of them, and shall be directed to the said person and shall be served in the same manner as subpoenas to appear and testify before the court." Section 43 of the English Arbitration Act reads (in part): "A party to arbitral proceedings may use the same court procedures as are available in relation to legal proceedings to secure the attendance before the tribunal of a witness in order to give oral testimony or to produce documents or other material evidence. This may only be done with the permission of the tribunal or the agreement of the other parties." Where the cooperation of a tribunal with a party's efforts may be implied from the actions of the arbitrators, Hong Kong courts have tended to waive the requirement of formal approval. *Vibroflotation v Express Builders, supra* n. 163.

167 *Jardine Lloyd Thompson v Western Oil Sands, supra* n. 135.

168 As noted by the *ad hoc* committee in the *Wena Hotels v Egypt* ICSID annulment application: "The Applicant tries to turn the discretionary nature of the rules on evidence to their contrary when it asserts the existence of an obligation on the tribunal to call for evidence on any item critical to the outcome of the dispute . . . The Applicant fails to demonstrate the existence of a fundamental rule of procedure which would have put the tribunal under an obligation to call for further evidence concerning Mr. Kandil [an alleged witness]." *Wena Hotels Ltd v Arab Republic of Egypt*, ICSID Case No. ARB/98/4, Decision on Annulment, para. 73 (2002). See also: the comments to art. 3.2.

A tribunal's authority over ancillary evidence gathering

3.106 The tribunal is vested with authority over evidentiary procedure within the boundaries of the *lex arbitri* and the agreement to arbitrate. In light of this basic presumption, article 3.9 (and its predecessor article 3.8 of the 1999 Rules) has been interpreted to restrict a party's right to unilaterally seek assistance from a court without permission from the tribunal. This issue comes to the fore when a party seeks to utilise domestic laws that allow it to seek assistance directly from a court in securing evidence from a relevant party.

3.107 One of the most wide-ranging laws permitting a court to assist a party in gathering evidence for potential use in international arbitration is the often discussed section 1782 of Title 28 of the *United States Code*.[169] This provision permits federal courts in the United States to potentially order wide-ranging US-style discovery on behalf of a party to an international arbitration. To the extent that this law or other similar laws permit a party to petition a court on its own, the question has arisen in the past whether article 3.9 requires a party to first seek approval from a tribunal before approaching local courts for assistance.[170]

3.108 Article 3.8 of the 1999 version of the Rules made no specific reference to unilateral attempts by a party to approach a court for the purpose of obtaining evidence, and in fact stated that the rule was to apply where a party needed assistance in obtaining evidence it could not obtain on its own (the same language appears in the new article 3.9). However, article 3.9 in the 2010 Rules now states that, in addition to petitioning a tribunal for help in obtaining court-assisted disclosure, a party "may . . . seek leave from the Arbitral Tribunal to take such steps itself". In a similar vein, article 3.9 states in its final sentence that "The Arbitral Tribunal shall decide on this request and shall take, authorize the requesting Party to take, or order any other Party to take, such steps as the Arbitral Tribunal considers appropriate . . .". The additional wording appears to presuppose that a party to the arbitration may not act without the prior acquiescence of the tribunal.[171]

---

169 28 USC § 1782(a): "The district court of the district in which a person resides or is found may order him to give his testimony or statement or to produce a document or other thing for use in a proceeding in a foreign or international tribunal, including criminal investigations conducted before formal accusation. The order may be made pursuant to a letter rogatory issued, or request made, by a foreign or international tribunal or upon the application of any interested person and may direct that the testimony or statement be given, or the document or other thing be produced, before a person appointed by the court. By virtue of his appointment, the person appointed has power to administer any necessary oath and take the testimony or statement. The order may prescribe the practice and procedure, which may be in whole or part the practice and procedure of the foreign country or the international tribunal, for taking the testimony or statement or producing the document or other thing. To the extent that the order does not prescribe otherwise, the testimony or statement shall be taken, and the document or other thing produced, in accordance with the Federal Rules of Civil Procedure. A person may not be compelled to give his testimony or statement or to produce a document or other thing in violation of any legally applicable privilege."

170 See: *Re the Republic of Ecuador*, No. C 11-80171 CRB, 2011 WL 4434816, at *2 (N.D. Cal. 23 September 2011): "A district court may grant an application under 28 U.S.C. § 1782 where (1) the person from whom discovery is sought resides or is found in the district of the district court to which the application is made; (2) the discovery is for use in a foreign tribunal; and (3) the application is made by a foreign or international tribunal or "any interested person." 28 U.S.C. § 1782. Respondents do not dispute that these statutory requirements have been met." See also: *Re Broadsheet LLC*, No. 11-CV-02436-PAB-KMT, 2011 WL 4949864, at *2 (D. Colo. Oct. 18, 2011): The Court also "may take into account the nature of the foreign tribunal, the character of the proceedings underway abroad, and the receptivity of the foreign government or the court . . . abroad to U.S. federal-court judicial assistance. [. . .] Finally, although the subpoenas request many categories of documents, the Court does not find that on their face the requests are "unduly intrusive or burdensome."

171 The official comments of the Review Subcommittee state that: "Ultimate oversight and control over this process should remain with the arbitral tribunal. However, there may be circumstances under which a party is

3.109 In *Methanex v United States of America*, an UNCITRAL arbitration, the investor-party announced its intention to seek court assistance in securing documents via section 1782, without first obtaining the permission of the tribunal. In this instance, it was clear that the investor-party interpreted article 3.8 of the 1999 Rules as not requiring a party to seek prior approval from a tribunal before unilaterally petitioning a court for assistance.[172] In that case the tribunal agreed with the investor-party's understanding of article 3.8, adopting the view that the qualifying language in article 3.8 "from whom the Party cannot obtain the Documents on its own", assumed that a party was free on its own to file an application such as the one under section 1782.[173]

3.110 The *Methanex* interpretation was not followed in a federal district court decision that interpreted article 3.8 of the 1999 Rules in regard to a petition filed in connection with the ICSID arbitration, *Caratube v Republic of Kazakhstan*. In this case the investor-party initiated a parallel section 1782 application to obtain further evidence from the state-party.[174] The tribunal was presented with the investor's decision to begin the section 1782 application *post facto*, when it received the state-party's request to order the investor-party to desist from its application to the court. The tribunal declined to do so, but noted that "whilst the tribunal might have been minded to find that its prior consent should have been sought by Claimant before the presentation of its Section 1782 petition, the Tribunal concludes that it is not necessary for it to order Claimant to cease and desist from the US action."[175]

3.111 The matter was then heard by the US District Court for the District of Columbia. In its decision denying the application, the District Court noted that Caratube's unilateral petition had "side-stepped" article 3.8, thus undermining "the Tribunal's control over the discovery process."[176] In a footnote to the decision, the court further interpreted article 3.8 of the 1999 version of the Rules:

> Although Caratube does not make this argument in its briefs, it previously contended in a letter to the Tribunal that the IBA Rules anticipate that parties may seek unilateral discovery via a section 1782 petition. Specifically it noted that IBA Rule 3.8 applies only to discovery from entities 'from whom the party cannot obtain documents on its own', and asserted that this text anticipates that parties may file section 1782 petitions to obtain such discovery. The Court disagrees: the better reading, given the context of this rule, is that the sentence refers to efforts to obtain documents without legal process.[177]

---

better positioned to undertake such steps, including, for example, due to presence in the country in question." *Commentary on the revised text of the 2010 IBA Rules, supra* n. 61, p. 11.

172 *Methanex v United States of America, supra* n. 7, Final Award II, chapter G, para. 21.

173 *Ibid.*

174 *Re application of Caratube International Oil Co*, 730 F. Supp. 2d 101, Case No. 10-0285 (US Dist. D.C. 2010).

175 *Ibid.*, p. 104.

176 *Ibid.*, p. 108.

177 *Ibid.* See also: the decision by the Illinois Court of Appeals, where the court was seized of the issue, *inter alia*, of whether it ought to approve a petition for discovery by a party who had a dual role as a litigant in a pending ICC arbitration and in state court proceedings. In consideration of whether it should order the discovery, the court specifically took note that it would be tantamount essentially to side stepping the rulings of the arbitral tribunal: "In this case, if the circuit court permitted discovery in the declaratory judgment action prior to the resolution of the Underlying Action [the ICC Arbitration], plaintiffs would then be allowed to 'lay the groundwork' for both a later denial of coverage and circumvent the discovery rulings made in the Underlying Action [the ICC Arbitration]. This result unfairly would benefit the dual-role Reinsurers participating both as plaintiffs in this case and as Underlying Claimants." *Certain Underwriters at Lloyd's London et al. v Boeing et al., supra* n. 44, p. 50. See also:

3.112 According to the *Caratube* court, therefore, the reference in article 3.8 of the 1999 Rules to documentary evidence which a party cannot "obtain . . . on its own", is best understood as referring to documents which cannot be obtained by means other than legal process (e.g., voluntary production). This is, of course, a more restrictive ruling than that given by the *Methanex* tribunal.

3.113 However, it is arguably more consistent with the 2010 version of this article. As article 3.9 states that a party may "seek leave from the Arbitral Tribunal to take such steps itself", or "The Arbitral Tribunal shall decide on this request and . . . authorize the requesting Party to take . . . such steps", this language presumes that any attempt by a party to gain evidence through the courts (e.g., through section 1782) should fall under the authority of the tribunal.[178]

Treatment of evidence obtained by unauthorised ancillary legal process

3.114 The tribunal in *Caratube* considered how it might treat evidence obtained through a non-authorised ancillary legal process. The tribunal commented that it would have to consider whether any evidence could be admitted "having regard to its obligation to accord procedural fairness . . .", particularly the need to allow the opposing party to

---

the decision of the Singapore High Court in relation to a request by a party to a SIAC arbitration to unilaterally subpoena a witness to appear at an arbitral hearing. Here the court also noted that to act on the petition would in fact side-step the tribunal's authority: "In my view, from the aforementioned express provisions under Procedural Order No. 1, IBA Rules and the correspondence between both the parties and the Arbitrator, it was clear that the parties had contractually agreed on the procedure to be adopted with regard to the calling of witnesses. These were agreed procedural terms by which both parties entered in good faith, and to circumvent and sidestep these directions seemed to obviate the very purpose of entering into such detailed directions with the Arbitrator in the first place." Michael Hwang and Zihua Su, "*ALC v ALF*, SGHC Case No. 231 (2010)", *A Contribution by the ITA Board of Reporters*, para. 29. For an opposite result, however, see *Re Ecuador*, where in 2011 a US district court considered a request for assistance under s. 1782, to obtain documents held by an expert retained by a party to an UNCITRAL arbitration. The court found in this instance that rule 3.9 permitted a party to take measures on its own to obtain documents via a s. 1782 application. The relevant portion of the court's reasoning is as follows: "There is no provision in the UNCITRAL Rules for production of documents from a non-party. Article 3, of the Rules adopted by the 'Members of the IBA [International Bar Association] Rules of Evidence Review Subcommittee,' which the tribunal may consult on an advisory basis, only applies to the process of obtaining documents from a non-party '*from whom the Party cannot obtain the Documents on its own . . .*', and the party may only ask the Tribunal to 'take whatever steps are *legally* available'. Ecuador can obtain documents from Dr. Hinchee by means of *§ 1782*. Thus, on its face this rule is not available to Ecuador to obtain documents from Dr. Hinchee." *Re Ecuador, supra* n. 78. Therefore, the court reasoned that this rule does not prevent a party from taking measures on its "own", such as lodging an application under s. 1782, to obtain documents (the opposite conclusion to what was reached in *Caratube*). Further, the court took note of the above mentioned position adopted in *Methanex* to find that the arbitral tribunal would not consider that a s. 1782 application should first be approved by the tribunal. In the view of the court, the *Methanex* precedent indicated that it was the inclination of the arbitrators to permit the courts in the US to determine the propriety of such applications.

178 In the case *Re Rhodianyl*, a US district court denied an application under s. 1782 even where the petitioning party argued that the evidence it was seeking had been ordered by the tribunal to be disclosed, and was being withheld by the adverse party in breach of its procedural duty to observe the tribunal's procedural order directing disclosure. The district court still denied the application, noting that the tribunal had the necessary authority to compel production or otherwise draw an inference, because the party from whom the discovery was sought was a party to the arbitration: "While applicants allege that respondents have refused to comply with discovery orders of the Arbitral Tribunal, the applicants also have an effective remedy for such alleged violations by seeking an adverse inference from the Tribunal. And indeed, applicants have followed this route, and requested such inference. The court finds that the requested information is not "unobtainable absent § 1782 aid." The clear inference to be drawn by the court's view is that the tribunal's authority over the process was sufficient for the petitioning party to obtain procedural relief for its complaint, and thus, unless the tribunal sought the s. 1782 assistance, the court was not prepared to assist the party seeking the documents. *Rhodianyl, supra* n. 56, p. 52.

respond to such documents and produce counter-evidence.[179] This comment pinpoints two key considerations: procedural economy and fairness to the opposing party.[180] These grounds are both stated within the revised article 9.2(g) as a basis for excluding documents from a procedure, empowering a tribunal to refuse the fruits of the ancillary legal process if a tribunal regards such an attempt as a violation of its authority under article 3.9 (see Chapter 9). Moreover, a tribunal may under article 3.1 set time frames. Therefore, a failure to file evidence obtained through court assistance within the procedural timetable may be grounds for exclusion of those documents.[181] Nevertheless, even in this respect a tribunal would most likely consider the potential probative value of such evidence before ruling to exclude it.[182]

General powers of a tribunal to order disclosure

Article 3.10 2010 IBA Rules:	At any time before the arbitration is concluded, the Arbitral Tribunal may (i) request any Party to produce Documents, (ii) request any Party to use its best efforts to take or (iii) itself take, any step that it considers appropriate to obtain Documents from any person or organisation. A Party to whom such a request for Documents is addressed may object to the request for any of the reasons set forth in Article 9.2. In such cases, Article 3.4 to Article 3.8 shall apply correspondingly.
Other Statements of the Rule Article 27(3) UNCITRAL Rules:	At any time during the arbitral proceedings the arbitral tribunal may require the parties to produce documents, exhibits or other evidence within such a period of time as the arbitral tribunal shall determine.

---

179 See: generally comments to art. 3.11.

180 See: generally comments to art. 9.2(g).

181 See: the example of an UNCITRAL tribunal sitting in Switzerland, which ordered in relation to all documents obtained through an ancillary discovery process under s. 1782, that such evidence, "would have to be produced according to the procedural timetable, as provided by Procedural Order No. 2", as reported in *CEH Lempa v Nejapa Power*, *supra* n. 9. See also: the procedural rule adopted by the tribunal in ICC Case No. 12279 where the tribunal informed the parties of their obligation to submit any evidence obtained from third-parties by use of subpoenas prior to any hearing. "The Parties acknowledge the possibility of subpoenas being necessary to obtain documents from third parties which are not parties to the present arbitration. The Parties should endeavor to obtain such documents in advance of the hearing, so that documents are available prior to written submissions and do not cause unnecessary delay." ICC Case No. 12279, *supra* n. 66.

182 It may also be that a tribunal regards unilateral petitions to local courts in violation of art. 3.9 to be in "bad faith", thus invoking the powers granted to arbitrators in art. 9.7 to award the costs of the arbitration against a party it believes "has failed to conduct itself in good faith in the taking of evidence". Other tribunals have adopted similar approaches but have left the door open to challenges to the admissibility of such documents, referencing objections based on article 9.2(g) of the IBA Rules. "[T]he Tribunal does not believe that it should summarily reject – in advance of their filing – all the Section 1782 documents that the Claimant may one day submit, for the sole reason that they have been procured though court proceedings. Once the documents are before the Tribunal, the Respondent will be able to object to them on the basis of the IBA Rules on the Taking of Evidence or any other applicable rules of arbitral procedure . . . Finally, the Tribunal agrees with the Respondent's request that further efforts by the Claimant to obtain evidence on Section 1782 be pursued exclusively under the supervision of the Tribunal." Charles H. Brower II, *Mesa Power Group, LLC v Canada*, Procedural Order No. 3, High Court, 28 March 201', A contribution by the ITA Board of Reporters, (Kluwer Law International).

General discussion

3.115 The principle aim of article 3.10 is to empower the tribunal to initiate requests for document production of its own accord.[183] Under article 3.10 the arbitral tribunal's may *sua sponte* (1) request a party to produce documents, (2) request a party to use its best efforts to procure or obtain documentary evidence from a non-party, or (3) itself take steps it deems appropriate to obtain documents from persons or organisations that are not a party to the proceedings. The earlier version of this article, article 3.9 of the 1999 version of the Rules, merely authorised tribunals to request a party to produce documents that were deemed relevant and material; however, non-parties and related entities were not addressed.

3.116 The tribunal's powers in this article should be distinguished from that set forth in the preceding article 3.9 which also grants the tribunal the right to petition a court for assistance in obtaining production of documents. Whereas article 3.9 is directed towards obtaining documentary evidence from third parties based upon a party's request for production, article 3.10 empowers a tribunal of its own initiative to seek to obtain evidence from one of the parties presently before them in the arbitration or to take appropriate measures to obtain documents from a third-party, which may include seeking court assistance.[184]

3.117 Under subparagraph (ii), a tribunal may also request a party to use its best efforts (including ancillary legal process) to obtain documents. Presumably a tribunal would direct a request to a party only if it felt comfortable with the burden such a request would impose (see comments to article 9.2(c)).

---

183 See: *Bear Creek Mining Corporation v Republic of Peru*, ICSID Case No. ARB/14/21, Procedural Order No. 1, §16.4 (2015): "The Tribunal may call upon the Parties to produce documents or other evidence in accordance with ICSID Arbitration Rule 34(2)." See also: *South American Silver Ltd v The Plurinational State of Bolivia*, PCA Case No. 2013-15, Procedural Order No. 2, §19 (2014): "Section 6.1 of Procedural Order No. 1 provides that the Tribunal may use as a guideline the IBA Rules on the Taking of Evidence in International Arbitration 2010 (the "IBA Rules") . . .". See also: *Cortec Mining Kenya Ltd, Cortec (Pty) Ltd and Stirling Capital Ltd v Republic of Kenya*, ICSID Case No. ARB/15/29, Procedural Order No. 1 (2016), §15.10: "The Tribunal may call upon the Parties to produce documents or other evidence in accordance with ICSID Arbitration Rule 34(2). In that case, the documents shall be submitted to the other Party and to the Tribunal in accordance with §16 below and shall be deemed on record." See also: *David Aven et al. v The Republic of Costa Rica*, Arbitration Proceeding Under Chapter 10 of the Dominican Republic-Central America-United States Free Trade Agreement and the UNCITRAL Arbitration Rules (2010) (UNCT/15/3), Procedural Order No 1 (2015), §15.4: "The Tribunal may call upon the parties to produce documents or other evidence within such a period as the tribunal shall determine."

184 See: *X.____ (International) v A.____, 4A_596/2012*, a civil appeal from an International Chamber of Commerce (ICC) Award filed before the First Civil law Court of the Swiss Federal Tribunal. The Swiss Federal Tribunal stated that "in the Procedural Orders under appeal, the Arbitral Tribunal ordered the production of a document under the control of the Appellant. In doing so, it relied on Art. 20 (4) of the rules of arbitration of the ICC (hereafter: the ICC Rules) and on Art. 3 (10) of the IBA Rules on the Taking of Evidence in International Commercial Arbitration." On adverse inference, the Swiss Federal Tribunal stated that "[i]f a party fails to produce a pertinent document without satisfactory reasons after the other party requested its production or when it was ordered by the Arbitral Tribunal and has not objected in due time, the Arbitral Tribunal may infer according to Art. 9 (5) of the IBA Rules that such document would be adverse to the interests of that party." Finally, the Swiss Federal Tribunal stated that the IBA Rules are exclusively procedural in nature and not substantive, and, "consequently, it is not a decision that can be appealed within the meaning of Art. 77 BGG." Because the production of evidence was not a matter capable of appeal, the civil appeal before the Swiss Federal Tribunal was rejected.

A tribunal's right to request document production from a party

3.118 Article 3.10 essentially confirms a power which is generally considered to be inherent to a tribunal's wider authority.[185] The power given to a tribunal to order the production of documents, pursuant to either a request from a party or *sua sponte*, is also confirmed in certain institutional rules.[186] Moreover, a tribunal has the authority to order specific evidence to be submitted by one party without opening the procedure to a new round of evidence production.[187]

3.119 The customary time frames that apply in international arbitration for the taking of evidence (see comments to articles 3.1 and 3.2) do not circumscribe the tribunal's authority to reopen the document production phase of the proceedings at any stage it deems appropriate.[188] This includes after the hearing, during which the tribunal may allow the parties to produce (or request) evidence, or order the disclosure of evidence *sua sponte* if it is deemed

---

185 See generally the comments to art. 3.4. "[T]he fact finding powers of international courts represents an essential part of their adjudicative function, and so where the power is not expressly included in the constitutive instrument, international courts arguably have an inherent power to request the production of further evidence." Chester Brown, *A Common Law of International Adjudication, International Courts and Tribunal Series*, p. 104 (2007). See also: Poudret and Besson, *supra* n. 1, s. 650, "Even in the absence of such a rule, it is recognized that such powers results from the general powers of the arbitrators to lay down rules for the arbitral proceedings." See the decision of the tribunal in ICC Case No. 13504, sitting in consideration of a dispute over a price review provision of an energy agreement, to call the parties to submit additional evidence because neither had adequately substantiated their positions. In this instance, the tribunal considered that to exercise its right to call *sua sponte* for additional evidence to be produced would facilitate the procedure: "The Arbitral Tribunal clearly sees the difficulties that the Parties are faced with initially when to substantiate or to dispute a price review request . . . Accordingly, the Arbitral Tribunal considers that it is appropriate to allow or request the Parties to later provide further information in order to refine the substantiation of their claims, counterclaims or documentation related to previously claimed factual market developments during the review period. In accordance with this view, the Arbitral Tribunal requested both parties to submit updated information . . .". ICC Case No. 13504, Final Award, *ICC Bulletin*, Vol. 20, No. 2, p. 107 (2009). See also: the determination of another tribunal, in ICC Case No. 14403, to order, on its own motion, the claimant to submit documents concerning a bid review, audit certifications, and other relevant documents. This procedural order was made following the oral hearing, and after the tribunal had determined that certain relevant evidence was in the possession of the claimant which, if produced, would be useful for determining the outcome of the case. ICC Case No. 14403, Final Award, para. 9 (2008) (unpublished).

186 See, for example: ICC Rules, art. 25(5). See also: *Mesa Power Group LLC v Government of Canada*, PCA Case No. 2012-17, Procedural Order No. 1, §12.4 (2012): "In addition, the Tribunal may of its own motion order a Party to produce documents at any time."

187 As the *ad hoc* committee noted in *Enron v Argentina*: "The Committee does not consider it inconsistent with any fundamental rule of procedure for a tribunal to give one party an opportunity to present specific additional evidence on a particular point where the tribunal finds that there are circumstances that justify this." *Enron Creditors Recovery Corp v Argentina*, ICSID Case No. ARB/01/3, Decision on the Application of Annulment, para. 192 (2010). See also: where the Madrid Court of Appeals did not consider that a decision by a tribunal to admit extra submissions by one party, where the other was not allotted any further opportunities to do so, was an annullable error. The court noted that the extra submissions "merely supplemented and clarified" the record. F. M. Serrano, "22 June 2009 Madrid Court of Appeals", *A Contribution by the ITA Board of Reporters*. Tribunals should give consideration to due process, specifically each party's right to be heard is ordering such a measure.

188 ICC Case No. 6192, Partial Award, *ICC Bulletin*, Vol. 8, No. 2, p. 6, paras 19–21 (1997): "l'arbitre a demandé aux parties, lors de l'audience du 4 décembre 1989, la production de pieces complémentaires" (unofficial translation) "the arbitrator requested the parties, at the hearing on 4 December 1989, to produce additional documents." See also: ICC Case No. 11367, Final Award, *ICC Bulletin*, Vol. 17, No. 2, p. 94, paras 16–17 (2006): "On 17.01.2002 the Arbitrator sent a letter to the parties, stating: As a consequence of [Company X]'s letter dated 9.11.2001, in which [Company X] rejects the Equipment, a number of new issues have arisen, which require additional evidence, in order to ascertain the reasons why [Company X] has taken such decision, and its possible impact on the contractual relation between Claimant and Defendant."

necessary to do so. A tribunal may request the production of evidence at any moment prior to the termination of the proceedings, or until it is otherwise *functus officio*.[189]

3.120 Because the parties are to be treated equally, and must be afforded the same opportunities to provide comments on disclosure requests, irrespective of whether they come from a tribunal on its own motion or from another party, a tribunal must give the party ordered to submit the evidence an opportunity to object to any proposed disclosure. For this reason, a tribunal should follow the procedure in articles 3.4 to 3.8 before ordering the production of documentary evidence.

3.121 Finally, non-compliance with a tribunal's order for the disclosure of evidence, irrespective of whether such order was issued directly by the tribunal or in response to another party's request, carries with it the same risks. Namely, that a tribunal will draw an adverse inference,[190] or find that a party's refusal has been made in bad faith, hence affecting its decision on the costs of the arbitration. Also, as discussed below, non-compliance may lead a tribunal to seek judicial assistance in the taking of evidence.

*A tribunal's authority to compel a party to use "best efforts" to obtain
evidence held by "any person or organisation"*

3.122 The authority described in article 3.10(ii) affords a tribunal the right to request a party to use best efforts to obtain documents that are in the possession of "any person or organisation", which is most often applied to entities related to one of the parties. It has been previously held that parties may be legitimately expected to produce documents from companies with which they maintain a significant relationship.[191] What "relationship" means is not entirely clear, but in the view of this author it would encompass any affiliation through which a party could be reasonably expected to exert or have significant influence over another entity. Parties which plead that a document is outside of their control because it is in the possession of a parent or subsidiary company may be requested to make "best

---

189 *El Paso Corp v La Comisión Ejecutiva Hidroelectrica Del Rio Lempa*, LEXIS 17596, 341 Fed Appx 31, pp. 5–6 (US App. 2009). In this case the court took express notice of the right which a tribunal has to reopen a proceeding after a hearing, and receive additional evidence: "Under [the] UNCITRAL arbitration rules, an 'arbitral tribunal may, if it considers it necessary owing to exceptional circumstances, decide, on its own motion or upon application of a party, to reopen the hearings at any time before the award is made'. If CEL discovers new evidence from its § 1782 application, it may ask the arbitral tribunal to reopen the evidentiary hearing to consider the evidence. Though this might be unlikely given the arbitral tribunal's expressed disapproval of CEL's discovery efforts in the United States, the possibility is enough to prevent the appeal from becoming moot." *Id.*

190 See: *Adel A Hamadi Al Tamimi v Sultanate of Oman*, ICSID Case No. ARB/11/33, Procedural Order No. 9, (2014), pp. 3–4, §10: "Since the parties are represented by high-quality and reputable legal firms with very ample resources, the Tribunal takes the view that if an assertion of a good faith search has been made, then generally that will be accepted by the Tribunal unless and until an opposing party is able to demonstrate, by the reference to other specific evidence or documents, that the assertion of a good faith search is clearly suspect or unfounded. Of course, if such an assertion of good faith is made but it turns out at the hearing that a party has not conducted itself in good faith in the disclosure process, any such failure may be taken into account by the Tribunal. For example, the Tribunal may infer that the documents that were not produced would have been adverse to the interests of the party to whom the request was made (IBA Rules, Artile 9(6)), and the Tribunal may also take such failure into account in the allocation of the costs of the arbitration, including costs arising out of or in connection with the production of evidence (IBA Rules, Article 9(7))."

191 See: comments to art. 3.3 above. See also the discussion of *Perenco* in footnote 193, *infra*.

efforts" to obtain and produce the document as per the express powers of article 3.10. Failure to do so may lead a tribunal to draw a negative inference.[192]

A tribunal's power to take "any steps"

3.123 As noted above, under IBA Rules article 3.9, a tribunal may take "any step that it considers appropriate to obtain documentary evidence from any person or organisation", which may involve seeking the assistance of a court.[193] This principle is embodied in the *lex arbitri* of many jurisdictions, such as in laws similar to article 27 of the UNCITRAL Model Law, or in laws such as section 7 of the US Federal Arbitration Act. The range of options available to a tribunal will be determined by the limits upon court assistance imposed by the relevant arbitration law.

3.124 In most instances, a tribunal's decision to seek judicial assistance will be directed to the court that exercises supervisory jurisdiction over the arbitration at the seat. However, a tribunal's options are not so restricted. In fact, a tribunal may under the laws of some countries approach courts in jurisdictions other than where the tribunal is seated to seek assistance (see discussion on section 1782 in comments to article 3.9).

3.125 To the extent that a tribunal will petition a court to subpoena or order a party to the arbitration to provide evidence to the tribunal, such an action should not be viewed as a breach of the principle of impartiality. A decision to approach a court by a tribunal would in most instances follow only after a tribunal has taken the necessary steps leading to such a request; which are, first, determining after receiving the comments from the parties that the evidence is relevant and material, and, second, issuing a procedural order requesting a party to produce the evidence. In this situation, a tribunal's decision to seek judicial assistance to compel a party to produce documentary evidence should be viewed in the same light as a decision by a tribunal to draw an adverse inference, that is, not as an act of partiality towards one party but as an appropriate response to the non-compliance with a procedural order.

---

192 See: *Mother company of joint venture corporation shareholder (US) v venture corporation shareholder (Mexico)*, Final Award, ICC Case No. 15248, International Court of Arbitration of the International Chamber of Commerce (2013), in Albert Jan van den Berg (ed.), *Yearbook Commercial Arbitration 2013* – Volume XXXVIII, Kluwer Law International (2013), pp. 127–173: "The arbitrators first noted that Respondent failed to comply adequately with procedural orders regarding document production and that the conduct of Respondent and the members of the XYZ family in the arbitration was generally uncooperative. This, reasoned the tribunal, had adverse consequences for the Respondent's case when weighing the evidence; however, the tribunal would not rely solely on those adverse consequences." *Ibid.*, p. 128.

193 This does not always have to be the case. Consider the actions taken in ICSID arbitration *Aguas del Tururi v Bolivia*, where the tribunal wrote, on its own motion, to the Netherlands Foreign ministry to obtain information regarding the interpretation of the Dutch/Bolivia BIT. See also: the decision of the ICSID tribunal in *Perenco v Ecuador* where the tribunal directed the parties to use their best efforts to obtain the *travaux préparatoires* of a BIT between Ecuador and France: "The Tribunal therefore invites the Parties to jointly communicate to the French authorities the Tribunal's interest in receiving any *travaux préparatoires* that may shed light on the fact that this Treaty appears to differ from other French treaties in terms of the deletion of the words 'directly or indirectly' from the definition of art. 1(3) (ii) and their insertion in art. 1(1). In particular, The tribunal wishes to understand the process through which the phrase 'directly or indirectly' was deleted from art. 1(3)(ii) and was inserted into art. 1(1)." *Perenco Ecuador Ltd v Republic of Ecuador and Empresa Estatal Petróleos del Ecuador*, ICSID Case No. ARB/08/6, Decision on Jurisdiction, p. 18 (June 2011). In the above two examples, it is clear that arbitrators interpreted their own fact finding authority to include seeking evidence from third parties, by either direct request from the tribunal to the party (see, for example, art. 4.10 in regard to witnesses), or by placing the onus on the parties to obtain specific documents relevant to the case.

Offering supplemental or rebuttal evidence

Article 3.11 2010 IBA Rules: **Within the time ordered by the Arbitral Tribunal, the Parties may submit to the Arbitral Tribunal and to the other Parties any additional Documents on which they intend to rely or which they believe have become relevant to the case and material to its outcome as a consequence of the issues raised in Documents, Witness Statements or Expert Reports submitted or produced, or in other submissions of the Parties.**

General discussion

3.126 Unless otherwise agreed beforehand, it is customary for a party to be afforded an opportunity to provide rebuttal evidence answering arguments or claims brought by its opponent.[194] The Swiss Federal Tribunal has referred to the right to introduce rebuttal evidence as fundamental to *le principe du contradictoire*, or a party's right to a contradictory proceeding.[195] It is widely affirmed in international arbitration practice that a party must generally be allowed to react to adverse evidence presented in the case, which may include the opportunity to produce rebuttal evidence.[196] Article 3.11 restates this rule

---

194 See: *David Aven et al. v The Republic of Costa Rica*, Arbitration Proceeding Under Chapter 10 of the Dominican Republic-Central America-United States Free Trade Agreement and the UNCITRAL Arbitration Rules (2010) (UNCT/15/3), Procedural Order No 1 (2015), §15.1: "The written pleadings shall be accompanied by the documentary evidence relied upon by the parties. Further documentary evidence of a responsive nature relied upon the parties may be submitted in rebuttal with the Reply and Rejoinder."

195 "7 janvier 2004 – Tribunal fédéral, Ire Cour civile (4P.196/2003)", *ASA Bulletin*, Vol. 22, No. 3, pp. 600–601 (2004): "Enfin, le principe de la contradiction, garanti par les mêmes dispositions, exige que chaque partie ait la faculté de se déterminer sur les moyens de son adversaire, d'examiner et de discuter les preuves apportées par lui et de les réfuter par ses propres preuves" (unofficial translation) "Finally, the principle of contradictory proceedings, guaranteed by the same provisions, requires that each party have the possibility to evaluate the arguments of their opponent, to review and discuss the evidence produced by him [the opponent] and to refute them with his own evidence."

196 *Rice Trading (Guyana) Ltd v Nidera Handelscompagnie BV*, District Court The Hague, in Albert Jan van den Berg (ed.), *Yearbook Commercial Arbitration*, Vol. XXIII, pp. 732–733 (1998): "It is established that the documents at issue are the five documents, until then totally unknown to Nidera, submitted by Rice Trading with its statement of 6 June 1996, which Rice Trading itself describes as 'new' documents in its statement, of which four are dated later than the date on which Nidera submitted its statement of claim and one just before that date. This means that, for us to conclude in the present case that Nidera waived its right, based on the fundamental procedural principle of contradictory proceedings, to comment on these documents either orally or in writing, it would be necessary at least that Nidera explicitly agreed that it would not react, either orally or in writing, on the documents, unknown to Nidera, which were to be submitted in the proceedings by Rice Trading in its statement, on 10 June 1996 at the latest. Neither is such an agreement alleged, nor does it appear [to exist]. Hence, the President correctly concluded that the arbitral tribunal violated the fundamental right to contradictory proceedings to Nidera's disadvantage." See also: *Fraport AG Frankfurt Airport Services Worldwide v The Philippines*, ICSID Case No. ARB/03/25, Decision on the Application for Annulment, para. 133 (2010): "The right to present one's case is also accepted as an essential element of the requirement to afford a fair hearing accorded in the principal human rights instruments. This principle requires both equality of arms and the proper participation of the contending parties in the procedure, these being separate but related fundamental elements of a fair trial. The principle will require the tribunal to afford both parties the opportunity to make submissions where new evidence is received and considered by the tribunal to be relevant to its final deliberations." Furthermore, the same committee held that after The Philippines were allowed to introduce new evidence, Fraport should have been awarded the opportunity to make submissions thereon and that failure to do so by the Arbitral Tribunal resulted in a serious departure from a fundamental rule of procedure. *Ibid.*, §246. Based on such failure, the Award was annulled in its entirety. *Ibid.*, §247. See also: *Paklito Investment Ltd v Klockner East Asia Ltd*, Supreme Court of Hong Kong, High Court, in Albert Jan van den Berg (ed.), *Yearbook Commercial Arbitration*, Vol. XIX, pp. 670–674 (1994). See also: the

by entitling the parties to submit additional documentary evidence in support of submissions, contentions and/or arguments aimed at contradicting arguments or evidence introduced by a counterparty.

3.127 In addition to the right to submit rebuttal evidence, article 3.11 widens the tribunal's scope to allow for documents intended as supplemental evidence to be submitted within the "time ordered by the Arbitral Tribunal". Whereas the 1999 version of the article required a party to submit a document that had become relevant and material, parties arbitrating under the 2010 version may submit additional documents if they merely intend to "rely" on them – which obviously casts the net considerably wider.

3.128 In this respect, article 3.11 simply lays down a broad right. However, a tribunal may, through adoption of a procedural rule, structure the proceedings to require evidence to be submitted in accordance with different issues, at various stages, or require the parties to submit primary evidence during the initial stages. If such a procedural rule is adopted, it would limit opportunities for general production of evidence during the later phases of a proceeding.

3.129 Moreover, consistent with a tribunal's authority over the procedure, it may determine to reject evidence that does not meet the definition of "rebuttal" evidence, if such is submitted in the proceedings.[197] Indeed, a tribunal may be required to make such a determination to prevent new evidence coming into the record which would require affording the non-producing party a further opportunity to submit evidence in response. Therefore, a tribunal may instruct the parties to limit supplemental production to purely rebuttal evidence for reasons of economy or other compelling reasons.[198] Rebuttal evidence has been understood in international arbitration to mean "material submitted in response to specific evidence previously filed."[199]

---

considerations of a CAS tribunal where it was held that procedural fairness meant affording a party the right to produce rebuttal evidence: "The Claimant proposed to call a witness, whom it would have tendered as an expert in matters of sponsorship. The panel did not agree to hear the witness, due in part to the lack of sufficient notice of intention to call him. It would not have been fair to the Respondent in the circumstances to have had to deal with such a witness with no prior notice and no chance to call rebuttal evidence." *International Triathlon Union (ITU) v Pacific Sports Corp Inc*, Award of 4 August 1999 – CAS 96/161 in Matthieu Reeb (ed.), *Digest of CAS Awards II 1998–2000*, p. 5.

197 See the following ruling of the Iran-US Tribunal: "It is evident that all of the material contained in these items was available to Iran and could have been submitted to the Tribunal with Iran's earlier filings. As such, the Tribunal finds that these items do not constitute proper items of rebuttal, which the Tribunal has described as 'material submitted in response to specific evidence previously filed'. The Tribunal concludes that all exhibits submitted . . . are inadmissible." *Eastman Kodak Co v the Government of Iran*, Award No. 514-227-3, para. 6 (1 July 1991).

198 *Uiterwyk v The Islamic Republic of Iran, supra* n. 25, Partial Award, p. 7, para. 21. The tribunal in *Azinian et al. v United Mexican States* noted the following in regard to evidence offered in rebuttal: "It should be enough for the Tribunal to exhort the parties to ensure that their respective final Memorials are responsive to their opponent's previous submissions, and be organized in such a way that this responsive character is plain to see. The same reasoning applies to evidence in support of the Reply or Rejoinder." *Azinian et al. v United Mexican States*, ICSID Case No. ARB(AF)/97/2, Decision of the Tribunal Concerning the Filing of a Reply and Rejoinder, p. 1, paras 3–4. See: the following procedural ruling of the Iran-US Claims Tribunal: "In its Order of 27 April 2006, the Tribunal stated that "any arguments and evidence filed by the Respondent on 1 March 2006 . . . that is not submitted in response to the Claimant's documents shall be declared inadmissible." *Islamic Republic of Iran v United States of America*, Partial Award No. 601-A3/A8/A9/A14/B61-FT, (17 July 2009), p. 16. See further: the general comments to art. 9.2(g).

199 *Ibid., Uiterwyk*. See also: the decision of the US Court of Appeals for the Third District which noted that a tribunal sitting in Switzerland under the UNCITRAL Rules had made the following procedural ruling, "all documentary evidence relied upon by the parties was required to be produced with the parties' first submissions

3.130 Domestic courts have affirmed the principle that arbitrators are not required to receive every piece of relevant evidence which a party may offer.[200] Indeed, as long as the parties have been given an equal and fair opportunity to present their evidence, a tribunal is generally empowered to reject evidence for procedural reasons, such as that it does not conform to rebuttal evidence.[201]

Originals, copies, forgeries and translations: the authenticity of documentary evidence

Article 3.12 2010 IBA Rules: With respect to the form of submission or production of Documents:

    (a) copies of Documents shall conform to the originals and, at the request of the Arbitral Tribunal, any original shall be presented for inspection;

    (b) Documents that a Party maintains in electronic form shall be submitted or produced in the form most convenient or economical to it that is reasonably usable by the recipients, unless the Parties agree otherwise or, in the absence of such agreement, the Arbitral Tribunal decides otherwise;

    (c) a Party is not obligated to produce multiple copies of Documents which are essentially identical unless the Arbitral Tribunal decides otherwise; and

    (d) translations of Documents shall be submitted together with the originals and marked as translations with the original language identified.

General discussion

3.131 In the modern practice of international arbitration, it is often presumed that copies of relevant documentary evidence will be produced as opposed to originals, and that unless

---

(i.e., Claimant's August 21, 2008 Statement of Claim and Respondent's October 31, 2008 Statement of Defence and Counterclaims) . . . as provided by Procedural order No. 1, Section F.1 the parties may only produce new documents with their Submission insofar as necessary to respond to an argument or allegation of the other party." *CEH Lempa v Nejapa Power Co LLC, supra* n. 9.

200 *Century v Certain Underwriters, supra* n. 45, p. 558: "Every failure of an arbitrator to receive relevant evidence does not constitute misconduct requiring vacature of an award; a federal court may vacate an award only if the panel's refusal to hear pertinent and material evidence prejudices the rights of the parties to the arbitration proceedings." The court went on to say, "not surprisingly, application of this 'extremely deferential standard' generally results in the confirmation of an arbitration award . . .". See also: the decision of the Court of Appeals in Bizkaia, Spain in *Norplanet v Transportes Bilbainos Vizcaya Audencia Provicial de Bizkaia*, where it was held, ". . . arbitral tribunals are under no obligation to admit all and any evidence offered by the parties . . . a parties' right to be heard is not breached by a court or Arbitral Tribunal's decision not to admit evidence." F. S. Mantilla, "Decision of 29 May 2009 ", *A Contribution by the ITA Board of Reporters.*

201 *Ibid., Century v Certain Underwriters*, pp. 558–559. The court further stated on the issue of admissibility of evidence, an arbitrator "need only grant the parties a fundamentally fair hearing." As an example of a typical procedural order limiting evidence, *Chevron Corp (United States of America) and Texaco Petroleum Co. (United States of America) v The Republic of Ecuador*, UNCITRAL, Interim Award, p. 28, para. 5.3 (1 December 2008): "New factual allegations or evidence shall not be any more permitted after the respective dates for the Rebuttal Memorials indicated in the above Timetable unless agreed between the Parties or expressly authorized by the Tribunal."

there is a challenge to the accuracy of a copy, it will be regarded as an accurate reproduction.[202] Therefore a copy of a document is generally regarded as satisfying the obligation to produce the best evidence in support of an allegation.[203] It is not uncommon for parties to submit copies even where an original is available and could otherwise be submitted. Moreover, tribunals have traditionally accepted facsimiles without requiring production of original correspondence.[204]

3.132 The modern practice is a departure from the early procedures adopted by tribunals and commissions of the nineteenth and twentieth centuries. As was stated in a case before the United States-Venezuelan Mixed Claims Commission of 1885, arbitrators presumed that originals would be submitted as evidence, "It seems to us in a case like this, the best evidence reasonably attainable should be required before an international tribunal . . ."[205] To the extent that copies were submitted in early arbitral procedures, it was often required they be "duly certified" or otherwise have their accuracy verified by an official competent to attest to it.[206] A tribunal may also have required testimony or explanation concerning the reasons why a copy was made or needed, and/or an explanation as to why the original

---

202 As an example, in a procedural order in ICC Case No. 16249, *supra* n. 24, the tribunal ordered that, "all documents submitted as photocopies or electronic copies shall be deemed to be authentic, unless disputed by the other party." Another panel of well-known arbitrators, also constituted under the ICC rules, rendered the following formulation of this rule, "All documents submitted to the Arbitral Tribunal are deemed authentic and complete, including those submitted in copy form, unless the other party disputes their authenticity and/or completeness." ICC Case No. 14069 (unpublished). See also: the following ruling of a WIPO Panel: *Sanofi-Aventis v New Health Care Inc*, WIPO Administrative Panel Decision, Case No. D2008-1881, at chapter 6, Part A (2009), "Although the trademark certificates supplied are not certified as identical to the original, in the context of these expedited UDRP proceedings and noting also the absence of any challenge from the Respondent, they are deemed to be authentic copies." See also: *Mesa Power Group LLC v Government of Canada*, PCA Case No. 2012-17, Procedural Order No. 1, §11.8 (2012): "All documents, including both originals and copies, submitted to the Tribunal shall be deemed to be authentic unless disputed by the other Party."

203 The "best evidence rule" is defined as follows: "The evidentiary rule providing that, to prove the contents of a writing (or a recording or photograph), a party must produce the original writing (or a mechanical, electronic, or other familiar duplicate, such as a photocopy) unless it is unavailable, in which case secondary evidence – the testimony of the drafter or a person who read the document – may be admitted." Bryan A. Garner (ed.), *Black's Law Dictionary*, p. 181 (9th edition, 2009). As applied in international arbitration, the best evidence rule has come to mean, "Where evidence of a better quality should be available and its non-production is not satisfactorily explained, this will weigh against the party whose allegations may either be proved or disproved by such evidence." Bin Cheng, *supra* n. 1, p. 321. The modern practice is that copies should be regarded as of sufficient quality to satisfy this principle unless challenged. See: the rule adopted by the tribunal in ICC Case No. 13046 which is reflected in art. 3.12: "All documentary evidence submitted to the Arbitral Tribunal shall be deemed authentic and complete, including evidence submitted in the form of copies, unless a party disputes its authenticity of completeness." ICC Case No. 13046, Procedural Order of 19 May 2004, *ICC Bulletin, 2010 Special Supplement: Decisions on ICC Arbitration Procedure, supra* n. 7, p. 91; See also: the decision of the Iran-US Claims Tribunal in *Benjamin Isaiah v Bank Mellat* in which the tribunal relied upon the copies of several important documents in combination with testimony from witnesses to find that a prima facie case had been established by the claimant: "The Tribunal has copies of (a) [listing several documents]. These documents, buttressed by credible testimony at the hearing, constitute a prima facie case that the money represented by the check was Isaiah's money and that he has held the claim for that money from the time the check was dishonored. In the absence of evidence to the contrary, that evidence is decisive." *Benjamin R. Isaiah and Bank Mellat*, Award No. 35-219-2, Iran-USCTR, Vol. 2, p. 238–239 (1983).

204 See: ICC Case No. 3779, Final Award (1981), in Sigvard Jarvin and Yves Derains (eds), *Collection of ICC Arbitral Awards*, Vol. I, 1974–1985, pp. 140 and 143, and, Zürich Chamber of Commerce arbitration, Final Award, *ASA Bulletin*, Vol. 25, No. 4, p. 764 (2007), where faxed copies were admitted as evidence.

205 Sandifer, *supra* n. 3, para. 3.01.

206 *Ibid.*

could not be produced. Consider the following rule of procedure taken from the United States-Spanish Mixed Claims Tribunal concerning the admission of secondary evidence, or copies, "Secondary evidence will be admitted upon proper foundation, according to recognized rules of evidence."[207]

3.133 Given that tribunals of this era did not generally have the benefit of modern photocopying and digital technology it is understandable why such a rigid view in opposition to secondary evidence was taken. In fact, the development of technology to allow for better reproductions was a key reason why some early international tribunals began to take a more liberal approach to admitting copies into the record. As an example, a decision of the United States-French Mixed Claims Commission observed in support of admitting a photographic copy of a pertinent document as evidence that such technology allows for reproductions that "so exactly resemble the originals that they may well be used when the original cannot be had for the purpose."[208] In the modern era of electronic communications, photocopying, scanning and other technological advances, which allow for the accurate and complete reproduction of originals, a presumption that only originals will suffice as evidence in a procedure is seemingly outmoded.

3.134 Article 3.12 of the IBA Rules sets forth the widely accepted and basic requirements for the form in which documents are to be produced or submitted in modern international arbitration practice. As in the 1999 version, article 3.12 of the 2010 Rules presumes that copies of original documentary evidence will be submitted into a procedure, and provides that copies of documents must conform to the originals, which must be available for inspection at the request of the arbitral tribunal. Article 3.12 also considers the submission or production of electronic documents in the form most convenient or procedurally economical and reasonably usable by the recipients, and the exemption from the obligation to submit multiple copies of essentially identical documents. These aspects of the rule simply reflect modern practicalities, and highlight the emphasis on efficiency in international arbitration. Further, article 3.12 also restates the common practice in international arbitration of requiring a translation of a document to be submitted together with an original thus permitting all Parties to view the translation.[209]

---

207 *Ibid.*
208 *Ibid.*
209 See: ICC Case No. 6192, *supra* n. 188, para. 1.11: "par lettre du 19 février 1990, l'arbitre ordonna la production d'une traduction française, par traducteur juré, d'un document en langue arabe produit par les défenderesses en annexe à leur note de plaidoirie du 23 novembre 1989, et reporta la clôture des débats jusqu'au 22 mars 1990 afin de permettre aux parties de formuler des observations, de prendre d'autres ou plus amples conclusions et de déposer éventuellement des pièces nouvelles" (unofficial translation) "by letter dated 19 February 1990, the arbitrator ordered the production of a French translation by a certified translator, of a document in Arabic produced by the defendants with their pleading of 23 November 1989 and delayed the closure of the hearing until 22 March 1990 in order to allow the parties time to prepare their comments, to draw new or supplementary conclusions and finally to file any new evidence." See also: *S.A.R.L. BLOW PACK v WINDMOLLER ET HOLSCHER KG*, CA Paris – 2 avril 2013 – n° 11/18244, Jurisprudence/Décision commentée ou cite: "considérant d'une part qu'en permettant à WINDMOLLER de produire des pièces partiellement traduites à sa seule discrétion sauf à BLOW PACK à en traduire le surplus et d'autre part en s'autorisant en la personne de son président à procéder lui même à des traductions partielles sans fixer aucun critère quant à leur mode de sélection alors que ta langue de l'arbitrage était le français, le tribunal arbitral qui s'est fondé pour rendre sa sentence exclusivement sur un rapport d'expertise auquel étaient annexées des pièces partiellement traduites, a violé le principe de la contradiction en ne mettant pas la société tunisienne en mesure de discuter utilement l'intégralité des pièces portées à la connaissance du tribunal arbitral et de la société allemande, en

Questions concerning the accuracy of a reproduction

3.135 Under the 1999 version of article 3.12, copies were required to "fully" conform to an original when introduced as evidence. The word "fully" was dropped from this article in the 2010 version.[210] Such a rule would appear to be consistent with the approach that international arbitrators frequently use insofar as evidence produced in an arbitration should have material conformity to an original, but minor and/or irrelevant discrepancies (such as irrelevant notes in the margins which do not feature on the original) should not bar a copy from being introduced as evidence.[211]

3.136 An example of this principle may be taken from a recent ICSID arbitration whereby the claimant challenged the accuracy of a copy of an important document submitted into evidence by the respondent. The claimant argued that since notes appearing at the top of the page (which read "Annex 2A") did not appear on the original, the evidence submitted by the respondent was unreliable. As a consequence, claimant argued that only those versions of the document submitted by it could be relied on as evidence. The tribunal did not dismiss the copy because of the incidental markings because in all material respects it appeared to conform to the original version.[212]

3.137 The materiality of a defect may be proved by means other than comparing the original to the copy. If it can be shown that inconsistencies in the evidence provide solid reasons to doubt the completeness of the copy, or its accuracy, there may be reasons to doubt the documents' probative value. As an example, in ICSID arbitration *EDF (Services) Inc v Romania*, the tribunal was confronted with questions over the authenticity

---

l'absence d'acquiescement de sa part . . ." (unofficial translation) "Jurisprudence/Decision commented or cited: "considering, on the one hand, that allowing WINDMOLLER to produce partially translated documents in its sole discretion, exempted BLOW PACK from having to translate the surplus and, on the other hand, authorized the President to carry out partial translations himself without setting any criteria as to their mode of selection, while the language of the arbitration was French, the arbitral tribunal which relied on its decision exclusively on an expert opinion to which were annexed partially translated documents violated the adversarial principle by not allowing the Tunisian society to discuss effectively all the documents brought to the attention of the Arbitral Tribunal and the German company, in the absence on an agreement in its part . . .".

210 Somewhat confusingly, the official comments of the Review Subcommittee still state in relation to art. 3.12, that: "Of course, the copies must fully conform to the originals (art. 3.12(a), formerly art. 3.11)." *Commentary on the revised text of the 2010 IBA Rules.*

211 As was held by a panel of the Iran-US Claims Tribunal, mistakes or other discrepancies which demonstrate poor record keeping are not proof of the inauthentic or forged nature of the evidence. "In light of the foregoing, the Tribunal finds that the Respondents' expert evidence on forgery is inconclusive. Irregularities in the corporate documentation of closely held corporations do not amount to proof of forgery. The Tribunal concludes that the Respondents' expert evidence relating to the share certificates and the stock transfer ledger is not sufficient to dislodge the presumption that Gulf Associates' company records are as they appear on their face." *Gulf Associates, Inc v The Islamic Republic of Iran et al.* Award No. 594-385-2, para. 49.

212 See the following consideration by an UNCITRAL tribunal of an immaterial non-conformity in a copy: "[Claimant] asserts that the document presented by [one of the Respondents] to this Tribunal on 13 October 2006 is not a 'true' copy of the SCA executed by [Claimant] because it is labelled 'Annex 2A' at the top, while the version signed and returned by [Claimant] on 11 October 2006 did not have such label. However, contrary to the documents submitted by [Claimant] on 6 October 2006, which differed in substance from the SCA submitted by [the Respondents] on 8 September 2006, the copy of the SCA submitted by the [Respondent] to this Tribunal on 13 October 2006 appears to have a content that is identical to the one signed and returned by Mr. Feldman on [Claimant's] behalf on 11 October 2006." *Canfor Corp v United States of America, Tembec et al. v United States of America and Terminal Forest Products Ltd v United States of America*, NAFTA/UNCITRAL, Joint Order on the Costs of Arbitration and for the Termination of Certain Arbitral Proceedings, p. 54, para. 119 (2007).

of a recording introduced into the proceedings.[213] At the outset of its analysis the tribunal affirmed that it would presume the recording conformed to the original. This presumption was overcome when it was shown that the copy of the recording was missing a portion of the original soundtrack, hence indicating some manipulation had taken place.[214] Consequently, the tribunal determined that the burden had shifted to the claimant to show that the relevant portions of the copy had not been improperly tampered with in a material fashion. In the end the tribunal determined this burden could only be discharged by producing the original recording.[215]

3.138 As the *EDF* example shows, once a discrepancy that raises serious doubts or calls into question the accuracy of the operative or relevant portion of the copy, a tribunal may then take the approach that the copy should be excluded. This presumption may be overcome, however, if a party is able to demonstrate that the relevant portion of the copy is accurate, despite the apparent discrepancies.

Allegations of forgery

3.139 In some instances a party may seek to disqualify evidence from consideration by alleging that the documents in question are "forgeries". To secure an arbitral award through the use of forged documentation may be a breach of due process, and thus arbitrators are required to give serious consideration to such a charge.[216] When confronted with challenges to evidence based on an allegation of forgery, customarily

---

213 *EDF (Services) Ltd v Romania*, ICSID Case No. ARB/05/13, Procedural Order No. 3 (29 August 2009). See also: where a panel of the Iran-US Claims Tribunal found that a party's own previous, but conflicting, statements concerning the origin of a letter introduced as evidence called into question its authenticity. It refused to assign any evidentiary weight to it, but found it unnecessary to rule on whether it had been forged: "The Tribunal notes that the explanation regarding the letter offered by the Claimant at the Hearing is in sharp contrast with the statements contained in his brief according to which "this notarized letter was obtained in a totally straightforward way, by inquiry addressed to the notarial office." Given the obscurity surrounding the true origin of this letter and the fact that not even the Claimant knows whether a genuine request for information was ever addressed to Notary Public Office No. 328, the Tribunal cannot accord any evidentiary value to this document. In view of this determination, the Tribunal need not address the arguments advanced by the Respondent in support of its position that the letter is forged." *Reza Said Malek v The Islamic Republic of Iran*, Final Award No. 534-193-3 of 11 August 1992, p. 45.

214 *Ibid.*, *EDF v Romania*, Procedural Order No. 3, para. 13.

215 *Ibid.*, para. 35. "The absence in the recording of a substantial part of the conversation between Mr. Katz and Ms Iacob and the possibility that the recorded part was manipulated, make the audio file unreliable in the absence of authentication through the original recording."

216 As an ICC tribunal noted regarding breaches of natural justice, "it is arguable that some taints, e.g., the use of fraudulent evidence to secure a judgment or an award, would always make it vulnerable to attack." *Licensor v Licensee*, Final award in ICC Case No. 6363 of 1991 in Albert Jan van den Berg (ed.), *Yearbook Commercial Arbitration*, Vol. XVII, pp. 186, 196 (1992). Although, it may also be said that the mere presence of a document in a proceeding that is tainted by an allegation of forgery is not in and of itself a basis for challenging the validity of an award. If the document is not material to the disposition of the case, the tribunal may decide that it is not necessary to determine the allegation of forgery, as was the case in an arbitration held under the rules of the Zurich Chamber of Commerce: "Although it was never entirely clear, it appears that NKAP was angling that if it could be determined that it was not a shareholder of the Hungarian company then its parallel obligation to supply it with aluminum would also fall. But the Arbitral Tribunal had already ruled that the investment and supply obligations of the framework agreements were severable, and that the supply obligation was not impugned by the alleged forgery. Furthermore the alleged forgeries, far from being part of a fraud on NKAP, had all been on documents that aided NKAP in being duly registered as a shareholder for the participation it had purchased." As summarised by Nicolas C. Ulmer in "Soinco v NKAP: A War story", 13–3 *Mealey's Int'l Arb Rep* 15 (1998).

arbitrators begin with the presumption that the evidence is authentic,[217] and require a high or enhanced standard of proof be met by the party alleging the forgery before disqualifying the evidence from the record. An analysis of this issue by a panel of the Iran-US Claims Tribunal is instructive:

> The allegations of forgery in these Cases seem to the Tribunal to be of a character that requires an enhanced standard of proof. Consistent with its past practice, the Tribunal therefore holds that the allegation of forgery must be proved with a higher degree of probability than other allegations in these Cases. [Internal citations omitted.] The minimum quantum of evidence that will be required to satisfy the Tribunal may be described as 'clear and convincing evidence', although the Tribunal deems that precise terminology less important than the enhanced proof requirement that it expresses.[218]

3.140 This enhanced standard of proof has been applied in recent arbitral case law. In one instance a respondent relied on indirect evidence adduced from related arbitrations to challenge the authenticity of certain share certificates relevant to the matter. The tribunal rejected this evidence as insufficient to satisfy the higher standard of proof required to disqualify the certificates as forgeries.[219] In other cases, an allegation of forgery, supported by scant indirect evidence, or merely the presence of a discrepancy, was not enough to establish

---

217 See the following decision of a panel of the Iran-US Claims Tribunal considering an allegation of forgery: "the key issue before the Tribunal is whether the three Sabet children owned the shares in Gulf Associates from 7 May 1979, the date the claims in this Case arose, until 19 January 1981, the date of the signing of the Algiers Declarations. The appropriate starting point for this determination is whether Gulf has provided prima facie evidence of the Sabet children's ownership of its shares from 31 October 1977. If not, that is the end of the matter. If, on the other hand, Gulf has provided that proof, the question becomes whether the Respondents, in turn, have carried their burden of proving that the documents Gulf submitted relating to the children's ownership were forged." *Gulf Associates Inc, Claimant v The Islamic Republic of Iran, supra* n. 211, para. 23. This presumption is only justified where a minimum of indicia [customary markings, signatures or other indications] corroborating the authenticity of the document is present. If, from the surface, it appears that there are problems with a document's authenticity, then a tribunal may not begin with such a presumption. Moreover, this holds true especially with documents that are claimed to have been officially issued by a government authority. See: the findings of an Iran-US Tribunal Panel in regard to this issue, "It follows, in the view of the Tribunal, that not every document that, at first glance, gives the impression that a Notary Public somehow may have been involved in its preparation warrants a presumption of authenticity. To trigger the presumption, there must be a minimum of indicia suggesting that the document indeed was prepared by a government official (a Notary Public) in accordance with that government official's legal authority as well as applicable laws and regulations. These considerations should not be read to imply that it must be demonstrated that, to be presumed authentic, the document and the transaction it incorporates must comply in every respect with all applicable regulations. Nevertheless, if the omissions reflected in a document purportedly of such a nature or number that the document on its face does not inspire the 'confidence and security' normally associated with an instrument of that kind, the document in question, in the Tribunal's view, may not be an official document entitled to a presumption of authenticity." *Abrahim Rahman Golshani v The Islamic Republic of Iran*, Award in Case No. 812 (546-812-3) of 2 March 1993 in Albert Jan van den Berg (ed.), *Yearbook Commercial Arbitration*, Vol. XIX, pp. 428–429 (1994).

218 *Dadras v The Islamic Republic of Iran, supra* n. 8, pp. 123–124.

219 "The Respondent questioned the authenticity of the temporary share certificates submitted by the Claimant, suggesting, *inter alia*, that they were postdated for the purposes of bringing the present arbitration. However, the Respondent did not go as far as making a claim of forgery, leaving the Tribunal with a number of allegations based on assumptions drawn from indirect evidence discussed in other arbitrations. When challenged directly by counsel for the Respondent, the Claimant was consistent in his denial of any tampering with the documents. The Tribunal considers that the burden of proof of any allegations of impropriety is particularly heavy. This burden of proof was not met in the present case. Consequently, the Tribunal accepts the Claimant's submission as to the dates of the transfer of the temporary certificates to the Claimant." *Mr Saba Fakes v Republic of Turkey*, ICSID Case No. ARB/07/20, Final Award, paras 130–131 (14 July 2010).

the claim.[220] This is especially true where there is circumstantial evidence supporting the authenticity of a document.[221]

3.141 Therefore, an allegation of fraud or forgery is one which can be proven only by meeting an enhanced burden of proof. A tribunal in most cases must be convinced of the falsity of a document before excluding it from the record.[222]

The tribunal's authority to order production of an original

3.142 It is generally accepted that international arbitral tribunals have the power to order parties to make originals available for inspection when questions concerning the accuracy of a copy have been raised or forgery is alleged and the tribunal is satisfied there is evidence to support the allegation.[223] This principle is incorporated in article

---

220 See: the decision of a CIETAC tribunal in a dispute between the buyer and seller of goods, to accept evidence proffered by a Chinese seller in the form of an invoice, which the buyer claimed was forged. Here, a reviewing Japanese district court considered that a challenge to the final award could not be sustained on such grounds since the simple fact that an original invoice had different prices than a copy submitted to the tribunal did not mean that forgery was the cause of the discrepancy. This case indicates again, that the mere presence of differences between two documents is not sufficient to cause the tribunal to find that forgery had occurred. *Zhong Guo Hua Gong Jian She Qing Dao Gong Si v Color Chemical Industry KK*, in Albert Jan van den Berg (ed.), *Yearbook Commercial Arbitration*, Vol. XXVII, p. 515 (2002).

221 See the following reasoning from an ICC tribunal on this issue: "respondent alleges that the stamped contract pages are mere forgeries and are not signed by respondent. The tribunal could not determine that the Exhibits 2a and 4a are forgeries. Besides the allegation that the documents in question are forgeries, respondent provided in addition to the mere denial of the document's authenticity, no evidence that could lead to the conclusion that the documents are forged. Respondent could have provided a copy of its original stamp so that the tribunal could have compared the original stamp with the stamp appearing on the Exhibits 2a and 4a. Furthermore, both Exhibits show a signature (however in different places) in the stamp of respondent. Regarding this signature, respondent also provided no original signatures of its representatives for the purpose of comparison. Thus, the provided information and evidence by respondent is not sufficient to establish that the Exhibits 2a and 4a are forgeries. It is the tribunal's finding that they are authentic telefax receipts, evidencing respondent's acceptance of the two contracts here in question (first possibility) or offers for the conclusion of the contracts here in question (second possibility)." ICC Case No. 10274, Final Award (1999), in Albert Jan van den Berg (ed.), *Yearbook Commercial Arbitration*, Vol. XXIX, pp. 95–99 (2004).

222 See: *Churchill Mining PLC and Planet Mining Pty Ltd v Republic of Indonesia*, ICSID Case No. ARB/12/14 and 12/40, Procedural Order No. 12 (2014). In an Application for Dismissal of Claimants' Claims Based on the Forged and Fabricated Ridlatama Mining Licenses (the "Application"), the Tribunal noted that "[t]he resolution of the issues raised in the Application will require several procedural steps, including briefings, possibly document production and new document inspection, before the matter can proceed to a hearing. The fact that a hearing is not feasible within the next 30 days does not, however, do away with the more general request to deal with the Respondent's Application as a preliminary issue separate from the remainder of the merits. [. . .] The Tribunal is not convinced that a decision in favor of the Respondent on document authenticity would lead to a complete dismissal of the claims before it. While it is true that the document authenticity issue may go to the heart of the question whether the revocation of the mining licenses was wrongful, other claims regarding, for instance, the alleged denial of justice before Indonesian courts would *prima facie* survive. As a result, bifurcated proceedings on liability would unnecessarily protract the proceedings and create additional costs for all Parties involved. [. . .] As a result, the Tribunal comes to the conclusion that, for reasons of efficient and cost-conscious case management, it is best to deal with the authenticity issue together with the other issues pertaining to the merits. This solution not only complies with good management, it also respects both Parties' due process rights, as both are given a fair opportunity to address the issues relevant to the resolution of this dispute." *Ibid.*, pp. 14–15, §§46–49.

223 As an example, in the procedural history of the final award in *Dadras v Iran*, *supra* n. 8, para. 14, the tribunal notes that it had made provision for the following inspection of originals of documents that had been submitted into the proceedings: "On 30 November 1992 the Respondents filed a request for examination of the originals of certain of the Claimant's documents. The Claimants did not object, and the Tribunal accordingly ordered that the inspection of documents take place at the Tribunal's registry three days before the hearing."

3.12(a). Ordering the disclosure of an original may at times be the course of action that is needed to clarify such an important issue. Failure by a party to produce an original when requested by a tribunal to do so may not only lead to the exclusion from the record of a copy, but also a decision to draw an adverse inference.[224] In some instances tribunals have in the past ordered that evidence should be submitted to a forensic expert to resolve questions over authenticity.[225]

3.143 The power of a tribunal to order the production of an original does not mean, however, that it should do so whenever a question is raised concerning a document in evidence. It would seem, based upon the examples discussed above, that the more prevalent approach in international arbitration is that an original should be compelled into production once a tribunal has been persuaded to the requisite standard that the evidence has been, or has potentially been, corrupted in a material way. Where there is no evidence that a copy is not a correct representation of an original, a tribunal may accept that the copy is accurate.[226]

3.144 Such a presumption would not necessarily hold for that documentary evidence the authenticity of which is highly material to the dispute.[227] Where the dispute in question centres primarily on the authenticity of a document which, for example, would prove ownership of an investment, a tribunal may expect that the original of such a document would be submitted in the course of the proceeding, or otherwise made available for inspection, and verification.

---

224 *Europe Cement v Turkey*, *supra* n. 36, Final Award para. 152: "If the originals of the share transfer agreements existed so that they could have been copied in order for copies to be included with the Claimant's Memorial on Jurisdiction and Liability on 15 May 2008, why could they not be produced when ordered to be so by the Tribunal on 29 May 2008? In his letter of 4 December 2008, Mr. Biserov alluded to the 'legacy of the previous management' and in his letter of 24 March 2009, the inability to produce the documents was referred to as a 'circumstantial hindrance', but no further explanation was provided. Thus, in the Tribunal's view there is a strong inference that the documents were not produced either because Europe Cement did not have them or because they would not withstand forensic scrutiny."

225 See: *Libananco v Turkey*, *supra*, n. 33, Decision on Preliminary Issues, pp. 43–44 (23 June 2008): "By July 1, 2008, the Claimant must deliver to an Escrow Agent ('the Escrow Agent') the originals of the documents requested under Prayer 1 of the First Request ('the Share Certificates') . . . (3.2.2.) The Escrow Agent will be appointed by the Claimant subject to the approval of the Tribunal after the Tribunal has heard the views of the Respondent, but must hold the Share Certificates to the order of the Tribunal and must take instructions only from the Tribunal . . . (3.2.5.) After the Escrow Agent has taken custody of the Share Certificates, the Respondent will be at liberty to employ forensic experts (at its expense) to examine the Share Certificates, but such examination must not destroy or damage the Share Certificates in any way. The Claimant must be given adequate advance notice of such examination so as to enable it to appoint its own forensic experts to monitor such examination when it is conducted by the Respondent's forensic experts. Such examination must be completed within 3 months after the appointment of the Escrow Agent. The Escrow Agent must not without the written consent of the Tribunal permit the Share Certificates (or any of them) to leave the place of custody designated by the Escrow Agent and approved by the Tribunal."

226 See, for instance, the determination of an ICC tribunal that a copy of an original Russian language contract was accurate in the absence of any compelling evidence to the contrary: "The arbitral tribunal has not been provided with the original of any version of the contract. The file contains only copies of both versions. There is no evidence that the copy of the Russian language contract including the ICC arbitration clause would be a forgery; each page is initialed by Mr. X, representative of defendant, and the last page bears his signature as well as Mr. A's signature, representative of claimant; one can see the stamps of the two companies; both signatures and stamps are the same as those appearing on the other version of the contract." Final Award in ICC Case No. 8790 of 2000 in Albert Jan van den Berg (ed.), *Yearbook Commercial Arbitration*, Vol. XXIX, p. 15 (2004).

227 See, for instance: the situation in *Libananco v Turkey*, *supra* n. 33, where the authenticity of certain bearer shares was generally agreed to be material to the jurisdictional issues in the arbitration by the parties and the willingness of the owner of the shares to submit them to inspection persuaded the tribunal to order their inspection.

Confidentiality of disclosed documents

Article 3.13 2010 IBA Rules:	**Any Document submitted or produced by a Party or non-Party in the arbitration and not otherwise in the public domain shall be kept confidential by the Arbitral Tribunal and the other Parties, and shall be used only in connection with the arbitration. This requirement shall apply except and to the extent that disclosure may be required of a Party to fulfil a legal duty, protect or pursue a legal right, or enforce or challenge an award in bona fide legal proceedings before a state court or other judicial authority. The Arbitral Tribunal may issue orders to set forth the terms of this confidentiality. This requirement shall be without prejudice to all other obligations of confidentiality in the arbitration.**
Other Statements of the Rule Principle 16.5 UNIDROIT/ ALI Principles:	A person who produces evidence, whether or not a party, has the right to a court order protecting against improper exposure of confidential information.

General discussion

3.145 While many parties may assume that confidentiality is an inherent aspect of international arbitration, in fact, there is no general rule that supports this assumption.[228] Some procedural rules specifically provide for confidentiality while others do not, and certain jurisdictions have either a rule of confidentiality expressly included or otherwise implied in their *lex arbitri;* however, this is not universally the case.[229] Therefore, as a general rule

---

228 See the following distinction between privacy and confidentiality reportedly drawn by the Swedish Supreme Court: "Accepting that arbitral proceedings are fundamentally private, and that such privacy constitutes one of the perceived advantages of arbitration, the Supreme Court nevertheless distinguished between privacy and confidentiality as follows: 'However, this advantage does not mean that it is a precondition that a duty of confidentiality prevails for the parties. The real meaning of this, compared with judicial proceedings, is instead obviously that the proceedings are not public, i.e. that the public does not have any right of insight by being in attendance at the hearings or having access to documents in the matter. . . . There is no contradiction in the parties simultaneously being entitled to disclose information to outsiders concerning the arbitration proceedings.'" Constantine Partasides, "Bulbank – The Final Act ", 15–12 *Mealey's Intl Arb Rep* 12 (2000). See also: "The universally accepted right to privacy, inherent in arbitration, does not entail an implied obligation of an arbitrating party to keep confidential the information disclosed during an arbitration." Antonio Dimolitsa, "Institutional Rules and National Regimes Relating to the Obligation of Confidentiality on Parties in Arbitration", in *ICC Bulletin, 2009 Special Supplement: Confidentiality in Arbitration*, p. 5. As an example, the UNCITRAL Model Law contains no provision concerning confidentiality. See also: Michael Hwang and Katie Chung, "Defining the Indefinable: Practical Problems of Confidentiality in Arbitration", *Journal of International Arbitration*, Vol. 26, No. 5, pp. 636–637 (2009). This being said, it is often thought that "confidentiality" is one of the natural advantages of international arbitration. See: Geneva Chamber of Commerce and Industry arbitration, Interim Award (1999) in *ASA Bulletin*, Vol. 19, No. 2, p. 265 (2001): "The [agreement] relates to the payment of a consultancy service fee by a German Company to [a citizen of country W resident in country Y] in connection with the settlement of a dispute between the German Company and the [W] Government. This is typically the kind of matter which the parties usually agree to submit to arbitration for a number of reasons, in particular the need for confidentiality . . .".

229 As an example, one could compare the rule stated in art. 30 of the LCIA Rules expressly stating that a party has a right to confidentiality with the ICC Rules of Arbitration, the ICSID Rules of Procedure for Arbitration Proceedings and the UNCITRAL Arbitration Rules, which are all silent on the issue. As examples of jurisdictions, the United States and Sweden are two jurisdictions which do not recognise a general right to confidentiality in arbitral proceedings, where as England does. For the English view see: *Dolling-Baker v Merrett* [1990] 1 WLR 1205, as quoted in Dimolitsa, *supra* n. 228, 18 "[the fact that] the obligation [of confidentiality] exists in some

one should look specifically for a right to confidentiality in the agreement to arbitrate, the relevant procedural rules or the *lex arbitri*, to determine whether the parties should treat the proceedings as confidential, but such should not be assumed.[230]

3.146 However, even in the absence of an express confidentiality agreement, or a confidentiality provision in the procedural rules or the *lex arbitri*, one should not assume licence to disclose details of the arbitration at will. Consider the following statement taken from one of the leading cases to analyse this issue, the ICSID arbitration *Giovanna A Beccara and Others v The Argentine Republic*: "if it is true that there is no general duty of confidentiality, this is not to be understood as a 'carte blanche' entitling a Party to disclose as it deems fit any kind of information or documents issued or produced in this proceeding."[231]

3.147 The view in *Beccara* would seem to explain why, in the absence of a universal rule of confidentiality, the drafters of the IBA Rules could confidently include article 3.13 as a general restatement of arbitral practice. It would seem that the view taken in article 3.13 is supported by the application of procedural principles other than a rule of confidentiality, such as procedural good faith and the case-management authority of the tribunal.[232]

---

form appears to me to be abundantly apparent. It is not a question of immunity or public interest. It is a question of an implied obligation arising out of the nature of arbitration itself". See also: *John Forster Emmott v Michael Wilson & Partners Ltd* [2008] EWCA Civ 184, para. 129.

230 In consideration of a request for an interim measure declaring the proceedings confidential, the arbitral tribunal in an ICSID case *World Duty Free v Kenya*, provided the following recitation of the accepted view on whether there exists a "general" rule on confidentiality, absent a confidentiality agreement or an express rule found in an applicable law or set of rules: "The Request raises the question as to whether there exists any general principle of confidentiality that would operate to prohibit public discussion of the arbitration proceedings by either Party. Neither the ICSID Convention nor the ICSID Arbitration Rules contain any express restriction on the freedom of the Parties in this respect. Though it is frequently said that one of the reasons for recourse to arbitration is to avoid publicity, unless the agreement between the Parties includes such a restriction, each of them is still free to speak of the arbitration. Especially in an arbitration to which a Government is a Party, it cannot be assumed that the Convention and the Rules incorporate a general obligation of confidentiality which would require the Parties to refrain from discussing the case in public." *World Duty Free Co Ltd v Republic of Kenya*, ICSID Case No. ARB/00/7, Final Award, para. 16 (4 October 2006). See also: the decision of a US court which rejected the arguments that the ICC Rules contain a confidentiality obligation and that a "general understanding" that the proceedings were confidential was sufficient to prevent disclosure of the arbitration documents. *United States of America v Panhandle Eastern Corp*, 118 FRD 346 (D Del 1988). On the other hand, in following the English case law on this issue, the High Court in Malaya (Kuala Lumpur) made the following observation concerning confidentiality under its arbitration law: "On confidentiality, I need to refer to the case of *Dolling-Baker v Merrett*, at 1213 [1991] 2 All ER 890, [1990] 1 WLR 1205 at 1213, CA, cited in Dimolitsa, *supra* n. 228, which held that in the absence of an express term in an arbitration clause providing for confidentiality, then the presumption of confidentiality arises as an implied term by the very nature of the arbitral process itself . . . It is now accepted, by all and sundry, that arbitrations are private and confidential." *Malaysian Newsprint Industries Sdn Bhd v Bechtel International Inc*, High Court in Malaya (Kuala Lumpur), 5 MLJ 254, paras 56–60 (2008).

231 *Giovanna A Beccara v The Argentine Republic*, ICSID Case No. ARB/07/5, Procedural Order No. 3, para. 79 (2010). See also: the qualifier attached by the *World Duty Free* tribunal to its ruling that there is no "general" rule of confidentiality: "The Tribunal nevertheless directs the Parties to avoid any action that would aggravate or exacerbate the dispute. The Tribunal further directs that any public discussion should be an accurate report." *Ibid.*, *World Duty Free v Kenya*, para. 16.

232 As a further example of this principle, see: ICC Case No. 12242. Here the tribunal considered whether it should impose confidentiality on the proceedings by restricting one party from communicating with the press. In consideration of the principles set forth by previous tribunals, in particular the ICSID tribunal in *Amico Asia Corp v Republic of Indonesia*, the tribunal noted that in the absence of a strict rule of confidentiality, it may still order that the parties restrict their communications to third-parties in the interest of preventing the exacerbation of the dispute. In affirming that the ICC Rules (1999) did not contain a strict rule on confidentiality, the tribunal considered the following principle: "En resume, les arbitres n'ont pas estimé pouvoir reconnaitre l'existence

3.148 In one of the decisions on this issue, ICSID arbitration *Biwater Gauff v Tanzania*, the tribunal of experienced arbitrators observed the following regarding the administration of a fair procedure in the context of whether confidentiality ought to be imposed on the parties:

> [The Tribunal's] mandate and responsibility includes ensuring that the proceedings will be conducted in the future in a regular, fair and orderly manner (including by issuing procedural directions to that effect). Among other things, its mandate extends to ensuring that potential inhibitions and unfairness do not arise; equally its mandate extends to attempting to reduce aggravation and exacerbation of the dispute, which necessarily involves probabilities, not certainties.[233]

3.149 Fears concerning the widespread dissemination of sensitive business documents, policy statements or other materials reflecting the operations of a participant to arbitration, may lead a party to withhold evidence otherwise necessary for presenting its case if the proceedings are not covered by a rule imposing confidentiality. Moreover, without a duty of confidentiality of some type, an adverse party may feel uninhibited to release documents submitted by its opponent in an effort to apply external pressure or cause public embarrassment. As noted by the *Biwater Gauff* tribunal, this would only serve to aggravate matters, and does not assist in the administration of a fair and efficient procedure.

3.150 These and other practical problems which would arise from a policy that imposes no limitations on the use of documents submitted in an arbitration supports the imposition of a framework for confidentiality. In this regard, reference may be had again to the decision in *Biwater Gauff* where the tribunal fashioned the following rule:

> However, in the interest of procedural integrity, the Tribunal does consider it appropriate to restrict publication or distribution of documents that have been produced in the arbitration by the opposing party. The interests of transparency are here outweighed, since the threat of wider publication may well undermine the document production process itself, as well as the overall arbitration

---

d'un devoir explicte de maintenir la confidentialite mais seulement une obligation implicite de ne pas exacerber le différend." (unofficial translation) "In summary, the arbitrators are not able to find an explicit obligation to maintain confidentiality – but only an implied duty not to exacerbate the dispute." On this basis the tribunal found grounds to limit one side's communications with the press. ICC Case No. 12242, Procedural Order of 11 July 2003, *ICC Bulletin, 2010 Special Supplement: Decisions on ICC Arbitration Procedure*, p. 41. It would seem clear that art. 3.13 recognises the general potential for misuse (or exacerbation of the dispute) that would be created if documents submitted as evidence into the proceedings were not required to remain confidential, and thus, following along similar reasoning, considers that a rule imposing confidentiality on such evidence is appropriate.

233 *Biwater Gauff v Tanzania, supra* n. 38, Procedural Order No. 1, para. 145. See also: the decision of *Casado v Chile* where the tribunal commented as follows: "aucune règle d'arbitrage CIRDI ni aucun principe général du droit de l'arbitrage n'interdit la publication par une partie des documents de la procédure mais qu'il y a lieu seulement de concilier les besoins de la transparance avec l'intérêt d'un bon déroulement de la procédure arbitrale ainsi qu'avec l'obligation des parties de s'abstenir de démarches propres à aggraver le litige ou faire obstacle à son bon règlement. Rappelant l'obligation générale de toute partie à une procédure arbitrale de s'abstenir de démarches susceptibles soit d'aggraver le différend soit d'en rendre la solution plus difficile et regrettant le manque de sérénité des parties dans la procedure." (Unofficial translation) "no ICSID rule of arbitration nor any general principle of arbitration law prohibits the publication by a party of documents from the case, but there is a need to balance the needs of transparency with the interest of a well-run procedure as well as with the obligation of the parties to abstain from taking steps to aggravate the case or place obstacles in the way of its resolution. Recalling the general obligation of all parties to an arbitration to refrain from steps susceptible either to aggravate the dispute or to render finding a resolution more difficult and regretting the lack of serenity of the parties to the procedure." *Victor Pey Casado v The Republic of Chile*, ICSID Case ARB/982, Procedural Order No. 13 (24 October 2006).

procedure. The production of documents by a party, whether in response to a disclosure request or otherwise is made for the purpose of resolving the parties' dispute and the presumption is that materials disclosed in this manner should be used only for such purpose.[234]

3.151 This approach has been adopted in other arbitrations, where tribunals confronted with the lack of an express agreement on this issue, but nevertheless desirous of ensuring that there is an effectively run procedure, have imposed restrictions on the use and disclosure of documentary evidence outside of the arbitration.[235] This is also reflected in the position adopted by some domestic courts that have recognised that documentary evidence exchanged in an arbitral procedure is worthy of a higher level of protection than a final award, or other ruling.[236] As has been widely recognised, there are any number of legitimate reasons why details of a final award may require publication (e.g., inclusion in yearly accounts), which do not apply to documentary evidence exchanged during a proceeding.

3.152 Therefore, an exception to the overarching rule that confidentiality should not be implied into an arbitral procedure in the absence of specific agreement or provision in the *lex arbitri* or governing rules, has been developed covering documentary evidence exchanged during the proceedings, as is reflected in article 3.13.[237]

3.153 IBA Rules article 3.13 sets forth the limitations that are generally accepted on the use of documentary evidence and exceptions to it. Those exceptions will be discussed further below, however, one fundamental principle bears mentioning; article 3.13 does not set any limitations on the right of a party to use their own documents. The rule is strictly limited to the documents submitted by an adverse party, or a non-party (such as an expert or third party who has been called to provide evidence such as in the case of article 3.9) and would not place limitations on a party's right to do as it wishes with information it has in its own possession or is in the public domain.

Transparency in international investment arbitration and confidentiality

3.154 It is quite often the case that investor-state arbitrations will be public or semi-public proceedings, meaning that often submissions exchanged, witness statements, expert

---

234 *Biwater Gauff v Tanzania, supra* n. 38, Procedural Order No. 3, para. 157.

235 See: *Beccara v Argentina, supra* n. 231, Procedural Order No. 3, para. 110: "a Party shall not publish or otherwise disclose to third parties the documents produced by the opposing party and shall use them only for the purpose of participating in the arbitration, except where documents are already in the public domain or the opposing party expressed its consent to their disclosure." In *Marvin Roy Feldman v United Mexican States*, the tribunal noted that: "As regards documents, testimony and other evidence produced in the proceeding, the Tribunal considers that each party is entitled to the treatment of such evidence by the other party as confidential." *Marvin Roy Feldman Karpa (CEMSA) v United Mexican States*, ICSID Case No. ARB(AF)/99/1, Final Award (2002).

236 "Commercial arbitrations are essentially private proceedings and unlike litigation in public courts do not place anything in the public domain. This may mean that the implied restrictions on the use of material obtained in arbitration proceedings may have a greater impact than those applying in litigation. But when it comes to the award, the same logic cannot be applied. An award may have to be referred to for accounting purposes or for the purpose of legal proceedings (as Aegis referred to it for the purposes of the present injunction proceedings) or for the purposes of enforcing the rights which the award confers (as European Re seek to do in the Rowe arbitration)." *Associated Electric & Gas Insurance Services Ltd v European Reinsurance Co of Zurich*, Court of Appeal of Bermuda, in *ASA Bulletin*, Vol. 21, No. 4, p. 20 (2003).

237 While the decisions cited in this section are largely taken from investor-state arbitrations, this principle is equally applicable to international commercial arbitration as there is at least equal potential for a commercial arbitration to be derailed by disclosure or the threat of disclosure of documents exchanged during arbitration.

reports, procedural orders and awards may be made available to the public. An international investment tribunal's determinations on confidentiality may be guided by arguments based on public interest, the need for transparency of governmental action and other issues of policy.[238] To the extent that a tribunal does rule that the proceedings are open for public view, there will often be a restriction imposed on the use of documentary evidence, that is to say, documents exchanged between the parties.[239] It will be in most instances for the party who asserts a claim of confidentiality to notify its counterparty and the tribunal of the claim and the evidence it pertains to.[240] Unless challenged, such claims to document confidentiality are often accepted prima facie as credible.

3.155 In a NAFTA arbitration, *Chemtura v Canada*, which was conducted under the UNCITRAL Rules the tribunal issued a procedural order covering documents it deemed to be sensitive information subject to business confidentiality. Broadly speaking, the tribunal regarded documentary evidence containing trade secrets, technical, financial and commercial information, which a party may be able to demonstrate has been consistently treated as confidential, and/or information which a party can demonstrate would cause it financial detriment if released, as covered by confidentiality.[241] Here, as mentioned above, the rule adopted by the tribunal required the party who claimed the right to confidentiality to assert it in the proceedings,[242] and for the designation to remain unless it was challenged (this approach has been adopted in more than one investor-state arbitration).[243]

3.156 The rule adopted in *Chemtura* was narrower in application than the wider, blanket protection afforded by article 3.13 which covers all documents produced in a proceeding. The narrower approach seems to be motivated by the objections raised to confidentiality in this case by the Canadian government owing to its transparency obligations concerning disputes brought under the NAFTA treaty. Other NAFTA tribunals have also restricted their confidentiality orders to documents defendable as "business confidential". Nevertheless, despite this narrower construction than what is set forth in article 3.13, these rulings affirm that the assertion of confidentiality over documents produced into an arbitration is still widely accepted.[244]

---

238 For one of the first major discussions of this issue by a court see: *Esso Australia Ltd v The Honourable Sidney James Plowman (Ministry for Energy and Minerals)* (1995) 128 ALR 391 (High Court of Australia).

239 *Biwater Gauff v Tanzania, supra* n. 38, Procedural Order No. 3 and Procedural Order No. 5, at paras 65, 66 (2007).

240 "Where counsel for either disputing party reasonably expects that information, whether documentary or oral, designated by a disputing party as confidential information shall be referred to during the course of any hearing held by the Tribunal, then such portion of the hearing as is reasonably necessary to protect that confidential information shall be conducted in camera and may only be attended by those persons designated in this Order." *Merrill & Ring Forestry LP v Government of Canada, supra* n. 55, Confidentiality Order, para. 28 (21 January 2008).

241 *Chemtura Corporation (formerly Crompton Corporation) v Government of Canada, Ad Hoc NAFTA Arbitration under UNCITRAL Rules*, Confidentiality Order (21 January 2008).

242 "A disputing party may designate information as confidential as set out in paragraph 1. The disputing party shall clearly identify on each page of the document containing such information the notation, 'Confidential' or 'Confidential Information – Unauthorized Disclosure Prohibited'. And shall take equivalent measures with respect to information contained in other material produced in electronic and similar media." *William Ralph Clayton et al. v Government of Canada*, UNCITRAL, Procedural Order No. 2 (Confidentiality Order), para. 2 (4 May 2009).

243 *Ibid.*, para, 6: "6. Disputes related to a disputing party's designation of confidential information may be submitted to the Tribunal for determination . . ."

244 "While procedural orders as well as pleadings and minutes of meetings may contain information of potential importance to the public, it seems that the risks of disrupting the procedural integrity of the process

Limitation on confidentiality: use of documentary evidence in connection with the arbitration

3.157 That documentary evidence produced in international arbitration may be disclosed to non-parties for the purposes of conducting the arbitration is a recognised exception to the rule of confidentiality that would otherwise apply. The phrase, "in connection with the arbitration" in article 3.13, is understood to encompass disclosure of the evidence received from an opponent to independent third-party witnesses and experts who reasonably would need to review it in the course of preparing their testimony.[245]

3.158 Whether a party is acting consistently with its obligation of confidentiality when it reveals the documents in question to third-party witnesses is generally judged by whether the disclosure is made, "in good faith to witnesses who are reasonably expected by the disputing party to offer evidence in the arbitration and only to the extent that such information is relevant to their expected testimony."[246] As applied to third-party consultants or experts, the expectation must be similar, insofar as the disclosure must be made pursuant to the expert's role in the arbitration proceedings, and the disclosure is proportional to the subject matter of the expert's advice or report. One would also expect that the expert should also agree to be bound by the same obligation of confidentiality as the disclosing party.

Exceptions to confidentiality: where confidential information is disclosed to "fulfil a legal duty"

3.159 A legal compulsion to disclose information or documents is a general exception to the duty to maintain confidentiality of evidence submitted in an arbitration. The scope of what constitutes a "legal duty" exception to confidentiality is generally subject to a restrictive interpretation and encompasses acts that require governments to make available information to the public (e.g., freedom of information acts).[247] Aside from such statutory

---

will frequently outweigh the interest of publication. Therefore it is appropriate to exempt not only documents revealing business secrets or other confidential information from a potential public disclosure but also to prohibit the publication of any other information which might aggravate disputes before investment tribunals." Christine Knahr, August Reinisch, "Transparency versus Confidentiality in International Investment Arbitration – The *Biwater Gauff* Compromise", *The Law and Practice of International Courts and Tribunals*, Vol. 6, pp 97–118 (2007).

245 In reviewing the conduct of a party who had shared information from a HKIAC proceeding with third-party witnesses in order to interview them regarding their recollections of the case, the reviewing court noted that this was a perfectly normal, and an accepted exception to the confidentiality rule: "In the present case, the HA does not dispute that Sui Chong would be entitled to speak to (and communicate with) Mr. Andrew Tsui and Mr. Patrick Cheong (both of whom were previously involved with the management and handling of the Contract, though both of them are now with Winfoong and not with Sui Chong) for the purpose of collecting evidence from them. In the course of doing so, Sui Chong may have to provide information or documents to these two persons to refresh their memory and to put any inquiries (to be made with them) in context. The HA does not have any problem with this; rightly so, in my view. Any contrary position would be untenable." *Hong Kong Housing Authority v Sui Chong Construction & Engineering Co Ltd* [2008] 1 HKLRD 84, para. 19.

246 *Chemtura v Canada, supra* n. 241, Confidentiality Order, para. 5.

247 See, for instance, the interim order issued by an ICSID tribunal in *Mondev v United States of America* whereby the United States had notified the tribunal that it intended to release written submissions and other documents exchanged during the arbitration pursuant to a Freedom of Information Act request: "On 13 December 2000, the Respondent informed the Tribunal that it had received and intended to comply with a request under the [Freedom of Information Act] for the release of certain of the Respondent's written submissions to the Tribunal and of certain letters that it had addressed to the Claimant and the Tribunal. By letter of 28 December 2000, the Claimant informed the Tribunal that it objected to such release and stated its grounds for that objection. Each

laws incumbent upon state-parties, it may be that a party also receives a subpoena requiring it to reveal documentary evidence it obtained in the course of the arbitration. A subpoena in such circumstances is generally not considered to constitute a "legal duty" requiring disclosure until it is confirmed by a judicial authority.[248]

3.160 The customary practice in international arbitration is for a party who claims that it is under a legal duty to disclose the confidential information, to provide notice of such impending disclosure to the tribunal (provided it is not *functus officio*) and the party who originally disclosed the documents. In providing the notice, a party may be required to provide details concerning the legal duty, and to also take steps, if so requested, to prevent further disclosure beyond the strict scope of its legal duty.

Exceptions to confidentiality: disclosure where needed to "protect or pursue a legal right"

3.161 Another exception to the rule of confidentiality laid down in article 3.13 is that a party may disclose documentary evidence it has received during the arbitration if such is needed to pursue or protect a legal right. Often this issue arises in connection with a desire to disclose evidence received in an arbitration procedure in a subsequent proceeding, although it may also be prompted by regulatory requirements.[249] Where the subsequent proceeding involves the same parties, there is arguably little reason why a confidentiality order in the first proceeding should prevent evidence from being used in the second. However, this issue becomes far more complicated when the second proceeding involves different participants.

3.162 An often-cited example of this scenario is the *Ali Shipping Corp v Shipyard Trogir* case out of the English courts, where it was held that a party may disclose evidence in subsequent proceedings if the need arises due to one of several court-defined exceptions to confidentiality, the most relevant to the present discussion being, "where it was reasonably necessary for the protection of the legitimate interests of the party to the arbitration."[250] In

---

party subsequently made written submissions in support of its contentions regarding such proposed release. On 25 January 2001, the Tribunal issued an order and interim decision in which it expressed the view that in general terms the ICSID (Additional Facility) Rules did not purport to qualify statutory obligations of disclosure which might exist for either party. Since it appeared that the FOIA created a statutory obligation of disclosure for the Respondent, the Tribunal rejected the Claimant's request for the Tribunal to prohibit the Respondent from releasing its submissions and correspondence in the case pursuant to the FOIA. By letter of 31 January 2001, the parties asked the Tribunal to clarify its order on the question of whether, in the absence of any statutory obligation of disclosure, the ICSID (Additional Facility) Rules would require the parties to treat as confidential documents such as parties' submissions made to the Tribunal and letters between the parties regarding the conduct of the arbitration. In response, the Tribunal issued on 27 February 2001 an order and further interim decision regarding confidentiality. In view of Articles 14(2), 24(1), 39(2) and 44(2) of the Arbitration (Additional Facility) Rules, and of Annex 1137.4 to chapter 11 of NAFTA, the Tribunal ordered the parties to treat as confidential until the conclusion of the proceedings such submissions and correspondence that, exempting any applicable statutory obligation of disclosure, do not already exist in a public register held by the Secretariat." *Mondev International Ltd v United States of America*, ICSID Case No. ARB(AF)/99/2, Final Award, para. 29 (11 October 2002).

248 As noted in language quoted by a US district court: "disclosure in the absence of a court order may place a party at considerable risk of being accused at a later date by other participants in the arbitration of improper disclosure. In light of this reality, the Court understands why Karteria has sought review of Magistrate Shushan's order prior to disclosing the relevant documents." *Caringal v Karteria Shipping* as quoted in *Contship Containerlines Ltd v PPG Industries, Conti Zweite Cristallo Schiffarhrts GmbH & Co*, Lexis 6857, p. 5 (SDNY 2003).

249 For a discussion of this issue, see: George Burn and Alison Pearsall, "Exceptions to Confidentiality in International Arbitration", *ICC Bulletin, 2009 Special Supplement: Confidentiality in Arbitration*, pp. 24–35.

250 *Ali Shipping Corp v Shipyard Trogir* [1999] 1 WLR 314, 327 (CA).

this sense the rule laid down in *Ali Shipping* is broader than what is permitted by the IBA Rules, which only permits in article 3.13 for confidentiality to be set aside to pursue or protect a "legal right". A "legitimate interest" at first blush would appear to be a broader concept. Nevertheless, as this principle has been interpreted in later case law, "interest" may best be understood as, "the establishment or protection of an arbitrating party's legal rights vis-à-vis a third party in order to found a cause of action against that third party or to defend a claim, or counterclaim, brought by that third party."[251] It is interesting to note that the court in *Ali Shipping* ruled that "only if a right could not be enforced without disclosure of the confidential material would the duty of confidentiality cease to apply."[252]

3.163 In the *Ali Shipping* case, a respondent in an arbitration sought to disclose information from an earlier arbitration with a different claimant including transcripts of the claimant's witnesses' oral evidence, the claimant's first submission and the final award. The respondent advanced a plea of issue estoppel claiming that the disclosure of the confidential information from the earlier arbitration was reasonably necessary to establish that the issues before the arbitrator in the second arbitration had already been addressed in the earlier case. The court did not permit disclosure of the confidential arbitration documents because, *inter alia*, it determined that the issue estoppel argument could not be reasonably expected to succeed. However, this begs the question whether the court would have ordered disclosure of the documents if the argument had had a better chance of succeeding?

3.164 In an *ad hoc* international arbitration seated in Ontario, Canada, a well-experienced tribunal was asked to exclude evidence which had been submitted in a previous arbitration involving different parties. The theory under which the documents were presented to the *ad hoc* tribunal was, again, one of issue estoppel. Here, because of the admitted relevance of the information (the objecting party had earlier admitted the relevance of the evidence) and also because the question of issue estoppel was predicated on whether the previous arbitral tribunal's ruling was of any effect, the tribunal admitted the evidence to the record even though the other proceedings had been covered by a confidentiality agreement.[253]

3.165 As opposed to the substantive legal theory of estoppel, it would appear clear that the use of documents (including expert reports) from another arbitration for the purpose of countering witness testimony in a second arbitration, does not constitute a legal right exception.[254] The tribunal in *Beccara v Argentina* evaluated a request by the respondent to introduce written testimony and other documents submitted in previous arbitrations by the same experts for the purpose of revealing their contradictory testimony. The tribunal, in

---

251 *Emmott v Wilson, supra* n. 229, para. 100.

252 Burn and Pearsall, *supra* n. 249, pp. 28–29. The court in *Ali Shipping* went on to define "necessity" as follows: "When the concept of reasonable 'necessity' comes into play in relation to the enforcement or protection of a party's legal rights, it seems to me to require a degree of flexibility in the court's approach. For instance, in reaching its decision, the court should not require the parties seeking disclosure to prove necessity regardless of difficulty or expense. It should approach the matter in the round, taking account of the nature and purpose of the proceedings for which the material is required, the powers and procedures of the tribunal in which the proceedings are being conducted, the issues to which the evidence or information sought is directed and the practicality and expense of obtaining such evidence or information elsewhere." *Ali Shipping, supra* n. 250.

253 The decision of the tribunal in Procedural Order No. 3(e) was recorded by the reviewing court in, *Telesat Canada v Boeing Satellite Systems International Inc* [2010] OJ No. 5938, paras 64, 65, Ontario Superior Court of Justice.

254 See: *Beccara v Argentina, supra* n. 231, Procedural Order No. 3, paras 148–150.

an extensive consideration of the issue, determined that the use of such documents would have limited value and, thus, the confidentiality order originally issued by other tribunals covering the use of those documents should not be overruled.

3.166 The conclusion of the *Beccara v Argentina* tribunal to not breach the confidentiality covering the earlier expert witness reports would appear to be correct in almost all instances. The evidence that an expert witness will give will be highly dependent upon the particular instructions given, the scope of advice that is sought, the fact and other matters he is asked to assume, the particular questions that lead to his conclusions in oral testimony, and a variety of other matters. Thus the pertinence of expert witness testimony, or written opinions, from one arbitration to another will likely be of limited value as was the situation in the *Beccara v Argentina* case. However, in respect of fact witnesses, such testimony is not generally shaped by the matters outlined above. One would, under normal circumstances, expect a consistent recollection of facts from a fact witness from one arbitration to another. Therefore, while confidentiality of earlier arbitrations should in most instances not be breached to introduce earlier expert witness testimony, as was the ruling in *Beccara v Argentina*, the same ruling may not be appropriate in respect of earlier fact witness testimony where such can be shown to be clearly inconsistent.

Exceptions to confidentiality: "to enforce or challenge an award"

3.167 One would expect under typical enforcement provisions (such as those reflected in the *Convention on the Recognition and Enforcement of Foreign Arbitral Awards 1958*) that enforcement of an award should be achieved with a minimum of evidence from the hearing being presented, if any at all. However, if such an award is subject of a setting-aside application or enforcement is challenged, it is possible that a party may need to submit evidence which was exchanged during the hearing to establish its right to enforce or set aside an award. In such a circumstance, it is generally accepted that to present evidence from an arbitration, irrespective of whether a confidentiality order was issued, is not considered a violation of such an order.

A tribunal's authority to enforce confidentiality

3.168 The question may arise as to what power, if any, a tribunal has to ensure that its orders on confidentiality are observed. It is rare in international arbitration for a tribunal to impose a penalty upon a party for failure to abide by a procedural order on confidentiality. Many jurisdictions do not permit the tribunal such authority in their *lex arbitri*,[255] and even where it is possible under a particular arbitration law,[256] it is not an approach commonly adopted in international arbitration. However, a tribunal may take note of a party's failure to abide by its order on confidentiality in the determination of costs.[257] Certainly, the failure by a party to observe the confidentiality of documentary evidence submitted into the

---

255 See: Poudret and Besson, *supra* n. 1, para. 3.01.

256 See: Netherlands Arbitration Act, art. 1056.

257 *Marvin Roy Feldman Karpa v Mexico, supra* n. 235, Procedural Order No. 5, para. 11 (2000): "the tribunal points out that it may take into account any such non observance [of confidentiality of evidence] for the purpose of determining how the costs and expenses of the proceedings are to be borne . . .".

arbitration could be viewed as a breach of good faith, and grounds for awarding costs against it.

3.169 A tribunal may also anticipate the issue by providing relevant provisions within the procedural order authorising a party to approach a local court to seek injunctive relief in order to prevent the disclosure of evidence. Such a condition within a procedural order will generally assert that the damage incurred by a disclosure of such evidence will cause irreparable harm.

Terms of a procedural order on confidentiality

3.170 Despite the default rule in article 3.13, situations may arise where it is unclear when and how a party may use documents "in connection with" the arbitration. In those cases where there is ambiguity, or where the parties themselves disagree on the extent of confidentiality, a tribunal may issue a specific procedural order setting forth more detailed rules concerning the terms of confidentiality.[258] In this respect, article 3.13 confirms the authority of a tribunal to issue such procedural orders.

3.171 An example of a scenario where a tribunal acted to facilitate the hearings by issuing a confidentiality order may be taken from the approach used in 2004 by an ICC tribunal in a dispute between an Asian company and a European company.[259] In that instance, the parties were concerned about the confidentiality of the technical "know-how" which was described in two expert witness reports. The tribunal, on the other hand, wanted to facilitate the procedure by asking the opposing experts to meet and confer on points of agreement between their two reports, and discuss the evidence. In order to protect their respective trade secrets, the tribunal issued a procedural order inviting the expert witnesses themselves to enter into a "confidentiality undertaking" before moving forward with the procedure.

3.172 The terms of a confidentiality order will obviously vary according to the needs of the case, the agreement of the parties and the willingness of the tribunal to consider these matters. In 2010, Michael Hwang SC developed a model confidentiality order following on a study and publication of an article giving thorough treatment to this issue.[260] This model order (hereinafter the "Hwang Model Confidentiality Order") has been recently revised and considers a number of the issues that often arise in dealing with questions concerning the confidentiality of evidence produced in an arbitration and in this respect is a template from which arbitrators and counsel may work to develop an appropriate confidentiality framework.[261] The whole of the order may be reviewed in Appendix 3 to this book, however some particular issues concerning this and other model orders which are often used, are considered below.

---

258 ICC Case No. 13507, Final Award, in Albert Jan van den Berg (ed.), *Yearbook Commercial Arbitration*, Vol. XXXV, p. 159 (2010): "Subsequently, in view of the reservations expressed by First Respondent regarding the confidentiality of information and documentation to be supplied as evidence in the arbitration and the failure of the parties to reach an agreement in this respect, the Sole Arbitrator circulated among the parties a draft confidentiality agreement; the draft was later incorporated into a Protective Confidentiality Order."

259 ICC Case No. [redacted], Procedural Order No. 7 (2004) (unpublished).

260 Hwang and Chung, *supra* n. 228, pp. 609–645. See also: Hwang S.C., Michael & Thio, Nicholas. 'A Proposed Model Procedural Order on Confidentiality in International Arbitration: A Comprehensive and Self-Governing Code'. *Journal of International Arbitration* Vol. 29, No. 2, pp. 137–169 (2012).

261 See: Appendix 3 to this book for a full reprint of the Hwang model confidentiality order.

3.173 As the Hwang Model Confidentiality Order treats "any evidence" supplied to the arbitral tribunal as confidential, whether documentary or other, it would cover witness statements.[262] While for standard international commercial arbitrations such an all-encompassing approach may pose no particular issue, where the dispute involves a public interest component such as in investor-state arbitration, this approach may be too broad. In this regard, for some investor-state arbitrations (e.g., NAFTA chapter 11) a procedural order will have to take into account whether the information will fall under the often used "business confidentiality" designation.

3.174 The Hwang Model Confidentiality Order also addresses itself to the issue of the communication of confidential information to third parties and individuals assisting the preparation of the case such as advisors and expert witnesses.[263] The Order adds the condition that disclosure to such third parties should be covered by a separate confidentiality undertaking entered into by the individual or entity to whom disclosure may be made.[264] The terms of such separate confidentiality undertaking should be agreed in advance by the party opposing disclosure or as determined by the arbitral tribunal.[265] The confidentiality undertaking will often require the expert to agree to maintain the confidential information and not disseminate it to persons other than those inside their organisation who need to use the information in connection with the arbitration, to undertake to observe the conditions of the procedural order on confidentiality, and to otherwise acknowledge that a party may seek injunctive relief to prevent dissemination of the evidence.[266]

3.175 Finally, the Hwang Model Confidentiality Order provides an answer to the question of how a confidentiality order may be enforced after the tribunal has rendered an award and is *functus officio*. As article 3.13 of the IBA Rules lays down a blanket prohibition on the use of documents exchanged in the proceedings for reasons other than participation in the arbitration, it does not impose any time limitation on this prohibition.[267] One would assume that this prohibition would exist even after the rendering of a final award. However, the means to enforce such a prohibition may be difficult. The solution to this issue, as proposed under the Hwang Model Confidentiality Order comes about by essentially inserting a choice of forum clause that binds the parties to the jurisdiction of the appropriate supervisory court at the seat of the arbitration.[268]

3.176 It may be somewhat cumbersome for parties who are not normally subject to such a court's jurisdiction (in other words, their business or daily operations are in another jurisdiction) to be required to approach a judge at the seat of the arbitration after the proceedings are completed. Moreover, the court which exercises direct supervision over a party who attempted to wrongfully disclose such information (such as the court in their home jurisdiction) may be the more appropriate court to petition for assistance.

---

262 See: Appendix 3, para. (2)(c).
263 See: Appendix 3, para. (3)(f).
264 See: Appendix 3, para. (5).
265 See: Appendix 3, para. (5).
266 See: *Chemtura* Confidentiality Order, "Confidentiality Undertaking" at Appendix 4.
267 This may be for good reason. Where a tribunal finds a confidentiality duty should be required of the parties in order to prevent the aggravation of the dispute, and to conduct an orderly arbitration, it may see no need to impose any requirements on the parties to maintain confidentiality after the conclusion of the proceedings. See: *Biwater Gauff v Tanzania, supra* n. 38, Procedural Order No. 1, para. 140.
268 See: Appendix 3, para. (9).

Either way, there does not seem to be any easy answer to the issue of maintaining confidentiality of documents exchanged during the arbitral proceedings after the tribunal is *functus officio.*

Different phases of document production

Article 3.14 2010 IBA Rules: **If the arbitration is organized into separate issues or phases (such as jurisdiction, preliminary determinations, liability or damages), the Arbitral Tribunal may, after consultation with the Parties, schedule the submission of Documents and Requests to Produce separately for each issue or phase.**

General discussion

3.177 Tribunals often find it necessary to bifurcate an arbitration procedure around certain issues. For instance, questions over jurisdiction may be handled as a preliminary matter, followed by a second phase covering the merits. Article 3.14 is a new addition to the IBA Rules which affords tribunals presiding over bifurcated proceedings the express authority to organise documentary production in different phases.

3.178 In connection with this issue, a party who objects to the jurisdiction of the tribunal may also object to an order that it produce documents for what it considers to be an invalid procedure. Nevertheless, tribunals have found that the raising of a jurisdictional objection does not excuse a party from producing documents in the arbitration.[269] The following quote from an order issued in an unreported ICC arbitration provides an example of the position often adopted in arbitration on this issue:

> [Respondent] is part of the proceedings because it was named as a responding party by Claimant. [Respondent] may dispute the jurisdiction of the Arbitral Tribunal, but it cannot escape the fact it is presently a party to this arbitration.[270]

3.179 The view expressed by the tribunal in the quote above is impliedly found in article 3.14, as under this article a tribunal may organise a procedure into separate phases to consider different issues, yet still retain the authority over evidentiary procedure granted by the IBA Rules (in particular articles 3.7 or 3.10).

Document disclosure based on a substantive right

Clause 4.10 FIDIC Red Book:[271] The Employer shall have made available to the Contractor for his information, prior to the Base Date, all relevant data in the Employer's possession on sub-surface and hydrological conditions at the Site, including environmental aspects. The

---

269 See, for instance: *UPS v Canada, supra* n. 120, Decisions relating to Document Production and Interrogatories, para. 3.72, where the tribunal noted: "Canada is not to refuse to produce documents because they allegedly raise jurisdictional issues. The test is whether the document is relevant to an allegation in the revised Amended Statement of Claim or the Statement of Defence; and document production is to proceed on that basis."
270 ICC Case No. 14069, *supra* n. 202, Procedural Order No. 2 (unpublished).
271 FIDIC, *Construction Contract*, 1st edition, 1999 (Red Book).

> Employer shall similarly make available to the Contractor all such data which comes into the Employer's possession after the Base Date . . .

General discussion

3.180 Through the course of an arbitration a tribunal may be confronted by a petition for the production of documents based not upon a procedural right, but instead a contractual provision, such as the one quoted above, or other substantive right. It is not uncommon that, as part of a commercial arrangement, parties will undertake to provide each other with documents pertaining to their respective activities. In this situation, a tribunal is faced with a request that calls for a different analysis than that which is applied to a standard procedural request for disclosure. When confronted with such a request, a tribunal should consider that it may be bound, in most instances, to apply a standard different to that which would normally be applied to a request based upon a procedural right. There may also be differences in the manner in which a tribunal orders such disclosure.

Application of substantive law standard

3.181 A request for document production based upon rights in a contract or other substantive basis, requires an analysis of the request based upon the relevant substantive law and not procedural legal standards. In this respect, the IBA Rules have no part to play in the analysis unless a tribunal finds it useful to apply them by analogy. As an example, the following excerpt from a decision of a tribunal sitting under the Swiss Rules of International Arbitration sets forth the considerations:

> As this request is grounded on the contract, the power to deal with it is vested in the Tribunal by the contract itself. The Tribunal has the power, and the duty, to address the merits of the dispute. The Claimants' request pertains to the merits. The arguments of the Respondent, which are grounded on procedural considerations and the IBA Rules (which are also of a procedural nature), are inapposite. The Claimants have a contractual right to receive the information identified in the Agreement.[272]

3.182 Therefore, the applicable standard considers the relevant right to document production arising from the contractual conditions as a matter of substantive law.[273] It follows from this that objections to the production of such documents should not be based on procedural rights, but on the contract and substantive law.[274]

---

272 Scherer (2010), *supra* n. 17.

273 The standards that are applied to a request for documentary evidence under a substantive right may allow for a broader amount of disclosure if the contractual right claimed as a basis for the request permits it. Craig, Park and Paulson recall the following scenario arising from an ICC arbitration which indicates that the tribunal was willing to grant a wider right of disclosure if it was based under a contractual as opposed to procedural right: "There are cases, however, where broad production orders are justified. In one ICC arbitration seated in Switzerland, involving several billion of U.S. dollars claim, the arbitrators, relying on the Rules and the claim by one of the parties that it had a contractual right as a joint venture partner to examine the documents in the hands of the other partner, issued an order of production which had the result of permitting the requesting party to examine 18,000 pages of documents . . .", Craig, Park, Paulsson, *supra* n. 71, para. 3.38.

274 *Ibid.*, para. 3.38, "The IBA Rules do not limit, and should not be used to restrict production of documents to which the party seeking productions is entitled as a matter of statutory law and/or contract."

3.183 This approach accords with the view taken in a judgment by a High Court in Singapore which had been requested on the basis of a provision of the civil procedure law, to order documents to be produced prior to the initiation of a SIAC arbitration. The court, in rejecting the application for discovery, noted that the right to receive the documents was contractual, and not a matter of civil procedure.[275] Therefore, in the court's view, this substantive right (along with other substantive claims) could only be determined in accordance with the arbitration clause.

Award or procedural order

3.184 As a request for the production of documents based upon a right in contract involves substantive rights, a tribunal may feel that an order compelling production should take the form of a partial award as opposed to a procedural order. This approach is consistent with the notion that a tribunal is ruling, in essence, on a substantive and not procedural right, and may allow for the enforcement of the document production decision before a relevant court.[276, 277] However, whether this is necessary or not is questionable, and in this regard, a tribunal may view it as less disruptive to a procedure to frame its findings in the form of a procedural order.[278]

Document disclosure and interim measures

Article 26(2)(d) UNCITRAL Rules:	An interim measure is any temporary measure by which, at any time prior to the issuance of the award by which the dispute is finally decided, the arbitral tribunal orders a party, for example and without limitation, to:
	. . .
	(d) Preserve evidence that may be relevant and material to the resolution of the dispute.

---

275 *Equinox Offshore Accommodation Ltd v Richshore Marine Supplies Pte Ltd.*, Singapore High Court, SGHC Case No. 122, para. 33 (2010): "The plaintiff's counsel also failed to persuade me that ordering the discovery prayed for in this application was necessary to dispose of the matter fairly or to save costs. The category of documents for which discovery was sought mirrored the class of documents covered by clause 3(iii) of the Agreement. The plaintiff had a contractual right to the inspection of those documents, and there was no necessity of a court order. If, as the plaintiff asserted, the defendant was wrongfully denying its contractual right of inspection, the plaintiff's recourse ought to be, as contractually provided for, to enforce that right by the process of arbitration."

276 See, for example: the decision of the US 7th Circuit where a decision issued by an UNCITRAL tribunal ordering the disclosure of tax records was rendered as a partial award, and enforced by the US courts. *Publicis Commun. v True North Communs. Inc*, 206 F.3d 725 (7th Cir. Ill. 2000). The extent to which this decision may be relied upon to support the argument that a partial or interim awards are enforceable has been questioned by Besson and Poudret, *supra* n. 1, ss. 640–641.

277 Award rendered by a tribunal sitting under the Swiss Rules, "The tribunal's decision must take the form of an award since the matter is one of substance. It will be noted, however, that even if the document production request were of procedural nature, the Tribunal could issue an award." As quoted in Scherer (2010), *supra* n. 17, p. 196.

278 As an example of a situation where a tribunal ordered a party to turn over documents based upon a provision of a Shareholder's Agreement, see: ICC Case No. 8879, Interim Award (1998), *ICC Bulletin* Vol. 2, No. 1 (2000).

General discussion

3.185 One of the accepted grounds on which a party may petition a tribunal to provide interim relief, is the need to preserve evidence. This principle is found implicitly in various rules, but is expressly set forth in UNCITRAL Rules, article 26(2)(d). Unlike interim measures aimed at preventing the loss of property or a right, which are primarily concerned with ensuring the effectiveness of a final award, a request to the tribunal to take action regarding the preservation of evidence is concerned with maintaining a party's ability to present its case. Access to evidence is something which international arbitrators have considered on previous occasions as necessary to ensuring the fairness of the proceedings, or more specifically the equality of arms.[279] Therefore, it is theoretically consistent with this principle for a tribunal to issue emergency, or preliminary, orders if necessary to preserve vital evidence for use during the proceedings. As will be discussed more fully below, the purpose and standards applied to interim orders concerning document production require different considerations than those normally applied to interim or provisional orders in other matters.

The purpose of provisional measures relating to documentary evidence

3.186 A request for an interim measure to preserve evidence may require a party to sequester documents, undertake to retrieve evidence from a location it controls, preserve electronic evidence (for instance, undertake to back-up relevant files) or otherwise ensure that the relevant evidence is kept for later use in the procedure. Such a procedure is intended to maintain the status quo of the evidence, and ensure that documents (or other evidence) already in existence are not lost or otherwise rendered unusable in the arbitration.

3.187 In principle, requiring actual disclosure of the evidence to an adverse party, by virtue of ordering a provisional measure, gives rise to a theoretical inconsistency. Much like ringing a bell, an order for the production of evidence can hardly be unrung or undone once complied with, which undermines the notion that the interim measure is in any way "provisional" (or "temporary" as the language in UNCITRAL Rules, article 26(2)(d) states).[280] The more consistent approach is for provisional measures to be permitted only

---

279 See: generally comments to art. 9.2(g). Where a party had complained that due process would be violated if the tribunal moved forward with the arbitration, due to the fact that criminal proceedings ongoing in France would hamper the respondent's ability to prepare its case, the arbitrators noted that such a consideration was moot where access to the evidence in question was equal to both parties. "Furthermore, the Tribunal notes that neither Claimant nor Defendants are a party to the criminal proceedings, that there is no third-party criminal liability (responsabilité pénale pour autrui) under French criminal law, and that neither Party to the arbitration faces charges in the criminal proceedings. The Tribunal has been informed that officers and/or employees of both Parties have access to the criminal file, which means that each Party faces the same restrictions with respect to accessibility to the criminal file and compliance with the secret de l'instruction [confidentiality in the preparatory investigation]. The question of how each Party chooses to disclose, use or rely on the information it retrieves from the criminal file rests with each Party." Final award in ICC Case No. 11961 in Albert Jan van den Berg (ed.), *Yearbook Commercial Arbitration*, Vol. XXXIV, pp. 32, 38 (2009).

280 Born makes no distinction between preserving evidence and ordering it to be produced, however, he states a similar point regarding the inconsistency in calling a measure requiring the production of evidence "provisional": "an order requiring preservation or production of evidence cannot be usefully understood as 'provisional' relief: such an order does not require one party to take particular action, subject to subsequent revision in a final award, but instead simply gives directions regarding disclosure and evidentiary matters as part of the tribunal's fact-finding process." Born, *supra* n. 33, p. 2007.

for the purpose of securing and maintaining evidence, but not necessarily disclosing it.[281] This being said, it is not unheard of for tribunals to overlook such inconsistency, and treat a request for provisional measures as a document request.[282]

The standard applicable to requests for interim measures aimed
at obtaining or preserving evidence

3.188 Generally, a party applying for an interim measure must provide justification to the tribunal as to why action is needed before the rendering of a final award. Thus, grounds of urgency must be demonstrated showing that the need for the measure is immediate. To the extent that a party is seeking the actual disclosure of documents via a provisional measure, the test of "urgency" would require the moving party to demonstrate why its request cannot wait for the scheduled document production phase.[283] In addition to this, it should be shown that such a measure is needed to prevent the occurrence of irreparable or serious injury to a party. Finally, such a measure must be capable of being ordered without causing the tribunal to prejudge the merits of the case.[284] These standards have long been considered appropriate for requests seeking security for the costs of the arbitration, or the claims themselves, and other measures relating to the subject matter of the dispute.

3.189 There may be reason to question whether provisional measures that are sought for the purpose of preserving documentary evidence should be subject to the same standard as

---

281 See the following analysis from the tribunal in the ICSID arbitration *Biwater Gauff v Tanzania*, where the tribunal noted the theoretical difference between the power to order interim measures under art. 47 of the ICSID convention, and art. 43 which authorises a tribunal to order the production of documents: "This is a more controversial issue when framed as an application for provisional measures under art. 47 of the ICSID Convention. Actual production is not usually considered within the ambit of such interim relief, partly because preservation is usually sufficient to protect the rights in question, and partly because actual production is catered for by other rules (in particular art. 43 of the ICSID Convention and Rule 34 of the ICSID Arbitration Rules). Indeed, the two procedures are aimed at different issues: art. 47 is designed to ensure that the Arbitral Tribunal can properly discharge its mandate, whilst art. 43 is one element in a range of provisions that structures how the mandate is to be discharged." *Biwater Gauff v Tanzania*, supra n. 38, Procedural Order No. 1, para. 100. See also: the comments made by the tribunal in *Libananco v Turkey*, an ICSID arbitration where the tribunal noted that early requests for disclosure of evidence posed a particular risk of allowing a "fishing" expedition: "The Tribunal would have been in a better position to deal with the applications covered by the present Decision had it already been in possession of the formal lines of argument adopted by both Parties. The Tribunal, like any other arbitral tribunal in a similar position, could not allow its process to be used as the cover for a mere fishing expedition launched in the hope of uncovering material to serve as the foundation for an argument (preliminary or substantive) not yet formally advanced before it." *Libananco v Turkey*, supra n. 33, Decision on Preliminary Issues, p. 31.

282 As an example, where an arbitrator had been called upon to interpret art. 38 of the NAI Rules, and more specifically whether a provisional order could be issued for the production of evidence, the tribunal regarded art. 38 as available grounds for issuing a document production order. NAI Case No. 3643, supra n. 25.

283 The *Phoenix v Czech Republic* tribunal observed the following on this point: "This is not to say a request for production of documents can never be made in a request for provisional measures. However, the granting of such provisional measure requesting one of the parties to produce documents or other evidence is only warranted if it is necessary in order to protect evidence that could otherwise – without the provisional measure – be lost or jeopardized." *Phoenix Action Ltd v Czech Republic*, ICSID Case No. ARB/06/5, Decision on Provisional Measures, para. 18 (2007).

284 Julian D. M. Lew, "Commentary on Interim and Conservatory Measures in ICC Arbitration Cases", *ICC Bulletin*, Vol. 11, No. 1, p. 23 (2000): "In the context of merely proceeding to determine whether or not to grant the relief sought, it would appear from the practice of several tribunals that there are mainly three requirements for the granting of an interim measure: no pre-judgment of the merits of a case, urgency, and irreparable or substantial harm."

described above. Some have suggested that the real issue in regard to requests concerning evidence centres on relevance, not the issues of urgency, harm and prejudice.[285] Nevertheless, it is possible to apply the traditional standards to requests seeking the preservation of documentary evidence. For example, "urgent" action may be needed to enjoin a party from destroying evidence, where it is established that there is a policy indicating that the evidence will soon be lost.[286] As to the "serious harm" prong, it may be argued that a provisional measure is necessary to prevent the loss of vital evidence necessary to establish a claim or defence. It is a legitimate fear that a party will lose an opportunity to prove its case if key documents are lost.

3.190 However, it cannot be denied that underlying the above considerations is the issue of the actual relevance of the evidence that is sought. The real aim of any preliminary measure is to preserve the evidence for later use in the proceeding, thus the threshold question is whether the target of a requested provisional measure could potentially be the subject of a disclosure order.[287] As an example, see the following observation from a panel of experienced arbitrators, who denied an interim measures request for disclosure of alleged "secret files":

> The Tribunal does not see what right of the Claimant such a vague and general request is deemed to protect. It should be emphasized that this last request is an application for disclosure of unspecified evidence rather than a proper request for provisional measures. This seems to be analogous to what is sometimes called a "fishing expedition".[288]

---

285 Born, *supra* n. 33, suggests the following at p. 2007: "With regard to orders for the sampling, it makes little sense to consider matters of urgency, irreparable harm, or prejudgment of the merits. Rather, the relevant inquiries are whether the materials in question appear relevant to the issues that are in dispute and are properly (or potentially) subject to disclosure under the parties' arbitration agreement and any applicable procedural rules."

286 See, for example: *Railroad Development v Guatemala, supra* n. 65, Decision on Provisional Measures, para. 35, where the tribunal noted that it would only act on a showing of a behaviour or policy indicating that the evidence would soon be lost: "As evidence, the Claimant has presented mainly news reports which refer to document destruction in 2004. As regards the change of government in 2008, the evidence presented refers to the disorder found in government offices when the new administration took over. No evidence has been presented that during the course of 2008 documents have been destroyed or lost by the current government of Guatemala or that the destruction of relevant documents is imminent because of the existence of this arbitration. A change of government in the normal course of constitutional transfer of power from one administration to another does not justify the recommendation of provisional measures for preservation of documents."

287 As the *Biwater Gauff* tribunal noted in Procedural Order No. 1 with regard to requests that tread the line between document production (ICSID Convention, art. 43) and interim measures (ICSID Convention, art. 47): "In the Arbitral Tribunal's view, it is appropriate to analyse the precise nature of the relief that BGT seeks, in order to assess whether each element falls within the ambit of art. 47 – or, alternatively art. 43. In so far as it falls out with art. 47, but within art. 43, the issue is then whether there are case management or other reasons to justify the issuance of an order under art. 43, ahead of the planned document disclosure exercise in this case." The tribunal went further in its analysis of this question by noting: "This is a more controversial issue when framed as an application for provisional measures under art. 47 of the ICSID Convention. Actual production is not usually considered within the ambit of such interim relief, partly because preservation is usually sufficient to protect the rights in question, and partly because actual production is catered for by other rules (in particular art. 43 of the ICSID Convention and Rule 34 of the ICSID Arbitration Rules). Indeed, the two procedures are aimed at different issues: art. 47 is designed to ensure that the Arbitral Tribunal can properly discharge its mandate, whilst art. 43 is one element in a range of provisions that structures how the mandate is to be discharged." *Biwater Gauff v Tanzania, supra* n. 38, Procedural Order No. 1, para. 3.20.

288 *Phoenix v Czech, supra* n. 283, Decision on Provisional Measures, para. 17.

3.191 As the tribunal noted above, because a fishing expedition would not be allowed in a normal document production request, so it should not be permitted in a request for interim measures. Issues such as relevance, burden (or overly broad requests) or possibly equal treatment and fairness, may be grounds for resisting the requested provisional measure.[289]

---

289 See, for example: *Railroad Development v Guatemala, supra* n. 65, Decision on Provisional Measures, where the tribunal denied a request for an interim measure ordering the preservation of evidence on the basis of the burden it would have imposed upon the respondent party. This being said, a tribunal may reserve determinations concerning objections based on legal privilege for its eventual decision to order the disclosure of such evidence.

CHAPTER 4

Witnesses of fact

Introduction

4.01 The general preference for documentary evidence notwithstanding, fact witnesses are often relied on in international arbitration as a means of presenting evidence. The procedures for taking witness testimony have evolved over time and it would seem that the modern practice for admitting witness evidence follows three basic assumptions: (1) a party has the right to be given notice of the identity of a witness and the subject matter of their testimony-in-chief before a hearing; (2) a witness who has provided testimony should be available to answer questions of the opposing party and/or the tribunal based upon that testimony; and (3) a tribunal's right to freely consider and weigh the evidence before it means that there are very few restrictions on who may offer testimony as a witness.

4.02 In order to accommodate these expectations, it has become common practice for a written witness statement to be used as the means of conveying a witness' testimony-in-chief. Earlier jurisprudence indicates that the witness statement was not as widely used as it is today; however, in modern practice it is rare to find instances where witnesses have not prepared and submitted a written version of their primary testimony prior to an oral hearing. A statement's form and the general requirements for its content also follow a widely used format.

4.03 There are variations in practice, and there are still instances where a witness statement may not be used. Exceptions notwithstanding, as article 4 makes clear, there are a number of generally recognised rules that provide guidance for the introduction and use of written witness testimony. The following chapter considers those rules, and the manner in which they have been applied in practice. Included in this section, among other topics, is a discussion of who may be a witness, the timing and content of a witness statement, the rules concerning the interviewing and preparation of witnesses prior to their testimony and the implications of a witness' failure to appear for an oral hearing. Specific matters regarding the oral testimony of witnesses are considered more thoroughly in Chapter 8, which covers hearing procedure. For a discussion of the particular issues arising out of the use of expert witnesses the reader is directed to Chapters 5 and 6.

Identification of witnesses

Article 4.1 2010 IBA Rules: **Within the time ordered by the Arbitral Tribunal, each Party shall identify the witnesses on whose testimony it intends to rely and the subject matter of that testimony.**

General discussion

4.04 It is widely accepted that a party has the right to be informed of the witnesses who have offered testimony in support of the adverse party.[1] Article 4.1 restates this principle, and also requires that a party who intends to present a witness should provide an indication of the subject matter of their testimony. In principle, the duty to provide such notice is satisfied by the filing of witness statements in the arbitration (see comments to article 4.4). Notice, whether it be in the form of a witness statement or otherwise, should be provided within the time frames set forth by the tribunal.

Failure to give notice of witness within the specified time

4.05 Failure to provide notice to the tribunal and the adverse party of a proffered witness within the prescribed time frames may result in the exclusion of both the written and oral testimony[2] of that witness.[3] As with documentary evidence submitted after the passing of a deadline, a tribunal may exercise its discretion to admit such evidence despite its tardiness. However, before doing so, it is customary for a tribunal to consider whether any prejudice or undue delay will result from the failure to observe the deadline, as well as the possible evidentiary value of the testimony (see also comments to articles 3.1 and 9.2(g)).

4.06 With regard to particular problems raised by witness evidence offered late, a tribunal may often be required to consider whether the belated submission of testimony

---

1   See: the comments to art. 8.1, with regard to the duty incumbent upon a party to provide notification to the adverse party prior to the hearing of the witnesses it intends to present. See also the instruction of the tribunal in ICC Case No. 12761; "the testimony of individuals who have not been identified by the Parties in their respective evidential proposal writs will not be admitted unless it has been shown, to the satisfaction of the Arbitral Tribunal, that it is newly-discovered." ICC Case No. 12761, Procedural Order of 12 March 2004, *ICC Bulletin, 2010 Special Supplement: Decisions on ICC Arbitration Procedure*, p. 73.

2   See: *Burimi S.R.L and Eagle Games SH.A, Claimants, v Republic of Albania*, Respondent, ICSID Case No. ARB/11/18, Procedural Order No. 3 of 9 January 2013: "In accordance with Procedural Order No. 1, paragraph 14(a), the Tribunal finds that written submissions were to include 'all of the evidence on which they [the Parties] intend to rely in support of the legal arguments advanced therein, including written witness statements, expert witness reports, documents, and all other evidence in whatever form.' The Claimants did not submit any witness statements with their memorials. Therefore, there are no witnesses tendered by the Claimants to be heard. In light of the above, the Tribunal confirms its Decision of December 12, 2012, that it will not permit the Claimants to present and examine witnesses at the hearing who have not previously submitted written statements as required by Procedural Order No. 1." See also: the decision of the Paris Court of Appeal rejecting a challenge to an ICC award because the arbitrator had rejected written witness statements submitted four days late. The challenging party sought to set the award aside claiming that the procedural decision of the arbitrator was overly formalistic and violated the *principe de la contradiction*. The award was upheld and the challenge rejected on the basis that the arbitrators decision was consistent with the aforementioned principle. *S.C.S. GE Medical Systems v Albanna Group for General Trade*, Court de Appel de Paris, Arret du 28 Janvier 2014, no. 12/20550.

3   See: *Harris International Telecommunications Inc v The Islamic Republic of Iran*, Case No. 409, Partial Award No. 323-409-1, Iran-USCTR, Vol. 17, pp. 64–67 (1987): "Affidavits constitute documentary evidence which must be submitted in accordance with the time-limits set in the Tribunal's orders so that the other Party is able to respond." See also: *Norman Gabay, also known as Nourollah Armanfar v The Islamic Republic of Iran*, Case No. 771, Award No. 515-771-2 of 10 July 1991, fn. 2, p. 4 where it was noted, that only four days before the hearing, the claimant requested the introduction of his cousin Rafiolaah Gabai as a rebuttal witness. This request was rejected by the Tribunal's Order of 26 April 1991: "[i]n view of the fact that the Respondent [had] notified no witness aside from its document expert, the lateness with which the Claimant notified Mr. Rafiolaah Gabai as a rebuttal witness for the Hearing, and the lack of any explanation as to why this notification could not have been made earlier".

will require rebuttal witnesses to be brought forward by the adverse party.[4] If so, then the question of whether the adverse party has sufficient time to both organise the attendance of rebuttal witnesses and to prepare an examination of the new witness may also have to be addressed.[5]

4.07 Underlying all of these concerns is the probative value of the proffered testimony, a question which requires consideration both as to whether the evidence is relevant to the presenting party's burden and material to the outcome of the case.[6] If a tribunal is of the opinion that the probative value of the witness testimony is of such a nature that it should make exception to hear the witness, it is within the tribunal's discretion to admit the statement after the deadline. However, to ensure that a party's right to a fair hearing is observed, arbitrators may be required to provide additional time to the adverse party to prepare its questions for the new witness, allow for rebuttal testimony to be provided or, at the very least, allow for the observations of the adverse party on the new witness testimony to be communicated in writing to the tribunal. Where previously unannounced witnesses have appeared at a hearing, reviewing courts have said that the adverse party suffered prejudice since they did not have the opportunity to prepare questions or introduce counter witnesses,[7]

Who may be a witness

Article 4.2 2010 IBA Rules:	**Any person may present evidence as a witness, including a Party or a Party's officer, employee or other representative.**
Other Statements of the Rule Article 27(2) 2010 UNCITRAL Rules:	Witnesses, including expert witnesses, who are presented by the parties to testify to the arbitral tribunal on any issue of fact or expertise may be any individual, notwithstanding that the individual is a party to the arbitration or in any way related to a party. Unless otherwise directed by the arbitral tribunal, statements by witnesses, including expert witnesses, may be presented in writing and signed by them.

---

4   *OKO Osuuspankkien Keskuspankki Oyj v Republic of Estonia*, ICSID Case No. ARB/04/6, Procedural Order No. 4, p. 1.

5   With regard to timing in general, a tribunal may continue with agreed time-lines as long as they will allow reasonable time for case preparation. See the decision of the Swiss Federal Tribunal in regard to an ICC Arbitration, where it upheld the refusal of a tribunal to grant time extensions in advance of a hearing. Georg von Segesser, "Swiss Federal Court, 14 December 2004, 1st Chamber", *A Contribution by the ITA Board of Reporters*. See also: *Brunswick Bowling & Billiards Corp v Shanghai Zhonglu Industrial Co Ltd*, Hong Kong High Court, Court of First Instance, Case No. HCCT66/2007, para. 88 (10 February 2009), where the court noted that when it is necessary to ensure that a party has a fair hearing, an international arbitral tribunal is within its power to adjust the time frame of a hearing, or otherwise, in order to "take steps to conduct the arbitration in such a manner that could redress the problem instead of being constrained by an unworkable agreement of the parties."

6   *Ibid.*, *Brunswick Bowling v Shanghai Zhonglu*. See also: the decision of the Iran-US Claims Tribunal regarding late filed evidence in which in addition to ascertaining the reason for the delay, the tribunal also considered the potential probative value of the evidence before determining to admit it: "[i]n determining whether a document presented at this stage of the proceedings is, in the particular circumstances, admissible, the Tribunal considers the character and contents of the submission." *Grune & Stratton v the Islamic Republic of Iran*, Case No. 10059, Award No. 359-10059-1 of 15 April 1988, p. 4.

7   See the judgment of the Netherlands Supreme Court where a final award was set aside because the tribunal allowed a witness not previously notified to the adverse party to give testimony at a hearing. *PJ Spaanderman v Anova Food*, Hoge Raad, Decision of 25 May 2007, in *RvdW*, No. 504, para. 3.6 (2007).

General discussion

4.08 In some jurisdictions the witness testimony of a party or an individual bearing a significant relationship to that party may not be admitted into evidence.[8] This principle derives from policy considerations or legal traditions; however, these restrictions generally do not apply in international arbitration. The customary approach taken by international tribunals has been to admit the testimony of witnesses into a proceeding irrespective of the connections, be they financial, social, familial or employment-related, which that witness may have with a party. This principle is restated in article 4.2 where it is made clear that "any person" may tender a witness statement in an international arbitration. Ultimately, as the arbitral tribunal is charged with weighing the value of the evidence, as set forth in article 9.1, it is up to the arbitrator to determine what, if any, probative value may be assigned to the statements made by a witness who maintains connections of some type with a party or otherwise has an interest in the outcome of the proceedings.

Testimony by witness with a connection to a party

4.09 In international arbitration a tribunal may admit the testimony of a witness who has an interest in the outcome of the arbitration, or is otherwise connected to one of the parties. This customary rule thus permits the testimony of persons bearing the following types of relationships to a party: (1) the claimant or respondent themselves;[9] (2) the shareholder of a party;[10]

---

8 For instance, it is reported that before the courts in numerous Swiss cantons the rules of evidence prohibit a person who has an interest in the outcome of the proceedings from giving evidence as a witness. Christian Oetiker, "Witnesses before the International Arbitral Tribunal", *ASA Bulletin*, Vol. 25, No. 2, p. 253 (2007).

9 In some of the earliest arbitral decisions this practice was accepted. Consider the following statement from a Mexico-US Mixed Claims Commission arbitration regarding the admission of a party's witness testimony into the record: "[Counsel] for the United States referred to the statement in the Mexican brief that 'Arbitral commissions with obvious prudence refuse to hear the claimant when he alone speaks or to take his statements literally'. . . . An arbitral tribunal cannot, in my opinion, refuse to consider sworn statements of a claimant, even when contentions are supported solely by his own testimony. It must give such testimony its proper value for or against such contentions. Unimpeached testimony of a person who may be the best informed person regarding transactions and occurrences under consideration cannot properly be disregarded because such a person is interested in a case. No principle of domestic or international law would sanction such an arbitrary disregard of evidence." *Daniel Dillon (United States of America) v United Mexican States*, 3 October 1928, 4 RIAA 370-371. It may be further noted that a connection between a witness and a party may also be an "adverse" connection. In this regard reference may be had to the ICSID case, *Libananco v Turkey*, where the respondent, the governmental party, argued that four witnesses who had absconded from Turkey to flee judicial investigation should not be permitted to testify. "The Respondent submitted that, in these circumstances, it would be wrong as a matter of law and judicial propriety to permit the four witnesses to testify, and requested that their statements be stricken or disregarded." After taking advice from the administering institution, the tribunal rejected this motion, and arranged to hear the witnesses. *Libananco Holdings Co Ltd v Republic of Turkey*, ICSID Case No. ARB/06/8, Final Award, paras 65–77 (2011). See also: Court de Appel de Paris, Arret du 10 Janvier 2012, no. 10/212671, a 2012 decision of the Paris Court of Appeal rejecting a challenge to a final award rendered in an ICC arbitration based upon the decision to allow a party to the proceeding to testify as a witness.

10 See a reported arbitration between a US company and a Chinese company, where an SCC tribunal ordered an oral hearing to be held even though it was not requested by the parties in order to hear *inter alia* the testimony of the owner of the claimant corporation. "Final Arbitral Award Rendered in SCC Case/090/2004", *Stockholm International Arbitration Review*, Vol. 2, No. 1, p. 211 (2007).

(3) spouse or other family member of a party;[11] (4) legal counsel (both internal and external);[12] (5) employee (including corporate officer);[13] and (6) business partners.[14] In certain instances, a tribunal has also accepted the party acting as its own expert.[15] The aforementioned list is not exhaustive but it does establish the fundamental principle that the relationship between a party and a fact witness does not disqualify the witness from giving valuable evidence.

---

11 "The Claimant's witness list includes the Claimant and her spouse. It is the long-standing practice of the Tribunal that such persons are allowed to testify as party-witnesses. Therefore, the Respondent's objection in respect of these persons cannot be accepted." *Frederica Lincoln Riahi v The Islamic Republic of Iran*, Case No. 485, Chamber 1, Order of 4 May 2000, para. C. See also: Iran-US Claims Tribunal Case No. 193, where the testimony of a number of family members was taken by the tribunal and considered in the final award. *Reza Said Malek v The Government of the Islamic Republic of Iran*, Award 534-193-3 of 11 August 1992 in Albert Jan van den Berg (ed.), *Yearbook Commercial Arbitration*, Vol. XVIII, pp. 283–291 (1993).

12 See the decision of a US court recorded in Donald Francis Donovan, Catherine M. Amirfar *et al.*, "2 November 2007 – United States District Court for the Southern District of New York", *A Contribution by the ITA Board of Reporters*, where it is noted that the in-house legal counsel of one of the parties was permitted to provide testimony regarded the drafting history of the contract in contention. See also the unusual situation of *Pac Rim Cayman v El Salvador* where the tribunal allowed the outside counsel representing the respondent in the arbitration to testify to certain key facts during the jurisdictional phase of the proceedings. *Pac Rim Cayman LLC v Republic of El Salvador*, ICSID Case No. ARB/09/12, Hearing on Jurisdiction, Transcript, pp. 324–325 (Washington DC, Day 2, 3 May 2011). See also: where an attorney which formally acted for a party was allowed to testify as to certain factual issues before the Iran-US Claims Tribunal in *General Petrochemicals Corp v The Islamic Republic of Iran*, Case No. 828, Award No. 522-828-1 of 21 October 1991.

13 See: *Highland Insurance Company v The Islamic Republic of Iran*, Case No. 435, Award No. 491-435-3 of 12 October 1990, in which an objection brought against a witness who had tendered testimony based on the general proposition that he was the officer of a company affiliated to claimant was rejected as the tribunal did not consider the witness' status as relevant to its right to consider the evidence. See also the final award in an UNCITRAL Rules arbitration where the former chief executive officers of the claimant were accepted as witnesses: "CME's two former CEOs, rendered extensive written and oral witness statements in the first stage of the proceedings and were cross-examined at length at the hearing in Stockholm." *CME Czech Republic BV v The Czech Republic*, UNCITRAL, Final Award, para. 69 (2003). See also: the decision of a Cairo Regional Centre for International Commercial Arbitration tribunal to call engineers in the employ of the parties to provide evidence: "The Arbitral Tribunal allowed several engineers working with each party to appear and bear witness upon the facts." *An African Construction Co v A Real Estate Investment Co*, Case No. 133/1999, Final Award of 31 January 2000, in M. E. I. Alam Eldin (ed.), *Arbitral Awards of the Cairo Regional Centre for International Commercial Arbitration II 1997–2000*, pp. 97, 99 (2003). See also: the reliance of an ICC tribunal upon the fact testimony of an employee of a party to the arbitration in the Final Award of 1999 in ICC Case No. 10188, in Albert Jan van den Berg (ed.), *Yearbook Commercial Arbitration*, Vol. XXVIII, p. 86 (2003). See also: Final Award in ICC Case No. 13676, in Albert Jan van den Berg (ed.), *Yearbook Commercial Arbitration*, Vol. XXXV, p. 168 (2010), where the tribunal took detailed consideration of the witness statement offered by an individual described as the "Assistant Vice President of Claimant". See also: an UNCITRAL arbitration where the tribunal relied upon the fact testimony of the chief financial officer of the claimant to determine that the claim presented considered properly the discount value of future cash flows. *Himpurna California Energy Ltd v PT (Persero) Perusahaan Listruik Negara*, Final Award of 4 May 1999, in Albert Jan van den Berg (ed.), *Yearbook Commercial Arbitration*, Vol. XXV, p. 72 (2000). See also: where an LCIA tribunal heard testimony of the chief executive officer of a company related to the Claimant. LCIA Case No. 7875, Final Award, para. 47 (2008) (unpublished).

14 In this ICSID arbitration the tribunal admitted the testimony of a witness who held himself out to be the strategic business partner of the claimant in the matter. John Beechey, "*Inceysa Vallisoletana SL v Republic of El Salvador*, ICSID Case No. ARB/03/26, 2 August 2006", *A Contribution by the ITA Board of Reporters*, para. 127.

15 *Frederica Lincoln Riahi v The Islamic Republic of Iran*, Case No. 485, Award No. 600-485-1 in Albert Jan van den Berg (ed.), *Yearbook Commercial Arbitration*, Vol. XXVIII, p. 52 (2003): "With respect to the value of the horse, Pishdad, the Claimant relies on her own expert knowledge. The Tribunal is not persuaded that the Revolution in Iran adversely affected the market and the value of horses in Iran. Moreover, the Respondent has not offered any evidence or opinion regarding the value of Pishdad. The Tribunal, therefore, accepts the Claimant's valuation, and finds that she is entitled to US$ 2,800."

Persons interested in the outcome of proceedings to be treated as a witness

4.10 The practice adopted by some international tribunals with regard to admitting testimony from fact witnesses with an interest in the outcome of the proceedings, has been to allow such statements to be submitted as part of the proffering party's case, but not as witness testimony.[16] It would seem that under this approach the individual is not treated as a "witness" or given the opportunity to offer "testimony" in a manner similar to other witnesses, although the tribunal will allow their oral and written assertions to be part of the record.[17]

4.11 This practice is unsatisfactory for a number of reasons. From a procedural standpoint, this method is less desirable as it leaves in doubt the exact nature of the statement that has been submitted and its evidentiary value (if any). A party in such a circumstance may be justifiably confused as to whether the statement should be regarded as evidence or simply argument. Moreover, this scenario creates uncertainty as to whether a tribunal may rely on a statement of this type, and if the person submitting the statement should be subject to cross-examination as a witness normally would be.

4.12 The IBA Rules do not adopt this approach. As noted above, article 4.2 sets forth a broad and liberal definition of "witness." In this regard, the IBA Rules have followed the principle that arbitrators are free to appreciate the evidence before them and, thus, consider whether the ties between a witness and a party should require less weight to be assigned to the testimony.[18]

---

16 See the decision of an ICC tribunal to admit the testimony of the directors of a corporation as part of the party's presentation and argumentation, and not as witnesses: "I would like to clarify that a party, including its legal representatives is not to be regarded as a witness in this arbitration. Indeed, in this respect I may refer to art. 14 paragraph 1 of the ICC Rules of Arbitration where a distinction is made between the hearing of the parties on the one hand, and the hearing of any other person, on the other hand. When using the term 'witness statements' in the Terms of Reference, I considered witnesses as being any person other than the party itself and its legal representatives. . . . If I decide to hear Messrs X and Y, this will be regarded as the hearing of the parties and not as the hearing of witnesses." ICC Case No. 7319, Procedural Order of 30 October 1992, in Dominique Hascher (ed.), *Collection of Procedural Decisions in ICC Arbitration 1993–1996*, p. 97 (2nd edition, 1998).

17 See the decision of an Iran-US Claims Tribunal panel regarding the admission of testimony from corporate officers. Here the tribunal admitted the evidence as part of a party's presentation of its case, but did not administer an oath or declaration: "The Tribunal notes that Mrs. Phillis Ball is the corporate secretary of the Claimant company and Mr. Richard T. Blancato is the corporate attorney of the Claimant company. Accordingly, Mrs. Ball and Mr. Blancato may be presented by the Claimant as part of the presentation of the Claimant's Case, but they will not be requested to make the declaration provided for in Note 6(a) to art. 25 of the Tribunal Rules." *Kaysons International Corp v The Islamic Republic of Iran*, Case No. 367, Order of 8 October 1992, pp. 1–2.

18 This approach has enjoyed wide support in international arbitration as a general rule. See also the decision of an ICC tribunal seated in Geneva, whereby in a procedural order it was noted that: "there is no restriction as to the qualification of the 'witness'. In this procedure, a person is called a witness irrespective of his links with one or the other party. The Tribunal is free in its appreciation of the witnesses' statement." "Documents" in *ASA Bulletin*, Vol. 11, No. 2, p. 317 (1993). See also the following rule, adopted by an ICC tribunal seated in Paris in ICC Case No. 9001, which captures the preferred approach to this issue: ". . . the claimant announced that its managing director would present part of its case at the hearing on the merits. The respondents did not object to this, but they claimed the right to cross-examine the Managing Director on the grounds that he was deeply implicated in the events giving rise to the dispute. In effect, by making a statement at the hearing, the Managing Director would be giving evidence as a witness. The claimant resisted this on the grounds that the Managing Director would be making a statement as a party representative rather than giving evidence as a witness. The arbitral tribunal correctly decided that, if the statements of a party representative at the hearing constituted testimony on the facts, the opposing party would be allowed to cross-examine the representative." As reported in Michael Bühler and Carroll Dorgan, "Witness Testimony Pursuant to the 1999 IBA Rules of Evidence in International Commercial Arbitration – Novel or Tested Standards?" *Journal of International Arbitration*, Vol. 17, No.1, p. 9 (2000). This being said, the approach adopted historically by international arbitrators has been to favour the testimony of a witness without interest in the outcome of the case, over those bearing a connection to a party: "personal interest of the deponent and the uncontrolled character of his affirmation

Such flexibility is consistent with the general approach to procedure in international arbitration.[19]

Witnesses who have legal obligations of confidentiality to a party

4.13 Difficult procedural issues may arise where a fact witness bears a relationship to a party which carries with it certain legal duties, such as a responsibility to maintain the confidentiality of certain information. The most obvious example being a witness who is also a legal counsel to the party and has a duty to maintain the confidentiality of privileged communications. Where this situation comes about a tribunal is presented with the difficult task of admitting the factual evidence into the record, while simultaneously observing the duty (to the extent that the tribunal accepts such privilege as binding) not to reveal privileged information. Where such issues have arisen in the past, arbitrators have drawn distinctions for the witness as to what areas are outside the scope of their privilege obligations. In particular, such instructions generally note that matters of fact, such as what occurred at a relevant (but non-privileged) meeting, may be disclosed, whereas legal advice rendered in relation to that meeting, may not.[20] It may be in these circumstances that a tribunal will have to communicate clear guidelines ahead of the hearing to the parties in order to clarify the issue to both the examining party and the witness.

4.14 Where a witness' confidentiality obligations render their testimony so incomplete that the examining party is simply unable to properly challenge or question the testimony, a tribunal should take such factors into consideration in determining the weight assigned to such testimony. Moreover, a tribunal may be wary of a fact witness using privilege as a sword, as well as a shield, insofar as a witness reveals partially the facts of a situation to support one party's case, but refuses to answer questions which would probe the veracity

---

are, therefore, important considerations which generally deprive a claimant's affidavit of much of its probative force." Bin Cheng, *General Principles of Law as Applied by International Courts and Tribunals*, p. 311 (1987).

19 The reasoning set forth below, from a well experienced arbitrator at the Iran-US Claims Tribunal, outlines the possible risks of applying a rigid rule of exclusion: "Respondent has contended that neither the affidavit of claimant's mother nor an affidavit of a cousin of a claimant should be given any consideration by the Tribunal. However, while family relationships and ties of friendship are factors to be considered in weighing the probative value of testimony, it goes entirely too far to suggest that no weight can be given to the testimony of relations and friends. The present Case is a dramatic illustration of where such a rigid approach would lead. Here, the claim relates to properties within a family compound. The parental home which was located at the central point of the compound is one of the subjects of the claim. It is difficult to imagine anyone better qualified to testify from personal experience of the events than Mrs. Roghieh Malek, who lived in the compound throughout the period in question. To suggest that her evidence must be disregarded borders on the absurd. The same can be said of Mr. Vossough, whose mother lived in the parental home and who personally observed the changes in the compound during the crucial period. If a degree of skepticism is in order concerning the attitudes of close relatives and friends, such skepticism would ordinarily come into play where testimony offered by the other party directly contradicts the testimony of the 'interested' witness. In this Case Respondent has provided no testimony that clashes with the testimony of Mrs. Malek, Mr. Vossough and Mr. Boini." *Reza Said Malek v The Islamic Republic of Iran*, Case No. 193, Concurring and Dissenting Opinion of Richard C. Allison of 11 August 1992 regarding Award No. 534-193-3, para. 15.

20 Consider the instruction given by an experienced ICSID tribunal when confronted with the testimony of the outside counsel appearing on behalf of his client as a fact witness during the proceedings: "Well, I think we have to divide your role and be very careful. We are not asking you here to give evidence about what you do or don't do as a legal representative of the Respondents, but you are here as a fact witness. Now, if you can testify, to the best of your recollection, truthfully what [Mr A] said to you, and you are going to be asked that question, as we understand, by counsel for the Claimant, you should answer that question as a fact witness." *Pac Rim Cayman LLC v Republic of El Salvador*, *supra* n. 12, Transcript.

of that recollection.[21] If the obligation preventing a witness from fully testifying as to the facts of a matter is not rooted in a recognised duty of confidentiality, or otherwise has been waived, a tribunal may order a party to instruct the witness to fully cooperate in regard to matters which the witness has already partially testified to.[22]

Preparing witnesses

Article 4.3 2010 IBA Rules: **It shall not be improper for a Party, its officers, employees, legal advisors or other representatives to interview its witnesses or potential witnesses and to discuss their prospective testimony with them.**

General discussion

4.15 Some jurisdictions regard it as unethical for a party or its lawyer to interview its witnesses prior to the giving of testimony. The difference in approach to witness preparation between domestic jurisdictions does not run strictly along civil law and common law divides. Even among countries that share similar legal heritages there is divergence as to the extent and quality of contact between legal counsel and witness considered permissible.[23] National rules which dictate acceptable levels of witness preparation have not been adopted in international arbitration, as is made plain by the simplicity of the rule set forth in article 4.3. It is generally accepted that lawyers appearing before international tribunals may interview and work with witnesses prior to the submission of witness statements and the appearance of the witness at a hearing.[24]

---

21 See: comments to art. 9.3(d), and the discussion concerning the waiver of privilege in relation to the selective use of privileged information.

22 For instance, in the *CME v Czech Republic* arbitration, the tribunal took a dim view of one party's attempt to selectively release two former officers of the corporation from their confidentiality obligations to testify on only discreet issues: "The Tribunal is of the view that the Claimant is not entitled to waive its confidentiality rights in respect to the two witnesses only for certain selected parts of the proceedings. The Respondent is free to interview the two witnesses on the basis of art. 4.2 and art. 4.3 of the IBA Rules of Evidence. The Claimant is ordered to instruct the two witnesses that the Claimant's confidentiality rights are waived except to the extent that the witnesses are not obligated to disclose Claimant's and/or CME's information which might be privileged . . .". *CME v Czech Republic supra* n. 13, Final Award, para. 69. As an example of the difference between a privilege which is accepted on its face once shown to apply, such as attorney-client privilege, and those claims to a right of confidentiality where a tribunal must balance whether the application of such a right is compelling, see the following distinction drawn by an UNCITRAL tribunal between governmental privilege and attorney-client privilege: "The Arbitral Tribunal finds that, unlike cases in which solicitor-client privilege is pleaded, it must take into account Claimant's interests in the production of said documents in order to determine whether Canada's interests in withholding the documents are outweighed." *Vito G. Gallo v Government of Canada*, NAFTA/UNCITRAL, Procedural Order No. 3, p. 14 (2009).

23 Two prominent examples being the differences between the rules governing witness preparation found in England versus what is permissible in the United States.

24 As an example, the following rule of procedure was adopted by a panel of arbitrators (the chairman of which was a prominent international commercial arbitrator) sitting over disputes arising out of the America's Cup: "It shall not be improper for counsel, with or without party representatives, to meet with witnesses and potential witnesses for the purpose of establishing the facts relevant to the hearing, preparing witness statements and preparing for hearings." +39 Challenge, Decision in Cases Nos ACJ005 and ACJ006, 14 June 2005, in Henry Peter (ed.), *The 32nd America's Cup Jury and its Decisions*, p. 209 (2009). See further the procedural direction given by an ICC tribunal in Case No. 12169 positively affirming the right of counsel and representatives of the party to contact and interview potential witnesses: "It shall be proper for the representative of the parties, including

4.16 The evident difference in approach to witness preparation taken by varying jurisdictions has led some to consider whether more detailed transnational rules and guidelines should be proposed to cover this issue.[25] Arguing that an uneven playing field may result where one party retains a lawyer from a jurisdiction which imposes little to no restriction on witness preparation, and the other side retains counsel that is under considerable restraint, some are tempted to regulate this possible imbalance. It is suggested that such a situation may require the tribunal to impose a general rule of conduct on the parties at the outset of the arbitration to deal with such issues.[26] From where that rule would be derived is unclear; however, a tribunal may consider a choice of law analysis to lead it to an applicable rule.[27]

4.17 The IBA Rules do not adopt this view. The Rules in one sense have already set forth a "transnational" standard, to the extent that one may be identified, in article 4.3. This rule covers what is generally agreed to be permissible conduct in international arbitration, but goes no further by, for instance, proscribing witness coaching or indicating what level of contact may exist between counsel and witness. Moreover, article 4.5 does not impose upon the fact witness the duty to disclose a relationship or contacts which a fact witness may have had with a legal counsel in the proceedings. This reflects that there is no transnational rule requiring disclosure of pre-hearing or pre-statement discussions between witnesses and counsel. The permissive approach of article 4.3 also restates the approach found in other prominent procedural rules.[28]

Ethical considerations for counsel

4.18 Following the release of the 2010 IBA Rules, the IBA Guidelines adopted a similar approach to article 4.3. Guideline 24 in essence reflects the same view as article 4.3, with some qualifications which are in line with the IBA Rules.[29] The adoption of this guideline further solidifies the view that interactions between counsel and witnesses concerning their future testimony are not *per se* inappropriate. The above being said, Guideline 23 makes plain that meetings or interactions with witnesses cannot be undertaken by counsel in order

---

Counsel, to interview prospective or potential witnesses whom that party considers calling." *ICC Bulletin, 2010 Special Supplement: Decisions on ICC Arbitration Procedure*, p. 35.

25 Fabian von Schlabrendorff, "Interview and Preparing Witnesses for Testimony in International Arbitration Proceedings: The Quest for Developing Transnational Standards of Lawyers Conduct", in M. A. Fernandez-Ballesteros and David Arias (eds), *Liber Amicorum Bernardo Cremades*, p. 1161 (2010). As noted by one commentator: ". . . in line with Article 4.3 of the IBA Rules on the taking of Evidence, tribunals are increasingly including in their procedural orders permission for counsel to have contact with their witnesses of fact." Ian Meredith, Hussain Khan, "Witness Preparation in International Arbitration – A Cross Cultural Minefield", 19–9 *Mealey's Int'l Arb Rep*, 4 (2011). See also the position adopted by the tribunal in ICC Case No. 12169: "It shall be proper for the representative of the parties, including Counsel, to interview prospective or potential witness whom that party considers calling." ICC Case No. 12169, Procedural Order of 12 May 2003, *ICC Bulletin, 2010 Special Supplement: Decisions on ICC Arbitration Procedure*, p. 35.

26 *Ibid.*, Schlabrendorff, p. 1178.

27 *Ibid.*

28 *Ibid.*, p. 1175. The author, in reviewing several sets of arbitral rules, notes: "Most rules of arbitration procedure recognize the arbitral tribunal's discretion to determine procedural rules, but they rarely deal with counsel witness relations. Only the LCIA Rules and the Swiss Rules, it appears, explicitly state that it is not improper for counsel to interview witnesses." *Id.*

29 IBA Guideline 24: "A Party Representative may, consistent with the principle that the evidence given should reflect the Witness's own account of relevant facts, events or circumstances, or the Expert's own analysis or opinion, meet or interact with Witnesses and Experts in order to discuss and prepare their prospective testimony."

to pressure a witness into giving false testimony.[30] Meetings with prospective witnesses are permitted in international arbitration in order to assist the fact-finding process, not hinder it.

Contacting adverse witnesses and ethical concerns

4.19 Article 4.3 considers communications between a party or its counsel and those witnesses it has or intends to present, but does not expressly apply to communications between party representatives and adverse or third-party witnesses. This is made plain by the text where it refers to a party interviewing "its witnesses". It might be said that a party who contacts an adverse witness with the hopes of convincing that witness to give information helpful to its case is, in effect, communicating with a "prospective" witness, which is generally sanctioned by the rule. This appears to be the view of an UNCITRAL tribunal which ordered that witnesses who had previously rendered testimony on behalf of the claimant be made available for an interview by respondent's counsel on the basis of articles 4.2 and 4.3.[31]

4.20 There are reasons to hold article 4.3 is not applicable to contact between a party and an adverse witness, in particular, because the rule gives no consideration to the issue of "witness intimidation", an allegation that may arise in the context of such communications. Arbitral tribunals in the past have issued orders prohibiting contact between a party and those witnesses testifying against it in the face of such accusations.[32] Thus, whether article 4.3 is sufficient in itself to govern cross-contact between a party or its legal counsel and an adverse witness merits further consideration.

4.21 A more detailed set of procedural rules governing requests to communicate with adverse witnesses may be taken from the *Azinian v Mexico* ICSID arbitration, where a tribunal of well-experienced arbitrators considered a request by the claimant to interview the respondent's witnesses. Here the tribunal found it permissible for a party to conduct such interviews, but set forth several conditions, which are summarised as follows:[33] (1) the witness should feel free to answer or not answer any questions; (2) the witness should be informed that his or her legal counsel may be present at the interview; (3) statements made during the interview are not to be admitted into the proceedings; (4) the only testimony to be given probative value is that contained in a written statement

---

30 IBA Guideline 23: "A Party Representative should not invite or encourage a Witness to give false evidence."

31 *CME v Czech Republic, supra* n. 13, Final Award.

32 The following excerpt from an ICSID arbitration describes such a scenario: "Respondent on 23 June 2009 asked the Tribunal to order Claimants to desist from contacting Respondent's current and former employees. The Tribunal on 25 June 2009 instructed Claimants to refrain from contact with Respondent's current employees. The Tribunal indicated that, with respect to former employees of Respondent, it would consider any applications on a case-by-case basis. The parties then exchanged further correspondence about Claimants' contacts with Respondent's employees, and Respondent's contacts with witnesses whose statements were submitted by Claimants. The Tribunal on 3 July 2009 issued an order instructing both parties to refrain from contacting each other's witnesses, and directing that any allegations of witness intimidation must be supported and documented." Dietmar W. Prager, Samantha J. Rowe *et al.*, *"Inmaris Perestroika Sailing Maritime Services GmbH v Ukraine*, ICSID Case No. ARB/08/8, 8 March 2010", *A Contribution by the ITA Board of Reporters*, para. 19.

33 *Azinian et al. v United Mexican States*, ICSID Case No. ARB(AF)/97/2, Letter from the Tribunal, 16 June 1998.

or orally given in the presence of the tribunal; and (5) it would not be required that the other party's representatives be present[34] at such an interview as long as the witness does not require it.

4.22 Some of the points raised by the *Azinian* tribunal have since been codified in the IBA Guidelines. There it is expressly set forth that counsel must identify themselves and make plain which party they represent when approaching a witness for the first time, as well as disclose the reason for seeking the interview.[35] The Guidelines also state that the witness must be made aware that they may have their own counsel present during the interview.[36] The Guidelines do not impose restrictions on the admissibility of evidence obtained when interviewing a non-cooperating witness, so long as the relevant ethical principles are observed.

The use of witness statements

Article 4.4 2010 IBA Rules: **The Arbitral Tribunal may order each Party to submit within a specified time to the Arbitral Tribunal and to the other Parties Witness Statements by each witness on whose testimony it intends to rely, except for those witnesses whose testimony is sought pursuant to Articles 4.9 or 4.10. If Evidentiary Hearings are organised into separate issues or phases (such as jurisdiction, preliminary determinations, liability or damages), the Arbitral Tribunal or the Parties by agreement may schedule the submission of Witness Statements separately for each issue or phase.**

General discussion

4.23 The customary practice within international arbitration is for each witness to submit a written statement recording their testimony.[37] This approach has become standard practice for a number of reasons, not least of which is procedural economy. Consider, for instance, the comments of one experienced arbitrator presiding over an *ad hoc* arbitration seated in Zurich, Switzerland: "What I would like to receive is from each prospective

---

34 This rule may change where the interview of a witness would result in admissible testimony. In one instance where an ICC tribunal allowed for the testimony of a witness to be taken in front of a notary public outside the view of the tribunal, it was expressly noted that both the claimant's and respondent's counsels should be allowed to be present and ask questions. ICC Case No. 7170, Procedural Order, in Dominique Hascher (ed.), *Collection of Procedural Decisions in ICC Arbitration 1993–1996*, p. 56 (2nd edition, 1998).

35 IBA Guideline 18.

36 IBA Guideline 19.

37 See the following observation of a well experienced arbitral tribunal comprised of mixed common law and civil law arbitrators: "It is standard practice in international arbitration to require the submission of direct testimony in the form of witness statements served in advance of the hearing as part of pre-hearing submissions. The practice ensures both the fairness and the efficiency of the proceedings by providing the parties full notice of the factual allegations advanced by the opposing party." *Jorf Lasfar Energy Co SCA v AMCI Export Corp*, UNCITRAL, Final Award, para. 50 (2005) (unpublished). See also: *SD Myers Inc v Government of Canada*, NAFTA/UNCITRAL, Explanatory Note to Procedural Order No. 16, para. 11 (2000): "Following the common practice in international commercial arbitrations, the Tribunal directed that the evidence-in-chief ('direct testimony'), the opening submissions and the trial exhibits should be delivered to the Tribunal and exchanged between the parties in advance of the substantive hearing."

witness a statement of what this witness will testify . . . This should facilitate hearing the witness since the witness direct testimony could simply confirm the witness statement as the witness direct testimony or evidence in chief."[38]

4.24 Witness statements also allow a tribunal to narrow the issues at an oral witness hearing. Various limitations on the scope of cross-examination may be used, but as a general rule arbitrators will limit the questioning of a witness to those issues described in the written statement and related issues (see comments to article 8.3).

4.25 An added advantage to the use of detailed, written witness statements is that it allows counsel or even the tribunal to determine which, if any, of the witnesses are useful to cross-examine and what subject matter should be traversed in the cross-examination. Further to the above, a tribunal may under the provisions of art. 4.4, call for witness statements to be limited to only specific issues presented during particular phases of the arbitration (see further the comments to art. 3.7).

Ethical issues for counsel and witness statements

4.26 The IBA Guidelines devote considerable attention to the interaction between counsel and witnesses. Counsel, whom are working with witnesses to prepare their written testimony, should be mindful of their ethical obligations while shepherding the preparation of their case. It is widely accepted in international arbitration practice for counsel to assist witnesses in the drafting of their statements. Some may argue that this practice undermines the weight of the statement[39] nonetheless, it is not regarded to be a breach of any internationally recognised ethical duty on the part of counsel.[40] The aforementioned notwithstanding, counsel should ensure that the statement reflects the witness' own words and recollections[41] and further work to prevent false testimony from being given.[42]

---

38 "Documents 31 through 40", *ASA Bulletin*, Vol. 11, No. 4, pp. 581–597 (1993). See also: Procedural Order No. 1 from an UNCITRAL arbitration: "In order to make most efficient use of time at the Hearing, written Witness Statements shall generally be used in lieu of direct oral examination though exceptions may be admitted by the Tribunal. Therefore, insofar as, at the Hearing, such witnesses are invited by the presenting Party or asked to attend at the request of the other Party, the available hearing time should mostly be reserved for cross-examination and redirect examination, as well as for questions by the Arbitrators," as quoted in Charles H. Brower II, "28 January 2008 – NAFTA Chapter 11/UNCITRAL", *A Contribution by the ITA Board of Reporters*, para. 14. It is often a pre-requisite that a witness has submitted a witness statement before he or she is permitted to give oral testimony. For example, see the procedural order of an ICC Tribunal, where it directed the parties as follows: "To avoid any misunderstanding, the tribunal points out, that without exception, only those witnesses and experts may be at the Hearing of which written statements (factual/or legal) have been filed with the submissions of the Parties." "ICC Case No. 7314 (1994)", in Dominique Hascher (ed.), *Collection of Procedural Decisions in ICC Arbitration 1993–1996*, p. 138 (2nd edition, 1998).

39 See: *Al Gaoud General Trading Est v SAAB Aktiebolag (pub.) Electronic Defense Systems*, Svea Court of Appeal, Judgment of 6 March 2014, (Svea HOVTR T4519-13) English translation available at www. arbitration.sccinstitute.com. In this case a party seeking to set aside an ICC award argued that the tribunal had erred because it permitted the counsel for one of the parties to testify concerning the process of drafting a particular witness' statement. It had been alleged that the witness statement was entirely the counsel's work and thus should be disregarded. The tribunal permitted counsel to testify as to the process of preparing the witness statement. The Svea Court of Appeal did not find that this prejudiced the complaining party's procedural rights.

40 IBA Guideline 20.

41 IBA Guideline 24.

42 IBA Guideline 10.

4.27 If incorrect testimony has been given, counsel must determine the best route to rectifying the record and work with their client and the witness in question to ensure that the false testimony is corrected. This duty of course presupposes that counsel is aware of any falsehoods, which may not always be the case.

A party's right to withdraw a witness statement

4.28 Article 4.4 (nor article 4 generally) does not directly address the situation where a party seeks to withdraw a witness statement it has previously submitted. Nevertheless, there is evidence that arbitral tribunals will accept this possibility.[43] Moreover, this is arguably the correct view if one applies the general principles of the Rules (as per article 1.5) to the question. It is a basic premise of article 4 that the admissibility of a witness statement is tied to the availability of the witness for cross-examination, as is made evident in article 4.7. Thus, it stands to reason that if a party is not able to, or does not wish to present the witness at the hearing, it may petition to withdraw the witness statement from the record. However, this principle is formulated without prejudice to the possibility that the withdrawn witness will be summoned to the hearing as per articles 4.9 and 4.10, or the possibility that the adverse party will reintroduce the withdrawn statement into the record as a document, in accordance with article 3 of the Rules. Furthermore, a tribunal may also consider the standard set forth in article 4.7 in determining that there is an exceptional reason for maintaining the witness statement in the record, even though the party which submitted it will no longer present the witness at the hearing.

The time frame for submitting a witness statement

4.29 As noted in the comments to article 4.1, a party must submit a witness statement within the time frames set by the tribunal or otherwise risk having the statement declared inadmissible. The customary time frames in international arbitration for the submission of witness statements are often linked to the dates for submitting the primary pleadings in the matter. Thus, the direct testimony of a witness will often accompany either the statement of claim or statement of defence, as the case may be.[44] Witness testimony offered in rebuttal will often be submitted along with the rebuttal or reply brief. This approach mirrors the

---

43 See: ICC Case No. 14069, in which the tribunal accepted a party's withdrawal of testimony from the record: "Mr [W] who filed a witness statement, was unable to appear and Claimant decided to waive his testimony, which implies that his written Witness Statement will not be considered in the context of this Interim Award." ICC Case No. 14069, Interim Award, para. 60 (2008) (unpublished).

44 This is generally consistent with the view that the parties should put their whole case upon which they intend to rely forward when called to do so. As was mentioned by an ICC tribunal, with its seat in Germany: "At each stage of the proceedings, each party shall come forward with all facts and legal arguments which it wishes to present and which at that time are within its reach." "Documents", *supra* n. 18, p. 314. See also the adherence to this practice of an LCIA tribunal: "Pursuant to Procedural Order No. 1, the Claimant submitted to the Tribunal and the Respondents a detailed Statement of Claim, with supporting exhibits, including witness statements, and the Respondent subsequently submitted to the Tribunal and the Claimant a detailed Statement of Defence and Counterclaims, with exhibits, including witness statements." LCIA Case No. 91244, Final Award, para. 10 (2010) (unpublished).

method often adopted for the introduction of written or documentary evidence insofar as the primary documents relied upon by a party in support of their case will often accompany the first substantive pleadings.

4.30 It is also customary in international arbitration for a tribunal to schedule a document production phase following the initial submission of witness statements. A request for production under article 3.2 of the IBA Rules (which often follows the presentation of the case-in-chief of both parties), could well be based on the assertions contained within a witness statement.

Contents of a witness statement

Article 4.5 2010 IBA Rules: **Each Witness Statement shall contain:**

    (a) **the full name and address of the witness, a statement regarding his or her present and past relationship (if any) with any of the Parties, and a description of his or her background, qualifications, training and experience, if such a description may be relevant to the dispute or to the contents of the statement;**

    (b) **a full and detailed description of the facts, and the source of the witness's information as to those facts, sufficient to serve as that witness's evidence in the matter in dispute. Documents on which the witness relies that have not already been submitted shall be provided;**

    (c) **a statement as to the language in which the Witness Statement was originally prepared and the language in which the witness anticipates giving testimony at the Evidentiary Hearing;**

    (d) **an affirmation of the truth of the Witness Statement; and**

    (e) **the signature of the witness and its date and place.**

General discussion

4.31 Article 4.5 sets forth the basic requirements of a witness statement in international arbitration. Subparagraph (a) of the article is part of an overall change that was instituted with the 2010 revision of the IBA Rules, in which the Review Subcommittee required both expert and factual witnesses to divulge any connection existing between a witness and a party. It has been debated to some extent whether it is necessary for a witness to divulge such facts, however, from a procedural standpoint it is undeniable that cross-examining counsel often will seek to expose these connections during questioning. Ensuring that such disclosures are included in the written statement in advance of a hearing may help to dispose of these issues quickly.

Disclosure of relationship to a party

4.32 As noted in the comments to article 4.2, the testimony of an individual who has a relationship to a party or interest in the proceedings may be admitted as witness evidence in international arbitration. The corollary to this principle is that a tribunal should be made aware of any relationship between a witness and a party to the proceedings so that such information may be considered when weighing the testimony. It is still often the case that tribunals will assign more weight to the testimony of witnesses who are independent of a party.[45] Therefore, the professional, familial or other ties that exist between a witness and a party is of considerable importance and, thus, article 4.5 requires full disclosure of such information.

Full description of the facts

4.33 As stated in article 4.5(b), a witness statement must provide a detailed recitation of the particular facts to which a party is attesting. This rule captures the approach commonly adopted by international tribunals, such as was described by an *ad hoc* tribunal seated in Dubai, United Arab Emirates:

> [T]he Respondent shall produce to the Claimant and the Arbitral Tribunal a statement indicating precisely the specific facts which Mr. D will relate (Witness Statement). Where the statement makes reference to any documents in the File, it will identify its reference. New documents referred to in the statement shall be attached to it.[46]

4.34 Failure to provide a sufficiently detailed statement that provides a clear account of a witness' testimony may be grounds for a tribunal to determine not to hear a witness.[47]

4.35 The practice most often adopted in international arbitration is for the written witness statement to be presented in the form of a first person narrative account, as was described by an UNCITRAL tribunal where it ordered that a statement, "Contain the evidence that the Party presents of that witness in the form of a narrative."[48] Such a narrative, as is indicated by article 4.5(b), will in most instances set forth a complete picture of the factual basis on which the statements therein are made, and whether the information has

---

45 "It is certainly not a rule of evidence that a statement made by a witness, not an employee of the party in question, cannot be binding for that party. The best witness is an objective witness – without relations to any of the parties." Final Award of 1999 in ICC Case No. 8547, in Albert Jan van den Berg (ed.), *Yearbook Commercial Arbitration*, Vol. XXVIII, pp. 27, 33 (2003).

46 "Documents", *supra* n. 18, pp. 314–333.

47 See the decision by a US court in *Intercarbon Bermuda v Caltex Trading*, where a tribunal refused to hear two witnesses who had submitted written statements. Here the court found that the quality of the witness affidavits was such that the refusal by the tribunal to hear the witnesses was justified, and was an appropriate anticipatory determination of the materiality of the testimony of the witnesses. *Intercarbon Bermuda Ltd v Caltex Trading & Transport Corp*, 146 FRD 64 (SDNY, 1993).

48 See: *GAMI Investments Inc v United Mexican States*, NAFTA/UNCITRAL, Procedural Order No. 1, paras 8.1–8.47.7 (2003). On the other hand, written testimony which is sufficiently clear and well articulated may be persuasive enough for a tribunal to rely on and use in the drafting of an award, as was noted by an *ad hoc* committee sitting in regard to an annulment application under the ICSID rules: "To further clarify its position, the *ad hoc* Committee also accepts that where a Tribunal agrees with one of the parties or with experts, it is not improper or unexpected for it to adopt the language used by them in the pleadings or in written testimony." Dietmar W. Prager and Samantha J. Rowe, *"Compañía de Aguas del Aconquija SA v Argentine Republic*, ICSID Case No. ARB/97/3, 10 August 2010", *A Contribution by the ITA Board of Reporters*, para. 250.

been ascertained by the witness based upon his or her own direct knowledge (e.g., eye witness account), the recollection of others[49] or review of documents.[50]

4.36 In this regard, a practice whereby a witness simply affirms what has been already set forth in another statement should be discouraged. Such statements add little value to the proceedings, as one tribunal commented:

> It is not denied that the statement of a person who confirms what another states in detail may have some value, but it is unquestionably true that in order to form a definite opinion each witness must set forth in his own manner the things he saw or knew since the comparison of different statements throws a light upon the facts equivalent to a confrontation of witnesses. . . .[51]

4.37 Furthermore, the historical position taken by international tribunals is that a witness statement which simply affirms legal pleadings of counsel is also of little probative value.[52] It would also seem that the spirit of article 4.5 is violated by such a practice. A witness statement is evidence and therefore should contribute to a tribunal's factual understanding of the case. However, a statement that is simply intended to verify the pleadings of legal counsel would not be consistent with the notion that the evidence should come from the honest, personal recollection of a witness, untainted by the influence of other individuals.

Documents accompanying the witness statement

4.38 Some tribunals have taken the view that a witness statement should be supported by corroborating evidence.[53] This approach does not appear to be widely followed.[54] Nev-

---

49 The mere fact that a witness statement contains hearsay evidence is rarely, if ever, a sole basis for excluding it from a proceeding. S. I. Strong and James Dries, "Witness Statements Under the IBA Rules of Evidence: What to Do About Hearsay", *Arbitration International*, Vol. 21, No. 3, pp. 307–308 (2005). Nevertheless, the tribunal may find that the witness statement should be barred on grounds of a lack of relevance or materiality, or another basis found in art. 9.2. However, the fact that a witness statement does contain hearsay evidence is a matter which the tribunal should consider when weighing the evidentiary value of the testimony. See as an example the following consideration by a panel of arbitrators of the Iran-US Claims Tribunal: "The Tribunal notes that on the issue of the alleged expropriation Mr. Banayan only testified that in 1986 he had been told that certain properties at issue in this Case, since the beginning of the Islamic Revolution, belonged to the Foundation for the Oppressed. The Tribunal considers this to be hearsay evidence, on which it cannot rely, unless the evidence is substantiated." *Jalal Moin v The Islamic Republic of Iran*, Case No. 950, Award No. 557-950-2 of 25 May 1994, p. 6. See the comments to art. 8.2 for further discussion.

50 See, for example, the directive given in a procedural order by an ICC tribunal, seated in Paris: "The Parties shall prepare and submit witness statements in writing by prospective witnesses, including expert witnesses. Witness statements shall consist of numbered paragraphs grouped by subjects. The basis of any statement (own perception or if on information received, from whom, when, and how) must be evidenced from the witness statement itself." "Documents", *supra* n. 18, p. 581.

51 *Pomeroy's El Paso Transfer Co (United States of America) v United Mexican States*, 8 October 1930, 4 RIAA, pp. 554–555.

52 "It was argued by counsel for the United States that, since the President of the company had sworn to the Memorial which includes a list giving the number, date and amount of the invoices of these goods, there was in fact before the commission an affidavit in support of the allegations respecting this item. Under the rules the Memorial must be accompanied by the evidence on which the claimant relies in support of the allegations contained in the Memorial. The fact that under the rules of the Commission as they existed when the memorial was framed it was required that the Memorial be verified by the claimant would not justify the Commission in sustaining the views of counsel in such a manner that its action would in effect constitute a precedent in the light of which a pleading might be regarded at once as a pleading and as evidence. This item must therefore be disallowed." *National Paper and Type Co (United States of America) v United Mexican States*, 26 September 1928, 4 RIAA, pp. 327–328.

53 According to the practice of some international tribunals, affidavits need to be supported by corroborating independent evidence. See, for example: *Robert R. Schott v The Islamic Republic of Iran*, Case No. 268, Award No. 474-268-1, Iran-USCTR, Vol. 24, p. 203, paras 56–57 (1990).

54 See, for example, the following decision of a panel of arbitrators under the Mexico-US Claims Commission, whereby the tribunal noted that the failure to produce corroborating evidence was not grounds

ertheless, the accepted practice before international arbitral tribunals often is that a reference to documents or supporting evidence in a witness statement should either be linked to previously admitted evidence, or the evidence should be appended to the statement. This practice has been codified in article 4.5(d).

4.39 The requirement that documents referred to in a statement should accompany it is helpful in terms of limiting the opportunity for surprise. It is not difficult to imagine that where a witness has alluded to various corroborating documents within his or her statement, but has not identified or produced said documents, the referenced evidence could surface at a hearing. If so, the opposing party will not have had an opportunity to review these documents when preparing the hearing, and therefore could be arguably surprised.

4.40 This situation occurred in the context of an Iran-United States Claims Tribunal hearing. The tribunal described its ruling as follows:

> Absent any convincing explanation by the Respondents, the Tribunal cannot accept a tactic that unveils previously existing evidence at literally the last movements of the hearing. Without prior notice having been given that the witness would testify, without showing that evidence is presented in rebuttal, and when the documents the witness proffered had not been included with – or even referred to in – the Respondent's various prior submissions. For procedural reasons the documents cannot therefore be accepted.[55]

4.41 The refusal by the panel of arbitrators to admit such evidence was clearly motivated by the failure of the party or the witness to provide it in advance of oral testimony. Under article 4.5(b) a tribunal would have grounds for denying the admissibility of the evidence, as well as per article 9.2(g). This is particularly the case if by admitting the evidence the adverse party would be prejudiced. However, the failure to submit evidence referenced in a statement is an issue that often goes to the weight given to the witness statement, and would not, in most instances, be a basis for excluding the statement itself.[56]

Witness affirmation

4.42 Article 4.5 confirms that a witness statement should include an affirmation that the facts reported therein are true. As is noted in the comments to article 8, the presence or use of an affirmation or an oath on a witness statement may be influenced by various procedural rules or the applicable *lex arbitri*. However, the formality with which such a declaration is made may not be cause for a tribunal to assign any further weight to the

---

for denying the probative value of an affidavit: "it seems to me that clearly the charge of mistreatment of Faulkner in the so-called 'downtown jail' cannot be said to have failed because of lack of substantiation in that it is supported merely by Faulkner's affidavit. Had it been desired to discredit the affidavit on this point it would doubtless have been possible to produce for that purpose evidence describing the condition of the jail." *Walter H. Faulkner (United States of America) v United Mexican States*, 2 November 1926, 4 RIAA, pp. 67, 72.

55 *Uiterwyk Corp v The Islamic Republic of Iran*, Case No. 381, Partial Award No. 375-381-1 (6 July 1988), p. 16.

56 In one instance, a claimant party moved to strike a witness statement from the record because documents referred to by the witness had not been introduced along with the statement or otherwise included within the record. The Tribunal rejected the application, noting that they would consider the absence of the referred to documents when it weighed the evidentiary value of the statement. ICC Case No. 11258, Final Award, para. 122 (2004) (unpublished).

testimony. As was noted in a decision of the US-Mexico General Claims Commission, the decision to formally "swear" a witness statement, or otherwise, may be influenced by domestic practice:

> this Commission is an international tribunal and it is its duty to receive and appraise in its best judgment, evidence presented to it in accordance with the arbitral agreement and international practice . . . When sworn statements instead of unsworn statements are employed in an international arbitration it is undoubtedly because the use of an affidavit in an arbitration is to some extent an approach to testimony given before domestic tribunals with the prescribed sanctions of judicial procedure . . . When sworn testimony is submitted by either party the other party is of course privileged to undertake to impeach it, and, further, to analyse its value, as the Commission must do.[57]

4.43 Therefore, the use of formal oaths or affirmations in international arbitration is a matter which may be influenced by a number of different factors. That being said, the prevalent approach is to admit unsworn witness statements. The fact that a statement is given under formal oath does not, in and of itself, have a strict effect upon the probative value of the statement in international practice.[58] Nevertheless, while the IBA Rules take no particular stance on whether it is appropriate for a statement to be given under formal

---

57 *GL Solis (United States of America) v United Mexican States*, 3 October 1928, 4 RIAA p. 359. Bühler and Dorgan state in regard to the duty to affirm a statement: "The rule does not require the witness statement to be sworn as an affidavit. Instead, pursuant to Article 4.5(c), the statement to shall contain an "affirmation of the truth of the statement". The witness who provides a written statement in an arbitration will normally appear at a hearing, where he will confirm the statement. The statement does not stand alone as evidence unless accepted as such by the parties. Thus, one of the principal reasons for swearing an affidavit is not present." Bühler and Dorgan, *supra* n. 18, p. 13. This approach seems to indicate a departure from the view of early international tribunals. Bin Cheng notes in regard to early practice, "an oath is regarded as a considerable safeguard of veracity". Bin Cheng, *supra* n. 18, p. 310. See further: the decision of a Society of Maritime Arbitrator's Tribunal which accepted unsworn witness statements as reliable evidence. The tribunal considered the unsworn testimony and determined that the veracity of such evidence could be accepted without limitation because the witness assertions were consistent with the facts established in the case by other evidence, "[o]ur arbitrator colleague, Mr. Murphy, is reluctant to rely on unsworn statements and wishes to voice his opinion in this regard. He does not discount them altogether in view of the complementary facts that are evident in the case which we, the other two arbitrators, feel dove-tail so neatly with these crew statements that they are deserving of full recognition and credibility, despite being unsworn." *In the Matter of the Arbitration Between, Amoco Overseas Oil Co and Amoco International Ltd and Ocean Couriers Inc, Owners of the S/T Avenger*, WL 372765, SMAAS (1977).

58 As one author observed: "[c]ontrary to English court proceedings where all testimony is taken under oath, the standard form of oral evidence in international commercial arbitrations – like in Continental European court proceedings – is the unsworn statement." Marianne Roth, "False Testimony at International Arbitration Hearings Conducted in England and Switzerland – A Comparative View", *Journal of International Arbitration*, Vol. 11, No. 1, p. 17 (1994). See also: the view expressed by a panel of the Iran-US Claims Tribunal, which noted that there were no special rules in its procedure regarding the probative value of a notarized affidavit. "The Tribunal has often been presented with notarized affidavits or oral testimony of claimants or their employees. [Rare] are the cases where such an issue does not arise. The probative value of such written or oral declarations is usually hotly debated between the parties, each of them relying on the pecul[i]arities of its own judicial system. . . . The Tribunal has, in the past, adopted a pragmatic and moderate approach towards this problem by deciding, on a case by case basis, whether the burden of proof has been properly sustained by each contending party, taking into consideration those declarations together with all other evidence submitted in the case, the particulars of the case and the attitude of both parties in the proceedings." *W. Jack Buckamier v The Islamic Republic of Iran et al.*, Award No. 528-941-3, paras 67–68 (6 March 1992), 28 Iran-USCTR 5. See also the following excerpt from an ICSID tribunal which followed similar reasoning in absence of any rule to the contrary: "As this provision does not call for a sworn affidavit, and as in many national jurisdictions non-sworn written witness statements are admissible and customary, the Tribunal is not prevented from giving evidentiary value to non-sworn written witness statements." *Tradex Hellas SA v Republic of Albania*, Decision on Jurisdiction of 24 December 1996 and Award of 29 April 1999, Case No. ARB/94/2, in Albert Jan van den Berg (ed.), *Yearbook Commercial Arbitration*, Vol. XXV, p. 240 (2000).

oath, it does strike the balance and make provision for a general affirmation by the witness that the information presented in the witness statement is true. For a further discussion of the consequences of perjury see the comments to article 8.4.

Signature of the witness

4.44 As per article 4.5(e), the signature of the witness should be appended to the witness statement. This is a formal requirement; however, the inadvertent omission of a signature is generally not grounds for striking the witness statement from the record if a tribunal believes that the statement has been endorsed by the witness.[59] If the reason for the missing signature is unclear, a tribunal may be required to take steps to have the statement confirmed by the witness; in the event the witness fails to do so, the statement should be disregarded.[60]

Rebuttal witness statements

Article 4.6 2010 IBA Rules: **If Witness Statements are submitted, any Party may, within the time ordered by the Arbitral Tribunal, submit to the Arbitral Tribunal and to the other Parties revised or additional Witness Statements, including statements from persons not previously named as witnesses, so long as any such revisions or additions respond only to matters contained in another Party's Witness Statements, Expert Reports or other submissions that have not been previously presented in the arbitration.**

General discussion

4.45 Under the IBA Rules the use of rebuttal witness statements is expressly allowed. This general principle recognises that issues raised in the testimony or submissions offered by an adverse party will often require a response. It is a widely recognised principle that a party, in order to be granted a fair hearing, should have the opportunity to respond to allegations or evidence which raises new issues.[61]

---

59 Where a CAS tribunal allowed an unsigned witness statement to remain in the record, the decision of the arbitrators was upheld by the Swiss Federal Tribunal. Tribunal Fédéral (unnumbered), Federal Supreme Court (27 May 2003), in Albert Jan van den Berg (ed.), *Yearbook Commercial Arbitration*, Vol. XXIX, pp. 206–231 (2004).

60 In an ICC arbitration between a Dutch and Italian party, seated in Switzerland, the Italian party submitted to the tribunal two witness statements taken from former employees residing in Milan, Italy. In the course of the proceedings, it was discovered that the witnesses had submitted two signed statements which were deemed unsatisfactory by the legal counsel for the Italian party. After consultation the witnesses agreed to review statements drafted by legal counsel. It was these second versions that were submitted to the tribunal; however, the witnesses never signed the statements because of dissatisfaction over their content. Upon becoming aware of this, the tribunal disregarded the witness statements. The decision was later challenged before the Swiss Federal Tribunal, which upheld the arbitrator's determination to disregard the statements. See: case summary of Swiss Federal Tribunal Decision No. 4A-539/2008 of 19 February 2009, in Mattias Scherer, "Introduction to the Case Law Section", *ASA Bulletin*, Vol. 27, No. 4, pp. 740–741 (2009).

61 See: *Fraport AG Frankfurt Airport Services Worldwide v The Philippines*, ICSID Case No. ARB/03/25, Decision on the Application for Annulment, para. 133 (2010): "The right to present one's case is also accepted as an essential element of the requirement to afford a fair hearing accorded in the principal human rights instruments.

4.46 In this regard, it is often assumed that rebuttal witness testimony will be filed and thus incorporated into the procedural schedule of an arbitration. However, the right to produce rebuttal testimony may also be invoked in relation to new evidence introduced at a late stage in the proceedings or in regard to a specific issue of which a witness has particular knowledge.[62] In such a situation, a tribunal may permit a witness statement to be filed which addresses only the specific and new issue that arose because of the additional information submitted to the procedure.[63]

4.47 The witness evidence to be submitted may come from witnesses who have already filed a report or statement in the proceedings or from entirely new witnesses, as the case may be. Witness testimony is, after all, evidence, and a strict rule permitting rebuttal evidence to come only from witnesses previously identified may unfairly cut off a party's right to submit the evidence needed to explain or rebut a new allegation. Where new witnesses are permitted to give testimony, they generally should constrain their statement to addressing the issue they have been called to rebut. Failure to do so may lead a tribunal to declare a witness statement inadmissible,[64] or at least those parts of the statement that go beyond simply rebutting an allegation.

This principle requires both equality of arms and the proper participation of the contending parties in the procedure, these being separate but related fundamental elements of a fair trial. The principle will require the tribunal to afford both parties the opportunity to make submissions where new evidence is received and considered by the tribunal to be relevant to its final deliberations."

62 "The Claimant also sought to introduce one of the two rebuttal witnesses as a general rebuttal witness. The Claimant further indicated that he wished to introduce 'Rebuttal Documents' at the Hearing. Finally, the Memorial addressed other aspects of the Case and its procedural history. By Order of 13 March 1995, the Tribunal notified the Parties that it would accept both witnesses indicated by the Claimant as rebuttal witnesses, with one of them being permitted to testify only on specific issues and the other being a general rebuttal witness." *Reza Nemazee v The Islamic Republic of Iran*, Case No. 4, Final Award No. 575-4-3 of 10 December 1996, p. 6.

63 For instance, consider the following procedural arrangement arrived at in the *Rumeli Telekom v Kazakhstan* ICSID arbitration where the tribunal permitted discreet witness evidence to be filed in response to an allegation which had arisen as a response to another party's submission of witness statements. "The Arbitral tribunal takes note that the parties agree that Respondent may file a witness statement by Judge Begaliev limited to the question of bribery raised in Mr. Agilonu's statement. The Tribunal decides that the filing of this witness statement must take place no later than October 5 and that Claimants will have the right to file a rebuttal witness statement by Mr. Agilonu, limited to the points covered by Judge Begaliev, no later than October." Dietmar W. Prager and Joanna E. Davidson, *"Rumeli Telekom AS and Telsim Mobil Telekomikasyon Hizmetleri AS v Republic of Kazakhstan*, ICSID Case No. ARB/05/16, 29 July 2008", *A Contribution by the ITA Board of Reporters*, para. 62. A caveat to this principle is where the newly introduced evidence or the issue itself, is regarded to have an unlikely effect on the non-proffering party's case. In this situation, the tribunal may not call for rebuttal evidence. See further the following observation from an ICSID tribunal: "While the evidence adduced by the Claimant at the oral hearing referred to in Paragraphs 132–133 above was objected to by the Respondents on the ground of late introduction, the Tribunal has referred to it to show that, even on the Claimant's best case, it could not establish its claim to have made an 'investment.' It has therefore not been necessary to call for any rebuttal evidence from the Respondent." Dietmar W. Prager and Constantinos Hotis, *"Malaysian Historical Salvors SDN, BHD v The Government of Malaysia*, ICSID Case No. ARB/05/10, 17 May 2007", *A Contribution by the ITA Board of Reporters*, para. 145.

64 As was noted by a panel of the Iran-US Claims Tribunal, evidence that is not responsive to an allegation or fact raised by the opposing party is not rebuttal evidence: "Mr. Kermani's statements did not address matters recently raised, and hence there was no reason why the Respondents could not have communicated their intention to call him by means of the ordinary art. 25 procedure. Accordingly, his statements are not admissible as rebuttal within the meaning of Note 2 to art. 25 of the Tribunal Rules." *William J. Levitt v The Islamic Republic of Iran*, Case No. 209, Award No. 297-209-1 of 22 April 1987, p. 9.

Disregarding witness statements

Article 4.7 2010 IBA Rules: **If a witness whose appearance has been requested pursuant to Article 8.1 fails without a valid reason to appear for testimony at an Evidentiary Hearing, the Arbitral Tribunal shall disregard any Witness Statement related to that Evidentiary Hearing by that witness unless, in exceptional circumstances, the Arbitral Tribunal decides otherwise.**

General discussion

4.48 The IBA Rules follow the principle that witness statements should be disregarded if the witness fails to appear for examination at a later evidentiary hearing without a valid reason. This rule is expressly stated in article 4.7, to which only minor changes have been made in the 2010 revision. The strict application of article 4.7 may be discomforting to tribunals should they be forced to disregard key witness testimony due to the non-appearance of a witness. Nevertheless, it is widely assumed that a party has a right to confront or otherwise challenge a witness' testimony during an in-person cross-examination, and for a party to be deprived of such a right may give rise to challenges based on lack of procedural fairness.

4.49 In 2004, the Swiss Federal Tribunal considered an application where a party complained that the arbitral tribunal had refused to let it cross-examine an expert witness.[65] The Federal Tribunal ruled that the arbitrator's decision to deny the request to cross-examine an expert did not violate the adverse party's right to be heard. The outcome notwithstanding, it is submitted that this case does not undermine the principle that witnesses who submit a statement should be made available for cross examination, which is generally adhered to by most tribunals.[66]

---

65 "Tribunal fédéral, 1re Cour civile, 7 Janvier 2004 (4P.196/2003)" (*W Ltd v D GmbH and E GmbH*), *ASA Bulletin*, Vol. 22, No. 3, p. 602 (2004).

66 *Ibid.* The decision seems to be based on the specific facts of the case, in particular, the wording of the Terms of Reference which reflected the tribunal's right to decide in their discretion whether witnesses should be called, the fact that the expert witnesses had already answered in writing extensive questions which had been put to them after the submission of their witness statements, and the fact that though the tribunal had agreed in the Terms of Reference to allow the parties to cross-examine witnesses, the tribunal had always maintained that expert witnesses may be treated differently. Finally, the Federal Tribunal pointed out that it must remain within the tribunal's discretion to modify the procedure as the proceedings evolve. See also the following decision of a tribunal constituted under the ICDR Rules for an example of the approach which is most often adopted: "Claimant had submitted witness statements by Francois Piette, John Bilbija, Thomas Dletzker, Michael Lohr, Michael Kessler, and Justin Sather, yet none of these witnesses were made available for cross examination at the hearing. Respondents had submitted witness statements from Brian Popiel and David Clark, and they also did not appear at the hearing to be cross examined. These written witness statements were therefore not accepted into evidence or considered by the Tribunal when deciding this case. Pursuant to Article 4.7 of the IBA Rules, which had been adopted as guidelines with the consent of the parties, written witness statements from individuals not made available to testify at the hearing are not admitted into evidence and will not be considered by the Tribunal. It would be unduly prejudicial for that written testimony to be accepted without giving the opposing side an opportunity to cross examine the witnesses to test their testimony. Neither Claimant nor Respondents presented any valid reasons for the failure of these witnesses to appear at the hearing and certainly no exceptional circumstances, as required by Article 4.7 of the IBA Rules, were shown. If these witnesses could not be in New York during the designated hearing days, the Tribunal demonstrated that it was willing to have witness testimony by video-link, which in fact occurred with two of the Claimant's witnesses, Mr. Bennett and Mr. Lecavalier, without any undue prejudice to

4.50 The approach most often used in modern practice was summarised by one well-experienced international tribunal as follows: "if a witness whose statement has been submitted by a party and whose examination at the Hearing has been requested by the other Party, does not appear at the Hearing, his statement will not be taken into account by the Tribunal. A Party may apply with reasons for the exception from that rule."[67] It is possible that this principle may be affected by the specific procedural rules adopted in a case, in that the parties (or the tribunal) may have afforded the arbitrators greater leeway to determine which witnesses will be heard, as compared to what is provided for in article 4.7. Where a statement has been submitted but the witness does not appear for questioning a court may be reluctant to annul an award if the adverse party has been afforded an opportunity to question a witness in writing[68] rather than orally. Nevertheless, the general presumption remains that a witness who offers written testimony should be made available for an oral examination if the adverse party requests it.

---

either party." *Sexton v Karam* (Final Award), ICDR Case No. 50 148 T 00408 11, 28 July 2014, p. 26, *Arbitrator Intelligence Materials* (Kluwer Law International).

67 *Chevron Corp and Texaco Petroleum Corp v The Republic of Ecuador*, UNCITRAL/PCA, Interim Award, p. 19 (1 December 2008). See also the ruling in ICC Case No. 13046 setting forth the commonly accepted rule: "Where the witness duly summoned to appear at the Hearing is not able to attend for valid reasons, the Arbitral tribunal shall in principle not be entitled to consider his witness statement, except if extraordinary circumstances so warrant. In such event, the Arbitral Tribunal shall hear the Parties and decide by taking into account all relevant circumstances including the Parties' legitimate interests." ICC Case No. 13046, Procedural Order No. 1 of 19 May 2004, *ICC Bulletin, 2010 Special Supplement: Decisions on ICC Arbitration Procedure*, p. 92. See also the following version of this rule adopted by an LCIA tribunal: ". . . every witness and expert whom a witness statement or expert report was presented would be expected to attend the hearing for examination unless expressly released." LCIA Case No. 6827, Final Award, para. 64 (2008) (unpublished). See also the adherence to this rule by an ICDR tribunal: "[o]n 22 January 2007, the Arbitrator issued Procedural Order No. 5, ruling that the affidavit of [the witness] would be considered on the condition that [the witness] appears at the hearing for the purpose of cross-examination." ICDR Case No. 50154, Final Award, para. 21 (2007) (unpublished). While the aforementioned rule mirrors the standard set forth in article 4.7 above, other tribunals have taken a more lenient stance, nevertheless still maintaining the basic presumption that failure by a witness to attend a hearing will lead to the exclusion of the written statement. See also the position adopted in ICC Case No. 12990: "The Arbitral Tribunal may consider the witness statement of a witness who provides a valid reason for failing to appear when summoned to a hearing, having regard to all surrounding circumstances. The Arbitral tribunal shall not consider the witness statement of a witness who fails to appear and does not provide a valid reason." *Ibid.*, p. 86. See further, in regard to the decision of the tribunal in ICC Case No. 11904 to allow a witness to have written questions put to him in lieu of attending the hearing due to illness, the tribunal noted in its procedural direction that: "To fully guarantee the adversarial principle, the applicant must have the opportunity to put questions to Mr. C. The Tribunal also reserves this right." (unofficial translation). Ordonnance de référé pré-arbitrale du 6 février 2002, ICC Case No. 11904, *ASA Bulletin*, Vol. 22, No. 3, p. 520 (2004). Such a ruling would suggest that even where an exceptional situation occurs so that a witness is unable to attend the hearing, the tribunal should attempt to allow questions to be communicated to the witness in order to ensure that due process is observed. These views are broadly consistent with the approach adopted by early international tribunals. See further the rule adopted in the *Walfish Bay Case*, where the tribunal entertained the admission of a written statement of a witness not presented to the hearing for reasons accepted by the arbitrator, but nonetheless where it was noted that the failure to submit to cross-examination had significant impact on the value of the evidence: "As evidence alluded to has been produced out of court, in the sense that the arbitrator has not been able to conduct any cross-examination and without being disputed, inasmuch as the party prejudiced by it has not cross-examined the witness either, circumstances which, though they do not deserve blame and appear easily explicable to the present case, certainly diminish the value of the evidence." Bin Cheng, *supra* n. 18, p. 314.

68 In a decision of the Swiss Federal Tribunal, the decision of an arbitrator to allow written questions to be put to a witness in lieu of an actual hearing was upheld. *A v X Ltd*, DFC, 14 July 2003 [114/2003]. See, for a further discussion: Cesare Jermini, "Note – Witnesses and the right to be heard in international arbitration: some remarks on recent decisions of the Swiss Federal Court", *ASA Bulletin*, Vol. 22, No. 3 (2004).

4.51 Additionally, it may also be argued that a tribunal has an inherent right to evaluate the materiality of the written witness evidence prior to determining whether to allow a witness to be called at a hearing, and that this right presupposes the authority to decline to hear a witness in-person if in the considered view of the tribunal there would be little value in doing so.[69] In fact, this is directly reflected in the Swiss Federal Tribunal's decision discussed above and in article 8.2. This notwithstanding, an anticipatory weighing of the materiality of testimony should operate in normal circumstances to exclude a witness from an oral hearing because their testimony is immaterial. Such a preliminary exercise, though, should not work to shield possibly material evidence from being challenged under cross-examination. To admit evidence from a witness without affording the opposing side the opportunity to challenge that testimony at a hearing (or in another appropriate manner) would be tantamount to prejudging the witness' views to be virtually unassailable. To assign such weight to evidence prior to the closing of the evidentiary phase of the arbitration would in most instances appear to be unjustified.

4.52 In that regard, the approach adopted by article 4.7 is preferred. A witness should in most instances be made available for examination if a tribunal considers the written testimony to be material to a final award, and, in such case, the adverse party allowed to put

---

69 As an example of the general deference given to a tribunal's weighing of the evidence, see the decision of a US court in an arbitration between *Interdigital Communications Corp v Samsung Electronics*, where it was found that: "it is clear that vacature is not appropriate under Section 10(a) where the losing party in an arbitration merely takes issue with the weight accorded to certain evidence actually considered by the panel or with the panel's rejection of arguments related to such evidence. Rather, the losing party's assertion 'that the arbitrators failed to give the evidence the consideration it deserved' must be rejected as an improper attempt to probe the collective minds of the arbitrators as to how they reached their judgment." *Interdigital Communications Corp LLC et al. v Samsung Electronics*, 528 F.Supp 2d, p. 350 (SDNY, 7 December 2007). See also a decision of the Swiss Federal Tribunal to reject a challenge brought to a Zurich Chamber of Commerce award where the tribunal had in its decision refused to assign probative weight to one party's witnesses. The Federal Tribunal determined that the consideration of the evidence and reasoning offered for why the witness evidence could not be given weight by the arbitral tribunal sufficiently afforded the party proffering the evidence the opportunity to be heard. "Decision of 16 March 2004, 4p.14/2004," *ASA Bulletin*, Vol. 22, No. 4, p. 770 (2004). See also, regarding the refusal to hear a witness, the *Matthew v Papua New Guinea* decision, where the tribunal only considered a written description of what the witness may attest to, but decided against calling the witness: "[a]s noted above, the arbitrator in the subject proceeding issued a Scheduling Order requiring the submission of any and all evidence to be used in Petitioner's direct case and received an affidavit and evidentiary submissions from Matthew. The Final Award makes it clear that Matthew made a detailed written proffer as to the anticipated substance of the Prime Minister's testimony and also tendered other evidence upon which Matthew intended to rely. . . . In *Tempo Shain*, the Second Circuit found that an arbitral panel had made unwarranted assumptions that the testimony of a temporarily unavailable witness, who was the only person who could have testified as to certain communications, would have been cumulative. In the instant matter the arbitrator carefully considered the statements attributed to the Prime Minister by Matthew and deemed them to be insufficient to issue an award under a theory of *quantum meruit*. Accordingly, there was no denial of fundamental fairness." *Michael Z. Matthew v Papua New Guinea*, No. 09 Civ 3851 (LTS) 2009 US Dist. LEXIS 117274 (SDNY, 9 December 2009). The above being said, a tribunal's right to decline to hear a witness should always be viewed in the context of a party's right to challenge evidence adverse to its case. This right of challenge includes the right to question witnesses who have offered a written witness statement adverse to a party's case. See: ICC Case No. 12575, where a tribunal seated in Switzerland affirmed that the right to cross-examine an adverse witness was a fundamental rule of procedure: "When evidence is filed by a party, the other is entitled under the same principle to challenge such evidence an, affirmatively, to file evidence in rebuttal. Under these rules each Party is therefore entitled to challenge witness evidence submitted by the other and a breach of such principle may result in an arbitral award to be set aside under art. 190(2)(d) of the 1987 Act. In the Arbitral Tribunal's opinion this would suffice per se to establish the Claimant's right to cross-examine Mr. [x] and to dismiss the Respondent's objection." ICC Case No. 12575, Procedural Order of 16 December 2003, *ICC Bulletin, 2010 Special Supplement: Decisions on ICC Arbitration Procedure*, p. 67. See also ICC Case No. 11904, *supra* n. 67.

questions to that witness. Nevertheless, as article 4.7 indicates, there may be grounds for admitting a witness statement from a witness who has not appeared at a hearing, if the failure to attend comes about for a valid reason, or there are other exceptional circumstances. These exceptions to the rule will be discussed below.

Valid reasons for non-attendance at a hearing

4.53 Article 4.7 permits the tribunal to admit the written statement of a witness who, for a valid reason, is unable to attend a hearing. While what constitutes a "valid" reason may be largely a factual question, the analysis of this issue should be approached from the fundamental principle that the party offering the written testimony bears the duty to present the witness at the hearing and the consequent risk of having their testimony removed from the record if they do not. This principle has been affirmed by reviewing courts. Consider a decision of the Canadian courts with regard to a challenge to an ICC award, where it was noted: "the inability to produce one's witness before an arbitral tribunal is a risk inherent in an agreement to submit to arbitration and is not a basis for setting aside an award."[70]

4.54 If the duty to present the witnesses is inherently on the party who intends to benefit from testimony it stands to reason that party bears the consequence resulting from the non-attendance of the witness. As an example of how this principle may be applied in practice, reference may be had to *Vivendi et al. v Argentina* where an ICSID tribunal was confronted with the inability of the respondent to both make contact with, and arrange for the attendance at the hearing of, an expert who had been summoned for cross-examination.[71] After considerable discussion of the issue, it became apparent that the respondent was aware the expert had an appointment conflicting with the hearing date at the time of submittal of the witness statement. The tribunal, in applying the standard found in article 4.7, considered the reasons for non-attendance, and opined as follows:

> After consideration of the Parties' respective positions, the Tribunal denied Respondent's application to present Mr. Kavanaugh for cross-examination by video conference and granted Claimants' application to have Mr. Kavanaugh's witness statements stricken from the record. The Tribunal was influenced, *inter alia*, by the number of opportunities Respondent had been given to explain the whereabouts of Mr. Kavanaugh and his reasons for being unable to attend the oral hearing and the unwillingness of Claimants to depart from the prior agreement of the parties that statements

---

70 *Corporacion Transnacional de Inversiones SA de CV v STET International SpA*, 45 OR (3d), 183, p. 199 (1999). See also the ruling of a US court whereby it was noted in rejection of a claim that due process was violated because a tribunal did not delay a proceeding to hear a witness: "This attempt to state a due process claim fails for several reasons. First, inability to produce one's witnesses before an arbitral tribunal is a risk inherent in an agreement to submit to arbitration. By agreeing to submit disputes to arbitration, a party relinquishes his courtroom rights – including that to subpoena witnesses – in favor of arbitration with all of its well known advantages and drawbacks." *Parsons & Whittemore Overseas Co v Société Générale de l'Industrie du Papier (RAKTA)*, 508 F.2d, p. 975 (2d Cir. NY 1974). See also: *X Firm v Y Ltd*, Preliminary Award of 9 October 2008, in which an arbitrator in an ICC arbitration seated in Switzerland, disregarded a witness statement of a key witness on the issue of a document's authenticity because he was not presented for cross-examination: "Even though A's testimony will be disregarded as evidence for the Claimant's allegations with respect to the authenticity of the Amendment Agreement (pursuant to Procedural Order No. 3), the latter remain on record and I will examine them based on all the evidence and pleadings before me. In this regard, I will also assess the relevance of the Claimant's inability to make A available for cross examination." *X Firm v Y Ltd*, Preliminary Award, 09 October 2008, *ASA Bulletin*, Vol. 29, no. 4, p. 869 (2011).

71 Dietmar W. Prager and Joanna E. Davidson, *"Compania de Aguas Del Aconquija SA & Vivendi Universal SA v The Argentine Republic*, ICSID Case No. ARB/97/3 (2007)", *A Contribution by the ITA Board of Reporters*.

from witnesses who were not available for cross-examination at the oral hearing were not to be taken into evidence by the Tribunal.[72]

4.55 Thus, conflicting appointments,[73] inconvenience,[74] expense or other matters which are entirely within a party's control or assumption of risk at the time it submitted a witness statement do not, as a general rule, constitute reasons or excuses which would mitigate a party's duty to present a witness for cross-examination at a hearing.

4.56 An acceptable basis for excusing a party's failure to present a witness generally stems from the event preventing attendance having been unforeseeable at the time of proffering the written statement. For example, the legitimate and serious illness of the witness (often substantiated by affirming correspondence from a physician),[75] or death of the

---

72 *Ibid.*, para. 2.7.16. A related issue is the question of whether evidence recording a witness' testimony which was not prepared as a witness statement (e.g., a transcript recording a witness' statements from an unrelated procedure), should be disregarded if the individual who made the statement does not appear at an oral hearing for cross examination. This question arose before the tribunal in SCC Case No. 156, where it was determined to admit a transcript of testimony by an individual who had not appeared as a witness in the arbitration. The testimony had been taken during a criminal investigation. SCC Case No. 156, Final Award, para. 5 (2007) (unpublished). The tribunal had set forth a procedural rule similar in effect to art. 4.7. The decision by the tribunal to admit the evidence was later challenged, where it was argued that the admittance of the transcript, without requiring the individual whose statements were recorded to appear as witnesses, was a breach of the procedural rules and a violation of the challenging party's right to be heard (i.e., because it had not been able to cross examine the witnesses). The reviewing court did not reach a decision on this issue. *AO Techsnabexport v Globe Nuclear Services & Supply GNSS*, 404 Fed. Appx. 793 (4th Cir. Md. 2010). However, the observations of Hans Smit, submitted in an expert statement in the challenge proceedings, are instructive: "It is true that the Rules [governing the arbitration] provide that written statements submitted may not be considered unless the witnesses, upon request of an adverse party or the tribunal, can be heard in person or oral examination. This is a rule now universally followed by international arbitral tribunals. Clearly the records of the testimony of witnesses hearing in the Russian Criminal proceedings . . . are not witness statements of the kind covered by the [rules of procedure quoted above]. They were not prepared by the witnesses with the assistance of . . . counsel for submission to the tribunal, to take the place of direct examination in the proceedings." Expert Opinion of Hans Smit, paras 73–75 (5 December 2008) (unpublished).

73 *Parsons & Whittemore Overseas Co v Société Générale de l'Industrie du Papier (RAKTA)*, *supra* n. 70. Although mentioned with regard to the issue of enforcement, the court noted that refusal of a tribunal to extend a hearing to accommodate a witness who had a conflicting appointment did not violate due process.

74 In commenting on a complaint raised in relation to the failure of a witness (who was also a party) to attend hearings seated in Hong Kong before an HKIAC tribunal, a US district court reiterated this fundamental rule: "But the simple truth is that Defendant willingly did business with a Chinese company and agreed to arbitrate its disputes in Hong Kong. Thus, Mr. Chang's inconvenience in attending hearings held in that forum does not amount to a denial of Defendant's due process rights." *China National Building Material Investment Co Ltd v BNK International LLC* (US Dist – Tex 2009) LEXIS 113194. Not uncommon is the situation where a witness is faced with criminal proceedings affecting their ability to testify. In *Libananco v Turkey*, the tribunal considered that the threat of arrest and prosecution by governmental authorities of the respondent state against three witnesses should not excuse the witnesses from testifying via video conference and or in alternative locations. *Libananco v Turkey*, *supra* n. 9. In the UNCITRAL arbitration *Grand River Enterprises Six Nations Ltd v United States of America*, the claimant petitioned the tribunal to either delay a hearing or excuse the witness from testifying because the subject of his cross-examination could potentially elicit testimony prejudicial to his defence to a criminal indictment. The tribunal rejected the petition, and noted that it would be for claimant's counsel to object to any such questions during cross-examination. *Grand River Enterprises Six Nations Ltd v United States of America*, UNCITRAL/NAFTA, Final Award, paras 56–58 (2011). Consider also the approach adopted by the tribunal in ICC Case No. 12048, where the claimant petitioned the tribunal to permit the witness to testify by phone at a hearing in Accra, Ghana, concerning interim measures. The reason given for the request was that the witness had "concerns for his personal liberty arising out of an investigation conducted by the Serious Fraud Office of Ghana." The tribunal, in this instance, refused the request, and determined not to allow the witness to testify by phone. The claimant would subsequently withdraw the witness' written statement from the record. ICC Case No. 12048, Final Award, p. 13 (2003) (unpublished).

75 In light of the established jurisprudence above demonstrating that 'inconvenience' is not a basis for excusing attendance at the hearing, it would follow that some demonstration of serious illness would be required before

witness,[76] and/or the disappearance of a witness due to reasons unconnected to the arbitration, are all grounds which may excuse a party from the consequence of not presenting a witness at the hearing. There are of course others.

4.57 Moreover, a tribunal may also allow a written witness statement to be admitted, despite the non-attendance of the witness, where the adverse party has taken legal or other steps to impede that witness' participation in the hearing. In the *Enron Creditors Recovery Corp et al. v The Argentine Republic* arbitration, the ICSID tribunal was faced with the scenario where the respondent had obtained a court injunction preventing a fact witness presented by the claimant, from attending the hearing.[77] The respondent argued that the witness had legal obligations owing to it, which should have in good faith prevented him from giving adverse testimony in the arbitration. While not accepting this rationale for excluding his testimony, the tribunal noted that this was an issue between the witness and the respondent, and admitted the written testimony. When respondent then obtained a court injunction preventing the witness from attending the hearing, the tribunal (who had wished to question the witness) ruled in favour of keeping the written statement in the record. This example suggests that where a party prevents an adverse witness from attending the hearing, arbitrators are within their rights to admit the written testimony of the witness.[78]

Exceptional reasons for admitting the testimony of a non-attending witness

4.58 According to article 4.7, a tribunal may in certain circumstances find that irrespective of the reasons offered for the non-attendance of a witness, there are exceptional grounds for permitting the written statement to remain in the record. These grounds are most likely tied to the probative value of the statement and, in particular, as it relates to questions where a tribunal has little other evidence to consider. That being said, a tribunal would in most circumstances give careful consideration to the adverse party's

---

a tribunal dismisses a witness from attendance at a hearing. This being said, a tribunal may not always require a medical certificate, or conversely, may not regard a medical certificate as sufficient proof of the incapacity of the witness, whatever the circumstances may be. As an example of the latter, see the *Libananco v Turkey* ICSID arbitration where a tribunal disregarded the witness statement of a witness who had claimed illness prevented her from attending a hearing, and presented a medical certificate supporting her position. In this instance, the tribunal was also informed that the witness was currently in hiding, having fled an investigation by the Turkish legal authorities. Evidently, the tribunal simply did not accept the medical certificate as proof of her inability to attend, and determined in accordance with art. 4.8 of the 1999 rules (similar to 4.7), to disregard the witness statement. *Libananco Holdings Co Ltd v Republic of Turkey*, ICSID Case No. ARB/06/8, Final Award, paras 65–77 (2011).

76 As was the case in ICC Case No. 11258 (unpublished), *supra* n. 56, para. 120, wherein the tribunal allowed the witness statement of an expert who had died prior to the hearing to remain in the record, under the following proviso: "it being understood that this shall in no way limit the Tribunal's discretion in appreciating the weight and materiality of Mr. B's Witness Statement."

77 *Enron Creditors Recovery Corp Ponderosa Assets LP v The Argentine Republic*, ICSID Case No. ARB/01/3, Decision on the Application for Annulment of the Argentine Republic, paras 163–169 (30 July 2010).

78 *Ibid.*, para. 177. The *ad hoc* committee, in reviewing the decision of the tribunal in the light of Argentina's arguments that, *inter alia*, equality between the parties and the right to a fair hearing meant that the witness statement should have been excluded, commented as follows: "Argentina cites numerous authorities for the general proposition that the principle of equality of the parties, the right to defence, and right to fair treatment are fundamental rules of procedure. However, Argentina cites no authority for the proposition that it would amount to a serious violation of a fundamental rule of procedure for a tribunal to admit the witness statement of a witness in the circumstances described in the preceding two paragraphs." It should be noted that the tribunal limited its findings to the facts of the present situation only, that is, where a party had gone to lengths to prevent the attendance at the hearing of a witness presented by the adverse party, and declined to lay down a broader rule.

right to be heard on the issue and its ability to challenge the testimony. As a minimum due process requirement, a tribunal in such circumstances should allow for the adverse party to challenge the witness statement in writing and perhaps offer rebuttal evidence if needed.

4.59 Furthermore, different options may also be open to tribunals who are faced with this issue. A tribunal may in such circumstances agree to reschedule the hearing date or allow for a second hearing date in order to ensure that the witness' oral testimony (under cross-examination) is taken. Other options may include organising a video conference for the testifying witness. While not ideal, and perhaps increasing the cost of the hearing, such a procedure would be at times appropriate in order to ensure that an adverse party is given an opportunity to put questions to the witness.

Failure to call a witness to a hearing

Article 4.8 2010 IBA Rules: If the appearance of a witness has not been requested pursuant to Article 8.1, none of the other Parties shall be deemed to have agreed to the correctness of the content of the Witness Statement.

General discussion

4.60 The failure to call a witness to a hearing is not considered an admission of the veracity of the witness' testimony. As tribunals are often faced with issues of procedural economy, so too are parties and their counsel, who are afforded limited time in which to present their case. Thus, a decision by a party to not call a witness for cross-examination may be influenced by any number of factors, many of which may not have a direct relationship to the veracity or quality of a witness' testimony.

4.61 Nevertheless, to the extent that witness testimony is not challenged in cross-examination or in writing, a tribunal is naturally free to give full consideration to the testimony that is offered. The general rule was expressed in an ICSID arbitration as follows:

> In accordance with the parties' shared understanding, as expressed in the letters referred to above, the Tribunal will consider the written statements of those witnesses and experts who have not been called to testify at the hearing as part of the evidentiary record and evaluate those statements in light of the record as well as the oral testimony of the witnesses and experts called to testify at the hearing.[79]

4.62 Thus, the statement of a witness who has not been called is often considered as part of the record, and is not diminished by the mere fact that the witness was not asked to be present to give oral testimony. Evidence which contradicts the statement or corroborates it may lead to a decision by the tribunal to assign weight to or otherwise ignore it, as the case may be.

---

79 Dietmar W. Prager and Ana Frischtak, *"Duke Energy International Peru Investments No. 1, Ltd v Republic of Peru*, ICSID Case No. ARB/03/28, 18 August 2008", *A Contribution by the ITA Board of Reporters*, para. 29. See also the recognition by an LCIA tribunal that the decision by a party not to call a witness to appear was based on procedural economy, and not an acceptance of the correctness of the witness statement: "In the interests of expedition and cost saving, [Claimant] agreed not to call these witnesses for cross examination, expressly stating that such decision did not indicate acceptance of the accuracy of the propositions set forth in the Witness Statements." LCIA Case No. 5680, Final Award, para. 1.18 (2006) (unpublished).

Calling non-cooperating witnesses

Article 4.9 2010 IBA Rules: If a Party wishes to present evidence from a person who will not appear voluntarily at its request, the Party may, within the time ordered by the Arbitral Tribunal, ask it to take whatever steps are legally available to obtain the testimony of that person, or seek leave from the Arbitral Tribunal to take such steps itself. In the case of a request to the Arbitral Tribunal, the Party shall identify the intended witness, shall describe the subjects on which the witness's testimony is sought and shall state why such subjects are relevant to the case and material to its outcome. The Arbitral Tribunal shall decide on this request and shall take, authorize the requesting Party to take or order any other Party to take, such steps as the Arbitral Tribunal considers appropriate if, in its discretion, it determines that the testimony of that witness would be relevant to the case and material to its outcome.

General discussion

4.63 As with documentary evidence under article 3.9, a tribunal is expressly author-ised to render assistance to a party who seeks to obtain witness testimony through domestic courts. The issues surrounding the involvement of a court in the process of taking witness testimony are in some ways similar to the questions that arise in rela-tion to obtaining document disclosure through the courts (see comments to article 3.9). Nevertheless, the divide between common law and civil law approaches (common law courts, which are familiar with such procedures, tend to be more receptive to assisting tribunals with document production requests, whereas civil law courts reflect limited openness to such a notion) is considered when it comes to issues of document disclo-sure. This is not necessarily the same situation with regard to witness hearings, where the *lex arbitri* of a number of civil law jurisdictions expressly provide for a court to assist a tribunal in the taking of witness testimony. These issues and others are discussed below.

The tribunal's authority over the taking of witness testimony

4.64 Article 4.9 presupposes that a party will consult a tribunal prior to seeking a court issued subpoena, or other measure designed to compel the attendance of a witness at a hearing. Yet the question may arise as to whether unilateral steps taken by a party to secure the attendance of a witness at a hearing under the applicable law would be permitted. This question was addressed in a case arising out of a SIAC arbitration by the High Court of Singapore. In this particular case, the parties had agreed that the IBA Rules would apply to the proceedings. Over the course of the arbitration one of the parties became dissatisfied with the level of disclosure the adverse party had provided, and sought from the arbitrator permission to obtain oral testimony from some of its opponent's employees, concerning compliance with the disclosure order. The tribunal denied permission, explaining that it did not believe the matter worthy of deposing witnesses.

4.65 Following the ruling of the tribunal, the disappointed party applied to the local Singapore court for a subpoena compelling the witness in question to attend an oral hearing. The application was made without the support of the tribunal and it was opposed by the adverse party, who argued that the subpoena was abusive. The High Court took up the application and considered whether it should refuse the subpoena, and in doing so took direct notice of article 4.9. In interpreting the text of the rule, the High Court provided the following observations: "the IBA Rules expressly reserve the decision as to what legal steps a party should take in the event it wishes to adduce from a person who will not appear voluntarily at its request to the Arbitrator, and second, the party should write first to the Arbitrator, enclosing the grounds on which they seek such a witness's testimony and explain its relevance to the substantive case."[80]

4.66 Thus, the interpretation given to article 4.9 of the High Court affirms that the text of this rule should be seen as imposing a restriction upon a party's right to involve local courts, insofar as it requires that a party first seek and obtain an arbitrator's permission to such involvement before petitioning a court. The High Court further opined that to do otherwise would undermine the authority of the arbitral tribunal.[81]

4.67 Interestingly, this interpretation of article 4.9 mirrors the more recent interpretation given to article 3.9 by US courts, concerning the right to petition a court for assistance in gaining document disclosure (see comments to article 3.9). In this regard, therefore, it would seem that the prevalent interpretation of the IBA Rules is that they confirm the authority of the tribunal over evidentiary procedure, and, further, require parties to obtain an arbitrator's permission prior to petitioning a local court for assistance in the gathering of evidence.

Court assistance in the taking of witness testimony

4.68 Some *lex arbitri* will allow for a supervising court to assist a tribunal in the taking of witness testimony by, for example, confirming or issuing subpoenas/or summons to witnesses to appear before either the court or the tribunal to provide witness testimony. In the United States, under section 7 of Title 9 of the US Code, an arbitral tribunal is authorised to issue a subpoena to an individual to appear before it to give testimony.[82] If resisted by the potential witness, the tribunal may have the subpoena confirmed by the

---

80 Michael Hwang and Zihua Su, "*ALC v ALF*, SGHC, Case No. 231 (2010)", *A Contribution by the ITA Board of Reporters*, para. 29.

81 *Ibid.*, para. 49.

82 This provision reads in part: "The arbitrators selected either as prescribed in this title or otherwise, or a majority of them, may summon in writing any person to attend before them or any of them as a witness and in a proper case to bring with him or them any book, record, document, or paper which may be deemed material as evidence in the case . . .; if any person or persons so summoned to testify shall refuse or neglect to obey said summons, upon petition the United States district court for the district in which such arbitrators, or a majority of them, are sitting may compel the attendance of such person or persons before said arbitrator or arbitrators, or punish said person or persons for contempt in the same manner provided by law for securing the attendance of witnesses or their punishment for neglect or refusal to attend in the courts of the United States." Title 9, US Code, s. 7.

local court. Similar methods for compelling the appearance of witnesses are available in England.[83]

4.69 Some civil law jurisdictions provide for courts to assist in the taking of witness testimony.[84] In cases where a court summons a witness before it to provide testimony, the procedure for the taking of the evidence will often be similar to that found in normal court proceedings before the court. In such instances, the documented testimony given by the witness to a court will be entered into the record of the arbitral proceedings.[85]

Considerations prior to authorising court involvement/a tribunal is not obliged to act

4.70 The provisions of article 4.9 have been brought into line with similar articles (e.g., articles 3.9 and 3.10 of the IBA Rules) covering court assistance in the taking of documentary evidence by requiring that any such request comport with the requirements of relevance and materiality. In this respect, the relevance or materiality of the requested evidence would follow the analysis set forth in article 3.7 of the IBA Rules, and essentially require the tribunal to determine whether: (1) the witness testimony in question is likely to be necessary for a party to obtain in order to meet its burden of proof; and (2) the issue in connection with which the witness testimony is sought will actually impact a tribunal's final award. More generally, a party must also describe the subject matter of the proposed testimony, and in doing so may identify certain documents with regard to which the witness should be prepared to answer questions. Depending on the jurisdiction in question, a court may be willing to order the subpoenaed witness to disclose discreet documents relative

---

83 See: Section 43 of the English Arbitration Act 1996.

84 See, for example, the following order issued by a Swiss Court which notified a third party that it was obliged to appear before the court in order to assist in the taking of evidence in connection with an arbitration: "En application de l'article 27 du concordat intercantonal sur l'arbitrage qui prévoit qu'en cas de nécessité le Tribunal arbitral peut dans le cadre de l'administration des preuves requérir le concours de l'autorité judiciaire, je vous invite formellement à répondre au questionnaire qui vous a été adressé le 2 août 2000 ainsi qu'à la question complémentaire (selon annexe), ceci dans un délai de 20 jours. Si vous ne deviez pas donner suite à l'injonction ci-dessus, il y aurait lieu d'envisager de vous citer à une audience qui devrait alors être appointée ainsi que de vous infliger cas échéant une amende conformément à l'article 251 CPC qui sanctionne le témoin récalcitrant. Il vous est par ailleurs rappelé votre obligation de répondre conformément à la vérité aux questions posées, le faux témoignage étant sévèrement puni." (unofficial translation) "Pursuant to article 27 of the 'intercantonal concordat' on arbitration, which provides that in case of necessity the Arbitral Tribunal may in the context of the administration of evidence require the assistance of the judicial authority, I formally invite you to respond the questionnaire sent to you on 2 August 2000 and the supplementary questions (according to the annex), within 20 days. If you fail to comply with the above injunction, consideration should be given to summoning you to a hearing that should then be appointed, and imposing a fine, if any, in accordance with section 251 CPC, which sanctions recalcitrant witnesses. You are also reminded of your obligation to respond truthfully to the questions asked, and that false testimony will be severely punished." Letter of injunction of the Neuchâtel Civil Court of 16 February 2001 to Mr X, *ASA Bulletin*, Vol. 21, no. 1, pp. 142–143 (2003).

85 See the example of an ICC tribunal which permitted witness testimony taken in the presence of both parties and before a notary public, but outside the tribunal's presence, to be submitted into the record. ICC Case No. 7170, Procedural Order, Dominique Hascher (ed.), *Collection of Procedural Decisions in ICC Arbitration 1993–1996*, p. 55 (2nd edition, 1998). See also the procedural rule adopted in ICC Case No. 12279, in which the tribunal admonished the parties to meet and confer, and arrange for the deposition of any witness who had not been offered by a party, but whom was under control of a party, and which the adverse party wished to interview. The witness testimony was to be transcribed or otherwise recorded (by video), and the transcript entered into the arbitral record prior to the hearing. ICC Case No. 12279, Procedural Order of 31 July 2003, *ICC Bulletin, 2010 Special Supplement: Decisions on ICC Arbitration Procedure*, p. 42.

to his testimony.[86] Irrespective of the type of information that is sought, however, a party should satisfy the tribunal that any objections raised under article 9.2 or that are possible before the administering court,[87] would not be a barrier to adducing the sought after witness testimony (and/or ancillary documents).

4.71 A party may also need to provide the tribunal with reasons why it could not secure the voluntary appearance of the witness. Consistent with the general approach found with regard to documentary evidence, a tribunal will generally not render assistance to a party in the taking of evidence where it has not undertaken its own reasonable efforts to secure the voluntary testimony of a witness.[88] Moreover, an arbitral tribunal is under no duty to assist a party in obtaining witness testimony. Arbitrators enjoy a wide discretion in determining whether to issue orders for the taking of evidence or whether to assist a party in such a matter, and their decisions to abstain from rendering such assistance are generally not open to successful challenge.[89]

Other steps which are legally available to a tribunal to obtain witness testimony

4.72 A tribunal may take steps to obtain the testimony of a witness that do not involve a direct appeal to a supervising court. Tribunals have in the past simply written letters in support of a party's attempt to secure the testimony of a witness located in a jurisdiction other than of the seat of arbitration.[90] Another approach may see the tribunal develop a list

---

86 See, for example: *Tajik Aluminium Plant v Hydro Aluminum AS* [2006] 1 Lloyd's Rep 154.

87 See the example of the decision of an English court sitting in consideration of a witness subpoena that also sought the disclosure of certain key documents over which confidentiality was claimed: "The fact that the documents of which production is sought are confidential or contain confidential information is not an absolute bar to the enforcement of their production by way of witness summons; however, in the exercise of its discretion, the court is entitled to have regard to the fact that documents are confidential and that to order production would involve a breach of confidence. While the court's paramount concern must be the fair disposal of the cause or matter, it is not unmindful of other legitimate interests and that to order production of a third party's confidential documents may be oppressive, intrusive or unfair. In this connection, when documents are confidential, the claim that their production is necessary for the fair resolution of proceedings may well be subjected to particularly close scrutiny." Nicholas Fletcher, "26 June 2009 – High Court, Queen's Bench Division", *A Contribution by the ITA Board of Reporters*, para. 3. See also: the decision of an ICC tribunal which sat in consideration of a request for assistance in obtaining documents and witness testimony from a third party, wherein the tribunal considered the issue of confidentiality, the civil law approach to document production and other matters in determining whether assistance should be granted to the party seeking to petition a Geneva court. In concluding that the request should be denied, the tribunal noted: "whereas Art. 184(2) of the Act provides for the assistance of the Courts of the seat of the arbitration, such assistance may only be applied for and obtained for measures that conform with the law and practice of that Court." ICC Case No. 8238, in ICC Case No. 8238, Procedural Order, Dominique Hascher (ed.), *Collection of Procedural Decisions in ICC Arbitration 1993–1996*, p. 157 (2nd edition, 1998).

88 *Methanex Corp v United States of America*, NAFTA/UNCITRAL, Final Award, Part II, chapter H, para. 25 (3 August 2005).

89 As was noted by an English court in its consideration of a challenge to an LCIA award where a party complained of the tribunal's failure to order certain witnesses to be present at the arbitral proceedings: "The tribunal's decisions to decline to make such an order were unexceptional, and were certainly not unfair, and did not give rise to any irregularity." *Double K Oil Products 1996 Ltd v Neste Oil* [2009] EWHC 3380 (Comm). See also: the decision of a German court determining that the arbitral tribunal had not erred in refusing to assist a party to obtain the testimony of an unwilling witness when it was not clear that the witness testimony to be elicited was still of relevance to the case. "7 September 2005 – Oberlandesgericht (Court of Appeal), Hamm", in Albert Jan van den Berg (ed.), *Yearbook Commercial Arbitration*, Vol. XXXI, pp. 685–697 (2006).

90 See: *Corporacion Transnacional de Inversiones SA de CV v STET International SpA*, *supra* n. 70, where an ICC tribunal seated in Canada sent correspondence to a court in Cuba advising it of its support for a party's petition to hear a witness.

of questions to be put to the particular witness that are forwarded to a court that has jurisdiction over the witness. Tribunals may also simply address correspondence directly to a witness or organisation to elicit answers from the individuals on relevant issues in some circumstances.

4.73 Other steps that a tribunal can take to secure the testimony of a witness may include petitioning the local court to forward letters of request[91] or otherwise authorise a party as a commissioner *ad hoc* under the *Convention of 18 March 1970 on the Taking of Evidence Abroad in Civil or Commercial Matters* ("Hague Evidence Convention"). Whether a letter of request under the Hague Evidence Convention will achieve the desired result should be addressed by the petitioning party in the application to the arbitral tribunal, when seeking its authorisation or assistance.

Tribunal's power to call witnesses

Article 4.10 2010 IBA Rules: **At any time before the arbitration is concluded, the Arbitral Tribunal may order any Party to provide for, or to use its best efforts to provide for, the appearance for testimony at an Evidentiary Hearing of any person, including one whose testimony has not yet been offered. A Party to whom such a request is addressed may object for any of the reasons set forth in Article 9.2.**

General discussion

4.74 A tribunal may act *sua sponte* or on request from a party to direct another party to produce a witness over which it has a measure of control or influence. It may be that in any given situation, a tribunal seeks to hear individuals who have particular information concerning a dispute, but whom have not been formerly tendered as a witness in the proceedings. The IBA Rules in article 4.10 thus confirm this power as being inherent to an arbitrator's authority over the proceedings.

4.75 An example of how a situation such as this may come about may be taken from a Cairo Regional Centre for International Commercial Arbitration proceeding, where the arbitrators sat in consideration of a dispute between a European oil company and an African oil authority. In this instance, the tribunal sought to determine the quality of goods that were delivered in the course of a purchase agreement. The parties had agreed to submit samples of the goods to a testing facility, however, the parties had disagreed over the interpretation and weight to be given to the results. Neither party had tendered employees from the testing facility, but after consideration of the matter the tribunal ruled that the

---

91 Tribunals have been known to be open to such measures to obtain evidence. The moving party will need to demonstrate that such a procedure is possible under a relevant convention. See, for instance: the notation in a final award of a Geneva Chamber of Commerce Arbitration, where it was recalled: "The Arbitral Tribunal was unable to have Mr. D. examined as witness by letters *rogatory*, which would have been at its discretion under Art. 184 LDIP. The Claimant alleged, undisputedly, that there is at present no possibility between Switzerland and former Y. to obtain letters *rogatory*." "28 février 1994 – Arbitral Tribunal", *ASA Bulletin*, Vol. 13, No. 2, pp. 301–357 (1995).

representative of the inspection office should be present to give testimony. The actions of the tribunal were reported as follows: "it was decided to demand attendance of the witness before the Tribunal to listen to his testimony regarding the certificates drawn up thereby and to confirm that the seals of samples submitted by the Respondent are the same seals placed upon sample taking."[92]

4.76 It is inherent to a tribunal's authority that it may expect a party to cooperate in producing evidence to it.[93] Thus, article 4.10 simply confirms this principle by acknowledging an arbitrator's basic authority to request a party to present a witness to be heard that has relevant and material evidence.

"Best efforts"

4.77 Much like article 3.10, a tribunal may expect that an individual with whom a party has influence or exerts control over will be responsive to a request from it to provide evidence. This certainly extends to individuals in the employment of the party or with whom a formal business relationship exists.[94] It may also be presumed by a tribunal that an individual who has retired or was a former employee of a party will also be available to give evidence, as was the case in an ICC arbitration where the tribunal ordered that a retired quality control specialist be made available to answer questions over the sale of allegedly non-conforming goods.[95]

4.78 In these instances, a party will be asked to use its "best efforts" to obtain the acquiescence from the third party witness to provide testimony. Such efforts would include contacting the individual, arranging for the expenses to travel to the hearing, and otherwise taking reasonable steps to ensure their attendance at a hearing. Age, animosity and

---

92 "Cairo Regional Centre for International Commercial Arbitration, Final Award, Case No. 102/1997 (1998)", in Eldin, *supra* n. 13, pp. 3–10.

93 For example, article 34(3) of the ICSID Rules of Procedure for Arbitration Proceedings (Arbitration Rules) states that: "[t]he parties shall cooperate with the Tribunal in the production of the evidence .... The Tribunal shall take formal note of the failure of a party to comply with its obligations under this paragraph and of any reasons given for such failure." See also: *Sempra Energy International v. Argentine Republic*, ICSID Case No. ARB/02/16, Decision on the Claimant's REquest for Provisional Measures of December 22, 2005, as referred in the Final Award, p. 9, §37: "the Tribunal notes, in accordance with, ICSID Arbitration Rule 34(3) the parties shall cooperate with the Tribunal in the production of the evidence". See also: *William A. Parker (U.S.A.) v. United Mexican States*, Reports of International Arbitral Awards, Vol. IV, pp. 35-41 (1926), at p. 4: "EVIDENCE, DUTY OF BOTH PARTIES TO SUBMIT. It is the duty of the two Agents to co-operate in submitting to the tribunal all relevant facts. Each Agent should present all the facts that can be reasonably ascertained by him without regard to what their effect may be." See also: V.V. Veeder, "The Lawyer's Duty to Arbitrate in Good Faith", *Arbitration International 18*, no. 4 (2002).

94 "The Arbitral Tribunal considers that, in this respect, in addition to entities which may be controlled by a party, there may be entities or persons with whom a party has a relationship which is relevant for the purposes of this arbitral processing. The duty of production extends to the entities controlled by each party. Furthermore, good faith also imposes a duty of best efforts to obtain documents that are in the possession of entities or persons with whom or with which the party the subject of the request has a relevant relationship." *Gallo v Canada, supra* n. 22, Procedural Order No. 2, para. 8 (10 February 2009).

95 Final Award, ICC Case No. 8547, *supra* n. 45, "Conclusions can be drawn from the fact that claimant refused to produce the witness as asked by the arbitral tribunal. Had the witness been made available it could have been further investigated whether or not claimant had knowledge of a non-conformity. Claimant justified its refusal in its brief of 30 October 1998 by stating that the person in question has retired and furthermore is not an employee of claimant but of supplier."

infirmity are just some of the reasons why a witness may not respond to such entreaties, but where a tribunal believes that a reasonable opportunity exists for the testimony to be taken, it should be demonstrated that the party requested the witness to attend and has acted in good faith in attempting to secure the witness' attendance. Otherwise, the party runs the risk of an adverse inference being drawn against it.[96]

---

96 *Ibid.* An example of this outcome may be taken from an ICDR administered arbitration wherein the tribunal ordered a party to present certain witnesses with relevant knowledge. The party compelled to present the witnesses failed to do so; claiming instead that the witnesses refused to testify while a parallel criminal proceeding was taking place. The tribunal considered these factors, and US common law principles governing evidence, when arriving at its decision on whether to draw an adverse inference: "While the failure of certain [redacted] witnesses to appear may have been precipitated by the indictment and the denial of the stay, the operative fact is that certain witnesses with knowledge did not testify. For the reasons set forth above, this does not translate into an automatic win or loss by one party or the other. Instead, the failure of a witness to testify "may be considered by a jury in assessing the strength of evidence offered by the opposite party on the issue which the witness was in a position to controvert. [internal citation omitted]" ICDR Case No. 50181T0032108, Final Award, p. 26 (21 April 2011) (unpublished). See also: the following comments from authors commenting on the 1999 version of the IBA Rules: "If the witness whom the arbitral tribunal wishes to hear is a person that a party would reasonably be expected to be able to present for testimony (e.g., the person is an employee of the party) and that party has no valid excuse for failing to present the person in response to the tribunal's order, the arbitral tribunal would be entitled to draw an adverse inference from the non-appearance of that person." Bühler and Dorgan, *supra* n. 17, p. 17.

CHAPTER 5

Party-appointed experts

Introduction

5.01 There are essentially two modes of presenting expert testimony in an international arbitration. The first is through introduction by a party of an expert's testimony in support of their case. Such witnesses are often referred to as the "party-appointed" expert, a designation indicating that the expert is instructed and compensated by a party for his or her work. This approach is to be distinguished from the tribunal-appointed expert. As the phrase suggests, the tribunal-appointed expert is retained to work on behalf of the tribunal, and does not accept direct compensation for his work from either party, and is instructed by the tribunal. While chapter 6 will deal extensively with the use of tribunal-appointed experts, the following chapter is devoted to article 5 of the IBA Rules, which covers party-appointed expert witnesses.

5.02 The expert's opinion is generally given in regard to factual issues which present particularly difficult questions for a tribunal. Thus the role of the party-appointed expert in international arbitration is to contribute to establishing, through his or her specialist testimony, certain conclusions regarding aspects of a case. Often referred to as "technical issues", the questions submitted to an expert for consideration may in fact cover a wide variety of subject matter. In this respect, it is important to note that article 5 of the IBA Rules does not impose any limitations on which issues a party may submit expert testimony on. However, as is discussed in the comments to article 5.1, the tribunal is equally free to ignore an expert's report if it is immaterial to the final award.

5.03 In the modern practice of international arbitration, the use of party-appointed experts has eclipsed the use of tribunal appointed experts. This may be the case for any number of reasons, but it would seem there are grounds for both the parties and arbitrators to prefer party-appointed experts. For the parties, this may be the case because they have greater control over the matters that will be put to the expert for his or her opinion, which arguably pares down the potential for irrelevant testimony. For the tribunal, this approach may be preferred because it relieves the arbitrators of the logistical and procedural responsibility of appointing an expert.

5.04 The above notwithstanding, there are counter arguments against the use of the party-appointed expert. In particular, some commentators regret the development of the "battle of the experts", which is a reference to the situation where two opposing experts offer contradictory positions by relying on technical jargon that is seemingly irreconcilable. In such a case a tribunal may feel at a loss to determine which expert is correct. While such a possibility is accepted, as will be discussed in the comments below to article 5.4, techniques have been developed for aiding the Tribunal in dealing with this "battle".

Party-appointed expert's testimony in international arbitration generally

Article 5.1 2010 IBA Rules: party may rely on a Party-Appointed Expert as a means of evidence on specific issues. Within the time ordered by the Arbitral Tribunal, (i) each Party shall identify any Party-Appointed Expert on whose testimony it intends to rely and the subject-matter of such testimony; and (ii) the Party-Appointed Expert shall submit an Expert Report.

General discussion

5.05 The language in article 5.1, which includes the statement that "a party may rely on a Party-Appointed Expert as a means of evidence", confirms the widely accepted view in international arbitration that the use of such experts by parties to support their case is acceptable. While for common law lawyers an affirmation of this principle may seem unexceptional, since party-appointed expert testimony is widely used in such jurisdictions, those of the civil law tradition may not as readily accept such a proposition. It is reported that the use of a party-appointed expert remains controversial in some civil law jurisdictions.[1] Thus article 5.1 serves as an important reminder that such testimony is generally admissible in international arbitration.

5.06 It should be further noted, however, that the general admissibility of such evidence does not affect the tribunal's right to weigh and assign the appropriate value to expert testimony.[2] The weighing of expert evidence is a matter left to the discretion of the tribunal, as is stated in article 9.1 of the IBA Rules.[3] In this respect, arbitrators may adopt the findings of one party-appointed expert as opposed to another as they see fit.[4] It has been further

---

1 See generally the discussion of party-appointed experts in Denmark: Jacob C. Jørgensen, "Expert Witness Evidence in Danish Arbitration", *ASA Bulletin*, Vol. 26, No. 3, p. 479 (2008).

2 One commentator provided the following consideration of general approach to weighing evidence provided by party-appointed experts: "the opinion of party-appointed experts is not merely argument but has its own weight depending on the competence and credibility of the expert. The position of these experts, thus, can be situated somewhere between that of a witness of fact and that of the parties' counsel." Michael E. Schneider, "Technical Experts in International Arbitration" *ASA Bulletin*, Vol. 11, No. 3, p. 446 (1993).

3 Where an arbitrator appears to ignore critical expert evidence one once courts have found a breach of a party's right to be heard. "The Appellant sets forth, with references, that on the basis of an expert report from a Mr. E._____, it stated in detail all of the elements constituting the price that the Respondent should have paid for acquiring the products at issue. [. . .] According to the Appellant, the Arbitrator totally overlooked this argument, merely taking into consideration the basic price of USD 30 per metric ton. It must be found that the Appellant is right. Indeed it appears from the award under appeal that while specifically mentioning the deductions proposed by expert E._____ (n. 101) and by the Appellant in agreement with him, the Arbitrator totally overlooks them, without giving the least explanation in this respect. [. . .] However the problem of the allocation of the acquisition costs of the products does not appear to have caught his attention. At least he did not give any explanation from which the reason for which he overlooked the issue could be asserted. In conclusion the Appellant is right to argue a violation of its right to be heard in this respect." *X.____ v Y.____*, 4A_669/2012. The original decision is in French. The text is available on the website of the Federal Tribunal: www.bger.ch.

4 This has been affirmed in a decision of an *ad hoc* annulment committee. In this instance, where the tribunal appeared to endorse one party-appointed expert's view over another, the *ad hoc* committee noted that to assign such weight did not constitute a departure from a fundamental rule of procedure: "In the view of the *ad hoc* committee, a Tribunal may rely in this connection on expert and other testimony with which it agrees and may disregard other testimony. That is one of its principal tasks. . . . It is generally accepted that a Tribunal has in these matters substantial discretion and does not need to explain expert views. To further clarify its position, the *ad hoc* Committee also accepts that where a Tribunal agrees with one of the parties or with experts, it is not improper or unexpected for it to adopt the language used by them in the pleadings or in written testimony." *Compañiá de*

considered that it is not inappropriate for the tribunal to adopt an expert's choice of terms and expressions in the final award, if the tribunal is persuaded that such terminology is useful to their determinations.[5]

Identifying the expert

5.07 Under article 5.1 the parties are required to identify any expert on whose testimony they intend to rely within the time frames set by the tribunal. In practice, such identification will often occur when the expert submits the first report in the case in accordance with the filing schedule set by the tribunal. However, under article 5.1 a tribunal is permitted to exclude testimony from an expert that is not identified in accordance with the established time frame.[6] This may be particularly the case where a party reveals an expert witness just prior to the hearing. In such circumstances, a tribunal may, after considering the merits of the proposed testimony, rightly determine that to admit the testimony of an expert, only recently proffered, would cause the adverse party to suffer unfair surprise.

The expert report

5.08 Article 5.1 states that experts retained by parties are expected to provide a written report. The IBA Rules do not appear to contemplate testimony from an expert that is only provided orally. For many reasons this approach is advisable. As the expert report will often be quite complex and cover issues of a highly technical nature, both the tribunal and the opposing party should be provided with the report in advance so that they may consider its contents fully and prepare questions.

5.09 Similar to articles 3.1 and 4.1 of the IBA Rules in regard to documentary evidence and fact witnesses, the timing for the submission of the expert's report is usually identified in the schedule set by the tribunal. The customary timing for the submission of an initial expert report intended to support a case-in-chief or defence-in-chief is with the filing of the statement of claim or defence, as is the case with the filing of documentary evidence and fact witness testimony.[7] However, a tribunal may exercise its discretion to admit expert

---

Aguas del Aconquija SA and Vivendi Universal v Argentine Republic, ICSID Case No. ARB/97/3, Decision on Request for Annulment, p. 62 (20 August 2007).

5   *Ibid.*

6   This rule implicitly covers the duty to identify a fact witness who may provide expert testimony as well. See the following description of an ICDR case, where a tribunal disregarded the expert report of a witness who had not previously been identified as an expert by the party presenting his testimony. Having already imposed a deadline for the submission of expert testimony, the tribunal refused to permit the expert analysis of the witness who had been presented as a fact witness. "[T]he Arbitrator issued Procedural Order No. 2, ruling that paragraphs 5 to the end of the witness statement of [the witness] constituted expert testimony submitted after the due date of the submission of expert reports, and would not be considered by the arbitrator." ICDR Case No. 15054T, Final Award, p. 3 (2008) (unpublished).

7   As an example, see the procedural direction given in the following case in regard to the filing of the statement of claim and defence: "the Parties shall indicate in their written submissions to the Arbitral Tribunal the nature of evidence relied upon (exhibit(s), witness testimony, expert opinion, specifically designated documents to be produced by the other party, etc.) by providing, with reasonable specificity, references to the exhibits and witness statements submitted in support of their allegations." ICC Case No. 13046, *ICC Bulletin, 2010 Special Supplement: Decisions on ICC Arbitration Procedure*, p. 94. See also: the following excerpt from the procedural history in *Duke Energy v Ecuador*, "On 2 September 2005, the Claimants submitted their Memorial in Chief accompanied by supporting documents as well as . . . the expert reports of [the five experts]." Dietmar W. Prager

reports filed after the deadline where it considers it appropriate to do so,[8] and equally, it may reject an expert report that is belatedly filed if the circumstances would warrant it.[9]

The contents of the expert report

Article 5.2 2010 IBA Rules: The Expert Report shall contain:

(a) the full name and address of the Party-Appointed Expert, a statement regarding his or her present and past relationship (if any) with any of the Parties, their legal advisors and the Arbitral Tribunal, and a description of his or her background, qualifications, training and experience;

(b) a description of the instructions pursuant to which he or she is providing his or her opinions and conclusions;

(c) a statement of his or her independence from the Parties, their legal advisors and the Arbitral Tribunal;

(d) a statement of the facts on which he or she is basing his or her expert opinions and conclusions;

(e) his or her expert opinions and conclusions, including a description of the methods, evidence and information used in arriving at the conclusions. Documents on which the Party-Appointed Expert relies that have not already been submitted shall be provided;

(f) if the Expert Report has been translated, a statement as to the language in which it was originally prepared, and the

---

and Ana Frischtak, *"Duke Energy Electroquil Partners and Electroquil SA v Republic of Ecuador*, ICSID Case No. ARB/04/19, 18 August 2008", *A Contribution by the ITA Board of Reporters*, para. 81. See also Schneider's confirmation of this principle: "The opinions of party-appointed experts often are expressed in writing and produced with the pleadings." Schneider, *supra* n. 2, p. 447.

8   See the affirmation of this principle by an *ad hoc* committee in regard to an ICSID tribunal's power to admit late evidence: "The Committee has no doubt that under these provisions, a tribunal has the power to accept the filing by a party of an expert report after the deadline fixed for such filing, if the tribunal considers that there are good reasons for so doing." *Enron Creditors Recovery Corp v Argentine Republic*, ICSID Case No. ARB/01/3, Decision on the Application for Annulment of the Argentine Republic, para. 188 (2010).

9   See the rule adopted by the tribunal in ICC Case No. 12761: "The technical opinion of the individuals who have not been identified as experts by the parties in their respective evidential proposal writs, or whose Expert Report has not been presented on the abovementioned date, will not be admissible." ICC Case No. 12761, *ICC Bulletin, 2010 Special Supplement: Decisions on ICC Arbitration Procedure*, p. 74. See also KCAB case no. 7, *Claimant (Counter-Respondent) Laboratories Ltda. (New Zealand) v Respondent (Counter-Claimant) Softgel Ltd. (Korea), in* "KCAB Arbitral Awards", an arbitration administered by the Korean Commercial Arbitration Board and seated in Seoul, Republic of Korea, in which the tribunal allowed the production of post-hearing documents substantiating the quantum claimed by the Claimant, but not additional argument nor additional explanation of from any witness on the parties' closing submissions on quantum. In this regard, the tribunal there reasoned that: "Although the Claimant produced further documents on quantum after the hearing with the agreement of the Respondent, the Respondent objects to the Claimant attempting to substantiate and add additional components to its estimation other than those already contained and set out in the Statement of Claim and the Mr. F's Report, in particular paragraph . . . of the technical report. The respondent pointed out that the purpose of the statement of quantum was to substantiate the components and work envisaged as contained in the Statement of Claim and the Mr. F's Report. The agreement and liberty to submit further documents on quantum were for the purpose of firming up the quotations and cost estimates that the Claimant had not done up to the conclusion of the oral hearing. I agree with the Respondent. It cannot be right that, after the close of the oral hearing, the Claimant submits claim amounts based on specifications that neither the Claimant nor Mr. F had previously submitted for the purpose of examination or clarifications during the oral hearing." *Id.* at [35], p. 146.

> language in which the Party-Appointed Expert anticipates giving testimony at the Evidentiary Hearing;
>
> (g) an affirmation of his or her genuine belief in the opinions expressed in the Expert Report;
>
> (h) the signature of the Party-Appointed Expert and its date and place; and
>
> (i) if the Expert Report has been signed by more than one person, an attribution of the entirety or specific parts of the Expert Report to each author.

General discussion

5.10 Article 5.2 of the IBA Rules sets forth the general criteria according to which an expert report should conform. These standards may be followed as a means of ensuring that the information necessary for the tribunal to assess the validity and weight of the expert's conclusions is included in the report, and to afford the adverse side, including its own experts, the fair opportunity to respond. In regard to the latter point, there is also a case to be made that the efficiency of the proceedings is enhanced when the parties adhere to the format set forth in article 5.2. This is so, because cross-examination of party-appointed experts may be conducted with greater efficiency if background information is included with the report in advance of the hearing as such disclosure may limit the need for foundational questions.

5.11 While some of the subparagraphs of article 5.2 are included for reasons that are self-evident, such as a requirement that the expert provide his or her full name under subparagraph (a), other requirements have from time to time given rise to controversy. Issues that have led to debate include, the duty incumbent on the expert to describe their instructions in subparagraph (b), the statement of independence set forth in subparagraph (c) (and the duty to disclose relevant relationships under 5.2(a)) as well as the duty to disclose the documents relied on in subparagraph (e). In regard to the subparagraph (b) and the requirement to disclose instructions, the question of whether the communications between a retained expert and legal counsel are covered by privilege may arise. Further, the required statement of independence set forth in subparagraph (c) may also be controversial insofar as it is often debated whether a party-appointed expert may be considered independent and, if so, to what extent does a perceived or real lack of independence impact upon the admissibility and weight to be given to a report. These and other issues are discussed more fully below.

The independence of a party-appointed expert

5.12 In regard to the independence of party-appointed experts, it is instructive to compare the requirements set forth in article 6 of the IBA Rules concerning tribunal-appointed experts and those pertaining to the party-appointed expert in article 5. Whereas article 6.1 pre-supposes that the tribunal-appointed expert will be independent, no such pre-requisite is noted in article 5.1. Instead, in article 5.2 a party-appointed expert is required to provide a "statement of independence from the Parties, their legal advisers and the Arbitral Tribunal" and to disclose details of relationships with any of the parties or legal advisers as per 5.2(a). This statement is to be included in the report itself, indicating that a determination that the party-appointed expert is sufficiently independent is not a pre-requisite for admitting the report into the record. Here too a contrast can be made to article 6.2, where the tribunal-appointed expert is required to disclose any details affecting his or her independence prior to being appointed, and before any testimony is to be admitted.[10]

5.13 The divergent approach to independence found in articles 5 and 6 derives from the different roles performed by the two types of expert. For the tribunal-appointed expert, a lack of independence may be grounds for terminating his or her appointment because independence is central to such expert's duty to remain neutral mandate.[11] Where the tribunal-appointed expert has a connection to a party or its advisers, that may be a cause of justifiable doubts concerning whether he or she is capable of acting for the tribunal. As a result, due process may require the tribunal to appoint a different expert.

5.14 Concerning the party-appointed expert, it is obvious from the outset that this expert is acting as per the instruction of a party.[12] It is not unethical for counsel or a party to pay to the expert (reasonable) fees charged for his or her time.[13] Therefore, it would appear inconsistent for a tribunal to consider the "independence" of an expert who is paid and instructed by a party, in a manner similar to a tribunal-appointed expert.[14] The more workable interpretation of article 5.2(c) (and the disclosure requirements of 5.2(a)), would be to view

---

10 Speaking in regard to art. 5 generally, Jones notes the following: "Article 5 now requires the party-appointed expert's report to contain a statement of independence from the parties, from their legal advisors and from the arbitral tribunal. This requirement is not as robust as that for tribunal-appointed experts who must provide a statement of independence before appointment, thereby ensuring the expert's mind is focused upon his or her paramount duty to the tribunal before he or she has a chance to identify with the case of either party." Doug Jones, "Party Appointed Experts: Can They be Usefully Independent?", *Transnational Dispute Management*, Vol. 8, No. 1, p. 7 (February 2011).

11 See, generally: comments to art. 6.2. Noting that under English procedural law experts owe a duty of independence to the court, which is defined as meaning that the expert witness would provide the same opinion if given the same instructions by another party, Gaffney and O'Leary make the following observation: "The authors suggest that this principle does not find expression in the IBA Rules, at least insofar as party-appointed experts are concerned. . . . The position is arguably different in the case of tribunal-appointed experts." John Gaffney, Gillian O'Leary, "Tilting at Windmills? The Quest for Independence of Party Appointed Expert Witnesses in International Arbitration", *Asian Dispute Review*, July 2011.

12 Tribunals have in the past pre-supposed that a party-appointed expert was acting "for" a side, going so far as to consider the expert as part of a party's team. See the following position adopted by an *ad hoc* tribunal constituted in Dubai, UAE: "At the opening of his examination, each expert must state the extent to which he confirms as expert witness the explanations which, as a member of a Party's team, he has given to the Arbitral Tribunal during May 1991 Hearing." "Documents 15–30", *ASA Bulletin*, Vol. 11, No. 3, p. 465 (1993).

13 See: IBA Guideline 25.

14 See the following comments of Harris regarding art. 5.2(c) and 5.2(a): "In opting to focus more strongly on the independence of the expert than his or her impartiality, the IBA subcommittee has preferred the (possible) outward manifestation of the partiality over tests which focus on the arguably more relevant but less tangible state of mind of the expert. Whilst that is legitimate per se, and is indeed the route taken by some notable institutional rules and arbitration laws, the disclosure of connection in this way is a rather blunt instrument, as it is the quality of those connections which is really of more importance. Indeed there is an inherent tension between the concept of independence and a relationship of retainer, such as the relationship between a party and the expert it appoints and pays." Christopher Harris, "Expert Evidence: The 2010 Revisions to the IBA Rules on the Taking of Evidence in International Arbitration", *International Arbitration Law Review*, Vol. 13, No. 5, p. 212 (2010). The view that there is a different intent as to independence with respect to tribunal-appointed experts as compared to party-appointed experts, may not be shared by all, as is evident in an article by Sachs and Schmidt-Ahrendts: "By aligning the requirements for a party-appointed and tribunal-appointed experts, the 2010 IBA Rules stress that both type of experts, at least in principle, are subject to the same standards of quality, accuracy and independence", and further, ". . . art. 5.2(a) and (c) highlights the fact that the party-appointed expert has to be impartial and independent." Dr. Klaus Sachs, Dr. Nils Schmidt-Ahrendts, "Expert Evidence Under the 2010 IBA Rules", *International Arbitration Law Review*, Vol. 13, No. 5, pp. 217–218 (2010).

these conditions as relevant to a tribunal's weighing of the probative value of the expert report, and not as a matter of admissibility. Indeed this is an approach commonly adopted in international arbitration, as the comments of one well-experienced tribunal chairman, who possesses a civil law background, indicates:

> [W]hen counsel in an arbitration starts to question the independence of experts, I always say there are no independent experts from the moment they are paid by the parties. That's an objective point. From the moment you are paid by a party, objectively you are not independent. The problem is the reliability of your report.[15]

5.15 This view captures the approach widely adopted in modern practice. In international arbitration, a tribunal may admit and give weight to testimony provided by experts who have a commercial relationship with a party, including one of employment[16] or, previous and on-going consultancy.[17] This principle also holds true in regard to connections

---

15 NAI Case No. 3702, Comment of 18 May 2011 [Hearing Transcript] (unreported). See also Harris' general agreement with this approach although he acknowledges that the wording of art. 5.2(c) may support the view that the disclosure statement regarding independence could give rise to challenges on the question of admissibility: "One particular concern is whether the new disclosure requirements will lead to challenges being made to experts appointed by the other party. . . . Whilst the better view is that the purpose of disclosure of such relationships is to enable the tribunal to take these matters into account for the purpose of determining the weight to give to an expert's evidence, the disclosure requirements give credence to the suggestion that such matters may properly form the basis for a challenge." Harris, *supra* n. 14, p. 213. On this point one may have further reference to the Chartered Institute of Arbitrators approach to the question: "An expert's opinion shall be impartial, objective, unbiased and uninfluenced by the pressures of the dispute resolution process or by any Party." Chartered Institute of Arbitrators, *Protocol for the Use of Party-Appointed Expert Witnesses in International Arbitration* ("CIArb Protocol"), art. 4.1. Conspicuously absent from the requirement is that the witness is "independent". Nevertheless, the CIArb Protocol does contain a disclosure requirement similar to art. 5.2(c) as well as an express statement in art. 4.2 that the mere fact that an expert is paid for his or her analysis does not "vitiate an expert's impartiality". One may consider that the Protocol's view is that impartiality and not independence is the issue which the tribunal should be most concerned. By analogy, one may further consider that the disclosure statement in art. 5.2(c) should be viewed as ultimately establishing the impartiality of an expert, or lack thereof.

16 See the view of a panel of the Iran-US Claims Tribunal which rejected the challenge by the respondent to the claimant's expert arguing that the report was per se unreliable because the expert was an employee of the claimant: "Mr. Thorne is a leading officer of the Claimant company and the President of SISA. In that last capacity he was ultimately responsible for the maintenance of the rigs. Although the Tribunal in principle does not accept NIOC's objection to Claimant's experts as unreliable because of their alleged master-servant relationship with Claimant, Mr. Thorne's close affiliation to Claimant and SISA could quite naturally have caused a certain subjectivity (which must be distinguished from bad faith) to taint his assessment." *Sedco Inc v Iranian National Oil Co and the Islamic Republic of Iran*, Award No. 309-129-3, para. 75 (7 July 1987). Although noticeably reserved in its comments, the following Danish Building and Construction Arbitration Board tribunal provides an interesting consideration of this issue: "The disputed exhibits contain among other things descriptions of observations made by the employees of the contractor in connection with the repair, as well as descriptions of the measures taken in the remedying of the works. Those of the contractor's employees who participated in remedying the defects can in any event be cross-examined about these issues. Even though the reports contain assessments as to the underlying causes of the defects, the claimant should not be prevented from submitting the reports, in a situation where a joint expert survey is no longer possible and where the arbitrators have technical insight. This said, we have not decided on the evidential value of the exhibits." Jørgensen, *supra* n. 1, p. 482.

17 In an LCIA arbitration the tribunal received an expert report from an accounting expert who disclosed that he had previously provided services on behalf of a shareholder to one of the parties. These services had impacted upon an agreement that was relevant to the proceedings. The tribunal, considering the nature of the work the expert had performed, noted the following: "[The Expert] explained his view, 'this background knowledge had not been of relevance to the instruction to carry out the production of [his] expert report and subsequent addenda and that the work has not prevented [him] in any way from forming an independent view on the matters set forth' in that report and addenda. The tribunal concludes that [the expert's] independence has not been impaired by virtue of that connection." LCIA Case No. 81079, Final Award, para. 138 (2009) (unpublished).

between an expert and an adverse party[18] and to some extent, connections between a party-appointed expert and the arbitral tribunal.[19] Reviewing courts in some jurisdictions have gone so far as to affirmatively state that the mere existence of a relationship between the expert and the party presenting his or her testimony does not constitute grounds for excluding the expert's evidence.[20] Therefore, a party-appointed expert's relationship with the appointing party should generally not be a basis for barring such a report from the record.

5.16 Further to the above, it appears uncontroversial in international arbitration that an expert's relationship with a party or its legal advisers may be considered as a factor in assessing the weight that should be given his or her conclusions. This does not mean that such ties, or a lack of them, will be determinative of whether the expert has shown independence in performing his or her work. A tribunal may be far more interested in the

---

18 In *Jan de Nul v Egypt*, an ICSID tribunal was requested by the claimants to strike from the record a report submitted by an expert for respondent, because the expert had previously been a member of the board of directors for one of the claimants, and was not impartial. Here the tribunal noted as follows: "Whereas the Tribunal is mindful of the Claimants' allegations and of their significance, it believes that they are not of such nature as to make the report co-authored by Mr. Taillé inadmissible at this stage. The Tribunal first notes that Mr. Taillé is just one of two co-authors of the report and that no objection was presented against his co-author Mr. Brossard. The Tribunal further takes into account that the Claimants will have an opportunity to cross-examine Mr. Taillé at the hearing. On the basis of such oral testimony, the parties may then comment on the value of Mr. Taillé's evidence and the Tribunal will be in a better position to assess such value and to decide what weight to give to Mr. Taillé's evidence, if any. This ruling is made without prejudice to any later determination on the evidentiary weight or relevance." *Jan de Nul & Dredging International v the Arab Republic of Egypt*, ICSID Case No. ARB/04/13, Final Award, para. 28 (2006). The tribunal's emphasis on the ability of a party to cross-examine the expert in question, is consistent with the overall principle that any ties between an expert and a party do not automatically disqualify the expert from rendering testimony, but rather go to the weight to be assigned his or her report. See also: *Helnan v Egypt*, where an ICSID tribunal noted an allegation that an expert was or had been an employee of the party which proffered his testimony, but refused to exclude the report: "[o]n 27 September 2007, Claimant requested the Tribunal to strike Mr. Mounir Doss's [Respondent's expert witness] expert witness statement from the record and preclude him from testifying. Claimant claimed that Mr. Mounir Doss was a former employee of Helnan who was working for the Respondent's legal team making him unqualified to testify as an independent expert witness. On 28 September 2007, the Centre, on behalf of the Tribunal, requested Respondent to provide its comments in regard to Claimant's request relative to its expert witness. On 2 October 2007, the Centre communicated the Respondent's reply. Respondent stated that Mr. Mounir Doss had left Helnan employment under favourable circumstances and contested the allegation that he now worked for Respondent. On 3 October 2007, the Tribunal stated that it would accept Mr. Mounir Doss' witness statement while taking into consideration the Parties' observations." Dietmar W. Prager and Joanna E. Davidson, "*Helnan International Hotels A/S v The Arab Republic of Egypt*, ICSID Case No. ARB/05/09, 7 June 2008", *A Contribution by the ITA Board of Reporters*, paras 39–42.

19 In *World Duty Free v Kenya*, the tribunal admitted into the procedure an expert opinion by Lord Mustill on English law, even though the expert shared chambers with a member of the tribunal. While accepting Lord Mustill's statement on the law, the tribunal noted that it would not accept any representations by Lord Mustill concerning the facts or legal outcome of the case based on the facts. *World Duty Free Co Ltd v Republic of Kenya*, ICSID Case No. ARB/00/7, Final Award, paras 50 and 163 (2006). Because connections between a party and an arbitrator are fertile ground for challenges of bias brought against the arbitrator, or a final award, a cautious approach to the contacts between a party-expert and an arbitrator is warranted.

20 See, for example, the view of the English courts: "On the question of independence, Mr. Brazier had no connection with Mr. Black prior to his retainer for the purposes of the arbitration, but in any event there is no rule of law that an expert witness may not be connected with a party. I have no doubt that a court or arbitral tribunal has jurisdiction to refuse to hear an expert witness on grounds of lack of independence, but it is essentially a procedural matter. For example, in small claims it is not uncommon for a party to use an in-house expert so as to save costs. The evidence of such a witness may carry less value in the eyes of the tribunal, but that is a matter for the tribunal." *Brandeis Brokers Ltd v Black*, 2001 WL 513189 (QB 2001) p. 14. See further the view of the US courts whereby a US district court noted that failure to disclose an underlying business relationship between a party-appointed expert and the party that proffered his testimony was not a reason to set aside a final award. *Trevino Hernandez, S de RL de CV v Smart & Final Inc*, Lexis 60755 (SD Cal. 2010).

professionalism with which the expert conducted the analysis,[21] and the consistency in his or her testimony, when determining whether an expert is truly independent.[22] Thus the statement required by article 5.2(c) and 5.2(a), may be only one of several factors considered by the tribunal when appraising the independence and impartiality with which experts approached their mission.[23]

Factual assumptions and documents relied upon

5.17 Essential for the critical evaluation of an expert's testimony is a full description of the factual basis upon which his or her conclusions rest.[24] Typically, an expert will have reviewed considerable documentation over the course of reaching his or her conclusions. It is a customary rule in international arbitration that relevant information should be produced if relied upon by the expert to reach his or her conclusions. This is reflected by articles 5.2(d) and 5.2(e). Such evidence should be disclosed even where the expert has considered documents which are publicly available, or, at the very least a party should provide details allowing the adverse party and the tribunal to locate

---

21 In ICC Case No. 7365, the tribunal seated in Zurich, Switzerland, reviewed the method applied by the party-appointed expert to determine that requisite thoroughness and professionalism had been demonstrated, permitting the tribunal to regard the report as "evidence" of certain conclusions. "Although the [experts] acted as party-appointed experts, their professional competence and the approach justify to accept the [expert's] reports not merely as argument, but as evidence, subject to the Tribunal's assessment of the credibility of the experts' opinion with respect to the various factual elements." ICC Case No. 7365, Final Award, para. 14.5 (1997) (unpublished).

22 See the following considerations of a Society of Maritime Arbitrator's tribunal: "Mr. Sykes' testimony and preferred method for calculating fair market rates differed from that used by Seacor's other experts. Indeed, there were instances where Mr. Sykes both contradicted himself and brought his claimed "independent" and "expert" status into question. Rather than rely upon his own expertise and independent research to form his opinion, Mr. Sykes used operational data supplied to him by Seacor and then modified his calculations based upon opinions offered by Seacor's other experts." *Seacor Offshore Inc Ltd v US Bancorp Leasing*, Decision as to Motion to Dismiss, Final Award SMAAS, WL 34461643 (2002). See also the considerations of the tribunal in ICC Case No. 12706, seated in Singapore, in which the technical testimony of an employee for the claimant was given dispositive weight: "CW4, who is the technical services manager of the Claimants, is in my view, a credible and reliable witness who gave straightforward answers to questions asked of her during cross-examination." ICC Case No. 12706, Parial Award, para. 10.32 (2005) (unpublished).

23 Kantor provides a useful consideration of the independence criterion as it relates to expert witnesses. He identifies that the following duties are inherent to the notion of "independence" as it exists under the IBA Rules: "(1) a duty to disclose material relationships with respect to the parties, their affiliates, counsel or the dispute, including compensation arrangements; (2) a duty to provide 'full information' even if adverse: to include in any written and oral evidence all material information, whether supportive or adverse to the professional analyses and conclusions found in that expert's evidence; and (3) a duty to assess reasonableness (4) a duty to use diligence to assess, to the extent the expert has the professional background to do so, the reasonableness of assumptions provided by counsel or a party on which that expert relies in the expert evidence." "A Code of Conduct for Party-Appointed Experts in International Arbitration – Can One be Found?", *Arbitration International*, Vol. 26, No. 3, p. 374 (2010).

24 Consider the following determination of an ICDR tribunal to reject an attack on the sufficiency of a party-appointed expert's report, based upon the description of the information considered by the expert: "Respondents' broadly assert that the 'documentation remains insufficient' to justify the claims made in this arbitration. This is apparently a criticism of [the expert] . . . [the expert] and his staff spent many hours investigating, analyzing and documenting the payment of [the project] expenses. They then incorporated their findings in a comprehensive report supported by detailed schedules. Backing up the text and schedules are literally boxes of documentation gathered from third parties. Respondent's vague claim that all of this is somehow inadequate is rejected." ICDR Case No. 50168, Final Award, p. 18 (2006) (unpublished).

the publicly available information.[25] While a tribunal may admit a report that does not append relevant documents to it,[26] failure by a party to produce the relevant documents after being ordered to do so, may be cause to disregard the expert report, as was the situation in the Iran-US Claims Tribunal case, *Fredrica Riahi v Iran:* "The Tribunal cannot give credence to a party's valuation report premised on evidence that that party refused to produce. This is especially true where, as here, the Tribunal specifically ordered the production of that very evidence."[27] All may not follow this approach; nevertheless, a failure to produce underlying documentation could have a potentially negative effect upon the weight assigned to the report.[28]

5.18 There are few objections that are open to the party seeking to resist production of the documents that its own expert has relied on. In the past, some have resorted to raising claims of burden where the information is arguably voluminous. Tribunals have generally rejected such objections, reasoning that a party's right to examine the evidence used by an expert to arrive at his conclusions outweighs the burden imposed in producing it.[29] This view accords with basic notions of procedural fairness which require that the adverse party should at all times be adequately allowed to challenge an expert's conclusions if they are potentially material.

Disclosure of an expert's instructions

5.19 Generally, the inclusion of an expert's instructions in a report is helpful for the tribunal and the adverse party to have a sense of the scope of the expert's analysis. In this regard,

---

25 In the *Methanex v US* case, the UNCITRAL tribunal was confronted with a refusal by the claimant to produce documents relied upon by the proffered expert. Arguing that the information which had been relied upon was voluminous and public information, with the exception of one internal survey, the claimant sought to be excused from this provision of the IBA Rules. The tribunal responded as follows: "Whilst the Tribunal accepts the reluctance of Methanex at this stage of the proceedings not to burden the Tribunal unnecessarily 'with voluminous and often highly technical scientific papers and reports on which [Methanex's] expert reports rely . . .', that consideration does not apply to the USA currently studying Methanex's Expert Reports. Accordingly, as regards the USA, Methanex's Expert Reports must comply fully with the requirements of the IBA Rules and the Tribunal's orders; (A) As regards the 'public information', the identification of this information should be provided by Methanex to the USA and its designated experts, as requested by the USA; and (B) As regards the 'survey', access to this documentation should be provided to the USA and its designated expert witnesses, as requested by the USA." *Methanex Corp v United States of America*, NAFTA/UNCITRAL, Order of 10 October 2003, p. 1.

26 As was noted by the tribunal in ICC Case No. 11258, when faced with a request to strike witness statements from the record for failure to include documents cited to by the witnesses: ". . . it is not for a tribunal to determine on the content of declarations made by third parties to the arbitration, namely witnesses." ICC Case No. 11258, Final Award, para. 120 (2004) (unpublished).

27 *Frederica Lincoln Riahi v The Government of the Islamic Republic of Iran*, Interlocutory Award No. ITL 80-485-1, para. 517 (10 June 1992).

28 See the decisions in the Iran-US Claims Tribunal case *INA Corp v Iran:* "INA argues that the Tribunal has been furnished with insufficient information as to the basis of the Amin valuation, the principles on which it was undertaken and the documents and data on which it was based, for it to be accorded any evidential value. The Tribunal's Order of 21 January 1983 required production *inter alia* of the material which had been made available to Amin & Co but no such material was filed and the Respondent contended at the hearing that it was too voluminous to be conveniently assembled. The tribunal decided to admit the Amin Report as evidence but to take account of the lack of supporting documentation in assessing the evidential weight to be accorded to it." *INA Corp v Islamic Republic of Iran*, Award No. 184-161-1, para. 6 (13 August 1985).

29 *Ibid.* See also: ICC Case No. 11258 where the respondent resisted the request for the production of documents relied upon by its expert witness claiming that they would be burdensome to produce. The tribunal responded by rejecting such an argument and ordering production. ICC Case No. 11258, *supra* n. 26, Procedural Order No. 4, p. 5 (2003) (unpublished). Discussed further in the comments to art. 9.2(c).

article 5.2(b) calls on the expert to include a "description" of the instructions provided to him or her. Thus this reference to instructions should be seen as a general requirement to provide an overview of the scope of the instructions under which the expert prepared his or her report – a line by line recitation of the instructions is not generally required.

5.20 In some circumstances however, it may be appropriate under article 5.2(b) for an expert to reveal their instructions in greater detail. In this respect the Chartered Institute of Arbitrators' *Protocol for the Use of Party-Appointed Expert Witnesses in International Arbitration* ("CIArb Protocol") is helpful.[30] Article 5 of the CIArb Protocol states that while instructions and terms of appointment shall not be regarded as "privileged", a tribunal should not, unless there is good cause, allow or require those instructions, or appointment documents to be disclosed or further permit the questioning of the expert witness on this issue.[31] Moreover, article 5(2) of the CIArb Protocol also makes clear that drafts, working papers or other documentation created by an expert for the arbitration should be regarded as privileged. In order to reconcile article 5 of the CIArb Protocol with article 5.2(b) of the IBA Rules, one could take the approach that a description of an expert's mandate is appropriate for inclusion with his or her report, but further questioning or investigation of that point should not be allowed unless a bona fide issue has been raised as to the suitability of the expert's instructions. In this way a balance between allowing the consideration of the expert's instructions, while preventing irrelevant and unnecessary questioning to occur, can be achieved. It should also be noted that where privilege questions are considered, a tribunal must take account of the mandatory ethical or legal impediments which a party may be required to adhere to under IBA Rules article 9.2(b).

Affirmation of an expert's genuine belief in the opinions expressed

5.21 The 1999 version of the IBA Rules required the party-appointed expert to affirm the truth of the report. This approach has been modified in the 2010 version of the rules to reflect the fact that an expert's role is often to provide a genuine analysis, and not to attest to the truth of certain facts. In this context it may be considered that one should not be held to guarantee the correctness of the facts underlying an analysis. Rather, it is for the expert to provide a reasoned view that applies, in good faith, his or her expertise to the question at hand. Thus the correction to the affirmation set forth in the 2010 version of article 5.2(g), which now requires the expert to assert his or her genuine belief in the opinions expressed in the expert report, was welcomed as a better reflection of current practice.[32] This change should not, however,

---

30 Chartered Institute of Arbitrators, *supra* n. 15. While a number of points in this chapter are taken from the CIArb Protocol, the reader is advised that this document, taken as a whole, may not be considered as indicative of international arbitration practice. See, for instance, the view of Kantor, who notes the criticism the CIArb Protocol has received for: "following too closely the practice of English Courts", Mark Kantor, *supra* n. 23, p. 332. However, the CIArb Protocol does contain some helpful suggestions, even if to adopt the entire document may not be consistent with general arbitral practice.

31 While not concerning "instructions" per se, in ICC Case No. 11258 a tribunal of well-experienced arbitrators of mixed civil and common law backgrounds declined to order the production of an expert's notes that had been made during an interview with the instructing party's representatives. ICC Case No. 11258, *supra* n. 26, para. 116.

32 Harris notes that: "whilst witnesses of fact give evidence of fact from their own knowledge, and therefore an affirmation of truth of that evidence is appropriate, for expert witnesses what is important is the opinions they state represent their genuine professional views and have not been unduly influenced by the party instructing them." Harris, *supra* n. 14, p. 213. However, it should be noted that some tribunals did follow the previous

be seen to lower, or call into question the duty incumbent on experts to provide accurate descriptions of the facts they are informed of, and have relied upon, and to answer questions concerning their report with truthfulness. The duty to act with honesty in the presentation of their findings remains binding upon experts under the IBA Rules.[33]

5.22 The utility of oaths, or formal affirmations in international arbitration, has been questioned by some.[34] Nevertheless, a general consensus on this issue has not yet been achieved. There are notable examples of situations where tribunals have required experts to affirm the genuineness of their testimony, or otherwise provide the expert report under oath.[35] This issue may be influenced largely by the legal culture of the parties or the members of the tribunal, or the requirements of the *lex arbitri* and procedural rules. These influences notwithstanding, it would seem that where an affirmation is required, the formula set forth in article 5.2(g) is to be generally preferred in respect of expert witnesses unless mandatory law would require another formulation.[36] Additionally, there is a discernable practice in international arbitration in favour of requiring experts to affirm a duty to assist the tribunal in establishing the facts of the case. An example may be drawn from an LCIA arbitration, where the following description of an expert's statement on this point was included: "[The Expert] made a declaration in his Expert Report, and again before the Tribunal, in which he recognized that his duty to the Tribunal overrides

---

formula as found in the 1999 version of the IBA Rules. See, for example: *Nobel Ventures v Romania*, Procedural Order No. 2, referred to in the final award: "[u]nless otherwise agreed by the Parties: Examination of witnesses and experts presented by Claimant. For each: a) Affirmation of witness or expert to tell the truth." Dietmar W. Prager, "*Noble Ventures Inc v Romania*, ICSID Case No. ARB/01/11, 12 October 2005", *A Contribution by the ITA Board of Reporters*.

33 In the *Chantiers de l'Atlantique SA v Gaztransport & Technigaz SAS* case before the English courts, it was considered whether a witness who had acted as a quasi-expert, had deliberately mislead the arbitral tribunal constituted under the ICC Rules who had also applied the IBA Rules to the proceedings. The specific issue was whether in his written report, and in his presentation at the hearing, the expert had made misleading statements, improperly enhancing the probative value of certain test results that were favourable to his findings, and also had concealed the existence of test results demonstrating inconsistent conclusions. It was demonstrated before the court that the expert was aware of the inconsistencies in his statements at the time of making them. Upon reviewing the written analysis which the expert had provided, as well as the power-point presentation which had been made to the tribunal, the court found that indeed the expert had misled the arbitrators concerning these facts underlying his analysis: "[t]his was serious deception of the tribunal by the head of the Research and Development Department of GTT who had been deputed to present GTR's technical case to the tribunal. That is fraud by GTT as a party to the arbitration for the purposes of section 68(2)(g) of the Arbitration Act." *Chantiers de l'Atlantique SA v Gaztransport & Technigaz SAS* [2011] EWHC 3383 (Comm), para. 291. While in this instance the expert was affiliated closely with a party, it is submitted that a similar result could occur where an outside expert colludes with a party to misrepresent aspects of the technical analysis presented to the tribunal. Thus the IBA Rules should be read as consistent with the universal requirement that experts testify with honesty regarding their findings and the basis for their conclusions.

34 Kantor reports the following in regard to oaths administered to experts: "Many international arbitrators do not in any event consider the administration of an oath to be part of international arbitration." Kantor, *supra* n. 23, p. 327.

35 See the procedural instruction in ICC Case No. 12761: "The Expert Report will be sworn on oath and shall: (a) state the name and address of the expert, their relationship with the Parties and a curriculum vitae which evidences their technical knowledge; (b) be signed by the expert, indicating the place and date of the signature." ICC Case No, 12761, *supra*. n. 9, p. 74. See also: the admonition by the chairman of the tribunal in ICC Case No. 14069, provided in accordance with Swiss law. "You will be heard today as an expert witness before a private arbitral tribunal . . . it is my duty to draw your attention to the fact that false testimony is a criminal offence under Swiss law, and I would like you to confirm to the audience that you will tell the truth?" ICC Case No. 14069, Transcript, pp. 469–470 (2009) (unpublished).

36 See: comments to art. 8.4, which contain a further discussion of the use of oaths and affirmations in oral hearings.

his obligation to the party who engaged him".[37] While this practice may be influenced by common-law procedure, the use of such statements in international arbitration have gained acceptance amongst some civil-law arbitrators as well.[38] Although such affirmations may be applied congruently with the IBA Rules, it should be noted that art. 5.2 does not impose this requirement.

Ethical guidance for counsel regarding expert witness reports

5.23 As is the case with fact witnesses, the IBA Guidelines contain several provisions relevant to the presentation of expert witness. Similar to fact witnesses, guideline 11 requires counsel to avoid the submittal of false expert statements. Per the sub-paragraphs of this guideline, counsel should advise experts to testify truthfully, take reasonable steps to prevent the submission of knowingly false statements, and urge experts to correct the record where prior statements are discovered to have been incorrect.

5.24 Guideline 22 reflects in part the duty of counsel to ensure that the statement in IBA Rules article 5.2(g) is truthfully given. For counsel, working with an expert means striking the delicate balance between ensuring that the expert's mandate is both understood and fulfilled, while refraining from unduly influencing the analysis or conclusions that are reached. Where guideline 22 advises that, "A Party representative should seek to ensure that an Expert Report reflects the Expert's own analysis and opinion" it places an ethical duty on counsel to ensure that the statement given pursuant to article 5.2(g) is reflective of the process leading to the final report.

5.25 The above notwithstanding, the IBA Guidelines also establish that it is not wrong for counsel to assist experts in the preparation of their report. Guideline 20 makes specific provisions for this in relation to both fact witnesses and experts. Further to this point, guideline 24 confirms that counsel may meet with an expert to "discuss and prepare their prospective testimony." Even though these guidelines apply to both types of witnesses, the level of assistance that would be appropriate for counsel to give to an expert, as compared to a fact witness, will likely vary.

Rebuttal expert reports

Article 5.3 2010 IBA Rules: **If Experts Reports are submitted, any Party may, within the time ordered by the Arbitral Tribunal, submit to the Arbitral Tribunal and to the other Parties revised or additional Experts Reports, including reports or statements from persons not previously identified as Party-Appointed Experts, so long as any such revisions or additions respond only to matters contained in another Party's Witness Statements, Expert Reports or other submissions that have not been previously presented in the arbitration.**

---

37 LCIA Case No. 81079, *supra* n. 17, para. 138.

38 See the following admonition of the chairman of an NAI tribunal: "I also insist to say that you are here to assist not the parties but the Arbitral Tribunal to reach a solution to the issues in dispute." NAI Case No. 3702, *supra* n. 15, p. 374, ln. 1–12.

General discussion

5.26 Article 5.3 addresses the submission of expert reports after the initial filing of a report in support of the case-in-chief or defence-in-chief. As in the case with rebuttal documentary evidence and fact witness statements, such latter submissions will often be restricted to reports that fit the category of rebuttal or reply evidence. This is made evident by the wording of article 5.3 which requires such reports to "respond only to matters contained in another Party's Witness Statements, Expert Reports or other submissions".

5.27 The rule set forth in article 5.3 generally affirms the tribunal's right to insist that responsive expert reports be narrowly tailored to points of rebuttal.[39] In some instances, a tribunal may be inclined to accept an expert's statement to the extent the report is responsive to a previous statement, but otherwise reject those aspects that are not.[40] Naturally, a party should be afforded the opportunity to respond to material points raised by the adverse side, thus a tribunal will often consider that fairness will require it to permit expert testimony to be revised, and resubmitted if needed to address a technical point that has been raised.[41] For a further consideration of rebuttal evidence, the reader is directed to the comments to article 3.11.

---

39 See, generally: comments to art. 3.11, which discuss what is considered "rebuttal" evidence in international arbitration. As a general example of the exercise of this procedural discretion, see the following procedural determination of the tribunal in an NAFTA/UNCITRAL arbitration: "By July 5, 2007, the Claimants file their Rebuttal Memorial on Jurisdiction with any further evidence (documents, witness statements, expert statements), but only in rebuttal to Respondent's Reply memorial or regarding new evidence." *Consolidated Cases Concerning the Border Closing Due to BSE Concerns (Canadian Cattlemen for Fair Trade v United States of America)*, Award on Jurisdiction, UNCITRAL/NAFTA, para. 14. (2008). See also: *Burimi SRL and Eagle Games SH.A v Republic of Albania*, ICSID Case No. ARB/11/18, Procedural Order No. 3, dated January 9, 2013: "Regarding the request for exclusion of the Respondent's expert reports: Pursuant to Procedural Order No. 1, paragraph 14(b), the Tribunal concludes that the expert reports submitted by the Respondent with its Rejoinder are admissible because they are responsive to arguments made by the Claimants in their Reply of October 17, 2012. Therefore, the Tribunal denies the Claimants' request to exclude such reports."

40 The past practice of international tribunals has often been to evaluate the nature of the evidence that was submitted to determine that it meets the standard of "rebuttal evidence". It follows that where particular evidence does not meet that standard it should be excluded, and conversely, where it does it should be admitted. See: the following ruling of the Iran-US Tribunal: "It is evident that all of the material contained in these items was available to Iran and could have been submitted to the Tribunal with Iran's earlier filings. As such, the Tribunal finds that these items do not constitute proper items of rebuttal, which the Tribunal has described as "material submitted in response to specific evidence previously filed. The Tribunal concludes that all exhibits submitted . . . are inadmissible". *Eastman Kodak Co v the Government of Iran*, Award No. 514-227-3, para. 6 (1 July 1991). See also the ruling of the Iran-US Claims Tribunal in *Teichman Inc v Hamdan Glass Co*: "On examination, much of what it contains does not appear to fall within the definition of "rebuttal" as being material page submitted in response to specific evidence previously filed. It consists largely of new material, presented in support of Hamadan's defence and counterclaims, and seemingly unrelated to any of the documents filed in evidence by Teichmann. The admission of such a document so close to the hearing date would effectively deprive the opposing party of an opportunity to examine and rebut a large body of new material. The Tribunal, therefore, decides not to admit this document in evidence." *Henry F. Teichman Inc v Hamdan Glass Co*, Award No. 264-264-1, para. 23 (12 November 1986).

41 See the following affirmation of this principle by a CAS tribunal applying Swiss law: "[u]nder the Swiss *Private International Law Act*, the right to be heard in adversarial proceedings specifically guarantees each party's right to participate in the evidentiary proceedings, to rebut allegations made by the opposite party, to examine and criticize evidence adduced by the opposite party and to bring its own evidence in rebuttal before an award is rendered to its detriment." *S. v Fédération Internationale de Natation (FINA)*, Award of 19 October 2000 – CAS 2000/A/274 in Matthieu Reeb (ed), *Recueil des sentences du TAS/Digest of CAS Awards II 1998–2000*, p. 400.

Ordering party-appointed experts to meet and confer

Article 5.4 2010 IBA Rules: **The Arbitral Tribunal in its discretion may order that any Party-Appointed Experts who will submit or who have submitted Expert Reports on the same or related issues meet and confer on such issues. At such meeting, the Party-Appointed Experts shall attempt to reach agreement on the issues within the scope of their Expert Reports, and they shall record in writing any such issues on which they reach agreement, any remaining areas of disagreement and the reasons therefore.**

General discussion

5.28 As noted at the outset of this chapter the utilisation of party-appointed expertise creates a propensity towards the so-called "battle of the experts". It has been rightly noted that this outcome does not serve the search for truth very well, as a tribunal's understanding of the technical nature of a case may not helped by the submission of conflicting expert reports on matters of a technical nature.[42]

5.29 To deal with such situations, various procedural tools have been developed for wading through the technical mire. One such tool is restated in article 5.4 where it is noted that a tribunal may require the experts to meet and confer in regard to their respective reports. This simple but useful procedural mechanism permits arbitrators to narrow the issues by directing the experts to determine in a joint report where the differences between their respective positions lie, as well as points of common ground.[43] It is the rare situation that two experts are utterly unable to find any points of agreement between their respective analyses.

5.30 Article 5.4 may be used in combination with other procedural approaches to further disentangle the experts in an arbitration. One common approach is to require the party-appointed experts to appear during the hearing to testify jointly.[44] Under IRA Rules article

---

42 "Indeed, one of the criticisms of this system is that the result is a battle of experts of doubtful neutrality, or even of declared partiality, the prize going to the more articulate and convincing one, not necessarily to the one telling the truth, the whole truth and nothing but the truth." Giovanni De Berti, "Experts and Expert Witnesses in International Arbitration: Adviser, Advocate or Adjudicator?" *Austrian Yearbook on International Arbitration*, Vol. 2011, p. 54 (2011).

43 See: *SD Myers v Canada*, whereby the tribunal ordered the following procedure, appointing an expert to analyse the dispute between two party-appointed experts: "As soon as practicable thereafter, and in consultation with the Disputing Parties, the Tribunal will decide whether a Tribunal expert should be appointed pursuant to art. 27(1) of the UNCITRAL Rules to assist in the determination of issues that are outstanding as between the Disputing Parties' expert witnesses; and, if so, the Terms of reference of any such Tribunal expert." *SD Myers v Government of Canada*, NAFTA/UNCITRAL, Procedural Order No. 17, p. 3 (26 February 2001).

44 See the discussion of witness conferencing in the comments to art. 8.3. See also: *William Ralph Clayton, William Richard Clayton, Douglas Clayton, Daniel Clayton and Bilcon of Delaware Inc v Government of Canada*, UNCITRAL, PCA Case No. 2009-04, Procedural Order No. 18, p. 4: "5.1 Expert reports shall stand in lieu of direct examination during the oral hearing. Accordingly, experts shall appear for testimony at the oral hearing only if they are called by the opposing Party or the Tribunal for cross-examination. By April 26, 2013, each Disputing Party shall notify in writing to the other Disputing Party, with a copy to the Tribunal, the names of the experts it wishes to cross-examine at the hearing. By May 22, 2013, each Disputing Party may amend its notification in light of the other Disputing Party's comments on any submissions from the Governments of Mexico or the United States of America. 5.2 The provisions of Sub-sections 4.2, 4.3, and 4.5 [regarding examination of witness] shall apply mutatis mutandis to the evidence of experts. 5.3 In addition to, and following, cross-examination of experts by the Disputing Parties, the Tribunal may require experts with corresponding areas of specialization to

8.3(f) a tribunal may determine that following the issuance of an article 5.4 joint report, the experts should appear together for further questioning concerning their respective views at the hearing. Many have found it useful to observe and question experts at the same time in the environment of an oral hearing.[45]

5.31 Tribunals may also require experts to meet and confer as a precursor to the appointment of a tribunal-expert. Tribunals have found in the past that by requiring the experts to work towards narrowing the issues between them, allows for the tribunal-appointed expert to deal discreetly with only the most relevant points in contention. From a cost as well as procedural economy stand-point, requiring party-appointed experts to meet and confer in advance of the appointment of a tribunal-appointed expert has obvious merit.

5.32 The general duty on behalf of the parties to cooperate in the taking of evidence applies equally to the party-appointed expert appointed under article 5.4.[46] The tribunal is free to take into consideration any lack of cooperation by a party, or its expert, in this exercise. As noted in other chapters, the failure by a party to fully cooperate in the taking of evidence may result in the drawing of an adverse inference, or have negative repercussions in the awarding of costs.

Summoning a party-appointed expert to an evidentiary hearing

Article 5.5 2010 IBA Rules:	**If a Party-Appointed Expert whose appearance has been requested pursuant to Article 8.1 fails without a valid reason to appear for testimony at an Evidentiary Hearing, the Arbitral Tribunal shall disregard any Expert Report by that Party-Appointed Expert related to that Evidentiary Hearing unless, in exceptional circumstances, the Arbitral Tribunal decides otherwise.**
Article 5.6 2010 IBA Rules:	**If the appearance of a Party-Appointed Expert has not been requested pursuant to Article 8.1, none of the other Parties shall be deemed to have agreed to the correctness of the content of the Expert Report.**

General discussion

5.33 Article 5.5 adopts a position which mirrors that of article 4.7 pertaining to fact witnesses, providing that the failure of a witness to attend a hearing is generally regarded as grounds for disregarding that expert's report. In addition, article 5.6 also reflects the general position taken on fact witnesses by noting that a decision to not call a witness is not to be interpreted as an acceptance of that expert's testimony. While much of the rationale

---

give evidence concurrently and to discuss any areas of disagreement between them in the presence of the Tribunal (expert conferencing)."

45 See: Wolfgang Peter, "Witness 'Conferencing'", *Arbitration International*, Vol. 18, No. 1, p. 47, for a general discussion of witness conferencing in international arbitration. See also the comments of the chairman of an ICDR tribunal in response to a question from an expert as to why she would be heard together with the adverse party's expert: "Well, we were informed in advance of what your position would be. It is my wish to have both witnesses declaring at the same time to see how one reacts to the questions of the other." ICDR Case No. 50T180, Transcript of 2 October 2002, p. 83, ln. 11–13 (unpublished).

46 See, generally: comments to art. 9.7.

behind these rules is discussed in chapter 4 in the comments to the corresponding portions concerning fact witnesses, the comments below consider some particular issues as they relate to party-appointed expert witnesses.

Failure by an expert to attend a hearing

5.34 While it may be true that cost and scheduling are factors will lead to difficulties in presenting an expert witness at a hearing, it is generally considered that such problems regarded as risks borne by the party proffering the expert's testimony in support of their case. The position adopted in international arbitration was summarised by the ICSID tribunal in *Aguas del Tunari SA v Republic of Bolivia* in response to a complaint by the claimant that it would incur considerable expense should it be forced to present its experts for examination at the hearing:

> The Tribunal observed that it is, in its view, customary in international arbitration that such witnesses, whether they are experts in law or witnesses of fact, be made available for examination if so requested.[47]

5.35 This customary rule accords with norms of procedural fairness, as there is little doubt that a party has a right to challenge evidence presented against it. As this principle translates to expert evidence, it naturally implies that a tribunal should afford a party a procedurally fair opportunity to challenge an expert on his or her report.[48] It follows therefore that where an expert who has proffered a statement in the arbitration does not appear at the hearing, the consequence should be that the statement is excluded from the proceedings.

5.36 The above notwithstanding, there are known instances where tribunals have not enforced this rule against experts, despite otherwise applying it to fact witnesses.[49] The reasons for this deviation from the standard rule may vary, but one possible explanation may be that a tribunal will often determine the weight to be assigned to an expert report based

---

47 *Aguas del Tunari SA v Republic of Bolivia*, ICSID Case No. ARB/02/3, Decision on Respondent's Objections to Jurisdiction, paras. 40, 41 (2005).

48 See the determination of an UNCITRAL tribunal that a proper opportunity to cross-examine an expert was required in order to safe-guard an equal opportunity to present one's case: "In response to the Claimant's request dated August 20, 2002 for clarification of the Tribunal's Order No. Q 13, the Tribunal advised the parties that Order No. Q 13 does not change the Tribunal's prior orders directing that each party has half of the allocated hearing time. The Tribunal advised that it may deviate from this principle, if appropriate, to safeguard each party's being given an equal opportunity to present its case in an appropriate manner. This shall apply in particular in respect to the cross-examination of the parties' experts . . .". *CME Czech Republic BV v The Czech Republic*, UNCITRAL, Final Award, para. 80 (2003). See also: *Adel A Hamadi Al Tamimi v Sultanate of Oman*, ICSID Case No. ARB/11/33, Procedural Order No. 8, April 18, 2014, p. 2, in which Claimant refused to present its party-appointed expert for cross-examination and asked to withdraw its expert report. Respondent objected to the withdrawal and requested that: "the [expert] Report should remain in the record and the Tribunal should draw from it whatever inferences it concludes are warranted in the circumstances." The Tribunal held that: "The Respondent's Application is therefore granted by consent. [The expert] shall not appear for cross-examination, but its report shall remain in the record and the Tribunal, after receiving further submissions, if any, during the proceedings, may draw whatever inferences, if any, it considers are warranted in the circumstances." *Id.*

49 See the rule adopted in the following award: "In case a witness whose presence at the hearing was requested does not show up, his or her written statement shall be disregarded. This rule will not apply to expert reports." *Karaha Bodas Co LLC v Perusahaan Pertambangan Minyak Dan Gas Bumi Negara*, as reported in David D. Caron, Lee M. Caplan, Matti Pellonpää, *The UNCITRAL Arbitration Rules*, pp. 649–650 (2006).

on whether the expert's conclusions logical, and follow the relevant facts.[50] These issues may, in some circumstances, be sufficiently challengeable in writing by rebuttal experts and to this extent the need for an in-person hearing is somewhat mitigated. This may not be so in the case of fact witnesses. A fact witness' credibility will often turn on whether they appear, under the pressure of cross-examination, to be believable regarding what he or she claims to have witnessed. The most widely accepted means of testing the memory of a fact witness is in-person cross-examination. Thus, where an expert is not testifying from memory, but a fact witness is, an in-person cross-examination is difficult to dispense with in the case of a fact witness.

5.37 The above notwithstanding, it is far from clear that this distinction would be largely accepted in international arbitration. Rather, it seems that tribunals in many instances are perfectly willing to enforce the rule set forth in article 5.5 where an expert, without good cause, fails to appear at a hearing.[51]

Determining not to call or cross-examine an expert witness

5.38 Article 5.6 adopts a rule generally accepted in regard to fact witnesses and applies it to expert testimony, which is to say that the failure to call an expert witness to a hearing should not be deemed an acceptance of that expert's conclusions. This rule is not controversial in international arbitration, but the corollary point that a failure to challenge a witness, or an expert, may be taken note of by the tribunal when weighing the unchallenged report, is often missed. Consider the following statement by an UNCITRAL tribunal seated in Miami, Florida, where this rule was articulated:

> While (the respondent) has not agreed that the witness statements it did not specifically challenge in cross-examination are to be considered true and accurate, it did not take advantage of the opportunity to test the veracity of the witnesses and only sought to challenge their evidence indirectly and (the claimant) has been very emphatic throughout that it considered unchallenged witness statements to be admitted as truthful and undisputed. Further, (the respondent) did not lead specific, detailed contrary evidence. In these circumstances, direct, probative witness statements will normally be accepted by the Tribunal unless there is a valid basis for discounting them. With respect to witness evidence central or critical to a claim, there is generally considered to be an onus on a party to challenge the witness in cross-examination, particularly if the party is challenging

---

50 Where a report provided a full analysis of the facts used to arrive at the conclusions set forth, it was noted in *ADC et al. v the Republic of Hungary* that: "The Tribunal would like to point out here that the LECG reports are, in the Tribunal's view, an example as to how damages calculations should be presented in international arbitration; they reflect a high degree of professionalism, clarity, integrity and independence by financial expert witnesses." *ADC Affiliate Ltd and ADC & ADMC Management Ltd v The Republic of Hungary*, ICSID Case No. ARB/03/16, Final Award, para. 516 (2006). See also: *Adem Dogan v Turkmenistan*, ICSID Case No. ARB/09/9, Decision on Annulment, 15 January 2016: "[T]he Respondent argues that it was denied the opportunity to be heard regarding the forgery of the Participation Agreement. The Tribunal refused to consider an Expert Report submitted by the Respondent 'which proves beyond any doubt that this document is inauthentic.' Yet, the Tribunal relied primarily, if not exclusively, on the Participation Agreement as evidence of the Claimant's interest in the Farm. Without going into the details of the Tribunal's assessment of the evidence, the Committee is of the view that the Tribunal duly considered the above issues in the light of the available evidence. The Tribunal identified the evidence it considered relevant to reject the allegation of forgery of the Participation Agreement, found that the Claimant had financed the equipment for the Farm and was not a seller of the same, and examined the different position that the Claimant had taken before the Turkmen courts. In conclusion, the Respondent's request for annulment of the Award on the ground of a serious departure from a fundamental rule of procedure is rejected."

51 See the discussion of *Vivendi et al. v Argentina* in the comments to art. 4.5.

that witness's credibility. This is particularly so when the witness is available and is cross-examined on other issues.[52]

5.39 A tribunal is free to accept the unchallenged conclusions included in the report where it deems it appropriate to do so. This being said, tribunals should consider the entire context of the expert report before accepting its conclusions to determine whether it is complete, logical and consistent with the evidence on record and circumstances of the case.[53]

---

52 As reported in Poupak Anjomshoaa and John Bellhouse, "The Implications of a Failure to Cross-Examine in International Arbitration", 23–6 *Mealey's Int'l Arb Rep* 19 (2008).

53 In this regard, a tribunal may consider the standard often applied to tribunal-appointed experts, which may be also applied to a party-appointed expert's report. "It is certain that the opinion of the expert does not bind the Commission which must decide according to its own conviction. But taking account of the facts and evaluation techniques, there is no reason for the court not adopting as its own the conclusion of the expert, unless his argumentation is in contradiction with the facts of record, with the legal provisions of the rules or logic." Durward V. Sandifer, *Evidence Before International Tribunals*, Procedural Aspects of International Law Series, Vol. 13, p. 327 (1975). Citing to the *Héritiers de SAR Mgr le Duc de Guise* decision. See also an articulation of this principle by an ICSID tribunal: "In accordance with the parties' shared understanding, as expressed in the letters referred to above, the Tribunal will consider the written statements of those witnesses and experts who have not been called to testify at the hearing as part of the evidentiary record and evaluate those statements in light of the record as well as the oral testimony of the witnesses and experts called to testify at the hearing." Dietmar W. Prager and Ana Frischtak, "*Duke Energy International Peru Investments No. 1 Ltd v Republic of Peru*, ICSID Case No. ARB/03/28, 18 August 2008", *A Contribution by the ITA Board of Reporters*, para. 29.

CHAPTER 6

Tribunal-appointed experts and inspections

Introduction

6.01 Civil-law jurisdictions have historically made great use of court-appointed experts. One may further observe that in the practice of international arbitration such procedures are permitted as well,[1] and are more generally accepted as part of international judicial procedure.[2] This method of adducing evidence is inquisitorial in nature as it is carried out at the direction of the tribunal, and not the parties.[3] In this respect, the tribunal-appointed expert is an individual who advises the tribunal through the creation of a report, and perhaps also through oral testimony that is entered into the evidentiary record of the arbitration. The process of appointing an expert poses several issues for consideration, in particular the manner of appointment and the instructions to the expert, the means and method of compiling a report, and the extent to which the expert's findings may be adopted by the tribunal.

6.02 Another procedure that is inquisitorial in nature and is a well-established feature in international arbitration is the inspection or site visit.[4] This method of adducing evidence calls for the tribunal, or the expert on behalf of the tribunal, to undertake a visit to a site[5] or area (such as a boundary) or to otherwise inspect an item (such as machinery), which is relevant to the arbitration. The underlying rationale for a site visit is to allow the tribunal

---

1 Sandifer recalls that: "Evidence furnished by expert witnesses or obtained through an inquiry by experts (*expertise*) normally stands in high repute in the procedure of civil law countries, being second in importance only to so called authentic documents." Durward V. Sandifer, *Evidence Before International Tribunals*, p. 197 (rev. edition, 1975). See further the comments to art. 6.1 in regard to the use of experts in international arbitration.

2 *Ibid.*, p. 335, where Sandifer discusses the use of court appointed experts before the PCIJ and the ICJ, in particular citing to the *Corfu Channel* case.

3 Sanders notes that: "In the civil law tradition, the trier of facts takes an active role in determining matters requiring expertise, including readily appointing its own expert on technical matters. In the common law approach, the parties are primarily responsible for presenting their cases, including the presentation of expert witnesses. Although the trier of fact can appoint its own experts, or special masters, usually the parties present their cases at their own risk; that is, they suffer the consequences of failing to make our their cases and the court rarely steps in." P. Sanders, "commentary on UNCITRAL Arbitration Rules", P. Sanders (ed.), *Yearbook Commercial Arbitration*, Vol.II, p. 204 (1972). Poudret and Besson note that: "In civil law countries, expert opinions are usually given by an independent expert who is appointed by the court and who acts in accordance with the judge's directions." Jean-François Poudret and Sébastien Besson, *Comparative Law of International Arbitration*, p. 560, para. 662 (2nd edition, 2007).

4 Consistent with the "inquisitorial" nature of an inspection or site visit, Bin Cheng makes the following connection to the taking of judicial notice: "In this connection it may be mentioned that the information obtained by a tribunal through an inspection of the places concerned in the proceedings (*descente sur les lieux*), a procedure which has sometimes been applied in international arbitral and judicial proceedings, presents considerable affinity with judicial notice." Bin Cheng, *General Principles of Law as Applied by International Courts and Tribunals* (1987).

5 As an example of a large-scale site visit, see the Order on Interim Measures recalling the decision of the tribunal in the *Indus Waters Kishenganga Arbitration*, whereby the tribunal undertook a six-day tour of a hydroelectric dam project and inspected relevant waterways by helicopter. *Islamic Republic of Pakistan v Republic of India (Indus Waters Kishenganga Arbitration)* (23 September 2011).

or the expert to obtain a first-hand understanding of an important issue in the case. This purpose notwithstanding, because the conduct of a visit or inspection is something which involves the active participation of the tribunal in the process of adducing evidence, reflection on whether the process will afford the parties a fair and equal opportunity to be heard on the matter is generally warranted.

6.03 The IBA Rules cover both of these issues. In particular, article 6 of the rules provides the procedure for appointing an expert as well as guidelines concerning the content of the report and other rules affirming the tribunal's control over the procedure. Inspections and site visits are mentioned in articles 6.3 and 7 of the IBA Rules, and provide guidance on the conduct of such procedures. These and related issues are further discussed below.

Appointment and mandate of tribunal-appointed expert

Article 6.1 2010 IBA Rules:	**The Arbitral Tribunal, after consulting with the Parties, may appoint one or more independent Tribunal-Appointed Experts to report to it on specific issues designated by the Arbitral Tribunal. The Arbitral Tribunal shall establish the terms of reference for any Tribunal-Appointed Expert Report after consulting with the Parties. A copy of the final terms of reference shall be sent by the Arbitral Tribunal to the Parties.**
Article 26(1)(a) UNCITRAL Model Law:	(1) Unless otherwise agreed by the parties, the arbitral tribunal: (a) may appoint one or more experts to report to it on specific issues to be determined by the arbitral tribunal;

General discussion

6.04 International arbitrators tend to involve the parties early on in the process of appointing an expert.[6] This is made clear by article 6.1 wherein the tribunal is directed to appoint an expert "after consulting with the parties"; an admonition that is both practical, and which some consider a requirement of due process.[7] The subjects under discussion

---

6 Two examples drawn from arbitrations concluded under the ICC Rules demonstrate how tribunals may solicit input on this process early. See: ICC Case 13490: "D. The parties are granted a period [of two weeks] to agree on a joint nomination of an expert, or alternatively to each submit a list of maximum three expert candidates. Unless an expert is proposed by both parties, the Tribunal is at liberty to designate the expert." ICC Case No. 13490, Procedural Order of July 2006, in *ICC International Court of Arbitration Bulletin Vol. 25/Supplement – 2014*, p. 8. See also: *Bangladesh Petroleum Exploration & Production Company Ltd ("Bapex"), and Bangladesh Oil Gas and Mineral Corporation ("Petrobangla")* (ICSID Case Nos. ARB/10/11 and ARB/10/18), Procedural Order No. 7, of October 17, 2014, p. 3: "The Parties are invited to propose expert(s) for these subject matters. Failing agreement on such experts, the Tribunals may seek proposals from the International Centre for Expertise of the International Chamber of Commerce or may identify the expert(s) by any other means. Before appointing the expert(s) the Tribunals will give the Parties an opportunity to comment. The Tribunals will not be bound by these comments and will make the appointment in their considered discretion."

7 See the considerations of the WTO Appellate Body in the *Canada – Continued Suspension* case: "Scientific experts and the manner in which their opinions are solicited and evaluated can have a significant bearing on a panel's consideration of the evidence and its review of a domestic measure, especially in cases like this one involving highly complex scientific issues. Fairness and impartiality in the decision-making process are fundamental guarantees of due process. Those guarantees would not be respected where the decision-makers appoint and consult experts who are not independent or impartial. Such appointments and consultations compromise a panel's ability to act as an independent adjudicator. For these reasons, we agree with the view of the European

during such a consultation customarily include the relative need for an expert to be appointed, and may also extend to the question of who the expert ought to be. The former is discussed more fully below. In regard to the latter, the common practice is to call for the comments of the parties on the identity of a prospective expert,[8] and also the number of experts to be appointed.[9] The practical benefit to arbitrators in following this approach is that it may assist the tribunal in identifying a candidate that is sufficiently neutral and acceptable to both sides, as one tribunal constituted under the ICC Rules noted:

> Whether an individual person could "fit the bill" is really highly questionable. It might seem best for counsel to both sides to reflect on a highly reputable and experienced engineering firm which, under its roof, might have a specialist for the technical/ engineering issues and a specialist on the economic side. In any event, the Independent Expert should be seen, and accepted, by both sides, as being truly neutral. It will mean that such Independent Expert will not be seen as having a closer relationship with either one of the Parties. This may not be very easy to find, given the broad networks of the claimant companies.[10]

6.05 While it is accepted that great weight may be given to the opinion of an expert appointed by the tribunal, arbitrators and the parties must resist the tendency to view the work of the tribunal-appointed expert as an outsourcing of the arbitrator's duties. The tribunal remains, at all times, the finder of fact and of the law, and thus the obligation to render a determination must remain solely within its control. In contrast, the expert is to assist the tribunal's work by the production of a report that is to be considered as evidence. Thus, far from outsourcing its decision-making and deliberative tasks, the tribunal and the parties should regard the expert's report as evidence that will assist the tribunal to complete its mandate. This distinction is relevant for determining whether a "specific issue" has arisen within the meaning of article 6.1, as is discussed further below.

6.06 Lastly, the tribunal should consider input from the parties on the content of the terms of reference under which the expert will fulfil his or her function.[11] The terms of reference define the expert's mandate, and will often contain directives on the issues to be

---

Communities that the protection of due process applies to a panel's consultations with experts. This due process protection applies to the process for selecting experts and to the panel's consultations with the experts, and continues throughout the proceedings." *Canada – Continued Suspension of Obligations in the EC-Hormones Dispute*, WT/DS321/AB/R, adopted 16 October 2008, para. 436. See also: Poudret and Besson: "The right to be heard can play a role not only with regard to the duty of an arbitral tribunal to accede to a request for the nomination of an expert. It also confers on the parties the right to be consulted before the expertise, namely to comment on the choice of the expert and the expert's terms of reference." *Supra* n. 3, p. 562.

8   See, for instance, the procedure that was adopted by a panel of the Iran-US Claims Tribunal whereby the tribunal sought from each party nominations, under sealed envelope, of three experts. The tribunal's intention was to appoint the expert that would have appeared on both lists. In case there wasn't a common choice, the tribunal had further directed the parties to meet and confer on the matter. *Arco Exploration Inc v National Iranian Oil Co*, Case No. 21, Chamber One, Order of 7 December 1989, p. 1.

9   *Ibid.*

10   ICC Case No. 14079, Procedural Order of May 2007, in *ICC International Court of Arbitration Bulletin Vol. 25/Supplement – 2014*, p. 10.

11   This may be done through an early case management conference. See, e.g.: ICC Case No. 14079: "The Hearing Dates . . . should likewise remain blocked in everybody's calendars. In fact, based on the discussion in Chapters II-IV, those Hearing Dates could be used for a one- or two-day Experts' Terms of Reference Meeting, or for a Kick-Off Meeting with the Independent Experts (in case the Terms of Reference can be settled beforehand)." ICC Case No. 14079, Procedural Order of May 2007, in *ICC International Court of Arbitration Bulletin Vol. 25/ Supplement – 2014*, p. 12.

considered, the evidence to be taken into account, and other matters.[12] As article 6.1 makes clear, the parties must be provided with a copy of these terms once finalised, but it is also the case that their views will be considered in the drafting phase. The terms of reference and the contents included in them are more fully discussed below.

Determining when "specific issues" have arisen

6.07 The appointment of an expert is a matter of significant consequence to the arbitral procedure because, amongst other things, the cost involved may be considerable; and the impact, decisive. Therefore, the decision by a tribunal to appoint an expert is one that must not be taken lightly. The tribunal, as the finder of fact, is traditionally afforded a wide discretion in its decision to appoint an expert.[13] An appointment is only appropriate where a tribunal will be assisted by the additional expertise; according to the wording of article 6.1, a "specific issue" must have arisen for which an expert's assistance is required. It is the widely accepted practice, and it is expressly stated in article 6.1, that the tribunal should consult the parties on the need for the expert before moving forward with the appointment, although this does not mean a tribunal may not take this decision *sua sponte*.[14]

---

12 See: ICC Case No. 13490. As an example of the delimitation of the expert's mission with regard to a software dispute, the Tribunal there stated that: "The expert's mission is: (1) To verify whether the software procured by [Respondent] is fit for the purpose and is exclusively substituting the software to be delivered under the Contract; (2) To indicate whether the software supplied by [Claimant] is operational, and if not, to state the reasons therefore and to which party these reasons are attributable; (3) To indicate whether the costs borne by [Respondent] in procuring the replacement software are justified and in line with market conditions or whether it would have been possible for [Respondent] to procure the replacement software at a lesser expense and if so at which cost." ICC Case No. 13490, Procedural Order of July 2006, in *ICC International Court of Arbitration Bulletin Vol. 25/Supplement – 2014*, p. 8.

13 See: Poudret and Besson: "The arbitral tribunal can also refuse to appoint an independent expert, or even refuse to accept the report or the testimony of private experts, if it considers this measure inappropriate." Poudret and Besson, *supra* n. 3, p. 561. That being said, it is generally agreed that tribunals tend to follow the principle set forth by the International Court of Justice in the *Corfu Channel* Case in regard to the appointment of experts, in that they will only make such an appointment where an expert is needed by the tribunal to obtain, "technical information that might guide it in the search for truth." As recalled by Michael Schneider in, "[t]echnical Experts in International Arbitration", *ASA Bulletin*, Vol. 11, No. 3, p. 449 (1993). Reviewing courts in Switzerland have reinforced the Tribunal's discretion to decide to appoint an expert: "[t]hus it was held in the field of arbitration that each party had the right to express its views on the facts essential for the decision, to present its legal arguments, to propose evidence on pertinent facts and to participate in the hearings of the arbitral tribunal (ATF 127 III 576 at 2c; 116 II 639 at 4c p. 643). As to the right to adduce evidence, it must have been exercised timely and according to the applicable procedural rules (ATF 119 II 386 at 1b p. 389). The arbitral tribunal may refuse to adduce evidence without breaching the right to be heard if the evidence is unfit to base a decision on, if the fact to be proved is already established, if it is without pertinence or if the tribunal, by assessing the evidence in advance, reaches the conclusion that it is already convinced and that the evidence proposed would not change its conviction (judgment 4A_440/20106 of January 7, 2011 at 4.1)." *Federation X.____ v European Chess Union*, 4A_274/2012. The original of the decision is in French. This quote is taken from an unofficial translation. The text is available on the website of the Federal Tribunal: www.bger.ch.

14 See the following rule adopted by a NAFTA/UNCITRAL tribunal in regard to the appointment of an expert: "Subject to NAFTA Article 1133, the Arbitral Tribunal may, on its own initiative or at the request of a disputing party, appoint one or more experts. The Arbitral Tribunal shall consult with the disputing parties on the selection, terms of reference (including expert fees) and conclusions of any such expert. The Arbitral Tribunal may, on its own initiative or at the request of any disputing party, take oral evidence of such expert(s)." *Chemtura Corp v Government of Canada*, UNCITRAL/ NAFTA, Procedural Order No. 1, para. 59 (21 January 2008). See: ICC Case No. 13046: "[t]he Arbitral Tribunal may appoint one or more experts on its own

6.08 As a general principle, the mere existence of *lacunae* in the evidentiary record is not a "specific issue" within the meaning of article 6.1 giving rise to the appointment of an expert;[15] it is each party's responsibility to produce the evidence necessary to establish its allegations. Furthermore, a tribunal will likely refrain from appointing an expert if it would appear that to do so would primarily assist one side in establishing their case.[16]

6.09 In connection with the above, the substantiation of an allegation by prima facie proof is generally a pre-requisite to determining that a legitimate "specific issue" has arisen for which expert guidance is necessary.[17] If prima facie evidence has established a substantive dispute between the parties on a point of fact, the customary practice of international tribunals is to determine first whether an expert's report will truly assist

---

initiative or at the request of a Party. Before appointing an expert or fixing his terms of reference, the Arbitral Tribunal shall hear the Parties on the issue. The expert appointed by the Arbitral Tribunal shall in principle submit a written report and, at the request of one of the Parties or of the Arbitral Tribunal, may be asked to appear at a hearing to be heard in person; each Party shall be entitled to examine the expert." ICC Case No. 13046, Procedural Order No. 1 of 19 May 2004, in *ICC Bulletin, 2010 Special Supplement, Decisions on ICC Arbitration Procedure*, p. 93 (2011). See also: ICC Case No. 13490, "The Arbitral Tribunal is of the opinion that the resolution of the dispute requires additional information and has therefore decided to appoint an expert for the determination of issues relating to (i) the allegedly still missing documents, and (ii) the allegedly incomplete and/or inoperative software supplied by [Claimant] and the software procured in replacement by [Respondent]." ICC Case No. 13490, Procedural Order of July 2006, in ICC International Court of Arbitration Bulletin Vol. 25/Supplement – 2014, p. 8.

15 See the decision of the umpire in the US-German Mixed Claims Commission case, *Lehigh Valley Railroad Co, Agency of Canadian Car and Foundry Co Ltd and Various Underwriters (United States of America) v Germany*. In that arbitration, the umpire noted that in regard to the authenticity of documentary evidence before him he was confronted with the contradictory testimony of the experts retained by the respective sides. Both sets of experts urged the tribunal to conduct its own experiments on the documents to test their views on the authenticity of the evidence. The umpire ultimately declined to render a decision on such a basis, grounding his award instead on the burden of proof, wherein he noted that the lack of confidence in the evidence ultimately worked against the party whom had had the burden of establishing that the document was written and sent at the time claimed. Thus, the tribunal determined that the evidence was not authentic. *Lehigh Valley Railroad Co, Agency of Canadian Car and Foundry Co Ltd and Various Underwriters (United States of America) v Germany*, 3 December 1932, 8 RIAA, p. 121.

16 As an ICC Tribunal noted: "[t]he Tribunal is aware of the difficulties Respondent experienced in establishing that it suffered damages following deficient information in technological matters. It finds it, nevertheless, unjustified to appoint an expert with such a general mission, so as to alleviate the burden of proof upon the counter-claimant. It is preferable that the Arbitral Tribunal adjudicates on the basis of all the materials that it could receive at the conclusion of a full and complete evidentiary process." (Unofficial English translation) Final award in ICC Case No. 8264, *ICC Bulletin*, Vol. 10, No. 2, p. 62 (1999). See also the following observation by the Iran-US Claims Tribunal: "In the Tribunal's view, the question whether to appoint an expert need only be reached in a case where the party requesting the appointment has sufficiently substantiated its claims or defense. It is not the task of an expert appointed by the Tribunal to argue a party's case. As discussed in more detail below, the Ministry has not carried its burden to sufficiently substantiate its defenses to the Claim during these proceedings. Therefore, considering the circumstances of this Case, the request for the appointment of an expert is denied." *Rockwell International Systems Inc v The Government of the Islamic Republic of Iran (The Ministry of National Defence)*, Award No. 438-430-1 of 5 September 1989 in Albert Jan van den Berg (ed.), *Yearbook Commercial Arbitration*, Vol. XV, p. 239–240 (1990).

17 A panel of the Iran-US Claims Tribunal noted the following in denying a request to appoint an expert: "With regard to the Respondent's request to appoint an expert to determine the value of the shares of the Zamzam Companies, the Tribunal finds that the Respondents have not sufficiently explained or substantiated that request. In support of their allegations . . . the Respondents submitted an affidavit of the auditor of the Foundation for the Oppressed Accounting Institute. However, this quite general affidavit . . . related to only one of the Zamzam Companies and was unsupported by any financial statements or specific analysis. The Tribunal finds that this evidence is inadequate to support the Respondents' allegations and does not form a sufficient basis to warrant appointment of an expert." *PepsiCo Inc v The Islamic Republic of Iran, Zamzam Bottling Co Azerbaijan*, Case No. 18, Award No. 260-18-1 of 13 October 1986, in Albert Jan van den Berg (ed.), *Yearbook Commercial Arbitration*, Vol. XII, p. 253 (1987).

its function. The following position adopted by an ICC tribunal summarises the general approach:

> The arbitrators are at liberty to decide whether such an appointment is necessary for the solution of the case. Such an expert may be useful or even necessary for technical questions. In the present situation, such utility is in no way established. On the contrary, the questions which are typically in the field of activity of an expert have already been covered by the [first expert's] report. This report describes the work done by the defendant party and is necessary for the determination of the payment claimed by the claimants. Other questions such as the ones quoted by respondent are to be resolved by the arbitrators. Moreover, it is their duty to interpret the contractual documents and evidences filed by the parties. To appoint a second expert would lead to a replacement of the arbitrators by an expert.[18]

6.10 The above decision provides the essential rule that the appointment of an expert by the tribunal should not encroach upon the latter's duty to weigh the evidence and use its discretion[19] to arrive at appropriate conclusions.[20] As the tribunal above noted, to appoint an expert to review contract documents or other evidence for their legal significance would be to delegate to the expert a role normally fulfilled by arbitrators.[21] Thus, before any expert is appointed, it is customary to consider whether a Tribunal truly lacks the needed expertise to decide the matter, and the nature of the questions the expert will be asked

---

18 *Contractor (European Country) v Owner (Middle Eastern Country)*, Final Award in ICC Case No. 4629, in Albert Jan van den Berg (ed.), *Yearbook Commercial Arbitration*, Vol. XVIII, p. 14 (1993).

19 See, for example, the decision of an ICC tribunal, where the tribunal did not believe that the factual record would be clarified by an expert report, and thus concluded that the matter was better handled using its discretion: "In the case at hand one way would be to appoint an expert. In light of the documents in the file and taking into consideration the testimonies in the hearing the Arbitral Tribunal doubts that an expert would be able to establish the factual basis for the decision it has to make. It deems [it], therefore, more appropriate not to decide on the basis of an item by item evaluation but by using the judicial discretion . . .". Final award in ICC Case No. 11440 of 2003 in Albert Jan van den Berg (ed.), *Yearbook Commercial Arbitration*, Vol. XXXI, p. 142 (2006).

20 Caron, Caplan and Pellonpää in commenting on UNCITRAL Rules, art. 27 state the following: "The main task of the expert is to produce a report containing opinions that may guide the arbitral tribunal's decision making. In fulfilling this task, the expert must conduct his investigation in strict accordance with his terms of reference without treading upon the adjudicatory functions of the tribunal." David Caron, Lee Caplan and Matti Pellonpää, *UNCITRAL Arbitration Rules, A Commentary*, p. 673 (2006). See also: Blackaby *et al.*, "It is a well-established principle of most national systems of law that, unless authorised to do so by the terms of his appointment, someone to whom a duty has been delegated must not delegate that duty to someone else. So long as it is plain, however, that the arbitral tribunal is merely taking advice from an expert (and not attempting to delegate its task to him) it is difficult to see any objection in principle to the appointment of an expert by an arbitral tribunal." Nigel Blackaby *et al.*, *Redfern and Hunter on International Arbitration*, p. 406 (5th edition, 2009).

21 See, for example, the decision by the Italian *Corte de Cassazione* regarding a challenge to a final award where the tribunal, which was composed of non-jurists, had appointed an expert to determine matters of law. The following summary of the holding is instructive regarding the issue of delegation by the tribunal of its decision making powers to an expert: "The issue is whether Italian procedural law allows arbitrators in arbitration ritual to delegate [to] an expert, to decide legal issues which are essential to the decision-making process. This question must be answered in the negative. . . . Under Italian procedural law it does not seem possible to allow [tribunals who are mandated to apply the law] to delegate a third person to assess the legal issues which are relevant for the decision-making process." 7 June 1989 – Corte de Cassazione, No. 2765 in Albert Jan van den Berg (ed.), *Yearbook Commercial Arbitration*, Vol. XVI, p. 157 (1991). See also: *Brandeis Brokers Ltd v Herbert Black* [2001] 2 Lloyd's Rep 359, para. 68, where the reviewing English court noted that it would be a serious breach of fundamental due process if a tribunal "effectively delegated their decision making on important questions to [the Expert]."

to consider.[22] The following position adopted by an ICC tribunal summarises the general approach:

> Based on such Hearing the Arbitral Tribunal will then form its own view in respect of what it should learn and conclude from the Independent Experts' Opinion (after testing at the occasion of the Hearing).In any event, the Tribunal will be free to appreciate the probative value, weight and significance to be given to the Independent Experts' Opinion, quite in the same way as the Tribunal has the authority and task to assess and adjudicate the weight and significance on any other evidentiary matters.[23]

6.11 In considering which issues ought to be referred to the expert, and which should not, it is useful to recall that a tribunal is ultimately required to determine whether the evidence meets the requisite standard of proof, or rather, "does the evidence, tested against human experience and common sense persuade [the arbitrator] or does it not."[24] If the tribunal is unable to apply its common sense and inherent experience to the evidence to make this determination for reasons owing to a lack of technical understanding or specialty knowledge, then it may find the assistance of an expert is required.[25]

6.12 Where the tribunal determines that a controversy over "technical questions" exists, it may determine that an expert would be of use. In this respect, "technical questions" would include matters requiring scientific or specialist skills of some type, such as knowledge or skills acquired in a profession such as medicine or engineering, that range beyond what one would be presumed to understand as a result of general knowledge.[26] Before such an appointment is made, the tribunal should be reasonably convinced that

---

22 See the observations of a sole arbitrator presiding in an *ad hoc* arbitration seated in Zurich, Switzerland wherein the following was communicated to the parties: "In the briefs I find repeated reference to the possibility that I may appoint an expert 'in order to solve the technical questions'. Which technical questions? I would need a list: I would need to know on what basis of which documents the expert should answer these particular technical questions. I would need to know what the expertise is that the expert should have (and which I may well lack). Consequently, I would need to know which profile the expert should match. Before I have the answers to these questions and before I have duly heard both Parties on the subject, I am in no position to decide what, if anything, I should do about expertise." "Documents 15–30," *ASA Bulletin*, Vol. 11, No. 3, p. 487 (1993). See also the determination of an ICC tribunal seated in Zurich, Switzerland: "Iran, although confirming its request that a neutral expert be appointed, failed however to specifically list the critical points which an expert should review in its opinion. Iran's comments were, with respect of quantification, vague and unspecific . . .". ICC Case No. 12257, Final Award, p. 68 (2004) (unpublished).

23 ICC Case No. 14079, Procedural Order of May 2007, in *ICC International Court of Arbitration Bulletin Vol. 25/Supplement – 2014*, p. 11.

24 The standard adopted by one tribunal in a noteworthy arbitration, as reported by Robert von Mehren, "Burden of Proof in International Arbitration", in Albert Jan van den Berg (ed.), *ICCA Congress Series No. 7* (Vienna, 1994), p. 127 (1995).

25 See the comments of von Wobeser which considers the appointment of a tribunal expert in regard to due process: "The right to an expert, derived from the right of due process, does not exist outside the necessity for such, or at least the utility thereof, for establishing the facts of the case." C. von Wobeser, "The Arbitral Tribunal-Appointed Expert", in Albert Jan van den Berg (ed.), *ICCA Congress Series No. 13* (Montreal, 2006), p. 807 (2007).

26 As an example, one may note the consideration of a panel of arbitrators under the rules of the Great Britain-Mexico Mixed Claims Commission commenting on the appointment of a medical doctor to examine the claimant in regard to claims of injury and lost earning potential: "so serious a statement as the measuring of the permanent effect on a man's earning capacity of events which occurred eighteen years ago, could only be accepted when given by independent medical experts of high standing, appointed by the Commission." *William McNeil (Great Britain) v United Mexican States*, Decision No. 46, 19 May 1931 (British-Mexican Claims Commission), 5 RIAA 168.

the technical issue under consideration is material to the outcome of the final award.[27] The tribunal may also consider whether the location, state or nature of the evidence upon which the expert would likely rely would lend itself to a useful report.[28] If these threshold queries are answered in the affirmative, an expert may be appointed to establish an independent view on the technical questions. Frequently, each side's case will have previously been substantiated by a report of its own expert.[29] In this scenario, the tribunal may determine that the issues to be decided are limited to only those matters upon which the party-appointed experts disagree.[30]

---

27 "The Arbitral Tribunal has taken into consideration the appointment of an expert. It came to the conclusion that – based on its just explained view on claimant's policy – an expertise is not necessary. It is not necessary to decide whether the method . . . the claimant used to make its electronic devices Y2K safe was the cheapest or easiest way from a view of an expert. Instead the Arbitral Tribunal has to decide whether the measures taken were [to correct problems that were] Y2K caused and whether the costs claimed have actually been spent in connection with that problem and for its solution. With regard to the costs and said purpose claimant has the burden of proof." *Supra* n. 15, p. 142. See also the decision of a panel of arbitrators of the Iran-US Claims Tribunal in the *Bechtel v The Islamic Republic of Iran* case whereby it was noted that findings on substantive issues in the case had rendered the need for the appointment of an expert unnecessary: "On 22 December 1978, a final invoice and a summary of all amounts billed was sent to IDRO. The aggregate amount still owing was $407,285.45. As required by the Agreement, the final invoice was accompanied by a statement of Coopers & Lybrand, OBI's auditors, certifying that the invoice was accurate and in conformance with the Agreement. No objection was made to this invoice until the present proceedings. According to the Agreement, the amounts became due within thirty days after receipt of the final invoice by IDRO. The Tribunal finds that, as sought by the Claimants, OBI is entitled to payment of $407,285.45 from IDRO as of 1 February 1979. In view of this finding, the Tribunal sees no need for an audit of OBI's books or for appointment of an expert to determine the value of the services rendered by OBI under the Technical Services Agreement." *Bechtel Inc v The Islamic Republic of Iran*, Case No. 181, Award No. 294-181-1 of 4 March 1987, p. 16.

28 See the ruling of an ICC tribunal: "Le tribunal arbitral considère en outre qu'une nouvelle expertise serait inutile et très vraisemblablement irréalisable, en raison notamment du fait que les barres ne peuvent pas être individualisées avec certitude et qu'il ne pourrait être prouvé que les barres objet d'une éventuelle expertise à venir seraient bien les barres objet du contrat" (unofficial translation) "The arbitral tribunal further considers that a new expertise would be useless and very likely impracticable, in particular because the bars cannot be individualized with certainty and it could only be proven that the bars subject to a possible expert report would be the same bars object of the contract". ICC Case No. 6653 (1993) reprinted in Jean-Jacques Arnaldez, Yves Derains and Dominique Hascher (eds), *Collection of ICC Arbitral Awards*, Vol. III, 1991–1995, pp. 522–523 (1997). See also the decision of a CIETAC panel not to order an expert report because the equipment in question was degraded to such a state that it required restoration at considerable cost before an expert could consider it: "Concerning the claimant's request to the arbitration tribunal to appoint experts to check and evaluate the problem . . . it would be meaningful for the arbitration tribunal to arrange for experts to check and evaluate only if the claimant could restore the equipment [to the] technical state as at the time of delivery in 1987. Despite the fact that it was technically possible to restore the equipment [to] the technical state, as five years ago, it was difficult and costly. In case experts were appointed in these circumstances, it would not be fair to both parties." "Award on dispute relating to non-textile cloth production equipment" CIETAC Awards (1993), p. 325.

29 See: ICC Case No. 14079: "31. It is of course clear that the Parties would in no way be prevented to use their own Experts, even if the Tribunal decided to mandate an Independent Expert." ICC Case No. 14079, Procedural Order of May 2007, in *ICC International Court of Arbitration Bulletin Vol. 25/Supplement – 2014*, p. 9.

30 Having to decide which of the experts before it is correct as to a technical point of fact can prove a daunting task to the arbitrator. One commentator recounted the following scenario which illustrates the point: "Faced with a genuine difference of opinion between experts as to the cause of a landslip he admits to feeling 'like a rather unintelligent first year undergraduate asked to decide a difference of opinion between two of his professors'. Had the case not settled during the lunch adjournment he would have seriously considered appointing a technical assessor." Ian Menzies, "Satisfying the Burden of Proof: A Layman's Approach", in The Standards and Burden of Proof in International Arbitration, Edward Eveleigh *et al.*, *Arbitration International*, Vol. 10, No. 3, p. 357 (1994). See also the decision in *SD Myers v Canada*, whereby the tribunal ordered the following procedure, appointing an expert to analyse the dispute between two party-appointed experts: "As soon as practicable thereafter, and in consultation with the Disputing Parties, the Tribunal will decide whether a Tribunal expert should be appointed pursuant to art. 27(1) of the UNCITRAL Rules to assist in the determination of issues that are outstanding as

6.13 Technical questions are not the only "specific issues" which may lead to the appointment of an expert. Where an issue arises requiring an industry practice or standard to be established, a tribunal may require the assistance of an individual familiar with the relevant business sector to assist it.[31] Moreover, arbitrators have been known to request the expert assistance of accountants to help undertake matters such as verifying corporate accounts,[32] the ownership of an entity based upon share certificates and other documentation[33] and valuations of assets or entities.[34] Tribunals have also been known to appoint experts to assist in the quantification of damages[35] where there are particularly challenging questions of economic theory, or other complex issues which the tribunal finds would be better handled through a report prepared with an individual possessing expertise in the area.[36] Thus,

---

between the Disputing Parties' expert witnesses; and, if so, the Terms of reference of any such Tribunal expert." *SD Myers v Government of Canada*, NAFTA/UNCITRAL, Procedural Order No. 17, p. 3 (26 February 2001). See also the determination of an ICSID tribunal to appoint an independent expert to evaluate the financial expert reports, submitted by the parties: "By letter dated 18 May 2005, the Tribunal informed the parties of its decision to appoint an independent expert to assist the Tribunal in evaluating the expert financial evidence. By letter of 14 September 2005, the ICSID Secretariat transmitted the report on the findings of the independent expert to the parties and invited them to comment on the report by 5 October 2005. The parties filed their observations with the Tribunal on that date." Dietmar W. Prager, "*LG&E Energy Corp, LG&E Capital Corp v The Argentine Republic*, ICSID Case No. ARB/02/1, 3 October 2006", *A Contribution by the ITA Board of Reporters*.

31 As noted by the tribunal in the Iran-US Claims Tribunal case *Harza v The Islamic Republic of Iran*, in response to objections from the claimant as to the appointment of an expert to testify on business practice in Iran: "[d]espite the fact, stressed by Claimant, that the claim for payment of fees due does not raise strictly technical issues, it appears from the pleadings and the substantiating evidence submitted by both Parties that the reasons for the disagreement between the Parties need to be clarified to the Tribunal by an expert familiar with business practices and administration of important consulting engineering contracts such as the 1965 contract concluded between Harza International and the Ministry of Energy." *Richard Harza et al. v The Islamic Republic of Iran*, Case No. 97, Chamber Two, Interlocutory Award No. 14-97-2, pp. 4–5 (23 February 1983).

32 In the *Société Ouest-Africaine des Bétons Industriels v The Republic of Senegal* ICSID arbitration, the tribunal appointed an expert to review certain accounts of the claimant to determine which costs were rightly attributable to the investment which the claimant argued had been lost. The appointment of the expert came about after the respondent had argued that the evidence was not sufficient to show that the funds spent were actually connected to the relevant investment. The claimant agreed to the appointment of an expert to review its accounts. *Société Ouest-Africaine des Bétons Industriels v The Republic of Senegal*, ICSID Case No. ARB/82/1, Award of 25 February 1988, in Albert Jan van den Berg (ed.), *Yearbook Commercial Arbitration*, Vol. XVII, p. 65 (1992).

33 *Bechtel v The Islamic Republic of Iran*, *supra* n. 27, p. 10: "In an Order issued after the hearing, the Tribunal requested the Claimants to make available for inspection by Peat Marwick Nederland, a firm of certified public accountants, such corporate books and records of these three corporations or other evidence, sufficient to show that fifty percent or more of their stock during the relevant periods was beneficially owned by natural persons who are citizens of the United States."

34 See: *Shain Shain Ebrahimi* and *The Islamic Republic of Iran*, Case Nos 44, 46 and 47, Chamber Three, Order of 20 July 1992, p. 1, where the tribunal appointed an expert to ascertain the value of an asset for which the claimant sought compensation: "The Tribunal has decided to appoint an expert in accordance with art. 27 of the Tribunal Rules to render a report as to certain matters relating to the valuation of Gostaresh Maskan Company as of 13 November 1979 . . .".

35 See: ICC Case No. 14079: "Claimants' counsel . . . submitted that the Tribunal should indeed appoint an Independent Expert for the purpose of evaluating the [liquidated damages] and [. . .] counterclaims." ICC Case No. 14079, Procedural Order of May 2007, in *ICC International Court of Arbitration Bulletin Vol. 25/Supplement – 2014*, p. 9.

36 See the following example where a tribunal in ICC Case No. 5294 appointed a quantity surveyor to consider the costs of completion of a project: "While claimant gave the above details of expenditure as per cost category, its bookkeeping system would not allow it to correlate costs to the individual items of work remaining to be done according to the [quantity surveyor's] report. On the other side, it is readily apparent that the cost expended by claimant to complete the job (on which work had already been performed) substantially exceeded the total sum contractually allotted to the performance of all the civil works. . . . In these circumstances it was necessary to check the appropriateness of the expenses incurred. For that purpose, Mr. . . . a chartered quantity surveyor, was appointed by the arbitrator as expert to produce an estimate of what the cost of completing the items

it is difficult to identify which subject areas may call for the appointment of an expert, and which would not, given that the question of whether an expert is needed will largely turn on the facts of the individual case.[37] Moreover, in some instances, the appointment of the expert may be partially or wholly justified on procedural economy grounds; which is to say that the appointment of the expert would greatly assist the tribunal in managing, cataloguing and/or otherwise analysing voluminous amounts of information.[38]

6.14 A "specific issue" may also arise in relation to the determination of foreign law. Tribunals who are asked to consider the application of a law in which none of the members of the tribunal are qualified, may consider it necessary to call in an expert to opine on selected issues concerning the foreign law in order to assist their deliberations.[39] Questions over foreign law remain a legitimate ground for appointing an expert; however, modern trends suggest that arbitrators are less inclined to appoint an expert in this instance, relying instead on the parties to "prove" the foreign legal principles.[40]

Applying the tribunal's own expertise to determine "specific issues"

6.15 While the majority of tribunals in international arbitration will be composed of jurists, with the possible exception of commodity or other specialised arbitral forums, it is not uncommon for arbitrators to also have specialist, technical expertise. Even where the tribunal is composed entirely of those possessing a legal background, a member of a tribunal may have specialty knowledge of a technical nature or of a foreign law or other matter relevant to the questions before the tribunal. That a tribunal member has special expertise relevant to determining difficult factual issues in the case is of consequence to whether a "specific issue" requiring the appointment of an expert is deemed to have arisen under article 6.1. This is so because the expert arbitrator, unlike the jurist arbitrator, may decide an issue applying his or her own technical or industry knowledge. But caution in this scenario

---

listed in column 3 of the [first quantity surveyor's] report would have been if done by an Egyptian civil contractor and, alternatively, if done by an international civil contractor." *Danish firm v Egyptian firm*, Final award in ICC Case No. 5294 of 22 February 1988 in Albert Jan van den Berg (ed.), *Yearbook Commercial Arbitration*, Vol. XIV, p. 137–145 (1989). See also: ICC Case No. 5008, where the tribunal appointed where an expert in matters of finance relating to shipping were appointed to assist the tribunal's determination of damages. As reported in, Olivier Cachard, "Maritime Arbitration under the ICC Rules of Arbitration", *ICC Bulletin*, vol 22, No. 1, p. 38 (2011).

37 Recalling the practice of the Iran-US Claims Tribunal, Mosk notes that: "The Tribunal appointed experts on such subjects as 'geology, petroleum, engineering, accounting, valuation, inventory and linguistics'." Richard D. Mosk, "The role of facts in international dispute resolution", *Recueil Des Cours*, Vol. 304, p. 128 (2003).

38 See, for example: *Luzon Hydro Corp (Philippines) v Transfield Philippines Inc* [2004] 4 SLR 705, where an ICC tribunal appointed an expert to assist it in administrative matters. Conversely, procedural economy and cost may also be grounds for determining not to appoint an expert. See the ruling in *American Bell International Inc v Islamic Republic of Iran*, wherein the tribunal noted: "With regard to the necessity of experts, the Tribunal notes that the Parties have had more than adequate time to prepare their case and engage their own experts. Having studied the case, the Tribunal concludes that any possibly benefits to be derived from the appointment of an expert are not in proportion to the delays and consequential prejudice to all parties which would ensue." As reported in Schneider, *supra* n. 13, p. 453.

39 See: ICC Case No. 5418, as an example of the considerations undertaken by the tribunal in relation to the appointment of an expert to report on Hungarian law. ICC Case No. 5418, in Sigvard Jarvin, Yves Derains and Jean-Jacques Arnaldez (eds), *Collection of ICC Arbitral Awards*, Vol. II, 1986–1990, p. 135 (1995).

40 *Ibid.* Where the tribunal refused the appointment of an expert on matters of Hungarian law. McIlwrath and Savage observe that: "A tribunal that counts lawyers among its members will be unlikely to appoint an expert to assist it on issues of law." Michael McIlwrath and John Savage, *International Arbitration and Mediation: A Practical Guide*, p. 305 (2010).

is warranted. The arbitrator should be wary not to engage in an investigation in a manner similar to an expert witness.

6.16 In order to determine whether an arbitrator with specialty expertise should rely on his or her own expertise to make a determination or should appoint an expert, one must first understand the key difference between the roles of the witness and arbitrator. Namely, the expert witness is charged with producing evidence whereas the arbitrator is to make a determination on the evidence before him or her. The expert witness' evidence comes in the form of the report, and sometimes testimony, the report or testimony results from an investigation of information, not limited to the evidence submitted into the record, and the application of relevant industry or technical modes of analysis which may not have been discussed in the pleadings, or for which no evidence has been produced. In other words, the expert witness may look beyond the evidence filed in an arbitration to prepare his or her report, whereas the tribunal is confined to the file before it. This is why the expert's report is submitted into the proceedings as evidence for consideration and for debate (see IBA Rules, article 6.4 and article 6.5). In contrast, an arbitrator does not generate evidence, and intra-tribunal deliberations are not open to the parties.

6.17 Therefore, referring to the language of article 6.1, the question of whether a "specific issue" has arisen for which the arbitrator possessing relevant expertise may engage an independent expert, may turn on whether the expert arbitrator is able in the circumstances to apply his or her own technical understanding to the evidence without requiring reference to technical materials not in the record.[41] This distinction has been cast by some reviewing courts to be the difference between relying on one's general background expertise to understand a technical issue, as opposed to extraneous specific knowledge of issues in dispute, to decide the case.[42] The former exercise is considered appropriate for the expert arbitrator to engage in, whereas the latter implies that the arbitrator is relying on specific evidence not in the record and in relation to which the parties have a right to be heard.[43] Moreover,

---

41 In an *ad hoc* arbitration in which an arbitrator with computer engineering expertise was appointed to hear a matter along with two jurist arbitrators, the final award was later challenged because the expert arbitrator had reviewed source code and prepared factual but not analytical summaries of the evidence for his fellow panellists. In finding that these activities did not cause any due process problems, the reviewing Canadian court noted that: "In my view, there seems little point in having an individual with technical expertise [on the tribunal] unless that individual can use his or her background in assessing the evidence before the tribunal. That is indeed one of the hallmarks of commercial arbitration as opposed to courtroom adjudication. There is a difference between an individual who because of his or her expertise is in a position to assess technical evidence that is before the Panel and an expert who relies on evidence from other sources outside the evidence and only available to that expert and not disclosed to the parties." *Xerox Canada Ltd v MPI Technologies Inc* [2006] OJ No. 4895, para. 85.

42 In reviewing the decision of an expert arbitrator under the New Zealand Arbitration Act of 1996, the following observations were offered by the High Court at Auckland: "Even without express agreement on the subject, it is presumed that [expert] arbitrators can draw on their knowledge and experience for general facts, that is to say facts which form part of the general body of knowledge within their area of expertise as distinct from facts that are specific to the particular dispute. An arbitrator appointed for his or her special knowledge or skill, or expertise, is entitled to draw upon those sources for the purpose of determining the dispute and need not advise the parties that he or she is doing so. . . . In the absence of an agreement to the contrary, not even experts may rely upon their extraneous knowledge of the specific events in question, whether or not derived from independent work or investigations they may have carried out." *Methanex Motunui Ltd v Spellman* [2004] 1 NZLR p. 95, paras 156–157.

43 See, for example the holding of an English court on this issue: "I fully accept and understand the difficulties in which an expert finds himself when acting as an arbitrator. There is an unavoidable inclination to rely on one's own expertise and in respect of general matters that is not only not objectionable but desirable and a very

the case law seems to consistently hold that if an expert arbitrator is inclined to apply a methodology that the parties have not been made aware of or have not previously made submissions on, as opposed to merely declining to accept the methodology proposed by one or more of the parties, here too, the tribunal should seek submissions on the matter it proposes to take into account.[44] Hence, where the expert arbitrator believes an investigation into the matters is required so that fresh facts may be adduced, including an investigation into technical standards or specific facts not in the record, it may be said that a "specific issue" has arisen. Under article 6.1 this would justify the appointment of an expert, even if the arbitrator holds specialist knowledge or skill on the issue in question.[45]

When a tribunal-appointed expert is required by mandatory law

6.18 The general discretion afforded to arbitrators notwithstanding, there is support for the proposition that a tribunal may, in some limited circumstances, be required to appoint an expert in order to pay due respect to the parties' right to be heard. It has been recognised by more than one reviewing court that where a tribunal does not possess the requisite expertise to determine a specific issue in the case, and that this issue must be decided in order to deliver a final award, further expertise should be obtained to assist in determination of the issue.[46] Such a situation may not necessarily require the tribunal

---

large part of the reason why an arbitrator with expert qualifications is chosen. Nevertheless, the rules of natural justice do require, even in an arbitration conducted by an expert, that matters which are likely to form the subject of decision, in so far as they are specific matters, should be exposed for the comment and submissions of the parties . . . If he is to any extent relying on his own personal experience in a specific way then that again is something that he should mention so that it can be explored. It is not right that a decision should be based on specific matters which the parties have never had the chance to deal with, nor is it right that a party should first learn of adverse points in the decision against him." *Zermalt Holdings SA v Nu-Life Upholstery Repairs Ltd* [1985] 2 EGLR 14. See also: ICC Case No. 9142, where it is reported that an arbitrator possessing particular expertise in the maritime industry determined damages owed to a party, by applying his own general knowledge of the market: "On the basis of an analysis of the market and his own experience, the arbitrator awarded compensatory damages corresponding to the shortfall between the income that would have resulted from the aborted contract and that earned from the substitute contract." Cachard, *supra* n. 36, p. 38.

44 While affirming this principle, the Swiss Federal Tribunal has noted that disclosure of any technical or other standards which the arbitrator intends to apply in deciding the matter may cure any due process problem: "However according to doctrinal opinion, the arbitrator who is specialized and who has access to sources of knowledge which are not always at the disposal of the parties, has the obligation to bring in advance to the attention of the parties the fundamental technical elements [upon] which his decision will be based." *Chrome Resources SA v Leopold Lazarus Ltd*, 8 February 1978 – Tribunal Fédéral.

45 In application of this standard to the question of whether a legal expert need be appointed by a tribunal, reference may be had to ICC Award No. 5418, where a tribunal was requested to appoint an expert on Hungarian law. Given that the tribunal already had on its panel a qualified Hungarian lawyer, and noting that the parties had submitted materials on the law to the tribunal, translated into English, the tribunal reasoned that the matter was one of interpretation and application of the legal principles already before the tribunal (it also noted that there appeared to be no Hungarian judicial precedent on point). In particular, the tribunal noted that it had performed its own research, and discussed it with the parties at an oral hearing during which they were able to present their views. Thus, it was determined that no need for the appointment of an expert was present. ICC Case No. 5418, *supra* n. 39, p. 135.

46 See, for instance, the following holding of a Hong Kong court of first instance which found that the tribunal's failure to call for expertise on Chinese law was a procedural irregularity leading to partial annulment of an award, since none of the arbitrators had expertise in that area: "I readily agree that in the process of fact finding arbitrators must have autonomy in drawing inferences as they deem fit and in that respect they are entitled to depart from the positions advanced by the parties. However, on primary factual disputes, they have to act on evidence and give reasonable opportunity to the parties to put forward their respective case on such evidence. In my judgment, given that we are dealing with an arbitration in Hong Kong, the requirement of contractual validity

to appoint an expert so much as it may call on the parties to submit their own expert reports. However, it is generally thought that where a party has specifically requested the appointment of an expert in time, and has undertaken to pay the additional costs of obtaining an expert, a tribunal may be compelled, if it is objectively necessary, to accede to such request.[47]

Expert's terms of reference

6.19 As article 6.1 points out, the tribunal is charged with providing the terms of reference for the tribunal-appointed expert.[48] The IBA Rules follow the view held generally in international arbitration that the instructions given to the expert should be put to the parties for comment, and reduced to writing. In this regard reference may be had to the *Hussman (Europe) v Al Ameen Development & Trade Co* decision arising out of an arbitration held under the rules of the Euro-Arab Chamber of Commerce. In that case, a decision by the tribunal to instruct an expert witness orally, without notifying the parties of the content of the instruction, was challenged as a procedural irregularity. Because of the complaining party's general agreement to afford the tribunal considerable latitude,

---

under PRC law has to be decided on the evidence before the Tribunal." *Brunswick Bowling & Billiards Corp v Shanghai Zhlu Industrial Co Ltd and Chen Rong* [2009] HKCU 211, para. 26. See also the 1992 ruling of the Swiss Federal Tribunal in which the decision by an ICC tribunal against ordering expert evidence on a technical matter was considered to be in error because the tribunal clearly could not decide the matter on the evidence before it, and did not have the expertise to determine the issue on its own. The court noted as follows: "even in the absence of a request by a party, arbitrators who do not have specialized knowledge must mandate an expert if they need clarification on certain technical problems which are decisive for the determination of the dispute". "Tribunal Fédéral, 1ere Cour Civile", *ASA Bulletin*, Vol. 10, No. 3, p. 381 (1992). Translation of this quote taken from Besson and Poudret, *supra* n. 3, p. 561.

47 Georg von Segesser provides the following succinct review of the Swiss Federal Tribunal's position on the necessity of an expert: "The parties have a right to the appointment of an expert by the tribunal (such right being a part of their right to submit evidence and be heard) if the following preconditions are met: (i) the party who intends to rely on this right must have expressly requested the appointment of an expert; (ii) the request must be made in proper form and in a timely manner; (iii) if required by the tribunal, the requesting party must advance the costs of such expertise; (iv) the expert evidence must relate to facts relevant for rendering of the award; and (v) the expert evidence must be necessary and proper for proving such relevant facts." Georg von Segesser, "A right to a tribunal appointed expert", *Kluwer Arbitration Blog* (9 August 2011). See also: Poudret and Besson on the Swiss position: "There is no right to an expert opinion flowing from the right to be heard unless such opinion is necessary and capable of establishing facts which are relevant to the outcome of the dispute." Poudret and Besson, *supra* n. 3, p. 561.

48 The position adopted by the ICC tribunal in ICC Case No. 14079 regarding Experts' Terms of Reference is instructive for setting out a generally acceptable approach: "Once the Independent Expert is identified, the next step will be to define more precisely the mandate to be given to the Independent Expert (or Experts' Team). This, again, is an exacting task and involves a significant number of issues. In all probability, it will be necessary to hold a one- or two-day Experts' Terms of Reference Meeting for devising the road map to be followed by the Independent Expert. The points to be agreed, obviously, consist of the files to be constituted for review by the Experts, the more precise scope of review of the Experts, and a series of questions how to carry out their mission, including the basic timetable, the modalities of receiving further information from the Parties, or from one of them, further fact-finding requirements, site visits with or without participation of the other Parties, with or without the Tribunal etc. Experience shows that such issues can hardly be solved by written communications, but require an oral interaction between the Parties, their representatives, their counsel, the Arbitrators and the Expert(s); hence a further Meeting will be required. As part of the Terms of Reference, a calendar for the several steps of the Experts' mission should be fixed, including the time when the Experts should come up with the written Experts' Opinion." ICC Case No. 14079, Procedural Order of May 2007, in *ICC International Court of Arbitration Bulletin Vol. 25/Supplement – 2014*, p. 11.

the court did not find a serious irregularity on the facts of the case, but noted the following general principle:

> In my view the correct course to have been followed by the tribunal was to have asked the parties whether there were any points where the law of Saudi Arabia differed from the law of England and Wales or to have itself raised with the parties specific points on which they might need assistance. Certainly it would have been better if the tribunal had sought the views of the parties on the issue raised before instructing Dr Al-Qasem and discussed with the parties the terms in which he should be instructed.[49]

6.20 Certainly the court's admonition is one worthy of note. As some jurisdictions take the view that a party's right to comment on the instructions given to the expert is integral to the right to be heard[50] the approach advocated by the *Hussman* court is a rule that should be generally adhered to.

6.21 The terms of reference will vary depending on the type of expertise that has been requested, but general practice in the appointment of an expert will call for the following points to be included in the terms of reference:

General admonition to remain neutral and independent: As is noted in article 6.2 of the IBA Rules, a tribunal-appointed expert is required to remain neutral and objective in the conduct of his or her investigation. An expert's terms of reference may contain a general admonition to this effect, similar to the following: "[the Tribunal] invites the experts to, at all times, adhere to the principle of contradictory proceedings, which notably implies that the two parties be informed of each communication of the expert to either party, of each and every request for information, that each interview takes place in the presence of both parties and that each party be placed in the position of submitting their observations and suggestions."[51] As is discussed below, neutrality is a vital aspect of the expert's engagement, without which, the report may be rendered unusable.

Descriptions of the issues and/or questions to be considered: Questions which the expert should consider in the preparation of the report may be broad or narrow depending on the nature of the expertise, the stage during which the expert is requested to act,[52] and the extent to which the tribunal and the parties may agree on the scope of the report. The terms of reference will generally include questions for the expert to consider which have been developed by the tribunal after consultation with the parties and may include certain assumptions which the expert should base the analysis on.[53] If the expert feels that it is

---

49 *Hussman (Europe) Ltd v Al Ameen Development & Trade Co* [2000] App LR 04/19.

50 See: Besson and Poudret, *supra* n. 3, p. 562, para 665.

51 ICC Case No. 5715, Procedure Order (1989), in Dominique Hascher (ed.), *Collection of Procedural Decisions in ICC Arbitration 1993–1996*, p. 145 (2nd edition, 1998).

52 As an example, in an ICC arbitration the tribunal defined the issues to be put to the expert by reference to an interim award that had already set forth a number of 'failures' identified by the tribunal and attributable to Claimant: "the Expert was asked, *inter alia*, to determine the extent of the delay for which Claimant is responsible, taking into account all relevant circumstances, in particular Claimant's failures referred to in the Third Interim Award as well as other subcontractors' delays and Respondent's own conduct. The Expert's Terms of Reference specified on the one hand that the findings of the Arbitral Tribunal as expressed in its Third Interim Award were binding on the Expert and on the other hand that he shall draw his own conclusions within the limits of such findings." Final Award in ICC Case No. 5835, in *ICC Bulletin*, Vol. 10, No. 2, p. 33 (1999).

53 As was noted in one procedural order issued in an ICC arbitration seated in Paris: "[s]uggestions that the Arbitral Tribunal summon its own expert must be accompanied by a separate list of the questions that [it] is suggested the expert should answer and the profile that it is suggested the expert should match. Before appointing any expert the Arbitral Tribunal shall hear both Parties, but the Terms of reference of any tribunal-appointed

necessary to expand, or change the scope of his mandate to include additional issues, it should only be done in consultation with the tribunal.[54]

Instructions concerning the evidence and investigation: Often, prior to the appointment of an expert, the parties together with the tribunal will have considered the parameters of the proposed investigation. In order to avoid any objections to requests for information from the expert, it is advisable that the parties, working with the tribunal, try to identify common ground as to the files and types of information that will be made available to the expert. This may not always be possible, hence a tribunal may therefore define the parameters quite broadly, in line with article 6.3, in terms of the volume and type of information that the expert may request.[55]

A time frame for the report: Clearly, an expert's appointment is intended to facilitate the fact-finding mission of the tribunal, not delay it. Thus the terms of reference will customarily include a time frame for the delivery of the report. The tribunal in accepting the terms of reference will have accepted the duty to deliver the report within the time frame as part of his mandate.[56]

Request to attend the hearing and general availability: As noted in article 6.6, the tribunal expert will be required to attend a hearing to answer oral questions from the parties and the tribunal. The hearing is a vital part of the expert's performance of his duties, thus the expert's agreement to attend a hearing is often thought of as a pre-requisite to his appointment.

Instructions concerning the report: The tribunal should request the expert to prepare a report that describes not only his or her conclusions, but also the methods used to reach

---

expert shall be fixed by the Arbitral Tribunal." "Documents 15–30", *supra* n. 22, p. 466. See also: *Arco Exploration v National Iranian Oil Co*, Case No. 21, Chamber One, Order of 7 December 1989, p. 1, where the tribunal instructed the expert who had been retained to provide a report on the annual production of crude oil from fields which the claimant alleged had been illegally seized, to assume the following, "The expert is instructed to assume, in preparing its report, that the Parties would have fully complied with their obligations throughout the term of the Joint Structure Agreement . . ."

54 See: *Behring International Inc v The Islamic Republic Iranian Airforce, Iran Aircraft Industries and The Government of Iran*, Case No. 382, Chamber Three, Decision No. DEC 27-382-3 (19 December 1983), where the amendment, requested by the claimant, broadened the expert's mandate, and also included the provision that the report be submitted first to the parties in draft form, prior to submitting it in final form to the tribunal.

55 See, as an example of the wide discretion afforded an expert, the directive given by an ICSID tribunal seated in The Hague: "[t]he Expert shall also be entitled to obtain from any Party all documents which he deems necessary for his investigation. Each Party shall without delay give the other Party a copy of any documents which it gives to the Expert. The Parties have the ability to apply to the Arbitral Tribunal if doubts should arise as to the relevance and/or difficulty of furnishing information which the expert seeks to obtain." "Documents 15–30", *supra* n. 22, p. 471 (1993). See also, for an example where a narrowly defined mandate was afforded to the expert, the order of 13 June 1990 in *Arco Exploration v National Iranian Oil Co*, Case Nos 20 and 21, Chamber One, Order of 13 June 1990, p. 2, whereby the tribunal issued precise directions to the expert detailing the information which he was allowed to consider. The scope in this instance was expanded, after the tribunal had received further submissions by the parties relaying their views on the necessary scope of production. See also the instruction by the Iran-US Claims Tribunal panel in *Harza v The Islamic Republic of Iran* whereby the tribunal broadly provided permission to the expert to request documents he believed "necessary" for the report: "After familiarizing himself with the Preliminary Report . . . and with the documents filed by the Parties and necessary to performance of his task, [the Expert] shall give his opinion on the following." *Harza v The Islamic Republic of Iran*, *supra* n. 31, p. 5.

56 In an interesting approach to this issue, the tribunal requested the expert to commit to a timeline for his report once he had reviewed the initial materials: "[t]he Expert is invited to familiarise himself with the documents filed by the Parties and submit thereafter to the Parties and the Arbitral Tribunal his plan of work, the estimate of the time he considers necessary to accomplish his mission and the approximate amount of his fees, as well as any proposal (with reasons) regarding possible modifications of the foregoing Terms of Reference which he deems necessary to permit the preparation of a proper report." "Documents 15–30", *supra* n. 22, p. 471.

them. This instruction is necessary for ensuring that the report complies with articles 6.3 and 6.4 which, based upon due process requirements, call for the expert to conduct his or her investigations with equal input from the parties and to notify them as to the methodologies and assumptions used in arriving at their conclusions. The following excerpt from terms of reference rendered in an ICC arbitration seated in Paris provides an example:

> Your report should set out not only the results of your investigation, but describe very precisely what method you selected to reach those results, why you selected this method rather than another method, which data you used, and in which publications the method followed and the data used are described more fully. If you make an assumption, please state clearly what it is and why you are making the assumption. The purpose of this is to ensure that the Parties (who have their own experts) can see exactly what you have done, and if they so wish, may challenge one or the other of the methods that you have selected, the data that you have accepted or assumption that you made.[57]

Compensation and other aspects of an expert's terms of reference: A question of practical significance when appointing an expert is the payment of his or her costs.[58] Generally, a tribunal will only appoint such an expert where a sufficient advance is paid to cover the anticipated costs of the expert. Nevertheless, the tribunal will often notify the expert of his or her duty to inform the tribunal if it is anticipated that the costs of the expert report will likely exceed the deposited advance.

6.22 It is accepted that the particular terms of reference used within a procedure may include extra or fewer provisions than what is described above. Nevertheless, the purpose of the terms of reference is served when the tribunal includes a precise description of the expert's role, thus ensuring that the expert's role does not encroach upon the tribunal's mandate and is clearly understood by the parties.[59]

Formalities that accompany the expert's appointment and time for raising objections

Article 6.2 2010 IBA Rules: **The Tribunal-Appointed Expert shall, before accepting appointment, submit to the Arbitral Tribunal and to the Parties a description of his or her qualifications and a statement of his or her independence from the Parties, their legal advisors and the Arbitral Tribunal. Within the time ordered by the Arbitral**

---

57 "Documents 15–30", *supra* n. 22, p. 469.

58 See: ICC Case No. 14079: "At the occasion of the Experts' Terms of Reference Meeting, the Tribunal and the Parties will not only have to consider the time budget and all other elements, but also the financial budget for the expertise procedure. The Independent Expert will be asked to make a quote, for submission to the Parties, and the funding and administration of that budget will also be a matter for discussion. It is unlikely that the Expert(s) can or even should start work prior to having settled the budget." ICC Case No. 14079, Procedural Order of May 2007, in *ICC International Court of Arbitration Bulletin Vol. 25/Supplement – 2014*, pp. 11–12.

59 See further: ICC Case No. 14079: "In the Chairman's experience, after having settled the Experts' Terms of Reference, and after a time sufficient for the Expert to familiarize with the incumbent tasks and mission on the basis of the (probably) voluminous files to be provided to him by the Parties, it will not only be useful but indeed necessary to hold such a Kick-Off Meeting for discussing and settling the further 'road map' along which the Expert will be expected to proceed. In the Chairman's experience, such Kick-Off Meeting may require two full working days." ICC Case No. 14079, Procedural Order of May 2007, in *ICC International Court of Arbitration Bulletin Vol. 25/Supplement – 2014*, p. 12, fn. 5.

Tribunal, the Parties shall inform the Arbitral Tribunal whether they have any objections as to the Tribunal-Appointed Expert's qualifications and independence. The Arbitral Tribunal shall decide promptly whether to accept any such objection. After the appointment of a Tribunal-Appointed Expert, a Party may object to the expert's qualifications or independence only if the objection is for reasons of which the Party becomes aware after the appointment has been made. The Arbitral Tribunal shall decide promptly what, if any, action to take.

General discussion

6.23 One of the clear conceptual differences between a party-appointed expert and the tribunal-appointed expert is the notion of independence. While it is generally understood in arbitration that the former is retained by a party in support of its case and thus the degree of independence such an expert has is an issue that goes to the probative value of his or her report, the latter should have no meaningful connection with the parties or with its counsel that would call into question his or her impartiality. Moreover, as the tribunal-appointed expert is called to consider often highly technical or difficult specialist questions, the qualifications of the expert are naturally important.

6.24 The issues of independence and qualifications are customarily put to the parties before the appointment of the expert is approved. If after the proposed expert has been vetted for these issues, the tribunal, and the parties decide to move forward with the appointment, this in theory should be the end of the matter. Nevertheless, as has been known to happen, questions concerning the expert's independence or qualifications for the case at hand may arise after the appointment. As is set forth in article 6.2, such objections should only be heard in the narrow circumstance where the information leading to the objection was discovered after the expert's appointment. These, and the other issues covered within article 6.2, are discussed in the following section.

Independence of the expert

6.25 Article 6.2 follows the general practice in international arbitration which calls for the tribunal-appointed expert to provide assurances of his or her independence prior to being appointed.[60] The purposes underlying this requirement are in some ways similar to the reasons behind the disclosures required for party-appointed experts (article 5.2) and fact witnesses (article 4.4). However, the treatment which each will receive if there is a suspected failure of independence is significantly different. Whereas ties between a

---

60 Chartered Institute of Arbitrators, Practice Guideline 10: Guidelines on the use of Tribunal-Appointed Experts, Legal Advisers and Assessors, para. 3.4.2 notes the following: "[t]he tribunal-appointed expert should be asked, before accepting [his or her] appointment, to submit to the tribunal and to the parties a statement of his or her independence from the parties and/or disclose any material connections that he or she may have with the parties. The tribunal should invite the parties to state whether they have any objections to the proposed expert's independence." See also the consideration of the general principle in *Canada – Continued Suspension* that parties should be afforded full disclosure by a tribunal-appointed expert: "While panels should insist that self-disclosure requirements . . . and while parties are entitled to full self-disclosure by experts . . ." *Canada – Continued Suspension of Obligations, supra* n. 7, para. 451.

witness or a party-appointed expert and a party, its legal counsel or the tribunal, may provide fertile grounds for questioning the probative value of his or her report, in the case of a tribunal-appointed expert, such ties would may result in the termination of the appointment.[61] This is so because the tribunal-appointed expert's function is to provide an unbiased view of certain discreet questions to assist the tribunal's analysis of the issues. These discreet questions have been briefed to the expert because they are outside of the tribunal's expertise and the expert is engaged to provide an unbiased assessment to the tribunal. This means that without the observance of strict neutrality the value of such a report is negated, and the rationale for the expert's appointment is lost. Thus where a fact witness or a party-appointed expert's statement will often be treated as admissible even where there is a connection of one kind or another between the witness and a party or a legal counsel, in the case of a tribunal-appointed expert such a relation could cause the tribunal to terminate the appointment.

6.26 The above notwithstanding, it would be incorrect to assume that a tribunal will disqualify an expert based purely upon an allegation of bias from a party.[62] Objections must be reasoned, and raise "justifiable doubts" as to the expert's ability to provide an unbiased report.[63] Commercial ties (including historical ones) and other substantial links between a

---

61 See: comments to art. 5.2. See also: the comments of McIlwrath and Savage: "Experts appointed by tribunals tend to be similar in profile to those appointed by the parties, although independence from the parties is critical in the case of a tribunal-appointed expert, not simply desirable as in the case of party-appointed experts." McIlwrath and Savage, *supra* n. 40, p. 305. See the following considerations of the Appellate Body in the *Canada – Continued Suspension* case: "[E]xperts consulted by a panel can have a decisive role in a case, especially when it involves highly complex scientific questions such as this one. The Panel in this case said 'the role of the experts was to act as an "interface" between the scientific evidence and the Panel, so as to allow it to perform its task as the trier of fact.' Experts appointed by a panel can significantly influence the decision-making process. If a panel does not ensure that the requirements of independence and impartiality are respected in its consultations with the experts, this can compromise the fairness of the proceedings and the impartiality of the decision-making. In these circumstances, the practical difficulties that a panel may encounter in selecting experts cannot displace the need to ensure that the consultations with the experts respect the parties' due process rights. . . . The appointment and consultations with Drs. [experts' names] compromised the adjudicative independence and impartiality of the Panel." *Canada – Continued Suspension of Obligations, supra* n. 7, para. 480.

62 See the considerations of a WTO panel in the *Australia – Measures Affecting the Importation of Apples from New Zealand*: "A panel is responsible for ensuring that the selected experts have the necessary qualifications and expertise, and comply with the requirements for independence, impartiality and avoidance of conflicts of interest. Conversely, it is not enough for a party to simply assert an objection regarding the selection of a particular expert. Any party raising such an objection is expected to explain in what manner the expert's independence or impartiality have been or may be compromised." *Australia – Measures Affecting the Importation of Apples from New Zealand*, WT/DS367/R, adopted 9 August 2010, para. 7.32. See for example, the unsuccessful challenge to an appointed expert by a party during a CAS arbitration: "On 8 January 1999, the CAS informed the parties that it intended to invite Dr. Laurent Rivier to testify as an expert witness and requested the parties to bring forward any statement of objection before 12 January 1999. On 13 January 1999, M.'s legal counsel raised doubts about Dr. Rivier's independence and suggested to appoint Prof. Wilhelm Schänzer. On 18 January 1999, the CAS confirmed that the Panel had decided to accept the expert testimony of Dr. Rivier. . . . At the beginning of the hearing the President of the Panel confirmed the appointment of Dr. Rivier and stated that the Panel was thoroughly convinced of the expert's competence and independence." *Union Cycliste Internationale v M & Federazione Ciclistica Italiana*, Award of 24 February 1999, CAS 98/212 in Matthieu Reeb (ed.), *Digest of CAS Awards II 1998–2000*, p. 275 (2002).

63 The standards applicable to determining a tribunal-appointed expert's independence are not codified in international arbitration. There is some support for referencing the *IBA Guidelines on Conflicts of Interest in International Arbitration*, however, these guidelines are applicable to arbitrators and were not developed for experts. The following excerpt from the WTO Appellate Body decision in *Canada – Continued Suspension* discusses the "justifiable doubt" standard: "Disclosure should not lead to automatic exclusion. Whether the disclosed information is likely to affect or give rise to justifiable doubts as to the person's independence or

party and a proposed tribunal-appointed expert may suffice as grounds for disqualifying the proposed expert, as will evidence that the expert may be biased against one party's arguments.[64] Moreover, consultations between the expert and one of the parties prior to an appointment should be disclosed, in particular if they have touched upon specific aspects of the case.[65]

The expert's professional qualifications

6.27 The IBA Rules do not state who may serve as an expert, or what qualifications will cause one to be considered an expert. It is an issue that is open to consideration in each case.[66] A common approach to finding the requisite expertise is to refer the

---

impartiality must be objectively determined and properly substantiated. In the case of an expert, the panel should assess the disclosed information against information submitted by the parties or other information that may be available. It should then determine whether, on the correct facts, there is a likelihood that the expert's independence and impartiality may be affected, or if justifiable doubts arise as to the expert's independent or impartiality. If this is indeed the case, the panel must not appoint such person as an expert." *Canada – Continued Suspension of Obligations, supra* n. 7, para. 256. See also a case in which an objection was raised to an expert report because an individual who had assisted an appointed expert had once been nominated as an arbitrator in the matter. The tribunal there rejected that the prior, arbitral nomination of an individual associated with the report would taint his neutrality: "Respondent also complains that Mr. [X] [the expert's collaborator] was first nominated as arbitrator by the Claimant. It must be noted that, in accordance with the ICC Rules, the parties do not 'nominate' their arbitrators and having refused the offer at the time for personal reasons [it] cannot be held against Mr. [X]. An arbitrator is, by nature and by his office, impartial and chosen on the basis of that attribute and his competence in relation to that specific dispute. The same goes for the expert." Award in ICC Case No. 2444 of 1976, in Sigvard Jarvin and Yves Derains (eds), *Collection of ICC Arbitral Awards*, Vol. I, 1974–1985, p. 286.

64 In the *Canada – Continued Suspension* case the Appellate Body considered two different types of conflicts of interest. In the first instance, the tribunal considered possible commercial ties between an expert and pharmaceutical companies, and noted that while some such companies had funded prior research conducted by the expert, there was no evidence that the companies involved in producing the products directly affected by the case before the panel had done so. Thus, the Appellate Body found no fault with the dispute panel's decision to dismiss the complaints raised on this point. "The European Communities did not present evidence indicating that the companies from which [the expert] received funding had links with other companies producing veterinary drugs or the hormones at issue. Thus, we consider that the Panel did not exceed its authority in dismissing the European Communities' objections." Next, the Appellate Body considered possible conflicts of interest which were not of a commercial nature, but instead, evidenced possible bias towards the positions of the parties involved in the matter. In this respect the Appellate Body analysed ties between the appointed experts and an institution that had issued an influential report on the subject-matter of the dispute. The Appellate Body considered the fact that this scientific study on the use of the hormone treatments in question, the conclusions of which were heavily criticised by one of the participants in the dispute before the panel, raised serious questions concerning the experts' ability to be impartial. The Appellate Body noted as follows: "[a]n expert could be very qualified and knowledgeable and yet his or her appointment could give rise to concerns about his or her impartiality or independence, because of that expert's institutional affiliation or for other reasons." *Canada – Continued Suspension of Obligations, supra* n. 7, paras 227–270. See also the decision of a CRCIA tribunal in which it was noted that a previously appointed expert on maritime works had been disqualified when it was revealed that he had previously served on the board of directors of one of the parties: "Final award of 30 June 1999, Cairo Regional Centre For International Commercial Arbitration," M. E. I. Alam Eldin (ed.), *Arbitral Awards of the Cairo Regional Centre for International Commercial Arbitration*, Vol. II, 1997–2000, pp. 212–213 (2003). By analogy, reference may be had to well-known guidelines on arbitration neutrality to evaluate an expert's independence.

65 See: Award on Preliminary Issues of 11 November 2003, ICC Case No. 12171, *ASA Bulletin*, Vol. 23, No. 2, p. 257 (2005), where a tribunal was critical of the consultations held by a party with the expert prior to appointment as a breach of the right to equal treatment.

66 Mosk notes the following concerning American practice in his comments regarding experts in international arbitration: "There is no specific definition of who is an expert. Expertise is dependent on the subject. A person

issue to an institution or body capable of providing profiles of potential candidates.[67] Another approach is to put the question to the parties for their own proposals on possible candidates.[68]

6.28 For the appointment of an expert by the tribunal to be of maximum utility, the qualifications of the expert must match the mandate as prepared by the tribunal in consultation with the parties.[69] The question of whether an expert is truly capable of rendering the type or quality of reporting required to be of probative value should be answered early in the proceedings. The following excerpt from an Iran-US Claims Tribunal case, the *Starrett Housing Corp v Islamic Republic of Iran* makes this point:

> In determining the weight to be given to the Expert's Report, the Tribunal must first consider his qualifications. It is noteworthy that no issue arose between the Parties on this point. While the Respondents contested a number of aspects of the Expert's investigation and Report, none of the Parties questioned his qualifications. The Tribunal, which had reviewed the Expert's background and experience before appointing him, finds that its initial impressions have been fully confirmed by the high professional quality and impartiality evident in his work. . . .[70]

6.29 In this respect, the tribunal is obliged under article 6.2 to communicate any information it may have on the expert's qualifications to the parties for comment. As in regard to questions regarding independence, the tribunal should disregard dilatory and baseless objections, otherwise intended to frustrate the process. However, true questions as to the expert's professional capacities may be grounds for seeking clarifications from the candidate or otherwise refusing the appointment.

---

with special knowledge, skill or experience in an occupation, trade or craft may be qualified as an expert in his or her field." Mosk, *supra* n. 37, p. 126.

67 Mosk further notes in relation to the practice of the Iran-US Claims Tribunal that: "[e]xperts were selected in a variety of ways ranging from agreement between the parties to selection by the Tribunal based upon recommendations of professional associations or the Tribunal's Chairman." *Ibid*

68 As an example, reference may be had to the following procedural order rendered by the Iran-US Claims Tribunal where after providing a general description of the needed expertise, the tribunal directed the parties to develop a joint proposal: "Two experts shall be appointed. Expert No. 1 shall be an engineer experienced in the field of hydro-electric power plant construction. Expert No. 2 shall be an accountant experienced in the business practices and administration of important consulting engineering contracts. Such experts shall, if possible, be chosen by agreement between the Claimant and KWPA. Should those two parties fail to mutually select the experts by 1 October 1983, the Tribunal shall make the appointments." *Chas T. Main International Inc v Khuzestan Water and Power Authority (KWPA) and the Ministry of Energy of the Islamic Republic of Iran*, Case No. 120, Interlocutory Award No. 23-120-2 of 27 July 1983, in Pieter Sanders (ed.), *Yearbook Commercial Arbitration*, Vol. IX, p. 261 (1984). See: ICC Case No. 14079: "[t]he Parties are expected to inform the Tribunal regarding any agreement they may have been able to reach in respect of a suitable "candidate" to serve as the Independent Expert [within two weeks]. The Tribunal may extend the time limit upon request, as there would be a strong preference that the Parties themselves reach an agreement on the Independent Expert (rather than seeking proposals from the ICC Centre of Expertise)." ICC Case No. 14079, Procedural Order of May 2007, in *ICC International Court of Arbitration Bulletin Vol. 25/Supplement – 2014*, p. 11.

69 See: ICC Case No. 14079: "The Tribunal has decided that an Independent Expert (or Team of Experts) should be mandated to assist the Tribunal in its tasks. The Expert or the Team of Experts should be capable and knowledgeable to examine (i) the technical issues as well as (ii) the economic issues in respect of the rehabilitation project." ICC Case No. 14079, Procedural Order of May 2007, in *ICC International Court of Arbitration Bulletin Vol. 25/Supplement – 2014*, p. 12.

70 *Starrett Housing Corp, Starrett Systems Inc, Starrett Housing International Inc v The Islamic Republic of Iran, Bank Omran, Bank Mellat*, Final Award No. 314-24-1 of 14 August 1987, 16 *Iran-US Claims Tribunal Reports* 112, p. 125 (1987).

Raising objections after the expert has been appointed

6.30 Save for the instance where new information comes to light after the expert's appointment calling his or her qualifications or independence into question, a party should not raise challenges to the expert after their confirmation. This is a well-accepted rule that applies to challenges brought to the mandate of the expert, in addition to objections raised in regard to the expert's independence or qualifications. For a party to raise such issues after the appointment would generally be considered as bad faith, and dilatory. Consider the excerpt from an arbitration under the ICC Rules reproduced below. In this matter, the agreed methodology for the expert's mission was challenged after the appointment:

> It is now too late for claimant to request a modification of Procedural Ordinance No. 3. In particular, the arbitral tribunal understands that, instead of allowing the expert to examine completely the account in question during a number of months as specified in the Ordinance, claimant proposes to choose themselves the debits which would allegedly correspond to the credits mentioned. This proposal is unacceptable.
>
> The arbitral tribunal considers therefore that, by their letter claimant now refuses to co-operate with the expertise, as decided in Ordinance No. 3. Consequently, such expertise will not take place. The arbitral tribunal will take account of these circumstances in its final Award.[71]

6.31 As implied by the quote above, a tribunal may consider objections to an expert which are raised late into the process, whether they be to qualifications independence or mandate, as constituting a failure to cooperate with the procedure and thus procedural bad faith. If so, it will be open to the tribunal to draw a negative inference from such non-cooperation (article 9.6), or take the dilatory actions into account in awarding costs against the uncooperative party (article 9.7).

Investigations by tribunal-appointed expert and inspections generally

Article 6.3 2010 IBA Rules: Subject to the provisions of Article 9.2, the Tribunal-Appointed Expert may request a Party to provide any information or to provide access to any Documents, goods, samples, property, machinery, systems, processes or site for inspection, to the extent relevant to the case and material to its outcome. The authority of a Tribunal-Appointed Expert to request such information or access shall be the same as the authority of the Arbitral Tribunal. The Parties and their representatives shall have the right to receive any such information and to attend any such inspection. Any disagreement between a Tribunal-Appointed Expert and a Party as to the relevance, materiality or appropriateness of such a request shall be decided by the Arbitral Tribunal, in the manner provided in Articles 3.5 through 3.8. The Tribunal-Appointed Expert shall record in the Expert Report any non-compliance by a Party with an appropriate request or decision by the Arbitral Tribunal and shall describe its effects on the determination of the specific issue.

---

71 "Final Award in ICC Case No. 6497 of 1994", Albert Jan van den Berg (ed.), *Yearbook Commercial Arbitration*, Vol. XXIVa, p. 77 (1999).

Article 7 2010 IBA Rules: **Subject to the provisions of Article 9.2, the Arbitral Tribunal may, at the request of a Party or on its own motion, inspect or require the inspection by a Tribunal-Appointed Expert or a Party-Appointed Expert of any site, property, machinery or any other goods, samples, systems, processes or Documents, as it deems appropriate. The Arbitral Tribunal shall, in consultation with the Parties, determine the timing and arrangement for the inspection. The Parties and their representatives shall have the right to attend any such inspection.**

General discussion

6.32 It is a well-established practice of international arbitral tribunals to appoint a tribunal expert to "report" on specific issues if such is deemed necessary.[72] The expert's mandate may cover evaluating evidence already submitted into the proceedings, as well as evidence not in the record, but which is uncovered through an investigation. As an example of the historical acceptance of the investigatory role of an expert, reference may be had to the *Walfish Bay Boundary Case of 1911*, between Great Britain and Germany:

> The Arbitrator may employ any necessary help and in particular, if he thinks fit, either with or without the previous request of one of the parties, he may appoint an expert officer to proceed to the post and make any survey or examination or receive any oral evidence which he may consider necessary to enable him to arrive at a decision.[73]

6.33 The principle that an expert may be employed by a tribunal to both investigate, as well as analyse the evidence, has been recognised in article 26(1) of the UNCITRAL Model Law as well as in article 6.3 of the IBA Rules wherein it is assumed that the tribunal-appointed expert may seek to obtain evidence from a party. As this article makes plain, the parties are under the same duty to cooperate with the expert in supplying relevant information as they are vis-à-vis the tribunal. In this respect, the duty of collaboration and procedural good faith[74] extends to working with the expert.

6.34 An issue connected with the parties' duty to cooperate in the production of evidence is the obligation of the expert to observe the principle of equal treatment and the right to be heard in the course of conducting the investigation. Failure to observe standards of due process may render the expert's report subject to challenge and call into question the tribunal's ability to rely on it. These duties also apply when an expert or the tribunal conducts an inspection, pursuant to articles 6.3 and 7. This means that the tribunal or expert should take care to ensure that both parties are afforded the opportunity to attend the inspection, and are privy to the information that is provided to the expert or the tribunal.[75]

---

72 See, for example the procedural rules of the Netherlands-Japanese Property Commission, art. 15: "The Commission may appoint an expert to submit in writing his opinion on factual matters." *Case of the Netherlands Steamship Op ten Noort-Decisions I and II* (Netherlands-Japan),16 January 1961, 14 RIAA, p. 505.

73 See: art. VI, Declaration between Great Britain and Germany referring the Delimitation of the Southern Boundary of the British Territory of Walfish Bay to Arbitration, signed at Berlin, 30 January 1909, *Walfish Bay Boundary Case* (Germany, Great Britain), 23 May 1911, 11 RIAA, p. 266.

74 See: comments to art. 9.7.

75 See, as an example the following instruction issued by a tribunal constituted under the ICC Rules: "Power and duties of the expert: The expert is to visit the site (the place of location of the documents and the software)

The production of evidence at the request of the expert

6.35 The text of article 6.3 makes plain that disputes over whether evidence ought to be produced by a party are to be held to the standards set forth in articles 3.5–3.8, in a manner similar to requests for adverse document disclosure. The introductory language of article 6.3 incorporates the objections stated in article 9.2 as grounds for a party to resist the disclosure requested by the expert which is consistent with past arbitral decisions on this issue.[76] Where article 6.3 states that the "authority of the expert shall be the same as the authority of the Arbitral Tribunal", it should be understood that although the expert operates with the approved authority of the tribunal to order evidence to be made available or to draw an inference, the scope of the authority is limited so that the ultimate right to determine disagreements over the expert's requests is retained by the tribunal.[77] To consider otherwise would be to violate one of the basic rules concerning tribunal-appointed experts, which is that the expert's function is that of witness and not specialist arbitrator.[78]

6.36 Thus, if the expert should seek documents which a party protests are irrelevant or immaterial to the outcome of the case, the tribunal should determine the matter based not only on whether the documents are necessary for the report, but also on whether they are relevant to the case and material to its outcome. Therefore, if an expert is seeking documents which he or she believes will assist his or her report, but which the tribunal believes go beyond the mandate given to the expert, it should restrict disclosure to those narrowly defined issues set forth in the expert's terms of reference, in keeping with the needs of the case at large. More generally, if an expert has submitted a request to a party which is wide ranging, potentially encompasses sensitive or privileged information or otherwise violates a principle of article 9.2, as per the express conditions of article 6.2 above, a tribunal should seek to either refine the request, or otherwise relieve a party of the burden of responding to it.

---

and the plant. He has the power to obtain from the parties all explanations required, to request all documents needed and make any and all verifications necessary to accomplish his mission. For that purpose the expert may also require information from any third parties, including third-party suppliers. When carrying out his mission, the expert may be assisted by any person he deems appropriate. He is to secure equal treatment of the parties and their rights to be heard, and in particular to avoid any unilateral communication with either party in the absence of the other. In case of difficulties, the expert is to contact the Chairman of the Arbitral Tribunal." ICC Case No. 13490, Procedural Order of July 2006, in *ICC International Court of Arbitration Bulletin Vol. 25/Supplement – 2014*, p. 8.

76 See the Dissenting Opinion of Richard Mosk to the interim award of the Iran-US Claims Tribunal, Chamber 3 in *Behring International v The Islamic Republic of Iran*, determining to appoint an expert: "The Tribunal provided that the expert is entitled to obtain from the parties documents 'he deems necessary', without any restriction. I assume this provision does not permit requests for documents that would be privileged or requests which would be burdensome and oppressive. Compliance with the decision may entail expenses to the Claimant, but the Tribunal has made no effort to determine the nature, extent and ultimate responsibility for such expenses. Moreover, the Tribunal's $30,000 figure for an advance of costs is not based on any information or investigation." *Behring International v The Islamic Republic of Iran, supra* n. 54, Dissent of Richard M. Mosk, mentioned also in Caron, Caplan and Pellonpää, *supra* n. 20, p. 673.

77 Commenting on art. 27(2) of the UNCITRAL Rules which is similar in formulation to art. 6.3, Caron, Caplan and Pellonpää note the following: "Although the expert may request information from the parties, only the tribunal possesses the right to enforce such demands for the provision of information." Caron, Caplan and Pellonpää, *supra* n. 20, p. 672.

78 See: comments to art. 6.1.

Right to be heard and impartiality in the conduct of an investigation

6.37 The tribunal-appointed expert is required to observe due process in carrying out the mandate set forth in the terms of reference. This is particularly true as it relates to the process of adducing evidence from the parties. A failure by the expert to treat the parties impartially calls into question the tribunal's ability to rely on a final report, as was noted by an ICC tribunal in rendering its instructions to the expert:

> We do not exclude that you might have to ask questions or hear explanations, and perhaps inspect plant and equipment on the spot, but in the experience of some this is somewhat tricky. It is essential to safeguard the integrity of the entire expertise procedure. Any irregularity could jeopardize the validity of your conclusions and of the decisions that the Arbitral Tribunal might take based on your report, all at considerable loss of time and money.[79]

6.38 Tribunal-appointed experts should avoid *ex parte* meetings or interviews with parties or party representatives unless conducted in accordance with an agreed schedule of consultations between the parties.[80] Interviews, if they do take place, will often be recorded by the expert, and notified to the tribunal.[81] Another principle that is derived from the expert's duty to observe equal treatment and the right to be heard in the conduct of compiling a report is the obligation to provide both sides the opportunity to inform him or her of the evidence in the case. The expert must afford both parties the opportunity to produce what they deem to be relevant.[82] The above notwithstanding, the expert is customarily

---

79 "Documents 15-30", *ASA Bulletin supra* n. 22, p. 469.

80 See also an ICC arbitration which presented the unusual scenario where an arbitral tribunal was asked to consider whether the activities of an expert, in the context of rendering a binding expert opinion were consistent with arbitral due process. In this regard, the tribunal noted that the expert had breached standards of the right to be heard and equal treatment when it had conducted four interviews with the claimant, without notifying the respondent. The expert argued that this was necessary to obtain information. However, the tribunal noted the following: "In order to observe equal treatment of the parties, Mr. H. H. should at least have offered to have a meeting with B. too, yet such offer was never made . . . therefore the equal treatment of the parties was violated by Mr. H. H.'s *ex parte* communications with K." "Award on Preliminary Issues of 11 November 2003, ICC Case No. 12171", *supra* n. 65, p. 257. See also the following instruction of an ICC tribunal which specifically ordered the expert not to engage in *ex parte* communications of any kind: "[the tribunal] orders that the expertise be conducted while strictly adhering to the equality of the parties and the principle of contradictory proceedings, in such a way that the two parties be informed of each written communication of the expert to either party, of each and every request for information, that the parties are put in the position of presenting their observations, and that no procedural action, even in the form of a simple interview, be conducted without that the parties have been called or informed on time." "ICC Case No. 6057, Procedural Order, (1990)", in Dominique Hascher (ed.), *Collection of Procedural Decisions in ICC Arbitration 1993–1996*, pp. 32–38 (2nd edition, 1998).

81 The following direction rendered by an ICSID tribunal is instructive concerning the duty to refrain from one-sided communications: "The Expert shall be entitled to hear any person with knowledge of the project, if he deems it appropriate and after the Parties have been duly invited to attend such a meeting. The Parties will be given at least two weeks' notice, unless, in view of exceptional circumstances, the Expert is authorized by the Chairman of the Arbitral Tribunal to shorten such period. He shall inform the Arbitral Tribunal of such invitations. He shall keep Minutes of such meetings." "Documents 15-30", *ASA Bulletin supra* n. 22, p. 469.

82 See, for instance, the following rule adhered to by an ICC tribunal: "A second point violating the principle of equal treatment and the right to be heard lies in the fact that Mr. H. H. did not ask B. to supply him with documents, whereas he had received and accepted documents from K. . . . . It is thus [the expert's] duty to indicate to the parties the right point of time when they have to supply him with documents and information." ICC Case No. 12171, *supra* n. 65, p. 263. It follows from this principle that the expert may not receive documentary evidence from one side without transmitting copies of the evidence to the other. See the decision of an ICC tribunal in Case No. 9151 to refuse the appointment of a tribunal expert because one party represented that it would only produce evidence to the expert and not the adverse party. "Claimants have referred to this provision [on confidentiality] as

afforded wide latitude to determine which documents, or evidence generally is considered probative, and useful for his report, and which is not.[83]

Equal treatment and the right to be heard in the conduct of an inspection

6.39 As noted in both articles 6.3 and 7, a tribunal or an expert may conduct an inspection of a relevant site or piece of equipment if to do so would have probative value. An inspection or site visit is generally to be considered an opportunity for the tribunal or the expert to obtain knowledge relevant to the case by means of its own observations, and not an opportunity for one side or the other to proffer its own argument and evidence. This is the historically accepted purpose of a site visit or inspection. One former justice of the Permanent Court of International Justice noted the approach that the court took in relation to a request from Belgium to engage in a site visit in the course of the well-known *River Meuse* case of 1937:

> The Court viewed the Belgian suggestion, not as an offer to present evidence but as an offer to the Court to procure its own information.[84]

6.40 It is accepted practice that attendance at an inspection should be open to both parties. The failure by a tribunal to inform a party fully of what transpired during a site visit has been found in the past to be tantamount to a breach of "natural justice", a term which implicates fundamental due process.[85] In a decision on a challenge to the enforcement of an award rendered under the CIETAC Rules of Arbitration by the Hong Kong Court of Appeal in *Polytek Engineering v Hebei*, the situation was considered where both the chairman of a tribunal and the tribunal-appointed expert had inspected the claimant's equipment over the course of the proceedings. Of initial consequence is the fact that the respondent had not

---

an explanation of their difficulties to submit evidence in support of their own claims and have instead offered to make the evidence available to the Arbitral Tribunal or to an independent expert, but not to the Respondents. The motion of the Claimants for the appointment of such an expert was rejected by the Arbitral Tribunal on the basis that a fair trial necessitates that all evidence be made available to both parties." *ICC Bulletin*, Vol. 20, No. 2, p. 73 (2009). See further: the comments to art. 6.5 below.

83 See: *Starrett Housing*, *supra* n. 70, p. 128, where the tribunal noted with approval the expert's decision to reject materials he considered irrelevant from consideration.

84 Reporting the comments of Justice Manley O. Hudson in *River Meuse case (Netherlands v Belgium)*, 28 June 1937, in Bin Cheng, *supra* n. 4, p. 304, n. 12. Cheng further comments that: "The procedure may thus be regarded as a means for edifying the judicial knowledge."

85 "*Polytek Engineering Co Ltd v Hebei Import & Export Corp*, High Court, Court of Appeal Hong Kong, No. 116 of 1997, 16 January 1998," in Albert Jan van den Berg (ed.), *Yearbook Commercial Arbitration*, Vol. XXIII, p. 666 (1998). This judgment would be reversed by the Hong Kong Court of Final Appeal but on grounds related to the Respondent's failure to raise the issue of ex parte communications and inspection before the tribunal. Despite the reversal, the Court of Appeals criticism of the practices of the tribunal in this instance are instructive as demonstrating conduct that would potentially violate the right to equal treatment and to present one's case. A.N. Mason NPJ, writing for the majority of the Court of Final Appeal, stated the following: "With respect to the argument arising from the communications to the Chief Arbitrator, the holding of the inspection at the end user's factory and the presentation by the technicians *in the absence of the respondent* were procedures which in Hong Kong might be considered unacceptable. But once the respondent received the report and the letter of 4 January 1996, it was in a position to explore the significance of what had happened. It failed to do so. It did not apply for a re-inspection in the presence of its representatives. It did not apply for removal of the Chief Arbitrator. It simply proceeded with the arbitration as if nothing untoward had happened. In these circumstances, the respondent has not established that the communications to the Chief Arbitrator gave rise to a case falling within s.44(3) of the Ordinance (Article V. 2(b) of the Convention)." [1999] 1 HKLRD 665; [1999] 2 HKCFAR 111. Available at www.judiciary.gov.hk.

been notified of the inspection, and therefore did not have a representative in attendance. The court noted as follows, "It would seem that such an inspection was very much part of the arbitration proceedings during which both parties should be present. In our view, the defendant should have been notified and allowed to be present at the inspection."[86] Both articles 6.3 and 7 require that all parties be permitted to attend any inspection conducted by the tribunal, and the tribunal-appointed expert, which is in essence an important aspect of maintaining equality between the parties. Should a party fail to nominate a representative to attend or otherwise fail to attend an inspection after receiving notice, it may be regarded as having waived its rights in this respect.[87]

6.41 It is quite clear that during the conduct of an inspection, the tribunal often will receive information concerning the case from relevant personnel or employees in attendance. Information that is received during an inspection should be made known to both sides. This was at issue in *Polytek* where during the investigation the employees of the claimant had conducted certain "seminars" on various technical aspects of the case, however, this information was not made known to the respondent. The court noted as follows:

> It is therefore quite clear both from the Tribunal's own reply and the expert's report that during the inspection, there were indeed "seminars" given by the plaintiff's technicians to the inspectors, including the Chief Arbitrator. There is of course no evidence before the court of any "records of seminars". It is immaterial as to whether such record or minutes existed, why the defendant has not asked for them or why they were not provided by the Tribunal or the plaintiff. The significance of the reference to the seminars and the record and minutes thereof in the Tribunal's reply and the expert's report is that the Tribunal in the course of the proceedings and deliberations, did receive communications from only one party in the absence of the other.[88]

6.42 The court would go on to find that even though the expert's report had been provided to the adverse party, the fact that one party was not aware of what had occurred during the inspection gave rise to a strong inference of bias on the part of the expert and even the tribunal. In its reasoning the Hong Kong court noted further that an oral hearing allowing for the expert to be questioned, if conducted, could possibly have cured the taint of bias by allowing the adverse party the ability to ask questions about, and respond to the information that had been delivered during the meeting.[89]

---

86 *Ibid.*, p. 678.

87 See: ICC Case No. 12171, where the tribunal ruled on the complaint by one party that the expert had acted in breach of equal treatment by inspecting a vessel in the company of the other party's personnel: "It is undisputed that Mr H. H. was at no time escorted by a person from B. when paying his two visits to the M. O., but that the second time he was accompanied by a service engineer ordered by K. (Minutes p. 153). However, one has to bear in mind that B. was fully informed about the visits of Mr H. H. and even assisted him in organizing his embarking. Mr M. M. was questioned in the Witness Hearing why he did not tell Mr H. H. that they wanted to give him their view on the issues once they knew that he was supposed to visit the M.O. . . . . Since B was informed about Mr H. H.'s inspections on the M.O., yet did not feel the need to send one of its own people, it has waived its right to claim that, based on this fact, it was not equally treated." ICC Case No. 12171, *supra* n. 65, pp. 261–262.

88 *Supra* n. 85, p. 679.

89 *Ibid.*: "In the peculiar circumstances of this case, we think that the Tribunal should have held further hearings with regard to the matters which had arisen from the inspection and the expert's report." p. 681. See the note above on the Court of Final Appeal's decision to reverse the Court of Appeal judgment on the basis that the party suffering the alleged breach of its right to be heard did not raise the matter before the tribunal.

6.43 Site inspections are common-place in international arbitration. In a recent ICC arbitration which arose out of a major infrastructure project in the Middle East,[90] the approach taken by the tribunal is instructive for the purposes of avoiding the type of due process concerns raised in the above-mentioned CIETAC arbitration. Initially, the tribunal invited the parties to share their views on the need for a visit, to which general agreement was reached that it would be useful. After doing so, the tribunal directed the parties to meet together and agree on the "rules" governing the visit.[91] These rules included: (1) restrictions on the number of individuals from each party who would be allowed to accompany the tribunal in its visit (including which legal counsel could be present); (2) the route the visit was to take and the technical aspects of the site which the tribunal was to review; (3) who, from each party, would be allowed to make a technical presentation and on what subject-matter; and (4) a general admonition that the site visit was to allow the tribunal to "familiarize itself with the site conditions", and not for each party to, "use the opportunity to justify or argue their case".[92]

A party's right to review and comment on the expert report and related matters

Article 6.5 2010 IBA Rules: The Arbitral Tribunal shall send a copy of such Expert Report to the Parties. The Parties may examine any information, Documents, goods, samples, property, machinery, systems, processes or site for inspection that the Tribunal-Appointed Expert has examined and any correspondence between the Arbitral Tribunal and the Tribunal-Appointed Expert. Within the time ordered by the Arbitral Tribunal, any Party shall have the opportunity to respond to the Expert Report in a submission by the Party or through a Witness Statement or an Expert Report by a Party-Appointed Expert. The Arbitral Tribunal shall send the submission, Witness Statement or Expert Report to the Tribunal-Appointed Expert and to the other Parties.

General discussion

6.44 The result of the investigation by the expert is the expert report. As the report itself is to be considered evidence, unless agreed otherwise, the tribunal must, as it would with any other piece of relevant evidence, inform the parties of the report by transmitting it to them.[93] Failure on the part of the tribunal to notify the parties of the expert report may

---

90 ICC Case No. 16249, Procedural Order No. 3 (15 February 2010) (unpublished).

91 *Ibid.* See also the direction of the tribunal in the *Indus Waters Kishenganga Arbitration*: "Having considered the Parties' respective communications concerning the site visit itinerary, the Court issued Procedural Order No. 3, deciding, *inter alia*, the itinerary of the proposed visit, the size of the delegations, matters concerning the confidentiality of the site visit and the manner in which the costs were to be apportioned between the Parties." *Indus Waters Kishenganga Arbitration, supra* n. 5, p. 5.

92 *Ibid.* Whether a site visit by a tribunal-appointed expert without the attendance of the tribunal would require such formality as described above may be questioned. However, even where a more practical, and less formalistic approach may be applied, the underlying rule that both parties' right to be heard in relation to the matters inspected and reviewed by the expert remains applicable.

93 The position adopted by the ICC tribunal in ICC Case No. 14079 summarises the general approach regarding access to the Experts' Opinion: "The Experts' Opinion, when prepared, will normally be submitted to the

prevent the tribunal from relying upon the findings found therein. Thus, article 6.5 provides for a principle of due process that must be observed.

Failure to allow the parties to respond to an expert's report

6.45 A reported case concerning a CIETAC arbitration demonstrates the dangers of failing to communicate the full details of an expert report to the parties. Here the tribunal commissioned an expert report to be compiled by an appointed expert, over the protests of the respondent party.[94] The expert report, which had been provided to the tribunal, was delivered to the parties seven days before the final award. In the intervening period, the respondent had notified the tribunal that it wished to submit counter evidence and comments on the report, nevertheless, without permitting such the tribunal issued its award shortly thereafter. The High Court of Hong Kong refused enforcement of the award, noting the following:

> I have no doubt whatsoever that a serious procedural irregularity occurred and that on reflection the Arbitral Tribunal would recognize it as such. The defendants had taken the stand throughout that inspection reports made many months after delivery were of no assistance in ascertaining whether at the time of delivery the goods were defective . . . It is clear that the Tribunal relied on these reports and that the defendants were given no chance to deal with this very different case which suddenly presented itself. The defendants should have been given an opportunity to deal with this new evidence. They asked for such opportunity but the award came too soon and they never received an answer for their request. Taking all the matters canvassed by both sides into account I have come to the very clear conclusion that the defendants were prevented from presenting their case and they have thus made out the grounds . . . The defendants were denied a fair and equal opportunity of being heard.[95]

6.46 In the above example, illustrates the dangers of failing to afford each party the right to be heard as to the findings of the expert.[96] This basic aspect of due process means that where a tribunal has commissioned an independent expert, it must provide the opportunity to the parties to present their views on this potentially decisive evidence.[97]

Parties for comments, and of course the Independent Experts' Opinion may be commented on by each side's own technical and commercial experts. Hence, Parties will be given time limits to comment on the findings of the Independent Expert." ICC Case No. 14079, Procedural Order of May 2007, in *ICC International Court of Arbitration Bulletin Vol. 25/Supplement – 2014*, p. 11.

94 "Paklito Investment Ltd v Klockner East Asia Ltd, Supreme Court of Hong Kong, High Court, 15 January 1993", Albert Jan van den Berg (ed.), *Yearbook Commercial Arbitration*, Vol. XIX, p. 665 (1994).

95 *Ibid.*, p. 671.

96 See the holding of an ICSID annulment committee confirming this principle: "The right to present one's case is also accepted as an essential element of the requirement to afford a fair hearing accorded in the principal human rights instruments. This principle requires both equality of arms and the proper participation of the contending parties in the procedure, these being separate but related fundamental elements of a fair trial. The principle will require the tribunal to afford both parties the opportunity to make submissions where new evidence is received and considered by the tribunal to be relevant to its final deliberations." *Fraport AG Frankfurt Airport Services Worldwide v The Philippines*, ICSID Case No. ARB/03/25, Decision on the Application for Annulment, para. 133 (2010).

97 See, as an example, the 2006 judgment of the Dubai Court of Cassation in which the court approved of the decision of the arbitrator to invite a party who had raised objections to the reports of the tribunal-appointed legal and accounting experts to submit a full memorandum on the report. The arbitrator also convened a hearing to allow the parties a further opportunity to question the expert concerning his report. In noting these steps had been taken by the arbitrator, the court rejected a challenge to the final award based on alleged violations of due process.

6.47 The above notwithstanding, reference should be further had to the case of *Luzon Hydro Corp v Transfield Pipelines*, a dispute arising out of an ICC arbitration that was heard before a High Court of Singapore.[98] The tribunal in this case had determined to appoint an expert whom, it was anticipated, would provide a written report. Subsequently, and after the expert had participated in the proceedings, the tribunal determined that an expert report would not be needed, but that the expert would continue to assist the tribunal with administrative matters. The tribunal's position notwithstanding, the fact that the expert had continued to advise the tribunal after the hearing was raised by Luzon as a procedural irregularity. It was Luzon 's position that the expert's activities constituted advice to the tribunal, and in the circumstances Luzon had not been afforded the opportunity to provide comment on such advice, thus its right to be heard had been breached. The Singapore High Court, in rejecting the challenge, found that the work performed by the expert had not been tantamount to rendering advice, but was correctly characterised by the tribunal as administrative assistance.[99]

6.48 Thus, article 6.5, supported by jurisprudence such as the above example taken from Hong Kong, posits the following rule of general practice: the parties should be provided an opportunity to comment on expert advice relied upon by the tribunal. This being said, the *Luzon* case does raise the possibility that not all work performed by an expert may be characterised as "advice" or in the language of article 6.5, as an "Expert Report".

6.49 To ensure that the various due process rights are observed, the following procedural order taken from an ICC arbitration provides a useful approach:

> The respondent shall submit a Memorandum on the Expert's findings (the "Memorandum") within 4 weeks from the date on which the Expert submits his/her final report, in accordance with the Terms of Reference . . . The Claimant shall submit a reply to the Respondent's Memorandum (the "Reply") within four weeks from the date on which the Respondent submits its Memorandum.[100]

6.50 Article 6.5 expands upon the above example by permitting the parties the right to submit counter evidence in addition to simply providing comments. This approach is to be recommended over limiting a party's right of rebuttal to simply comments as the right to be heard is often considered to include the right to produce counter evidence.[101] As article 6.5 makes clear, the party wishing to respond to the expert report must generally do so within the time frame set by the tribunal.[102]

"1 July 2006, Court of Cassation", in Jalal El Ahdab (ed.), *International Journal of Arab Arbitration*, Vol. 1, No. 4, p. 159 (2009).

98　*Luzon v Transfield, supra* n. 38.

99　*Ibid.,* para. 16: "I did not find much substance in Luzon's complaints . . . there was little reason to believe that he had gone beyond the bounds of assisting the tribunal in sorting out the evidence and understanding technical terms and identifying which part of the evidence was relevant to the various issues that were being considered by the tribunal."

100　ICC Case No. 11250, in *ICC Bulletin*, vol. 10, No. 2, p. 17 (1999).

101　See: comments to art. 3.11.

102　See an ICC arbitration seated in Jordan where the tribunal closed the evidentiary record because the parties had not abided by the time frame for submitting comments. There, the tribunal noted the steps it took to ensure the parties had been provided with a right to comment, but ultimately closed the proceedings when the parties failed to observe the deadline: "As no comments or request for the Expert's examination were given from the Parties on the Report by August 11, 2003, the Tribunal forwarded a reminder to both Parties giving them a final date for submitting their views concerning the Report no later than Saturday August 16, 2003. The Respondent gave some comments on the report and requested an additional period to provide comments. The prevailing

The right to review the information relied upon by the expert

6.51 In addition to access to the report itself, article 6.5 requires the parties to be afforded an opportunity to review the materials and evidence considered by the expert in preparing his report. In a practical sense, such access is needed by the parties in order to respond and/or comment on the report.[103] Thus, this principle should be respected as a basic requirement for affording a party the right to be heard. It should also be noted that article 6.5 establishes that a party has the right to review any information which the "Appointed Expert has examined", not just "relied upon" in preparing the report. Some jurisprudence supports the position that it is not a breach of due process if an expert fails to divulge documents that were received over the course of the investigation, so long as the expert did not rely upon them in reaching his conclusions.[104] Article 6.5, in requiring all documents examined by the expert, and not just those relied upon by the expert, thus may be said to expand the scope of a Party's right of review beyond what has previously been considered necessary.[105]

6.52 Further, it should also be noted that article 6.5 does not regard the communications between the expert and the tribunal to be subject to confidentiality. By contrast, in the *Luzon* case of the Singapore High Court, the court upheld the confidentiality of communications between the expert and the tribunal on grounds that these communications, like those between the arbitrators, are confidential.[106] Article 6.5 appears not to follow this approach, as communications between a tribunal-appointed expert and the arbitrators are

---

judgment of the Tribunal was that the Parties [had received] their opportunity to present their case and that the case was ready for deliberation and issuing of the award. Consequently, on August 17, 2003, the Tribunal declared the procedure closed for deliberation." "5 April 2004 Award in C Case", in Jalal El Ahdab (ed.), *International Journal of Arab Arbitration*, Vol. 2, No. 2, p. 301 (2010).

103 See the procedural rule adopted by an ICC tribunal requiring copies of documents submitted to the expert to be provided to both sides: "The Expert shall also be entitled to obtain from any Party all documents which he deems necessary for his investigation. Each Party shall without delay give the other Party a copy of any documents which it gives to the Expert. The Parties have the ability to apply to the Arbitral Tribunal if doubts should arise as to the relevance and/or difficulty of furnishing information which the expert seeks to obtain. "Documents 15–30", *ASA Bulletin*, Vol. 11, No. 3, p. 470 (1993).

104 See the *Unichips v Gesnouin* decision of the Paris court of appeal in which the enforcement of a final rendered in Switzerland was challenged based upon *inter alia* that the challenging party's right to be heard had not been respected because the tribunal-appointed expert had not divulged certain documents he had received in the course of the investigation. The court dismissed the challenge noting that: "In these circumstances, neither the expert nor the arbitral tribunal took into account documents that were not known to Unichips." "Cour d'appel, Paris, 12 February 1993" (*Société Unichips Finanziaria SpA SA and Unichips International BV, Netherlands v François et Michèle Gesnouin)*", in Albert Jan van den Berg (ed.), *Yearbook of Commercial Arbitration*, Vol. XIX, p. 659 (1994).

105 The view taken by art. 6.5 is to be preferred. It is not only relevant what an expert considers in preparing his report, but it may also be material what was ignored or not included in preparing the expert report. In the interest of thoroughness, a party should be afforded an opportunity to understand the full spectrum of information that the expert had available in preparing the final report. See the position taken by Schneider who comments as follows: "It is of course important that each party knows which documents have been communicated to the expert by its opponent. Some arbitrators, therefore, take care to prescribe that the other party and the arbitral tribunal must be informed of such communications by the copy of the documents or otherwise." Schneider, *supra* n. 13, p 459. See also: the discussion of ICC Case No. 9151, *supra* n. 82.

106 Speaking as to the expert's terms of reference the court noted, "The engagement did not provide that parties should have a copy of other communications between the tribunal and Mr. Shorland. These were confidential in the same way that communications between members of the tribunal itself would be confidential." *Luzon Hydro Corp v Transfield Philippines Inc*, *supra* n. 38, para. 19.

not afforded secrecy.[107] Rather, it would appear that the Rules take the position of the court in the *Hussman v Al Ameen* case where it was found that it was not proper for the tribunal to engage in discussions with the expert outside the view of the parties.[108]

Opportunity to examine the tribunal-appointed expert

Article 6.6 2010 IBA Rules:	**At the request of a Party or of the Arbitral Tribunal, the Tribunal-Appointed Expert shall be present at an Evidentiary Hearing. The Arbitral Tribunal may question the Tribunal-Appointed Expert, and he or she may be questioned by the Parties or by any Party-Appointed Expert, on issues raised in his or her Expert Report, the Parties' submissions or Witness Statement or the Expert Reports made by the Party-Appointed Experts pursuant to Article 6.5.**
Article 26(2) UNCITRAL Model Law:	Unless otherwise agreed by the parties, if a party so requests or if the arbitral tribunal considers it necessary, the expert shall, after delivery of his written or oral report, participate in a hearing where the parties have the opportunity to put questions to him and to present expert witnesses in order to testify on the points at issue.

General discussion

6.53 Article 6.6 follows the well-accepted principle that the tribunal-appointed expert should make him or herself available for a hearing upon request from the parties or the tribunal.[109] This principle is also found in the UNCITRAL Model Law in article 26(2). Notably both article 26(2), the specific provision dealing with experts, and article 24(2), which addresses the right to an oral hearing more generally, use the mandatory language of "shall". This means that upon a request from a party, the expert witness must make him

---

107 One might suppose that the view of the Singapore High Court would be different had the expert performed the normal task of an appointed expert and issued a report that the tribunal would have considered. There, in acting in his full capacity as an expert, the court may have seen the need to follow the principles of art. 6.5 and required all communications to be divulged since the parties should in that circumstance have the right to comment on the circumstances connected to the delivery of the expert report.

108 See: paras 45 and 46 of *Hussman v Al Ameen*, *supra* n. 49. The court noted that: "The point was taken that in the meeting with Dr. Al-Qasm, the tribunal was not taking evidence and so the provisions of s. 37(1)(b) did not apply; I do not agree. They were plainly discussing with him the law of Saudi Arabia and the content of his report; in my judgment the provisions of the section were applicable to this meeting at which this evidence was discussed . . . Although it was accepted on behalf of the Respondents that to have this meeting had been unwise on the part of the tribunal, they submitted it was not an irregularity. I do not agree."

109 See: ICC Case No. 14079: "Thereafter, i.e. after Submissions dealing with the Parties' comments to the Independent Experts' Opinion, the Tribunal will most likely schedule a Hearing for which one entire week should be reserved. The purpose of the Hearing will be for the Experts to be examined orally on their findings, quite in the sense of examination and cross-examination. It is not possible, at this time, to determine whether such further oral examination will be a short exercise, or whether it will be an exercise to be carried out during one or two or more days. Thereafter, time will be needed to reflect on where we stand, including oral post-hearing arguments on the "lessons to be learned" from the examination of the Expert(s). Hence, one week is to be reserved." ICC Case No. 14079, Procedural Order of May 2007, in *ICC International Court of Arbitration Bulletin Vol. 25/Supplement – 2014*, p. 11.

or herself available to attend a hearing.[110] This is consistent with the notion that an expert's report should be provided to the parties for comment and challenge as a necessary requirement in order to uphold a party's right to be heard – a party must have the right to review, consider and challenge the expert's findings. The above principles are of course subject to the caveat that a party, expressly or by conduct, may waive such a right.[111] Moreover, it should be considered that a party's right to examine the expert is limited to those subject areas described in article 6.6.

6.54 A review of the procedural practices of various arbitral tribunals confirms that articles 6.6 and 26(2) reflect a customary practice that is routinely adopted.[112] The hearing provides a useful means for examination of the assumptions, methods and conclusions of the expert by the parties, potentially with the assistance of their own experts.[113] The tribunal also may intervene to ask questions if necessary. The issues and means of conducting a hearing discussed in respect of article 8 are equally applicable to the hearing of the expert. Although not specifically stated in the Rules, a failure by an expert to appear for an oral hearing may require the tribunal to disregard the written report. In this respect, a tribunal may consider, by analogy, the standards set forth in articles 4.7 and 5.5.

Weighing the probative value of the expert report

Article 6.4 2010 IBA Rules: The Tribunal-Appointed Expert shall report in writing to the Arbitral Tribunal in an Expert Report.
The Expert Report shall contain:

(a) the full name and address of the Tribunal-Appointed Expert, and a description of his or her background, qualifications, training and experience;

---

110 See, for example, the comments of Holtzman and Neuhaus in their report on the drafting history of UNCITRAL Model Law, art. 26(2): "The Fourth Draft required that in every case the expert after presenting his report 'shall' participate at a hearing. That approach was rejected, presumably because there may be cases in which neither the arbitral tribunal nor any party considers the hearing of the expert is necessary. The Working Group adopted the more flexible formulation that appears in the final text, providing for a hearing only where either a party requested one or the tribunal considered it necessary." Howard M. Holtzman and Joseph E. Neuhaus, *A Guide To The UNCITRAL Model Law on International Commercial Arbitration, Legislative History and Commentary*, p. 720 (1989).

111 See: ICC arbitration, *supra* n. 102. where the tribunal closed the evidentiary procedure without receiving comments of the parties on an expert's report because of the parties' failure to observe the necessary time limits. See also: for an extreme example of this principle, the finding in, *International Standard Electric Corp v Bridas Sociedad Anonima Petrolera, Indus. y Comercial*, 745 F.Supp. 172 (SDNY 1990), here an ICC tribunal determined to appoint an expert on New York substantive law, but proposed not to inform the parties of his identity, nor permit cross-examination. Later, at the enforcement stage, the resisting party argued that the procedure breached due process, however, because it had not raised an objection to the tribunal's proposed plan, it was deemed to have accepted the appointment of the anonymous expert, and hence lost its right to object before the enforcing court.

112 See: Poudret and Besson, who note the following: "The parties must however be able to comment freely on the contents of the expert's report and several laws and sets of arbitration rules expressly grant them the right to put questions to the expert at a hearing, possibly accompanied by their own experts." Poudret and Besson, *supra* n. 3, p. 562, para. 665.

113 See: ICC Case No. 14079: "The examinations of the Independent Expert(s) can be done by counsel of the Parties, and/or – under control of counsel and of the Tribunal – by the Parties' own experts (who may be better placed to discuss truly technical or other issues than counsel with no technical or other engineering degrees)." ICC Case No. 14079, Procedural Order of May 2007, in *ICC International Court of Arbitration Bulletin Vol. 25/ Supplement – 2014*, p. 11, fn. 4.

(b)   a statement of the facts on which he or she is basing his or her expert opinions and conclusions;

(c)   his or her expert opinions and conclusions, including a description of the methods, evidence and information used in arriving at the conclusions. Documents on which the Tribunal-Appointed Expert relies that have not already been submitted shall be provided;

(d)   if the Expert Report has been translated, a statement as to the language in which it was originally prepared, and the language in which the Tribunal-Appointed Expert anticipates giving testimony at the Evidentiary Hearing;

(e)   an affirmation of his or her genuine belief in the opinions expressed in the Expert Report;

(f)   the signature of the Tribunal-Appointed Expert and its date and place; and

(g)   if the Expert Report has been signed by more than one person, an attribution of the entirety or specific parts of the Expert Report to each author.

Article 6.7 2010 IBA Rules: Any Expert Report made by a Tribunal-Appointed Expert and its conclusions shall be assessed by the Arbitral Tribunal with due regard to all circumstances of the case.

General discussion

6.55 Article 6.4 sets forth a number of minimum requirements for the content of the expert report. This is a standard, non-exhaustive formula that provides a structure for the expert to follow. If adhered to, these guidelines should render the report's reasoning sufficiently clear so that the tribunal and the parties will be able to weigh its probative value.

6.56 In weighing the probative value of the report, article 6.7 calls for the tribunal to consider the report in light of all the elements of the case. The expert report is evidence which may be treated like any other witness statement, documentary evidence or other expert report submitted into the record of the proceedings (subject to the proviso that it may be accorded more weight than party submissions since it is a non-partisan document).[114] There is little doubt that a tribunal may ignore partially or wholly the findings of the appointed expert, if it deems it prudent to do so.[115]

---

114 "It is important to clarify that the Experts' Opinion as such is not binding upon the Arbitrators, but is subject to the Arbitrators' appreciation, as expressed in this paragraph. Obviously, the Tribunal's task will be to put the technical and economical findings (as may be submitted to them by the Independent Expert) into the contractual and legal perspective. Hence, the determinations to be made by the Independent Expert(s) is [*sic*] only one stone in the overall 'mosaic' to be considered and appreciated by the Tribunal." ICC Case No. 14079, Procedural Order of May 2007, in *ICC International Court of Arbitration Bulletin Vol. 25/Supplement – 2014*, p. 11.

115 See, for instance, the statement of the tribunal in an ICC arbitration: "The Parties are reminded that the Arbitral Tribunal is not bound by the conclusions of the experts, but that it may assess them freely and with due consideration of all factual and legal circumstances." (unofficial translation) "Il est rappelé aux parties que le Tribunal arbitral n'est pas lié par les conclusions des experts, mais qu'il les apprécie librement en tenant compte de toutes les circonstances de fait et de droit." Award in ICC Case No. 2444 of 1976, *supra* n. 63, pp. 285–286. See also the position of a CRCICA tribunal: "The Arbitral Tribunal said that, in line with the judgments of the Court of Cassation, the expert's report is not binding on the court (or the arbitrator) since it

The above notwithstanding, it is not uncommon for a tribunal to adopt large parts of an expert witness' report, if not the entire set of findings, where it deems it appropriate to do so.[116] The probative value of a tribunal-appointed expert's findings may be high if the report is considered to be reliable and consistent with other evidence. Some standards by which a tribunal may judge the conclusions of an expert are considered further below.

Attributes of a report

6.57 Beyond those minimum requirements identified above, the report of the expert will have content which varies depending on the needs of the case. In terms of form, article 6.4 describes the content which should be included in the report, and provides both substantive and formal requirements. Of immediate note is that the introduction to article 6.4 states that the report of the expert is to be reduced to writing. The word "shall" as used in this article is an express indication that oral reports are not contemplated under the IBA Rules.[117] This has not always been the practice in arbitration with respect to some types of experts, though the instances where a written report has not been required are limited.[118] Where a tribunal deviates from this rule it should at the very least require the

---

is a mere opinion and an element of evidence to be assessed by the court (Case No. 333 of the judicial year 21, hearing of 3 May 1955). The court may uphold a part of such a report and disregard the rest (Cassation No. 41 of the judicial year 13, hearing of 9 March 1944). The court is not bound by such a report and can exclude it; it is enough to give reasons for such an exclusion (Cassation No. 240 of the judicial year 22, hearing of 15 December 1955). The statement of a party before the expert may not be considered an acknowledgement if it was stated as argument and discussion of a claimed right, because in such a case the acknowledgement of such right is not pure and express (Cassation No. 15 of the judicial year 34 hearing of 6 June 1967)." Final award of 25 September 2000, Cairo Regional Centre for International Commercial Arbitration in M. E. I. Alam Eldin (ed.), *Arbitral Awards of the Cairo Regional Centre for International Commercial Arbitration*, p. 201 (2003). The following summary captures customary practice: "The expert's report is but one factor that the tribunal considers in light of the totality of the circumstances of the case. The report is not legally binding on the arbitrators who may pick and choose from its contents as they deem appropriate." Caron, Caplan and Pellonpää, *supra* n. 20, p. 674.

116 As an example, see the following decision by an ICC tribunal accepting the findings of the final report by an appointed expert: "We have, on the other hand, found that the [product] did not, in April 1984, comply with Annex I in certain respects some of which were quite serious, e.g., the characteristics referred to in p. 8 of Mr. X's report. We accept in this regard the Reports of Mr. X. (whose evidence was not in our view seriously challenged by either side)." "Final award in ICC Case No. 4975 of 1988", in Albert Jan van den Berg (ed.), *Yearbook Commercial Arbitration*, Vol. XIV, pp. 122, 132 (1989).

117 See: ICC Case No. 13490: "The expert is expected to submit his report to the Arbitral Tribunal [within two months]. This deadline may be extended by the Arbitral Tribunal if necessary." ICC Case No. 13490, Procedural Order of July 2006, in *ICC International Court of Arbitration Bulletin Vol. 25/Supplement – 2014*, p. 8.

118 For instance, the Chartered Institute of Arbitrators *Practice Guideline No. 10: Guidelines on the use of Tribunal-Appointed Experts, Legal Advisers and Assessors* notes that in respect of "assessors" appointed by a tribunal to give guidance on technical issues, often a formal report is not prepared though they may informally advise the tribunal. However, as many arbitration laws require the parties to be made aware of the evidence delivered to the tribunal, and afforded an opportunity to react, the tribunal is best advised to have any reporting by an assessor put in writing, as the following quote from the *Guideline* notes: "5.4. . . . Where assessors give advice to the tribunal following the conclusion of the oral hearing, a convenient mode of ensuring that the parties have an opportunity to comment on that advice is to reduce it to writing and to send it, together with a draft of the proposed technical sections of the award, to the parties for their comments before the award is issued." In this respect, art. 6.4 takes a conservative approach and calls for all reporting to be done in writing, and in light of the common expectation in international arbitration that a party will be made privy to any information presented to the tribunal, the correctness of this approach must be accepted.

expert to give an oral report at a hearing with the parties and their experts, to the extent they have appointed one.[119]

6.58 Subparagraphs (b) and (c) provide a guideline for the substance of the report, and are crucial for the tribunal to follow the reasoning adopted by the expert. In terms of weighing the report, the tribunal must have confidence in the thoroughness, impartiality and logic of the expert's analysis. The following example drawn from the *Starrett Housing* case provides an example of a report that was given considerable weight due to its thoroughness:

> In this massive submission, the Expert set forth not only his conclusions but also cited the evidentiary support for them and described the positions of the Parties on each significant issue. He included full texts or quotations of relevant portions of the documents upon which he relied. His credibility is enhanced by his candour. Thus, where he drew inferences or made subjective judgments, he pointed them out and explained his reasons. Where he considered that he may have made a judicial interpretation, he identified the point and referred it to the Tribunal for final decision. Where he considered a matter beyond his terms of reference, he specifically called attention to it.[120]

6.59 The more closely the expert works with the parties to ensure they have a full view of the case the more persuasive his or her report is likely to be.

Adopting the full findings of the expert

6.60 In applying article 6.7, the tribunal is required to consider whether the full or partial adoption of the expert's conclusions is warranted. The jurisprudence of international tribunals suggests that the common standard applied to whether a tribunal-appointed expert's findings should be adopted is captured by the following statement from the Franco-Italian Conciliation Commission:

> It is certain that the opinion of the expert does not bind the Commission which must decide according to its own conviction. But taking account of the facts and evaluation techniques, there is no reason for the court not adopting as its own the conclusion of the expert, unless his argumentation is in contradiction with the facts of record, with the legal provisions of the rules or logic.[121]

6.61 This standard is implicitly found within article 6.7, as it is surely correct to consider that the comparison of the report's findings to the "circumstances of the case" will inevitably invite an evaluation by the tribunal of whether the report's findings are consistent with the facts and its interpretation of the law. In applying this standard, some arbitral tribunals may decline to accept the expert's findings for reasons of equity, estoppel and other legal doctrines.[122] Moreover, a tribunal may consider that there are factual

---

119 See, generally: comments to art. 6.6.

120 Quoted in *Starrett Housing v Iran, supra* n. 70, p. 274.

121 Sandifer, *supra* n. 1, p. 327, citing to the *Héritiers de SAR Mgr le Duc de Guise* decision.

122 Poudret and Besson make the following valuable contribution regarding a tribunal's discretion to not accept the findings of an appointed expert: "The arbitrators are not bound by the findings of an expert, even if he has been appointed by the arbitral tribunal . . . If the arbitral tribunal departs from the opinion of an independent expert, it should give reasons. Such reasons are not 'so much destined to convince the appellate court or the court or the enforcement judge, which cannot review the facts, but rather to avoid the accusation of an oversight, or worse a violation of the right to be heard." Poudret and Besson, *supra* n. 3, p. 562, para. 666.

considerations, such as intervening circumstances or other issues, which the expert was not aware of, did not take into consideration or which were beyond his or her mandate that require the tribunal to reject some conclusions. Equally, the expert's reasoning simply may not be persuasive to the tribunal in light of the evidentiary record or the logic adopted.

Costs of tribunal-appointed expert

Article 6.8 2010 IBA Rules: **The fees and expenses of a Tribunal-Appointed Expert, to be funded in a manner determined by the Arbitral Tribunal, shall form part of the costs of the arbitration.**

General discussion

6.62 The principle that the expert's costs are to form "part" of the costs of the arbitration is consistent with the basic notion that the expert performs their duties for both or all of the parties and thus they are jointly and severably liable for the fees associated with the expert's work. See for example the following comments which lay out the applicable rule:

> Normally, a tribunal-appointed expert has both parties . . . as his contract parties. This rule also applies where one of the arbitrating parties has objected to the tribunal appointing an expert . . . This view holds true when only one of the parties has paid the entire advance on costs into the account of the chairman of the arbitral tribunal or the administering organisation. The liability must be joint and several.[123]

6.63 This is the basic principle conveyed by article 6.8. Like arbitrator's fees and other costs for administering the arbitration, the fees of the tribunal-appointed expert are part of the administrative costs of the case, and in general, are paid in advance by the parties by depositing equal portions of the advance into a designated account.[124] By extension, this also means that the tribunal may award in the final award a refund of the costs of the expert as part of the arbitration costs to one party or the other taking into consideration the appropriate circumstances of the case.[125]

---

123 Peter F. Schlosser, "Generalizable Approaches to Agreements with Experts and Witnesses Acting in Arbitration and International Litigation" *Global Reflections on International Law, Commerce and Dispute Resolution, Liber Amicorum in honour of Robert Briner*, p. 776 (2005).

124 "The Tribunal further decides, in accordance with Tribunal Rule 41(2), that the Claimant shall deposit within two months from the date of this Award the sum of Twenty-Five Thousand United States Dollars (US$25,000) into account number 24.58.28.583 at Pierson, Heldring and Pierson, Korte Vijverberg 2, 2513 AB The Hague, in the name of the Secretary-General of the Iran-United States Claims Tribunal (Account No. II), as an advance for the costs of expert advice. The account shall be administered by the Secretary-General of the Tribunal, who shall consult with the Tribunal. The Tribunal further retains jurisdiction to request from the parties such other amounts as may be required from time to time in connection with the expert's work, or to decide any disputes which may arise in connection with that work." *Chas T. Main International Inc v Khuzestan Water and Power Authority (KWPA) and the Ministry of Energy of the Islamic Republic of Iran*, supra n. 68, p. 263. See also: ICC Case No. 13490, "E. Fees and costs: Each party shall advance the fees and costs of the expert in equal shares." ICC Case No. 13490, Procedural Order of July 2006, in *ICC International Court of Arbitration Bulletin Vol. 25/Supplement – 2014*, p. 8.

125 This will only be the case where the agreed rules of procedure would permit such an award.

CHAPTER 7

Assessing the evidence, burden of proof, adverse inferences and procedural good faith

7.01 It is generally recognised that arbitrators have great freedom to determine the admissibility of evidence and weigh its probative value in the light of the circumstances of the case and arguments of the parties. The deference given to arbitrators notwithstanding, there remain outer limits on a tribunal's authority to weigh and admit evidence as defined by principles of due process. The initial portion of this chapter considers the general grant of discretion as set forth in article 9.1 of the IBA Rules, with regard to due process issues, and also discusses commonly accepted principles utilised by tribunals in the weighing of evidence.

7.02 An issue not considered under the IBA Rules, but yet still one of considerable interest in international arbitration is that of the burden of proof. The phrase "burden of proof" itself may lead to confusion, as it is often used in different contexts and with varying meanings. It is a subject to which commentators, practitioners and arbitrators alike often apply interpretations based upon their own domestic legal backgrounds which has led to a variety of opinions on how the burden of proof may be allocated in international arbitration. Yet despite what may seem like a great diversity of views on this topic, a review of the case law reveals that consistent and widely accepted principles relating to this issue. These rules will be discussed further below.

7.03 A topic closely connected to the issue of the burden of proof is adverse inferences. An adverse inference is a tool available to arbitrators that has the dual function of both enforcing procedural discipline as well as serving as a means for arriving at specific findings on the merits of the dispute. IBA Rules articles 9.5 and 9.6 consider the issue of adverse inferences and are discussed further in this chapter.

7.04 While adverse inferences may be used to sanction a party for failing to abide by its duty to provide evidence to the tribunal, so too may awards on costs. In 2010, the Review Subcommittee included article 9.7 in the revised Rules, which affords the tribunal the right to award costs against a party because of a failure to participate in good faith in the taking of evidence. "Good faith" is a phrase that is prone to wide-interpretation; therefore, the final portion of this chapter considers some of the inherent evidentiary procedural principles integral to that concept.

The general authority of the tribunal to admit and weigh evidence

Article 9.1 2010 IBA Rules: **The Arbitral Tribunal shall determine the admissibility,**
Related Rules   **relevance, materiality and weight of evidence.**

Article 19(2) UNCITRAL Model Law:	Failing such agreement, the arbitral tribunal may, subject to the provisions of this Law, conduct the arbitration in such manner as it considers appropriate. The power conferred upon the arbitral tribunal includes the power to determine the admissibility, relevance, materiality and weight of any evidence.

General discussion

7.05 Article 9.1 confirms the principle that the authority over evidentiary procedure ultimately rests with the tribunal. This power is circumscribed only by the agreement to arbitrate and mandatory law. Most modern arbitration rules affirm a tribunal's latitude to determine the admissibility, relevance, materiality and weight of evidence. In this respect, article 9.1 of the IBA Rules follows accepted practice and is relatively uncontroversial. As many of the issues broadly highlighted in article 9.1 are dealt with in detail in Chapter 9, the section below discusses the general authority vested in the tribunal to weigh, exclude or admit evidence.

A tribunal's general authority to determine admissibility and the limits of discretion

7.06 As article 9.1 affirms, an international tribunal is vested with authority to determine the admissibility of evidence.[1] It is widely accepted that an arbitral tribunal is not constrained by rules of court procedure practised in the jurisdiction of the seat, nor those jurisdictions where the parties have their domicile. This is particularly true with regard to questions over the admissibility of evidence, as was affirmed by an ICC arbitral tribunal when it ruled to admit the diaries of a relevant witness over the objections of the adverse party:

> This is an international arbitration procedure. The strict rules of evidence, as they apply in England where the Tribunal is sitting, or in India, do not apply. In accordance with the power given

---

1   This principle was affirmed by an ICSID *ad hoc* committee in consideration of a challenge to a final award in the *Duke Energy v Peru* arbitration. In that case, the committee noted that it did not have the power to review a decision by the tribunal not to hear the oral testimony of a witness: "[i]t is the Tribunal that is *'the judge of the admissibility of any evidence adduced and of its probative value'*. It is no part of the mission entrusted to an *ad hoc* committee under Article 52 to review those judgments." Dietmar W. Prager and Rebecca Jenkin, *Duke Energy International Peru Investments No. 1, Ltd v Republic of Peru*, ICSID Case No. ARB/03/28, *A Contribution by the ITA Board of Reporters*, (2011), para. 258. Similarly, reviewing courts have also accepted this principle when considering challenges to awards rendered in international commercial arbitrations. See also the following statement from the Paris Court of Appeal: "In particular, the arbitrators have no obligation to admit all evidence offered by the parties, just the evidence they deem relevant to the outcome of the dispute." "France 44. Cour d'Appel [Court of Appeal], Paris, 10 January 2008", Albert Jan van den Berg (ed.), *Yearbook Commercial Arbitration*, Vol. XXXIII, p. 482 (2008). This rule has been accepted by WTO panels as a bedrock principle of international adjudication: "[A] panel established by the DSB, and engaged in a dispute settlement proceeding, [has] ample and extensive authority to undertake and to control the process by which it informs itself both of the relevant facts of the dispute and of the legal norms and principles applicable to such facts. That authority, and the breadth thereof, is indispensably necessary to enable a panel to discharge its duty imposed by Article 11 of the DSU to 'make an objective assessment of the matter before it, including an objective assessment of the facts of the case and the applicability of and conformity with the relevant covered agreements . . .'". *United States – Import Prohibition of Certain Shrimp and Shrimp Products ("United States – Shrimp")*, WT/DS58/AB/R, adopted 6 November 1998, para. 114.

to the arbitrators in the Terms of Reference, and under the ICC Rules, the Tribunal has the right to determine whether and what evidence shall be admitted. The Tribunal considers that the diary notes of Dr. Y and Dr. V are admissible. They were used as an aide memoire by Dr. Y as to what occurred and were explained to the Tribunal. P had the opportunity to cross-examine him on that evidence. It is up to the Tribunal to give to those diary notes whatever credence and weight it considers appropriate. The notes are not in themselves proof of what was discussed, but do indicate and support the evidence given by Dr. Y. Furthermore, and in any event, the Tribunal does not consider that the Indian Evidence Act has any relevance to the conduct of and the admission of evidence in this arbitration.[2]

7.07 In a manner similar to article 9.1, the ICC tribunal above affirmed that its authority to admit evidence is not subject to local court rules of evidence,[3] unless such rules have been incorporated by agreement into the procedure. Moreover, some tribunals have opined that the discretion given to an international tribunal implies it is not constrained by rules emanating from substantive law that would bar the consideration of certain types of evidence, as the following quote from a panel of the Iran-US Claims Tribunal observed:

> Under Iranian law, a contract not in writing and involving an amount exceeding over 500 rials in value cannot be proved by oral or written testimony alone. In the present case the Claimants rely on contemporaneous documents recording the understandings reached with TRC, and demonstrating part performance of the contract. It appears that acceptance of part performance can be proof of a binding contract under Iranian law. Moreover, although the governing law of the contract itself must be taken to be that of Iran, each forum applies its own procedural and evidentiary rules to the disputes before it, and it is arguable that the type of evidence admissible to establish a contract is a procedural or evidentiary matter.[4]

7.08 As illustrated by the cases cited above, arbitrators will often adopt a certain liberality with regard to questions of admissibility; however, it is also the case that a tribunal may determine to exclude evidence from the record.[5] A tribunal's authority in this respect

---

2   *Technical know-how buyer P v Engineer/seller A*, Final Award in ICC Case No. 7626 of 1995, in Albert Jan van den Berg (ed.), *Yearbook Commercial Arbitration*, Vol. XXII, p. 132 (1997). See also: "International tribunals are not bound to adhere to strict judicial rules of evidence. As a general principle the probative force of the evidence presented is for the tribunal to determine . . .". *Tradex Hellas SA v Republic of Albania*, ICSID Case No. ARB/94/2, Decision on Jurisdiction of 24 December 1996 and Award of 29 April 1999, in Albert Jan van den Berg (ed.), *Yearbook Commercial Arbitration*, Vol. XXV, p. 241 (2000).

3   In this regard, it was reported that an AAA panel admitted evidence to the record even though it was largely based on hearsay, which would have rendered it inadmissible before a US court: "The arbitrators endorsed Defendant's argument that Claimant's case was largely based on hearsay evidence, which might not be admissible in a court of law. However, an arbitration proceeding is not governed by strict evidentiary requirements. Section 30 of the American Arbitration Association Rules, adopted by Clause 15 of the Commercial Operating Agreement, makes it clear that: '[T]he Arbitrator shall be judge of the relevancy and materiality of the evidence offered and conformity to the legal rules of evidence shall not be required'". Awards in Case No. 1310-0417-78 of 4 January 1980, in Pieter Sanders (ed.), *Yearbook Commercial Arbitration*, Vol. VIII, pp. 166, 168 (1983).

4   *DIC of Delaware Inc, Underhill of Delaware Inc v Tehran Redevelopment Corp, The Government of the Islamic Republic of Iran*, Case No. 255; Award No. 176-255-3 of 26 April 1985, in Albert Jan van den Berg (ed.), *Yearbook Commercial Arbitration*, Vol. XI, pp. 332, 333 (1986). See also the decision of the South African Supreme Court of Appeal in *Telcordia Technologies Inc v Telcom SA Ltd*, BCLR, Vol. 5, 503 (2007), where the court dismissed a challenge to an ICC award which was brought because the arbitrator had exercised his discretion to admit evidence which the losing party argued should not have been considered under the relevant substantive law. The court, in considering the matter determined that the arbitrator's discretion was wide, and he had not committed prejudicial error in his various rulings on evidence (including admitting the disputed evidence).

5   See, for example, the decision of the Austrian Supreme Court where it was ruled that the denial of the right to be heard is not established simply because a tribunal refused to admit evidence proffered by one side or the other. James Castello, "31 March 2005 – Supreme Court of Austria", *A Contribution by the ITA Board of Reporters*. See also the decision of an Argentine court of appeals rejecting a petition to annul an award based a

is circumscribed only by the agreement to arbitrate and mandatory law, the most often implicated principle of which is a party's right to be heard.

7.09 It is generally considered that a tribunal's determination to exclude evidence will fall afoul of mandatory law when a ruling has seriously and unfairly impaired the ability of a party to present its case. Instances where an exclusionary ruling has given rise to successful challenges to an award would include cases where arbitrators declined to admit highly relevant and material witness testimony without proper motivation,[6] refused to appoint or hear experts where an issue to be determined is clearly not within a tribunal's professional competence,[7] and where arbitrators have allowed for material evidence to be submitted

---

challenge to the weight assigned to the evidence by the tribunal: "it is important to point out that both the case law, as well as legal scholars' opinion and even the most modern regulatory legislation of Arbitration set forth that the evidence issue depends on the arbitrator's decision and that this is not a sufficient reason to bring any matter for consideration." Federico Godoy, "10 March 2005 – Formosa's Civil and Commercial Court of Appeals", *A Contribution by the ITA Board of Reporters*.

6 *Tempo Shain Corporation et al. v Bertek Inc*, 120 F.3d 16 (2nd Cir. 1997). This decision of the US 2nd Circuit Court of Appeals was rendered in relation to a domestic arbitration, and determined that a tribunal had erred where it refused to extend a hearing in order to receive testimony from the only witness who was able to testify to a material issue in the case. The witness had been unable to testify due to an emergency health problem suffered by his wife. In later rulings concerning the propriety of an arbitrator's actions in the context of an international arbitration, the courts have applied *Tempo Shain*, but rarely found that the standard necessitated setting aside an award. In particular, the *Yonir Techs Inc v Duration Systems* decision which followed *Tempo Shain* and considered an international arbitral tribunal's decision not to hold a hearing, relied upon the following summary of the *Tempo Shain* rule in determining to uphold the arbitrator's discretion: "The essential proposition for which *Tempo Shain* stands is that, absent a reasonable basis for its decision, a refusal to grant an adjournment of a hearing, due to a medical emergency, constitutes misconduct under the [F.A.A.] if it excludes the presentation of evidence material and pertinent to the controversy thus prejudicing the parties in the dispute and making the hearing fundamentally unfair." *Yonir Technologies Inc v Duration Systems Ltd*, 244 F.Supp 2d 195, p. 209 (SDNY 2002). See also: Richard H. Kreindler, "30 May 2008 – Higher Regional Court Hamburg (Hanseatisches Oberlandesgericht or OLG Hamburg)", *A Contribution by the ITA Board of Reporters*. In that instance, the tribunal refused to hear a witness who was offered to substantiate a challenge to the jurisdiction of the arbitrator: "[t]he Higher Regional Court disagreed with the arbitral tribunal's holding. According to the court, the arbitral tribunal could not reasonably have concluded that Claimant had capacity to enter into a valid arbitration agreement without further inquiry into the matter. "See also: the decision of a Netherlands Court of Appeal setting aside an NAI award because the tribunal had ruled to exclude witness testimony offered in lieu of documents no longer available. The holding there is summarised as follows: "The decision of the Tribunal not to allow Pastoe to provide evidence of its allegation that Van den Nieuwelaar had no copyright resulting in the decision to reject the claim, was based on the consideration that 'Pastoe would not be able to provide testimony that would outweigh what could have become apparent from the missing minutes'. The Court held that this reasoning did not contain any sort of persuasive explanation of the relevant decision. Apart from the fact that the Tribunal's decision prejudges the evaluation of evidence, this reasoning is defective because it is unclear why witness testimony does (never) outweigh what could be derived from (unknown) documentary evidence." Jacomijn J. van Haersolte-van Hof, "14 October 2004, Court of Appeals", *A Contribution by the ITA Board of Reporters*.

7 Where a tribunal did not call (or allow) for evidence to be given on the application of People's Republic of China law and none of the arbitrators had experience with or were qualified in that law, the Hong Kong High Court, Court of First Instance, partially set aside an award. The court opined as follows: "I readily agree that in the process of fact finding arbitrators must have autonomy in drawing inferences as they deem fit and in that respect they are entitled to depart from the positions advanced by the parties. However, on primary factual disputes, they have to act on evidence and give reasonable opportunity to the parties to put forward their respective case on such evidence. In my judgment, given that we are dealing with an arbitration in Hong Kong, the requirement of contractual validity under PRC law has to be decided on the evidence before the Tribunal." *Brunswick Bowling & Billiards Corp v Shanghai Zhonglu Industrial Co* [2009] HKCU 211, para. 26. See also the 1992 ruling of the Swiss Federal Tribunal in which the decision by an ICC tribunal against ordering expert evidence on a technical matter was considered to be in error because the tribunal clearly could not decide the matter on the evidence before them, and did not have the expertise to determine the issue on their own. "11 mai 1992 – Tribunal fédéral, 1ère Cour Civile", *ASA Bulletin*, Vol. 10, No. 3, pp. 381–401 (1992).

while not permitting a party against whom the evidence is construed the opportunity to produce counter-evidence.[8]

7.10 The above examples notwithstanding, it is often the case that where a tribunal's exclusionary ruling is given with reasonable regard for the alleged probative value of the evidence (see comments to article 9.2(a)), such a determination will be left undisturbed by a reviewing court.[9] Moreover, where a tribunal applies correctly, and with requisite consideration, the grounds set forth in article 9.2, a determination to exclude evidence will likely be considered as consistent with due process.

Weighing the evidence

7.11 The weight ultimately assigned to evidence is directly tied to whether it contributes to establishing a relevant fact. Therefore, the persuasiveness of that evidence may be judged only in the context of the case.[10]

7.12 It is thus up to the tribunal to use its discretion to weigh the evidence.[11] A reviewing court will rarely overturn an award because a tribunal incorrectly weighed the factual evidence before it,[12] or because it found one party's evidence more persuasive than

---

8 Where an ICSID tribunal received material evidence following the closure of the evidentiary portion of the proceedings and failed to provide the party against whom the evidence was construed an opportunity to provide counter evidence, and/or comment, an *ad hoc* annulment committee found that a serious procedural error had occurred. *Fraport AG Frankfurt Airport Services Worldwide v The Philippines*, ICSID Case No. ARB/03/25, Decision on the Application for Annulment, para. 133 (23 December 2010). See generally the comments to art. 3.11.

9 See the following summary of a Swiss Federal Tribunal decision: "The dismissal of requests for the production of documents and the refusal to hear witnesses, even if contrary to an earlier procedural order made by the court, were held not to violate the claimant's right to be heard where the arbitral tribunal had concluded that the parties had already established all the facts necessary for it to make its decision regarding jurisdiction." Georg von Segesser, "September 2005 – Swiss Supreme Court, 1st Civil Chamber", *A Contribution by the ITA Board of Reporters*. See, e.g.: Decision of the ad hoc Committee on the Application for Annulment in the case of *Impregilo S.p.A. v Argentine Republic*, ICSID Case No. ARB/07/17, §176: "The Committee concludes that the Tribunal evaluated the evidence submitted by both parties on the amount of compensation, and reviewed the conclusions presented therein. There is, therefore, no serious departure from fundamental rules of procedure as Argentina has had the opportunity to present its defenses and evidence on this matter and the Tribunal established the amount of compensation in a reasonable manner. There is no requirement whatsoever for arbitral tribunals to indicate in an award the reasons why some types of evidence are more credible than others. Discretionary authority that is reasonable and reasoned is the rule in this regard, and it is clearly not within the purview of Annulment Committees, which do not have direct and immediate access to the evidence submitted by both parties, to determine whether the determinations made in an award were correct. Attempting to do so would involve a subsequent assessment of the conclusions of arbitral tribunals, which would destroy the basic principles of the institution of arbitration and outside the power of ad hoc Committees."

10 In the *Island of Palmas* case, the arbitrator noted: "The value and weight of any assertion can only be estimated in the light of all the evidence and all the assertions made on either side, and of the facts which are notorious for the tribunal." *The Island of Palmas Case (USA v Netherlands)*, Final Award, 4 April 1928, 2 RIAA pp. 827, 840. See also: Amy F. Cohen, "Options for Approaching Evidentiary Privilege in International Arbitration", in T. Giovannini and A. Mourre (eds), *Dossier VI: Written Evidence and Discovery in International Arbitration*, p. 433 (2009): "The assessment of relevance and materiality requires no special agreement, and the analysis can only be undertaken on the basis of the knowledge of the case at the time."

11 *Asian Agricultural Products Ltd v The Republic of Sri Lanka*, ICSID Case No. ARB/87/3 Final Award, in Albert Jan van den Berg (ed.), *Yearbook Commercial Arbitration*, Vol. XVII, p. 122 (1992): "International tribunals are not bound to adhere to strict judicial rules of evidence. As a general principle the probative force of the evidence presented is for the Tribunal to determine."

12 See the following summary of a ruling by the Hanseatic Court of Appeal of 14 May 1999: "The court stated that such a right [a right to be heard] only requires that a tribunal take into account arguments brought forward

another's.[13] To rule as such would require a supervising court to essentially reconsider all of the elements of the case, both legal and factual; a level of review that exceeds what is contemplated under most modern *lex arbitri*, such as the UNCITRAL Model Law, or, in the enforcement context, what is permitted by the New York Convention. The rare exception to this principle seems to lie in cases where a tribunal has unfairly penalised a party for a failure to produce evidence, when the omission results from directions given by the tribunal.[14] In limited circumstances such as these, a reviewing court may consider

---

by the parties but does not limit the right of the tribunal to evaluate the evidence presented." Hanseatisches Oberlandesgericht Hamburg, CLOUT Case No. 457 (1999), in Albert Jan van den Berg (ed.), *Yearbook Commercial Arbitration*, Vol. XXVIII, p. 265 (2003). See also the following summary of a decision by the Swiss Federal Tribunal, where a party challenged an ICC final award because the tribunal had not assigned what the party perceived to be the proper weight to the witness statements it had proffered. Georg von Segesser, "18 November 2004 – Schweizerisches Bundesgericht, I. Zivilabteilung (Swiss Federal Court, 1st Chamber), Case No. 4p.140/2004", *A Contribution by the ITA Board of Reporters*: "In particular the supplier [a party] claimed that the arbitral tribunal had not given the statements of its witnesses the same weight as the statements of the other party's witnesses, thereby violating the right to equal treatment. The Swiss Federal Court held that a party may not argue a violation of its right to equal treatment, when in reality, it is merely criticizing the weighing of evidence by the tribunal." See also the decision by the US District Court for the Southern District of New York, *Interdigital Communications Corp et al. v Samsung Electronics Co Ltd*, 528 F.Supp 340, p. 352 (SDNY 2007): "However, it is also clear that vacature is not appropriate . . . where the losing party in an arbitration merely takes issue with the weight accorded to such evidence . . . the losing party's assertion that the arbitrators failed to give the evidence the 'consideration it deserved' must be rejected as an improper 'attempt to probe the collective minds of the arbitrators as to how they reached their judgment'". See also a decision of the Netherlands courts where the President of the District Court of Zutphen rejected a challenge to the enforcement of an award based upon an argument that the tribunal had wrongly weighed the facts in favour of the party seeking an enforcement. The court found that it was not proper to second guess the assessment of the tribunal's weighing of the facts. *Tianjin Stationary & Sporting Goods Import & Export Corp (China) v Verisport BV (the Netherlands)*, Arrondissementsrechtbank, Zutphen, in Albert Jan van den Berg (ed.), *Yearbook Commercial Arbitration*, Vol. XXII, pp. 766–767 (1997). See also the position of the Canadian courts: "On a finding of fact, for which there is support in the evidence, the court must defer to the tribunal." *Marvin Roy Feldman Karpa v United Mexican States*, Court of Appeal for Ontario, Case No. C41169, para. 60 (2005).

13 See the following decision of the ICSID *ad hoc* committee: "The Arbitral Tribunal did not create a different standard of proof when it concluded that there was 'no conclusive evidence that Claimants defrauded KaR-Tel by causing it to enter into transactions with Telsim at excessive prices'. Rather, the Tribunal was merely expressing its failure to be convinced by the evidence put before it. On a fair reading of paragraphs 320–322 of the Award, the Tribunal is simply rejecting Kazakhstan's case of fraud on the evidence adduced by it." Dietmar W. Prager and Samantha J. Rowe, "*Republic of Kazakhstan v Rumeli Telekom AS*, ICSID Case No. ARB/05/16, 25 March 2010", *A Contribution by the ITA Board of Reporters*, para. 97.

14 In a dispute before an Iran-US Claims Tribunal panel, the claimant ("Avco") had been advised by the original tribunal that for procedural economy reasons it should not submit the whole of the evidence (invoices) in its possession on a particular issue, but instead provide audited accounts reflecting the invoices. Later, the tribunal, after two arbitrators were replaced, ruled against the claimant citing the lack of proper evidence for the claim, and in particular the failure to provide original invoices instead of the accounts: "At the pre-hearing conference, Judge Mangard specifically advised Avco not to burden the Tribunal by submitting 'kilos and kilos of invoices'. Instead, Judge Mangard approved the method of proof proposed by Avco, namely the submission of Avco's audited accounts receivable ledgers. Later, when Judge Ansari questioned Avco's method of proof, he never responded to Avco's explanation that it was proceeding according to an earlier understanding. Thus, Avco was not made aware that the Tribunal now required the actual invoices to substantiate Avco's claim. Having thus led Avco to believe it had used a proper method to substantiate its claim, the Tribunal then rejected Avco's claim for lack of proof. We believe that by so misleading Avco, however unwittingly, the Tribunal denied Avco the opportunity to present its claim in a meaningful manner. Accordingly, Avco was 'unable to present [its] case' within the meaning of Article V(1)(b), and enforcement of the Award was properly denied." *Iran Aircraft Industries v Avco Corp*, 980 F.2d 141 (2 nd Cir. 1992). See also the following discussion of the rules developed in the jurisprudence of the WTO Appellate Body concerning the limits upon a panel's right to weigh the evidence: "In *EC-Hormones*, the Appellate Body stated that '[t]he duty to make an objective assessment of the facts is, among other things, an obligation to consider the evidence presented to a panel and to make factual findings on the basis of that evidence'. Accordingly, the 'deliberate disregard of' or 'refusal to

it appropriate to question any reliance placed by the tribunal on such an omission in the record.

7.13 The predominant practice adopted in international arbitration is for the tribunal to provide reasoned explanations for the weight it has assigned to different pieces of evidence. Some principles which have been considered by international tribunals in their assessment of evidence are set forth below:

(i) A tribunal, in exercising its power to weigh the evidence before it, should consider and explain its reasons for accepting or rejecting objections raised as to the reliability of a particular piece of evidence. This is true only if that evidence is pertinent to the award.[15]

(ii) Prima facie evidence is evidence that may stand unless effectively controverted by countering evidence or argument.[16]

(iii) A tribunal may, within its discretion, give dispositive weight to circumstantial evidence.[17]

---

consider' evidence is incompatible with a panel's duty to make an objective assessment of the facts. . . . How a panel treats the evidence that is presented to it, including expert testimony, may affect the parties' substantive rights in a dispute as well as their rights to due process. A panel's choice not to discuss a piece of evidence that on its face appears to be favourable to the arguments of one of the parties might suggest bias or lack of even-handedness in the treatment of the evidence by the panel, even if in fact the panel is making an objective assessment of the facts. . . . The Appellate Body has, however, also clarified that, as the 'trier of facts', a panel enjoys a margin of discretion in the assessment of the facts, including the treatment of evidence . . . [a] panel enjoys a margin of discretion in assessing the value of and the weight to be ascribed to the evidence and that a panel is 'entitled, in the exercise of its discretion, to determine that certain elements of evidence should be accorded more weight than other elements'". *Australia – Measures Affecting the Importation of Apples from New Zealand*, WT/DS367/AB/R, adopted 29 November 2010, paras 268–271. In principle the duty to approach the evidence without bias is also applicable to the deliberations of international commercial arbitral tribunals. Nevertheless, such principles should not be seen to nullify a tribunal's right to exclude evidence from the record for the various reasons set forth in art. 9 or elsewhere within the IBA Rules, nor would the failure of an arbitral tribunal to deal with every part and parcel of evidence be definitive proof of its failure to afford equal treatment to the parties.

15 See: *Tradex Hellas SA v Albania*, in making use of its authority under ICSID Rule 34(1) to "be the judge . . . of its probative value", the Tribunal, in evaluating the respective evidence, shall take into account the objections raised by the Parties insofar as the Tribunal considers that the evidence objected to is relevant for the award on the merits. On the other hand, the Tribunal sees no need to deal with and decide on objections regarding evidence which, in the Tribunal's judgment, is not relevant for it in deciding on the claim before it. *Tradex Hellas SA v Albania*, ICSID Case No. ARB/94/2, Final Award, para. 83 (1999).

16 See further the discussion of prima facie evidence below.

17 "In general, international tribunals have given full weight to circumstantial evidence. Two independent factors are considered by Arbitral Tribunals when assessing the weight that should be given to such evidence '. . . the first factor is the party's attitude in the proceedings. If a party, as was the case with Respondent, does not comply with its obligations, for instance by refusing to produce the requested documents and witnesses, the Arbitral Tribunal is authorized to draw adverse conclusions from the party's behavior. The same applies when witnesses manifestly lack independence, as was the case with those produced by Respondent, [and] the second factor is whether direct evidence of fact is unavailable'". Dietmar W. Prager and Joanna E. Davidson, *"Rumeli Telekom AS and Telsim Mobil Telekomikasyon Hizmetleri AS v Republic of Kazakhstan*, ICSID Case No. ARB/05/16, 29 July 2008", *A Contribution by the ITA Board of Reporters*, para. 444. See also: the following consideration of "indirect" proof concerning a bribery claim by an ICC tribunal: "In the present case, bribery has not been proved beyond doubt. It is true that it is possible to prove something through indirect evidence and that Art. 8 of the Swiss CC does not exclude indirect evidence. However, it is necessary that a sufficient ensemble of indirect evidence be collected to allow the judge to base his decision on something more than likely facts, i.e., facts which have not been proven." *Broker v Contractor*, ICC Case No. 5622, Final Award, in Albert Jan van den Berg (ed.), *Yearbook of Commercial Arbitration*, Vol. XIX, p. 112 (1994).

  (iv) A tribunal may draw an adverse inference from a lack of evidence on the record.[18]

  (v) When two witnesses offer contradictory testimony, a tribunal should not, based solely on the testimony, give greater weight to one over the other if both accounts appear to be equally plausible and to be given in good faith. In such a case, a tribunal should consider circumstantial or other evidence in determining which testimony is more persuasive as to the veracity of a matter.[19]

  (vi) If witness testimony is contradicted by relevant documentary evidence, a tribunal need not automatically disregard such testimony.[20] Nevertheless, in considering the weight to assign to the testimony a tribunal should explain the effect that previous, contradictory statements, inconsistencies or omissions have on the credibility of the witness.[21]

  (vii) Exaggerations or misrepresentations of fact by a party or a party witness do not destroy the value of their primary contentions per se.[22]

  (viii) Witness testimony may be assigned probative value when the witness has first-hand knowledge of the information to which he or she is attesting, but may be disregarded or assigned lesser value if the testimony simply repeats facts originally heard or witnessed by another individual.[23]

  (ix) Unless expressly agreed to by the parties ahead of time, evidence submitted by one party should not be regarded as irrefutable proof of a contention barring the consideration of counter evidence.[24]

  (x) That a witness of fact bears a connection to a party of employment, familial relation, shareholding, or other significant business relation, does not disqualify that individual from giving testimony. A party to an arbitration that is a natural person may also give witness testimony.[25]

---

18 As an example of this principle, in ICC Case No. 5562 where a tribunal, noted the total absence in the arbitral record of correspondence which in normal circumstances would have been exchanged between the parties, drew the following factual conclusion: "These considerations lead us to believe that claimant saw its task as totally different from what was initially provided for in the Protocol of Agreement, that claimant informed defendant orally regarding its activities, that defendant did not in any way object to claimant's activities – which were different from those provided for in the Protocol of Agreement – and that, on the contrary, it even approved of it. . . . In fact, how else could it be explained that, during a period of three years, a company aiming at obtaining a major contract . . . neither worried about nor requested information on its broker's work? Such behaviour can only be logically explained if we admit that defendant tacitly approved of claimant's activity. The consequence of this approval – which is not necessarily the validity of the contract – will be examined below." *Ibid.*, ICC Case No. 5622, pp. 105, 117. See further below.

19 "Final Award in ICC Case No. 9333 of 1998", *ASA Bulletin*, Vol. 19, No. 4, p. 757 (2001).

20 See: *Plama Consortium Ltd v Republic of Bulgaria*, ICSID Case No. ARB/03/24, Decision on Jurisdiction (2005). The tribunal noted with respect to witness testimony certain inconsistencies with documentary records produced in the proceedings, but was not minded to reject the testimony as false. The tribunal did, however, take a more permissive standard in regard to the evidence, due to the general view that testimony may be accepted during a jurisdictional phase on face value, with greater scrutiny reserved for the merits phase.

21 *Dadras International et al. v The Islamic Republic of Iran*, Case Nos 213 and 215, Award No. 567-213/215-3 of 7 November 1995, para. 180.

22 *Francisco Mallén (United Mexican States) v United States of America*, 27 April 1927, 4 RIAA, pp. 173–174.

23 "ICC Case No. 4815, Procedural Order of 9 June, 1987", in Dominique Hascher (ed.), *Collection of Procedural Decisions in ICC Arbitration 1993–1996*, p. 130 (2nd edition, 1998). In this procedural order a witness was to testify only to those matters that he or she had personally witnessed as the tribunal limited testimony by noting that the witness "was invited to state orally before the arbitrators the facts of which he had personal knowledge". This being said, hearsay evidence is admissible in international arbitration. See: generally comments to art. 8.2.

24 ICC Case No. 9887, Final Award, *ICC Bulletin*, Vol. 11, No. 2, p. 109 (2000).

25 See: comments to art. 4.1.

(xi) Where it is reasonable that a party by virtue of circumstance does not have the ability to provide the 'best' or primary evidence of a factual contention, a tribunal is able to accept lesser or secondary evidence for the purposes of establishing that fact.[26]

7.14 This list should not be regarded as exhaustive, but rather as illustrative of some of the recognised principles applied in the past by various tribunals. Naturally, the discretion of the tribunal to weigh evidence is not limited to those rules set forth here, and may be exercised taking into account a variety of other factors or principles not mentioned above.

Burden of proof, standards of proof and shifting the burden

Article 27(1) UNCITRAL Rules: **Each party shall have the burden of proving the facts relied on to support its claim or defence.**

General discussion

7.15 A discussion of the "burden of proof" in international arbitration has the tendency to become complex, partly as a result of the varying terminology that is used. One finds that the phrase "burden of proof" is often used interchangeably with other phrases such as the *burden of persuasion, burden of production, burden of going forward, the legal burden* and *burden of allegation*. These concepts, primarily deriving from domestic practice, find awkward application in the international setting given that arbitral procedure often does not follow the national procedures that underlie their development. Additionally, as commentators and practitioners from varying jurisdictional backgrounds assign different meanings to these phrases, it soon becomes clear why the issue becomes obscured.[27]

7.16 The following section considers the burden of proof as it relates to evidence and more specifically the obligation to submit evidence and the risks associated with failing to do so.[28] The three key facets of the burden of proof that are given transnational recognition and application in modern arbitral procedure, and which are considered below, are as

---

26 *Frederica Lincoln Riahi v The Government of the Islamic Republic of Iran*, Case No. 485, Award No. 600-485-1, para. 415 (27 February 2003). "While the Claimant must shoulder the burden of proving the value of the expropriated concern by the best available evidence, the Tribunal must be prepared to take some account of the disadvantages suffered by the Claimant, namely its lack of access to detailed documentation, as an inevitable consequence of the circumstances in which the expropriation took place." See also: "In cases where proof of a fact presents extreme difficulty, a tribunal may be satisfied with less conclusive proof, i.e., prima facie evidence." *Asian Agricultural Products Ltd (AAPL) v The Republic of Sri Lanka*, Final award of 27 June 1990, Case No. ARB/87/3, in Albert Jan van den Berg (ed.), *Yearbook Commercial Arbitration*, Vol. XVII, p. 124 (1992).

27 Confusion as to the proper use of the term "burden of proof" is also common within domestic practice, as the following excerpt from a standard American text explains: "The phrase burden of proof as used by the courts, is one of double meaning, which circumstance has been the cause of confusion so great as to suggest the propriety of adopting a less objectionable term." Owens and Imodio (eds), *Corpus Juris Secundum: Complete Restatement of the Entire American Law as Developed by all Reported Cases*, 31A Evidence, s. 103.

28 Or as some may consider it, the 'burden of producing evidence'. While not necessarily endorsing this author's view on the classification of these concepts, Marossi provides an interesting consideration of the various aspects of the burden of proof question in, Ali Z. Marossi, "Shifting the Burden of Proof in the Practice of the Iran-United States Claims Tribunal", *Journal of International Arbitration*, Vol. 28, No. 5, p. 427 (2011).

follows: *onus probandi actori incumbit*, standards or proof, and the shifting of the burden of proof. Moreover, as is further discussed in this section, the substantive law may have an impact on the issue of the burden of proof.

The burden of proof: Onus Probandi Actori Incumbit

7.17 In 1930 the governments of Britain and France agreed to submit to arbitration claims arising out of the arrest by British authorities of a French national, a Mr. Chevreau, who had been detained in what was then known as Persia.[29] The agreement to submit the matter to arbitration omitted a number of procedural details, including any explicit allocation of the burden other than to say that both parties were expected to produce evidence in support of their respective allegations of fact. The French agent interpreted such a principle to mean that there was no respondent and no claimant in the matter, and thus there was no burden of proof. The British position was that France was the claimant, therefore, it bore the burden of producing evidence to support its case. The arbitrator, in weighing these arguments, took the following position:

> Although article 3 of the submission agreement imposed on both parties the "obligation to establish to the satisfaction of the arbitrator the authenticity of all issues of fact asserted for the purpose of establishing or denying liability", this provision was not . . . intended to exclude the application of the normal rules of evidence. It was merely intended to provide an additional obligation to prove the existence of facts alleged for the purpose of denying liability.[30]

7.18 Here, the tribunal drew a distinction between two aspects of the burden of proof. In the first instance, the tribunal acknowledged that both parties were under a procedural duty to provide evidence of the "existence of facts alleged".[31] Second, it clarified that this rule did not displace the "normal rules of evidence".

7.19 Taking the first, it is clear that the procedural burden of proof is incumbent on both parties, in a manner similar to the principle of *onus probandi actori incumbit* or *actori incumbit probatio:* he who asserts a fact must prove it.[32] The following discussion from an ICSID award in *AAPL v Sri Lanka*, further explains how this widely accepted formula is applied in practice:

> The term *actor* in the principle *onus probandi actori incumbit* is not to be taken to mean the plaintiff from the procedural standpoint, but the real claimant in view of the issues involved. Hence,

---

29 Summary of *Chevreau Claim* (United Kingdom and France), in P. Hamilton *et al.* (eds), *The Permanent Court of Arbitration: International Arbitration and Dispute Resolution*, p. 129 (1999).

30 *Ibid.*, p. 132.

31 Bin Cheng describes burden of proof as it relates to the obligation to produce evidence as follows: "The term burden of proof may, however, also be used in a more restricted sense as referring to the proof of the individual allegations advanced by the parties in the course of proceedings. This burden of proof may be called procedural." Bin Cheng, *General Principles of Law as Applied by International Courts and Tribunals*, p. 334 (2nd edition, 1987).

32 The ICSID tribunal in *Salini v Jordan* noted with approval the wide acceptance of *actori incumbit probatio* and considered also the application of the rule by the International Court of Justice: "The Permanent Court of International Justice and the International Court of Justice applied this principle in many cases and the Court stated explicitly in 1984 in the case concerning military and paramilitary activities in and against Nicaragua that "it is the litigant seeking to establish a fact who bears the burden of proving it." Dietmar W. Prager, "*Salini Costruttori SpA Italstrade SpA*, ICSID Case No. ARB/02/13, 31 January 2006", *A Contribution by the ITA Board of Reporters*, para. 72.

with regard to 'the proof of individual allegations' advanced by the parties in the course of proceedings, the burden of proof rests upon the party alleging the fact.[33]

7.20 While the burden of proof will often be thought to lie exclusively with the claimant, this is not completely accurate. From a procedural standpoint, the burden of proof
under the principle of *onus probandi actori incumbit* attaches to both the claimant and
respondent, who must substantiate their allegations.[34] For the respondent, this burden may
mean *inter alia* that it is charged with producing evidence where it has challenged the reliability of claimant's evidence, such as by alleging a piece of evidence is tainted by fraud,[35]
or where it alleges rebuttal facts.[36] As reflected from the discussion above, this principle
applies to both the substantive claim and defence.[37] Article 27.1 of the UNCITRAL Rules
restates this rule.

---

33 *AAPL v Sri Lanka, supra* n. 26, p. 121. The tribunal in this case was borrowing from Bin Cheng's formulation of this principle. Bin Cheng, *supra* n. 31, p. 332. See also where another tribunal noted with approval the
rule set forth in *AAPL*: "The Tribunal agrees with the standard articulated by the AAPL tribunal that, with regard
to 'proof of individual allegations advanced by the parties in the course of proceedings, the burden of proof
rests upon the party alleging the fact'." Dietmar W. Prager and Rebecca Jenkin, "*Alpha Projektholding GmbH v
Ukraine*, ICSID Case No. ARB/07/16, 8 November 2010", *A Contribution by the ITA Board of Reporters*, para.
170. See also the decision by an ICC tribunal which followed this principle: "The burden of proof for the conclusion of a contract is on the party claiming rights out of the contract. Since the arbitration clause is also a contract,
the same rules are applicable for the arbitration clause. Thus, in the case at hand the claimant must establish the
conclusion of the alleged contracts and of an arbitration clause for each alleged contract." ICC Case No. 10274 of
1999, Final Award, in Albert Jan van den Berg (ed.), *Yearbook Commercial Arbitration*, Vol. XXIX, p. 94 (2004).

34 See the following observations of the tribunal in ICC Case No. 7365: "the basic principle of proof '*actori
incumbit probatio*' relates to the determination of the tribunal of *disputed facts*, not to the final result of a dispute.
Accordingly the issue does not necessarily depend on the parties' role as a claimant or defendant." ICC Case
No. 7365, Final Award, para. 15.2 (1997) (unpublished). See the ruling of an ICC tribunal: "Any facts that are
favorable towards the position of the defendant must be proven by it." ICC Case No. 8547 of 1999, Final Award,
in Albert Jan van den Berg (ed.), *Yearbook Commercial Arbitration*, Vol. XXVIII, p. 35 (2003). See also: Mojtaba
Kazazi, *Burden of Proof and Related Issues: A Study of Evidence Before International Tribunals*, p. 221 (1996):
"According to this rule, which is rooted in Roman law and is applied in different legal systems of municipal law,
the burden of proof, as a point of departure, is on the '*actori*'. However, the '*actori*' is the party who alleges a fact,
not necessarily always the party who instated the proceedings."

35 In an Iran-US Claims Tribunal case, the tribunal explained: "The Tribunal believes that the analysis of the
distribution of the burden of proof in this Case should be centered around Article 24, paragraph 1 of the Tribunal
Rules which states that '[e]ach party shall have the burden of proving the facts relied on to support his claim or
defence'. It was the Respondent who, at one point during the proceedings in this Case, raised the defence that the
Deed is a forgery. Specifically, the Respondent has contended that the Deed, dated 15 August 1978, was in fact
fabricated in 1982. Having made that factual allegation, the Respondent has the burden of proving it." *Abrahim
Rahman Golshani v the Government of the Islamic Republic of Iran*, Award No. 546-812-3 of 2 March 1993, in
Albert Jan van den Berg (ed.), *Yearbook Commercial Arbitration*, Vol. XIX, p. 429 (1994).

36 See the determination of one *ad hoc* tribunal regarding the burden on the respondent: "[t]he seller of
guaranteed machinery does, according to common burden of proof principles, carry the burden of proving that
deficiencies which emerge during the guarantee period are not due to deficiencies which were there at the time of
delivery." *Owner of the Tanker Wingull v BMV (Norwegian supplier)*, Award of 10 April 1978, in Albert Jan van
den Berg (ed.), *Yearbook Commercial Arbitration*, Vol. XI, p. 108 (1986).

37 See the acknowledgement of this principle by an ICC tribunal as a general rule of law: "[o]ne can acknowledge the existence of a general principle according to which a claimant who seeks damages for non-performance
carries the burden of proving the existence and the contents of the obligation while it rests upon the defendant to
claim and to prove the fact that he has performed this obligation." Final Award in ICC Case No. 1434, *Journal du
Droit International*, p. 982 (1976). See further for the summary of the Swiss view on the matter: "in most cases,
each party shall bear the burden of proof for the facts on which it is basing its case (*actori incumbit probatio*)."
Georg von Segesser and Dorothée Schramm, "Swiss Private International Law Act (Chapter 12), Article 184
(Procedure: taking of evidence)", in Loukas A. Mistelis (ed.), *Concise International Arbitration*, p. 938 (2010).
See also the following position adopted by an ICC tribunal, as a classic example of where a party's failure to
meet the burden of proof resulted in an adverse finding: "In view of these contradictions and of the fact that the

7.21 The above notwithstanding, *onus probandi actori incumbit* only explains one part of how the burden of proof operates in international arbitration as it relates to the duty to produce evidence. The second part is what was described in the *Chevreau Claims* case as the burden of proof that was found to exist under the "normal rules of evidence"; that is, determining the party who bears the risk of failing to substantiate their case. There, the arbitrator noted that: "the burden of proof rested with the French Government, and that, following the rule established in analogous cases, Mr. Chevreau's allegations could not be considered as sufficient proof, absent other supporting evidence."[38] Thus, while noting that both parties had a procedural obligation to submit proof of their factual allegations, the tribunal found that the risk of failing to produce sufficient evidence rested initially with the party bringing the claim for relief.[39] This too was the position adopted by a panel of the Iran-US Claims Tribunal, who considered the interplay between a rule similar to article 27.1, which called on both parties to submit their evidence, and the allocation of the risk of failing to produce evidence: "the Tribunal believes the Claim . . . is best decided by reference to Article 24, paragraph 1 of the Tribunal Rules according to which '[e]ach party shall have the burden of proving the facts relied on to support his claim or defence.' It goes without saying that it is the Claimant who carries the initial burden of proving the facts upon which he relies."[40] Therefore, while both parties must

---

loan agreement concluded with the bank was not produced, nor any bank statements concerning the amount of the debts of the Plaintiff towards the bank, during the period under scrutiny, the Arbitral Tribunal considers that it is impossible to take into account the interests claimed by the Plaintiff, which has not brought the necessary proof although the burden of proof laid on it." ICC Case No. 6896, Final Award, in *ICC Bulletin*, Vol. 15, No. 1, p. 15 (2004). See also a decision of the High Court of Ireland approving this principle: "[i]t was also submitted on behalf of the respondent that the Danish Arbitration Board had wrongly refused to consider the counterclaims of the respondent when making its award. I consider this submission is misconceived and also unsupported by the facts. The award clearly indicated that the Board considered the respondent's counter claims, made in correspondence, but simply found that they were not proven in evidence. The burden of proof for any claim in an arbitration made by the respondent is obviously on that respondent. The Arbitration Board simply stated that the respondent had not proved the claims. This was the fact. There was no evidence before the Board. Therefore the claim could not be allowed. The principle of 'he who asserts must prove' is applicable. Furthermore, as is evident from the award, the written counterclaims were considered during the oral hearing as the applicant itself accepted two of the counterclaims, in fact even lowering its own claim because of these counterclaims – a matter mentioned directly in the arbitration award." *Kastrup Trae-Aluvinduet AS v Aluwood Concepts Ltd* in Albert Jan van den Berg (ed.), *Yearbook Commercial Arbitration*, Vol. XXXV, p. 406 (2010).

38 *Chevreau Claim* case, *supra* n. 29, p. 133.

39 See the following determination by an ICSID tribunal regarding the burden of proof pertaining to requests for interim measures: "While the Tribunal has a certain discretion whether it considers that it should recommend provisional measures, the party requesting provisional measures must be considered to have the burden of proof regarding its request." Dietmar W. Prager and Rebecca Jenkin," *Caratube International Oil Co LLP v Republic of Kazakhstan*, ICSID Case No. ARB/08/12, 31 July 2009", *A Contribution by the ITA Board of Reporters*, para. 75. See also: *Noble Ventures v Romania*, where the tribunal stated that while both parties were to bring their evidence, the claimant bore the initial duty to substantiate its claims. "Finally the Tribunal notes that, insofar as a Party has the burden of proof it is sufficient for the other Party to deny what the respective Party has alleged and then, later in the procedure, respond to and rebut the evidence provided by that respective Party to comply with its burden of proof. Dietmar W. Prager," *Noble Ventures Inc v Romania*, ICSID Case No. ARB/01/11, 12 October 2005", *A Contribution by the ITA Board of Reporters* (quoting from Procedural Order No. 1 at para. 5). In commenting on this case and the risk of non-production of evidence, Bin Cheng notes that: "The ultimate distinction between the claimant and the defendant lies in the fact that the claimant's submission requires to be substantiated, whilst that of the defendant does not." Bin Cheng, *supra* n. 31, p. 332.

40 *Reza Said Malek v The Government of the Islamic Republic of Iran*, Case No. 193, Award No. 534-193-3 of 11 August 1992, in Albert Jan van den Berg (ed.), *Yearbook Commercial Arbitration*, Vol. XVIII, p. 289 (1993). See a similar formulation used by a well-experienced panel of arbitrators in an NAI arbitration: "In the Tribunal's view Claimant has done nothing more than articulate the usual burden of proof standard, *i.e.* that Claimant must

produce evidence to substantiate their cases, the tribunal may, as influenced by the log-ical sequence of facts involved in a claim or as imposed by the substantive law or other circumstances of the case, allocate to one side or the other the risk of not producing the evidence in support of their case.[41]

7.22 If the tribunal will allocate to one party or the other the risk of failing to pro-duce sufficient supporting evidence, what is the purpose of the procedural rule *onus probandi actori incumbit* or article 27.1 of the UNCITRAL Rules? It may be said that *onus probandi actori incumbit* is a rule of procedural flexibility which accomplishes the following: (1) it places both parties on notice that they are bound to substantiate their factual allegations with evidence; (2) it makes clear that both parties may bear the risk of failing on their allegations if they do not do so; and (3) because the parties are on notice, a tribunal is not under the procedural duty to inform each side at various stages of the proceedings as to whether the risk of non-production of evidence is placed or has shifted to them.[42]

---

prove its claims and, if it does, Respondent bears the burden of proving its defenses." NAI Case No. 3702, Final Award, p. 37 (2011) (unpublished). See also where this standard was articulated in regard to jurisdictional claims: "Where an investment is owned and/or controlled by the investor/claimant through a series of corporations, typically the claimant will adduce evidence as to how it owns or controls such investment. In this case it is the investment rather than a French investor that has brought the claim and it has sought to adduce evidence of how it is controlled by four non-parties to the arbitration who are nationals of France. The burden of proof to establish the facts supporting its claim to standing lies with the Claimant." *Perenco Ecuador Ltd v Republic of Ecuador and Empresa Estatal Petróleos del Ecuador*, ICSID Case No. ARB/08/6, Decision on Jurisdiction, p. 18 (2011).

41 See also the considerations of the *Tradex v Albania* tribunal which after reviewing the requirements of the substantive law, noted as follows: "The wording of these provisions confirms what can be considered as a general principle of international procedure – and probably also of virtually all national civil procedural laws – namely that it is the claimant who has the burden of proof for the conditions required in the applicable substantive rules of law to establish the claim." *Tradex Hellas v Albania*, supra n. 2, Decision on Jurisdiction of 24 December 1996 as referred to in the Award of 29 April 1999, in Albert Jan van den Berg (ed.), *Yearbook Commercial Arbitration*, Vol. XXV, p. 239 (2000). The Swiss Federal Tribunal, in reviewing an arbitral award from the Court of Arbitration for Sport (CAS) in the case *Michel Platini v FIFA*, 4A_600/2016 (available at www.bger.ch), held that, in accordance with the applicable regulation in the case, "Art. 8 CC [the French Civil Code], under which each party must prove the facts it alleges in order to derive its right there from unless the law provides otherwise, is interpreted by the doctrine in that the burden of proving the facts giving rise to the right lies with plaintiff, while it is incumbent on the defendant to prove the facts that annul that right. In the present case, the fact that gives rise to the right is the existence of the written agreement of August 25, 1999, and the lack, *a priori*, of a ground for a remuneration higher than that the one provided for in the said agreement. The fact annulling that right is the existence of the oral agreement, which would serve as a basis for the higher remuneration according to Michel Platini. Given that FIFA denies that it had entered into such an agreement, Michel Platini had to prove its existence. There is therefore no reversal of the burden of proof in this case: FIFA must prove that Michel Platini violated the CEF [FIFA's Code of Ethics], because the payment he received was unfounded, while Michel Platini has to prove that such a basis existed."

42 For instance, it has been argued by some parties that a tribunal had the duty to notify the party it that its evidence was not sufficient to meet its burden of proof. In regard to a particular case before the Swiss Federal Tri-bunal, it was noted that: "[t]he Swiss Federal Supreme Court found there is no duty of a court or an arbitral tribunal to inform a party that the documents it has produced are not sufficient to establish the facts of the case. The right to be heard does not mean that an arbitrator has to draw the parties' attention to the facts which are decisive for his decision." Georg von Segesser and Andrea Meier, "9 January 2008, Federal Supreme Court", *A Contribution by the ITA Board of Reporters*. This being said, it is not unheard of for a tribunal to give indications on how it has allocated the burden in the case prior to the final award, in particular where arbitrators have called upon one or both sides to produce evidence. See the decision of an ICC tribunal, where it noted in the final award that a party had not met its burden of proof even though the tribunal had alerted it to its obligation to bring forth its evidence in an earlier ruling on document production: "[t]he Tribunal wants to add that it indicated quite clearly, in particular in Procedural Order No. 6, that Claimant bears the burden of proof for its allegations . . .: 'Since neither Respondent nor the Tribunal are yet sufficiently informed about the fulfilment of the State X Entity Contract and any replacement contract, it is in

7.23 Finally, it is generally considered that a tribunal has wide discretion in allocating the burden of proof as an inherent part of its function to weigh and assess the evidence under article 9.1 of the IBA Rules and other similar arbitration rules. Reviewing courts rarely will overturn a tribunal's determinations regarding the allocation of the burden as it relates to its procedural discretion,[43] with the possible exception of those jurisdictions where a tribunal's decision allocating the burden of proof may be reviewed for error of law.[44]

Substantive law and the burden of proof

7.24 The substantive law of some jurisdictions, particularly those of civil law countries, may contain presumptions or rules on the burden of proof.[45] This fact notwithstanding, the substantive law provisions relating to the allocation of the burden of proof will often require no more than for the claimant to produce evidence in support of its allegations, a result similarly found under the procedural principle of *onus probandi actori incumbit.*[46]

Claimant's own interest to submit any relevant document.'" ICC Case No. 13133, Final Award, in Albert Jan van den Berg (ed.), *Yearbook Commercial Arbitration*, Vol. XXXV, p. 142 (2010).

43 See the following observation of the *ad hoc* committee in the ICSID case *Continental Casualty Co v The Argentine Republic* in response to the Claimant's argument that the tribunal had wrongly applied the burden of proof, the *ad hoc* committee reasoned: "[t]he Committee notes that the ICSID Convention and the Arbitration Rules contain no provisions with respect to the burden of proof or standard of proof. Accordingly, there cannot be any requirement that a tribunal expressly apply a particular burden of proof or standard of proof in determining the dispute before it. Indeed, the tribunal is not obliged expressly to articulate any specific burden of proof or standard of proof and to analyse the evidence in those terms, as opposed simply to making findings of fact on the basis of the evidence before it." *Continental Casualty Co v The Argentine Republic*, ICSID Case No. ARB/03/9, Decision on the Application for Partial Annulment of Continental Casualty Company and the Application for Partial Annulment of the Argentine Republic, p. 51 and 52 (16 September 2011).The Swiss Federal Tribunal, in reviewing the case *X._____Corp v Y._____ Ltd*, 4A_330/2013 (available at www.bger.ch), found there was no public policy violation in the arbitral tribunal's decision of refusing to shift the burden of proof or draw any adverse inferences from the absence of specific evidence because it would have been incompatible with the circumstances of the case: "[t]o the extent that the Appellant additionally argues in its brief on the basis of Art. 8 ZGB and Art. 16(1) OR that, contrary to the view of the Arbitral Tribunal, the Respondent should have had the burden of proof with regard to the intent to be bound, it merely criticizes the award under appeal in an inadmissible manner, without claiming one of the grounds for appeal under Art. 190(2) PILA."

44 See, for instance, the decision of the English courts in *Milan Nigeria Ltd v Angeliki B Maritime Co* [2011] EWHC 892 (Comm), where the allocation of the burden of proof by a panel of the London Maritime Arbitrators Association was judged an error of law and a basis for setting aside the award under s. 69 of the Arbitration Act of 1996.

45 See the following example of an ICC tribunal's application of Portuguese substantive law on the burden of proof: "The Arbitral Tribunal deems that the participation of S in the tender for the exploitation of Plant I is a violation of paragraph 1 of the noncompetition provision of the 1989 Agreement. Defendant French parent company did not prove that this breach of the obligation to abstain from competition cannot be ascribed to it, although it has the burden of such proof under Art. 799 no. 1 of the Portuguese Civil Code." ICC Case No. 8423 of 1994, Final Award, in Albert Jan van den Berg (ed.), *Yearbook Commercial Arbitration*, Vol. XXVI, p. 160 (2001). See also KCAB case no. 8, *Claimant (Counter-Respondent) Energy Company (Korea) v Respondent (Counter-Claimant) Seller Company (Vietnam), in* "KCAB Arbitral Awards", an arbitration administered by the Korean Commercial Arbitration Board and seated in Seoul, Republic of Korea, in which the tribunal determined that, in general, the law governing the contract applies to the burden of proof: "It is necessary to identify the applicable law to the burden of proof. In general, the law governing the contract applies with respect to the burden of proof. For example, Article 18 of Rome I Regulation provides that '[t]he law governing a contractual obligation under this Regulation shall apply to the extent that, in matters of contractual obligations, it contains rules which raise presumptions of law or determine the burden of proof.' The burden of proof is to be decided by the applicable law to the substance. The parties expressly chose Vietnamese law as the applicable law in this case. The Arbitral Tribunal therefore could have reviewed Vietnamese law in regard to the burden of proof." *Id.*, pp. 168–169.

46 See, for instance, the decision of a tribunal under the rules of the Arbitration and Mediation Centre of Paris: "The sole arbitrator first noted that under the applicable French law the burden of proof is on the party making an

That being said, the impact of the substantive law on the burden of proof may affect the manner by which the tribunal determines who bears the risk of not producing evidence. The following example-taken from an ICC arbitration applying the Swiss Code of Obligations shows that the tribunal determined that the substantive law created a certain presumption based upon the occurrence of a prescribed event, effectively shifting the burden of not producing evidence to the respondent:

> The Arbitral Tribunal points out that according to Swiss law, when a broker performs a certain activity within the frame of a brokerage agreement and the contract with the third party has been concluded, there is a presumption in favour of the broker of the existence of the psychological link requested by art. 413 CO. The burden of proof shifts then to the principal to prove that such a psychological link does not exist.[47]

7.25 Still, it is generally the case that the procedural and substantive rules on the burden of proof are congruent. A tribunal may organise the arbitration procedure so as to call both sides to substantiate their allegations of fact with evidence, but determine in accordance with the substantive law that one of the parties bears the initial risk of not providing evidence under the substantive law.[48] Thus, the customary approach in international arbitration is for the tribunal to apply the procedural rules on the burden of proof chosen by the parties, but to also give regard to any provisions of the substantive law influencing allocation of the burden. [49]

Standard of proof

7.26 The standard of proof is used to determine whether the evidence a party has produced in support of its factual allegations is sufficient to establish the facts in question. The standard may be determined by the relevant substantive law, but in some instances tribunals will appeal to customary practice to devise the threshold standard of proof.

7.27 The standard predominantly applied is quite often the *balance of probabilities* test, as was confirmed by an ICSID tribunal composed of well-experienced arbitrators.[50] The balance of probabilities standard generally calls for a claim to be upheld if the tribunal is convinced by the evidence that the claim is more likely than not true. This standard has been applied to the great majority of categories of claims in international arbitration,

---

allegation." Award in Case No. 9926, in Albert Jan van den Berg (ed.), *Yearbook Commercial Arbitration*, Vol. XXXIII, p. 15 (2008).

47 As reported by Andreas Reiner, "Burden and General Standards of Proof", in Edward Eveleigh *et al.*, "The Standards and Burden of Proof in International Arbitration", *Arbitration International*, Vol. 10, No. 3, p. 333 (1994).

48 See, for example, the following allocation of the burden of proof, made in consideration of the substantive law of contract, by an ICC tribunal: "According to the basic rules of the contractual laws regarding sales of movable objects the supplier must prove that he has furnished additional samples and/ or material which correspond to an approved sample. The same is true for a contract of work. In particular this is the situation under German law which is applicable in the present case." *Ibid.*, cited at 333.

49 "The better view is that the tribunal should allocate the burden of proof in the light of its assessment of the applicable substantive law and procedures adopted in the arbitration. In so doing, the tribunal need not apply the burden of proof rules of any specific jurisdiction, but can instead fashion specialized rules in light of the particular substantive issues and procedures at issue in a specific instance." Gary B. Born, *International Commercial Arbitration*, p. 1857 (2009).

50 "The Tribunal finds that the principle articulated by the vast majority of arbitral tribunals in respect of the burden of proof in international arbitration proceedings applies in these concurrent proceedings and does not impose on the Parties any burden of proof beyond a balance of probabilities." Dietmar W. Prager and Samantha J. Rowe, "*Ioannis Kardassopoulos v The Republic of Georgia*, ICSID Case No. ARB/05/18 and ARB/07/15, 3 March 2010", *A Contribution by the ITA Board of Reporters*, para. 229. That being said, one should note that a tribunal has considerable discretion in this regard. See also: *Continental Casualty, supra* n. 43.

including causes of action arising from a breach of contract or other obligation,[51] interpretation of contractual clauses or the intent of the parties to the contract,[52] and claims based on breach of international treaties regulating the treatment afforded to investors (a modified prima facie standard of proof has been adopted in regard to jurisdictional objectives by some tribunals).[53]

---

51 See, for instance, ICC Case No. 12596 in regard to a sale of goods agreement: "It is submitted by the Tribunal that the balance of probabilities point, not only to the Respondent's failure to secure the goods with contractually prescribed on-board packing for what had been foreseen in the Contracts, but also to defects attributable to the manufacturing process. . . . The foregoing reasoning, anchored particularly in an assessment of the balance of probabilities as well as in logic as it is, is reinforced by contractual provisions making liability for damage to the goods falling on the Respondent's shoulders." ICC Case No. 12596, Final Award, *ICC Bulletin*, Vol. 21, No. 1, pp. 84, 85 (2010). See also: the following application of the balance of probabilities standard by a CAS tribunal in a dispute (not involving allegations of doping which typically require a higher standard of proof): "Were the question of fact in this regard to have been critical, the Panel would have concluded, on a balance of probabilities, that C. lived, grew up and played primarily in Houston, Texas, where C. Sr. played professional baseball with the Houston Astros, and that he visited Puerto Rico during vacation periods and played some, but not a great deal of, baseball in Puerto Rico on such occasions)." *Puerto Rico Amateur Baseball Federation (PRABF) v USA Baseball (USAB)*, Award of 15 March 1996, CAS 94/132, in Matthieu Reeb (ed.), *Digest of CAS Awards I 1986–1998*, p. 56 (1998). See also the decision in ICC Case No. 12257, in regard to a dispute over a finance agreement: "the Arbitral Tribunal concludes that Claimant's proof established, by a pre-ponderance of the evidence, each of the foregoing issues in their favor." ICC Case No. 12257, Final Award, p. 15 (2004) (unpublished).

52 See the application of this standard in an *ad hoc* international commercial arbitration on the question of the choice of law: "As the [Utopian] party bases itself on the applicability of the Constitution of its country as the law chosen by the parties, it was for them to show, at least on the balance of probabilities, the joint intention of the parties in this respect; did the parties wish to submit their contractual relations, and in particular the validity of the undertaking to arbitrate, to [Utopian] law, purely and simply, or to [Utopian] law 'in its evolution', in other words including future legislative or constitutional provisions which could nullify or paralyse the undertaking to arbitrate?" Award of April 1982, in Pieter Sanders (ed.), *Yearbook of Commercial Arbitration*, Vol. VIII, p. 107 (1983). See also the application of the standard in an NAI arbitration to the issue of contract interpretation: "Also, Respondent has argued that Claimant did not act in accordance with good faith and fair dealing in terminating the Agreement and, thus, should not be allowed to invoke its right, if any, to collect on its 24 November 2006 invoice. On the basis of the evidence presented, the Tribunal is not convinced that Claimant acted in an unreasonable way. This might have been different if Respondent's interpretation of the Agreement were clear beyond doubt, but the Tribunal is not in a position in summary proceedings to judge whether the Agreement is for ten seasons, as advocated by Respondent, or for nine seasons as defended by Claimant. This interpretation issue has divided the parties for almost eighteen months and the Tribunal in the context of summary proceedings, which do not relate to breach of contract except for a counterclaim that was filed one week before the hearing, on a balance of probabilities cannot decide that issue." Award in summary arbitral proceedings in NAI Case No. 3310, in Albert Jan van den Berg (ed.), *Yearbook Commercial Arbitration*, Vol. XXXIII, p. 162 (2008).

53 See the following excerpt from an ICSID award for a discussion of the standard of proof applicable to claims brought, *inter alia*, for a breach of fair and equitable treatment as to the merits: "As regards the standard, three possibilities have attracted support. First, the usual standard, which requires the party making an assertion to persuade the decision-maker that it is more likely than not to be true. Second, that where the dispute concerns an allegation against a person or body in high authority the burden may be lower, simply because direct proof is likely to be hard to find. Third, that in such a situation, the standard is higher than the balance of probabilities. As to these, the logic of the second appears questionable, for its consequence is that the person who makes the allegation may be entitled to succeed even if it is less likely than not that the allegation is true. Certainly, any sensible tribunal considering an allegation of this kind will recognise that the need to rely on circumstantial or secondary evidence does not necessarily tell against it, but this does not dispense with the need for evidence of one kind or another sufficient to take the proof over the barrier. As for the third possibility, which at the other extreme requires proof of more than the balance of probabilities where an allegation of gross misconduct is made against a highly placed person, here also there are serious logical problems. It surely cannot be the case that evidentiary requirements can be heightened purely on the grounds of deference or comity or otherwise. And if it is said that this is an example of the common sense principle that an inherently unlikely allegation requires stronger than usual supporting evidence before it is accepted, contemporary experience shows how unrealistic it can be to assume that important persons will not behave badly. We make no assumptions of this kind, one way or the other, in the present case, and shall approach the issues on the basis that in order to prove its case on the existence and causal relevance of a nayizd the Claimant must show that its assertion is more likely than not to be true." Yaroslav

7.28 A standard derived from civil law jurisdictions sometimes mentioned as an alternative to the *balance of probabilities test* is the *inner conviction* test. This test is centered on the personal reaction to the evidence given by the arbitrator and is a matter of whether the arbitrator regards the evidence to have reached a level where he or she is personally satisfied of the veracity of an allegation. It has been suggested that the *inner conviction* test may impose a somewhat higher level of proof than that which is often otherwise applied by international arbitrators;[54] however, this conclusion is debatable.[55] As noted, this test is

---

Petrov, Sergey Voitovich *et al.*, *"Tokios Tokeles v Government of Ukraine, 26 July 2007"*, *A Contribution by the ITA Board of Reporters*, para. 124. See further the prima facie standard as applied to jurisdictional objections raised in investment treaty arbitrations. Originating in the opinion by Judge Higgins, in what has become known as the *Oil Platforms* case, the following decision by an UNCITRAL tribunal describes the prima facie standard as it relates to disputes over jurisdiction: "In short, by that standard, the Tribunal is here required for jurisdictional purposes, at the early stage of this arbitration (i.e. before the Respondent has pleaded any defence on the merits, particularly in response to the Claimants' Memorial on the Merits), to assume that the facts pleaded by the Claimants in the Notice of Arbitration are true unless such factual pleading is incredible, frivolous, vexatious or otherwise advanced by the Claimants in bad faith. . . . The Tribunal specifically rejects as imposing too high a prima facie standard the Respondent's submission at the Jurisdiction Hearing that the Claimants must already have established their case with a 51% chance of success, i.e. on a balance of probabilities. . . . There is another feature of the prima facie standard . . . it would not be appropriate for the Tribunal here to found its jurisdiction on any of the Claimants' claims on the basis of an assumed fact (alleged by the Claimants but disputed by the Respondent) if that factual issue was never again to be examined by the Tribunal. . . . Accordingly, in summary, the Tribunal's general approach in deciding the Respondent's jurisdictional objections under the prima facie standard here requires an assumption of the truth of the relevant facts alleged by the Claimants in the Notice of Arbitration (subject to the qualifications described above), excluding however a disputed fact uniquely relevant to the existence or exercise of the Tribunal's jurisdiction." *Chevron Corp, Texaco Petroleum Co v The Republic of Ecuador*, Third Interim Award on Jurisdiction and Admissibility, UNCITRAL, pp. IV 3–4 (2012).

54 This standard is described in German law as the following: "The civil law tends to apply a stricter standard [than the common law]. According to German civil procedure law, a judge must be convinced that a particular disputed fact is true in order for his decision to be based on that very fact. This requires neither irrefutable certainty nor a degree of probability close to certitude (*an Sicherheit grenzende Wahrscheinlichkeit*), but the judge must be sure to a practically viable degree of certainty that puts doubts to silence without eliminating them entirely. Balance of probabilities will suffice only in exceptional cases where the standard of proof is reduced, by statute, to prima facie evidence (*Glaubhaftmachung*). The Austrian law follows a similar approach." Siegfried H. Elsing, "Procedural Efficiency in International Arbitration: Choosing the Best of Both Legal Worlds", *Zeitschrift für Schiedsverfahren*, No. 3, pp 120–121 (2011). The Swiss Federal Tribunal, in reviewing an arbitral award from the Court of Arbitration for Sport (CAS) in the case *Michel Platini v FIFA*, 4A_600/2016 (available at www.bger. ch), held that the arbitration agreement made reference to the standard of proof agreed upon between the parties: "As to the standard of proof, it is indeed the one provided for in Art. 51 CEF [FIFA's Code of Ethics], "personal conviction." This means that the Panel must be firmly convinced of the non-existence of the oral agreement in order to confirm a violation of the CEF [FIFA's Code of Ethics] and vice versa." Fifa's Code of Ethics, Art. 51, provides the applicable standard of proof: "The members of the Ethics Committee shall judge and decide on the basis of their personal convictions." *See* Fifa's Code of Ethics, available at https://resources.fifa.com/mm/document/affederation/administration/50/02/82/codeofethics_v211015_e_neutral.pdf.

55 "Neither the main institutional rules for international arbitration of which I am aware, nor the UNCITRAL rules fix a standard of proof. Rather, the standard of proof which is required is often expressed by international arbitrators in terms of the jurisdiction from which they come. Thus, the English lawyers may talk in terms of the standard of proof in civil cases in this country, namely, a balance of probability. The civil lawyers may talk in terms of the concept of the inner conviction of the judge ('l'intime conviction du juge', 'die richterliche Überzeugung', 'il libero convincimento del giudice'). In practice the result is the same." Arthur L. Marriott, "Evidence in International Arbitration", *Arbitration International*, Vol. 5, No. 3. p. 282 (1989). See also the following description of the practice in France and Belgium, which suggests that the inner conviction standard results in an outcome based on probabilities: "Authors who have studied the case law in France or in Belgium have reached the conclusion that the courts do not apply the rules concerning the burden of proof with a spirit of geometry. To satisfy the burden of proof means to establish the existence of a probability or likeness which is sufficient to convince the judge and when this result is reached, the judge gives the other party the opportunity to explain himself in order to create eventually in his turn a contrary likelihood. This is in fact the way the courts tend to act in Belgium and in France, although this approach remains contrary to the rules set up by the Cour de cassation, at least in Belgium."

customarily regarded as an alternative to the more widely used *balance of probabilities* standard.[56]

7.29 It is generally conceded that a tribunal may take note of the substantive nature of a charge brought against a party when fashioning the applicable standard of proof as a matter of international evidentiary procedure.[57] For those allegations of particular gravity, a tribunal may find it necessary to apply a higher standard of proof. One finds examples of this in sports arbitrations convened to consider questions over the use of performance-enhancing drugs, where tribunals often will, as a matter of practice, require more than the general balance of probabilities standard of proof applicable to most commercial and contract claims, but less than the standard of *beyond reasonable doubt* applied in criminal proceedings.[58] Other claims, such as those brought on the basis of fraud or forgery, will attract a higher

---

Bernard Hanatiou, "Satisfying the Burden of Proof: The Viewpoint of a 'Civil Law' Lawyer", in Edward Eveleigh *et al.*, *supra* n. 47, p. 352.

56 Elsing, *supra* n.54, p. 211, "National and Institutional arbitration rules do not define any standard of proof. Yet a practice seems to have emerged by which international arbitral tribunals require a degree of proof close to the 'balance of probabilities' or 'more likely than not' standard known from common law systems. This development is to be appreciated, mainly because it offers more flexibility than the continental systems do."

57 The following quote from the decision of the ICJ in *Bosnia and Hercegovina v Serbia* affirms this general principle in international law: "The Court has long recognized that claims against a State involving charges of exceptional gravity must be proved by evidence that is fully conclusive (cf. *Corfu Channel* (*United Kingdom v Albania*), Judgment, ICJ Reports 1949, p. 17). The Court requires that it be fully convinced that allegations made in the proceedings, that the crime of genocide or the other acts enumerated in Article III have been committed, have been clearly established. The same standard applies to the proof of attribution for such acts." Pieter Bekker, *"Bosnia and Herzegovina v Serbia and Montenegro*, ICJ Case No. 91, 26 February 2007", *A Contribution by the ITA Board of Reporters*, para. 209.

58 The following rule setting forth the standard of proof used in cases involving allegations of "doping" was adopted by an America's Cup *ad hoc* panel: "The hearing body shall have the burden of establishing that a Rule violation has occurred. The standard of proof shall be whether a Rule violation has been established to the comfortable satisfaction of the hearing body bearing in mind the seriousness of the allegation which is made. This standard of proof in all cases is greater than a mere balance of probability but less than proof beyond a reasonable doubt. Where these Rules place the burden of proof upon the Competitor's Crew Member or other Person alleged to have committed a Rule violation to rebut a presumption or establish specified facts or circumstances, the standard of proof shall be by a balance of probability." Simon Daubney, 'Case No. ACJ036, Decision on the Merits (26 September 2007)', in Henry Peter (ed.), *The 32nd America's Cup Jury and its Decisions*, p. 429 (2009). See also the following comment of a CAS tribunal, which noted that in doping cases the standard of proof is higher than in general commercial disputes: "The standard of proof is high. It is higher than the standard in ordinary civil cases but it is less than that in criminal cases." *H v Fédération Internationale de Motorcyclisme*, Award of 22 December 2000, CAS 2000/A/281, in Matthieu Reeb (ed.), *Digest of CAS Awards II 1998–2000*, p. 415 (2002). The Swiss Federal Tribunal, in reviewing an arbitral award from the Court of Arbitration for Sport (CAS) in the case *X._____ v The Football Federation of Ukraine*, 4A_362/2013 (available at www.bger.ch), held that criminal standards of proof, particularly the principle of *"in dubio pro reo,"* cannot apply to private disputes: "Relying on the evidentiary provisions of the Swiss civil and criminal procedural laws and on the presumption of innocence according to Art. 10 CCrP and Art. 6(2) ECHR, [Appellant] argued that the standard of evidence applied in the arbitral proceedings to determine the existence of a manipulation of the game was inaccurate. In this respect [Appellant] argues – inaccurately – that the Arbitral Tribunal disregarded the significance of the legal consequences for the people involved. The Arbitral Tribunal reasoned in an understandable way as to why it applied the principle used in doping cases to the assessment of a game manipulation as to the burden and the scope of evidence and pointed out, among other points, that the seriousness of the allegation was to be taken into consideration as well, which the Appellant does not address. Contrary to the view taken in the appeal brief, the reasoning of the CAS that the Respondent would have to show the existence of a manipulated game "to the comfortable satisfaction of the Panel" does not violate public policy. In doing so, the Arbitral Tribunal established the burden of proof and the scope of the evidence needed, by reference to the pertinent rules of the federation and its case law, which in private law – even when disciplinary measures of private sport federations are to be assessed – cannot be determined from the point of view of criminal concepts such as the presumption of innocence or the principle of *"in dubio pro reo,"* or on the basis of the guarantees arising from the ECHR, as the Federal Tribunal mentioned several times in particular in cases involving doping violations (citations omitted)."

standard of proof which is articulated as requiring evidence that is *clear and convincing* or higher.[59] The gravity of a claim is determined according to the nature of the allegation, not according to personage of the party against whom it is levelled.[60]

7.30 If a request for an interim measure is before a tribunal, the arbitrators may be influenced to apply a standard of proof that is lower. For instance, it has been the view of some tribunals that the standard of proof is lower than the balance of probabilities test for requests for interim measures such as security for costs.[61]

Prima facie evidence and shifting of the burden of proof

7.31 In international arbitral procedure, prima facie evidence has been described as evidence "which, unexplained or uncontradicted is sufficient to maintain the proposition affirmed."[62] More broadly, a case characterised as prima facie has been described in the following manner: "A prima facie case is a case sufficient to call for an answer."[63] Both definitions stand for the notion that prima facie evidence is proof that is sufficient, if not contradicted, to establish the contention – a position widely accepted in international arbitration.[64] Whether evidence will meet such a standard is a subjective question depending

---

59 See the following decision of an Iran-US Claims Tribunal panel: "In this regard, the Tribunal has held previously that allegations of forgery, because of their implications of fraudulent conduct and intent to deceive, must be proven with a higher degree of probability than other allegations. This enhanced standard of proof has been expressed as 'clear and convincing evidence'." *Gulf Associates Inc v The Islamic Republic of Iran, Zamzam Bottling Co et al.*, Case No. 385, Award No. 594-385-2 of 7 October 1999, p. 15. See also: the following summary of ICC case law by the tribunal in Case No. 12542, citing, *inter alia*, to decisions in ICC Case Nos 6401 and 5622 (see below) to support the position that, "it is commonly accepted by ICC arbitral tribunals that allegations of fraud call for a high standard of evidence" ICC Arbitration, Preliminary Award of 9 October 2008, *ASA Bulletin*, Vol. 29, No. 2, pp. 860–883 (2011). See also the following finding of an ICC tribunal which required evidence of bribery to be "beyond doubt": "In the present case, bribery has not been proved beyond doubt. It is true that it is possible to prove something through indirect evidence and that Art. 8 of the Swiss CC does not exclude indirect evidence. However, it is necessary that a sufficient ensemble of indirect evidence be collected to allow the judge to base his decision on something more than likely facts, i.e., facts which have not been proven (citations omitted) Thus, evidence of bribery has not been given and the indirect evidence is not sufficiently relevant." ICC Case No. 5622, *supra* n. 18, p. 11. See also the following considerations of an UNCITRAL tribunal that considered the standard of proof for actions based on "bad faith": "Although the Claimant has avoided formulating this allegation in such terms, the underlying idea is that the PMRA acted in bad faith and launched a review process for reasons unrelated to its mandate and to the international obligations of Canada. The burden of proving these facts rests on the Claimant, in accordance with well established principles on the allocation of the burden of proof, and the standard of proof for allegations of bad faith or disingenuous behaviour is a demanding one." Charles H. Brower II, *"Chemtura Corp v Government of Canada*, 2 August 2010", *A Contribution by the ITA Board of Reporters*, para. 137.
60 *Tokios Tokeles v Government of Ukraine, supra* n. 53.
61 "The standard of proof relating to the two requirements set out in the preceding paragraph was not the usual standard of the balance of probabilities applicable in the resolution of commercial disputes on the merits, but the lower standard of plausibility according to a prima facie examination, as was normally the case for interim measures." "ICC Case No. 12542, Procedural Order No. 1 on the Respondent's Request for Security of 19 December 2003", *ASA Bulletin*, Vol. 23, No. 4, p. 685.
62 *Lillie S. Kling v United Mexican States*, 4 RIAA, p. 585.
63 The definition approved in, Dissenting Opinion of Judge Brower, *International Ore & Fertilizer Corp v Razi Chemical Co Ltd*, Award No. 351-486-3, para. 1, fn. 1 (1988).
64 For instance, as regards to a request for security for costs, the following summary of arbitral practice in Switzerland was provided in an ICC case: "It is required that the facts supporting the request for interim measures have to be substantiated by prima facie evidence". "Interim Award of 1996, Case No. 8786", *ASA Bulletin*, Vol. 19, No. 4, p. 751 (1996). See also the recognition of this rule in a decision by Society of Maritime Arbitrators tribunal: "While it is true the strict rules of evidence do not apply to arbitration proceedings, there are nevertheless basic rules and standards which should be observed and applied. It is Neorion's burden to establish a prima facie case for the performance and pricing of the work it contends was done . . .". *In the Matter of an Arbitration*

on the facts and circumstances of the case; however, it is generally recognised that the evidence must not be open to several equally plausible and opposing interpretations if it is to be considered prima facie proof of a contention.[65] Similarly, while witness or expert testimony may be sufficient to establish a prima facie case on its own,[66] vague and uncorroborated recollections are often not considered probative to the degree of constituting prima facie evidence establishing a contention.[67] Generally, evidence that does little more than repeat an allegation, or allude to it, but does not independently corroborate it, will not sufficiently rise to the level of prima facie evidence.[68]

7.32 In international arbitration, it is generally considered that evidence that establishes a contention to a level of prima facie certainty is sufficient to move the burden of proof from one party to the other.[69] With respect to the production of evidence, the shifting of the

---

Between Neorion Shipyards Syros Ltd and Colonial Marine Industries Inc, Final Award, SMAAS, WL 16780022 (1994). See also the following explanation of the customary rule taken from a decision of the Iran-US Claims Tribunal panel in the *Flexi-Van v Iran* case: "Other tribunals which have adjudicated international claims in the past have also faced similar problems. They have required what they considered to be sufficient evidence and from that have drawn reasonable inferences. . . . 'A respondent is, of course, always free to produce evidence in rebuttal. However, as the Mexican-United States General Claims Commission held: '[W]hen the claimant has established a prima facie case and the respondent has offered no evidence in rebuttal the latter may not insist that the former pile up evidence to establish its allegations beyond a reasonable doubt without pointing out some reason for doubting.'" *Flexi-Van Leasing, General Motors Corp v The Islamic Republic of Iran, The Government of the Islamic Republic of Iran*, Case No. 36, Order of 20 December 1982, in Pieter Sanders (ed.), *Yearbook Commercial Arbitration*, Vol. IX, p. 242 (1984).

65 As an example, see the following ICC tribunal's decision in a dispute over a software distribution agreement. There, a party argued that a clause within the contract was self-evident or prima facie evidence of one of its primary contentions, thus operating to shift the burden: "[s]econd, the tribunal concludes that there is no persuasive evidence that software developer E violated any such secondary duties. Software distributor M argues that the burden of proving the fairness and suitability of the O Agreement's fee structure is on software developer E. Software distributor M relies in particular on the rule of prima facie evidence. The prima facie evidence rule is applicable if particular events could, according to ordinary experience, only have had a single cause. The requirements of the prima facie evidence rule are not satisfied in the present case. There are multiple possible explanations for the fee structure of the O Agreement and for the grant of free users." Final Award of 1999 in ICC Case No. 10188, in Albert Jan van den Berg (ed.), *Yearbook Commercial Arbitration*, Vol. XXVIII, p. 82 (2003).

66 See, as an example, the decision of an English court, which noted that acceptance by an *ad hoc* tribunal of one side's expert's testimony was a sufficient finding of prima facie evidence to shift the burden to the opposing side. "Reviewing the award, there was no suggestion that the arbitrators had reversed the burden of proof in the manner suggested by the charterers. They had gone no further than accepting the evidence of the owners' expert and noting that the charterers had failed to discharge the evidential burden of rebutting that evidence. It had not been held that in the absence of evidence the charterers' case failed. There was, accordingly, no error of law, and permission for an appeal would not be given." *Arbitration Law Monthly*, Vol. 3, No. 5, summarising *Bulfracht (Cyprus) Ltd v Boneset Shipping Co Ltd (The MV Pamphilos)* [2002] EWHC 2292 (Comm).

67 "It is not denied that the statement of a person who confirms what another states in detail may have some value, but it is unquestionably true that in order to form a definite opinion each witness must set forth in his own manner the things he saw or knew since the comparison of different statements throws a light upon the facts equivalent to a confrontation of witnesses. . . . In this case it appears that the evidence submitted by the claimant Government is not sufficient to establish a prima facie case, since it consists of a simple vague statement of one witness only without any support from documents contemporaneous with the facts . . .". *Pomeroy's El Paso Transfer Co (USA) v United Mexican States*, Decisions, 8 October 1930, 4 RIAA, pp. 554–555.

68 As is noted by Kazazi, it has been historically held that an allegation does not constitute prima facie evidence of a fact. Kazazi, *supra* n. 34. See also: *Chevreau Claim, supra*, n. 29.

69 This principle was accepted in ICC Case No. 7365: "Prima facie evidence and presumptions may alleviate the burden of proof." ICC Case No. 7365, *supra* n. 34, para. 15.2. See the following discussion of prima facie evidence and the shifting of the burden of proof in the decision of the ICSID *ad hoc* annulment committee *Soufraki v United Arab Emirates*: "Mr. Soufraki had submitted to the Tribunal certificates of Italian nationality, which were *prima facie* evidence of the existence of such Italian nationality. Therefore, it would appear that the burden of proving the contrary should have shifted to the Respondent. In the proceedings before it, however, the Tribunal

burden concerns the risk of non-production and does not displace the procedural duty on both parties throughout the arbitration to substantiate their allegations as per article 27.1 UNCITRAL Rules or the maxim *onus probandi actori incumbit*. This general principle concerning the shifting of the risk of non-production was explained by a well-experienced tribunal as follows:

> The Tribunal notes that the Parties do not seem to diverge on the principles governing the burden of proof. The Tribunal shall apply the well-established principle that the party alleging a violation of international law giving rise to international responsibility has the burden of proving its assertion. If said Party adduces evidence that prima facie supports its allegation, the burden of proof may be shifted to the other Party, if the circumstances so justify.[70]

7.33 Therefore, once the burden shifts, the party that has presented the evidence has passed the risk of non-production to its opponent,[71] and may prevail on its allegation unless sufficient rebuttal evidence or argument is produced.[72] The above notwithstanding,

---

was presented with facts sufficient to throw significant doubt on the accuracy of the certificates: (a) it appeared from the certificates themselves that they where granted by different Italian municipal and consular officials without examining Mr. Soufraki's situation; (b) there existed some textual gaps and possible inconsistencies between the different certificates, which were never explained by the Claimant; (c) the Claimant himself asserted he was Canadian in his dealings with the U.A.E.; and (d) the initial testimony of Mr. Soufraki did not mention residence in Italy. *Prima facie* evidence is indeed evidence which should stand unless effectively controverted by countering evidence or argument." Dietmar W. Prager and Constantinos Hotis, "*Hussein Nuaman Soufraki v The United Arab Emirates*, ICSID Case No. ARB/02/7, 5 June 2007", *A Contribution by the ITA Board of Reporters*, para. 109. See also: *Flexi-Van Leasing v Iran, supra* n. 64, where a rule taken from the jurisprudence of the Mexico-US Claims Commission regarding the claimant's duty to produce prima facie evidence in order to establish its claim is cited to with approval. See the decision by a Society of Maritime Arbitrator's tribunal which noted that prima facie evidence, while not irrefutable, was sufficient to require the opposing party to establish its case: "the panel finds Dow has provided sufficient evidence to have established its prima facie case. In having done this, however, some of the assertions employed in making its prima facie case are open to doubt and in order for the panel to make a final determination as to what caused the cargo to become polymerized, the panel must hear Stolt's arguments and defenses." *In the Matter of the Consolidated Arbitration Among Coral Navigation Co Inc and Stolt Tankers Inc and Asahi Shosehen Co Ltd and Tsurumi Yuso Co Ltd*, Final Award, SMAAS, WL 12602116 (1992). See also an ICC arbitration, where it was noted that one party's failure to produce evidence that could reasonably have provided prima facie proof of its contention resulted in the tribunal refusing to shift the burden to the other side. Final Award, ICC Case No. 6497 of 1994, in Albert Jan van den Berg (ed.), *Yearbook Commercial Arbitration*, Vol. XXIVa, p. 74 (1999).

70 Charles H. Brower II, "*International Thunderbird Gaming Corp v The United Mexican States*, 26 January 2006", *A Contribution by the ITA Board of Reporters*, para. 95. The allocation of the burden of proof in *International Thunderbird v Mexico* was later challenged before a US district court which ruled Against the challenge. See: *International Thunderbird Gaming Corp v United Mexican States*, 473 F.Supp 2d 80 (US Dist. D.C. – 2007). See also the following from another tribunal composed of experienced arbitrators who stated the following: "Various international tribunals, including the International Court of Justice, have generally and consistently accepted and applied the rule that the party who asserts a fact, whether the claimant or the respondent, is responsible for providing proof thereof. Also, it is a generally accepted canon of evidence in civil law, common law and, in fact, most jurisdictions, that the burden of proof rests upon the party, whether complaining or defending, who asserts the affirmative of a claim or defence. If that party adduces evidence sufficient to raise a presumption that what is claimed is true, the burden then shifts to the other party, who will fail unless it adduces sufficient evidence to rebut the presumption." *Marvin Feldman Karpa v United Mexican States*, ICSID Case No. ARB/99/01, Final Award, para. 177 (2002).

71 See also, as noted by one CAS tribunal, once a party has produced sufficient evidence to shift the burden, it is not required to foreclose all other possible scenarios: "It is clear that the submission of the Appellants that, notwithstanding the shifting of the burden, the sporting regulator is still obliged to eliminate all other possibilities must be rejected. Such a submission is consistent neither with the concept of a shifting burden nor with language of the provisions nor required by Swiss law." *N., J., Y., W. v Fédération Internationale de Natation (FINA)*, Award of 22 December 1998, CAS 98/208, in Matthieu Reeb (ed.), *Digest of CAS Awards II 1998–2000*, p. 248 (2002).

72 See: Decision on the Annulment Application of Caratube International Oil Company LLP in the case *Caratube International Oil Company LLP v The Republic of Kazakhstan*, ICSID Case No. ARB/08/12, in which

it should also be noted that the burden may be shifted because of a presumption found in the applicable law, contractual rules or standards[73] as well as due to the presentation of affirmative defences.[74]

7.34 There is some support for the notion that a tribunal may shift the risk of non-production to a party which has exclusive control over relevant evidence, but has refused to produce it.[75] Rather than this being a question of 'shifting of the burden' however,

---

the Committee decided that: "In accordance with the general rule of evidence *actori incumbit probatio* it is CIOC [Appellant/Claimant] who bears the burden of establishing that the requirements of the applicable legal tests have been met, since CIOC [Appellant/Claimant] is the one seeking to benefit from Mr. Hourani's US nationality and control. The Committee therefore finds no reason to question the Award's initial assumption that 'Claimant bears the burden of proof to establish that the Tribunal has jurisdiction over the present dispute.' As a next step, the Tribunal accepted that Mr. Hourani had met his burden of proving that he was the owner of a 92% stake in CIOC [Appellant/Claimant]. The Tribunal then added that, as a general rule, the majority owner of a company must be presumed to control it, this being a presumption already established in a number of previous awards. Having come to that conclusion, the Tribunal decided that, in the circumstances of the present case, the presumption of control could not be applied in Mr. Hourani's favour. Doubts on this matter were already expressed when the presumption was established ('it will have to be examined whether in the present case this presumption is a sufficient indication of control'), and the doubts were confirmed when the Tribunal in its subsequent reasoning unequivocally averred that, as regards control, 'Claimant has the burden of proof.' [. . .] The existence of special circumstances justifies in the present case that the Tribunal deviate from the general presumption that majority ownership of a company also entails its control. Consequently, in the absence of the presumption, whether Mr. Hourani controls CIOC [Appellant/Claimant] is a matter to be proven; and in accordance with the general rule of *actori incumbit probatio* it is for Mr. Hourani to do so.'" *Ibid.*, pp. 268–273.

73 See: ICC Case No. 14020, where a clause in a contract for the sale and import of goods required buyer's approval of the vessel to be used for transport. After considering the construction of the agreement, the tribunal determined that the agreement was intended to place the burden onto buyer to show that it had exercised its veto power over the choice of transport vessel in a reasonable fashion. "[the Tribunal] decides that in the absence of technical or age reasons related to the nominated vessel, the burden of proof shifts upon buyer to establish that it did exercise its power under Clause 6 of the contract reasonably." Final Award, ICC Case No. 14020, in Albert Jan van den Berg (ed.), *Yearbook Commercial Arbitration*, Vol. XXXVI, p. 126 (2011). See also the following decision of a CAS tribunal wherein it noted that the presumption found within the relevant rules resulted in a shift in the burden different to that which may normally be expected: "The FEI Regulations institute a system of legal presumption. The burden of proof, which is normally incumbent upon the person alleging the guilt of a third party, is reversed: for the person responsible to have a penalty imposed upon him or her, it is sufficient that the analyses performed reveal the presence of a prohibited substance." *G v Fédération Equestre Internationale (FEI)*, Award of 10 September 1992, CAS 92/63, in Matthieu Reeb (ed.), *Digest of CAS Awards I 1986–1998*, p. 115 (1998). See also the following decision of a WIPO panel considering a domain dispute in which the following presumption was applied: "As a matter of principle, registration of a mark is prima facie evidence of validity, which creates a rebuttable presumption that the mark is distinctive. The Respondent has the burden of refuting this presumption." *Sankyo Co Ltd v Zhu Jiajun*, Administrative Panel Decision of 23 March 2001, Case No. D2000-1791, in Matthias Lilleengen and Eun-Joo Min (eds), *Collection of WIPO Domain Name Panel Decisions*, p. 166 (2003).

74 See the following determination of the tribunal in NAI Case No. 3702: "In the context of this threshold defense, however, the Tribunal agrees with Claimant that the burden of proof is rather on Respondent, taking into account that: (i) it is Respondent that has asserted the threshold defense, such that (ii) if Respondent succeeds, the Tribunal will not even come to address Claimant's claim." NAI Case No. 3702, *supra* n. 40, p. 66. See also the following determination by the tribunal in an ICC arbitration: "The Respondent, having raise the point, has the burden of proof. It has failed to discharge its burden to adduce convincing evidence that a bill of lading was required." ICC Case No. 14113, *ICC Bulletin*, Vol. 22, No. 1, p. 87 (2011). See also as the allocation of the burden of proof by an ICDR tribunal to the respondent to prove its mitigation defense: "Respondent asserts that "the burden of proving that losses could have been avoided by reasonable effort and expense must always be borne by the party who breached the contract . . . to the extent it has been proven that Respondent's conduct occasioned Claimants' losses (addressed above), it is Respondent which bears the burden of proving that Claimants were able to avoid the losses so claimed and proven." ICDR Case No. (partially redacted 056-04), Final Award, WL 6346392 (2005).

75 See the following ICSID annulment decision: "The Tribunal undertook the task of determining the amount invested by P. T. Amco in the construction, outfitting and furnishing of the Hotel. This task was rendered difficult by the incompleteness of the evidence submitted by Amco as well as that submitted by Indonesia. The Tribunal

the better view may be that this principle permits a tribunal to accept the veracity of the primary evidence brought to support the allegation, if rebuttal evidence that should otherwise have been brought was not.[76]

7.35 The moment when the burden shifts is often not a formal event within the procedure. As explained above, each party has the burden of proving their factual positions. Therefore, if a party fails to provide sufficient evidence to substantiate its position, it runs the risk that it will not satisfy the tribunal of its case, be it claimant or respondent. For the responding party such a risk only comes alive once the alleging party has submitted evidence sufficient to be called prima facie proof of its allegation or a presumption exists permitting the tribunal to regard the allegation as established. It is self-evident than an allegation must be established before a responding party is liable for failing to substantiate its response to it.

7.36 Finally, it should be noted that the relationship between the prima facie evidence rule and the standard of proof in international arbitration may be best described as follows: prima facie evidence is evidence that provides the tribunal with the lowest level of certainty permissible to justify a finding that an allegation is more likely than not to be true. However, in many instances this may not be enough to establish the contention on the balance of probabilities where countervailing evidence or argument is produced or doubts are raised regarding the reliability of the evidence. Irrespective of how the evidence is characterised, it should not be forgotten that in order for a party to carry the ultimate burden of proof and prevail in the dispute, it must persuade the tribunal of the correctness of its case.

Adverse inferences in international arbitration

Article 9.6 IBA Rules:　　**If a Party fails without satisfactory explanation to make available any other relevant evidence, including testimony, sought by one Party to which**

---

did not find that P. T. Amco's records and accounts were stolen as P. T. Amco had claimed (Award, para. 104) but the fact remains that P. T. Amco was expelled from its business premises under circumstances imposing at least the risk of loss of records. Thus, documents which in the ordinary course of business should have been in the possession of P. T. Amco and presented by it to the Tribunal, were submitted by Indonesia instead. At the same time, however, important documents such as those relating to the registration or the registerability of foreign exchange supposedly infused into the project were not submitted to the Tribunal by P. T. Amco; a reasonably prudent foreign non-resident investor may be expected in the ordinary course of business to keep copies of such documents outside the host State. The incomplete character of the evidence submitted by Indonesia – e.g., the lack of copies of complete tax returns and financial statements by P. T. Wisma (a company wholly owned by Inkopad, itself controlled by the Government) and of investment reports of P. T. Amco – may also be noted. The relatively low capability of an administrative agency efficiently to store and monitor and enforce the submission of formally required documentation is commonly a reflection of the realities of developing countries, and not an indication of bad faith towards investors, domestic or foreign. It seems to the ad hoc Committee that the Tribunal was aware of all these difficulties and took them into account in distributing the burden of proof between the parties (Award, para. 236). Thus, the ad hoc Committee does not consider the claim of Indonesia (Reply, p. 31) of unequal treatment of the parties in the allocation of the burden of proof as successfully established and therefore does not regard annulment as justified in this respect." *Republic of Indonesia v Amco Asia Corp*, Annulment Decision of 16 May 1986, in Albert Jan van den Berg (ed.), *Yearbook Commercial Arbitration*, Vol. XII, pp. 143, 144 (1987). This follows the principle raised by Bin Cheng from the jurisprudence of the Mexico-US Claims Commission that: "in any case where evidence which would probably influence its decision is peculiarly within the knowledge of the claimant or of the respondent government, the failure to produce it, unexplained, may be taken into account by the Commission in reaching a decision". Bin Cheng, *supra* 31, p. 330.

76 Bin Cheng notes further regarding the failure to produce evidence by a party who could otherwise have been expected to do so, that the jurisprudence of the Mexico-US Claims Commission shows that the arbitrators were at times "satisfied with prima facie evidence whenever the allegations, if unfounded, could be easily disproved by the opposing party." *Ibid.*

the Party to whom the request was addressed has not objected in due time or fails to make available any evidence, including testimony, ordered by the Arbitral Tribunal to be produced, the Arbitral Tribunal may infer that such evidence would be adverse to the interests of that Party.

Article 9.5 IBA Rules: If a Party fails without satisfactory explanation to produce any Document requested in a Request to Produce to which it has not objected in due time or fails to produce any Document ordered to be produced by the Arbitral Tribunal, the Arbitral Tribunal may infer that such document would be adverse to the interests of that Party.

General discussion

7.37 The majority of the well-known international arbitration rules omit reference to a tribunal's right to draw an adverse inference from the failure of a party to produce evidence. Nevertheless, a tribunal's authority to take notice of, and draw an adverse inference from, a party's failure to produce evidence is considered inherent to its right to appreciate the evidence (or lack thereof) presented to it.[77] This was historically confirmed in the jurisprudence of the Mexico-US Claims Commission arbitrations in the *Parker Case*.[78] In

---

77 For an example of arbitral rules that do contain such a rule, see Article 21.9 of the ICDR International Arbitration Rules, amended and effective as of 2014: "In the event a party fails to comply with an order for information exchange, the tribunal may draw adverse inferences and may take such failure into account in allocating costs." See the decision of the Swiss Federal Tribunal in "28 March 2007–1ère Cour civile", *ASA Bulletin*, Vol. 25, No. 3, pp. 610, 616 (2007). In ICC Case No. 16090, Final Award, ICC Bulletin 2016, Issue 1, p. 147 (2016), an arbitration seated in Geneva, the Respondent alleged Claimant paid commission fees amounting to bribery and argued Claimant's lack of cooperation in the taking of evidence supported adverse inferences against Claimant. However, the arbitrator found that there were no circumstances justifying the allegations of bribery and cautioned that adverse inferences should not be drawn lightly, particularly in relation to corruption. "In the present case, the Sole Arbitrator first notes that the amount of the percentage commission, namely 2%, is not unusually high and does not constitute a 'red flag' indicating a case of bribery. Consequently, this Respondent's argument cannot be deemed as a circumstantial evidence." *Ibid.*, §§304–309. "Concerning the existence of a Swiss bank account, the Sole Arbitrator refers to the ICC Case *Westman* ([1994] Rev. Arb. 359 at 367) in which it has been ruled that the fact that payment is to be made to a bank account outside the broker's country is not decisive, even less when it is a Swiss bank account since in Switzerland one must ascertain the beneficial owner of any account, numbered or not." *Ibid.*, §310. "With respect to the Claimant's refusal to disclose information on its beneficial owner(s) and to produce banking documents, it is true that a party's refusal to allow the arbitral tribunal access to documentary evidence may lead the tribunal to draw an adverse inference (ICC Case No. 6497 (1999) XXIV Y.B. Com. Arb. 71; ICC Case No. 8891 (1998) J.D.I. – Clunet 4/2000, 1076). *Ibid.*, §312. "As it has been reminded, each party has a procedural duty to cooperate in the gathering and presentation of evidence as clearly provided by the Swiss Supreme Court (4A_2/2007, decision of 28 March 2007) and it cannot be disputed that the requested documents are not under the control of the Respondent." *Ibid.*, §314. "The Claimant stated that it could not produce the requested documents and took the view that it could not provide details about the beneficial owner for tax reasons and since it could not exclude that this information could be illegitimately used or disclosed to third parties. . . . The Sole Arbitrator regrets the lack of cooperation of the Claimant in the taking of evidence. Obviously, the Sole Arbitrator is not in a position to ascertain with a full degree of certainty whether the reasons relied upon by the Claimant for not accepting to provide information are the true and/or sole reasons. However, the Sole Arbitrator is of the view that the reasons invoked by the Claimant are justified." *Ibid.*, §§317–319. "Therefore, the Sole Arbitrator finds that the Claimant's refusal to disclose the requested information cannot be characterized as a sufficient indication of bribery. The Sole Arbitrator also finds that the Claimant cannot be held to have failed to provide 'satisfactory explanation' which might have led him to infer that such evidence would be adverse to its interests (Article 9, para. 4 [currently Art. 9, para. 5] of the IBA Rules on the Raking of Evidence in International Commercial Arbitration (version 1999) referred to in the Respondent's Post-Hearing Brief on p. 14 para. 50). The Sole Arbitrator is further of the view that in the context of allegation of bribery, an arbitral tribunal shall be particularly careful when applying such provision to draw adverse inference." *Ibid.*, §§321.

78 *William A. Parker (USA) v United Mexican States*, 31 March 1926, 4 RIAA, pp. 35, 39–41.

that case, the tribunal described the basic rule, which has subsequently been adopted and followed by arbitrators since: "In any case where evidence which would probably influence [the Commission's] decision in particular within the knowledge of the claimant or of the respondent Government, the failure to produce it, unexplained, may be taken into account by the Commission in reaching a decision."[79]

7.38 That such a consequence may result from a party's refusal to observe a procedural order directing it to produce evidence should be of no surprise.[80] Parties come to international arbitration with the obligation to cooperate with the tribunal's efforts to establish the facts of the case (see comments to article 9.7). Refusing to produce evidence that has been called for by the arbitrator may constitute a breach of that duty. That a party may suffer an inference drawn against it because of its non-observance of the duty to cooperate is a widely accepted result.[81]

Adverse inferences relate to the merits of the case

7.39 Drawing an adverse inference from the non-production of evidence means that a tribunal may adopt positions on the evidence that are contrary to the arguments of the party that has failed to comply with a procedural order. A tribunal may accept the existence or the non-existence of a fact that is adverse to the non-complying party as it relates to the merits of the case. Therefore, while an adverse inference may be seen as a negative consequence for procedural non-compliance, a decision to draw an adverse inference should be consistent with the evidence as a whole, and be a legitimate result of a tribunal's findings on the facts of the case.[82] This rule means that a tribunal will generally not draw an adverse inference during an early stage in an arbitration and then move forward through the remaining phases of the case as though the inference is established on a particular point in contention.[83] The determination of whether an inference ought to be drawn against a recalcitrant party is in practice reserved for the final award and is part of a tribunal's process of weighing the evidence, as per article 9.1 of the IBA Rules.

7.40 This is not to say that a tribunal may not warn a party of the consequences of its failure to produce the requested evidence at an early stage of the proceedings. As an example, in an LCIA arbitration the tribunal notified a respondent that its failure to produce evidence could lead to the drawing of an adverse inference against it, but declined to order

---

79 *Ibid.*, p. 39.

80 In ICDR Case No. 526-04, available in Grant Hanessian (ed.), *ICDR Awards and Commentaries*, JurisNet, LLC (August 27, 2012), pp. 272 et. seq.: "the Tribunal found that Respondents entirely failed to comply with the discovery order of the Tribunal issued during pre-hearing proceedings. These orders had directed Respondents to (*i*) produce key documents, including records of raw material purchases and of shipments to customers; and (*ii*) allow the Claimant to conduct site visits of Respondents' manufacturing plants, and to inspect all manufacturing molds used on those premises. As a result, "[t]he Tribunal ruled in favor of the Claimant on all the procedural and substantive issues before the Tribunal. On the procedural issues, the Tribunal: [. . .] (*ii*) drew adverse inferences from Respondents' non-compliance with discovery orders. [. . .]." *Ibid.*, p. 275.

81 See, for instance, the following statement of the rule by an ICSID tribunal: "Ultimate sanction for non-disclosure [of documents] is the drawing of an adverse inference against the non-disclosing party." *Waste Management Inc v United Mexican States*, ICSID Case No. ARB(AF)/00/3, Procedural Order concerning disclosure of documents, para. 6 (2000).

82 *Ibid.*, *Waste Management Inc v United Mexican States*, Procedural Order No. 2 (27 November 2002).

83 *Ibid.*

the production as the respondent had claimed that the documents in question were covered by privilege.[84]

Accepted rules for drawing an adverse inference

7.41 While article 9.6 of the IBA Rules empowers a tribunal to draw an adverse inference, it provides little guidance on when such an inference is justified. This gap in the rules has been filled by the development of case-based rules setting forth the considerations justifying the drawing of an adverse inference.[85] These principles are explained below:

(a) *An adverse inference should be corroborated by all available evidence held by the party requesting that the adverse inference be drawn.* A party who moves for an adverse inference to be drawn cannot itself withhold evidence that would normally corroborate the inference it seeks.[86] In this regard, tribunals are often reluctant to draw an adverse inference where the finding could have been established on actual evidence under the control of the party seeking the inference.

(b) *In order to justify an adverse inference the requested evidence must have been accessible to the non-producing party.* Under this criterion, a tribunal may approve a request for document disclosure only if it has been shown that the evidence was or should have been in the possession of the party who refused to procure it. The presumption that the party does possess or has access to the evidence may be drawn from the facts of the case and previous statements that have been made in the arbitral record. The following considerations of an ICDR tribunal which determined to draw a negative inference from the failure of a party to produce relevant records, provides a useful example of this approach:

> "Respondents did not comply with the Panel's May 10, 2005 Order, its June 13, 2005, Order, or its July 19, 2005, Order. Respondents did not produce relevant documents or allow site visits of Respondents' facilities (. . .) There is no question that additional documents were available to Respondents. Respondents admitted to the Panel that they had maintained records required (. . .) but no such records were produced. Respondents also admitted to the Panel that there existed documentation supporting the income statement that was produced, but no such supporting documentation was produced. Respondents are required by law to make various tax and other filings with

---

84 "On day one of the hearings, Double K asked the tribunal to determine the question before it took a position. On day two, the Chairman dealt with the matter by indicating that if the documents were said by Double K to be privileged, it would make not an order for production, but it would be for Neste to make submissions as to what inferences might be drawn." *Double K Oil Products 1996 Ltd v Neste Oil* [2009] EWHC 3380 (Comm), para. 50.

85 These rules originally appear in the following article by Jeremy Sharpe in which he reviews the case law of the Iran-US Claims Tribunal: Jeremy K. Sharpe, "Drawing Adverse Inferences from the Non-production of Evidence", *Arbitration International*, Vol. 22, No. 4, pp. 549–571 (2006).

86 *Ibid.*, pp. 555–556. Sharpe draws from the *William Levitt* and *Kathryn Jaye Hilt* cases before the Iran-US Claims Tribunal to support the basic premise that: "The crucial point, however, is that arbitrators will not draw adverse inferences leading to an adverse award against a party that has failed to produce discoverable evidence in its possession if the claiming party itself likely has access to evidence corroborative of the inference sought, but has failed to produce that evidence or adequately explain its non-production."

the government, documents which remain available to them and could have been produced."[87]

As shown by the tribunal's consideration of the legal or tax filing requirements incumbent upon the party, arbitrators may take note of known business practices to infer that the documents in question were in the possession of the party requested to produce them.[88]

When applying an assumption based on known business practices, however, the tribunal should be satisfied that intervening circumstances would not negate such an assumption.[89] Furthermore, in establishing whether a party has access to the relevant

---

[87] ICDR Case No. (partially redacted-526-04), Final Award, WL 6354057, para. 74 (2006). See also the following review of a decision by an *ad hoc* tribunal to draw an inference from the failure to produce witnesses under their control, a Canadian court reviewing the award of an *ad hoc* arbitral tribunal noted that a decision by the tribunal to draw a negative inference was appropriate because employee witnesses available to one party who had direct knowledge of a case were not called: "Mr Christiansen was not believed by the Panel. Neither were some of the other Xerox witnesses. The Panel was entitled to and did draw an inference from the failure of Xerox to call some of the others who had worked on both the MPI/ Xerox software and the Xerox software to deal directly with the issue of copying." *Xerox Canada Ltd v MPI Technologies Inc* [2006] OJ No. 4895. See also: the decision of an Iran-US Claims Tribunal panel, which noted that it need only be shown that the evidence was likely accessible to the party: "[t]he tribunal notes that it is an accepted principle that an adverse inference may be drawn from a party's failure to submit evidence likely to be at its disposal. In weighing the evidence before it, the Tribunal must therefore take into account the Respondents' omission to produce the directors' reports." *Arthur J Fritz & Co v Sherkate Tavonie Sherkathaye Sakhtemanie (Cooperative Society of Construction Companies)*, Case No. 276, Award 426-276-3 of 30 June 1989, in Albert Jan van den Berg (ed.), *Yearbook Commercial Arbitration*, Vol. XV, p. 215 (1990). Regarding site visits, the tribunal in *Adel A Hamadi Al Tamimi v Sultanate of Oman*, ICSID Case No. ARB/11/33, Procedural Order No. 2, Concerning the Claimant's Application for Access to Conduct a Site Inspection, stated that: "a site visit is, in general terms, justified and should be allowed [. . .] The parties shall confer with a view to agreeing a time and protocol for a site visit by the Claimant's experts and counsel. *Ibid.*, §§15–17. In a follow up Decision on the Claimant's Request (Concerning the Procedural Calendar of Order No. 2), the Tribunal in ICSID Case No. ARB/11/33 summed up the issue regarding the parties' cooperation regarding a site visit: "The Tribunal stresses that the Claimant is entitled to an inspection – the only question is and has been when it should occur and under what conditions."

[88] See the decision of a tribunal to draw an adverse inference because a party's denial of the existence of the documents was inconsistent with the known responsibilities of a party to legally comply with the Foreign Corrupt Practices Act: "L'inexistence de pièces produites étonne d'autant plus que la défenderesse affirme être soumise à la loi FCPA qui oblige en fait les sociétés concernées à tenir des livres très complets. Ces documents doivent être tenus à la disposition des autorités, la confidentialité et le secret des affaires étant limités par la loi FCPA. Leur existence supposée, on ne voit donc pas pour quelles raisons la défenderesse n'aurait pas pu produire, dans cet arbitrage, des documents appropriés pour soutenir sa thèse (le cas échéant selon des modalités garantissant une confidentialité encore accrue par rapport à la confidentialité habituelle caractérisant l'arbitrage)" (unofficial translation) "The non-existence of exhibits is surprising, especially since the defendant claims to be subject to the FCPA, which in fact requires the companies concerned to keep very complete books. These documents must be kept at the disposal of the authorities, the confidentiality and secrecy of the cases being limited by the FCPA. Their existence presumed, we therefore do not see why the defendant could not have produced, in this arbitration, appropriate documents to support its thesis (where appropriate, the present case would ensure greater confidentiality than the usual confidentiality characterizing the arbitration)". "Final Award in ICC Case No. 9333", *ASA Bulletin*, Vol. 19, No. 4, p. 769 (2001). See also the finding of a tribunal under the rules of the Hong Kong International Arbitration Centre: "Essentially, if a party says repeatedly that no more documents exist, there is little the arbitral tribunal can do in international arbitration. But if the requesting party can persuade the arbitral tribunal that such documents/information must or ought to exist, continuous non-disclosure may result in an adverse inference against the non-disclosing party." *Jung Science Information Technology Co Ltd v ZTE Corp* [2008] 4 HKLRD 776.

[89] In an ICC arbitration the tribunal noted that the passage of considerable time between when the dispute arose and the commencement of the arbitration explained the loss of evidence which would normally be expected to have been produced. In *Anthony LaPine v Kyocera Corp*, 2008 US Dist LEXIS 41172 (ND Cal., 22 May 2008), p. 28, the court held: "[h]ere, the panel found that LaPine had not made a showing as to 'where or under whose control [the missing] documents – if at all existing – could or would be'. The panel went further to note that 'such circumstances eloquently reveal once more the daunting evidentiary difficulties to be met if this case were tried

evidence a tribunal may have recourse to the standard set forth in article 3.3(c) (ii) of the IBA Rules. This same standard should be used to determine whether it is sufficiently proven that the non-producing party had access to the evidence, and should be liable for an adverse inference due to its non-production.[90]

(c) *The inference must be reasonable and consistent with the facts in the record and logically related to the likely nature of the evidence withheld.* As the drawing of an adverse inference results in a substantive finding, the tribunal must be adequately assured that the inference will be consistent with known facts within the case. Naturally, such inferences may not be drawn where the arbitral record would contradict the inference or where the general circumstances of the case do not support it.[91] The tribunal should further be certain that the evidence is of the type which would normally contain information supporting the finding, before it draws the adverse inference.[92]

(d) *The party seeking the adverse inference must provide prima facie evidence of the facts supporting its claim.* The party seeking that an inference be drawn still retains the burden of proving that there is a factual basis for the allegation pursuant to which it seeks the inference to be drawn. Thus, it must provide prima facie

---

on the merits after having been dormant for over twenty years and the absence of even a prima facie record permitting that to happen'. Consequently, the panel's reasoned decision not to wait for these documents, which was well within their powers under the California Statute, does not offend due process nor is it a manifest disregard of the law."

90 As mentioned in the comments to article 3.3, the concept of "control", or access, is broader than simply whether the evidence in question is strictly within the party's direct possession. Control is generally interpreted to mean the following: "the Tribunal wishes to clarify that, for a party to claim that documents are not in its control, it must have made 'best efforts' to obtain documents that are in the possession of persons or entities with whom or which the party has a relevant relationship". *William Ralph Clayton, William Richard Clayton, Douglas Clayton and Bilcon of Delaware Inc v Government of Canada*, NAFTA/ UNCITRAL, Procedural Order No. 8, p. 1 (25 November 2009).

91 See the decision of the *Methanex v USA* tribunal not to draw an inference based on the inconsistency of the requested inference with the facts of the case: "That invitation [to draw an inference] is . . . rejected by the Tribunal on the facts of this case." *Methanex v Government of the United States of America*, Final Award, UNCITRAL/ NAFTA, para. 25 (2005).

92 See the decision of an Iran-US Claims Tribunal panel in *INA Corp v Iran*, where it drew an adverse inference against the respondent because it had not submitted evidence referred to in its expert report. The arbitrators noted that to draw the adverse inference from the non-production of such evidence was consistent with their view as to the general inadequacy of the report itself: "[i]n assessing the evidentiary weight of the Amin report, the Tribunal must draw negative inferences from the Respondent's failure to submit the documents which it was ordered to produce. In sum, the Amin report is so qualified and limited, and so influenced by unexplained, specially adopted (and not generally accepted) accounting techniques, that it cannot be considered to reflect the value of Shargh at the time of nationalisation." *INA Corp v The Government of the Islamic Republic of Iran*, Case No. 161, Award No. 184-161-1 of 13 August 1985, in Albert Jan van den Berg (ed.), *Yearbook Commercial Arbitration*, Vol. XI, p. 314 (1986). See also the *Frederica Riahi* case before the Iran-US Claims Tribunal, whereby a decision not to draw an inference was explained as follows: "With respect to the Claimant's request that the Tribunal draw an adverse inference from the Respondent's failure to produce Khoshkeh's share register, the Tribunal notes that the matter in respect of 510 shares concerns bearer shares and that Iranian law does not require that transfers of bearer shares be entered into share registers of the companies. In addition, Article 10 of the Articles of Association of Khoshkeh provides that only the transfer of registered shares requires the approval of the board of directors and recording in the share register. The Tribunal therefore is not convinced that the share register or other requested corporate records of Khoshkeh would show that the Claimant owned these 510 bearer shares and that the transfer of those shares from her spouse took place before his shares were expropriated. Accordingly, the Tribunal finds no need to consider the issue of whether the Respondent has complied with the relevant Tribunal Orders as far as Khoshkeh is concerned." *Riahi v Iran, supra* n. 26, p. 472.

evidence of its claim.[93] Moreover, where a party seeks an adverse inference from the non-production of evidence it must establish that the evidence that has not been produced would likely have been material.[94]

(e)   *An adverse inference is not permissible if the party alleged to have failed to produce evidence was not made aware of its duty to produce that evidence.* Generally a party will be notified that it is expected to produce evidence of a certain type through a finding on document production or by a request from the tribunal to present a witness.[95] A procedural order inviting a party to produce evidence on a certain point is sufficient notice that an adverse inference will be drawn against it if it persists in its failure to produce the requested evidence. Of the rules set forth above, the "notification principle" is expressly set forth in articles 9.5 and 9.6 of the IBA Rules,

---

93   See, for example, the finding of an Iran-US Claims Tribunal panel that correspondence evidence had sufficiently established a contention to which counter-evidence should have been produced: "[t]he tribunal acknowledges that in this Case, some evidentiary gaps remain. However, after reviewing the evidence as a whole, the Tribunal finds that it is justified in concluding that the Respondent has not introduced any evidence adequate to rebut the substance of Mr Behbahani's letters. Thus, the Respondent has not rebutted the Claimant's evidence of serious interference with, and, as a result of that, the deprivation of, their ownership rights in the real property at issue in this Case. Moreover, in the circumstances of this Case, the failure of the Respondent to produce evidence available to it justifies the Tribunal's drawing inferences from that failure." *Edgar Protiva and Eric Protiva v The Government of the Islamic Republic of Iran*, Case No. 316, Award No. 566-316-2 of 12 October 1989, para. 68.

94   See the decision of an LCIA tribunal not to draw an adverse inference from the failure of a party to present certain witnesses who had been requested by the claimant because there was a lack of evidence establishing what, if anything, the requested witnesses would have added to the evidentiary record: "[t]he Claimant asks the tribunal to draw adverse inference from the Respondent's alleged failure to call other witnesses including Messrs Loktyukhov and Koushnarev who attended the meeting [of 25 September 2007]. The tribunal does not consider it appropriate to draw the adverse inferences contended for by the Claimant: the three main witnesses were called and were fully questioned by Mr Shackleton; and the tribunal does not accept that anything substantial was lost by these additional persons not being called as witnesses." *Double K, supra* n. 84, para. 49. See further: where an ICDR tribunal considered the nature of the evidence, and determined it was likely to be supportive of Claimant's main contentions: "Respondents' failures to comply with the orders of this Panel support the inference that the documents and evidence that Respondents failed to produce were adverse to their interests, would have further substantiated Claimant's claims that Respondent 1 committed breaches of the Manufacturing Agreement, that all Respondents participated in such breaches and in violation of CLAIMANT trademark rights and in wrongful passing off of their products as Claimant licensed products, and that the transfers to Company 1 and Company 2 were and continue to be fraudulent shams arranged in an attempt to avoid Respondents' legitimate obligations." ICDR Case, *supra* n. 87, para. 86

95   See the decision below regarding the tribunal's determination not to drawn an inference because a party had not been ordered to produce the evidence which the adverse party accused it of withholding. Although applying a US standard, the panel, which was sitting in consideration of an international dispute, followed an approach that accords with the general rule found in international arbitration: "[w]ith respect to the requested adverse inference, the law requires that the party against whom the inference is sought had to have breached a duty to produce the documents requested. . . . In this case, the panel denied Ferrominera's request to require Transferven to produce the financial records relating to the repair and maintenance of the vessel after December 21, 2001, so it would be improper to draw an adverse inference." *In the Matter of an Arbitration Between Ferreos de Venezuela CA, F/N/A Transportes Ferreos II and Transferven Ltd and Segmar Ltd and CVG Ferrominera Orinoco, CA*, Final Award, SMAAS, WL 5911057 (2007). See also the decision of an ICDR tribunal not to draw an inference against a party because the party had not been ordered to produce the subject evidence. ICDR Case, *supra* n. 74. See also the decision of an ICC tribunal to draw a negative inference on certain key points of fact after the respondent had been notified in a procedural order on disclosure that production of certain important documents was requested: "Claimant had the opportunity to enlighten the Tribunal about these facts. It was even formally requested to do so in the frame of the discovery. The Tribunal moreover specifically drew Claimant's attention to the fact that non-compliance with the instructions in the discovery order would have serious consequences on the outcome of its claims. Claimant chose not to comply and thus did not dispel the doubts of the Arbitral Tribunal. . . . The members of the Arbitral Tribunal had the impression that there were many facts which Claimant did not tell and that there must have been reasons for not telling them. If they were not told, the only conclusion which can be drawn is that they would have stood in the way of Claimant's arguments." Final Award in ICC Case No. 13133, *supra* n. 42, pp. 129, 140–149.

where the drawing of an inference is expressly predicated on either the failure by the non-producing party to object to a request for production, or, on its failure to respond to an order from the tribunal inviting it to produce the evidence in question.[96]

7.42 The above principles are generally considered to be a list of criteria that should be satisfied in order for a tribunal to draw an adverse inference from the non-production of evidence by a party. Thus, it is the comparatively rare situation where one or two of the principles above is not present, yet the tribunal would still draw an adverse inference.

Procedural good faith

Article 9.7 IBA Rules: **If the Arbitral Tribunal determines that a Party has failed to conduct itself in good faith in the taking of evidence, the Arbitral Tribunal may, in addition to any other measures available under these Rules,**

---

96 In ICC Case No. 16391, Final Award, ICC Bulletin 2016, Issue 1, p. 150 (2016), an arbitration seated in Vienna regarding breaches of a distribution agreement, Respondent (the manufacturer) requested that Claimant (the distributor) be ordered to produce communications it had exchanged with a company X, with which it had secured a contract for the purchase of Respondent's products, allegedly through illicit means. Respondent requested that an adverse inference be drawn from Claimant's refusal to comply with the order. The sole arbitrator did not accede to Respondent's request, noting that local business practices made an adverse inference unjustified. "Respondent requests the Sole Arbitrator to draw adverse inference from the fact that despite being ordered to do so, Claimant in this arbitration did not disclose its communication with [X] in relation to the negotiations, implementation and service of contracts entered into between Respondent and [X] and facilitated by Claimant in the relevant timeframe." *Ibid.*, §268. "Claimant firstly stated that no such documents were in its possession. I, nevertheless [. . .] ordered the production of documents and requested detailed explanations why the requested documents could not be produced." *Ibid.*, §269. "Claimant reiterated that no such documents could be allocated [sic]. Up to this Final Award, no such documents were produced by Claimant." *Ibid.*, §271. Under the guise of Article 9.4 of the IBA Rules on the Taking of Evidence, the Sole Arbitrator stated "[t]he prerequisites for such an adverse inference are generally the following: (i) the party seeking the adverse inference must produce all available evidence corroborating the inference sought; (ii) the party requesting adverse inference must establish that the requested party has, or should have, access to the evidence sought; (iii) the inference sought must be reasonable, consistent with facts in the record and logically related to the likely nature of the evidence withheld; (iv) the party seeking the adverse inference must produce prima facie evidence; and (v) the inference opponent must know, or have reason to know, of its obligation to produce evidence rebutting the adverse inference sought." *Ibid.*, §276. "[D]espite my doubts about Claimant's explanations why it did not produce the documents requested, I cannot lightly assume that the documents to be produced would prove that Claimant indeed was involved in the illicit ASSF [after sales service fees] scheme for the following reasons. Western companies have detailed obligations to document in writing their business transactions and to keep books. US-based companies and in particular pharmaceutical and medical companies often even have very strict document retention policies. These regulations and practices are, however, not universally accepted. Particularly in the Middle East and Asia, less emphasis is put on documenting every detail of a business transaction in writing. This difference in business practices has to be carefully taken into account in international arbitration in order not to prejudice from the outset parties from certain cultural areas. I am therefore not prepared to draw claims not to be in the possession of certain documents which a European party would be expected to possess almost with certainty. Secondly, taking into account the evidence on file, in particular the witness testimony of both parties, as well as the circumstances in which the illicit ASSF scheme took place, it would be surprising to find direct written evidence of the Claimant's participation in this scheme in the documents which Claimant was ordered to produce. Therefore, I dismiss Respondent's request to draw adverse inference." *Ibid.*, §§278–281. See also KCAB case no. 5, *Claimant (Counter-Respondent) Construction Company (Korea) v Respondent (Counter-Claimant) Power Company (France), in* "KCAB Arbitral Awards", an arbitration administered by the Korean Commercial Arbitration Board and seated in Seoul, Republic of Korea, in which the tribunal determined that, while it had the authority to grant adverse inferences based upon Article 29(3) of the LCBA Rules and Article 9(5) of the IBA Rules on the Taking of Evidence in International Arbitration: "the Tribunal considers that it is appropriate to draw adverse inferences only in circumstances where the evidence is not produced or where evidence is not disclosed in due time. Here, the evidence was produced by the Parties prior to the hearing, and the evidence has been before the Tribunal for many months. The Tribunal therefore believes it is unnecessary to draw any adverse inferences and it is appropriate to proceed with the evidence on the record." *Id.* at [143], p. 98.

take such failure into account in its assignment of the costs of the arbitration, including costs arising out of or in connection with the taking evidence.

General discussion

7.43 Where a party has "failed" to conduct itself according to procedural good faith, a tribunal may apply article 9.7 and determine that the offending party should bear a portion or all of the costs of an arbitration. While this rule was added to the 2010 version, of the IBA Rules, it is a principle consistent with the general practice customarily long adhered to by arbitral tribunals. It is generally considered that the conduct of a party during a procedure as a whole (not just with regard to the taking of evidence) may influence the awarding of costs in international arbitration. An ICC tribunal succinctly stated the rule as follows:

> According to the general principles of international arbitration law, the arbitral tribunal must take into account for its decision on costs not only the results of the proceedings but also the behaviour of the parties during the proceedings. According to good faith, the parties to an international arbitration must in particular facilitate the proceedings and abstain all delaying tactics.[97]

7.44 Article 9.7 simply restates this rule as it relates to evidentiary procedure empowering the arbitral tribunal to impose a cost consequence as a result of bad faith behaviour in relation specifically to the taking of evidence. In application of article 9.7 the question may arise as to what constitutes "good faith". This issue becomes somewhat complicated in the realm of international arbitration because of the multitude of legal cultures that have the potential to meet during an arbitration. What may be considered simply as good, skillful advocacy in one jurisdiction, has the potential to offend the professional sensibilities of lawyers who hail from other backgrounds. Thus, what constitutes "procedural bad faith" should not be culturally motivated. It must be an objective standard so that no party is caught unawares by rules of procedural conduct that would appear parochial to some and foreign to others.

The duty to act in "good faith" and the "duty to cooperate"

7.45 The duty to act in "good faith" in international arbitration is closely aligned with the assumed obligation of a party to cooperate in the taking of evidence. The duty of cooperation, or as it is sometimes known, collaboration, is a general principle of international arbitration law that places upon a party the obligation to present evidence when called to do so, and more generally to employ due diligence in response to requests from the tribunal. This is a principle that has been widely accepted, as the quote below from one of the early, foremost experts on arbitral procedure, explains:

> It is incumbent on litigating States to cooperate in the submission of proof. This principle is of Anglo-Saxon inspiration. We have seen that in English law the obligation of the plaintiff is less that of proving than of commencing the proof. This principle passed very early into the law of international arbitration. It is today a major general principle of that law.[98]

---

97 ICC Case No. 7626, J. Arnaldez, Y. Derains and D. Hascher (eds), *Collection of ICC Arbitral Awards*, Vol. IV, 1996–2000, (2003) p. 331.

98 Unofficial translation taken from Witenberg, "La Théorie des Preuves Devant les Juridictions Internationales", as quoted in the dissenting opinion of Judge Holtzmann in Iran-US Claims Tribunal Case No. 244, Award

7.46 The above was historically confirmed in the early jurisprudence of the Mexico-US General Claims Commission,[99] and in modern practice it is generally recognised that the duty to cooperate is commensurate with procedural good faith.[100]

7.47 For a party to be in good faith it should take reasonable steps to cooperate with the tribunal and the opposing party in carrying forth the evidentiary procedure. Broadly speaking, this will require it to abide by the rules of procedure in the voluntary production of evidence, which means, among other things, identifying witnesses, experts and producing documents it intends to rely upon (or which a party may expect will be necessary for the adjudication of the claim) in accordance with the procedural timetable (articles 3.1, 4.1 or 5.1 of the IBA Rules).[101] A party should also be expected to cooperate with a tribunal-appointed expert once its views on the appointment have been properly heard.

7.48 It may be generally said that it is incompatible with good faith for a party not to comply fully with a tribunal's procedural order. This does not mean that a party may not petition for a reconsideration of an order if the circumstances would justify it. Nevertheless, when receiving a directive from the tribunal to produce or sequester evidence, a party

---

No. 57-244-1 of 15 June 1983, in Pieter Sanders (ed.), *Yearbook Commercial Arbitration*, Vol. IX, p. 292 (1984). This rule is incorporated into the IBA Rules by virtue of para. 3 of the preamble: "The taking of evidence shall be conducted on the principles that each Party shall act in good faith and be entitled to know, reasonably in advance of any Evidentiary Hearing or any fact or merits determination, the evidence on which the other Parties rely."

99 In the *Parker Case* the tribunal noted: "The duty of the respective Agencies to co-operate in searching out and presenting to this tribunal all facts throwing any light on the merits of the claim presented." *Parker v United Mexican States, supra* n. 78, p. 39.

100 "It is indeed another basic principle of international commercial arbitration that the parties have the duty to co-operate in good faith in the performance of their agreement as well as in the arbitral proceedings. . . . Arbitral institutions and arbitrators have therefore a correlative obligation to make sure that the duty of good faith is respected by the parties." Bernard Hanotiau, "Complex Multicontract-Multiparty Arbitrations", *Arbitration International*, Vol. 14, No. 4, p. 373 (1998). See the following general statement of this rule by an ICC tribunal: "All arbitration agreements must be implemented by the parties in good faith. A provision in an arbitration agreement must never be abused as a tool to delay the proceedings. On the contrary, arbitration proceedings require the bona fide cooperation of both parties." *Seller v Buyer*, Interim Award, ICC Case No. 6149 of 1990, in Albert Jan van den Berg (ed.), *Yearbook Commercial Arbitration*, Vol. XX, p. 48 (1995): See also: the description of this duty to both, (1) participate in good faith in the proceedings and, (2) honour the final award, described by an ICSID *ad hoc* committee: "There is no evidence that Georgia was in breach of its procedural obligation of loyalty inherent to a fair trial and that its comportment in the arbitration proceeding is now an indication to renege on its obligation to comply with the Award under Article 53 of the ICSID Convention if the applications for annulment are rejected." Dietmar W. Prager and Samantha J. Rowe, "*The Republic of Georgia v Ioannis Kardassopoulos AS*, ICSID Case No. ARB/05/18; ARB/07/15, 12 November 2010", *A Contribution by the ITA Board of Reporters*. The duty of procedural good faith naturally includes a professional obligation by counsel to the parties to provide accurate answers in regard to matters of evidentiary procedure. This point was affirmed by the UNCITRAL tribunal in *Himpurna v Indonesia*, where it was noted that a party's counsel should provide good faith answers as to when and if it received a submission: ". . . as a matter of principle Counsel should consider whether they do not have a professional duty, when appearing before any tribunal, to abide by standards of consistency and faithfulness to the record. Naturally the Arbitral Tribunal considers that such standards apply equally to both sides." *Himpurna California Energy Ltd v Republic of Indonesia*, Interim Award of 26 September 1999 and Final Award of 16 October 1999, in Albert Jan van den Berg (ed.), *Yearbook Commercial Arbitration*, Vol. XXV, p. 116 (2000).

101 "In its Decision on Jurisdiction (para. 238), the Arbitral Tribunal criticized Claimant for not having earlier disclosed to Respondent the details of the ownership and structure of the PCL PHL EMU group. That failure of disclosure certainly added to the costs of Respondent during the jurisdictional phase, which have been taken into account by the Tribunal." Dietmar W. Prager, Joanna E. Davidson et al., "*Plama Consortium Ltd v Republic of Bulgaria*, ICSID Case No. ARB/03/24, 27 August 2008", *A Contribution by the ITA Board of Reporters*, para. 316.

should undertake with the requisite best effort to comply with it – and to the extent it is unable to do so, provide reasoned explanations for its non-compliance.[102] Moreover, the manner of producing the evidence, and the timing in doing so, should also be undertaken so that the adverse party and the tribunal may make proper use of the evidence.

7.49 A party's duty to cooperate further requires it to undertake procedural objections or applications in good faith. In general, for a party to repeatedly raise baseless objections to the disclosure or admissibility of evidence, in particular after a tribunal has ruled on the matter, may be considered dilatory and in breach of good faith.[103] Actions generally that are taken for the purpose of delaying the administration of the evidentiary procedure will often be considered a breach of procedural good faith.[104] Moreover, a party will have breached its obligation to cooperate when it negligently or knowingly submits forged documents or other corrupted evidence, or does not take reasonable steps to ensure that its translations of evidence are accurate.

---

102 In the *Himpurna v Indonesia* UNCITRAL arbitration, the tribunal noted that a party's unilateral but sincere assumption that its procedural posture is correct, does not shield it from complying with the tribunal's directives. When overruled by the tribunal, a party's duty of good faith should require it to comply in good faith and adapt its procedural position accordingly. "The Arbitral Tribunal finally reminds the Republic of Indonesia that it would have been unacceptable for it to base its course of conduct on the unilateral presumption that the procedural contentions it has raised before the Arbitral Tribunal are well founded. If the Arbitral Tribunal holds to the contrary, the Republic of Indonesia is hereby put on formal notice that it will then be required to file the documentary evidence . . .". *Himpurna California Energy Ltd v Republic of Indonesia, supra* n. 100, p. 138. See also: the decision on the challenge to the arbitrator of the LCIA court in Case No. 3431. Here, the division of the LCIA court addressed the repeated objections and complaints lodged by a party concerning the procedural directions given by the tribunal. After examining the record, the division noted that such complaints were not brought on proper grounds and thus were a breach of good faith. ". . . Respondent's constant complaints and objections had amounted to an increasingly vexatious attempt to hinder the proceedings. . . . Respondent had failed in its obligation to do everything necessary for the fair, efficient and expeditious conduct of the arbitration." LCIA Court Challenges to Arbitrator's Reference No. 3431, 3 July 2003, 18 December 2003 and 18 February 2004, *Arbitration International*, Vol. 27, No. 3, pp. 361–362 (2011).

103 For example, as an ICC tribunal noted, raising procedural objections, whether in relation to evidentiary matters or are otherwise baseless, will be considered procedural bad faith: "The arbitral tribunal notes that, in objecting to the jurisdiction of this tribunal, the defendant does not raise any valid argument, so that its position appears to be dilatory." *Distributor v Manufacturer*, Partial Award, ICC Case No. 7920 of 1993, in Albert Jan van den Berg (ed.), *Yearbook Commercial Arbitration*, Vol. XXIII, p. 80 (1998). See also: the determination of an ICC tribunal concerning acts it noted consistently led to delays and were in bad faith: "First defendant's conduct herein was dilatory from the beginning until the end of the proceedings and that conduct was obstructive, and it was calculated to be obstructive, of the Tribunal in carrying out its task. Much extra and unnecessary work was caused thereby for everyone concerned. First defendant must bear and pay the entire costs of this arbitration . . . and also the entire legal costs of claimant and out of pocket expenses of counsel to claimant save for a reasonable reduction from such legal costs in respect of the issues of termination of the contract and retrospectivity of the Act in which first defendant succeeded." *Agent v (1) Principal*, Final Award, ICC Case No. 7453 of 1994, in Albert Jan van den Berg (ed.), *Yearbook Commercial Arbitration*, Vol. XXII, p. 124 (1997).

104 As an ICC tribunal noted: "[h]owever, the issue of general legal costs, fees and expenses should be viewed differently and in light of other fairness considerations. Claimant has succeeded in overcoming numerous and repeated applications by both Respondents to obtain a stay of these arbitral proceedings and to challenge the jurisdiction of the Sole Arbitrator to hear this case. Such applications – proven without merit – substantially slowed down the pace of these arbitral proceedings and unnecessarily delayed, among other things, the completion of the Terms of Reference and the general organization of this arbitration, including the timing for the submission of memorials, production of evidence and scheduling of a hearing on the merits. It is not to be excluded that had such disruptions not taken place, these arbitral proceedings would have ended by a final award on the merits before or shortly after the initiation of the liquidation of First Respondent. Under such circumstances, the Sole Arbitrator concludes that each Party shall support its own general legal costs, fees and expenses." Final Award, ICC Case No. 13507, in Albert Jan van den Berg (ed.), *Yearbook Commercial Arbitration*, Vol. XXXV, p. 166 (2010).

7.50 The question still may arise whether it is possible for a party to refuse certain aspects of cooperation in the taking of evidence and to remain in good faith. Some have suggested that the provisions of the IBA Rules requiring parties to meet and confer at the invitation of the tribunal and other so-called duties of "increased cooperation", may be resisted without falling into "bad faith",[105] though this may depend largely on the facts of the particular case. A single refusal to voluntarily undertake an act for which a tribunal has expressed a preference may not give rise to an adverse finding on costs, whereas a consistent pattern of failure to cooperate in implementing expedient and voluntary solutions to procedural issues may be considered a lack of good faith.

The duty of good faith and the equality of arms

7.51 Another principle of procedure that ties into the observance of good faith in the taking of evidence includes the obligation to refrain from actions aimed at disturbing the equality of arms between the parties. As it relates to evidence, this principle requires parties to refrain from acting in a way which would impede or threaten a party's access to evidence.[106] Examples of where such violations have occurred include instances in which state parties have used their police powers to disrupt the investor's ability to interview witnesses or gain access to needed documents, or acts by private parties to obtain evidence that violate a criminal law.[107] Attempts to illicitly obtain privileged communications are also generally considered "bad faith" procedural behaviour.[108]

7.52 In determining whether such acts as described above would give rise to a finding that a party had acted with procedural bad faith, a tribunal will often consider whether the act itself was pursued under legitimate pretence. For example, arbitrators sitting in consideration of investment disputes will often give deference to the legitimate exercise of police powers by the state, even if in doing so a private party's ability to prepare its case is hampered. Nevertheless, the true test of whether the act undertaken was legitimate will often be whether the party that took the complained of action is willing to mitigate its consequences to the arbitration and take reasonable steps to make available the evidence or witnesses it has in some manner impeded access to.[109] Failure by the party to take such steps may be considered bad faith, and the basis for an adverse award on costs.

---

105 Cohen, *supra* n. 10, p. 163, notes the following: "The revised IBA Rules also foresee increased co-operation among the parties in the taking of evidence. This raises the question of whether the duty of good faith should be interpreted to define or prescribe a particular level of co-operation. One interpretation is that the increased co-operation requirements in the IBA Rules should be regarded as being separate and apart from the duty of good faith on the notion that co-operation appears to be largely optional under the IBA Rules, whereas good faith is binding."

106 See the discussion of *Methanex v United States* in the comments to art. 9.2(g).

107 *Ibid.* See also the discussion of *Libananco v Turkey* in the comments to art. 9.2(g).

108 *Ibid.*

109 As an example, in the *Caratube v Kazakhstan* ICSID arbitration, the tribunal noted the following regarding the raids conducted by police on the offices of the investor-party: "In view of the particular importance of procedural equality between the parties in an arbitration proceeding and that all parties can use and rely on the same evidence, the Tribunal notes with pleasure that, during the hearing, considerable progress and agreement could be reached in the discussion between the Parties and the Tribunal." The Tribunal also noted that: "the Parties have an obligation to conduct the *procedure* in *good faith* and that this obligation includes a duty to avoid any unnecessary aggravation of the dispute and harassment of the other party". Dietmar W. Prager and Rebecca Jenkin, "*Caratube International Oil Co LLP v Republic of Kazakhstan AS*, ICSID Case No. ARB/08/12, 31 July 2009", *A Contribution by the ITA Board of Reporters*, paras 100, 120.

Document production generally and costs

7.53 Some commentators have suggested that the costs borne by a disclosing party in conformity with a document production order may be recouped once it is determined that the evidence was not material to the final award.[110] Such a decision may indeed be taken by arbitrators; however, the basis for awarding the costs against a party would in most instances be motivated by the outcome of the award or other considerations, and not based solely on the fact that a party sought disclosure which ultimately was not determinative of the case. To find otherwise would be to say that a request for disclosure, if it fails to reveal material evidence, was made in bad faith, which is not an outcome that is consistent with the right of a party to petition for evidence it reasonably believes to be relevant to the case and material to its outcome.

---

110 "When assessing costs in the final award, the tribunal should establish whether the documents one party requested from the other were material for the outcome of one or more claims." Michael Bühler, "Costs of Arbitration: Some Further Considerations", in *Global Reflections on International Law, Commerce and Dispute Resolution, Liber Amicorum in Honour of Robert Briner*, ICC Publication 693, p. 186 (November 2005). This was also alluded to by the tribunal in *Azurix Corp v Argentine Republic*, ICSID Case No. ARB/01/02, Procedural Order No. 3 (24 May 2004).

CHAPTER 8

Evidentiary hearing

Introduction

8.01 In the vast majority of international arbitrations, the balance of the evidence will be taken before holding an evidentiary hearing. The exchange of documents, submission of fact witness statements, and expert reports will often be submitted over the course of the arbitration, before a scheduled hearing is held.

8.02 From the standpoint of taking evidence, a hearing is often the place where the record is both challenged and refined through the questioning of witnesses. Usually arbitrators will attempt to avoid raising new issues and/or allegations at the hearing by insisting that the parties refrain from last minute submissions of new evidence, whether it be witness statements or documents. It is often the intention that the parties and the tribunal will come to a hearing well versed in the issues and evidence, so that the scheduled time will be spent honing in on the important questions left to be answered.[1]

8.03 The approach set forth above leads to the fact that a hearing in international arbitration often takes on different characteristics to one held in domestic legal systems. For instance, the practice of international arbitration has developed so that the predominant purpose of the evidentiary hearing is not to hear the direct testimony of witnesses and experts, but rather to allow for the questioning of witnesses and experts by the tribunal and/or the adverse party. Thus, the hours spent on direct examination of witnesses and experts in the courtrooms of common law jurisdictions is avoided in international arbitration. Also, whereas in some civil law jurisdictions the judge will take the leading role in questioning witnesses and experts, in the modern practice of arbitration it is the counsel who will do most of the questioning of witnesses and experts.

8.04 Of course there are exceptions; nevertheless, the rules set forth in article 8 generally support the above described practices. The following chapter considers these issues and the other questions which arise in regard to the organisation and conduct of an evidentiary hearing.

---

1   In *Zeevi Holdings v The Republic of Bulgaria et al.*, UNCITRAL Arbitration Case UNC 39/DK, the Tribunal issued Procedural Order No. 15 dealing with the details of the Final Hearing. *Inter alia*, the Tribunal clarified the "intention and scope of the hearing": "In view of the many and voluminous submissions and documents filed by the Parties before the Hearing, there is no need to repeat such presentations at the Hearing. As only a selected number of these exhibits will be used in the limited time available at the Hearing, to avoid that all exhibits have to be transported to Vienna and to avoid delays for search of documents at the Hearing, the members of the Tribunal intend to bring to the Hearing the major contractual and selected other documents, but invite the Parties to prepare and provide at the Hearing to each member of Tribunal and to the other party 'Hearing Binders' (a) one containing the statements of those witnesses and opinions and reports of those experts for which the Parties will notify their examination at the Hearing under Section 3.a. above, (b) containing copies of those further exhibits or parts of exhibits to which they intend to refer in their oral presentations at the Hearing. If possible, the contents of the Hearing Binders shall also be handed over on a CD." *Ibid.*, pp. 56–57, §55.

Notification of witnesses and the right to a hearing

Article 8.1 2010 IBA Rules:	**Within the time ordered by the Arbitral Tribunal, each Party shall inform the Arbitral Tribunal and the other Parties of the witnesses whose appearance it requests. Each witness (which term includes, for the purposes of this Article, witnesses of fact and any experts) shall, subject to Article 8.2, appear for testimony at the Evidentiary Hearing if such person's appearance has been requested by any Party or by the Arbitral Tribunal. Each witness shall appear in person unless the Arbitral Tribunal allows the use of videoconference or similar technology with respect to a particular witness.**
Other Statements of the Rule Article 24(1) UNCITRAL Model Law:	Subject to any contrary agreement by the parties, the arbitral tribunal shall decide whether to hold oral hearings for the presentation of evidence or for oral argument, or whether the proceedings shall be conducted on the basis of documents and other materials. However, unless the parties have agreed that no hearings shall be held, the arbitral tribunal shall hold such hearings at an appropriate stage of the proceedings, if so requested by a party.

General discussion

8.05 Practically speaking, an evidentiary hearing may not always be required. Given the extent to which written submissions are used in international arbitration, it is quite possible that a tribunal will be able to adequately decide the matter without oral witness testimony. Nevertheless, the parties, or even the arbitrators, will often seek to hold an evidentiary hearing for the purpose of hearing witnesses. Article 8.1 therefore presupposes that the tribunal has informed the parties of the respective dates for the hearing, and imposed deadlines by which notice of the witnesses expected to attend the hearing should be given. The above notwithstanding, whether a party has a right to a hearing, and, if so, who may call the witnesses, as well as whether the witness must appear in person (as opposed to via video-conference) are all questions which may arise, and are addressed below.

Right to a hearing

8.06 The position historically adopted in international arbitration is that an oral hearing should generally be afforded to the parties in the event that it is requested.[2] This practice is reflected in many of the well-known procedural rules as well as in the Model Law.[3] The

---

2 Article 15, UNCITRAL Rules.

3 See, for example: art. 24(1), Model Law. See also: art. 19.1, LCIA Arbitration Rules: "Any party which expresses a desire to that effect has the right to be heard orally before the Arbitral Tribunal on the merits of the dispute, unless the parties have agreed in writing on documents-only arbitration." See further: art. 20(2), ICC Arbitration Rules: "The Arbitral Tribunal may decide the case solely on the documents submitted by the parties unless any of the parties requests a hearing."

general presumption is that arbitrators will in most instances be compelled to hold an oral hearing of some type when one is requested.[4]

8.07 The above notwithstanding, a party's right to a hearing is not without limits. The practice reflected in the Model Law is that where a previous agreement has been reached to waive the right to a hearing by either the adoption of rules that restrict a party's right to a hearing or by express agreement, a subsequent request for a hearing by a party may be denied.[5] Moreover, as the right to an oral hearing pertains to the hearing of witnesses, the authority vested in the tribunal over the proceedings implies that it has the right to determine the extent to which witnesses should be heard (see comments on article 8.2).[6]

---

4 There appears to be more latitude for an arbitrator to refuse to hold a hearing in the United States even if a party requests one. Decisions challenging such an exercise of discretion typically analyse whether such decision was tantamount to misconduct, or caused a party to be deprived of a fair opportunity to present its case. When considering whether a refusal by a tribunal to consider the oral testimony of witnesses should justify the cancelling of an award, a US district court noted the following: "[i]n other words, a panel's erroneous refusal to hear 'pertinent and material' evidence will only provide a basis for vacature if the decision deprives a party of a fundamentally fair arbitration process." *Interdigital Communications Corp & Interdigital Technology Corp v Samsung Electronics Co Ltd*, 528 F.Supp. 2d 340, p. 352 (SDNY 2007). Other jurisdictions are far stricter on this issue as is indicated by a 2010 decision of the Austrian Supreme Court, where the court ruled that under the New Austrian Arbitration Law (which largely follows the Model Law) an arbitrator's refusal to grant a hearing to a party who had repeatedly requested one was a breach of their right to be heard. G. J. Horvath, "*Austrian Ltd Liability Company v Austrian Incorporated Association* (Austrian Supreme Court 30 June 2010)", *A Contribution by the ITA Board of Reporters*. See also a 2004 decision of the Supreme Commercial Court of the Russian Federation where an UNCITRAL award rendered in London was denied enforcement because a party was not aware and was not given a chance to protest the decision of the tribunal to determine the matter without a hearing. Case No. 3253/04, summarised in, I. Nikiforov, "Interpretation of art. V of the New York Convention by Russian Courts", *Journal of International Arbitration*, Vol. 25, No. 6, pp. 787, 803 (2008). Petrochilos summarises this issue as follows: "Subject to contrary party agreement and upon party request, a hearing should take place, for legal argument and/or presentation of evidence." G. Petrochilos, *Procedural Law in International Arbitration*, p. 219 (2004).

5 See the decision of a Hong Kong court rejecting a challenge to a HKIAC final award brought by a party who complained that it had not had an opportunity to cross-examine the opponent's witnesses. The court noted that as the parties had agreed to a "documents only" procedure, it was not open to the challenging party to complain that the tribunal had been unfair if the tribunal did not heed its later request for a hearing of the witnesses: "The submission that [there] was no evidence from the respondent is fallacious. Neither party's witness statement was under oath, neither witness statement was in the form of an affidavit. Neither were required to be either on oath, or in the form of an affidavit. The parties agreed upon the procedure, and agreed upon the absence of cross-examination, and the applicant cannot now complain about that procedure." *Taigo Ltd v China Master Shipping Ltd*, High Court of the Hong Kong Special Administrative Region of First Instance for Construction and Arbitration Proceedings, Case No. 22 of 2010, Reasons for Decision, para. 11 (17 June 2010). See also the drafting history of art. 24 of the Model Law which reveals: "The Commission, however, was split as to whether an agreement by the Parties that no oral hearings would be held should be equally binding on the tribunal. According to one view, parties should never be deprived of the right to have an oral presentation of their case, so that a party that previously agreed that no hearings would be held should still have the right at a later stage to request that the tribunal hold oral hearings. In the end a compromise was accepted: as the provision now stands, each party will have the right to request the tribunal to hold oral hearings, which will be binding upon the tribunal. However, this right will be available to each party only if the parties have previously failed to make arrangements on oral hearings. Otherwise, an agreement by the parties that no oral hearings will be held will be binding upon them, and preclude them from requesting oral hearings at a later stage." Stavros Brekoulakis and Laurence Shore, "United Nations Commission on International Trade Law (UNCITRAL) Model Law on International Commercial Arbitration", in Loukas A. Mistelis (ed.), *Concise International Arbitration*, pp. 630–631 (2010).

6 See the following procedural order taken from an *ad hoc* arbitration as a standard example of the reservation of the right by a tribunal to not hear witnesses: "The Procedural Rules require witness statements. Those statements, pursuant to Procedural Order No. 1, must be filed with the Statement of Claim or Defence. The Tribunal may consider a witness statement even if the witness, although summonsed, fails to attend the hearing for

Broadly speaking, a tribunal may choose not to hear certain witnesses as part of the legitimate exercise of its authority.[7] As is noted in the comments to article 8.2, however, arbitrators must be mindful of whether a decision not to hear a witness will, depending on the facts of the case, violate a party's right to be heard.[8]

8.08 A party's right to request a hearing is also circumscribed by a tribunal's authority to impose notice periods. The 2010 version of the IBA Rules, article 8.1, presupposes that the tribunal has provided a time frame within which a party must notify the tribunal and its adverse party which witnesses they wish to hear. Furthermore, article 8.1 is drafted in mandatory language reflecting that if a party fails to satisfy the notice obligation, such a failure may be construed as a waiver of the right to hear a particular witness or to have a hearing.[9] The

---

a valid reason. In instances specified, the Tribunal may refuse to hear a witness or prohibit the right of a party to examine a witness." *Telesat Canada v Boeing Satellite Systems International Inc*, Ontario Supreme Court [2010] OJ No. 5938, para. 64 (unpublished).

7 Commenting on the French language version of the ICC Rules, one tribunal wrote: ". . . the arbitrator has a wide discretion in matters of procedure, for instance, he has the right to proceed with the hearing of the case 'by all appropriate means' (cf. art. 20 French text which is somewhat more precise than the English text), having the power (but not the duty) of hearing witnesses, if he believes that this is useful." ICC Case No. 1512 (1971), in Pieter Sanders (ed.), *Yearbook Commercial Arbitration*, Vol. I, p. 128 (1976).

8 In *Ukio Banko Investiciné Grupé UAB et al. v Rual Trade Ltd*, Case No. T-6238-10, Judgment dated 24 February 2012, SVEA Court of Appeal, Department 02, Division 020109, an appeal on a challenge of an arbitration award rendered in Stockholm on 21 April 2010, the SVEA Court of Appeals in Stockholm ruled on the issue of the Tribunal's authority to reject a Party's right to a hearing for oral witness statements. In that case, the Tribunal rejected a request from Ukio Banko Investiciné Grupé UAB and the other respondents for a hearing for oral witness examination because the arbitration was based on the Expedited Rules of the Arbitration Institute of the Stockhold Chamber of Commerce and the arbitrator simply: "[d]oes not think it necessary to call for an oral hearing and to summon witnesses in order to finally resolve the dispute." *Ibid.*, pp. 4–5. In rejecting the challenge to the arbitral award, the SVEA Court of Appeal stated that: "[a]rbitration proceedings are different from court proceedings in that, amongst other things, the parties themselves choose who shall settle their dispute. The arbitrator is further not bound by the principles of concentration, immediacy and orality. The possibility to deviate from these principles means that the proceedings can be streamlined and tailored to the nature of the dispute and the wishes of the parties." *Ibid.*, p. 8. In particular, the Court held that the parties "agreed that possible disputes related to the settlement shall be resolved under the Expedited Rules for Arbitration of the Arbitration Institute of the Stockholm Chamber of Commerce [and] the [applicable] law provides a rule whereby, when fully applicable, no evidence other than the parties' written agreement is permissible and may be considered (the parol evidence rule)." *Ibid.*, p. 9. Further, "[t]he arbitrator applied the rules that the parties in the arbitration proceedings had themselves had agreed upon [allowing] the arbitrator to not hold a hearing or to not allow the requested witnesses." *Ibid.* Thus, the Court of Appeals found that there was no breach of fundamental principles of Swedish law or procedural error and rejected the challenge. *Ibid.*

9 "If a party or parties (as the case may be) after due consultation, deliberately chose not to bring further evidence and expresses this clearly or demonstrates it by conduct, this might be deemed to be a material or procedural waiver of rights that a party is fully entitled to even if the omission is against his interests." Matti S. Kurkela, Santtu Turunen and Conflict Management Institute, *Due Process in International Commercial Arbitration*, p. 177 (2nd edition, 2010). See also the determination of a well experienced UNCITRAL tribunal seated in Paris, France, not to hear a witness nor hold a hearing, for which no witness statement was given, following a party's belated request to hear a new witness. In this instance, the party seeking to present the witness was required by the terms of Procedural Order No. 4 to present the written statement of their witnesses in advance of the hearing. No such witness statement was given. "The Respondent in its submission . . . did not submit any witness statement nor did it request that [the witness] be heard as a witness. This new request is therefore clearly inadmissible as it was for the first time raised [after the deadline for submitting witness statements]. The request that a hearing be held to present (the Respondent's) arguments and to have a 'real debate' is not convincing. The Respondent was invited by Procedural Order No. 4 to submit [by a deadline] its arguments and thereby continue the debate by answering the arguments and allegations of the Claimant. It did, however, not submit any further arguments as it stated that it chose to 'fully maintain (its) points as presented [on an earlier occasion] and by this letter reiterate those points.' The Arbitral Tribunal is therefore at a loss to understand what an oral hearing could at this stage add to the debate . . . the Arbitral Tribunal will therefore decide the case based on the written submission of the Parties." *Jorf Lasfar Energy Co SCA v AMCI Export Corp*, UNCITRAL, Procedural Order No. 7 (2005) (unpublished). When

above being said, it is imperative that the tribunal ensures that reasonable notice is afforded to the witnesses summoned.[10]

8.09 The duty to abide by the procedural time frames for the notification of witnesses to be heard correlates to the tribunal's authority and control over the arbitral procedure, which is often given considerable deference by reviewing courts.[11] Thus, rules of procedure or arbitration laws which grant a party the right to a hearing, should be read as providing for such a right subject to the case management authority of the tribunal to determine when the hearing will be held and when notice of the witnesses is to be provided. This point was addressed by an Iran-US Claims Tribunal panel in the *World Farmers Trading Inc v The Islamic Republic of Iran* case in relation to a party's failure to abide by the proper notice period:

> WFT did not file a request for Hearing by the 18 February 1987 deadline established by the Tribunal's Order filed 4 August 1986. Eleven months after the deadline, however, WFT requested a Hearing. Article 15(2) of the Tribunal Rules . . . states that a party may request a Hearing at "any stage of the proceedings". This provision should be interpreted, in the light of the particular circumstances of the case, to mean that hearings are to be held upon the reasonable request of a party made at an appropriate stage of the proceedings. The Tribunal determines that, in light of all the circumstances of this Case, WFT having failed to request a Hearing within the deadline set by the Tribunal's Order, WFT's request is not reasonable or appropriate at this stage. Therefore the Tribunal will decide the remaining jurisdictional issues and the merits on the basis of the documents that have been submitted without holding a Hearing.[12]

---

this determination by the tribunal was later challenged before a US court on the grounds that the denial of the opportunity to present witness testimony at a hearing was a breach of due process (public policy), the enforcing court noted: "AMCI requested an oral hearing only after indicating that it would be available for any hearing that the Tribunal decided to call in the matter. Regardless of whether AMCI waived its right to a hearing by making that statement, the uncontested fact is that, under the rules and procedures established by the Tribunal, AMCI would have had no evidence to present at the hearing. Although AMCI has argued elsewhere in this case that it would have presented substantial evidence at a hearing regarding 'the facts of the force majeure events' . . . and other matters, all such evidence would have been excluded because it was not submitted in accordance with Procedural Order No. 4. [internal citations omitted]. The requirements of Procedural Order No. 4 are clear, reasonable, and common in international arbitration practice." *Jorf Lasfar Energy Co SCA v AMCI Export Corp*, 2006 US Dist. LEXIS 28948, pp. 8–9 (WD Pa. 2006).

10 In *Subway International B.V. v Mr. B [information omitted]*, Case No. Ö 5300-12, Judgment dated 20 September 2013, SVEA Court of Appeal, Department 02, Division 020108, an application for the enforcement of an arbitral award rendered by the International Centre for Dispute Resolution in New York on 24 August 2011, the SVEA Court of Appeals in Stockholm ruled on the issue of a Tribunal's duty to properly notify the parties of the scheduling of the main arbitration hearing. In that case, Mr. B notified the ICDR and provided a physician's certificate that, due to illness, Mr. B could not participate in the main hearing. *Ibid.*, p. 2. The main hearing was postponed and new summonses for a main hearing were sent. Mr. B did not participate in the main hearing. Later, Mr. B alleged he never received a new summons for the new date of the main hearing. As per the documents provided with the application for recognition and enforcement of the award, there was no evidence that e-mail correspondence had been sent to Mr. B in anticipation of the hearing. *Ibid.*, p. 6. As a result, the SVEA Court of Appeals found that Mr. B was notified of the main hearing with only four days in advance of the hearing, including a weekend. This was not "adequate advance notice" and Mr. B did not have the opportunity to argue his case. *Ibid.*, p. 7. As a result, the SVEA Court of Appeals found "there are impediments to recognize and declare the relevant arbitral award enforceable in Sweden. Thus, Subway's application for recognition and enforcement shall be rejected." *Ibid.*

11 "As long as an arbitrator's choice to render a decision based solely on documentary evidence is reasonable, and does not render the process, 'fundamentally unfair', the arbitrator is acting within the liberal sphere of discretion." *British Insurance Co of Cayman v Water Street Insurance Co*, 93 F.Supp. 2d 506, p. 517.

12 *World Farmers Trading Inc v The Islamic Republic of Iran*, Award No. 428-764-1 (7 July 1989), in Albert Jan van den Berg (ed.), *Yearbook Commercial Arbitration*, Vol. XV, p. 267 (1990). See also the decision of the *Glamis Gold v United States* tribunal in response to a late notification by a party to hear a witness: "With respect

8.10 The above decision affirms the principle that a party's right to a hearing carries with it the obligation to abide by the procedural notice periods. Furthermore, as noted by the tribunal in the *WFT v Iran* case, the right to a hearing does not require that a tribunal schedule multiple hearings upon each new request from a party.[13] Rather, what is required is that the tribunal provides an opportunity for a hearing at a stage in the proceedings it deems appropriate and the parties have the correlative obligation to ensure that their witnesses attend at the specified time.[14] Moreover, new developments in the case, or simply the discovery of new evidence, does not require additional or new witness hearings to be scheduled if the tribunal is satisfied that the parties have had an adequate opportunity to present their oral evidence and that the arbitrator's understanding of the issues would not be helped by a new hearing.[15]

---

to Claimant's request that Mr. Robert W. Anderson be made available by Respondent for testimony at the hearing, the Tribunal observes that the production phase of this proceeding was completed substantially prior to this point, and that, absent exceptional circumstances, it is not appropriate for new testimony to be offered at the hearing. No exceptional circumstances have been offered in support of this request. The Tribunal denies Claimant's request that Respondent make Mr. Anderson available for testimony at the hearing." *Glamis Gold Ltd v United States of America*, NAFTA/UNCITRAL, Procedural Order No. 11, para. 21 (9 July 2007).

13 See: LCIA Case No. 6827, where two respondents petitioned the tribunal for a new hearing following the originally scheduled hearing which they had not attended. The rationale underlying the request was that the two respondents, having appointed legal counsel late in the proceedings, following the hearing, would now present new, relevant evidence for consideration. In denying the request, the tribunal provided the following analysis: "The [respondents] were given every opportunity to attend this hearing. The tribunal does not accept the claim, in [counsel for respondent's] letter . . . that in the absence of proper legal representation the [respondents] 'were under the impression that it was not necessary for them to attend the hearing in London.' Respondents are sophisticated commercial businesses. They had their own in-house counsel . . . who wrote to the Tribunal that witness statements were being prepared and counsel would be appointed. . . . The Tribunal considers that it would be unfair to now reopen this matter and rehear this arbitration. The instruction of [counsel] cannot change the process. Furthermore, and in any event, the Tribunal does not consider, on a prima facie basis, that the evidence which the [respondents] now wish to adduce, as stated in [counsel's] letters would now change the Tribunal's conclusions on the merits as stated in this Award." LCIA Case No. 6827, Final Award, paras 136–142 (2008) (unpublished). This was also confirmed in the following Canadian case, where the court noted, ". . . any decision-maker has to balance the prejudice that might result from delay with the duty to hear all material evidence". *Corporacion Transnacional de Inversiones SA de CV v STET International SpA* (1999) 45 OR 3d 183, p. 197.

14 The Italian Supreme Court decided that the refusal to adjourn a hearing by an arbitral tribunal seated in Lugano, Switzerland was not unreasonable because no relevant explanation as to why the witness who had been scheduled to attend could not be present was given. *Cass.* 18 October 1997, n. 10229, as reported in Piero Bernardini and Marco Perrini, "New York Convention of June 10, 1958: The Application of art. V by the Courts of Italy", *Journal of International Arbitration*, Vol. 25, No. 6, p. 713 (2008).

15 See: *Compagnie de Saint Gobain-Pont v The Fertilizer Corp of India Ltd*, Cour d'Appel, Paris, 10 May 1971, in Pieter Sanders (ed.), *Yearbook Commercial Arbitration*, Vol. I, p. 184 (1976). See also a recent decision of the Swiss Federal Tribunal determination not to permit the revision of a final award rendered by a CAS tribunal. In this instance the party moving to revise the award had discovered that that one of the adverse experts whom had testified during the hearing had subsequently changed his opinion. The tribunal was petitioned to reopen the proceedings to hear the expert's revised views, which it refused to do, instead confirming a final award against the petitioning party. The Swiss Federal Tribunal, in consideration of the decision by the tribunal not to reopen the proceedings to hear the expert again, found that: "it was for a party to ensure that all the evidence in support of its case was available in the arbitration." Furthermore, the Swiss court noted that it was not clear that the new evidence would have altered the outcome of the case. Case No. 4A_144/2010 of 28 September 2010 as reported in, Matthias Scherer, "Introduction to the Case Law Section", *ASA Bulletin*, Vol. 29, No. 1, p. 76 (2011). See further Berger's reflections on the application of art. 15(2) of the 1976 UNCITRAL Rules wherein he notes that this provision, "should not be interpreted as an unlimited right to have separate hearings on all kinds of procedural or preliminary questions as they may arise." Klaus Peter Berger, 21–4 *Mealey's Int'l. Arb. Rep.* 19 (2006). Of note, the revised art. 17(3) of the 2010 UNCITRAL Rules contains the corresponding provision. Additionally, in *EMFESZ Elsö Magyar Földgáz és Energiakereskedelmi és Szolgáltató Korlátolt Felelösségü Társaság v Rosukrenergo AG (Emfesz v RUE)*, Case No. T-2737-11, Judgment dated 21 December 2012, SVEA

8.11 The above-mentioned points notwithstanding, arbitrators should proceed with a certain degree of caution when enforcing strict deadlines, if to do so would result in fundamental unfairness to one side or the other. A tribunal that insists on moving forward with a hearing without considering mitigating circumstances that render a party unable to adequately present its case could cause the final award to be susceptible to successful challenge.[16]

Hearing of witnesses after submission of a written witness statement

8.12 It is customary in international arbitration that a witness appears at a hearing following the submission of a detailed written statement of their testimony. The primary purpose of the oral hearing, in this respect, is to allow the tribunal and the parties to question the witness about his or her written statement and matters related to it. The following order taken from an ICC arbitration seated in Zurich, Switzerland, captures the standard approach:

> In general, evidence and argument submitted shall be in written form. A written statement of a witness that has been verified by that witness shall be admissible in evidence, subject to the right to require the witness to attend to be cross-examined. If such a witness attends for such purpose,

---

Court of Appeal, Department 02, Division 020101, an appeal on a challenge of an arbitration award rendered in Stockholm on 17 March 2011, the SVEA Court of Appeals in Stockholm ruled on the issue of the tribunal's authority to not postpone a hearing and not hear new witnesses. Following the issuance of a USD 527 million dollar award, Emfesz requested that the Court of Appeal to annul the award because, *inter alia*, of the Tribunal's failure to postpone the hearing and to hear new witnesses deprived Emfesz the possibility to answer RUE's claims in an appropriate manner. *Ibid.*, p. 3. Emfesz argued that two weeks before the planned main hearing in the arbitration, RUE submitted extensive evidence and new circumstances, which led Emfesz to request the Tribunal to either postpone the main hearing or to reject parts of the new material. *Ibid.*, p. 7. RUE argued postponement would entail great costs and delay, which were not justified because the allegedly new evidence and new circumstances were in fact not new and should have been produced in accordance with the Tribunal's order of discovery. *Ibid.*, p. 9. The Tribunal rejected Emfesz's request, but allowed Emfesz to complement its case with additional witness testimony from its witnesses already scheduled to appear. *Ibid.* The Court of Appeal held that Emfesz did not specify which witnesses they wished to hear in the case and that Emfesz had an opportunity to effectively present its case. *Ibid.*, p. 11. In rejecting Emfesz's application, the Court of Appeals further stated that: "[while] the arbitrators shall conduct the procedure impartially, adapted to its purposes and fast [. . .] the arbitral tribunal has, observing the rules and the parties' agreements, a great liberty to conduct the procedure in the way which the arbitral tribunal finds appropriate." *Ibid.*

16 In a case from the Supreme Court of Sweden, a Swedish party seeking to resist enforcement of a final award rendered under the rules of International Arbitration Court of the Chamber of Commerce of the Russian Federation successfully argued that it had not been given a fair opportunity to present its case when the tribunal had proceeded to hold a scheduled hearing over its protests. Here, the parties to the arbitration had repeatedly informed the tribunal that they were attempting to resolve their dispute using amicable means and sought postponements. By the forth procedural hearing with the arbitrators, the Russian side changed its view and reported that the attempts at negotiation had failed, and requested that the tribunal move immediately ahead with the hearing. The Swedish side protested that they had not had a chance to prepare a defense. The tribunal obliged the request, proceeded to hearing and rendered an award against the Swedish party. The Supreme Court upheld a lower court's decision to refuse enforcement, finding: "The arbitral award as well as the remainder of the investigation clarify that only in connection with the fourth scheduled date of the main hearing did it become clear that the parties had failed to reach an amicable settlement. Until that point, [the respondent] was justified in assuming that the dispute would not be reviewed on its merits at the hearing. When [the claimant] requested at the hearing that the arbitral tribunal proceed to review the dispute, the circumstances changed again. Therefore, the arbitral tribunal ought to have given [respondent] a reasonable respite to finally prepare its case on the merits and invoke evidence. The arbitral tribunal has disregarded basic principles of due process of law in international arbitrations, which entailed that [the respondent] did not have the opportunity to present its case." *Belaya Ptitsa-Kursk v Robot Grader AB*, Högsta Domstolen [HD] [Supreme Court] 2018–05–04, Ö 3626-17 (Swed.).

with the permission of the Arbitral Tribunal oral evidence from such witness may be adduced by the party calling that witness. The Arbitral Tribunal, and counsel for the adverse party, shall have the right to cross-examine any witness who is called at any hearing but a reasonable time, as determined by the Arbitral Tribunal, shall be allocated to each of the parties for the examination of a witness or witnesses. The examination and cross-examination of any witnesses shall at all times remain under the entire control of the Arbitral Tribunal.[17]

8.13 Where written witness statements are not used or not required, as a bare minimum the party who is presenting the witness will have provided some summary indication of the subject matter of the expected testimony prior to the hearing.[18] As an example, in an ICC arbitration seated in Cologne, Germany, the tribunal ordered the parties who intended to present witnesses at the hearing to produce a list of those witnesses, and "their precise address and the subject of their evidence will be indicated by the party concerned at least 3 weeks before the witnesses are heard by the Arbitral Tribunal."[19]

---

17 ICC Case No. 14925, Procedural Order No. 1, para. 5, (2007).

18 Under the rules of the Iran-US claims tribunal, special provision was given for the introduction of rebuttal witnesses who were called to respond to testimony provided prior to the hearing by an adverse witness. Nevertheless, it was still anticipated that a written summary or indication of the testimony would be given in advance of the hearing, if possible. "Under the provisions of the rules applied by the tribunal, it is pre-supposed that such a witness has not had an opportunity to give a normal statement or other indication of its testimony, and thus is required to provide the written notice of the subject on which the witness will testify as soon as possible before the hearing. Notes to Article 25 state with respect to art. 25(2): 'The information concerning witnesses which an arbitrating party must communicate pursuant to paragraph 2 of art. 25 of the Tribunal Rules is not required with respect to any witnesses which an arbitrating party may later decide to present to rebut evidence presented by the other arbitrating party. However, such information concerning any rebuttal witness shall be communicated to the arbitral tribunal and the other arbitrating parties as far in advance of hearing the witness as is reasonably possible.'" *Harris International Telecommunications Inc v The Islamic Republic of Iran*, Partial Award No. 323-409-1, in Albert Jan van den Berg (ed.), *Yearbook Commercial Arbitration*, Vol. XIV, paras 103–105 (1989). See also a procedural order taken from an ICC arbitration wherein the arbitrators noted, "If witnesses are to be heard, the tribunal should assure that a list of the witnesses to be heard and the subject of their proposed testimony is communicated in advance to the tribunal and the other party." ICC Case No. 7170, in W. Laurence Craig, William W. Park and Jan Paulsson, *Annotated Guide to the 1998 ICC Arbitration Rules*, p. 125 (1998). See also the decision of an ICSID tribunal in *Spyridon Rousallis v Romania* where a party submitted a request to admit new direct testimony at the hearing of two witnesses who had not previously tendered a witness statement. In the absence of a written statement, the tribunal rejected the new testimony of the two proffered witnesses, as it violated the rules of procedure. *Spyridon Rousallis v Romania*, ICSID Case No. ARB/06/1, Final Award, p. 4 (2011). See also the following rule adopted by the tribunal in ICC arbitration No. 12206 as an example of a typical procedural rule limiting hearing testimony to only witnesses who offered a written statement: "Witnesses may be called by the party who wishes to cross-examine him or her. Only witnesses who have given witness statements shall be called." *ICC Bulletin, 2010 Special Supplement: Decisions On ICC Arbitration Procedure*, p. 37. See further a decision of the US Courts in *Al-Haddad Commodities v Toepfer*. In this instance a tribunal permitted a witness to testify by telephone at the witness hearing despite the fact that the witness did not submit a written statement in advance. The tribunal had previously determined that only those witnesses having submitted written statements fourteen days in advance of the hearing could testify at the hearing, thus the decision by the chairman to permit the telephonic appearance at the last moments prior to the hearing was a departure from the tribunal's earlier rule. These actions were later criticised by a US district court in the context of an enforcement proceeding as both arbitrary and concerning. Nevertheless, as no prejudice to the adverse party stemming from this procedural decision could be shown, the court did not regard it as a basis for refusing to enforce the award. *Al-Haddad Commodities Corp v Toepfer Int'l Asia Pte Ltd*, 485 F. Supp. 2d 677 (E.D. Va. 2007). It should be noted that if a tribunal has considered the offer of testimony of a witness who has not previously provided a witness statement, and found it possibly material to the outcome of the arbitration, it may generally choose to hear the witness irrespective of the rule discussed above. However, in choosing to do so, the tribunal should ensure that the adverse party is afforded an opportunity to respond to the new evidence and further, make arrangement for the witness to provide some manner of indication as to the nature of testimony that will be offered in advance of the hearing, if possible.

19 *"Documents"*, in *ASA Bulletin*, Vol. 11, No. 2, p. 314 (1993).

8.14 Thus, it is generally the case that the testimony of witnesses to be called at hearing will be reduced to writing in the form of a witness statement, or in the very least through a summary of the subject matter of the testimony. This rule holds true also with respect to rebuttal witnesses, who are simply called to refute a point raised by an adverse witness, to the extent there is enough time to permit submission of a written statement.[20] In reviewing the logistical challenges involved in organising an international arbitration hearing, and the duty to treat the parties with equality, as well as the common practice of arbitral institutions, an American court, when considering an application to challenge an award, affirmed this basic practice by noting that, "in international cases, it is important that parties be able to anticipate what will transpire at the hearing."[21]

8.15 An exception to this approach may come about where a party seeks to call to the hearing witnesses who are not cooperative, and whom have been identified in the proceedings as having relevant information.[22] As an example, a party may summon an individual whom the adverse party has referred to in their submissions even if they have not provided a witness statement.[23] In this comparatively rare situation, it may be that an written summary of the testimony of that witness will not be provided in advance of the hearing (see comments to article 4.4).

Which party may call witnesses?

8.16 While article 8.1 makes no distinction as to which party may request a witness to attend a hearing, it is a common practice in international arbitration that it is primarily up to the party who has not presented the written statement of the witness, namely, the adverse party, to call him or her to appear at the hearing.[24] This practice derives from the general rule that the witness statement itself should serve as the primary, or main portion of any "direct" testimony offered into the record (see comments on articles 8.2 and 8.4).[25]

---

20 *Harris v Iran, supra* n. 18. See: comments to art. 4.4.

21 *Industrial Risk Insurers et al. v MAN Gutehoffnungshutte GmbH et al.* 141 F.3d 1434, p. 1443 (US Ct App. 11th Circ. 1998).

22 Article 4.4 of the IBA Rules notes that a witness statement is not required of witnesses who appear by compulsion of court order, or who are otherwise requested to attend a hearing on the motion of the tribunal.

23 See, for example: John Beechey "*Brandeis (Brokers) Ltd v Herbert Black*, LME Arbitration, Queen's Bench Division (Commercial Court)", *A Contribution by the ITA Board of Reporters*, para. 7.

24 As the witness has already in essence provided his direct testimony in the form of the written statement, the utility in asking that witness to appear at the hearing may in many if not most circumstances be very limited if the adverse party does not wish to cross-examine them. See. for example, the following excerpt from the procedural record of an ICC arbitration held in Geneva, Switzerland, where the arbitrators adopted the standard approach of calling to the hearing only those witnesses whom the adverse party wished to cross-examine: "[t]his agreed procedure was followed subsequently throughout the course of the arbitration. The only occasions on which witnesses for the respondents did not give their evidence in person were when the claimants elected not to require their attendance for cross-examination. Thus, on 6 January 1986 the claimants' solicitors wrote: 'In accordance with the tribunal's Order dated 18 September 1985 we enclose in triplicate copies of the following documents . . . (3) Bundle of witness statements'. In their letter of 18 April 1986 the claimants' solicitors themselves referred to 'the advantages of the reduction of the case to writing' and referred to the proposal that the parties identify witnesses for cross-examination at the September hearing by a defined date as 'a very helpful suggestion'." Final award ICC Case No. 4975 of 1998, in Albert Jan van den Berg (ed.), *Yearbook Commercial Arbitration*, Vol. XIV, p. 122 (1989).

25 "In order to make most efficient use of time at the Hearing, written Witness Statements shall generally be used in lieu of direct examination though exceptions may be admitted by the Tribunal. Therefore, insofar as, at the Hearing, such witnesses are invited by the presenting Party or asked to attend at the request of the other Party,

8.17 A tribunal may be interested in hearing further oral, direct testimony of a witness if the issues in the arbitration have matured or changed so that the individual has probative information to offer in addition to what is found within his or her original written statement. Moreover, it is not uncommon for a tribunal to allow limited, extra direct testimony to be given by a witness if he or she has been called to the hearing to be cross-examined. It is for the tribunal in many instances to judge what is appropriate, however, for a witness to be present at a hearing for the predominant purpose of offering additional direct testimony is an exception to general practice.[26] A hearing is most often called for the purpose of allowing the adverse party, and the tribunal, to examine witnesses concerning the positions they have adopted in their witness statements.

Testifying by video conference

8.18 The use of video conferencing technology to conduct witness examinations has become more widely accepted in recent years. The improvement of the technology, the need for expedited procedures and the general convenience afforded to witnesses who may offer their testimony without having to travel to the hearing, are all factors militating in favour of using such technology. If a witness is permitted to testify by video, the testimony is usually given full weight as if the witness had appeared in person.[27]

8.19 With the possible exception of international sports arbitrations, where expedited procedural schedules are often used, witness examinations using video conference technology are still by far the exception as opposed to the rule. The principal concerns around video-conferencing are ensuring the integrity of the testimony received, as well as lingering issues over the reliability of the process and logistical complications.[28] For example,

---

the available hearing time should mostly be reserved for cross-examination and re-direct examination, as well as for questions by the Arbitrator." *TCW Group Inc & Dominican Energy Holdings LP v The Dominican Republic*, CAFTA/UNCITRAL/PCA, Procedural Order No. 2, p. 11, para. 6.2 (2008).

26 Commenting on the customary approach to witness hearings, Cremades confirms that the general approach is to use the hearing to afford the adverse party the opportunity to cross-examine the witnesses presented by the opposing side: "A specific form of this compromise which has by now become substantially generalized is the practice of receiving evidence-in-chief by way of written brief, with little or no direct examination of witnesses. The important functions of the oral hearing are therefore cross-examination, the opportunity for counsel to make oral submissions to the tribunal, and for the tribunal to question counsel and witnesses about specific issues." Bernardo M. Cremades, "The Oral Presentation of Fact Witnesses in International Commercial Arbitration", in Albert Jan van den Berg (ed.), *ICCA Congress Series No. 13*, (Montreal, 2006), p. 646. As an example of the aforementioned, the following except from a procedural order issued in an ICDR Rules arbitration sets out the typical approach to direct examination: "The Party who has presented the witness may briefly examine the witness (in principle, not more than 10 minutes without leave from the Sole Arbitrator) for purposes of asking introductory questions, including to confirm and/or correct that witness's written statement, and to address matters which have arisen after such statement was drafted ("direct examination")." ICDR Case No. 01-17-0004-2264, (unpublished), Procedural Order No. 3

27 "The Panel allowed the Evidentiary Hearing to be conducted by videoconference. No objections were raised by Defendant and the witness statement had full evidentiary value." *Bray v FINA*, Award of 22 March 2002 – CAS 2001/A/337, in Matthieu Reeb (ed.), *Digest of CAS Awards III 2001–2003*, p. 206 (2004).

28 In a challenge to the sole arbitrator's appointment pursuant to Article 10.4 of the London Court of International Arbitration (LCIA) Rules 1998, LCIA Reference No. 122039, Decision Rendered on 10 October 2013 (available at www.lcia.org//challenge-decision-database.aspx), the arbitrator's independence and impartiality were challenged for siding with Respondent on issues pertaining to videoconferencing. Claimant argued the Sole Arbitrator showed a lack of impartiality because the Sole Arbitrator acceded to Respondent's request to have a representative present while the testimony was being given through video-link. *Ibid.*, p. 5, §45. The Sole Arbitrator's considerations at the Jurisdictional Hearing were as follows: "[w]hat is clear is that the Respondent, for

before agreeing to testimony by video, the tribunal should be satisfied that the witness is not coached or otherwise influenced in his or her testimony by individuals or lawyers off-screen. Moreover, as cross-examination within arbitration will often require a witness to be questioned using documents from the record, the tribunal would need to ensure that satisfactory logistical arrangements are made to ensure that those documents are provided to the witness, and that the party conducting the cross-examination is not unfairly disadvantaged as a result of the video testimony. These and other logistical as well as substantive challenges posed by the use of remote video conferencing are some of the reasons why it is still regarded as preferable to have the witness attend the hearing in person.[29] Without a valid reason as to why the witness cannot attend the hearing in person, arbitrators will often deny a request to use video conferencing.[30]

---

very understandable reasons, will only accept video link conference evidence if it can have its own representative present in [the witness' country] when that evidence is given, and I cannot see how as a matter of fairness I can prevent the respondent doing that. Given those circumstances, we need to factor in flights, hotel arrangements, visas and so on and the parties are going to discuss this at lunchtime so this aspect will be dealt with after lunch." *Ibid.*, p. 6, §46. The LCIA rejected the challenge to the Sole Arbitrator and held that: "In considering the Sole Arbitrator's stance, it is necessary to bear in mind that the Claimant's proposal that the witness be heard over video was made late. The Jurisdictional Hearing was scheduled to start in the morning of Monday, 9 September 2013, and the Claimant sent an email on Sunday, 8 September, at 22:31, requesting that, because of certain commitments of the witness, she testify on Tuesday afternoon, 10 September, by video or audio link. The message did not make it clear that the witness was not in London as expected. Only during the Hearing on Monday morning the Claimant clarified that the witness should testify from [the witness' country] [. . .]. In those circumstances, and given the highly contentious nature of the disputed facts that were to be addressed by the testimony and the fact that the witness accounts of those facts diverged, it is understandable that the Sole Arbitrator showed deference to the Respondent's position that the video-link testimony could proceed only if there was a member of the Respondent's team present in [the witness' country] during the testimony and that the timing of the testimony had to take into account the travel arrangements that were to be made on short notice. In my view, the Sole Arbitrator's decision was within the bounds of his discretion and does not give rise to justifiable doubts as to his impartiality." *Ibid.*, p. 6, §47.

29 *Aguas del Tunari SA v The Republic of Bolivia*, ICSID Case No. ARB/02/3, Decision on Respondent's Objections to Jurisdiction, para. 41 (21 October 2005) "On December 31, 2003, the Tribunal issued Procedural Order No. 3 ('Order No. 3'). 'The Tribunal observed that it is, in its view, customary in international arbitration that such witnesses, whether they are experts in law or witnesses of fact, if need be, it may be acceptable to examine witnesses via videoconference or other such means. However, the Tribunal found it presumptively preferable that witnesses appear in person.' The Tribunal thus granted Bolivia's motion that witnesses relied upon be made available for examination at the hearing."

30 The procedural history recited in the second award after the annulment of the first award in *Vivendi v Argentina* describes a scenario where a request for testimony to be given by video was denied: "Prior to the commencement of the oral hearing . . . Respondent applied to the Tribunal, *inter alia*, for an order permitting one of its expert witnesses . . . to testify [via video] instead of attending in-person at the oral hearing. Claimants made their position known on Respondent's application . . . having considered the parties respective positions, the Tribunal denied Respondent's application, noting that no reason had been provided for the proposed non-attendance at the oral hearing of Mr. K. The Tribunal indicated its willingness to reconsider Respondent's application if Respondent substantiated, for good reason, why Mr. K could not make himself available to attend." *Compañía de Aguas del Aconquija SA and Vivendi Universal SA v Argentine Republic*, ICSID Case No. ARB/97/3, Award pp. 30–31 (20 August 2007). The above notwithstanding, where a witness is unable to attend the hearing for a valid reason a party should endeavor to arrange for telephonic or video attendance if the testimony is relevant to its case. Failure to do so means that the party may not argue later that the witness' absence was tantamount to a violation of due process. See the following consideration from a US court in *Consorcio Rive v Briggs of Cancun* where it was established that the party claiming a due process violation had not made any attempt to secure attendance of a party-representative at the hearing by telephone: "[i]n the instant case, the Court finds that Briggs of Cancun was not 'unable to present its case,' because Briggs of Cancun could have participated by means other than David Briggs's physical presence at the arbitration. For instance, Briggs of Cancun could have sent a company representative to attend; could have sent its attorney to attend; or David Briggs could have attended by telephone." *Consorcio Rive, SA de CV v Briggs of Cancun Inc*, 134 F. Supp. 2d 789, 796 (E.D. La. 2001).

A tribunal's control over the hearing

Article 8.2 2010 IBA Rules: The Arbitral Tribunal shall at all times have complete control over the Evidentiary Hearing. The Arbitral Tribunal may limit or exclude any question to, answer by or appearance of a witness, if it considers such question, answer or appearance to be irrelevant, immaterial, unreasonably burdensome, duplicative or otherwise covered by a reason for objection set forth in Article 9.2. Questions to a witness during direct and re-direct testimony may not be unreasonably leading.

General discussion

8.20 Article 8.2 restates the rule that a tribunal is vested with control over the hearing, which inherently includes authority to determine how the oral questioning of witnesses is conducted.[31] In exercising this authority, a tribunal will often determine the manner of questioning, when it is appropriate to begin putting its own questions to witnesses, and what type of limits must be set on the examination of witnesses.[32] This authority is generally accepted in arbitral practice, as the following order from an UNCITRAL arbitration reflects:

> Witnesses giving oral evidence shall first be asked to confirm the truth of their written statements. Each witness shall then be examined by counsel for the opposing Party ("cross-examination"), and subsequently by counsel for the Party offering the witness, with respect to matters that arose during cross-examination ("re-direct examination"). The Arbitral Tribunal shall have the right to pose questions during or after the examination of any witness. The Arbitral Tribunal shall at all times have control over oral proceedings, including the right to limit or deny the right of a Party to examine a witness when it appears to the Arbitral Tribunal that such evidence for examination is not likely to serve any further relevant purpose.[33]

8.21 The authority to limit witness testimony must be tempered by a tribunal's duty to afford the parties a fair opportunity to present their case. Whenever a tribunal limits the

---

31 One example is found in *Windstream Energy LLC v Government of Canada*, an arbitration under Chapter Eleven of the North American Free Trade Agreement and the 2010 UNCITRAL Arbitration Rules registered under the Permanent Court of Arbitration, the Tribunal clarified in Procedural Order No. 1 that: "The Tribunal shall at all times have complete control over the procedure for hearing a witness. In particular, the Tribunal may, at its discretion: (1) refuse to hear a witness if it considers that the facts with respect to which the witness will testify are either proven by other evidence or are irrelevant; (2) limit or refuse the right of a Party to examine a witness when it appears that a question has been addressed by other evidence or is irrelevant; or (3) direct that a witness be recalled for further examination at any time." *Ibid.*, p. 7, §10.13.

32 A good example of a procedural order laying out the organisation of a hearing may be found in *Mesa Power Group, LLC v Government of Canada*, an arbitration under Chapter 11 of the NAFTA and the UNCITRAL Arbitration Rules, PCA Case No. 2012-17, Procedural Order No. 14, dated 3 October 2014. In that case, a well-experienced tribunal set out organisational and procedural matters for the Hearing, comprising of: (1) witness and expert examinations, including which witnesses and experts were to be examined, the sequence of examinations, and sequestration of witnesses, rules applicable for examination/cross-examination of the witnesses and experts, and witness and expert document bundles; (2) opening and closing arguments; (3) allocation of hearing time between the Parties; (4) confirmation of the dates, location and schedule of the hearing; (5) arrangements to deal with confidential/restricted access information at the hearing; (6) logistical arrangements, including special equipment for presentation, documentary issues such as copies of presentations and demonstratives exhibits, broadcasting; and other logistical and procedural issues.

33 *GAMI Investments Inc v Government of the United Mexican States*, NAFTA/UNCITRAL, Procedural Order No. 1, para. 8.6 (2003).

ability of a party to produce or present evidence, it naturally runs a risk that by doing so it unfairly inhibits that party from putting forth the essential aspects of its case.

8.22 Thus the limitations imposed on the conduct of witness examinations should support the fundamental purpose of the evidentiary hearing, which is to allow a face-to-face evaluation of the witnesses presenting testimony for the record, and to afford the participants in the arbitration an opportunity to ask relevant and material questions. This was noted by a panel of CAS arbitrators when registering their regret at not having an oral hearing:

> Finally we note that the agreement of the parties to dispense with an oral hearing means that the Panel has been deprived of the opportunity of evaluating the credibility of the witnesses from the way in which they presented their evidence face to face, and from having their evidence tested by cross-examination. However, our decision did not ultimately depend upon a resolution of conflicting versions of particular events.[34]

8.23 Given that hearings are most often convened for the purpose of allowing the credibility of a witness (expert or fact) to be tested, a tribunal should approach the issue over whether to impose limitations on the conduct of witness examinations by first determining whether if so doing would further this fundamental aim. Article 8.2 sets forth a number of grounds on which a tribunal may determine that examinations conducted within the hearing or the attendance of a witness should be subject to certain limitations. Those grounds, as well as the approach to objections raised during a hearing, will be discussed below.

Excluding witnesses from a hearing and due process

8.24 As noted in the comments to article 8.1, an arbitral tribunal is generally vested with the power to exclude a witness from a hearing. This power is specifically included in article 8.2. Nevertheless, there is jurisprudence to suggest that such a determination may result in a violation of a party's right to be heard in some instances (see comments to art. 4.7 regarding a party's right to challenge adverse witnesses).[35] Reported decisions where

---

34 *P v International Equestrian Federation*, Award of 25 September 1998, CAS-98/184 (1998), in Matthieu Reeb (ed.), *Digest of CAS Awards II 1998–2000*, p. 198 (2002).

35 See the *Tempo Shain* case, an often-cited decision of the US courts in which an award was successfully challenged on fairness grounds due to the determination of the arbitral tribunal not to hear a witness. In the view of the reviewing court, a tribunal's determination that witness evidence was cumulative was not reasonable, since the witness in question was allegedly the only individual who possessed the relevant information. "We find that there was no reasonable basis for the arbitration panel to determine that Pollock's omitted testimony would be cumulative with regard to the fraudulent inducement claims. Said differently, the panel excluded evidence plainly 'pertinent and material to the controversy', 9 USC § 10(a)(3). The panel did not indicate in what respects Pollock's testimony would be cumulative, but stated that there were 'a number of letters in the file' and that Pollock was 'speaking through the letters [he wrote], and the reports he received'. These letters and reports were not specifically identified by the arbitration panel." *Tempo Shain Corp et al. v Bertek Inc*, 120 F. 3d 16, p. 20 (2nd Cir. 1997). For the opposite view, see: *X.____ Ltf. v Y.____ GmbH*, 4A_76/2012, judgment of October 11, 2012, First Civil Law Court, Basel, Switzerland (original decision in German, available on the website of the Federal Tribunal: www.bger.ch). Here, the Court ruled on the issue of whether rejection of a party's request for a new hearing violates the right to be heard and to present one's case. There, the Court stated that: "The Arbitral Tribunal held that the interrogation of new witnesses was not necessary as the Respondent had relied on the price difference of EUR 1'120'000 before the hearing and after on the possible deductions from this amount had been discussed in the witness statements of A.____ and B.____; at the hearing of September 14 and 15, 2010, the Appellant had the opportunity to interrogate the witnesses as to these issues. The Appellant's right to be heard was complied with when it was given the opportunity to express its view as to the Respondent's submission of

arbitrators have refused to hear a witness without giving due consideration to the nature of the evidence that would be given by the presented witness have given rise to successful challenges to the final award.[36] Therefore, as article 8.2 suggests, a determination by a tribunal to exclude a witness from a hearing should be motivated[37] by one of the reasons set forth in this article so as to ensure that the parties, and a subsequent reviewing court, understand that the determination was made based upon due consideration of the proffered testimony and of the procedural requirements of the arbitration.[38, 39]

February 2, 2011, which it did thoroughly in its written submission of March, 14, 2011. The Appellant does not show to the Federal Tribunal which specific exhibits submitted by the Respondent would have required a new interrogation of witnesses. It merely argues sweepingly that the Respondent introduced many new arguments as to the computation of damages and new exhibits in its submission of February 2, 2011, which had not been made during the hearing on September 14 and 15, 2010. However, it does not show which specific submissions or exhibits would have been new and therefore could not have been addressed at the hearing. Neither does it show with reference to the record which of its arguments in the arbitral proceedings could have been proved by introducing witnesses and satisfies itself with the general allegation that hearing new witnesses would have made it possible for the Appellant to show that the loss claimed by the Respondent was inaccurate. This does not demonstrate a violation of the right to be heard (Art. 190 (2) (d) PILA)." *Ibid.*, p. 7.

36 See: Richard H Kreindler, "30 May 2008 – Higher Regional Court Hamburg (Hanseatisches Oberlandes-gericht or OLG Hamburg)", *A contribution by the ITA Board of Reporters*. In this instance the tribunal refused to hear a witness who was offered to substantiate a challenge to the jurisdiction of the arbitrator. The reviewing court ruled that: "The Higher Regional Court disagreed with the arbitral tribunal's holding. According to the court, the arbitral tribunal could not reasonably have concluded that Claimant had capacity to enter into a valid arbitration agreement without further inquiry into the matter."

37 With regard to reasoned procedural rulings, reference may be had to the admonition of Tomlinson J in *ABB v Hochtief* whereby it was stated that: "Whilst the court will never dictate to arbitrators how their conclusions should be expressed, it must be obvious that the giving of clearly expressed reasons responsive to the issues as they were debated before the arbitrators will reduce the scope for the making of unmeritorious challenges . . . ". *ABB AG v Hochtief Airport GmbH* [2006] EWHC 388 (Comm), para. 87 (8 March 2006).

38 See also the comments of Bühler and Dorgan, whereby they note that irrelevance is a reason for not hear-ing a witness: "However, it would be a very unusual case where the arbitral tribunal could properly decide not to hear witnesses, notwithstanding the request of a party to present a witness, unless the testimony of the witness were deemed to be manifestly irrelevant. In international arbitration, the arbitral tribunal is required to treat the parties equally and to give each party a reasonable opportunity to present its case. In practice, arbitral tribunals will hear virtually any witnesses whom the parties wish to present, although the arbitrators may actively exercise their power to limit witness testimony and/or to limit the testimony of a witness to a particular subject (e.g., they may limit the number of witnesses to avoid repetitious testimony or indicate the factual issues they consider to be relevant). This leads to a caveat: the arbitrators should not turn the hearing into a perfunctory exercise, conducted merely in order to fulfill the obligation to hear the parties. The arbitrators should not lightly presume that the parties' written submissions have adequately informed them regarding the relevant factual and legal issues. The arbitrators may conclude that a witness' testimony added nothing of value to the record, but normally they should do so only after hearing that witness." Michael Bühler and Carroll Dorgan, "Witness Testimony Pursuant to the 1999 IBA Rules of Evidence in International Commercial Arbitration – Novel or Tested Standards?", *Journal of International Arbitration*, Vol. 17, No. 1, pp. 3, 17 (2000).

39 In this regard reference may be had to the decision of the *ad hoc* annulment committee in ICSID case *Duke Energy International v Peru*. In one of the challenges brought by the respondent party to the final award it was alleged that the tribunal had committed a procedural error by not calling for the cross-examination of one of respondent's key expert witnesses. The respondent argued to the *ad hoc* committee that the tribunal should have called respondent's expert to testify at the hearing because, as was made evident in the final award, the tribunal had a number of reservations concerning the expert's report (in the final award the tribunal preferred the analysis of claimant's expert). In essence, the respondent's argument was that if the tribunal had reservations concerning the report, it should have given the expert an opportunity at the hearing to answer the questions or concerns of the tribunal under cross-examination. The *ad hoc* committee rejected the challenge, and noted the following: "A tri-bunal is not obliged to hear from all witnesses orally. On the contrary, it is empowered under ICSID Arbitration Rule 36 to admit evidence given by a witness or expert in a written deposition. It follows that it may also evaluate the probative value of the evidence given in such a form. This final ground for partial annulment of the Award is thus also rejected." Dietmar W. Prager and Rebecca Jenkin, *Duke Energy International Peru Investments No. 1, Ltd v Republic of Peru*, ICSID Case No. ARB/03/28, *A Contribution by the ITA Board of Reporters*, para. 258

8.25 It has been suggested that, save for exceptional circumstances, a tribunal should hear those witnesses that a party wishes to present at the hearing irrespective of reservations it may have over the usefulness of such an exercise.[40] This view seems overly restrictive, in that article 8.2 allows a tribunal to exclude the appearance of witnesses as long as this power is reasonably exercised; a position seemingly consistent with general practice.[41] A rule requiring arbitrators to hear all witnesses presented by the parties could possibly be burdensome, and at odds with an arbitrator's duty to provide for procedural efficiency.

Raising objections during an evidentiary hearing

8.26 It is comparatively rare for parties to an international arbitration to raise numerous objections to the questions posed to witnesses, such as one might find in the Anglo-American practice.[42] Most notably, the "hearsay" objection is not known in international

---

(2011). Thus one may consider that where a tribunal has received into evidence a written direct testimony of a fact or expert witness prior to the hearing, a determination by the tribunal to not hear the witness orally will in most cases not be reviewable for a violation of due process. This is so because the receipt and review by the tribunal of the written testimony will suffice to demonstrate that the arbitrators have given due consideration to the evidence, and in their exercise of discretion, have determined not to hear the witness orally. See: the following Procedural Order from an ICSID tribunal which ruled against the stated intention of a party to present its own witnesses for oral testimony, even though a written statement of their direct testimony had been submitted: "The Tribunal has decided not to allow the hearing of [witness 1] and [witness 2] at the oral hearing. In this respect the Tribunal notes that the Claimants did not wish to cross-examine either [witness 1] or [witness 2]. Therefore, in accordance with the agreement of the Parties recorded in item 16 of the Minutes of the First Session of the Tribunal, the witness statement and expert report of [witness 1] and [witness 2] shall stand as their evidence in chief." *OKO Osuuspankkien Keskuspankki Oyj v Republic of Estonia*, ICSID Case No. ARB/04/06, Procedural Order, para. 2 (13 September 2005).

40 See comments of Bühler and Dorgan, *supra* n. 38. See also the procedural order in ICC Case No. 5926, where the tribunal noted that it would hear certain witnesses despite its own determination that it was unnecessary to do so: "In making the above decision, the arbitral tribunal which so far does not see the necessity of the appearance of witnesses, thanks to the very thorough and complete briefs and documentation filed by the two parties, has been guided by the essential principle of offering to each party the full opportunity to present its case as it wishes while, at the same time, keeping up with the characteristic of arbitration of avoiding unnecessary delays." Dominique Hascher (ed.), *Collection of Procedural Decisions in ICC Arbitration 1993–1996*, p. 105 (2nd edition, 1998).

41 See: *Intercarbon Bermuda Ltd v Caltex Trading & Transport Corp*, 146 FRD 64, pp. 72–74 (SDNY 1993); and also *Weizmann Institute of Science et al. v Janet Neschis et al.*, 421 F.Supp. 2d 654, p. 681 (SDNY 2005). In both cases US courts approved of the decision of the tribunal to not have witnesses testify at hearing. As noted in *Weizmann*: "the tribunal's decision to forgo live testimony in favor of affidavits from some witnesses is common practice." See also the ruling of the Swiss Federal Tribunal: "[t]he dismissal of requests for production of documents and the refusal to hear witnesses . . . were held not to violate a claimant's right to be heard where the arbitral tribunal had concluded that the parties had already established all the facts necessary for it to make its decision regarding jurisdiction." Georg von Segesser, "20 September 2005 – Swiss Supreme Court 1st Chamber", *A Contribution by the ITA Board of Reporters*. See further the following view expressed in a dissenting opinion in Society of Maritime Arbitrators which summarises the general authority granted to arbitrators to decline witness testimony: "We, as arbitrators, have wide discretion to accept or exclude witnesses and hear the evidence we deem relevant. It has been said that parties who agree to arbitration must be content with the informalities of the system. However, this informality must still give way to the requirement of fundamental fairness afforded the parties. . . . *In the Matter of an Arbitration Between Triumph Tankers Ltd and Kerr Mcgee Refining Corp*, Final Award No. 2642, WL 10555671 (SMAAS 1990).

42 Consider the following admonition of the chairman of an ICDR tribunal in reaction to the use of US court-style objections: "[t]ry to leave the objections outside. I'm sorry. Arbitration proceedings run a little differently than courts are." ICDR Case No. 50T180, Transcript of 2 October 2002 Hearing, p. 29, ln(s) 17–20 (unpublished). The following comments of Hunter sum up the general approach to objections in international arbitration: "A lawyer will be aware that constant interruptions by him when his opponent is examining a witness will irritate the arbitrators, and he will normally try to keep his interruptions to a minimum. He will therefore not usually object

arbitration,[43] and arbitrators are generally not quick to chastise witnesses for failing to provide "yes" or "no" answers in response to leading questions, as long as the tribunal is satisfied that a good faith effort to address the question has been made.

8.27 Instead of relying upon compulsory powers, the influence that a tribunal most often exercises over the conduct of witness examinations derives from the inherent reality that it has the binding authority to weigh and determine the value of the evidence.[44] Therefore, if a witness is evasive or uncooperative with an examiner's questions, or if a questioning legal counsel is abusive in their line of examination, both sides run the risk of turning the arbitrator against their position. This is often all that is needed by a tribunal to keep the parties and their legal counsel in line with the purpose of the proceedings. For this reason, arbitrators typically do not control the examination of a witness closely, as in the manner of a common-law judge.

8.28 Nonetheless, even if there are rather limited instances where a tribunal will be required to lay down rules of limitation, such as to exclude testimony or prevent examinations from moving forward, it does not mean that a hearing in international arbitration will be free of such issues. Generally speaking, even where hearings are conducted by professionals working in good faith, differences of opinion may arise over whether a witness should be questioned or allowed to give testimony on a particular issue or topic. Moreover,

---

to irrelevant or repetitive questions being put. On the other hand, where a lawyer examining a witness seems to be trying to gain an advantage over the witness by asking unclear questions, or if the questions are in some way offensive or otherwise improper, then an objection will be made and a ruling will be asked from the tribunal." Howard M. Holtzmann and Professor Giorgio Bernini, "Hypothetical Case: N. Presentation of Oral Evidence", in Pieter Sanders (ed.), *ICCA Congress Series, No. 3*, p. 129 (New York, 1986).

43 See the reported ruling of a panel of AAA arbitrators sitting under the international ICDR rules, where the tribunal considered an objection raised by the respondent that the claimant's case was largely based on hearsay: "The arbitrators endorsed Defendant's argument that Claimant's case was largely based on hearsay evidence, which might not be admissible in a court of law. However, an arbitration proceeding is not governed by strict evidentiary requirements. Section 30 of the American Arbitration Association Rules, adopted by Clause 15 of the Commercial Operating Agreement, makes it clear that: '[T]he Arbitrator shall be judge of the relevancy and materiality of the evidence offered and conformity to the legal rules of evidence shall not be required'". Awards in Case No. 1310-0417-78 of 4 January 1980 in Pieter Sanders (ed.), *Yearbook Commercial Arbitration*, Vol. VIII, pp. 166, 167 (1983). See also: ICC Case No. 12124, declining to exclude hearsay portions of an expert witness testimony. *ICC Bulletin, 2010 Special Supplement: Decisions on ICC Arbitration Procedure*, p. 32. See also the following approach to the issue of hearsay evidence in an international arbitration under the rules of the Society of Maritime Arbitrators which was recorded in a dissenting opinion: "[a]lthough the majority refers to 'hearsay' evidence, I wish to make it clear that no evidence was excluded. On the contrary, in accordance with several rulings of the chairman, all offered evidence was admitted and given such weight as the individual arbitrators thought appropriate." *In the Matter of an Arbitration between Enron Gas Ltd and Petroloe Brasileiro SA (Petrobras)*, Final Award (Dissent of Arbitrator Siciliano), SMAAS, WL 34449953 (1996). The above notwithstanding, the absence of a formal objection to the admissibility of evidence based upon hearsay does not mean that the tribunals are prevented from noting the hearsay when weighing the evidence's probative value. See also the following consideration by a panel of the Iran-US Claims Tribunal: "[t]he Tribunal notes that on the issue of the alleged expropriation Mr. Banayan only testified that in 1986 he had been told that certain properties at issue in this Case, since the beginning of the Islamic Revolution, belonged to the Foundation for the Oppressed. The Tribunal considers this to be hearsay evidence, on which it cannot rely, unless the evidence is substantiated." *Jalal Moin v The Islamic Republic of Iran*, Case No. 950, Award No. 557-950-2 of 24 May 1994, p. 6.

44 "Effective advocacy requires advocates to choose their material and use their time wisely. The effective advocate has a discretion in the choice of fact witnesses, the choice of topics for questioning, and also the mode of questioning. In the private, full professionalized arbitration hearing room there is no need for further rules or guidelines on the questioning of witnesses. Abusive questioning of witnesses carries its own sanction: it does not convince and it wastes valuable time." Cremades, *supra* n. 26, pp. 645, 647.

in the more egregious situation where it appears that a party is employing tactics aimed at undermining the procedural economy of the hearing, or if a party's legal counsel appears to be attempting to intimidate a witness, action by the tribunal to keep matters on track may be required.

8.29 When objections are raised during a hearing a tribunal may take one of several approaches to handling them. As a general principle, international arbitrators often will seek to deal with an objection to a line of questioning by offering a chance to the examiner to explain the reasons for asking the question, and hopefully clarifying what, if any, problems exist with it. An example may be taken from the transcript of the cross-examination of an expert witness in the *Guyana v Suriname* boundary dispute arbitration where an objection was raised concerning the form of a question:

[EXAMINER]: Would you agree with me, sir, that if those assumptions are correct, there has been a significant accretion?

[OBJECTING COUNSEL]: Excuse me. Normally, when posing hypotheticals there has to be some basis, some evidentiary basis for posing the hypothetical. [*OBJECTING Counsel further elaborates and then concludes*:] But this continual belaboring of the point of shipwreck, we don't even know that that is a shipwreck. It may just be a ship . . . it seems to me that this is – it goes beyond the hypothetical to the – well, it goes beyond the hypothetical, let's just say that.

[EXAMINER]: Shall I respond?

[PRESIDENT of the TRIBUNAL]: Of course.

[EXAMINER]: The evidence to which I refer the Tribunal at this time – and there is going to be additional evidence during our case – the evidence to which I refer the Tribunal at this time is [a map in the record]. If you look at Tab 23 in the book that I gave you, [the map] was from Guyana's submission, and the witness told us this morning, without actually prompting from me, as you may remember, when I showed him that symbol, he said, oh, that's a shipwreck, and I said you anticipated my next question. [*EXAMINER goes on to further explain his question and concludes as follows*:] And all I'm asking the witness to do was to assume that those are correct, and I'm asking the witness whether or not if those three hypothetical facts are correct, there has been significant accretion in the coastline. That's my question, Mr. President.

[THE WITNESS]: Am I to answer?

[PRESIDENT of the TRIBUNAL]: Yes.[45]

8.30 In the above example the arbitrator provided considerable leeway to both the examining and objecting counsel to explain the objection, and the background to the line of questioning. This is an indication of the approach that is often followed in international arbitration.

8.31 Objections that are raised strictly in relation to the form of a question may in many instances be inappropriate for the setting of an international arbitration. Where the question is capable of being answered, the witness in many instances may be asked to answer it by the tribunal even if the query itself does not comport to technical rules

---

45 *Republic of Guyana v Republic of Suriname*, UNCLOS/PCA Case No. 2004-4, Transcript of Hearings, pp. 523–525 (Washington DC, Day 4, 11 December 2006).

used in domestic court systems. The following excerpt from an ICSID arbitration hearing demonstrates the point:

[EXAMINER]: When did you become aware of the possibility of arbitration under CAFTA?

[OBJECTING COUNSEL]: Objection. Vague.

[PRESIDENT of the TRIBUNAL]: If you can answer the question, please do so.[46]

8.32 There may be instances where a tribunal finds that it should rule immediately on an objection to an examination because the questioning is straying into an area that is obviously without merit. This is particularly true where a line of questioning should be ended because it is prying into matters that violate a rule of legal privilege, or where the questioning is intended to harass or intimidate the witness.[47]

8.33 Otherwise, if an objection is raised that an arbitrator does not believe is of such a level that it should cause the line of questioning to be halted, a tribunal would have the option to allow the questioning to move forward while simply noting, for the record, that an objection was raised. The effect of doing this is that the objection, which may in most instances go to the probative value (or lack thereof) of the questions put to the witness, is noted in the record of the hearing for the arbitrator to consider later when assessing the value of the oral testimony that was given.[48] In any case, within international arbitration there are but a few number of accepted objections which may be made during an oral hearing. They are in essence listed in article 9.2.

Irrelevant or immaterial questioning

8.34 Materiality and relevance stand for different issues with regard to the taking of evidence; relevance is a criterion dealing primarily with whether the evidence in question assists or is necessary for a party to meet its own burden of proof, whereas materiality goes to the issue of whether the tribunal regards the evidence to be of consequence to its final decision on the merits of the case. (See Chapter 3 for full discussion.) Article 8.2, in

---

46 *Pac Rim Cayman LLC v Republic of El Salvador*, ICSID Case No. ARB/09/12, Transcript of Hearing on Jurisdiction, p. 461 (Washington DC Day 3, 3 May 2011).

47 The following cautionary note was offered by the President of the tribunal in *Pac Rim Cayman LLC v Republic of El Salvador*, "PRESIDENT [of the TRIBUNAL]: '[You are] being asked about your own understanding and in answering that question, if you're minded to, please don't refer to anything that a lawyer may or may not have told you. Just for your own understanding. Can you answer this question?'" *Ibid.*, pp. 462, 463.

48 As an example of this principle, the following excerpt may be taken from an Iran-US Claims Tribunal award where an objection raised at the hearing was noted and then dealt with later during the subsequent award: "During that part of the Hearing devoted to the IACI cluster of claims, Iran objected to the presentation by the United States of Lt. Gen. William E. Odom (Ret.) as a witness to the extent he would give testimony on issues that had already been addressed during that part of the Hearing devoted to General Issues. The Tribunal considered and rejected this objection at the IACI Hearing, and Lt. Gen. Odom (Ret.) appeared as a witness before the Tribunal. At that point, Iran objected to the admissibility of his testimony. The Tribunal rules on this objection below. The Tribunal holds that, during that part of the Hearing devoted to Individual Claims, revisiting a general issue or issues was possible and, indeed, took place even before Lt. Gen. Odom (Ret.) testified. Accordingly, the Tribunal rejects Iran's objection as to the admissibility of his testimony." *The Islamic Republic of Iran v United States of America*, Partial Award No. 601-A3/A8/A9/A14/B61-FT, Full Tribunal, p. 50.

conjunction with article 9.2 restates the often affirmed principle that the tribunal may use either grounds to limit the answers, questions or appearances of a witness in a hearing.[49]

8.35 Where an examination of a witness strays into territory that is obviously irrelevant to a party's burden of proof, but is pursued for theatrical effect, or some other improper purpose, an arbitrator may prevent the questioning from moving forward.[50] An example of such a situation may be taken from an ICC hearing conducted in Paris, France, where the arbitrator stopped a line of questioning because it seemed to be aimed at exposing the witness' own personal liability.[51] As the arbitrator could not establish a connection between exposing the witness' personal legal liability and the questioning party's arguments in the case, he prohibited the examination of the witness from moving forward on those issues. On later challenge to the enforcement of the award, the reviewing court found such a limitation to have been appropriate because it had not affected the party's ability to present its case on the relevant matters at hand.[52] Irrelevance may be a ground for limiting the

---

49 "The Arbitral Tribunal shall at all times have control over oral proceedings, including the right to limit or deny the right of a Party to examine a witness when it appears to the Arbitral Tribunal that such evidence for examination is not likely to serve any further relevant purpose." *GAMI Investments v United Mexican States*, *supra* n. 33, Procedural Order No. 1, para. 8.6.

50 In commenting on the need for cross-examinations to be tailored to relevant information, Cremades notes the following: "[t]he preparation and professionalism of an arbitral tribunal mean that cross-examination should be limited by counsel to only the most important issues. It should also be conducted strictly to inform the tribunal; theatrical cross-examination or attempts to humiliate a witness should be avoided. There should be a clear relationship between the cross-examination of counsel and the oral submissions made by counsel." Cremades, *supra* n. 26, p. 646. See also the following rule adopted in ICC Case No. 13225: "[t]he sole arbitrator shall, at all times, have a complete right of control (in accordance with Article 182 par. 3 of the Swiss Private International Law Statute) over the procedure in relation to the examination of a witness, including the right to limit or refuse the right of a party to examine a witness when it considers that the factual allegation(s) on which the witness is intended to depose is sufficiently proven by exhibits or other witnesses or that the particular witness deposition as such is irrelevant." *ICC Bulletin, 2010 Special Supplement: Decisions on ICC Arbitration Procedure*, p. 99.

51 The arbitrator in this instance had been asked to allow further cross-examination of a witness, known as Mr H, who was an officer of a company named Athlone. While the business of Athlone and Mr H touched upon matters in the case, whether Mr H's personal liability (or that of his company) bore any relevance in this case was unclear to the arbitrator because it did not seem to relate to the examining party's burden of proof – which concerned the use of a licence to exploit certain pharmaceutical products. Therefore, the arbitrator terminated the line of questioning as follows: "I am not willing to expose Mr. H to any conceivable prejudice to his own position or to Athlone's position in circumstances where I do not believe this Tribunal is adequately provided with the evidence or the means to carry those things through to their proper and logical conclusion." The arbitrator had earlier also reasoned that: "I do not regard this arbitration as an appropriate forum for conducting any general inquiry into the quality, safety or consistency of the clomiphene tablets produced by Athlone. . . . I am therefore not disposed to allow this arbitration to be used as a vehicle for any general attack on those matters." When reviewing the arbitrator's decision to limit the cross-examination the Court of Appeals for the 9th Circuit (US) regarded the limitation as fair. *Generica Ltd v Pharmaceutical Basics Inc*, 125 F 3d 1123, p. 1129 (7th Cir. 1997). See also the procedural direction given by an UNCITRAL tribunal in consideration of cross-examination questions put to a witness which may implicate matters relevant to a criminal investigation: "On December 14, 2009, the Tribunal reaffirmed the dates of the February hearing, stating that it expected Mr. Montour to be present for cross-examination. The Tribunal stated further that 'if any questions directed to him at that time raise matters that in counsel's opinion may be prejudicial to his position in the pending criminal case, counsel may object, indicating the reason for the objection. The Tribunal will then make an appropriate ruling, always bearing in mind the need to avoid any prejudice to his position in the criminal case.'" *Grand River Enterprises Six Nations Ltd v United States of America*, UNCITRAL, Final Award, paras 56, 57 (2011). Thus the tribunal here considered that the potential exposure to matters relevant to the criminal liability of the witness may be grounds for limiting questions during cross-examination.

52 *Ibid.* It should be noted that the court did find that the arbitrator's decision to place less reliance on the direct evidence of that witness as a consequence of his decision to limit the cross-examination was an appropriate way to ameliorate any potential bias caused by his decision.

appearance of witnesses at the hearing as well. Where the tribunal is unconvinced that to call or recall a witness for oral testimony will have sufficient probative value to warrant the time and cost, it may decline to hear the witness. The following restatement of this rule taken from an international arbitration between an owner and charterer of a vessel:

> The Panel denies the request of Owner that Charterer not be permitted to recall any witnesses or review prior testimony in this arbitration. This ruling is subject to the caveat that it is the intention of this Panel during the continuation of this arbitration to deter irrelevancy or reconsideration of matters which, in its considered opinion, are unreasonable and will cause needless delay in arriving at a conclusion of the proceeding. Charterer will be required to show sufficient cause as to why it must be necessary to again present witnesses and evidence previously submitted to the Panel.[53]

8.36 If a tribunal believes that a party may be simply calling a witness in order to harass or intimidate the witness, or because the party intends to engage in a speculative fishing expedition, it may require the parties to give reasons as to why the examination is relevant, or refuse to hear the witness.

8.37 Immateriality is also a basis on which a tribunal may limit the questioning of a witness during a hearing. In this regard, the tribunal may have pre-judged, based upon the submissions in the case, the issues which it believes will be material to a final award and determine that it should limit the examination to only pertinent points.[54] This type of limitation may be influenced also by the competence of the witness. For instance, a tribunal may regard a certain fact witness as competent only to testify to the things he or she saw, or an expert witness' testimony to be material only to the narrow area of the witness' expertise.[55] If testimony outside of the limited subject matter will not be persuasive to the tribunal the arbitrators are free to set boundaries on the scope of examination to the material issues within the witness' competence.

8.38 Limitations on questions may be communicated in a pre-hearing order, or as an intervention by the tribunal during the examination. As an example of the latter, in the

---

53 *Compania Ulysses SA v Owner of the Ermoupolis & Maco of Panama SA*, Award No. 2077 (29 March 1985), *Journal of International Arbitration*, Vol. 2, No. 4, pp. 87, 92–93 (1985).

54 Inherent to this principle is that a tribunal may limit the questions put to a witness pertaining to that evidence, and those allegations, timely submitted. For instance, if a tribunal has prohibited a party from introducing new theories of the case, or allegations, prior to the hearing, it may exclude questioning on any such undeveloped theories. See, for instance, the position adopted by a tribunal sitting under the Geneva Chamber of Commerce and Industry Rules, wherein it observed that it was improper for a party to ask questions of a witness which went to establishing a new allegation which had not been admitted into the proceeding. "28 février 1994 – Arbitral Tribunal" in *ASA Bulletin*, Vol. 13, No. 2, pp. 301–357 (1995). See also the rule set forth in ICC Case No. 12206, limiting questions during the oral hearing to only those material issues, namely those set forth in the terms of reference: "[t]he parties shall address only the issues stated in the Terms of Reference and those necessary to the resolution of those issues." ICC Case No. 12206, *supra* n. 18.

55 In a reinsurance arbitration, the panel of arbitrators limited the testimony that they would hear from one side's witnesses. The party who would eventually lose the matter challenged the decision of the tribunal to limit the witness' testimony. The reviewing court found that such a limitation had not impeded the parties from presenting their case. "The Panel's actions do not rise to the level of misconduct, as there is nothing in the record to suggest that the Panel blocked OneBeacon's right to a full and fair hearing. Both of OneBeacon's witnesses were allowed to present the evidence they were competent to present. Mr. D, whom OneBeacon introduced as a fact witness rather than an expert witness, was allowed to testify as to matters of fact (that is, what he saw and heard), but not as to his opinions on the state of the industry. Similarly, Ms. H was allowed to testify on her experience with a similar treaty, but not on underwriting intent, an area in which she admitted to having no expertise." *OneBeacon America Insurance Co v Swiss Reinsurance America Corp*, Civil Action No. 09-CV-11495-PBS, Memorandum and Order, p. 11 (Mass D, 23 December 2010).

Guyana v Suriname case the President of the Tribunal intervened to provide the following cautionary limitation: "Thank you, Mr. [Examiner]. Before you go on, I just would like to make the point that the function of this expert witness is to deal with his report and questions on report, and it's not to be assumed that he knows much about what has been depicted here, so I would like you to bear that in mind."[56] This being said, it is also the case that tribunals often allow fact witnesses to be examined on matters that go beyond what is strictly within their written statements, if the question would otherwise reasonably fall within their scope of knowledge.[57]

8.39 Finally, it should also be said that a tribunal's determination not to hear a witness at all, or refusal to extend the schedule of a hearing to accommodate a witness' appearance also does not violate a party's right to be heard where the arbitrators have come to the reasoned view that the proffered evidence will not affect the outcome of the award.[58] Such a decision was taken by a panel of ICDR arbitrators seated in New York, where the tribunal determined that it was unnecessary for a prominent politician to give testimony concerning the quantum in dispute. Their decision not to require the witness was later challenged; however, as the prospective witness' testimony would not have materially affected the tribunal's analysis, the decision not to call the witness was deemed consistent with due process.

Avoiding duplicative testimony (direct testimony)

8.40 A tribunal is afforded the power under article 8.2 to impose limitations in order to avoid hearing redundant or duplicative witness testimony. The basis for this limitation is

---

56 *Guyana v Suriname*, *supra* n. 45, Transcript of Hearings, p. 510.

57 See the following limitation on the permissible scope of an examination taken from an ICC arbitration held in Geneva, Switzerland: "Subject to the above paragraph, the written witness statement shall be the basis for the oral examination of the witness. However, neither party shall use a written witness statement as an instrument to limit the scope of examination of the respective witness and to deprive the other party and/ or the Arbitral Tribunal from the possibility to ask questions on issues and matters not covered by the witness statement, if and to the extent [that] these issues and matters related to the dispute are of relevance. Likewise, the oral examination of the witness by a party shall not be used as a means to take the other party or the Arbitral Tribunal by surprise by confronting the witness with issues that go beyond the scope of those which the other party and the Arbitral Tribunal reasonably had expected in view of the written witness statement produced and by taking account of the subject matter of the dispute." ICC Case No. 14069, Procedural Order No. 1 (unpublished).

58 In *Matthew v Papua New Guinea*, the court affirmed that the decision of an ICDR tribunal to not call a witness, the Prime Minister of the country, to testify, did not cause prejudice to the claimant's case because the witness' testimony was immaterial to the final award. "The Final Award makes it clear that Matthew made a detailed written proffer as to the anticipated substance of the Prime Minister's testimony and also tendered other evidence upon which Matthew intended to rely. Even if the Prime Minister had appeared and testified in accordance with Matthew's proffers, the arbitrator would not have reached a different conclusion, as he had determined that the Prime Minister's valuation testimony was so intimately tied to the unenforceable contract claim that it could not be viewed as establishing the reasonable value of the services performed even if admitted as expert opinion or lay testimony." *Michael Z. Matthew v Papua New Guinea*, No. 09 Civ 3851 (LTS) 2009 US Dist. LEXIS 117274 (SDNY, 9 December 2009). See also the decision of a Stockholm Chamber of Commerce tribunal not to postpone the hearing to accommodate additional witnesses: "A hearing was scheduled for 14 June 1993. Counsel for respondent requested a postponement until September 1993 which was refused by the arbitral tribunal." *Licensor & Buyer v Manufacturer*, Interim Award (17 July 1992) and Final Award (13 July 1993), SCC Arbitration, in Albert Jan van den Berg (ed.), *Yearbook Commercial Arbitration*, Vol. XXII, pp. 197–210 (1997). See also the affirmation of this rule in ICC Case No. 7365, where the tribunal affirmed the following general principle of evidentiary procedure: "The tribunal may refuse to admit a party's offer of further evidence if it is convinced that the issue has been sufficiently clarified." ICC Case No. 7365, Final Award, para. 15.2 (1997) (unpublished).

derived from a tribunal's general authority to ensure that the proceedings are conducted with reasonable economy. To avoid duplicative testimony, tribunals will often limit direct testimony during a hearing to a short, "warm-up" round of questioning, with perhaps a limited amount of testimony supplementary to the testimony-in-chief submitted in the written witness statement. One NAI arbitration procedural order directed the parties as follows: "Each witness giving oral evidence shall first be briefly (for a maximum of ten minutes) examined in direct examination, but only to the extent that new matters have arisen since the witness submitted his or her written statements."[59]

8.41 Not all tribunals will necessarily limit the initial direct examination to matters that have arisen since the written testimony was filed, as it may be useful in some circumstances for the witness to be allowed to refresh the tribunal's memory of the subject matter of his or her statement. Nevertheless, the usual approach is that such direct testimony be limited in duration to a short period, often 10 minutes, given that a written statement has already been submitted.[60] A challenge to the fairness of this limitation by a disappointed party, which wished to conduct a longer oral direct examination, was dismissed by the supervising court.[61]

8.42 In an *ad hoc* international arbitration held in Liechtenstein, the tribunal decided to forgo witness examinations of some of the witnesses because the affidavits were complete, and the tribunal did not believe that oral examination would be of sufficient probative value.[62] The court seized of the enforcement of the award noted that, "The Tribunal's decision

---

59 NAI Arbitration, Case No. 3702, Procedural Order No. 1 (unpublished). See also the following order from UNCITRAL arbitration *Chevron v Ecuador* where the tribunal established the agenda for the hearing which specifically instructed the parties regarding witness testimony on direct examination (see point (b)): "3. Unless otherwise agreed by the Parties: Examination of witnesses and experts presented by Respondent. For each:

(1) Affirmation of witness or expert to tell the truth.

(2) Short introduction by Respondent (This may include a short direct examination on new developments after the last written statement of the witness or expert).

(3) Cross-examination by Claimants.

(4) Re-direct examination by Respondent, but only on issues raised in cross-examination.

(5) Re-Cross-examination by Claimants.

(6) Remaining questions by members of the Tribunal, but they may raise questions at any time.

Examination of witnesses and experts presented by Claimants. For each: vice versa as under (a) to (f) above." *Chevron Corp and Texaco Petroleum Corp v The Republic of Ecuador*, PCA Case No. 2009-23, Interim Award, p. 33 (1 December 2008).

60 See: *Pac Rim v El Salvador, supra* n. 46, Transcript of Hearing on Jurisdiction, p. 281 (Washington DC, Day 2, 3 May 2011), where the following objection to an extended direct examination was upheld by the tribunal: "we do object to Mr. P being given any additional time on direct. Everything that he has to testify on direct is already in his Witness Statement, and those were the rules of the game that were established by the Tribunal. There is no reason why he should be allowed to testify for longer on direct. And certainly he should not be allowed to testify on anything that is not within the scope of his Witness Statement that's already been tendered."

61 In the *OneBeacon* case, the challenging party complained of the Tribunal's decision to limit the witness' direct testimony in light of the fact that a written statement had already been offered into the proceedings: "[i]n the place of direct expert testimony, the Panel reviewed and accepted into evidence the written reports of both Ms. H and Swiss Re's expert. OneBeacon claims that Dwyer should have been entitled to testify about his knowledge of the contract, including how it was intended to be applied, how it actually was applied, and how other reinsurers applied similar contract language . . .". The reviewing court ruled that such an approach did not impinge upon a party's right to a fair hearing: "The Panel's actions do not rise to the level of misconduct, as there is nothing in the record to suggest that the Panel blocked OneBeacon's right to a full and fair hearing." *OneBeacon America Insurance Co v Swiss Reinsurance America Corp*, Civil Action No. 09-CV-11495-PBS Lexis 136039 (Mass D, 23 December 2010).

62 *Weizmann v Neschis, supra* n. 41, p. 681. The decision by the tribunal in this regard was recorded in the published decision, and is instructive. "It was possible to forgo taking the testimony of the witnesses and experts

to forgo live testimony in favour of affidavits from some witnesses is common practice."[63] The court went on to note that given the abundance of written materials, the tribunal had not offended due process by limiting the number of witness examinations.

Leading questions on direct examination

8.43 Questions which consistently call for a "yes" or "no" may be used during cross-examination. However, as noted in article 8.2 leading questions are not permissible in direct examination. To allow counsel for the party in support of which the witness has offered his or her testimony to lead that witness through their testimony obviously undermines the probative value of the oral evidence. The witness who has offered his or her views or recollection of facts should be able to give complete, voluntary answers in response to open questions in such a circumstance. Save for exceptional circumstances, where legal counsel attempts to control his or her own witness' answers by using leading questions, the tribunal will likely question the value of that testimony.

Sequestration of witnesses

8.44 An issue that may arise with regard to the taking of witness testimony is whether it is permissible to allow witnesses, in particular fact witnesses, to observe other witnesses giving their testimony. The obvious concern over such a situation is that the testimony of one witness may be influenced by what has transpired during another's testimony. This point was acknowledged by one experienced arbitrator who, acting as chairman of an *ad hoc* tribunal seated in Geneva, noted for the parties during the hearing that: "I very much see that this can influence the way witnesses are expressing their views. [A witness] may be inclined to say exactly the same thing as the witness before. Had he been out of the room he would have used his own words, which could be possibly different."[64]

8.45 To prevent the above-mentioned fear from materialising, a tribunal may decide to order witnesses to be sequestered outside the hearing room during the testimony of other witnesses. Part of such an order will most likely also prohibit the witness from discussing his or her evidence with anyone during the giving of such evidence and from discussing his or her evidence with witnesses who have not yet testified. Where proceedings are transcribed and made available to the parties, the witness should not review this transcript prior to giving their own evidence.

8.46 An arbitral tribunal's authority to organise witness appearances in such a manner derives from the control over the hearing vested in it, as is stated in article 8.2, and as has been affirmed by reviewing courts. Consider the following excerpt from a challenge to a CAS award in which the Swiss Federal Tribunal affirmed a tribunal's right to decide whether to sequester a witnesses:

The plaintiffs deplore the fact that the witnesses were allowed to be present at the hearing before they were questioned and that they were therefore inevitably influenced by preceding witnesses, the

---

offered by the Third Party Intervenors because the arbitration court admitted into evidence and evaluated the written statements of the proffered witnesses."
63 *Ibid.*
64 Excerpt from ICC arbitration in "Documents 31 to 40", *ASA Bulletin*, Vol. 11, No. 4, p. 593 (1993).

parties statements and the proceedings in general. They believe this to be a breach of procedural public policy. This argument is groundless. The plaintiffs do not refer to any provision of the Code which either prevents witnesses from attending the debates before they are questioned or, in particular, obliges them to retire while another witness is being questioned. . . . Furthermore it cannot be argued that this rule is essential to the fairness of the proceedings. Besides, arbitration rules generally leave it to the arbitral tribunal to decide whether a witness should retire during part of the proceedings, particularly during the testimony of other witnesses.[65]

8.47 Thus a tribunal is generally free to make determinations on sequestration as long as the rule it derives is applied fairly. While it may often be the case that witnesses are sequestered, it is by no means a certainty nor is it inherent to a party's right to a fair proceeding.

In camera *hearings*

8.48 One usually assumes that international arbitration is private and thus hearings would normally take place *in camera* away from the survey of the public. Interestingly, the IBA Rules do not take an express position on the issue although article 25(4) of the UNCITRAL Rules states that hearings shall be held *in camera*. Under such rule a tribunal does not have the discretion to open the oral proceedings to the public, save an agreement to the contrary reached by the parties.[66] In the NAFTA arbitration between *Methanex v United States of America*, the tribunal confirmed that though it had the power to accept *amicus curiae* briefs and such was not in contradiction with *in camera* hearing provision in article 25(4) of the UNCITRAL Rules, it could not allow the *amici curiae* to attend the hearing in the absence of the claimant's consent.[67]

8.49 The private nature of the arbitral hearing generally implies the default position that the parties are not to disclose transcripts of the hearing.[68] On some occasions tribunals have extended the reach of the "private hearing" rule to mean that documents prepared for the hearing, including witness statements, may also not be disclosed: "it would be artificial and might adversely affect the efficient organization of Chapter 11 proceedings if such materials were to be deemed to be less private merely because they were to be delivered in advance of an oral hearing, or even after to it in the form of post-hearing briefs. The same level of confidentiality that is conferred on the transcripts of the opening and closing submissions and witness testimony must logically be applied to equivalent written materials."[69] Whether this approach is followed by other tribunals may be influenced by the nature of the proceeding.

---

65 "Tribunal Federal, 27 May 2003", in Albert Jan Van den Berg (ed.), *Yearbook Commercial Arbitration*, Vol. XXIX, pp. 206–231 (2004).

66 "Article 25.4 is written in mandatory terms (Hearings shall be held . . . unless . . .). A close examination of the manner in which Section III of the Rules was crafted reveals that the drafters had the distinction between mandatory and permissive terminology in mind. Accordingly, the Tribunal takes the view that it has no authority to derogate from the provision contained in art. 25.4 in the absence of an agreement by the Parties." *SD Myers Inc v Government of Canada*, NAFTA/UNCITRAL, Procedural Order No. 16, para. 13 (13 May 2000).

67 *Methanex Corp v United States of America*, NAFTA/UNCITRAL, Decisions on Petitions From Third Persons to Intervene as "Amici Curiae", para. 41 (15 January 2001).

68 "In the instant case neither Party has submitted a request for the hearings to be open to the public, and no decision has been made in this respect by the Tribunal. Thus, the minutes and audio-recordings of hearings may not be disseminated to the public by one of the Parties." *World Duty Free Co Ltd v Republic of Kenya*, ICSID Case No. ARB/00/7, Final Award, para. 16 (31 August 2006).

69 *SD Myers Inc v Canada, supra* n. 66, Procedural Order No. 16, para. 12.

8.50 In the absence of a rule like UNCITRAL Rules, article 25(4), the question arises as to whether the parties would still have a right to a private hearing. The general consensus on this issue appears to favour an inherent right to a private hearing irrespective of whether such is included expressly within the arbitral rules. In this regard a distinction between a party's right to a private hearing, and the right to expect that the entire proceeding (written submissions, evidence, oral hearing and any interim and final awards) will remain confidential (see comments to article 3.13), should be made.[70] While there is an argument for the privacy of a hearing to be implied in international arbitration, the right to confidentiality does not carry the weight of a universal rule, particularly given the divergence in its treatment in institutional arbitrations rules.

The presentation of oral testimony

Article 8.3 2010 IBA Rules:	With respect to oral testimony at an Evidentiary Hearing:
	(a) the Claimant shall ordinarily first present the testimony of its witnesses, followed by the Respondent presenting the testimony of its witnesses;
	(b) following direct testimony, any other Party may question such witness, in an order to be determined by the Arbitral Tribunal. The Party who initially presented the witness shall subsequently have the opportunity to ask additional questions on the matters raised in the other Parties' questioning;
	(c) thereafter, the Claimant shall ordinarily first present the testimony of its Party-Appointed Experts, followed by the Respondent presenting the testimony of its Party-Appointed Experts. The Party who initially presented the Party-Appointed Expert shall subsequently have the opportunity to ask additional questions on the matters raised in the other Parties' questioning;
	(d) the Arbitral Tribunal may question a Tribunal-Appointed Expert, and he or she may be questioned by the Parties or by any Party-Appointed Expert, on issues raised in the Tribunal-Appointed Expert Report, in the Parties' submissions or in the Expert Reports made by the Party-Appointed Experts;
	(e) if the arbitration is organised into separate issues or phases (such as jurisdiction, preliminary determinations, liability and damages), the Parties may agree or the Arbitral

---

70 "The universally accepted right to privacy, inherent in arbitration, does not entail an implied obligation of an arbitrating party to keep confidential the information disclosed during an arbitration." Antonio Dimolitsa, "Institutional Rules and National Regimes Relating to the Obligation of Confidentiality on Parties in Arbitration", in *ICC Bulletin, 2009 Special Supplement: Confidentiality in Arbitration*, p. 5 (2009). See also the following from the International Law Association's report on confidentiality in international arbitration: "[t]he concept of privacy is typically used to refer to the fact that only the parties, and not third parties, may attend arbitral hearings or otherwise participate in the arbitral proceedings." Filip De Ly, Luca G.R. di Brozolo, M. Friedman, *ILA Report: Confidentiality in International Arbitration*, p. 4 (The Hague Conference, 2010).

Tribunal may order the scheduling of testimony separately for each issue or phase;

(f) the Arbitral Tribunal, upon request of a Party or on its own motion, may vary this order of proceeding, including the arrangement of testimony by particular issues or in such a manner that witnesses be questioned at the same time and in confrontation with each other (witness conferencing);

(g) the Arbitral Tribunal may ask questions to a witness at any time.

General discussion

8.51 In 2010 changes were made to article 8.3 to add subparagraphs (c), (d) and (e) to cover the approach tribunals should take to expert witnesses (both party-appointed and tribunal-appointed). The new subparagraph (e) expressly grants the tribunal the right to organise a hearing around particular issues in the arbitration. However, the traditional starting point for organising a hearing is restated in article 8.3(a) and (b) and follows the approach that the evidence in support of the case-in-chief, meaning the witnesses proffered by each party in support of their main contentions, should proceed first before rebuttal witnesses are heard. An example of the procedural format reflected in article 8.3 may be taken below from an Iran-US Claims Tribunal award:

> At the commencement of the hearing, the Chairman, outlining the established practices of the Chamber in conducting oral proceedings, emphasized that any testimony the Respondents wished to introduce as part of their case-in-chief, (that is, evidence directed to arguments and evidence presented by the Claimants in their written pleadings or in the first phase of their oral presentation), should be included in the 'first round' of the Respondents' presentation. The only testimony permissible during the second round would be material presented to rebut statements made in the course of the Claimants' second round (ie 'rebuttal' evidence).[71]

8.52 Modern arbitrations may contain numerous counter-claims involving similar fact patterns, or multiple parties as the case may be. Both the parties and the tribunal may find it more informative in such circumstances if the evidence adduced at the hearing is organised around issues as per subparagraph (e), and not the traditional approach described above. In this regard, arbitrators are free to deviate from the traditional model, as well as from the

---

71 *Uiterwyk Corp et al. v The Islamic Republic of Iran*, Partial Award, Albert Jan van den Berg, *Yearbook Commercial Arbitration*, volume XIV, p. 398 (1988). In *Windstream Energy LLC v Government of Canada*, an arbitration under Chapter Eleven of the North American Free Trade Agreement and the 2010 UNCITRAL Arbitration Rules registered under the Permanent Court of Arbitration, the Tribunal clarified in Procedural Order No. 1 that: "At any hearing, the examination of each witness shall proceed as follows: (1) the Party summoning the witness may briefly examine the witness for the purpose of introducing the witness, correcting, if necessary, any errors in the witness statement and addressing matters arisen after the witness statement was given, if any; (2) the adverse Party may then cross-examine the witness; (3) the Party presenting the witness may then re-examine the witness with respect to any matters or issues arising out of the cross-examination, with re-cross examination – limited to the witness' testimony on re-examination – at the discretion of the Tribunal; and (4) the Tribunal may examine the witness at any time, either before, during or after examination by one of the Parties." *Ibid.*, p. 7, §10.10.

practice predominantly used at the seat of the arbitration, provided that the parties are given a fair opportunity to be heard.[72]

Right to cross-examination

8.53 Article 8.3(b) expressly allows witnesses, presented at the hearing, to be questioned by all parties to the arbitration. This may lead parties to query whether this rule contemplates or gives rise to a right by a party to conduct a cross-examination. While it is the case that a party under the IBA Rules has a right to put questions to an adverse witness (see comments to article 4.7), the Rules do not prescribe the format in which the questioning should be conducted. Such latitude is appropriate as different forms of witness examination may be used within international arbitration. For example, some tribunals may decide to conduct the questioning themselves, and in doing so will ask the parties to provide them with their respective list of questions in writing. Other approaches may see arbitrators asking the bulk of questions of the witness, with counsel permitted to ask only limited follow-up questions which they deem necessary.[73] That being said, the traditional format allowing for cross-examining counsel to take the lead in questioning the witness followed by questions from the tribunal is predominantly employed. Under article 8.3(b) a tribunal may organise the witness testimony using different approaches, however rigidity is almost never an issue in international arbitration, as arbitrators generally use the flexibility afforded to them to work towards ensuring that the hearing will be as productive as possible.[74]

8.54 The common law method of cross-examination, which relies on the use of leading questions, is often used in international arbitration. As an example of

---

72 A challenge was brought to an LCIA arbitration award during which the hearing was conducted in a manner so that the claimant was not afforded the last opportunity to present oral evidence. The reviewing court noted: "[i]n common law practice, the plaintiff in a court case speaks last, on the basis that he carries the burden of proof. This means that the plaintiff will have two opportunities to make oral submissions, whilst the defendant has only one. In arbitrations this practice is not widely followed, since arbitrators tend to feel, instinctively, that due process is generally served only if the parties are permitted an equal number of opportunities to make oral submissions." And then later in the same judgment: "[i]ndeed, the procedure that was adopted was not unusual in an international arbitration . . .". And, "[i]n my judgment, what the arbitrator did was well within the scope of what he was empowered to do." *Margulead Ltd v Exide Technologies* [2004] EWHC 1019 (Comm) paras 30, 33. The above being said, it should be also noted that a right to cross-examine a witness has been affirmed as inherent to a right of due process (as is reflected by art. 8.3(b)). The implication of this is that whatever format is used for the conduct of a hearing in international arbitration, the tribunal should endeavor to ensure that a party has the right to put questions to those adverse witnesses which have offered testimony relevant to the final award. See further: ICC Case No. 12575, in which the tribunal affirmed that a party's right to challenge an adverse witness is implicated by art. 190(2)(d) of the Swiss PILA, thus further establishing "per se" the right to conduct a cross-examination. *ICC Bulletin, 2010 Special Supplement: Decisions on ICC Arbitration Procedure*, p. 67.

73 As was communicated to the parties in a procedural directive given in an *ad hoc* arbitration seated in Zurich: "[t]he witnesses will be questioned by the Chairman; the Arbitrators and the Parties' Counsel will be given the opportunity to ask further questions." "Documents", *supra* n. 19, p. 318.

74 As an ICC tribunal of mixed common law and civil law practitioners noted in a communiqué to the parties: "[w]ith respect to the examination and cross-examination the Tribunal, of course, reserves the right to control it. However, in principle it is left to the parties to conduct this examination and cross-examination with the right to of the Tribunal to put questions where necessary. Although we must, of course, proceed in an orderly manner the examination should not be bound by too much formality. The important thing is that we obtain as much information as possible." "Documents", *supra* n. 19, p. 327.

how leading questions may be permitted the following excerpt from the *Barbados v Trinidad* boundary dispute administered by the Permanent Court of Arbitration is reproduced:

"Q. Could you read the first name on there and the description of the role? A. "His Excellency [redacted], Leader."

Q. Could you please locate your name and your description as part of that delegation on that record?

A. My name is not listed here.

Q. I am sorry? Your name is not listed?

A. No, my name is not listed here.

Q. Were you at this first negotiating session?

A. Yes, I was at the first negotiating session.

Q. So the record of the joint report is incorrect, in your testimony.

A. Well, there is an absence of the name here, that is correct, yes. There is an absence of the name, but would not say the record is incorrect as far as the substantive areas are concerned.

Q. This session was held at the Crown Plaza Hotel, was it not? A. That is correct.

Q. And you have very clear recollections of being there, are you telling us?

A. I have said before, I was there at the Crown Plaza during these negotiations, that is correct."[75]

8.55 As the above example demonstrates, counsel may use this approach to walk witnesses through exhibits using short questions that call for "yes" or "no" answers. The above excerpt is from a state-to-state international arbitration, but certainly, cross-examination of this kind is often used in international commercial arbitrations as well.[76]

---

75 *Barbados v Republic of Trinidad & Tobago* UNCLOS/PCA, Hearing Transcript, p. 43 (London, Day 3, 20 October 2005).

76 The following example is taken from the transcript of an international maritime arbitration under the Society of Maritime Arbitrators Rules, *Buques Centroamericanos v Refinadora Costarricense de Petroleo* :

"Q. What was the state of the market in 1973; Charter markets?

A. '73.

Q. Yes, November, '73 when this contract was entered into.

A. The rates were very high. There was a great demand for tankers, especially of the kind we needed, small tankers.

Q. Are you telling this Panel that this company agreed to take any requirements of this company, of RECOPE, regardless of the amount per month? Is that your testimony in light of that testimony about the state of the market?

A. Yes.

Q. If RECOPE told BUCESA that it needed only 15,000 or 5,000 BUCESA would have to produce the vessel and carry 5,000; is that your testimony?

A. Yes.

Q. And you think they entered into an agreement along those lines that stipulated to that in clause N-3 in the state of that market? Is that your testimony?

A. Yes.

Q. I submit that's incredible, Mr. Villalobos.

(Transcript 182-83)." *Buques Centroamericanos SA v Refinadora Costarricense de Petroleo SA*, Award No. 2378 of 24 April 1987, Journal of International Arbitration, Vol. 4, No. 4, p. 150 (1987).

Examining witnesses using documents

8.56 Tribunals typically limit the documentary evidence which counsel may use to confront a witness to evidence already submitted within the procedure.[77] Customary practice is that witnesses should not be surprised with documents that have not been previously submitted into the record of the arbitration. Tribunals which are confronted with an attempt to introduce new evidence at the hearing will often exclude such documents unless the adverse party waives its objection.[78] The basic rule as it applies to witness testimony is that witnesses should not be confronted with documents for the first time at a hearing, as was explained by an ICC tribunal which noted disapprovingly of an attempt by counsel to present a witness with a document which had not previously been submitted to the record:

> It is obviously unsatisfactory for a witness to be confronted for the first time with a set of calculations during the course of a hearing and to be asked, in effect, to confirm their accuracy. It would have been very much more helpful to all concerned (including the Tribunal) if Counsel for Y had put Exhibit R1 to the Claimant's lawyers before the Hearing and asked them either to agree to it or to point out where they disagreed. This is the way in which an arbitration should be conducted – rather than springing a document on a witness at the last moment. . . .[79]

8.57 Exceptional circumstances may require that a tribunal modify this rule, in particular where a witness has introduced new factual testimony previously not known to the parties.[80] In such situations, it may be appropriate for a tribunal to allow a party to introduce new documents for the purpose of rebutting the witness testimony. Other situations may also give rise to a decision by the tribunal to admit new evidence at the hearing, such as where the existence of evidence is revealed for the first time only at the oral hearing. Finally, where the new evidence is highly probative, a tribunal may admit the evidence for use at the hearing with the caveat that the adverse side will be afforded an opportunity to respond.

---

77 A typical limiting order will usually take a form similar to the following: "[n]o new documents may be presented at the Hearing, unless agreed by the Parties or authorized by the Tribunal. But demonstrative exhibits may be shown using documents submitted earlier in accordance with the Timetable." *Chevron v Ecuador, supra* n. 59, Interim Award, p. 28.

78 The following quote from the *Harris v Iran* case of the Iran-US Claims Tribunal records just such an instance: "[f]or example, in *Bechtel Inc, supra*, para. 20, one of the Respondents submitted a document entitled 'Hearing Statement' at the Hearing which the attorney described as being a 'verbatim' transcript of the oral statements he intended to make. The Claimants objected to the admission of this document at such a late stage of the proceedings. The Tribunal permitted the distribution of the document, but did not accept it for filing, reserving its decision until after the Hearing. Upon examination of the document after the Hearing, the Tribunal discovered that the 'Hearing Statement' constituted in fact the Respondent's Hearing Memorial which had been due by 15 December 1985 and had not been submitted before the Hearing, which was held on 13 and 14 February 1986. The Tribunal found that this 'Hearing Statement' contained a detailed and partly new outline of factual allegations and legal arguments, 'the acceptance of which for filing would prejudice the Claimants, who did not have sufficient opportunity to comment on the document as a whole'. It refused to admit the document but stated that it 'takes note of arguments contained therein to the extent they were contained in and could be followed during the oral presentation' of the Respondent's attorney at the Hearing. The Claimant had the opportunity to respond orally to the Respondent's oral arguments." *Harris v Iran, supra* n. 18, Partial Award, endnote 3.

79 Final Award in ICC Case No. 11307 of 2003 in Albert Jan van den Berg (ed.), *Yearbook Commercial Arbitration*, Vol. XXXIII, p. 56 (2008).

80 For example, in the *Pac Rim v El Salvador* arbitration, the tribunal was confronted with a request to admit a new document at the hearing which had only recently become relevant due to the factual development of the case. After deliberation the tribunal allowed the document in. *Pac Rim v El Salvador, supra* n. 46, Hearing on Jurisdiction, pp. 571–575, 762, 763 (Washington DC, Day 3, 4 May 2011).

8.58 Limitations imposed on documentary evidence used at a hearing will generally not exclude demonstrative exhibits used to aid witness examination. Such exhibits often will not include new factual evidence and are useful only for the purposes of clarifying the questions put to the witness. As one tribunal noted in regard to the use of demonstrative aids, "as with other evidence, any means of explanation or clarification of previously submitted evidence during the Hearing is in principle admissible, unless new evidence is introduced in that way. As such, showing of slides is not objectionable as long as it conforms to these standards."[81]

Re-direct and re-cross-examinations

8.59 Article 8.3(b) takes the customary position that re-direct and re-cross-examinations are to be limited to the matters raised during cross-examination. This, too, is a basic organisational principle useful for maintaining the equal treatment of the parties during the proceeding. Each party's right to conduct questioning of the witness is limited in a similar manner, or in other words both parties are required to keep their questions narrowly tailored to issues which arose during the cross-examination.[82]

Examination of a tribunal-appointed expert

8.60 A tribunal-appointed expert will often be requested to appear at an oral hearing to provide an oral summary of his or her report and to answer questions regarding its contents. As article 8.3(d) implies, it is often the case that the first round of questioning of a tribunal-appointed expert witness will be conducted by the tribunal. Nevertheless, the parties are expressly granted an opportunity under this provision to put their own questions to the

---

81 *Oil Field of Texas Inc v The Islamic Republic of Iran*, Case No. 43, Final Award No. 258-43-1 of 8 October 1986, in Albert Jan van den Berg (ed.), *Yearbook Commercial Arbitration*, Vol. XII, p. 287 (1987). In *KBR, Inc v United Mexican States*, ICSID Case No. UNCT/14/1, an arbitration under Chapter 11 of the NAFTA and the UNCITRAL Arbitration Rules, the Tribunal issued Procedural Order No. 2, dated 5 September 2014, dealing with organisational issues for the hearing. Regarding the use of documents at the Hearing, the Tribunal stated: "(5.) Documents for Use at the Hearing: (5.1.) In accordance with the parties' agreement, demonstrative exhibits (such as Power Point slides, charts, tabulations, etc.) may be used at the Hearing, provided they contain no new evidence and are closely tied to the exhibits that are already on the record. (5.2.) Each party shall number its demonstrative exhibits consecutively, and indicate on each demonstrative exhibit the exhibit number of the document(s) from which it is derived. The party submitting such demonstrative exhibits shall provide them in hard copy to the other party, the Tribunal Members, the Secretary of the Tribunal, the court reporter(s) and interpreter(s) at the Hearing. (5.3.) The Tribunal takes note of the statement during the pre-Hearing organizational call that hearing bundles are not anticipated." *Ibid.*, p. 5.

82 See the expert from *Uiterwyk Corp et al. v Iran, supra* n. 71, para.23. See also: *Chevron v Ecuador* scheduling order quoted above, *supra* n. 59. See also the following order from ICC Case No. 12990 which limits the re-direct examination to issues raised during the cross-examination: "the party summoning the witness may then re-examine the witness with respect to any matters or issues arising out of the cross-examination." *ICC Bulletin, 2010 Special Supplement: Decisions on ICC Arbitration Procedure*, p. 88. See also the following ruling of an ICDR tribunal denying respondent an opportunity to redirect a witness. Consistent with the concept that a redirect is limited to subjects raised in the preceding cross-examination, in this instance, where claimant waived its right to perform a cross-examination, the tribunal did not permit the respondent to pursue further questioning. This was so, even though the tribunal itself did pose questions to the witness. "[T]he Claimant waived its right to cross examine witnesses [listing of names] and therefore the Respondent was not allowed to redirect those witnesses, and the tribunal proceeded to ask the questions it considered relevant to the resolution of the arbitration." ICDR Case No. 50181, Final Award, para. 88 (2009) (unpublished).

tribunal-appointed expert through counsel, or through their own party-appointed expert. Where experts or even the party representatives themselves are permitted to question the tribunal-appointed expert, legal counsel is still often asked to maintain overall control of the examination under the ultimate authority of the tribunal.[83]

8.61 Questions that are put to a tribunal-appointed expert will often go to the scope and substance of the expert's report. It should be noted, however, that it is appropriate for an expert to be questioned on the procedure that was adopted in arriving at the report. As is discussed more thoroughly in the comments to article 6, a tribunal-appointed expert is generally required to follow an approach in compiling his or her report that affords each party an equal opportunity to be heard on the issues covered.[84] Defects in the procedural method followed by an expert should be exposed for the tribunal's awareness so that they may be dealt with prior to the rendering of a final award.

Language of an evidentiary hearing

8.62 The language of an arbitral hearing will often be determined by the arbitration clause, or in the absence of agreement between the parties, in the first procedural order issued in the proceedings. Irrespective of the official language (or even in some cases languages) of the proceedings, the tribunal may need to make provision for witnesses and counsel who prefer to conduct examinations in a language other than that of the arbitration. Unless otherwise agreed amongst the parties, where the testimony of a witness is transcribed, it must be in the official language of the hearing. In such circumstances, generally only the interpretation and not the original language testimony of a witness will be admitted as evidence.

8.63 An example of a procedural order setting out the customary approach to such matters may be taken from an ICC arbitration as set out below:

> Claimant's Counsel requested [of] the Arbitral Tribunal that 'the next Hearing will be held as the previous Hearing in French' and said that it would take in charge the fees of the translator. The Chairman answered in the following terms: "The language of the Arbitration is English and not French. This cannot and will not be modified. The previous Hearing was held in English with Claimant speaking in French through an English translator. Only the English translation was taken into account and transcribed by the Court reporter".[85]

8.64 A tribunal will customarily desire to ensure that the oral proceedings remain consistent with the arbitration clause unless both parties consent to departure from it. Irrespective of the method chosen to accommodate testimony offered in a language other than that of the arbitral proceedings, a tribunal will in most circumstances arrange, or ask the

---

83 "Basically, examinations are conducted by the legal counsel of record. However, it is perfectly admissible that questions may also be put under the counsel's control, and under the overall control of the Arbitration Tribunal – witnesses of the party, or experts, or party representatives such as the in-house counsel, the CEO/CFO, or other members of the management of either Party." ICC Case No. 16249, Procedural Order No. 1 (2010) (unpublished).

84 See, for instance, the discussion of due process and expert reports provided in the final award rendered by an ICC tribunal seated in Zurich, Switzerland. ICC Case No. 12171, Award on Preliminary Issues, in *ASA Bulletin*, Vol. 23, No. 2, pp. 256–269 (2005).

85 ICC Case No. 13133, Final Award, in Albert Jan van den Berg (ed.), *Yearbook Commercial Arbitration*, Vol. XXXV, pp. 129, 137–138 (2010).

parties to arrange for the following issues to be dealt with: (1) the evidence (testimony offered under direct and cross-examination) is interpreted into and transcribed in the language of the proceedings;[86] (2) where a witness is questioned in a language other than the language of the proceedings, the tribunal and other parties are advised (by provision of interpretation services at the hearing) of the questions being put to the witness prior to answers being given; (3) the witness is given an opportunity to fully understand the issues being put to them;[87] and (4) the party not proffering the witness will have the opportunity to both examine and receive answers to its cross-examination questions in the language of the proceedings.

Questions by the tribunal

8.65 Article 8.3(g) grants the tribunal the express right to conduct its own questioning of witnesses at any time. In practical application of this rule a tribunal may schedule time following the examination of the witnesses by counsel to ask questions, and/or interject during counsel's questioning with its own queries to the witness. Likewise, the tribunal may choose to conduct the cross-examination itself by asking its own questions or questions prepared by each party's counsel.

> The Arbitral Tribunal may put questions to the witness or experts at any time during the Hearings, either before, during or after the examination by counsel; it may direct questions to other witnesses or experts attending the Hearing so as to clarify different or contradicting statements. Witnesses and Experts may be questioned by the Arbitral Tribunal on any matter deemed relevant, whether or not such matter had been covered in the written statement previously filed.[88]

8.66 Interjection by arbitrators during an examination may cause disruption to the flow of the examination conducted by counsel. Nevertheless, as control over the hearing is vested in the tribunal, arbitrators have great leeway to question the witnesses before them as they deem appropriate, provided that fairness should be afforded to the parties. If counsel's examination is interrupted by the questions of the tribunal, reasonable time should be allotted to allow a party to finish its planned examination. It does not violate the principles of equal treatment or fairness for arbitrators to engage in questioning of a particular witness or multiple witnesses on a particular issue, if they are of the opinion that to do so is of material value. In a challenge to an ICC award based partially on the fact that counsel for the losing party believed two of the arbitrators evinced bias because of their aggressive questioning of its witnesses during the hearing, the reviewing court noted the following:

> [Complainant] has not shown that it lacked the opportunity to respond to [the arbitrator's] comments and questions. A review of the transcript reveals that each of the panel members asked questions of the witnesses, often vigorously. The hearings involved highly technical and detailed

---

86 According to a case reported from Germany, it has been held that it is the responsibility of the party proffering the witness to provide the necessary translation services for participation in the hearing. "Germany No. 96. Oberlandesgericht, Celle, 2 October 2001", in Albert Jan van den Berg (ed.), *Yearbook Commercial Arbitration*, Vol. XXXII, p. 303 (2007).

87 In a 2001 ruling of the Russian Supreme Court an SCC award was set aside because, *inter alia*, the Russian witnesses were not allowed to consult their witness statement that had been originally authored in Russian, during the examination. Instead they were directed by the tribunal to use only the English language version. Nikiforov, *supra* n. 4, p. 807.

88   ICC Case No. 16249, *supra* n. 83.

subjects, about which the arbitrators had acknowledged substantive expertise and experience, as well as experience as arbitrators. There were a number of sharp disputes and disagreements. The transcript shows that a number of participants interrupted, questioned, and commented. The record does not support [complainant's] characterization of [the arbitrator's] behaviour as improper or as prejudicial.[89]

8.67 If a tribunal offers an opportunity to the parties to respond to an arbitrator's questions or follow-up with its own questions to the witnesses, it is often enough to cure any concern over fairness. Clearly, however, if an arbitrator conducts the examination of a witness, it should not per se give rise to claims of unfairness or bias if the questions have a reasonable basis in the facts of the case, are aimed at uncovering or clarifying material issues and are not meant to intimidate or harass a witness. Nor is it inappropriate for arbitrators to intervene to clarify the questions put to a witness, if it is done as part of a good faith effort to focus the hearing on the issues at hand.[90]

Witness conferencing

8.68 The use of witness conferencing has grown in popularity in international arbitration in recent years. Reduced to its basic elements, witness conferencing essentially allows a tribunal to question two witnesses who have proffered potentially adverse testimony at the same time. Prominently used in the Australian courts, the process of witness conferencing may allow tribunals to achieve a certain degree of procedural economy in determining the facts of a case.[91] The purpose of such an exercise generally is to allow for the testing of the

---

89 *Lummus Global Amazonas SA v Aguaytia Energy Del Peru SR Ltda*, 256 F.Supp. 2d 594, pp. 628, 629 (S.D. Tex. 2002). With respect to the role of the tribunal at a hearing, it is useful to consider the standard commonly adhered to by arbitrators when reviewing the evidence before them, as was noted by one LCIA tribunal as follows: "[Claimant] encourages the Tribunal to test the evidence before it with robust common sense and careful discrimination (in the sense of separating the evidential wheat from the evidential chaff). Again the Tribunal agrees that this is the appropriate approach." LCIA Case No. 7875, Partial Final Award, para. 93 (2008) (unpublished). Clearly, to accomplish this task, a tribunal may be required to interrupt a counsel's examination to question a witness and further follow-up a line of questioning with persistence, in order to obtain useful answers.

90 In a case before the Svea Court of Appeals brought as a challenge to an arbitration under the SCC Rules, the Court noted the following concerning questioning by the tribunal: "[e]ven if the main principle in arbitration, as the Court has described above, is that the parties have the responsibility for the evidence, there was therefore scope here for the tribunal to put questions during the examinations. In order for the tribunal not to be seen to be biased, however, the questions it puts should focus primarily on contradictory and incomprehensible information and circumstances that require simplification or summarising (internal citation omitted). In other words, an attempt to correct an ambiguous question falls within the scope of the tribunal's mandate and cannot normally be taken as a cause of bias." *Cypress Oilfield Holdings Limited v. China Petrochemical International Company Limited*, Svea Court Of Appeal, Case No. T 5296-14, Department 02, Division 020102, dated 19 February 2016, Stockholm.

91 "The fundamental difficulty facing a court hearing mega-litigation, however, is that the parties may decide, for whatever reason, to engage in a full-blown forensic battle in which almost every barely arguable issue is examined in depth. In these circumstances, the best efforts of the court to limit the scope of the dispute may amount to very little. . . . Similarly, I made a tentative suggestion, which Seven took up, that some of the experts might give concurrent evidence as a means of saving hearing time and encouraging a narrowing of the issues. However, the proposal was strenuously resisted by the Respondents and ultimately was not implemented." *Seven Network Ltd v News Ltd* [2007] FCA 1062, para. 25 (Federal Court of Australia, 27 July 2007). See also the following directive issued in ICC Case No. 13225: "The Sole Arbitrator reserves [the right] to hear several witnesses at the same time ("witness conferencing") if in the Arbitrator's opinion this would significantly facilitate the taking of evidence. The Arbitrator will consult with the Parties before making a respective decision." ICC Case No. 13225 *supra* n. 50. See also: *Libananco Holdings v Turkey*, where the tribunal directed the various party-appointed experts to be grouped according to discipline, and to produce joint reports covering areas of disagreement:

testimony proffered by both witnesses in order to discover (1) where areas of agreement may be found, (2) where the crucial points of disagreement are and (3) for the tribunal to gain a greater contextual understanding of the individual statements that are being offered.[92]

8.69 This method is most often used by tribunals in the assessment of expert testimony although fact witnesses too may be subjected to such a procedure. When applied to expert witnesses, a tribunal may ask the experts to meet to discuss areas of disagreement between their respective reports prior to appearing jointly before the tribunal. It may also be the case that a tribunal will use witness conferencing only as a follow up to a more traditional witness examination in which counsel for the parties have questioned the individual witnesses.

Hearing schedule

8.70 A common practice adopted by tribunals in determining the hearing schedule is to put the issue to the parties asking them to develop a draft schedule in consultation with each other, subject to the tribunal's approval. Obviously, such an approach will help avoid accusations of unfairness or bias in the scheduling of the hearing. Another method often employed is for a tribunal to use the "chess-clock" procedure, which allocates each party a certain number of hours which they may use for conducting their examinations (perhaps an even division of time). Each party is allowed to divide their time among the witnesses as they may wish; however, under such an arrangement the tribunal will keep a studious check on the time each party uses. Once one side's time allotment is depleted, that party should, in theory, bring their presentation to an end. A third scenario may see the tribunal scheduling a pre-hearing conference (often telephonic) in which the arbitrators and the parties work to develop an agreed time frame for the hearing.

8.71 Even where such practices are adopted, disputes over scheduling may still come about. Controversy may arise where, for instance, a party seeks additional time in excess of what was scheduled to conduct their examination, or where a party seeks to extend a hearing for a period of time. Such requests may arise for legitimate reasons; however, in dealing with them tribunals are usually mindful of the duty to treat the parties equally. Whether this principle requires each party to be given the exact same allotment of time to conduct witness examinations is a matter the tribunal must consider. Moreover, a tribunal may further be reluctant to alter a schedule which the parties have agreed to at the outset of the hearing.

8.72 Both considerations described above should not lead arbitrators to unduly limit the amount of time needed to conduct a thorough hearing. In a decision of the Hong Kong Courts regarding a challenge to a final award based, *inter alia*, on a complaint that one side had received 10 extra hours to examine witnesses than was agreed,[93] the court noted

---

"[a]mong other things, the Tribunal directed the Parties that it intended to implement witness conferencing and hear the Parties' forensic and computer experts in appropriate "conferencing groups" according to their respective discipline, and that each "conferencing group" prepare a joint report for the Tribunal by 16 October 2009." *Libananco Holdings Co Ltd v Republic of Turkey*, Final Award, ICSID Case No. ARB/06/8, para. 50. (2011);

92   See the following description of a witness conference conducted by an ICC tribunal: "[t]his was not a traditional examination through direct and cross-examination, but rather involved each of the legal experts sitting as a panel and answering questions from the tribunal and then from counsel. The purpose of the witness conference was to learn about Venezuelan law." ICC Case No. 15416, Final Award, para. 42 (2011) (unpublished).

93   In a decision of the Hong Kong High Court Special Administrative Region, Court of First Instance, a court approved of a tribunal's adjustment of a procedural schedule to allow one party more time to conduct their examination, in particular because that party had been required to examine 14 witnesses through translators.

that a tribunal should be primarily concerned with ensuring a fair opportunity to be heard is given each party.[94] The court further noted that if a tribunal believes that changes to the agreed procedure may be required, or more time must be allocated to one side in the interest of fairness, it should act to do so. The following excerpt from the court's reasoning is instructive:

> in a situation where the arbitrators discern potential problems with the opportunity to a party presenting his case fairly arising from a procedure agreed by the parties, they are obliged to raise it with the parties instead of following blindly what had been agreed. After hearing submissions from the parties, if the arbitrators were of the view that the procedure agreed by the parties would result in a breach of [the arbitration law's requirement for a fair hearing], they should take steps to conduct the arbitration in such a manner that could redress the problem instead of being constrained by an unworkable agreement of the parties. In my judgment, this is precisely what happened in this instance when the Tribunal made its decision on Day 24 and subsequently on the allocation of time for the three extended days. It follows that there is no breach under [the arbitration law] because in this particular instance, the slavish application of the chess-clock arrangement is in conflict with [the arbitration law requiring a fair hearing], as such the Tribunal was obliged to depart from it.[95]

8.73 With regard to the issue of equal treatment, in the above described instance the party allotted 10 hours less to conduct their examinations did not request additional time. Therefore, on this basis the court observed that the equal treatment principle had not been offended. Equal treatment has long been considered to necessitate an equal opportunity

---

Brunswick Bowling & Billards Corp v Shanghai Zhonglu Industrial Co Ltd (2009) HKCU 211. "The upshot was that as of the close of evidence, the respondents had used approximately 63 hours and the claimant had used approximately 73 hours. That has to be considered against the fact that 13 of the respondents' 14 factual witnesses gave evidence with interpretation, while only two of the claimant's witnesses required interpretation. The cross-examination of witnesses with interpretation inevitably took much more time and such time would be clocked as time taken up by the cross-examining party under the chess clock arrangement . . .". See also the decision of an ICSID tribunal to allow the respondent additional time in the examination of witnesses because the claimant had been allowed at the last minute to introduce new documentary evidence for use at the hearing: "[i]n Procedural Order No. 4 of March 14, 2009 ('Order No. 4'), the Tribunal decided, among other things, that it would permit the introduction of the New Documents but only under specified conditions. Depending upon the use to which Claimant would put the New Documents during the Hearing, the Tribunal expressed its intention to grant additional time to Respondent for the purposes of examining witnesses and experts, and commenting in its closing statement at the end of the Hearing." Dietmar W. Prager and Rebecca Jenkin, *"Alpha Projektholding GmbH v Ukraine*, ICSID Case No. ARB/07/16, 8 November 2010," *A Contribution by the ITA Board of Reporters*, para. 18.

94 *Ibid., Brunswick Bowling v Shanghai Zhonglu*, para. 92.

95 *Ibid.*, paras 87–90. See also the observations of an ICDR tribunal concerning a tribunal's discretion to change a hearing date. In this instance, it was argued that the tribunal could not extend the time frame for a hearing because it had previously been agreed by the parties. The tribunal, rejecting that argument, made the following relevant consideration regarding an arbitrator's case management powers: "In the final analysis, one should not lose sight of the fact that the sole thing at issue here is the Arbitrator's exercise of his discretion to grant a 12 week extension of the start of the hearing under circumstances where the parties had never agreed to the hearing date which was extended. Even if the parties had agreed to the prior date, however, it would still be contrary to any semblance of reason, logic or common sense to adopt a completely unworkable rule that once parties to an arbitration agree on an interim procedural matter, that matter is forever out of the Arbitrator's hands, regardless of what might thereafter occur. Suffice it to say that such a rule would wrongly deprive the arbitrator of the control and management of the arbitration process . . .". ICDR Case No. [partially redacted] 251-04, Final Award, WL 6346380 (2005), part VII. This tribunal's opinion is consistent with the view described in *Brunswick*. Both opinions place emphasis on the right of the tribunal to exercise its case management authority to ensure that a fair hearing occurs. Irrespective of what may have been agreed previously, a tribunal may alter prior arrangements for a hearing if in its discretion it is necessary to do so in order to ensure a fair hearing.

to present evidence, but not the mechanical application of the same time frames to both parties.[96]

8.74 The focus of a reviewing court in such a situation is generally on the reasonable use of discretion by the tribunal to ensure fairness, and equal treatment. This applies also to decisions by a tribunal to refuse to extend a hearing date. If, in its reasoned consideration such an extension is not required for a fair hearing there will be no breach of the fairness and equal treatment principles.[97]

Affirmations and confirmations

Article 8.4 2010 IBA Rules: A witness of fact providing testimony shall first affirm, in a manner determined appropriate by the Arbitral Tribunal, that he or she commits to tell the truth or, in the case of an expert witness, his or her genuine belief in the opinions to be expressed at the Evidentiary Hearing. If the witness has submitted a Witness Statement or an Expert Report, the witness shall confirm it. The Parties may agree or the Arbitral Tribunal may order that the Witness Statement or Expert Report shall serve as that witness's direct testimony.

---

96   "The principle of equality should not be given a strictly mechanical meaning; it does not mean that each party should have precisely the same number of days in which to prepare its submissions or exactly the same time to present its oral pleadings, for example. What matters is that a general balance be maintained and that each party be given an equal opportunity to present its case in an appropriate manner." Emmanuel Gaillard and John Savage (eds), *Fouchard Gaillard Goldman on International Commercial Arbitration*, p. 956 (1999). See further: comments to art. 9.2(9). This being said, it has generally considered that equality requires both parties to be granted access to the transcripts of the hearing testimony if a transcript is produced. Nevertheless, where a party does not raise any failure in this respect during the arbitration, it may not later raise the issue as a due process complaint. See the following summary of a Paris Court of Appeals decision which considered this issue: "M Schneider also contended before the Court of Appeal that the award should be set aside because the sole arbitrator violated due process. Specifically, M Schneider criticized the sole arbitrator for having (1) failed to communicate to the parties transcripts of the hearing that had been held in March 2008, and precipitously closed the proceedings in May 2008, thereby preventing the parties from commenting on the evidence and arguments presented at that hearing, all of which allegedly disappeared along with the transcripts. The Court of Appeal found that M Schneider had not requested copies of the hearing transcripts or raised any objection on this score during the arbitration and therefore could not complain about it now." D. Bensuade, J. Kirby, "View from Paris, December 2009", 24–12 *Mealey's Int'l Arb Rep* 17 (2009). The principle of equal treatment has also been interpreted to mean that a tribunal may not tamper with or alter a hearing transcript. See: the decision of the LCIA court on the successful challenge to a tribunal, on grounds of bias, because it had, *inter alia*, altered the transcript of a hearing by deleting certain portions. "LCIA Court Decision on Challenges to Arbitrators Reference No. UN3490", *Arbitration International*, Vol. 27, No. 3, p. 389 (2011).

97   See a decision of the US Second Circuit Court of Appeals approving a tribunal's decision not to postpone the hearing to allow respondent to engage in "third-party discovery", noting that the refusal to alter the schedule did not violate respondent's right to be heard. "10 June 2002 – United States Court of Appeals, Second Circuit" in Albert Jan van den Berg (ed.), *Yearbook Commercial Arbitration*, Vol. XXVIII, pp. 967–969 (2003). Some arbitrators may view the use of time during a hearing as within a party's strategic prerogative. If a tribunal subscribes to such a view, it may well see little reason to grant extensions. Consider the following procedural directive issued in ICC Case No. 12154. "Each Party is wholly responsible for the way it chooses to use the time available to it. Time is an immensely valuable resource, and its use is costly; a party's skill in presenting its case is reflected in the way it husbands this resource." *ICC Bulletin, 2010 Special Supplement: Decisions on ICC Arbitration Procedure*, p. 33.

General discussion

8.75 Article 8.4 sets forth procedural steps leading to the examination of individual witnesses. As the rule notes, when seated before the tribunal a witness may be asked to affirm that he or she will tell the truth during the questioning, or in the case of an expert witness their genuine belief in the testimony they are to give, and confirm that the witness statement previously submitted into the proceedings has been authored by the witness and is a correct representation of his or her testimony. The customary approach taken in international arbitration is for the written statement of the witness to be regarded as his or her direct testimony. The testimony taken during the hearing of a witness will be largely in response to questions from the adverse party or the tribunal (see comments to article 8.1 above). Article 8.4, therefore, restates the basic procedural steps that are taken in regard to the hearing of individual witnesses in an international arbitration.

The administration of affirmations or oaths to witnesses

8.76 The IBA Rules do not prescribe a specific oath or formula to be administered to witnesses when called to give oral testimony. This may be for a number of reasons; however, the issue of whether to administer and oath and what type of oath should be administered by a tribunal may be influenced by the arbitration law or rules that are applied. As an example, the ICSID Arbitration Rules require a specific oath be administered in proceedings administered under its rules.[98]

8.77 The fact that a witness has not taken an oath prior to giving testimony may have no effect on the probative value of the testimony. As a Dutch court noted in relation to testimony heard by a tribunal without administration of an oath, "in the court's judgment, testimony offered under oath and one given while not under oath should in principle be given the same weight."[99] Arbitrators expect witnesses to give their testimony in good faith, which

---

98 Article 35(2), ICSID Arbitration Rules. Where there are no specific rules or legal requirements requiring a particular oath to be administered, tribunals may formulate various affirmations that inform the witness of its duty of honesty. As an example of the types of witness affirmations used in international arbitration, consider the following except from an ICC award describing the practice of a tribunal comprised of experienced common-law and civil-law arbitrators: "Prior to testifying each witness and expert read either a '*witness declaration*' or an '*expert declaration*' aloud, as appropriate. The text of both declarations is provided for ease of reference. [Fact Witness Declaration] 'I am aware that in my testimony I have to tell the truth and nothing but the truth. I'm also aware that if I do not comply with this obligation, I may face severe legal consequences.' [Expert Declaration] 'I solemnly declare upon my honor and conscience that my statement will be in accordance with my sincere belief.'" ICC Case No. 15416, *supra* n. 92, para. 37.

99 *Rechtbank* Groningen (Groningen Court of First Instance), Case No. 49632/HA ZA 00-915 (24 January 2002). See also the decision of an ICSID tribunal concerning the admissibility of unsworn witness statements as an example of the weight, or lack thereof, given to the use of oaths in international arbitration: "As this provision does not call for a sworn affidavit, and as in many national jurisdictions non-sworn written witness statements are admissible and customary, the Tribunal is not prevented from giving evidentiary value to non-sworn written witness statements." *Tradex Hellas SA v Republic of Albania*, ICSID Case No. ARB/94/2, Decision on Jurisdiction of 24 December 1996 and Award of 29 April 1999, in Albert Jan van den Berg (ed.), *Yearbook Commercial Arbitration*, Vol. XXV, pp. 11, 240 (2000). See further the following comment concerning the approach to oaths in international arbitration, "The commitment within the US oath to 'tell the whole truth' indeed picks up the witness's obligation to provide a tribunal adverse, as well as supportive, information. . . . Still, practical experience teaches that witnesses too often only honour such an oath in the breach. Perjury prosecutions for giving false testimony in arbitrations are rare indeed. More importantly, the line between false testimony and advocacy is too

means an honest statement of those facts they recollect, or accurate professional opinions, irrespective of whether an oath has been administered. Thus, to some extent swearing in or asking witnesses to affirm the truthfulness of their testimony is a formality rather than a matter that goes to the weight which should be accorded to the testimony. Nevertheless, in some jurisdictions where criminal sanctions may be imposed upon a witness if they do commit perjury before an arbitrator, the administration of an oath may be a necessary warning to the witness.[100]

8.78 Irrespective of whether a witness is administered an oath prior to giving evidence, false witness testimony may well have adverse consequences for the party on whose behalf it was given. In the first instance, a tribunal may disregard such testimony or even draw adverse inferences from the fact that the witness lied.[101] If not caught during the course of the arbitration, a false testimony may be a basis for setting aside an award by the supervising court.[102]

---

hard to find for the standard witness oath to offer much clarity regarding the ethical responsibilities of an expert witness. Thus, the presence or absence of an oath (or truth affirmation) by a testifying expert is unlikely to afford arbitrators much practical direction regarding the ethical parameters for that witness's evidence." Mark Kantor, "A Code of Conduct for Party-Appointed Experts in International Arbitration – Can One be Found?", *Arbitration International*, Vol. 26, No. 3, p. 327 (2011); this being said the above approach may be contrasted to the view taken by tribunals of an earlier era, where it was considered that the administration of an oath provided a measure assurance that the testimony was true. Bin Cheng, *General Principles of Law as Applied by International Courts and Tribunals*, pp. 311–313 (2nd edition, 1987).

100 This was the case in Petition to Cassation No. 503 of 2003, issued on 15 May 2004 by the Dubai Court of Cassation. That case involved the development of a commercial and residential area in Dubai, which resulted in an international arbitration held in Dubai under the auspices of the Dubai Chamber of Commerce and Industry and in accordance with the UNCITRAL Arbitration Rules. The arbitrator in that case warned the witnesses of the following: "[b]e informed, in your capacity as a witness, that you are required to tell the whole truth or otherwise you will be held liable. Are you aware of this?" However, the arbitrator did not administer an oath. Article 41.2 of the UAE Evidence Law states that the testimony of a witness will be invalid if given without the administration of an oath with the following wording: "I swear to speak the whole truth and nothing but the truth." Article 211 of the UAE Civil Procedure Code provides that: "[t]he arbitrators should administer an oath on the witnesses and everyone who shall perjure before the arbitrators shall be considered a committer of the crime of perjury." Accordingly, Article 252 of the UAE Penal Code considers a person providing false testimony to have committed the offence of perjury as laid down by the law and the witness shall be penalised. The Dubai Court of First Instance annulled the award, as a direct result of the arbitrators' failure to take the oath during testimonies. On appeal from that decision, the Court of Cassation affirmed the lower court's decision to set aside the award because, "the arbitrator . . . heard the testimonies of witnesses without administering their oaths . . . said award has accordingly been deemed invalid." Among the reasoning is precisely the fact that Article 252 of the UAE Penal Code provides for criminal consequences to witnesses who commit perjury. Additionally, it is also interesting to note that the Court of Cassation was not persuaded by the fact that the local party did not object to the phrasing utilised by the arbitrator during the arbitration and also did not request that the witnesses take the oath in the wording prescribed under Article 41 of the Evidence Law. See: Hassan Arab, Lara Hammoud and Graham Lovett (eds), *Summaries of UAE Courts' Decisions on Arbitration*, ICC Publication No. 746E, pp. 41–44 (2013).

101 As an example, the following observations from an Iran-US Claims Tribunal panel concerning the apparent reversals and inconsistencies of a witness' testimony confirm a tribunal's right to candidly dismiss witness testimony when it appears to be less than truthful: "[i]n sum, then, the testimony of Mr. G at the Second Hearing was of such a quality that it reinforced the Tribunal's previous impression of Mr. G's lack of credibility, rather than bolstering the Tribunal's confidence in him as a witness. For the foregoing reasons, the Tribunal finds that Mr. G is not a credible witness and that it is unable to attach any evidentiary weight to the allegations contained in the G affidavit or to the testimony of Mr. G at the Second Hearing." *Dadras International et al. v The Islamic Republic of Iran et al.*, Award No. 567-213/215-3 of 7 November 1995; Iran-USCTR, Vol. 31, paras 158–162 (1995).

102 See also the finding of Flax J., in *Chantiers de l'Atlantique SA v Gaztransport & Technigaz SAS*, [2011] EWHC 3383 (Comm), para. 291, that the failure by a witness presenting technical evidence to disclose the existence of unfavourable test results was in fact fraud committed by a party under section 68(2) of the English Arbitration Act. Although, as in the other examples cited above, the court did not vacate the award because it was not evident that the fraud would have affected the outcome of the award. In a US case, the reviewing court noted

8.79 Even after the passing of the prescription period for challenging a final award, it may be that a party will still have recourse against an award tainted by perjured testimony.[103] However, in such instances the evidence of perjury will often be required to be quite compelling. A challenge may be mounted over false testimony in either the jurisdiction where the award was rendered (i.e., for those jurisdictions which allow an award to be revised) or before a court where the enforcement of the award is sought.[104]

8.80 In a well-known case where it was discovered after the final award was issued, that a key witness had perjured himself the Swiss Federal Tribunal revised the award of the ICC tribunal. A criminal investigation in France had established that the testimony of one of the key witnesses in the case was undeniably false.[105] In addition to demonstrating that a key witness had perjured himself, it was also proven to the satisfaction of the Federal Tribunal that had such been known to the arbitral tribunal, it may have likely resulted in the arbitrators arriving at a different result concerning the true nature of the contract in question, and the admissibility of the claims.[106] The request for revision (and annulment) was approved over 10 years after the final award had been rendered.

8.81 While the analysis of whether the presence of perjured testimony in an arbitration is sufficient to overturn the finality of an award will assume different forms depending on the jurisdiction seized of the matter, it would seem that reviewing courts will commonly look to at least two elements: (1) is there sufficient certainty that the witness testimony in question was in fact materially false; and (2) had the tribunal been aware of the false testimony, is there a reasonable possibility that the award would have been decided differently.

---

that fraud, within the meaning of s. 9 USC 10(a), may well encompass perjury. However, "the party relying on it must first show that he could not have discovered it during the arbitration, else he should have invoked it as a defense at that time". *Biotronik Mess- und Therapiegeraete GmbH & Co v Medford Medical Instrument Co*, 415 F.Supp. 133, p. 138 (D.N.J. 1976). Similarly in a case before the Singapore High Court, the court refused to set aside an award holding that it must be proved that the suppressed evidence could not have been discovered during the arbitration despite reasonable diligence and that such evidence would have been decisive in that it would have caused the arbitrator to rule in favour of the party petitioning for the setting aside. Michael Hwang SC, "*Swiss Singapore Overseas Enterprise Pte Ltd v Exim Rajathi Pvt Ltd* [2009] SGHC 231", in *A Contribution by the ITA Board of Reporters* (2010).

103 See, for example, the decision in *X AG v Y* before the Swiss Federal Tribunal, where a final award was revised and annulled when documents came to light which demonstrated that a key witness who had rebutted in his testimony the allegation that the underlying contractual arrangement was a money laundering scheme set-up to benefit certain Russian government officials, was in fact lying. Because the tribunal had relied on the false testimony, the Swiss Federal Tribunal annulled the award, and returned the matter to the tribunal to reconsider. 9 Mars 2005 – Tribunal fédéral, 1ère cour civil (4p 2206/2004) *ASA Bulletin*, Vol. 23, No. 3, p. 528 (2005).

104 In an English case it was noted that the court would not normally permit a party to challenge the enforcement of a foreign arbitration award on the grounds of fraud unless the evidence establishing the fraud was unavailable to that party at the time of the arbitration hearing. Furthermore, where perjury was the fraud alleged, the evidence had to be so strong that it would reasonably have been expected to be decisive at a hearing, and would necessarily have had that result if unanswered. *Westacre Investments Inc v Jugoimport-SDPR Holding Co Ltd* [2000] 1 QB 288. See also: *National Oil Corp v Libyan Sun Oil Co*, 733 F.Supp. 800, p. 813 (1990) in Albert Jan van den Berg (ed.), *Yearbook Commercial Arbitration*, Vol. XVI, p. 654, para. 7 (1991): "Intentionally giving false testimony in an arbitration proceeding would constitute fraud. 'But in order to protect the finality of arbitration decisions, courts must be slow to vacate an arbitral award on the ground of fraud.' Accordingly the fraud must not have been discoverable upon the exercise of due diligence prior to the arbitration hearing. The alleged fraud must also relate to a material issue."

105 Georg von Segesser and A. Meier, "*Thales v Y & Z*, Swiss Federal Tribunal, 6 October 2009", *A Contribution by the ITA Board of Reporters* (2009).

106 *Ibid.*: "[t]he Federal Tribunal reason that, had the arbitrators known the real purpose of the Contract, they would have held that corrupt influence peddling had rendered the Contract null and void and made inadmissible claims for remuneration pursuant to it."

If both of these elements are answered in favour of the challenging party, then it is possible that as a result of false witness testimony a final award will be annulled.

Confirmation of statement

8.82 The request that a witness confirm or deny his or her written statement generally affords an opportunity to correct any errors in the statement that have been discovered after it was initially issued. The purpose of the confirmation is to ensure that the witness stands behind the witness statement as true and accurate to the best of his or her knowledge. It is not uncommon that at the moment a witness is asked to confirm his or her statement, the witness will take that moment to correct incidental mistakes (i.e., typographical errors) or mis-statements discovered after it was initially filed.

Witness statements to serve as direct testimony

8.83 As previously stated in comments to articles 8.1 and 8.2, the predominant approach in international arbitration is that the written statement of a witness should be regarded as his or her primary direct testimony, thus eliminating the need for a long direct examination.[107] This common rule has a positive influence on procedural economy and allows the hearing to focus on the key points within a witness statement, bypassing testimony that covers the same ground as the written testimony. Although commonly accepted in modern practice, such a procedure is generally communicated to the parties at the outset of the arbitration. An example may be taken from an ICC arbitration seated in Belgium: "Every witness called shall first of all be invited by the Arbitrator to confirm or deny, as the case may be, his written statement. His written statement shall, in principle, be considered his direct testimony."[108]

A tribunal's authority to call a witness on its own motion

Article 8.5 2010 IBA Rules: **Subject to the provisions of Article 9.2, the Arbitral Tribunal may request any person to give oral or written evidence on any issue that the Arbitral Tribunal considers to be relevant to the case and material to its outcome. Any witness called and questioned by the Arbitral Tribunal may also be questioned by the Parties.**

General discussion

8.84 The arbitral tribunal is empowered under article 8.5 to call a witness to the hearing for the purpose of answering its questions. The manner in which a tribunal summons

---

107 Consider the observations on this point made by the tribunal in *SD Myers*, "Following common practice in international commercial arbitration, the Tribunal directed that the evidence-in-chief ('direct testimony') . . . should be delivered to the Tribunal and exchanged between the parties in advance of the substantive hearing." *SD Myers v Canada*, *supra* n. 66, Procedural Order No. 16, para. 11.

108 ICC Case No. 14106, Final Award (unpublished). See also: the following example taken from an ICC arbitration seated in Switzerland, "His [the witness'] written statement shall, in principle, be considered his direct testimony. However, the party summoning the witness may briefly examine the witness on issues contained in his or her written statement(s)." ICC Case No. 14069, *supra* n. 57, Specific Procedural Rules.

an individual to the hearing may be influenced by the *lex arbitri* and the powers granted by it to either issue its own subpoena or to request court assistance *sua sponte*. It may be a matter of the tribunal requesting a party to communicate the request to attend to a witness and the party using its best efforts to secure their attendance, or of the tribunal contacting the witness and requesting their voluntary attendance. In doing this, however, the tribunal may wish to be mindful of its obligations regarding confidentiality. As per other provisions of the IBA Rules allowing a tribunal to act on its own motion, the arbitrators should subject such a decision to comment from the parties, and allow for objections to be raised.

"Any person"

8.85 The tribunal may summon "any person" to appear and give testimony. While the text of the article casts the net quite widely, the authority in article 8.5 will often be used to summon a person whom the parties have identified in their pleadings as possessing relevant information, but whom, for one reason or another, they have not called as a witness.

8.86 An example of the authority expressed in article 8.5 may be taken from a decision by an international tribunal sitting under the AAA rules (now ICDR rules). In that case the tribunal summoned a witness to testify concerning his involvement in a redesign and construction of an industrial facility.[109] The individual in question had been an expert retained by the respondent to review the site and provide his analysis on the effect of a prior accident on the facility and the prospects of a new design. The respondent had refused to summon the individual and had objected to claimant's request to do so. The tribunal acted on its own motion and requested his attendance at the hearing. In a later challenge to the award, the respondent argued that the determination by the tribunal to call the expert had violated public policy prohibiting experts from testifying against a party who had previously retained them. The US Court of Appeals for the 11th Circuit found that the tribunal had acted within its powers and that calling the witness *sua sponte* was not unfair.

8.87 The above example affirms the basic authority which a tribunal has to call witnesses to a hearing. As article 8.5 makes clear, the objections listed in article 9.2 should be taken into consideration when a tribunal entertains making an order. However, the simple fact that one party does not wish the witness to be present at the hearing does not abrogate a tribunal's authority to act to hear the witness. It may also be that a tribunal will call a witness once tendered by a party, but which it later withdraws. Tribunals have in the past found that the withdraw by a party of a witness does not disqualify them from being called to give testimony before a tribunal.[110]

---

109 *Industrial Risk Insurers v MAN Gutehoffnungshutte GmbH*, 141 F.3d 1434 (11th Cir. Fla. 1998).

110 Arbitration under the Geneva Chamber of Commerce and Industry Rules, *supra* n. 54, p. 312 where the tribunal noted that: "There is no procedural objection against the Claimant's renouncing the witness whom it had originally named itself. Each party to an arbitration procedure is free to name and to renounce witnesses as it deems fit." The Arbitral tribunal would later engage in attempts to contact the witness and request their attendance at a hearing.

No duty to order attendance

8.88 It should also be mentioned that article 8.5 in no way binds a tribunal to call a witness to appear. This is true no matter how relevant a party may claim that the testimony of that potential witness will be. A tribunal is not obliged to call a witness on its own if it does not find that the witness would assist the tribunal's determinations.[111] In an LCIA arbitration where a party had urged a tribunal to call a witness which it complained should have been presented by the adverse party, the tribunal employed a relevance analysis in denying the request. The tribunal pointed out that it was for the adverse party to prove its own case, and the mere fact that its counter-party had failed to call a witness which may (or may not be) relevant to its burden of proof is not sufficient reason for the witness to be summoned to the hearing by the tribunal.[112] This example serves as a reminder that a party seeking to petition the production or presentation of evidence must demonstrate why the potential evidence is relevant to its "own" burden of proof, not its opponents'.

---

111 *Double K Oil Products 1996 Ltd v Neste Oil OYJ* [2009] EWHC 3380 (Comm).

112 *Ibid.*, p. 152, para. 39: "[i]t would not be an appropriate order, not least because the Respondent does not seek to rely on evidence from either of these persons. Whether any inferences are to be drawn from the fact that the Respondent does not produce evidence from either of these persons will be a matter on which submissions can if so wished be made at the substantive hearing."

CHAPTER 9

Disclosure and admissibility of evidence

Introduction

9.01. It is well accepted that international arbitrators tend to exercise a certain liberality towards the admittance of evidence. This principle has at times been carried to an extreme, insofar as there are historical examples where arbitrators were prohibited from excluding any evidence from consideration, as was the case of the Italian-Venezuelan Mixed Claims Commission of 1903:

> The commissioners shall be bound before reaching a decision, to receive and carefully examine all evidence presented to them by the Government of Venezuela and the Royal Italian Legation at Caracas, as well as oral or written arguments submitted by the agent of the Government or of the Legation.[1]

9.02 Modern practice is more nuanced. It is accepted today that there are grounds upon which evidence may be excluded from an international arbitration.[2] The contemporary approach notwithstanding, fairness and procedural propriety,[3] as opposed to a fear that the decision-maker will be improperly influenced, tends to guide decisions concerning the admissibility of evidence.[4]

---

1   Mixed Claims Commission (Italy-Venezuela), Protocol of 7 May 1903, 10 RIAA, p. 482. As a later decision of the Umpire to the tribunal confirmed, the duty to receive "all" evidence was correctly understood as not permitting the application of rules of exclusion. Opinions and Questions of Procedure, p. 488.

2   See Mosk's discussion of evidence before international tribunals where he comments: "[i]t is recognized that international tribunals are liberal in admitting evidence. But as Professor Reissman points out, that does not mean that everything is admissible: "[a]s I discussed, late-filed evidence has been rejected, as has been evidence that was not in the proper form, was delayed, constituted settlement discussions or was confidential. As illustrated by privileges, international arbitral panels can and do refuse to consider evidence." Richard Mosk, "The role of facts in international dispute resolution", *Recueil Des Cours*, Vol. 304, p. 120 (2003).

3   See: *Quiborax SA, Non Metallic Minerals SA, Allan Fosk Kaplún v Plurinational State of Bolivia*, Decision on Jurisdiction, ICSID Case No. ARB/06/2, 27 September 2012: "65. The Parties also disagree on whether evidence emanating from the Bolivian criminal proceedings should be admitted or not. The Claimants request that evidence arising from the Bolivian criminal proceedings be declared inadmissible. The Respondent opposes this request. 66. Arbitration Rule 34(1) reads as follows: 'The Tribunal shall be the judge of the admissibility of any evidence adduced and of its probative value.' Under this Rule, the Tribunal has ample discretion to rule on the admissibility of any evidence adduced. The Tribunal does not consider that declaring the evidence gathered in the Bolivian proceedings admissible would give the Respondent an undue advantage. Neither does it believe that admitting this evidence would harm the integrity of this arbitration. If and when it will have to consider any such evidence, the Tribunal will weigh its probative value taking into account other evidences on record as well as the circumstances surrounding this very evidence. In the exercise of its discretion under Arbitration Rule 34(I), it will then give this evidence more or less weight, or no weight at all. Therefore, the Tribunal concludes that the evidence from the Bolivian proceedings is admissible, being specified that its probative value will be addressed if and when necessary for the resolution of the issues before the Tribunal."

4   See *Mosk* supra n. 2, p. 114: "In sum, hearsay evidence generally may be submitted in international arbitration proceedings, but it is often viewed as evidence of little weight." See also: ICC Case No. 12124, whereby the tribunal rejected a motion to exclude hearsay evidence from the record: "The arbitral tribunal constituted pursuant to the ICC Rules of Arbitration and applying those rules in these proceedings, is not required to apply the strict

9.03 An issue closely related to the admissibility of evidence is the adverse disclosure of evidence. The modern practice of arbitration embraces the procedures surrounding document disclosure set forth in article 3 of the IBA Rules. Equally, article 9.2 sets forth the grounds on which it is widely accepted that document disclosure may be resisted.

9.04 The general acceptance of article 9.2 notwithstanding, the extent and manner to which these rules are applied may not always be clear from their text. This chapter considers each of the rules set forth in article 9.2 in greater depth. (The general authority of the tribunal to admit and weigh evidence under article 9.1 is discussed in Chapter 7.)

9.05 Of the rules considered in article 9.2, the issue of privilege presents one of the most persistently discussed problems in the modern practice of international arbitration. In the 2010 revision to the IBA Rules, the Review Subcommittee included within article 9.3 a list of factors an arbitral tribunal should consider when weighing this issue. These factors are reviewed in conjunction with the general discussion on privilege set forth below article 9.2.

Relevance and materiality objections to the admissibility of evidence

Article 9.2 2010 IBA Rules: The Arbitral Tribunal shall, at the request of a Party or on its own motion, exclude from evidence or production any Document, statement, oral testimony or inspection for any of the following reasons:

    (a) lack of sufficient relevance to the case or materiality to its outcome;

General discussion

9.06 Under article 9.2(a) a tribunal is permitted to exclude from the arbitral record, or deny a request for the production of any evidence that lacks sufficient relevance to the case or materiality to its outcome. The formula "relevant to the case" and "material to its outcome" is discussed above in Chapter 3 as it relates to requests for document production (see comment to article 3.7), therefore that material will not be reiterated here. In this section relevance and materiality are considered in the context of the admissibility of evidence generally.

9.07 A tribunal may declare evidence inadmissible due to a lack of relevance or materiality without necessarily violating a party's right to be heard. This principle has found support in various jurisdictions, such as a 2004 ruling by the Swiss Federal Tribunal in consideration of challenge to an ICC award.[5] The court described several instances in which a tribunal may bar evidence on the basis of relevance and materiality:

> The arbitral tribunal may refuse to admit evidence, without violating the right to be heard, if the evidence is insufficient to substantiate a contention, if the fact to be proven has already been

---

evidentiary rules of the place of arbitration. . . . The Arbitral Tribunal admit the impugned portions of the expert witness statements . . . whose relevance and materiality it shall assess in light of the other evidence tendered in the arbitration. The Arbitral Tribunal shall attribute to the impugned evidence the weight it concludes is appropriate in light of these factors." ICC Case No. 12124, *ICC Bulletin, 2010 Special Supplement: Decisions on ICC Arbitration Procedure*, pp. 33 and 34.

   5 "7 janvier 2004 – Tribunal fédéral, 1re Cour civile (4P.196/2003)", *ASA Bulletin*, Vol. 22, No. 3, pp. 592, 597 (2004).

established, if it lacks relevance or yet if the tribunal, having conducted an anticipatory evaluation of the evidence, comes to the conclusion that it is already convinced and the result of the requested probative measure would not modify its decision.[6]

9.08 It is often the case that international tribunals will adopt a liberal view with respect to the admissibility of evidence during the early phases of a dispute.[7] However, there are times when a tribunal may deny the admittance of evidence, even early on, because it is already clear that the proffered "proof" will not be helpful to resolving the dispute. Such rulings are covered by article 9.2(a) and are discussed further below.

Relevance to the case

9.09 The standard "relevance to the case" is often understood as implicating the probative value of certain evidence as it relates to a party's burden of proof. Therefore a tribunal's analysis as to whether evidence should be excluded because it is irrelevant may be strongly influenced by the allegations presented in the case.[8] If a tribunal has an objection before it as to the admissibility of evidence relevance, according the customary approach, calls for a consideration of whether the proffered information is likely to be necessary for a party to prove an allegation or defense.[9]

9.10 An example in which a tribunal considered the issue of relevance as it relates to admissibility may be taken from an ICC arbitration conducted in Paris, presided over by a sole arbitrator. During the hearing a witness had been called to give evidence concerning a licence to produce pharmaceutical products. In the course of oral testimony, after cross-examination had continued for a reasonable duration, the questioning turned to matters

---

6   *Ibid.*, "Le tribunal arbitral peut refuser d'administrer une preuve, sans violer le droit d'être entendu, si le moyen de preuve est inapte à fonder une conviction, si le fait à prouver est déjà établi, s'il est sans pertinence ou encore si le tribunal, en procédant à une appréciation anticipée des preuves, parvient à la conclusion que sa conviction est déjà faite et que le résultat de la mesure probatoire sollicitée ne peut plus la modifier" (unofficial translation) "The arbitral tribunal may refuse to allow certain evidence without violating the right to be heard, if the evidence is unfit to base a conviction, if the fact to prove is already established, if it is irrelevant or if the court, by making an advance assessment of the evidence, reaches the conclusion that its conviction has already been formed and that the result of the probationary measure requested can no longer modify that conviction."

7   ". . . [T]he admission of evidence before international tribunals has much in common with the approach of courts in countries of the civilian legal tradition in that there is a tendency to avoid a restrictive approach to the admissibility of evidence." Chester Brown, *A Common Law of International Adjudication, International Courts and Tribunals Series*, p. 91 (2009).

8   For example, reference may be had to the decision of an arbitrator under the ICC rules who in the course of the disclosure phase of the arbitral proceedings had determined that evidence of a French patent could not be introduced into the arbitration. The arbitrator deemed the evidence irrelevant to the arguments before him as it was related to another dispute in a separate arbitration. In a later phase, however, it became clear that one of the central arguments in the case turned on the existence of the patent. Therefore, the arbitrator was required to consider the factual support for the patent's existence, and hence allowed in evidence pertaining to it. ICC Case No. 5480, Final Award, *ICC Bulletin*, Vol. 4, No. 2 (1993).

9   In *A._____ v Nationale Anti-Doping Agentur Deutschland*, 4A_178/2014, the Swiss Federal Tribunal summarised the issue well: "the right to be heard is not without limit, even in arbitral proceedings. Thus, the arbitral tribunal is not forbidden from establishing the facts only on the basis of the evidence it considers suitable and relevant (citations omitted). The arbitral tribunal may waive the administration of evidence when the corresponding submission concerns facts that are not legally relevant, when the evidence is obviously inadequate or when the arbitral tribunal has already reached its opinion on the basis of the evidence already heard and may conclude on the basis of a preliminary assessment of the new evidence that introducing further evidence will not change its conclusion (citations omitted). The assessment of evidence in advance by an international arbitration tribunal may be reviewed in an appeal only from the limited point of view of a violation of public policy (citations omitted)."

which the arbitrator understood as relating to the witness' own liability. As the testimony that the cross-examining party was attempting to elicit was not clearly relevant to the arguments in the case, since the witness was not a party (or an employee of the party), the tribunal ruled that further questioning (and thus responses) would be inadmissible. The arbitrator set forth his reasons as follows:[10]

> I am not willing to expose [the witness] to any conceivable prejudice to his own position or to (Respondent's) position in circumstances where I do not believe this Tribunal is adequately provided with the evidence or the means to carry those things through to their proper and logical conclusion.[11]

9.11 The above example illustrates the authority arbitrators may exercise to exclude evidence on relevance grounds (see also the comments to article 8.2). As in the example quoted above, a tribunal may exercise this authority in order to stop the line of questioning on points that bear no direct connection to a contention a party is tasked with proving, determine not to hear certain witnesses,[12] or in relation to documentary

---

10 As quoted in the Court of Appeal's judgment: *Generica Ltd v Pharmaceutical Basics*, 125 F.3d 1123 (7th Cir. 1997).

11 *Generica, ibid.*, p. 1131. See also the rule adopted by the tribunal in ICC Case No. 12990: "[t]he Arbitral Tribunal shall at all times have complete control over the procedure for hearing a witness. The Arbitral Tribunal may in its discretion . . . limit or refuse the right of a party to examine a witness when it appears that a question has been addressed by other evidence or is irrelevant." ICC Case No. 12990, Procedural Order of 12 May 2004, *ICC Bulletin, 2010 Special Supplement: Decisions on ICC Arbitration Procedure*, p. 87. See also: "[l]ikewise the Arbitral Tribunal will have the right to limit or deny the Parties the right to examine an expert when they determine at their discretion that the experts do not contribute to establishing relevant technical questions." ICC Case No. 12761, Procedural Order of 12 March 2004, *ICC Bulletin, 2010 Special Supplement: Decisions on ICC Arbitration Procedure*, p. 74. As noted in this decision, the right to deny admission to evidence must also be balanced against the fair opportunity for a party to present their case. See also the following consideration of this issue under Swiss law in ICC Case No. 12575: "[d]ue process (*le droit d'etre entendu, Rechtliches Gehör*) both under art. 182(3) of the Swiss Federal Private International Law Act, 1987 ('the 1987 Act') and art. 15(2) ICC Rules includes the right of each Party to present its case by filing submissions and evidence. When evidence is filed by a party the other is entitled under the same principle to challenge such evidence and, affirmatively, to file evidence in rebuttal. Under these rules each Party is therefore entitled to challenge relevant witness evidence submitted by the other and a breach of, such principle may result in an arbitral award to be set aside under art. 190(2)(d) of the 1987 Act." ICC Case No. 12575, Procedural Order of 16 December 2003, *ICC Bulletin, 2010 Special Supplement: Decisions on ICC Arbitration Procedure*, p. 67.

12 See the decision of the Iran-US Claims Tribunal not to hear a witness because of his connection to a party: "[i]t was so decided that Mr. Jennings would not be heard as a witness, because he is the chairman of the board of directors of the Company and is therefore considered to be an interested party." *Economy Forms Corp v The Government of the Islamic Republic of Iran*, Award No. 55-165-1 of 14 June 1983 (Dissenting Opinion of M. Kashani). This view is now inconsistent with art. 4.2. See also the position adopted by a reviewing US court in regard to a decision by an international arbitrator not to hear oral testimony from some witnesses: "[a]rbitrators must give both parties to the dispute an opportunity to present their evidence and argument. An award can be vacated if an arbitrator refuses to hear material and pertinent evidence. However, arbitrators are not required to hear *all* of the evidence, and are afforded broad discretion in determining what evidence is necessary, as long as they allow each party an 'adequate opportunity to present its evidence and argument.'" (Internal citations omitted) *Yonir Technologies Inc v Duration Systems (1992) Ltd*, 244 F.Supp. 2d 195, 209 (SDNY 2002). In *Euroflon Tekniska Producter AB v Flexiboys I Motala AB*, Case No. Ö 1590-11, the Swedish Supreme Court stated that: "in order for a document to be considered to be of importance as evidence, it is required that it can be assumed that the document adds something to the existing evidence. The arbitral tribunal, which appears to have rather wide discretion to reach its decisions, can deny such a motion if the evidence relates to irrelevant circumstances or if the issue has been sufficiently clarified through the existing evidence. However, the arbitral tribunal is not entitled to deny such a motion in cases where the taking of evidence before a court is called for. Since the court shall try the matter with respect to its legality (citations omitted), the arbitral tribunal shall typically also try the matter in this respect, so as to avoid decisions that are rendered irrelevant." *Ibid.*, p. 6. Regarding the issue of discretion, the

evidence, it may decline to receive information it believes would not have sufficient probative value.[13] In connection with the above, one may also consider the issue of evidence introduced to impeach a witness. While nothing in the IBA Rules or arbitral practice in general would prevent a party from introducing evidence to attack a witness' credibility based on, for example, prior statements which are inconsistent with their proffered testimony, tribunals may exclude evidence they believe will not materially affect a witness' credibility.[14]

9.12 Finally, evidence introduced on a point which is no longer in contention may also fall into the designation of irrelevant. Where an issue has been conceded, a tribunal may declare that no further evidence on this point should be introduced under article 9.2(a), as was noted by the chairman of an ICC tribunal: "If a party concedes a fact asserted by the other side, there is normally no reason to order further evidence in the form of documents, witness statements etc . . .".[15]

Material to the outcome of the case

9.13 Unlike relevance, objections to the admissibility of evidence based upon a lack of materiality under article 9.2(a) invoke the tribunal's view of the case and not the party's burden of proof.[16] The issue under consideration here is whether the tribunal considers that the proffered evidence will affect its deliberations in reaching a final award.

Swedish Supreme Court has stated that: "[J]urisprudence holds an almost unanimous view that the courts should not review the decision of the arbitral tribunal that an order to disclose is reasonable." *Ibid.*, p. 6.

13 See the following decision of the Iran-US Claims Tribunal: "Claimant's request to submit minutes of witness testimony heard by the Experts in Boston and/or statements of these witnesses is denied. The Tribunal decides that notes taken by assistance clerks of testimony by witnesses before the Experts cannot be considered appropriate evidence." *Chas T. Main International, Inc v Khuzestan Water & Power Utility et al.*, Case No. 120, Order of 14 February 1986. See also the decision in a Society of Maritime Arbitrators case, where the tribunal would not consider documents establishing an agreed credit due to the charterer because it was connected to another transaction between the same parties. In the view of the tribunal, evidence relating to a separate agreement was not relevant to the party's individual cases, and thus the evidence was inadmissible. *Orient Shipping Rotterdam BV v Sealift Inc*, Final Award in Case No. 3309, SMAAS, WL 34483931 (1996).

14 In the ICSID arbitration *Giovanna a Beccara v Argentine Republic*, the tribunal excluded from the record legal opinions that had been rendered in prior arbitral proceedings by expert witnesses providing testimony in the matter before them. The intention of the respondent party in seeking to introduce the evidence was to impeach the experts currently adverse to its case with allegedly inconsistent testimony concerning the legal interpretation of the relevant international treaty. Present in the controversy over admissibility was the issue of the confidential nature of the documents since they had been given in a prior arbitration over which confidentiality had been ordered. But the tribunal's analysis of the admissibility question also considered the relevance the prior testimony would have in regard to the rebuttal of the present testimony of the witnesses. The tribunal considered the fact that experts often give opinions influenced by a particular set of instructions, and are relative to differing fact patterns, and thus to be relevant, context must be given to the prior opinion to determine whether it was truly inconsistent with the testimony in the present case: "[t]he exercise of putting the relevant expert opinions back into their original context would not only be a very time consuming exercise, but also a very delicate and difficult one . . .". *Giovanna a Beccara v Argentine Republic*, ICSID Case No. ARB/07/5, Procedural Order No. 3, para. 147 (27 January 2010).

15 ICC Case No. 6465, Procedural Order, Dominique Hascher (ed.), *Collection of Procedural Decisions in ICC Arbitration 1993–1996*, p. 82 (2nd edition, 1998).

16 See: *Euroflon Tekniska Producter AB v Flexiboys I Motala AB*, *supra* at 12: "[T]he actual purpose of an order to disclose is that the documents within the scope of the order should grant the tribunal access to evidence relevant for the review of the merits of the case. Thus, orders for disclosure serve to ensure the efficacy of arbitration proceedings and not to form the basis of any future review by the courts." *Ibid.*, p. 7.

9.14 It is axiomatic that for a tribunal to rule that evidence is immaterial to the outcome of the case, it must in most instances have formed a view on the arguments before it. This will often occur only after the case has substantially progressed and the parties have for the most part laid out their arguments. If evidence is offered at such a point in the procedure, it may be that a tribunal would in the words of the Swiss Federal Tribunal, "come to the conclusion that it is already convinced [of a legal result] and the result of the requested probative measure would not modify its decision."[17]

9.15 An example of this scenario may be taken from the *International Military Services Ltd v Modsaf* decision of the Netherlands Supreme Court.[18] In this instance, the court reviewed the conduct of an ICC arbitral tribunal which had denied the claimant's petition to introduce new expert, as well as documentary, evidence at an advanced stage of the procedure. The request to submit extra evidence was denied on the basis that the tribunal had issued a preliminary finding on the matters in relation to which the petitioning party sought to submit evidence. Moreover, the proposing party had not sufficiently explained what it hoped to prove with the additional evidence.[19] The Netherlands Supreme Court, confirming the decision of lower court, The Hague Court of Appeal, upheld the determination by the arbitral tribunal to refuse to admit the new evidence as consistent with due process.[20]

9.16 A similar example is found in an *ad hoc* arbitration concerning an international reinsurance dispute. At an advanced stage of the proceedings the respondent attempted to introduce witness testimony concerning the proper construction of a disputed agreement. In this instance, the tribunal noted that it had already determined that the agreement was clear and unambiguous, therefore further extrinsic evidence was not needed. The tribunal did, however, invite limited written comments from the parties as to their views on the additional evidence and whether it should be admitted. Their method for determining the admissibility of the new evidence was described as follows: "the panel considered Century's witness statements containing the evidence that it would proffer . . . and concluded that the evidence was irrelevant or, at the very least, of very little probative value to the resolution of the issues in dispute."[21]

---

17 *Supra*, n. 4. See also the decision of the Iran-US Claims Tribunal to disregard evidence, over which an objection had been made because it was filed late. Instead of ruling on an objection to the lateness of the filing, the tribunal instead disregarded the evidence because, in the tribunal's view, it was immaterial to the outcome of the case. "The Tribunal finds that both the evidence presented with Document 182 and the documents submitted by the Claimants at the Hearing are irrelevant to the decision in this Case. Accordingly, the Tribunal need not reach the question of their admissibility." *Watkins-Johnson Co v Islamic Republic of Iran*, Award 429-370-1, para. 64 (1989). The above being said, where a tribunal is constituted under a very limited mandate and scope of review, it may be in the position to note at the outset of the case that certain evidence will be immaterial to its final award even if it has not yet informed itself sufficiently of the matters before it. Additionally, see for example the following comments of an ICSID annulment committee: "[n]ew arguments or evidence on the merits will therefore be irrelevant for the annulment process, and therefore not admissible. It cannot be excluded, however, that evidence, particularly expert evidence, may exceptionally be accepted in annulment proceedings insofar it is specifically relevant for the annulment grounds listed in art. 52(1) of the Convention (insofar invoked by a party)." Dietmar W. Prager and Samantha J. Rowe, "*Sempra Energy International v Argentina*, ICSID Case No. ARB/02/16, 29 June 2010", *A Contribution by the ITA Board of Reporters*, para. 74. See further: comments to art. 9.1.

18 *International Military Services Ltd v Ministry of Defence and Support for Armed Forces of the Islamic Republic of Iran*, Hoge Raad, Case No. C07/202HR (2009).

19 *Ibid.*, para. 4.4.

20 *Ibid.*, para. 4.4.2.

21 *Century Indemnity Co v Certain Underwriters at Lloyd's*, 584 F.3d 513, 557 (3rd Cir. Pa. 2009). See also the decision by the tribunal in ICC Case No. 10416 not to hear additional witnesses proffered by the respondent.

9.17 In summary therefore, when a party proffers new "proof", and based on the nature of the issue which the evidence pertains to, a tribunal finds that it isn't likely[22] that such information would affect its final award, it is within its authority to deny admissibility of the evidence under article 9.2(a).

Evidentiary privileges

Article 9.2 2010 IBA Rules: The Arbitral Tribunal shall, at the request of a Party or on its own motion, exclude from evidence or production any Document, statement, oral testimony or inspection for any of the following reasons:

   . . .

   (b)   legal impediment or privilege under the legal or ethical rules determined by the Arbitral Tribunal to be applicable;

   . . .

Article 9.3 2010 IBA Rules: In considering issues of legal impediment or privilege under Article 9.2(b), and insofar as permitted by any mandatory legal or ethical rules that are determined by it to be applicable, the Arbitral Tribunal may take into account:

   (a)   any need to protect the confidentiality of a Document created or statement or oral communication made in connection with and for the purpose of providing or obtaining legal advice;

   (b)   any need to protect the confidentiality of a Document created or statement or oral communication made in connection with and for the purpose of settlement negotiations;

   (c)   the expectations of the Parties and their advisors at the time the legal impediment or privilege is said to have arisen;

   (d)   any possible waiver of any applicable legal impediment or privilege by virtue of consent, earlier disclosure, affirmative use of the Document, statement, oral communication or advice contained therein, or otherwise; and

---

In that dispute over a know-how license agreement, the respondent had argued, as a defense to its failure to render payment, that the know-how transferred to it was deficient. Finding that the evidence presented in the case established firmly that the know-how was not deficient, and moreover, determining that the witnesses to be proffered by the respondent would not have offered further witness testimony of contemporaneous facts on this point, but rather evidence as to industry practice, the tribunal regarded such testimony as immaterial to its decision on the issues before it. Thus the tribunal denied the respondent's application to hear the additional witness testimony. ICC Case No. 10416, Final Award, (2000) (unpublished). See further: *Phoenix Aktiengesellschaft v Ecoplas Inc*, 391 F.3d 433 (2d Cir. NY 2004), a decision of the US courts rejecting a challenge to the exercise of the arbitrator's discretion in ICC Case No. 10416 not to hear additional witnesses.

22 In the *William Ralph Clayton v Canada* arbitration, under the UNCITRAL Rules, the tribunal followed the following formula: "the tribunal does not consider that there is any *reasonable likelihood* that any negotiation documents that NAFTA Parties have kept confidential for about two decades would, if now produced, alter the Tribunal's interpretation and application of those provisions." *William Ralph Clayton et al. v Government of Canada*, NAFTA/UNCITRAL, PCA Case No. 2009-04, Procedural Order No. 8, p. 3 (2009).

> **(e) the need to maintain fairness and equality as between the Parties, particularly if they are subject to different legal or ethical rules.**

Other statement of the rule:	
Principle 18.1	Effect should be given to privileges, immunities, and
ALI/UNIDROIT Principles:	similar protections of a party or non-party concerning disclosure of evidence or other information.[23]

General discussion

9.18 The subject of evidentiary privileges has caused considerable debate amongst academics and practitioners of international arbitration as is illustrated by the comment of one prominent arbitrator when he said, "the only thing that is clear is that nothing is clear in this area."[24] The complexity this subject become obvious if one considers two equally true facts about international arbitration procedure: one, domestic rules of evidentiary procedure, including privilege, are not directly applicable to an international arbitration;[25] and two, a properly invoked evidentiary privilege constitutes grounds for either denying a request for disclosure or the admissibility of evidence.[26] As it is generally accepted that there is not at present an all encompassing and universal set of rules governing evidentiary privileges – owing to the widely varying approaches to the matter found in different jurisdictions – an international arbitrator is often left to determine the applicable privilege rule by sifting through various sources of law in an

---

23 This statement of the rule outside of the IBA Rules sums up a generally accepted approach. Some institutions have incorporated reference to issues of privilege and the general approach to this issue set forth in article 9.2(b) and 9.3 of the IBA Rules. See, for example: article 23 of the ICDR Rules.

24 As reported in Klaus P. Berger, "Evidentiary Privileges: Best Practice Standards versus/and Arbitral Discretion", *Arbitration International*, Vol. 22, No. 4, p. 515 (2006). The definition of evidentiary privileges may be taken from a rather influential article by Fabian von Schlabrendorff and Audley Sheppard from 2005, wherein the authors set forth a generally recognised understanding of evidentiary privileges: "[b]y evidentiary privileges, we mean those rules that allow a party to withhold a document or other evidence from the other side in contested proceedings, or from any one investigating or determining a complaint or dispute (e.g., police, regulatory authority, court or arbitral tribunal)." "Conflict of Legal Privileges in International Arbitration, an Attempt to Find a Holistic Solution" in Aksen *et al.* (eds), *Liber Amicorum in Honour of Robert Briner: Global Reflections on International Law, Commerce and Dispute Resolution*, p. 745 (2005).

25 See: comments to art. 9.1 (admissibility generally). See also the following comments from the tribunal in ICC Case No. 12169: "[t]he Tribunal is not bound by any strict rule of evidence. It may receive and rely upon any evidence it considers relevant and helpful and will determine the relevance, materiality and weight of the evidence before it," *ICC Bulletin, 2010 Special Supplement: Decisions on ICC Arbitration Procedure*, p. 35. See comments of the UNCITRAL tribunal in *Glamis Gold v United States of America* "The Tribunal observes that the law of the United States, both as to production of documents or to the privilege enjoyed by some set of documents, is not directly applicable to this arbitration. Rather document production in this arbitration is governed by art. 24 of the UNCITRAL Arbitration Rules and guided by the Parties' own agreements to production as evidenced in their February 24, 2005 letters." *Glamis Gold Ltd v United States of America*, NAFTA/UNCITRAL/ICSID, Decision on Parties' Requests for Production of Documents withheld on Grounds of Privilege, p. 3 (17 November 2005).

26 "The attorney-client privilege, which is widely applied in domestic legal systems, has been recognized in public international law and international commercial arbitration rules and arbitral awards. The privilege applies to corporate entities as well as to individuals; when claimed for corporate entities it obtains with respect to those who are authorized to participate in the decisions." *Dr Horst Reineccius et al. v Bank for International Settlements*, Tribunal Regarding the Bank for International Settlements/PCA, Procedural Order No. 6, p. 10 (11 June 2002).

attempt to find an appropriate solution to this issue.[27] Even with respect to the method for determining which source of law should provide an applicable rule of privilege, here too there has historically been diversity of opinion.[28] The above notwithstanding, and as discussed below, there has emerged international consensus on some aspects of this issue, but not all.

9.19 In this regard the IBA Rules are the primary body of principles providing guidance on this question. Article 9.2(b) of the 2010 IBA Rules reaffirms the accepted principle that a rule of legal impediment or privilege, if found to be applicable, does serve as a rule of exclusion. In the 1999 version of the Rules, article 9.2(b) was the only provision to address evidentiary privileges; however, in the 2010 revision, article 9.3 was added to provide further guidance on this issue.

Guiding principles in determining the appropriate rule of privilege

9.20 Evidentiary privileges in domestic practice may be an issue of procedural law, professional ethics or substantive law, depending on the jurisdiction.[29] The importance of this categorisation is somewhat muted in international arbitration because the issue of privilege is primarily treated as one of evidentiary procedure.[30] It follows from this

---

27 "The mosaic of cultures and legal regimes raises substantial questions when the time comes to determine how to deal with a privilege claim. The variety of domestic rules on privilege is so significant that disputes on applicable regimes or standards are frequently foreseeable. Faced with such questions, tribunals need to determine whether the party refusing disclosure holds an evidentiary privilege enforceable as such within the international proceedings." Guido S. Tawil and Ignacio J. Mirorini Lima, "Privilege-Related Issues in International Arbitration", in T. Giovannini and A. Mourre (eds), *ICC Publication Dossier VI: Written Evidence and Discovery in International Arbitration*, p. 30 (2009).

28 "Privilege determinations in international arbitration today are particularly complex because there are no established choice-of-law rules that govern these determinations . . .". Javier H. Rubinstein and Britton B. Guerrina, "The Attorney-Client Privilege and International Arbitration", *Journal of International Arbitration*, Vol. 18, No. 6, p. 590 (2001).

29 Speaking with regard to the civil law approach, Tawil and Lima summarise the situation as follows: "civil law countries generally speak of the attorney-client privilege in terms of 'professional secret'. It is deemed a procedural issue, rather than a substantive one, whose abidance is generally seen both as a legal and ethical obligation pertaining to counsel as a matter of public policy." Tawil and Lima, *supra* n. 27, p. 33.

30 The approach of the IBA Rules is generally in line with those who recognise the procedural ramifications of a rule of privilege, irrespective of how it may be cast in domestic laws: "[a]s far as privileges are concerned, it must be noted that even if characterized as issues of substantive law due to their underlying policy judgments, their effects are felt in the area of the taking of evidence." Berger, *supra* n. 24, p. 515. See also the following statement on protecting privileges in cross-border situations in the statement issued by Council of Bars and Law Societies of Europe, entitled *Protection of Confidences Between European Lawyer and Client*: "[c]onfidential communications between a client and a lawyer from one Member State, as a consequence of what has been mentioned, must be protected also in any other Member State as if such lawyer were a lawyer of such other Member State, regardless of how the protection is legally operated (right to deny testimony and protection of files against investigation and seizure by virtue of professional secrecy or confidentiality or legal privilege etc.). What matters is the result that, and not how, the protection is achieved." *Protection of Confidences between European Lawyer and Client* (December 2004). As an example of a professional rule of ethics applied as a procedural principle in arbitration see the excerpt quoted from ICC Case No. 6653, at n. 49 below. The above notwithstanding, some have suggested that some rules of privilege may be characterised as a matter of substantive law which may raise issues of party autonomy. See, for instance, the following comments of Mosk and Ginsburg: "[o]n the other hand, if privileges are considered to be substantive law, then the arbitrators might be required under principles of party autonomy to apply the governing law in determining what rules apply to the assertion of privileges." Although the authors go on to comment concerning privilege that: "they are not usually considered to be part of the substantive

principle that a mere choice of a substantive law in a contract does not extend to issues of privilege.[31]

9.21 Under article 9.2(b), a tribunal may apply either a legal or ethical rule of privilege to declare evidence inadmissible or protected from disclosure. Therefore, the classification of an evidentiary privilege as a rule of ethics or law (either substantive or procedural) in domestic law does not affect an international arbitral tribunal's right to apply it as a procedural rule of exclusion.

9.22 When determining whether a rule of privilege may apply, a tribunal must consider applicable mandatory law. In this regard, the tribunal will likely look to the *lex arbitri*, which in most cases will require, if nothing else, that a party has a right to a fair opportunity to state its case and to be treated with equality. Rules of mandatory law have implications for the determination and application of a rule of privilege as will be explored further below.[32]

---

law that governs the transaction." Richard Mosk and Tom Ginsburg, "Evidentiary Privileges in International Arbitration", *International & Comparative Law Quarterly*, Vol. 50, p. 377 (April 2001). Von Schlabrendorff and Sheppard, also note this point: "[t]his acknowledgement that legal privileges have a substantive character leads to the conclusion that international arbitrators do not have completely unfettered discretion in determining whether or not to recognize them." Fabian von Schlabrendorff and Audley Sheppard, "Conflict of Legal Privileges in International Arbitration: An Attempt to Find a Holistic Solution", in Aksen *et al.* (eds), *Liber Amicorum in Honour of Robert Briner: Global Reflections on International Law, Commerce and Dispute Resolution* (2005), p. 765. The authors quoted above generally seem to agree that privilege does pose procedural issues even where it is contained in the substantive law, and that arbitrators have flexibility in dealing with this issue. Mosk and Ginsburg conclude: "[a]s privileges have both procedural and substantive qualities, arbitrators must turn to other consideration in determining whether privileges should be accepted. The discretion generally accorded to international arbitrators with regard to evidentiary matters and the inherent power of arbitrators to run the proceedings provides some flexibility". *Id.*, at p. 377.

31 In *The Titan Corporation v Alcatel CIT SA*, Svea Court of Appeal, T 1038-05, 28 February 2005, an ICC arbitration held in Sweden, the Claimant (a US company) challenged the Award at the Svea Court of Appeal against Respondent (a French company). Regarding admissibility of evidence: "during the course of the Project, between 2000 and 2002 and before this arbitration started, there were many meetings and correspondence between representatives of Alcatel and Titan. These considered the ongoing relations between the parties, what actions were to be taken, problems and solutions were reviewed, and finance and outstanding payments were discussed. Both parties have referred to various of these meeting minutes and letters in support of their contentions in this arbitration." *Ibid.*, §118. Essentially, Respondents claimed that the documents regarding those meetings constituted "genuine attempts to settle the dispute that is the subject of this arbitration" and that "all offers made to settle the disputes were such that the non-recourse nature of the Project was preserved . . . and that the correspondence upon which Alcatel is attempting to rely is protected by the without prejudice rule." *Ibid.*, §112. The Sole Arbitrator found that the documents were admissible: "the issue of admissibility of evidence is not to be determined by the law governing the substantive issues in the dispute – here English law. This is an issue for the law governing this procedure and the law of the place of arbitration, i.e., Swedish law. Nothing was expressly agreed by the parties affecting the admissibility or nature of the letters in question. The ICC Rules according to which this arbitration is conducted require the arbitrator to determine the facts by 'all appropriate means'. (Article 20(1)) Furthermore, in this arbitration, the Sole Arbitrator has the power to determine the procedure to follow ' "in his absolute discretion' (Paragraph 60 Terms of Reference) and to determine 'the admissibility of evidence in his sole discretion' (Paragraph 13 Procedural Order No 1, 30 April 2003)." *Ibid.*, §115. In essence, the arbitrator held that "there was no express agreement that the meetings and correspondence were without prejudice and there is no basis to imply such an agreement." *Ibid.*, §116. Furthermore, the Sole Arbitrator found that "the six documents which Titan states should not be admitted in this arbitration are not significantly different to other documents in which Titan's liability to pay invoices has been acknowledged and arrangements for payment discussed". *Ibid.*, §118.

32 Berger notes the following: "[a]rbitral due process has thus a dual role to play in the taking and evaluation of evidence by the tribunal. On one side, in order to protect their award from annulment, international arbitrators are generally careful not to exclude evidence in a way that could arguably prejudice one side's right to present its case. On the other side, they are also reluctant to deny exclusion of evidence if such denial would amount to a clear violation of one party's right for fair and equal treatment." Berger, *supra* n. 24, p. 518.

9.23 The above notwithstanding, it is most often the case that neither mandatory law nor the arbitration law of the seat will contain a rule of privilege that is directly applicable to an international arbitration. Instead, a better source of guidance has emerged via various international authorities that have considered this question. Pursuant to this body of work, international practice yields the following principles that often frame a privilege analysis: (1) tribunals should accede to objections based on recognised rules of privilege where a party has legitimately invoked them; (2) tribunals should ensure that the legitimate reliance of a party on a privilege is upheld so as to avoid unfair surprise;[33] and (3) a tribunal's general duty to ensure procedural fairness and to avoid serious procedural irregularities also applies to the application of rules of privilege as between the parties.[34]

9.24 The subparagraphs of article 9.3 build upon these three principles and are to be read in conjunction with article 9.2(a).[35] The structure of article 9.3 suggests that subparagraphs (a) and (b) may be regarded as restatements of transnational or general rules of evidentiary privilege that may be applied on their own.[36] Where a tribunal finds that it is not appropriate

---

33 These first two principles are formulated in substantially the same manner by Berger, *supra* n. 24, p. 518: "[h]owever, we have seen that there is also consensus that international arbitrators should accede to an appropriate privilege objection raised in good faith." Also at p. 502: "As in any other field of international arbitration law, a 'trial by ambush', i.e., unfair surprise of parties who have relied on the protection standard of a certain evidentiary privilege, must be avoided." Moreover, in addition to what is described here, it should also be noted that tribunals confronted with privilege issues have considered the problem having regard to what they considered to be the unique context of international arbitration. For example, the following point raised by an ICSID tribunal where the procedure was governed by the UNCITRAL Rules in its analysis of privilege notes this factor: "[t]he Tribunal then used this information combined with the knowledge of an appreciation for the differences between court proceedings and international arbitration, to craft standards that can assist the Parties in assessing their claims of privilege and their objections to such claims." *Glamis Gold v United States of America, supra* n. 25, para. 20.

34 These three criteria are cited by Craig Tevendale and Ula Cartwright-Finch, "Privilege in International Arbitration: is it time to recognize the consensus?", *Journal of International Arbitration*, Vol. 26, No. 6, pp. 823–828 (2009). Von Schlabrendorff and Sheppard mention the following three similar points which they regard as guiding principles for determining the applicable privilege: "[t]he first expectation is that communications which are privileged when made will remain privileged . . . the second expectation of parties involved in international arbitration is that the arbitral tribunal's decisions are made on the basis of the applicable law . . . the third expectation is that parties that agree to resolve a dispute by arbitration will be treated by the arbitral tribunal in a fair and reasonable manner." Von Schlabrendorff and Sheppard, *supra* n. 34.

35 "The Subcommittee provided additional non-binding guidance on determining the applicable privileges in Article 9.3. Although the standard to be applied is left to the discretion of the arbitral tribunal, it is desirable that the tribunal take account of the elements set forth in Article 9.3." Review Subcommittee, "Commentary on the revised text of the 2010 IBA Rules on the Taking of Evidence in International Arbitration", p. 25 (2010) available at www.ibanet.org. In commenting on the potential form which rules on privilege could take in 2007, noted arbitrator Henri Alvarez stated: "[i]n order to achieve sufficient acceptance, any harmonized set of rules will have to be general in nature. This is particularly so in the case of privilege given the highly fact-intensive or specific nature of the circumstances in which privilege issues in international arbitration are likely to arise . . . any harmonized rules eventually developed will have to remain general and flexible in nature and arbitral discretion will continue to play an important role." Henri Alvarez, "Evidentiary Privileges in International Arbitration", in Albert Jan van den Berg (ed.), *Back to Basics? ICCA Congress Series 2006*, Montreal, Vol. 13, pp. 663, 684 (2007). It would appear that this is the approach which has been taken to the drafting of art. 9.3, insofar as the principles stated there are general and do allow for tribunals to exercise their discretion in applying them.

36 In commenting on art. 9.3(a), Berger states the following: "[t]he attorney-client privilege to which this provision refers, relates to communications between an attorney and his or her client in the course of, or in anticipation of legal advice. It is generally accepted today in many jurisdictions all over the world." Klaus P. Berger, "Evidentiary privileges under the Revised IBA rules," *International Arbitration Law Review*, Vol. 13, No. 5, p. 172 (2010). Berger also accepts that art. 9.3(b) is a transnational rule. The Review Subcommittee noted that the rule set forth in art. 9.3(a): ". . . seeks to encompass both the common law understanding of attorney-client

to apply the rules in subparagraphs (a) and (b), or that a more detailed rule is required, it may refer to the guiding criteria of subparagraphs (c) which calls for the consideration of the legitimate expectations of the parties. When deciding what those legitimate expectations might be, a tribunal may have recourse to accepted choice of law analyses (see comments to article 9.3(c) below). Furthermore, that a party may waive a privilege is accepted under article 9.3(d) as a principle of international arbitration procedure – nevertheless a tribunal may be required to consider various local or domestic rules on waiver when determining this issue. Finally, reference should also be had to fundamental procedural law when conducting a determination of this issue, as article 9.3(e) requires the tribunal to consider principles of mandatory law such as fairness and equality.

9.25 A point of procedure that also bears mention is that it is the party asserting the privilege who has the burden of proof.[37] This is true for both proving which legal on privilege is to apply and proving the factual basis for the assertion of privilege. Tribunals have in the past requested the moving party to produce a list of documents over which privilege is claimed, setting forth a description of the document (including a brief summary of the subject matter), the author and recipients, and the legal basis for the asserted privilege.[38] In cases where further investigation is merited, tribunals have asked for affidavits from the legal advisor who authored the document, or from witnesses who can attest to its purpose, as a means of establishing the facts around the asserted claim of privilege.[39]

---

privilege and the civil law understanding of the duty of professional secrecy," and in relation to art. 9.3(b) states, "art. 9.3(b) expresses a generalized understanding of the so-called 'without prejudice' or 'settlement' privilege, which is recognized in certain jurisdictions and relates to the contents of settlement negotiations." Review Subcommittee, *supra* n. 35, p. 25.

37 See the decision of the Iran-US Claims Tribunal in which it was noted that attorney-client privilege may not be presumed, but rather it is the party who seeks to rely on it: "who carr[ies] the duty to assert the alleged privilege in response to a timely request for information from the Respondent." *Edgar Protiva, Eric Protiva v The Islamic Republic of Iran*, Case No. 316, Award No. 566-316-2, para. 34 (12 October 1989). See the following ruling of the UNCITRAL tribunal in *Glamis Gold v United States of America*: "[t]he Tribunal notes that the party asserting the privilege has the burden of proving that such privilege applies to each document but, after that showing is made, the burden shifts to the other party to contest their privilege." *Glamis Gold Ltd v United States of America, supra* n. 25, Decision on Parties' Requests for Production of Documents withheld on Grounds of Privilege, p. 4.

38 "The Tribunal orders the Claimants to prepare a schedule of all the documents falling within the scope of the Respondent's request, taking into account the Tribunal's observations on relevance and materiality above, briefly setting forth the author and recipient, date and type of document and the basis for the privilege claimed in respect of each document." See the discussion in *Tidewater Inc et al. v Bolivarian Republic of Venezuela*, ICSID Case No. ARB/10/5, Procedural Order No. 1, para. 42 (29 March 2011). See also the decision of a Society of Maritime Arbitrators' tribunal, that set forth the basic requirement that a party must plead sufficient facts in order to avail itself of a privilege protection: "[a]s a general rule, the burden of establishing the existence of an attorney-client privilege rests with the party asserting it, Tidewater in this case. The privilege is strictly construed, and readily waived, because it tends to inhibit and limit the full benefit of discovery. A party asserting the privilege cannot carry its burden by asserting the right in a blanket fashion. The privilege must be specifically raised, and the party seeking to invoke it must demonstrate why the particular material being demanded should be afforded the protection sought." *Tidewater Marine Service CA v Gulf of Paria East Operating Co*, Final Award in Case No. 3847, SMAAS, WL 5658896 (2004).

39 See, for instance, the direction of the tribunal in *OKO Osuuspankkien Keskuspankki Oyj v Estonia* of 9 September 2005, whereby the tribunal ordered that the respondent party, who was asserting the privilege, to provide: "[a] written account by either the two lawyers or by the Chairman of the said boards – or both – including a written account of the reasons for the involvement of the said lawyers at each of the litigious board meetings." *OKO Osuuspankkien Keskuspankki Oyj v Republic of Estonia*, ICSID Case No. ARB/04/6, Procedural Order of 9 September 2005, p. 2.

Article 9.3(a): any need to protect the confidentiality of a document created or statement or oral communication made in connection with and for the purpose of providing or obtaining legal advice

9.26 Attorney-client privilege has largely gained acceptance within international arbitration as a transnational rule of procedural law.[40] Recent jurisprudence of the International Court of Justice has affirmed that attorney-client privilege in all likelihood exists as a general procedural rule of public international law, applicable to arbitration and inclusive of the related protections afforded to attorney "work product". In the matter of *Questions relating to the Seizure and Detention of Certain Documents and Data (Timor-Leste v Australia)* the issue of whether Timor-Leste had, as a general principle of law, the right to expect that its communications with lawyers representing it in an arbitration with Australia would remain confidential and free from the latter's interference was put to the Court wherein it opined as follows:

> If a State is engaged in the peaceful settlement of a dispute with another State through arbitration or negotiations, it would expect to undertake these arbitration proceedings or negotiations without interference by the other party in the preparation and conduct of its case. It would follow that in such a situation, a State has a plausible right to the protection of its communications with counsel relating to an arbitration or to negotiations, in particular, to the protection of the correspondence between them, as well as to the protection of confidentiality of any documents and data prepared by counsel to advise that State in such a context.[41]
>
> The reference in the Court's decision to both communications and "documents and data prepared by counsel" indicates an acceptance of the privileged nature of attorney "work product" as well as communications between counsel and client.[42] Other international arbitral tribunals have accepted this position as well. [43] In light of these precedents, it seems well supported that

---

40 See also the following from the tribunal's decision in *Vito Gallo v Canada*: "[t]he Arbitral Tribunal is of the view that Solicitor-Client Privilege and analogous concepts of confidentiality are widely observed in different States. Thus it cannot be dispensed with [in] a proceeding governed by international law on the ground that domestic law is not the governing law." *Vito G. Gallo v Government of Canada*, NAFTA/ UNCITRAL/PCA, Procedural Order No. 3, p. 13 (8 April 2009). The following definition of attorney-client privilege is listed as Principle XII.6 on the Central List of Lex Mercatoria: "[a]ny communication between a client and his attorney which is made in the course of or in anticipation of legal proceedings or which relates to the giving of legal advice, i.e., the seeking of advice as to legal rights and obligations as opposed to general business matters, and which originates in a confidence that it will not be disclosed, is privileged and may not be introduced as evidence in court or arbitration proceedings." Available at www.trans-lex.org/968600. See also: Principle 18.1 ALI/UNIDROIT Principles. See further the articulation of privilege by the Council of Bars and Law Societies of Europe, in the *Charter of Core Principles of the European Legal Profession and Code of Conduct for European Lawyers*, General Principle 2.3.1: "[i]t is of the essence of a lawyer's function that the lawyer should be told by his or her client things which the client would not tell to others, and that the lawyer should be the recipient of other information on a basis of confidence. Without the certainty of confidentiality there cannot be trust. Confidentiality is therefore a primary and fundamental right and duty of the lawyer."

41 *Questions Relating to the Seizure and Detention of Certain Documents and Data (Timor-Leste v Australia)*, Provisional Measures Order (Int'l Ct. Justice, 3 March 2014). Decisions and documents of the ICJ are available at www.icj-cij.org).

42 *Ibid.*

43 See: *William Ralph Clayton, William Richard Clayton, Douglas Clayton, Daniel Clayton And Bilcon Of Delaware Inc v Government Of Canada*, Permanent Court of Arbitration (PCA) Case No. 2009-04, Procedural Order No. 12 (2012): "[t]he Respondent claims work product privilege over notations placed on 11 documents for purposes of document review in this arbitration. The Investors challenge the Respondent's assertion of work product privilege on the basis that the Respondent has not established the notations were prepared in anticipation of any litigation. The Respondent submits that '[a]s the notations also constitute confidential communications between a representative of the Government of Canada and legal counsel for the Government of Canada, for

article 9.3(a)'s reference to "any document" made "in connection" with providing legal advice covers attorney work-product materials.

In the context of the IBA Rules, the ICJ's jurisprudence lends support to the inclusion of article 9.3(a) in the 2010 Rules without reference to domestic law, as an accurate expression of attorney-client privilege as it exists in general international arbitration procedural law.[44] It follows that the basic definition of attorney-client privilege may be applied as a stand-alone rule of procedure without reference to domestic law, as was the case in ICSID arbitration *Tidewater et al. v Venezuela*, whereby the tribunal ruled, "The tribunal considers that, in principle, documents which it might otherwise be necessary to produce may legitimately be privileged from production if they consist of confidential documents 'made in connection with and for the purpose of providing or obtaining legal advice'."[45] Article 9.3(a) expresses the rule of privilege in a basic form.

9.27 An arbitral precedent that further supports this view is the *Bank for International Settlements* arbitration. A question before the tribunal in this instance was whether shareholders of the bank had a right to the discovery of legal advice given to the bank's management, including memorandums authored by in-house counsel. The tribunal's analysis is partially reproduced below:

> The attorney-client privilege, which is widely applied in domestic legal systems, has been recognized in public international law and international commercial arbitration rules and arbitral awards. The privilege applies to corporate entities as well as to individuals; when claimed for corporate entities it obtains with respect to those who are authorized to participate in the decisions.
>
> At the core of the attorney-client privilege, which in both domestic and international law is the appreciation that those who must make decisions on their own or other's behalf are entitled to seek and receive legal advice and that the provision of a full canvas of legal options and the exploration and evaluation of their legal implications would be chilled, were counsel and their clients not assured in advance that the advice proffered along with communications related to it, would remain confidential and immune to discovery.
>
> *Ratione materiae*, the legal communications which are entitled to an attorney-client privilege must be related to making a decision that is in or is in contemplation of legal contention; *ratione personae*, the legal communications must be between an attorney (whether in-house or outside) and those who are afforded his or her professional advice for purposes of making or in contemplation of that decision.[46]

---

the use of legal counsel during document review, they are also subject to solicitor-client privilege.' The Tribunal agrees with the Respondent that the notations are protected by solicitor-client privilege as discussed above. Hence, the Tribunal need not decide whether the documents are also protected by work product privilege." *Ibid.*, p. 8.

44 The tribunal in *ACP Axos Capital GmbH v Republic of Kosovo* provided the following affirmation of this principle as it applies to external counsel: "[a]s a general principle, the Tribunal accepts the widely recognized principle that legal advice provided by external legal counsel is covered by privilege and does not need to be justified. Therefore, the documents falling within this description of the *legal privilege* are excluded from production. However, the Parties have also asserted other types of privilege, as well as differing characterizations of legal privilege that do not fall within the above-stated definition. To the extent either Party wishes to rely on any privilege, other than the above-defined *legal privilege*, the source of the privilege must be specified and each category falling within that privilege must be identified." *ACP Axos Capital v Kosovo*, ICSID Case No. ARB/15/22, Procedural Order No. 2 (6 March 2017), para. 3.

45 *Tidewater v Venezuela*, *supra* n. 38, Procedural Order No. 1, para. 35. See also Mosk and Ginsburg where the following is noted concerning privilege as a general principle of law: "[a]rbitrators can consider whether certain privileges constitute a general principle of law that ought to be applied in the dispute, even if the choice-of-law analysis does not require arbitrators to do so. The fact that certain privileges are widespread suggests that they may indeed constitute a general principle that should be generally applied." Mosk and Ginsburg, *supra* n. 30, p. 379.

46 *Reineccius v Bank for International Settlements*, *supra* n. 26, Procedural Order No. 6, p. 10. *See also Tidewater v Venezuela*, *supra* n. 38, Procedural Order No. 1, para. 42. In the *Pac Rim Cayman v Ecuador* CAFTA

9.28 The considerations set forth above identify some of the key principles of a transnational rule on attorney-client privilege. By way of synopsis, the criteria adopted by the *Bank for International Settlements* tribunal may be considered as follows: (1) confidential legal advice[47] should be protected from disclosure in an international arbitration if, (2) the advice is given by a legal counsel[48] (3) who has been called upon to provide such advice to authorised decision-makers, (4) in contemplation of taking or otherwise making a decision in respect of a legal contention.[49] Moreover, as set forth by the tribunal in its analysis, this rule applies to the work of in-house counsel.[50]

---

arbitration administered under the ICSID Rules, the tribunal was confronted with the unusual situation of an outside legal counsel offering factual testimony in support of his client's own case. Similar to the *Bank for International Settlements* tribunal, the *Pac Rim* tribunal recognised attorney-client privilege as applicable in the matter without giving particular reference to a domestic or national law. However, in addition to this, this procedural scenario provides an interesting precedent for tribunals who receive testimony from in-house legal counsel who are also restricted in what matters they may reveal and which are covered by attorney-client privilege. In this regard, the concern expressed by the tribunal in the quote below could easily apply to testimony given by legal counsel in the employ of a party. On the second day of the hearing the tribunal instructed the attorney witness as follows: "[w]ell, I think we have to divide your role and be very careful. We are not asking you here to give evidence about what you do or don't do as a legal representative of the Respondents, but you are here as a fact witness. Now, if you can testify, to the best of your recollection, truthfully what [Mr. A] said to you, and you are going to be asked that question, as we understand, by counsel for the Claimant, you should answer that question as a fact witness." *Pac Rim Cayman LLC v Republic of El Salvador*, ICSID Case No. ARB/09/12, Hearing on Jurisdiction Day 2, Transcript at pp. 324–325 (2006).

47 In the *Protiva* case the Iran-US Claims Tribunal noted that the attorney-client privilege in international arbitration attaches to all matters a legal adviser may or may not have witnessed, and thus only pertains to confidential legal advice: "the attorney-client privilege protects only information an attorney has gained from his client in confidence under no rule of law known to the Tribunal could mere events witnessed by Mr. Behbahani in 1979 and 1980 in Iran represent protected information which he was under the obligation, as the Claimants' attorney, not to reveal." *Protiva v The Islamic Republic of Iran, supra* n. 37, [Final Arival], para. 35.

48 Note the following point raised by the *Glamis Gold* tribunal in relation to legal counsel in the employ of the government: "[t]he Tribunal recognizes that, when asserting this privilege, it is important to make clear that the attorney is indeed acting as such and providing legal advice, and is not acting as a policy-maker or corporate officer." *Glamis Gold v United States of America, supra* n. 25, Decision on Parties' Requests for Production of Documents withheld on Grounds of Privilege, p. 4.

49 Whether the recipient of the alleged privileged document is an "authorised" decision-maker may be determined by reference to: "whether the recipients of these documents were authorised by the relevant legal regime to participate in making the decision with respect to which the legal advice had been prepared." *Bank for International Settlements, supra* n. 26, Procedural Order No. 6, p. 11.

50 In connection with whether the privilege attaches to the work of in-house counsel, other international arbitral tribunals have also recognised that attorney-client privilege covers advice rendered by lawyers working as employees of a party. In the *CME Czech Republic BV v The Czech Republic* arbitration conducted under the UNCITRAL Rules, for example, the tribunal determined that: "Claimant was not obliged to submit privileged documents such as documents originated by its in-house legal advisors to the extent that such legal advice is related to legal proceedings or disputes between the Claimant and the Respondent and/or agencies . . .". *CME Czech Republic BV et al. v The Czech Republic*, UNCITRAL, Final Award, para. 64 (2006). In the often discussed *Akzo Nobel* decision of the European Court of Justice, the application of attorney-client privilege was narrowly interpreted so as to exclude the work of in-house legal counsel. *Akzo Nobel Chemicals Ltd and Akcros Chemicals Ltd et al. v European Commission*, European Court of Justice (Grand Chamber) Case C-550/07 P (14 September 2010). This development has led to considerable speculation as to whether in the whole of the EU legal privilege is no longer available to in-house legal advisers. One view would be that the *Akzo Nobel* decision is limited in application to the context of European-Commission conducted investigations, and would not necessitate that in international arbitrations seated in EU countries, or otherwise involving parties from the EU, that legal privilege no longer attaches to the work of in-house counsel. Given that, in the published arbitral decisions (cited above) of truly international tribunals, privilege was still extended to cover the work of in-house counsel, it would seem that there is support for extending this privilege to cover the work of lawyers who are employed on a full-time basis by the party asserting the privilege – in the context of international arbitration.

9.29 Building upon the *Bank for International Settlements* precedent, the UNCITRAL tribunal in the *Vito Gallo v Canada* case also affirmed the applicability of attorney-client privilege in international procedural law.[51] The tribunal fashioned four specific transnational rules that may be applied as general principles. In defining attorney-client privilege for international arbitration, the tribunal set forth the following points: (1) the document has to be drafted by a lawyer acting in his or her capacity as a lawyer (thus, persons qualified as lawyers but acting in a quasi-commercial role may not be covered); (2) a solicitor-client relationship based on trust must exist as between the lawyer (in-house or external adviser) and the client; (3) the document has to be prepared for the purpose of obtaining or giving legal advice; and (4) the lawyer and the client when giving and obtaining legal advice, must have acted with the expectation that the advice would be kept confidential in a contentious situation.[52] The *Vito Gallo* criteria line up generally with those set forth in the *Bank for International Settlements* case, although they are worded differently.[53]

9.30 Where legal advice is incorporated into a larger, multi-purpose document, generally only the portions of the document are connected to the legal advice would attract privilege. For example, in the context of a board meeting held for the purpose of considering the legal advice, the presumption often is that only those portions of meeting minutes recording and discussing "legal advice" are covered by privilege, whereas aspects of the minutes recording unrelated business strategy or other issues do not fall under legal privilege.[54]

9.31 In summary, therefore, there is significant authority supporting the view that attorney-client privilege has been accepted as a rule of procedure applicable to international arbitration, and is expressed in its basic form in article 9.3(a). One observes, however, that

---

51 The *Vito Gallo v Canada* tribunal, after affirming the general applicability of privilege as a rule of international arbitral procedure, noted in particular the *Bank for International Settlements* precedent as follows: "[t]he Arbitral Tribunal agrees in this respect with the procedural order of the tribunal in *First Eagle SoGen Funds Inc v Bank for International Settlements*, where it was found that the 'attorney-client privilege, which is widely applied in domestic legal systems, has been recognized in public international and international commercial arbitration rules and arbitral awards'". *Vito Gallo v Canada*, *supra* n. 40, Procedural Order No. 3, p. 13. See also: *Pope & Talbot v Canada* the tribunal also found that privilege should be formulated in a manner similar to the description of the rule stated in the *Bank for International Settlements* case (internal citations omitted): "[t]he Tribunal, accepts in general, the conclusion by Canada, that solicitor-client privilege extends to communications for the giving or seeking of legal advice. It rejects the contention on behalf of the Investor that the privilege is confined to legal advice given in contemplation of litigation." *Pope & Talbot Inc v Government of Canada*, NAFTA/UNCITRAL, Decision on Crown Privilege and Solicitor-Client Privilege, para. 1.9 (6 September 2000).

52 *Vito Gallo v Canada*, *supra* n. 40, Procedural Order No. 3, para. 47.

53 The *Vito Gallo* tribunal added that the parties must have acted with the expectation that the advice would be kept confidential as a fourth criteria. However, this factor is implicitly considered in the *Bank for International Settlements* decision where the tribunal states that the advice must be confidential in the first place. Thus the *Bank for International Settlements* tribunal also considered it important that the party claiming privilege had remained consistent with such a claim by treating the communication as confidential.

54 See the directions given by the tribunal in the *OKO Osuuspankkien Keskuspankki v Estonia*, *supra* n. 39, Procedural Order of 9 September 2005, whereby the tribunal requested in reaction to an assertion of a privilege over board meeting minutes an explanation: "clarifying why at least a redacted version of the minutes could not be disclosed, excising only those passages said to be privileged from production in these proceedings". In some instances, a tribunal may direct that information which is privileged should be redacted from the document. Consider the guidance given by an ICC tribunal as follows: "[e]ach Party is entitled to redact truly irrelevant information of a sensitive or confidential nature as well as privileged information. If a document is redacted, it should to the extent possible, not redact the information which permits a reader to identify the author, recipient, document type and date of the document. In the event such information is redacted, the Party making the redactions must provide the information in question to the other Party so that the basis for the redaction can be appropriately tested." Virginia Hamilton, "Document Production in ICC Arbitration", *ICC Bulletin, 2006 Special Supplement: Document Production in International Arbitration*, p. 77.

the cases discussing the issue of privilege in the transnational context have developed more detailed applications of the rule in article 9.3(a).

9.32 These more precise expressions of attorney-client privilege should be given consideration when applying this and in particular the factors described in the *Bank for International Settlements* case, and the four factors set forth in *Vito Gallo v Canada*. Nevertheless, it is accepted that there are times when a tribunal may find it more appropriate to consider domestic notions of attorney-client privilege, in which case reference may be had to article 9.3(c).

Article 9.3(b): any need to protect the confidentiality of a document created or statement or oral communication made in connection with and for the purpose of settlement negotiations

9.33 Communications exchanged during negotiations conducted towards achieving an amicable resolution to a known dispute may be subject to what is commonly referred to as a *settlement privilege*.[55] The inclusion of a settlement privilege in article 9.3(b) follows upon a growing consensus that there exists a common protection of settlement communications as a matter of procedural principles governing international arbitration.[56]

9.34 The settlement privilege set forth in subparagraph (b) has been previously developed in international case law to include the following: "declarations, admissions or proposals which the parties may have made during direct negotiations between themselves, when such negotiations have not led to complete agreement."[57] This expression of the settlement privilege relays an important distinction, which is that the "communication" falling under the settlement privilege need not have been exchanged in relation to a negotiation that was in contemplation of a total settlement of the case, but may have been part of an attempt to only settle an allegation.

9.35 One example of the acceptance of a "settlement privilege" as a matter of international arbitration law may be taken from the decision of an ICC tribunal which found communications exchanged during a settlement negotiation to be inadmissible based not only on French law, but also in international procedural law:

> The arbitral tribunal also considers that it is customary, not only in French law – where the custom is equally a rule of professional conduct for *avocats* – but also in the field of international commerce, that exchanges of proposals between parties with a view to reaching an agreement aimed at resolving a dispute submitted to a tribunal – arbitral or not – are and must remain confidential. If the parties have tried in good faith to reconcile their positions, one of them cannot, in the event the negotiations fail, use for its benefit the proposals of the other to deduce an alleged admission of fault.[58]

---

55 "While in many cases the law applicable to such a privilege objection must be determined by classical conflict of laws analysis, the situation is different with respect to the settlement privilege. Here, a transnational privilege exists which protects settlement negotiations both with and without the presence of a third neutral." Berger, *supra* n. 20, p. 514.

56 Berger writes persuasively in favour of the inclusion of the settlement privilege amongst the principles of transnational procedural law in Klaus P. Berger, "The Settlement Privilege – A General Principle of International ADR-Law", *Arbitration International*, Vol. 24, No. 2, pp. 265 et seq (2008).

57 *Chorzów Factory* case *(Germany v Poland)*, PCIJ, Judgment No. 13 (1928).

58 ICC Case No. 6653, in Jean-Jacques Arnaldez, Yves Derains and Dominique Hascher (eds), *Collection of ICC Arbitral Awards*, Vol. III, 1991–1995, p. 512 (1997). Translated in Jason Fry, "Without Prejudice and

9.36 The settlement privilege is also established in the jurisprudence of the Iran-US Claims Tribunal. In the *Mobil Oil v The Islamic Republic of Iran* arbitration, the panel recognised in a similar manner to the ICC example, the existence of this exclusionary rule as a part of international arbitration procedural law:

> It is well settled that a tribunal, which must decide a case subsequent to the failure of the parties to arrive at a settlement by way of negotiations, need not take into account the proposals and concessions that either party might have made in the course of such negotiations. The reason for this rule is obvious: such proposals and concessions have no purpose other than to allow an agreement to be attained and may well be very far from what each party considered to be its rights. Since such proposals were rejected they have lost all validity and have become meaningless.[59]

9.37 The above examples demonstrate that settlement communications are generally regarded to be inadmissible in international arbitration, and therefore article 9.3(b) may be applied as a standalone principle. It may be further noted that this principle covers communications exchanged in the course of mediation.[60] Mediation privilege is arguably a subset of the settlement privilege given that mediation is a process in which an impartial third-party facilitates settlement negotiations. International model laws, European directives and commonly accepted rules such as the ICC ADR Rules, all adopt the position that communications exchanged or made during a mediation conducted with a third-party mediator are confidential and may not be used in subsequent contentious proceedings.[61] The ICJ in the *Qatar v Bahrain* boundary dispute case recognised the confidential nature of mediation as well.[62]

Confidential Communications in International Arbitration (When Does Procedural Flexibility Erode Public Policy?)", *International Arbitration Law Review*, Vol. 1, No. 6, p. 212 (1998).

59 *Mobil Oil Iran Inc et al. v Government of the Islamic Republic of Iran, et al.*, Cases Nos 74, 76, 81, 150, Partial Award No. 311-74/76/81/150-3 (14 July 1987), Iran-USCTR, Vol. 16, 3, p. 55. See the following decision of the full tribunal of the Iran-US Claims Tribunal in the case *Islamic Republic of Iran v the United States of America*: "[w]ith respect to point (a), and Iran's reference to settlement negotiations held in August, 1981, a court cannot take account of that which one party proposes to another in a confidential manner in an effort to achieve a resolution of their disputes". As reported in David Caron, Lee Caplan, Matti Pellonpää, *The UNCITRAL Arbitration Rules, A Commentary*, p. 638 (2006). See also where the Iran-US Claims Tribunal noted in the *Frederica Riahi* case that it would not admit evidence of a telex because it related to settlement discussions: "[i]n addition, the Tribunal finds the content of the telex questionable since it relates to the position taken by one party when seeking a settlement with the other party. The Tribunal has in several instances found that positions taken by the parties during settlement negotiations are without prejudice to their respective rights." *Frederica Lincoln Riahi v Islamic Government of Iran*, Award 600-485-1, para. 52 (2003). See also the following further consideration from the Iran-US Claims Tribunal: ". . . it is not this Tribunal's practice to permit parties to proffer the terms of attempted settlements or the positions underlying them as admissions by which opposing parties should continue to be bound." *International School Services Inc v Islamic Republic of Iran*, Award 290-123-1, para. 37 (1987). See also the decision by an Iran-US Claims Tribunal panel to deny a request for the disclosure of an amount paid by a claimant party pursuant to a settlement with a third party. The amount had been redacted from documents previously submitted. *Phelps Dodge Corp and Overseas Private Investment Corp v The Islamic Republic of Iran*, Case No. 99, Award No. 217-99-2, para. 17 (19 March 1986).

60 Mosk and Ginsburg note the following concerning mediation privilege: "[m]any systems will treat as privileged or inadmissible statements made in the course of settlement discussions and some include a privilege for statements made in mediations." Mosk and Ginsburg, *supra* n. 30, p. 362.

61 As an example, see: art. 4(1) of Directive 2008/52/EC of 21 May 2008. See also the consideration by the tribunal in *Noble Ventures v Romania* of documents created during settlement negotiations. In this instance the tribunal considered whether a binding settlement agreement had been reached by the parties and, if so, its consequence to the claims. *Noble Ventures Inc v Romania*, Final Award, ICSID Case No. ARB/01/11, para. 199 (2005).

62 In this case the ICJ referred to the rule of the *Chorzów Factory* case which regards settlement communications to be inadmissible, with regard to its application to negotiations conducted within the presence of a

9.38 International arbitral tribunals have applied the mediation privilege to exclude evidence subject to such privilege without reference to national law thus indicating its acceptance as a principle of international arbitration procedural law, going so far as to extend in some instances the privilege has been extended to cover mediation communications exchanged by third parties not involved in the arbitration. In an ICC arbitration where a party sought to introduce mediation statements made between two non-parties into the arbitration record, the tribunal ruled that the mediation evidence was inadmissible on the grounds that there was a general international public policy against introducing mediation statements into contentious hearings:

> The Tribunal considers that protecting the confidentiality of mediation proceedings is justified by public policy. In the tribunal['s] view, ordering the discovery of documents exchanged in the course of a mediation between two third parties implies a self-evident risk of jeopardizing mediation as an institution . . . This is similar to the well established international legal principle applied by the ICJ precluding the admittance of evidence of earlier efforts to settle the dispute.[63]

9.39 In the specific context of mediation, the policy considerations underlying the protection of these communications may be extended to their natural conclusion of protecting all communications created for and exchanged during mediation, irrespective of who was involved. Such a prohibition may also be said to exclude testimony about the mediation given by the mediator.

9.40 Arbitral tribunals have recognised some instances where the mediation and settlement privileges do not apply. In an Iran-US Claims Tribunal decision, the panel held that the mere acknowledgement of a debt that occurs in the course of normal business activity did not attract the settlement privilege.[64] This case therefore reflects the importance that the communication in question meets the requirement that a document or statement be created or made "in connection with and for the purpose of settlement" in article 9.3(b). Also, in certain instances, evidence concerning attempts at settlement or agreements may be required to be submitted into the procedure. For example, where the scope and enforceability of a settlement agreement is in controversy or attempts at settlement are a prerequisite to a tribunal's jurisdiction or an award on costs.[65] In such cases evidence of settlement or attempts to achieve settlement will likely be admissible.

---

third-party neutral. *Maritime and Delimitation and Territorial Questions between Qatar and Bahrain*, (*Qatar v Bahrain*) Jurisdiction and Admissibility Judgment, ICJ Reports 1994, pp. 112, 126.

63 ICC Case No. 11258, Procedural Order No. 2, p. 6 (2003) (unpublished). The above example demonstrates the willingness of international arbitrators to uphold the confidentiality of the mediation process based upon public policy grounds. See also the assumption from the following ICC tribunal seated in California that the mediation process would remain confidential if conducted as part of the overall dispute resolution process: "[t]he Tribunal strongly urges the parties to engage in a mediation with an experienced mediator. This is a complex matter that will be expensive to arbitrate, and the outcome is never certain. Mediation works and will give both sides the opportunity to manage their risk and to control the outcome in a confidential setting." ICC Case No. 12279, Procedural Order of 31 July 2003, *ICC Bulletin, 2010 Special Supplement: Decisions on ICC Arbitration Procedure*, p. 45.

64 A panel of the Iran-US Claims Tribunal found with regard to a letter that had been exchanged between the parties in the course of normal business, that contained an acknowledgement of a debt: "this letter is admissible as a normal business communication acknowledging the current status of outstanding accounts, and that is not . . . an offer of settlement that the tribunal must ignore." *PepsiCo Inc v The Islamic Republic of Iran et al.*, Case No. 18, Award No. 260-18-1of 11 October 1986, p. 32.

65 ICC Case No. 1149, Final Award, in *ICC Bulletin*, Vol. 19, No. 2, p. 97, ss. 7.1 and 7.6 (2008). In this instance, the tribunal ruled that the settlement offer would not be regarded as a *Calderbank offer*, because it failed to meet the criteria for such an offer as per the applicable case law. Generally speaking, such an offer would

Article 9.3(c): the expectations of the parties and their advisers at the time the legal impediment or privilege is said to have arisen

9.41 If reference to the general rules in articles 9.3(a) and 9.3(b) do not adequately provide a solution to disputes over privilege, a tribunal may be required to conduct a choice of law analysis to identify the specific legal principle of privilege that is applicable. Such an analysis is generally guided by an analysis aimed at ascertaining the legitimate expectations of the parties.[66]

9.42 There appear to be two leading methods that arbitrators increasingly rely on in this regard, the "closest connection" test (sometimes described as the "centre of gravity test") and the "survey method".

Closest connection test

9.43 It is often said that the most popular private international law method for determining the applicable rule of privilege is the "closest connection" test or the "centre of gravity test".[67] This approach points the tribunal towards a relevant domestic rule of privilege that may be justifiably transposed onto arbitration because of its proximity to the communication, the party, or attorney of the party in question. The closest connection or centre of gravity test, because of its wide acceptance within international commercial law,[68] may be seen as a reliable method for establishing the legitimate expectations of the parties.

---

generally have to be made under the understanding and marked *"Without Prejudice and Confidential Save as to Costs"*. It is customary in some national systems for a party to deposit with its opponent (or the court) a settlement offer for the purposes of determining the cost award in the arbitration – or what is known in some jurisdictions as a *Calderbank offer*. Where the final award is not more favourable than the settlement offer, the party having made the offer will likely receive some or all of its costs. A tribunal may admit exchanges concerning the offer of settlement for the purpose of determining costs if the offer was made with the intention that it would be subject to disclosure during the cost assessment, and that intention was clearly communicated at the time.

66 In their article on the topic, Von Schlabrendorff and Sheppard note that their preference for a choice of law analysis, *inter alia*, is led by the following consideration: "we are also led to this conclusion by other factors mentioned above, such as the generally recognized value of protected attorney-client communications, and the desirable objective of meeting the parties' expectations". Von Schlabrendorff and Sheppard, *supra* n. 30, p. 768. Clearly implied in any consideration of a party's expectations is that the expectation is legitimate. To ascertain the legitimate reliance on a legal principle, a choice of law analysis based on the application of specific private international law rules or general principles of law may be had.

67 The "centre of gravity" test has met with widespread acceptance in international adjudication with regard to substantive contract law issues, in addition to its application to questions of privilege. In ICC Case No. 2730 the manner in which the centre of gravity test may be applied to a contract for which the laws of different jurisdictions were considered was described. The quote below is instructive as to how tribunals apply this rule: "[t]he rules of Swiss, French and Yugoslav private international law today all refer to similar criteria to determine the law applicable to a contractual obligation. First of all, one has to determine the characteristic performance of the contract or contracts. Then, one has to determine with which territory this characteristic performance is most closely connected or, to use an expression of the Swiss Federal Tribunal, one has to localize the 'center of gravity' of the contract." ICC Case No. 2730, *Journal du Droit International "Clunet"*, Vol. 111, pp. 914 et seq (1984). See also: Peter Roscher, "The Application and Scope of Attorney Client Privilege in International Arbitration", *Stockholm International Arbitration Review*, Vol. 2, No. 1 (2007).

68 "Cependant, l'application cumulative des systèmes de conflit de lois intéressés au litige est utilisée par le tribunal arbitral pour mettre en lumière ce qu'il semble considérer comme un principe général du droit international privé: l'application du droit dans lequel le 'centre de gravité' du contrat est localisé" (unofficial translation): "However, the cumulative application of the systems of conflicts of laws relevant to the case is used by the tribunal to highlight what it considers to be a general principle of private international law: the application of the law in which the 'centre of gravity' of the contract is located." Yves Derains, Note to ICC Case No. 2730, *supra* n. 67, pp. 918 *et seq*. See also: ICC Case No. 4650: "The arbitral tribunal does not deem it necessary in this case to

9.44 In determining the correct rule of privilege, a tribunal may apply one or more of the following factors as part of a closest connection analysis:

(1) The law where the attorney with whom the communication took place is admitted to practice.[69]
(2) The law of the place where the attorney-client relationship has its predominant effects, whether or not the attorney is admitted to practice in that jurisdiction.
(3) The domicile of the party claiming the privilege.[70]
(4) The law of the place where the document is located or stored.[71]
(5) The law of the place where the document is created.[72]
(6) The law of the place to which the document was sent.[73]

9.45 Although the above factors are particular to the issue of attorney-client privilege, with adjustment they may be used to analyse other types of legal impediment.

9.46 Of all the factors named above, it is the first that appears to garner the widest support as the dominant factor to rely upon in determining the applicable privilege although the second factor is also often regarded as being persuasive.[74] Nonetheless, the principles set out above provide a framework for ascertaining the applicable rules of privilege. Because of their wide acceptance such criteria may be confidently applied within an arbitral procedure.

The "survey" method
9.47 To determine whether a common rule of privilege exists arbitrators may compare, or survey, relevant sources of law in order to discern commonly accepted

---

decide on a specific rule of conflict to designate the proper law of the contract in view of the fact that most major rules in some form or other point to the place of the characteristic or dominant work . . ." ICC Case No. 4650, *Yearbook Commercial Arbitration*, Vol. XXVII, pp. 111 *et seq.* (1987).

69 Born generally advocates for this factor as being the most persuasive. Gary B. Born, *International Commercial Arbitration*, Vol. II, p. 1913 (2009). See also, Von Schlabrendorff and Sheppard, where it is generally noted that: "[w]e consider that an appropriate connecting factor in many cases will be the law applicable at the lawyer's professional domicile (ie where he is admitted to practise)." Von Schlabrendorff and Sheppard, *supra* n. 30, p. 771.

70 Berger regards factor (3) as well as possibly (2) to be persuasive: "a tribunal must, absent a choice of law by the parties, apply the law of the jurisdiction which the events of the communication which form the subject of the evidence issue before it are most closely connected. This law can and will in many cases be different from the law applicable to the substance of the dispute and the law applicable to the arbitral procedure. It is the law of the jurisdiction where the party has its place of business at the moment the relevant communication took place and where most of the attorney-client contact occurred which will be applied in most of these cases." Klaus P. Berger, *supra* n. 36, p. 172. While affirming that this may be a possible connecting factor, Von Schlabrendorff and Sheppard note that: "in some cases, a real connecting link may be missing. And it seems illogical to us that all communications between a US company and its in-house counsel in France have the same privileged status as communications with its US in-house counsel, when the same communication between French in-house counsel and a French company would not be privileged." Von Schlabrendorff and Sheppard, *supra* n. 30, p. 770.

71 Von Schlabrendorff and Sheppard reject this factor. See: Von Schlabrendorff and Sheppard. *Ibid.*

72 Von Schlabrendorff and Sheppard note that the disadvantage to applying this principle is as follows: "due to advances in modern technology and the fact that lawyers increasingly give advice from laptop or handheld computers while travelling, the place of production may be difficult to determine and/or be wholly unrelated to any aspect of the transaction or advice". Von Schlabrendorff and Sheppard. *Ibid.*

73 The above factors are taken from Roscher, *supra* n. 67, p. 17.

74 "Where legal privileges are concerned, applying the law of the place where the lawyer is qualified to practice is generally the better solution, from the perspective of predictability and conforming to the parties' expectations." Gary B. Born, *International Commercial Arbitration*, Vol. II, p. 1913 (2009).

principles. The advantages to using this method are that it, (1) arguably considers more fully the expectations of the parties by determining the commonly held regional or multi-jurisdictional view on privilege which a party involved in cross-border business would have expected to encounter,[75] and (2) ensures that a rule that is widely held and, hence, affirmed by multiple jurisdictions as "fair" and not an anomaly to accepted practice is applied.

9.48 The survey approach requires a tribunal to first consider the possible relevant sources of law. For instance, when presiding over a dispute between parties who are both from similar legal heritages, a tribunal may consider the approach taken by relevant jurisdictions that have the same system of law. As an example, a tribunal sitting under the rules of the Austrian Federal Economic Chamber adopted the survey approach with regard to the laws found in a number of different civil law jurisdictions.[76] Their method was articulated as follows:

> Rather than applying any countries' specific law(s) to the question at hand, the Arbitral Tribunal will address the issue in accordance with general principles developed by civil law and in civil law arbitrations, general procedural rules on disclosure and due process and general standards of fairness applicable in international arbitration proceedings.[77]

9.49 This approach has also been applied by tribunals who considered the rule of privilege as found in various common law jurisdictions.[78]

9.50 Thus, a tribunal may focus its survey on jurisdictions that have as a common denominator a similar system of law (e.g., civil law). For jurisdictions that share a common supranational court system, such as the European Union, a tribunal may wish to consider principles articulated by those courts, such as the European Court of Justice, or other expressions of commonly accepted legal principles within that geographical region.[79]

9.51 Apart from national rules on privilege, a tribunal may also look to restatements of international or transnational legal principles to determine whether there is a generally accepted rule of evidentiary privilege which may be applied. The sources of law which a tribunal may survey in discerning the transnational rule may be predominant arbitral procedural rules, widely enacted model laws, decisions of the ICJ or, quite often, the pronouncements of other arbitral tribunals.[80]

---

75 As the *Glamis Gold v United States of America* tribunal described it, the survey method is useful for determining where there is consensus in order to identify what the parties may reasonably expect to encounter. "Thus, the Tribunal has reviewed the case law of numerous United States jurisdictions – including California and the District of Columbia, neither of which were found to be outliers – and attempted to identify general consensus between courts that might be helpful in defining what the Parties would reasonably expect to apply in this situation." *Glamis Gold v United States of America, supra* n. 25, para. 20.

76 Bernhard Meyer-Hauser and Phillip Sieber, "Attorney Secrecy v Attorney-Client Privilege in International Commercial Arbitration", *International Journal of Arbitration, Mediation and Dispute Management*, Vol. 73, No. 2, p. 170 (2007).

77 *Ibid.*

78 As both parties were from common law backgrounds, the Claims tribunal conducted a survey of common law rules of privilege: *Glamis Gold v United States of America, supra* n. 25. Decision on Parties' Requests for Production of Documents Withheld on Grounds of Privilege, para. 19.

79 As noted above, the European Court of Justice opinion that legal privilege did not extend to lawyers who work as in-house employees in that case has received considerable attention. See also: *Akzo Nobel Chemicals Ltd and Akcros Chemicals Ltd v European Commission, supra* n. 50.

80 For example, see: *Reineccius v Bank for International Settlements, supra* n. 26, p. 10.

9.52 Irrespective of whether a general rule of privilege is to be ascertained by analysing national or transnational principles of law, the analytical process generally appears to be the same. First, the relevant sources of law are determined; secondly, similarities between the various laws are considered with a particular emphasis on the policy objectives behind the various rules;[81] and finally, in determining the general rule, a tribunal will also consider the particular requirements of the international commercial and arbitration system.

Article 9.3(d): any possible waiver of any applicable legal impediment or privilege by virtue of consent, earlier disclosure, affirmative use of the document, statement, oral communication or advice contained therein, or otherwise

9.53 Determining to what extent an evidentiary privilege has been waived may be a complicated matter. This is the case in part because the ability to waive privilege is an issue very much tied to whom the right is vested in (e.g., one cannot waive a right which one does not have). This may be a question controlled by domestic laws on privilege.[82]

9.54 Nevertheless, that a party may waive a privilege is an accepted possibility in international arbitral procedure. In this respect, the non-exhaustive factors listed in article 9.3(d) are generally accepted grounds for determining whether a privilege has been waived. A review of these principles and how they have been interpreted in arbitral practice is set forth below.

Consent

9.55 Where a party knowingly and intentionally submits unredacted evidence into a procedure for which it has claimed (or may claim) privileged status, such an act is deemed to be a waiver of the privilege. Thus, a party may not proffer evidence and "reserve its rights"

---

81 Mosk and Ginsburg note the following in regard to the consideration of various rules of privilege: "[f]or an arbitral panel that must determine the character of particular evidentiary rules, one authority has suggested a useful approach by focusing not on an abstract distinction between procedure and substance, but rather on an examination of the policies underlying the evidentiary rules at issue." Mosk and Ginsburg, *supra* n. 30, p. 377.

82 As previously noted, one of the great differences between common law and civil law approaches to privilege is the party who is vested with the right to assert the privilege. In common law, it is generally the client who holds the privilege whereas in civil law jurisdictions, privilege is a matter of professional ethics, and thus remains with the lawyer. However, the application of civil law notions of privilege to the process of document production in international arbitration poses difficulties. Consider the following observation of Von Schlabrendorff and Sheppard: "[t]he more limited doctrine of privilege in the civil law needs to be seen, we suggest, in its context. The civil law has not needed to develop the same doctrine as is found in the common law, because the civil law has not developed a general requirement that a party produce documents it does not want to produce. The modern practice of international arbitration, at least where one common law party is involved, is to allow requests for production by each side and some non-voluntary disclosure. Applying civil law doctrines to document production of a common law kind is to do so wholly out of context." Von Schlabrendorff and Sheppard, *supra*, n. 30, p. 772. The described incongruity between civil law views on privilege and the practice of document production may lead one to query whether the factors listed in art. 9.3(d), which appear to be oriented towards the actions of the party, and not its lawyer, may be appropriate to apply in a case involving a party who hails from a civil law jurisdiction. Nevertheless, one may consider that the rule of privilege, even in certain civil law jurisdictions such as the Netherlands, is maintained in the client's interests. ("De advocaat is verplicht tot geheimhouding; hij dient te zwijgen over bijzonderheden van door hem behandelde zaken, de person van zijn client en de aard en omvang diens belangen." (Advocate Gedragregels 1992, Regel 6). Thus, if a party has demonstrated a disinterest in maintaining privilege over a document by, for instance, engaging in one or some of the factors listed in art. 9.3(d), then the tribunal may determine that the privilege is waived.

to maintain privilege over it at the same time. Nor may a party engage in an unauthorised *ex parte* submission of privileged evidence to a tribunal and expect that the document will remain inadmissible on grounds of privilege.[83] Actions in which a party intentionally reveals the communication into the proceedings will generally be regarded as consent to waiver of privilege.

Earlier disclosure

9.56 When a party has inadvertently disclosed evidence into the proceedings or publicised the document content, the adverse party may claim that such a disclosure should lead to a loss of privilege. With regard to inadvertent disclosure generally, however, the mistaken disclosure of a communication does not automatically lead to a loss of privilege.[84] Nevertheless, in determining this issue a tribunal may need to weigh the relevant actions that have been taken to determine whether the disclosure of the document was sufficiently inadvertent, and not a matter of recklessness.[85] Where the mistaken disclosure is part of a string of similar acts, demonstrating repeated failures to safeguard the relevant information, and/or the adverse party has had possession of the privileged material for a substantial period and has engaged in case preparation using the evidence in question, a tribunal may find that the disclosure, albeit unintentional, should lead to a loss of privilege.[86]

9.57 Intentional publication to those not entitled to receive legal advice may lead to a loss of privilege. For instance, the distribution of otherwise privileged materials within an organisation or group of related organisations to individuals other than authorised decision-makers is prima facie evidence that privilege has been waived.[87] If a document is

---

83 With regard to a decision by an LCIA tribunal to admit into evidence a document which was produced by a party who had reserved its right to maintain the confidentiality of the evidence, the reviewing court affirmed the view of the arbitrators that once produced intentionally, a party may not continue to maintain a legitimate claim of privilege. *Double K Oil Products 1996 Ltd v Neste Oil OYJ* [2009] EWHC 3380 (Comm).

84 "The Tribunal agrees with Canada that according to Canadian law (which is taken into account so much as it conforms to international practice) and also international law on the subject, where information that is covered by solicitor-client [privilege] is inadvertently disclosed, as a general rule there is no waiver of privilege." *Vito Gallo v Canada, supra* n. 40, Procedural Order No. 4, para. 27 (21 December 2009). See also the rule set forth by an ICC tribunal regarding privilege: "[t]he inadvertent production of any documents in this proceeding that are otherwise subject to the attorney-client privilege shall not result in the waiver or impairment of the privileged status of such documents. Such inadvertently produced documents and any copies thereof shall be promptly returned to the producing party upon a written request, subject to determination by the Tribunal in the event of any dispute as to the claim of privilege." Hamilton, *supra* n. 54, p. 76.

85 Citing to factors common in American practice, the *Glamis* tribunal considered the following as to whether an inadvertent disclosure over the course of the proceedings should lead to the loss of privilege over certain key documents: "[t]he Tribunal is assured that a proper attorney-client relationship did exist at the times of the communications and thus the privilege would ordinarily apply. Whether such privilege was waived by the inadvertent release of several documents must be determined by examining Respondent's actions surrounding the release. The Tribunal notes that a US judicial decision lists five factors to consider in determining whether an inadvertent production should amount to waiver: (1) the reasonableness of the precautions taken to prevent inadvertent disclosure in view of the extent of the document production; (2) the number of inadvertent disclosures; (3) the extent of the disclosure; (4) any delay and measures taken to rectify the disclosure; and (5) whether the overriding interests of justice would or would not be served by relieving the party of its error. The Tribunal finds these five factors to reflect considerations generally applicable to the analysis of waiver of privilege on the grounds of partial disclosure." *Glamis Gold v United States of America, supra* n. 25, Decision on Requests for Production of Documents and Challenges to Assertions of Privilege, para. 51 (21 April 2006).

86 *Vito Gallo v Canada, supra* n. 40, Procedural Order No. 4, paras 43–46.

87 *Reineccius v Bank for International Settlements, supra* n. 26, p. 11.

produced to participants of a meeting that is held in public then privilege is also generally deemed waived.[88]

Affirmative use

9.58 A party may not use the contents of a communication over which it claims privilege as a sword in furtherance of its arguments, while refusing to produce necessary aspects of the communication based upon the shield of privilege.[89] This is generally what is meant by "affirmative" use. Where a party partially or selectively uses information covered by privilege, it is generally deemed to have waived its right to protect the privileged aspects of the claimant from disclosure.[90]

9.59 While these principles may be deemed transnational in character, they may not always lead to a suitable solution to questions over privilege. In this regard, reference to other relevant sources of law, including domestic laws on privilege, may be required.

Article 9.3(e): the need to maintain fairness and equality as between the parties, particularly if they are subject to different legal or ethical rules

9.60 When applying an evidentiary privilege, it is not uncommon that an "equal treatment" and fairness issue may come about. The problem arises in connection with the application of different rules of privilege to the parties. If, for example, a tribunal uses a private international law analysis to determine that one rule of privilege applies to Party A's communication and a different rule to Party B's, it is effectively applying different standards

---

88 "If the Extraordinary General Meeting had been open to the public, communications made there would cease to benefit from the attorney-client privilege. There is no indication that any General Meetings are open to the public. Article 44 of the Statutes permits attendance only by nominees of the central banks or other financial institutions referred to in art. 14." *Reineccius v Bank for International Settlements, supra* n. 26, p. 12.

89 Reference was made to this principle in the *Reineccius v Bank for International Settlements* case as an act which would cause privilege to be waived. *Ibid.*

90 See: *Vito Gallo v Canada*, where the state-party had revealed in its statement of defence the existence of a legal advice which it had relied on, the tribunal regarded the right to privilege on this document to have been waived, and thus ordered the production of the advice. *Vito Gallo v Canada, supra* n. 40, paras 61, 62 and Procedural Order No. 4, paras 58–64. See also the *CME v Czech Republic* UNCITRAL arbitration where a party attempted to present witnesses for in-person testimony, but insisted that it maintained a right to restrict their testimony based upon a duty of confidentiality owed by the witnesses to that party. "The Tribunal is of the view that the Claimant is not entitled to waive its confidentiality rights in respect to the two witnesses only for certain selected parts of the proceedings. The Respondent is free to interview the two witnesses on the basis of art. 4.2 and art. 4.3 of the IBA Rules of Evidence. The Claimant is ordered to instruct the two witnesses that the Claimant's confidentiality rights are waived except to the extent that the witnesses are not obligated to disclose Claimant's and/or CME's information which might be privileged . . .". *CME v Czech Republic, supra* n. 50, para. 69. See further: the ruling of a tribunal under the rules of the Geneva Chamber of Commerce which rejected the selective invocation of governmental privilege over certain documents by a state-party because, *inter alia*, the state-party and its witnesses had referred to some of the same material in support of its case. Decision of 28 February, *ASA Bulletin*, Vol. 13, No. 2, p. 312 (1995). See also the finding of a tribunal under the rules of the Society of Maritime Arbitrators that select disclosure of correspondence between a client and their lawyer, by legal counsel, was not sufficient to constitute waiver of attorney-client privilege over related documents, because the disclosed correspondence had minimal relevance: "[d]uring the hearings the Panel was called on to decide whether submission of certain evidence by Owner was in fact a waiver of attorney-client and work product privileges. The Panel's majority, with Arbitrator Berg dissenting, found for Owner and felt the submission of a letter from the Owner's local attorney listing a group of pictures was insufficient to have created a waiver of attorney-client and work product privileges." *Endurance Bay Shipping Ltd v Panama Centroamericanan de Navigacione SA*, Final Award, SMAAS, WL 1095284 (1987).

between the parties. To the extent this results in one party obtaining greater protection for its communication than the adverse party, it is generally agreed by practitioners and scholars alike that a fairness and "equal treatment" problem has arisen.[91]

9.61 The widely accepted solution to this problem is to apply the 'most favourable privilege' rule.[92] This approach posits that the tribunal should apply the rule of privilege which affords the greatest, or widest protection, to both parties.[93] Formerly, it was the view of some writers that article 9.2(g) (considerations of procedural economy, proportionality, fairness or equality of the parties) could be used as the basis for applying the same rule of privilege to both parties.[94] However, with the addition of article 9.3 it is now expressly recognised that a tribunal may take this approach. It should be noted, however, that a clash of priorities may occur when a rule, which is perhaps unusual, is applied to both parties.

---

91 Tevendale and Cartwright-Finch, *supra* n. 34, p. 831, note that: "[i]ndeed, it is likely that there will be a number of different 'closest connections' for the other party to the dispute. There is, therefore, a risk that this approach may result in the application of different standards or privilege between the parties." This was noted also by the Review Subcommittee, which stated the following: "[t]he need to protect fairness and equality among the parties may arise when the approach to privilege prevailing in the parties' home jurisdictions differs. For example, one jurisdiction may recognise the settlement privilege, whereas another may not, or one jurisdiction may extend the attorney-client privilege to in-house counsel, whereas another may not. In such cases, applying different rules to the parties could create unfairness by shielding the documents of one party from production but not those of the other." Review Subcommittee Commentary *supra* n. 35, p. 25.

92 In proposing this rule, Von Schlabrendorff and Sheppard write: "[i]n cases where there is a conflict of privileges and the rules differ as significantly as they do between the common law and civil law systems, it does not appear acceptable to us, for practical as well as legal reasons, simply to rely on a choice-of-law analysis and to apply different rules of privilege to different parties. . . . For greater predictability, we propose that international arbitrators, after determining which privileges may be applicable based on the closest connection test, adopt an approach that allows any party to the arbitration to claim the same legal privileges as are available to any other party. This will generally mean, when a common law party is involved, that a civil law party can claim common law privileges. This will result in the application of the 'most favourable privilege'". Von Schlabrendorff and Sheppard, *supra* n. 30, p. 773.

93 For an example of how this principle is applied in practice, see: *Poštová banka, a.s. and ISTROKAPITAL SE v Hellenic Republic*, ICSID Case No. ARB/13/8, Procedural Order No. 6 (2014): "[t]he Commentary on the IBA Evidence Rules suggests that the need to protect fairness and equality among the parties may arise when the approach to privilege in their home jurisdictions differs, and quotes as a specific example the difference between applying the attorney-client privilege to in house counsel or not. The Commentary states that in such cases 'applying different rules to the parties could create unfairness by shielding the documents of one party from production but not those of the other'. The Tribunal notes that the laws of the Hellenic Republic offer a broader protection than those of the Slovak Republic in regards to the attorney-client privilege as applied to in-house counsel and that there is not certainty, and the Parties debate, as to the treatment that the communications between client and in house should be treated under Slovak law. The Tribunal is concerned that applying different standards on the matters of privilege could affect the balance and equality of treatment of parties in international arbitration. In this particular case, such difference in treatment could result in Claimants having to produce documents originating from in house counsel while the same type of documents would not have to be produced by Respondent, creating a clear imbalance in the treatment of the parties in the proceedings. Therefore, the Tribunal concludes that the Parties should be bound by the standard that affords the broadest protection and that protects the expectations of both parties in international arbitration. For the foregoing reasons, Respondent's request to direct Claimants to produce all communications that they have withheld on purported grounds of attorney-client privilege cannot be upheld." *Ibid.*, pp. 6–7. While some authors regard the "most favourable privilege" rule to be a manner or means of selecting a rule, it is the more widely accepted consensus that it is in fact a means of ensuring that the rule arrived at, through whatever approach is used in determining it, is equally applied between the parties. For instance Carter notes the following after describing the closest connection test: "[a]nd then there is another step: if a conflicts-of-law analysis produces a different privilege rule applicable to each party, arbitral tribunals can invoke an 'equality of arms' approach to avoid any unfair treatment." James H. Carter, "Privilege Gets a New Framework", *International Arbitration Law Review*, Vol. 13, No. 5, p. 178 (2010).

94 Hilmar Raeschke-Kessler, "The Production of Documents in International Arbitration – A Commentary on art. 3 of the New IBA Rules of Evidence", *Arbitration International*, Vol. 18, No. 4, p. 428 (2002).

In that instance, the parties may be afforded a wider or different measure of legal privilege than would normally be expected, and hence the consideration in article 9.3(c) (the contemporaneous expectation of the parties) is not met. At this point, the tribunal may be better advised to employ a survey approach to arrive at a rule of privilege given that the survey approach would identify common themes in privilege across jurisdictions and exclude any extreme aspects of such a rule.

9.62 A theory employing the opposite logic to the most favoured privilege approach provides that instead of applying the rule that affords greatest protection, the tribunal should apply the rule that provides the "least protection", or in other words a narrower standard providing less protection. This theory has come in for considerable criticism, and is not favourably regarded in current practice.[95]

Other approaches to determining an applicable rule of privilege

9.63 The above described methods for determining a law or rule of evidentiary privilege presuppose that the parties themselves have not designated an applicable rule. While comparatively rare, it is not unheard of for an agreement to be reached by the parties that a particular transnational or national rule of privilege is applicable. This may occur at various stages, but in the context of one known instance before an ICC tribunal, was decided at the drafting of the terms of reference.[96] Here the parties, in anticipation of possible issues of confidentiality and privilege, agreed on the general application of English law, even though neither side was from that jurisdiction, none of the legal counsel involved were qualified in English law, and the substantive law applicable to the matter was that of a Middle Eastern country. The underlying rationale for adopting such a rule was that this selection would afford the broadest protection – a line of reasoning consistent with the "most favourable privilege" rule described above.

9.64 Any pre-selection of a rule of privilege would have to be done carefully and with consideration of the source of the potential information that will come to light in the course of the proceedings. Naturally, taking such a decision before a dispute arises runs the risk of the illogical application of a rule of privilege to a communication which has no connection at all to the jurisdiction from which the rule was taken. Moreover, there is also the chance that settling upon a rule of privilege hailing from a particular jurisdiction in advance, will mean that unanticipated oddities of a domestic rule may be transposed onto the arbitration, leading to unintended surprise. However, if the parties are sufficiently comfortable with imposing onto the procedure a rule of privilege which they believe affords broad protection, it may make perfect sense for this to be agreed upon at the outset of the procedure.

---

95 "The alternative is the 'lowest common denominator' approach. This is considerably less popular. In any context, and particularly one such as arbitration where cooperation and goodwill play some part in procedural matters, if it really must be that 'everyone is the same', it is easier to 'mark up' than 'mark down'". Tevendale and Cartwright-Finch, *supra* n. 29, p. 834.

96 See: ICC Case No. 16249, Terms of Reference (2010) (unpublished). In that case, the parties had negotiated at the outset of arbitration on several procedural matters, and had come to the reasoned conclusion that English law was a suitable reference for the rule of privilege in that matter.

Objections to production based on burden

Article 9.2 2010 IBA Rules: **The Arbitral Tribunal shall, at the request of a Party or on its own motion, exclude from evidence or production any Document, statement, oral testimony or inspection for any of the following reasons:**

. . .

(c)   **unreasonable burden to produce the requested evidence;**

General discussion

9.65 It is accepted in international arbitration that a party may object to a request for disclosure if it would impose a burden of time or cost that would be unreasonable. This point notwithstanding, there is clear arbitral precedent that a party cannot escape its duty to provide evidence by simply claiming that the requested documents are "voluminous".[97] When applying article 9.2(c) a tribunal must determine whether the hardship caused by an order to disclose evidence is of sufficient magnitude to deny the requesting party the document production it seeks.

9.66 At first glance, it may seem that it is difficult to generalise as to what is unreasonably burdensome since this analysis may vary considerably from instance to another. The potential for subjectivity notwithstanding, there has developed a general approach to determining the reasonableness of the burden imposed by a document production request which is predicated on the principle of "proportionality", so that a tribunal will ask, "Is the probative weight of the requested evidence worth the apparent burden of producing it?" One ICC tribunal constituted of experienced arbitrators of mixed civil law and common law backgrounds articulated this standard:

> As a threshold matter, the Tribunal notes that, in and of itself, the burden on a requested Party does not represent a sufficient reason to disallow a request for production of documents. The burden imposed on the producing Party should be weighed against the potential use of the documents.[98]

---

97 *INA Corp v The Islamic Republic of Iran*, Award No. 184-161-1 (1985), in Albert Jan van den Berg (ed.), *Yearbook Commercial Arbitration*, Vol. XI, pp. 312, 314 (1986). See also the comments of the arbitrator in the *Rhine Navigation* arbitration in which he acknowledged that the work of producing relevant evidence could be burdensome, yet necessary: "[t]he work leading up to the determination of this grave problem has been most arduous for the two delegations as well as for the Arbitrator. The requests which he has had to make for information have been numerous and burdensome but have been cheerfully complied with in spite of other pressing duties characteristic of this difficult period of readjustment." *Rhine Navigation Case, France v Germany* decision, 8 January 1921, 1 RIAA, p. 78.

98 ICC Case No. 11258, *supra* n. 63, Procedural Order No. 4, p. 5 (2003). See also the considerations of the ICSID tribunal in *Noble Ventures v Romania* in regard to a number of document requests: "[t]he Tribunal further recognises that, on the one hand, ordering the production of documents can be helpful in the Tribunal's task of establishing the facts of the case relevant for the issues to be decided, but, on the other hand, (1) the process of discovery and disclosure may be time-consuming, excessively burdensome and even oppressive and that unless carefully limited, the burden may be disproportionate to the value of the result, and (2) Parties may have a legitimate interest of confidentiality." *Noble Ventures Inc v Romania*, ICSID Case No. ARB/01/11, Procedural Order No. 1 (3 June 2003) as cited in Dietmar W. Prager, "*Noble Ventures Inc v Romania*, ICSID Case No. ARB/01/11, 12 October 2005", *A Contribution by the ITA Board of Reporters*. See also the following rule in ICC Case No. 12279 adopting the proportionality principle: "[t]he Parties shall have the right to object to improper requests, including requests which are overbroad 'fishing expeditions', or requests for which the burden of production outweighs the probative value of the information." ICC Case No. 12279, *supra* n. 63, p. 45.

9.67 Therefore, the question is whether the documents will be useful to the resolution of the case as a whole.[99] Requests for documents which have a highly probative value as to an issue that is nonetheless viewed by the tribunal as minor or secondary, may not justify the burden imposed on the party asked to produce them. For instance some preliminary issues may not justify asking one party to go through the effort to locate and produce voluminous documents.[100] This is especially true where the tribunal is of the view that more information on this issue is not needed.[101]

9.68 To determine whether a request to produce evidence imposes an unreasonable burden an arbitrator may consider objective factors to assess the nature of the hardship imposed by the request, as discussed below. However, the final determination will often come down to whether it is reasonable to expect a party to endure such inconveniencies in light of the possible value of the evidence.[102]

Objective factors to consider when assessing the reasonableness of the burden

9.69 In order to determine the reasonableness of the burden of producing the requested documents, the volume or number of documents (or other type of evidence) requested, the timing of the request, as well as the relative accessibility of the information should be taken into account by the tribunal.[103] One could also add the cost of producing the

---

See also the following rule adopted in an UNCITRAL arbitration: "[t]he issue of whether a request should be rejected as unduly burdensome must, in the Tribunal's view, take into account both the time and effort required to produce the requested documents and the prospect that these documents will have probative value." *William Clayton v Canada, supra* n. 22, p. 3.

99 As an example, in an Iran-US Claims Tribunal case the claimant argued that respondent's request for the production of evidence imposed an unreasonable burden. The tribunal denied the request, stating that it did so after considering the case in whole. "Having noted the positions taken up by the Parties, the Tribunal now decides the Respondents' request of 28 April 1992. Considering the circumstances as a whole, the Tribunal does not deem it appropriate to require the Claimant to produce the evidence. However, the Tribunal points out that this decision is without prejudice to the Tribunal, if and when it eventually considers the merits of the case, weighing the evidentiary significance if any, that flows from the above mentioned Respondent's request for production of documents and the Claimant's position taken in their respective submissions." *Brown & Root, Inc v The Islamic Republic of Iran*, Case No. 50, Chamber One, Order of 4 Jan 1993, p. 1.

100 This may not be true for jurisdictional objections. See: *RosInvest Co v Russian Federation* arbitration, where the tribunal made provision for disclosure during the jurisdictional phase. *RosInvest Co UK Ltd v Russian Federation*, SCC Arbitration, Case No. V079/2005, Award on Jurisdiction, p. 19 (October 2007).

101 *El Paso Energy International Co v The Argentine Republic*, ICSID Arbitration No. ARB/03/15, Decision on Jurisdiction, p. 4 (2006). In that arbitration the tribunal denied respondent's request for disclosure because it was satisfied that it had enough documents before it to determine the issue of jurisdiction: "[t]he information in possession [was] sufficient to decide the jurisdictional issues raised by Respondent, and that, if the proceedings [would] reach the merits of the dispute it would be open to Respondent to reiterate the above document production requests."

102 "The Respondent has furnished neither the texts of such rules and directives nor the underlying documents, although it was ordered to do so. The Respondent's attempt to excuse its non-compliance with the Tribunal's Order by merely stating that the documents were 'voluminous' is not convincing. The Respondent did not raise this asserted excuse until the hearing, long after the date for submission of these materials had passed; even then, the Respondent gave no indication of the actual amounts of material involved or any description of the alleged problems involved which prevented submission of the materials by the Respondent or their inspection by INA." *INA v The Islamic Republic of Iran, supra* n. 97, p. 314. See also: *Waste Management Inc v United Mexican States*, ICSID Case No. ARB (AF)/00/3, Final Award, pp. 269, 271 (30 April 2004), where an ICSID arbitration tribunal denied discovery because the invoices sought by the respondent were prima facie too voluminous in number and the content of those invoices was largely not in dispute.

103 Review Subcommittee Commentary, *supra* n. 35, p. 16.

evidence requested.[104] Common sense and knowledge of business practices, often guides this analysis.

9.70 Arbitrators may also wish to consider the standard record-keeping activities of the industry when determining whether a request to retrieve and produce such records is truly burdensome. Other issues to consider would also include the manner and form in which the requested evidence is stored. Obviously, electronic documents for which there is relatively straightforward access pose less of a challenge then hard copies that may be scattered across several offices.

9.71 A tribunal may further wish to consider the contractual or legal duties incumbent upon parties to maintain records. Long-term projects often necessitate the maintenance of operational logs as a contractual duty. This consideration goes to the issue of the advance notice a party has of the possible need to produce the document.[105] If it is reasonable to expect that a party would have preserved such documents in an easily accessible format as part of a legal duty, tribunals may take note of this in determining whether it is appropriate to draw an adverse inference from their non-production.

9.72 Other factors notwithstanding, the proportionality rule weighs heaviest upon a tribunal's decision regarding what is unreasonably burdensome. Where the facts and issues regarding a dispute simply do not warrant an in-depth phase of document production, or where the issue pursuant to which the disclosure is sought does not merit in-depth disclosure, it may be appropriate to find that a request for production is unreasonably burdensome. Moreover, where it is shown that the type of evidence which is requested is not likely to yield material information, the tribunal may regard the effort to obtain the evidence as not worth the effort.[106] On the other hand, as it is widely known that some international arbitrations involving claims for large amounts will require thousands of pages of evidence to be disclosed, it is equally true that in the right context a tribunal may find it perfectly reasonable for disclosure involving a high volume of documents to take place.[107]

---

104 This factor may be mitigated to some extent if the costs of locating and reproducing documents can be recouped as part of a cost award at the end of the arbitration. Tribunals have in the past noted that the relevance (or lack thereof) of a particularly large production of documents as well as the costs involved in locating the documents may be considered in determining a cost award at the end of a procedure. *Azurix Corp v Argentine Republic*, ICSID Case No. ARB/01/02, Procedural Order No. 3 (24 May 2004).

105 In an ICC Arbitration, the tribunal noted that since a party had been aware for some time that it would be required to produce an original of an exhibit, it should not be surprised by the request to produce it and therefore it posed no unreasonable hardship upon them. Hamilton, *supra* n. 54, p. 74.

106 This position may be adopted by the tribunal in respect to certain types of information which the characteristics of, in and by themselves, suggest that the probative value of would be low. See for example the position adopted by the *CIARB Protocol for E-Disclosure in Arbitration* with respect to the disclosure of metadata: "[a] party requesting disclosure of metadata in respect of electronic documents shall be required to demonstrate that the relevance and materiality of the requested metadata outweigh the costs and burdens of producing the same, unless the documents will otherwise be produced in a form that includes the requested metadata." *Chartered Institute of Arbitrators Protocol for E-Disclosure in Arbitration*, Guideline 9 at www.ciarb.org.

107 As an example, in a reported ICDR arbitration between an Israeli party and a US party, the tribunal presided over a disclosure process that saw over 150,000 pages of documents produced by the parties. *Mofet Etzion Ltd v General Dynamics Land Systems Inc*, US Dist Ct, LEXIS 11362 (SDNY February 2008). It is also reported that in an arbitration seated in Switzerland involving hundreds of millions of US dollars in claims, the arbitrators issued an order that resulted in 18,000 pages of documents being disclosed to one of the parties. William L Craig, William Park and Jan Paulsson, *International Chamber of Commerce Arbitration*, p. 450, fn. 4 (3rd edition, 2000).

Vague or overly broad requests for the production of documents

9.73 Broad requests for "all documents" or for documents pertaining to undefined time periods, for example, are generally considered to be vague or overly broad. Such requests are often denied because either the location of the documents is difficult to identify or the effort required to obtain them is difficult to quantify. In an ICSID arbitration, *Railroad Development Corp v Republic of Guatemala*, the investor-party had petitioned for interim measures requiring the state-party to preserve what it considered to be important and relevant documents.[108] The requests that were submitted by the investor-party were judged to be overly broad by the tribunal. As a result, the tribunal denied the request determining that it was unclear how the requested party might go about obtaining the requested evidence. The tribunal made the following point in connection with the issue of burden: "The Tribunal is doubtful that such an all encompassing request, if recommended, can realistically be put into practice. In this respect, the Tribunal fails to see how the measures requested would suppose a merely 'ministerial task' for the government."[109] Thus, where a tribunal is unable to determine a reasonable means by which the requested evidence could be obtained, it may well regard the request to impose an unreasonable burden upon the producing party (see comments to article 3.4).

A party's jurisdictional background

9.74 A party's perception of burden may be heavily shaped by their legal culture. This is so because that party's customary preservation of evidence may be influenced by their familiarity with the process of adverse evidentiary disclosure. Some tribunals have taken this factor into consideration in determining the reasonableness of a party's objection to production.[110] As an example, in an ICC arbitration with its seat in Switzerland, the tribunal noted each party's jurisdiction in determining the scope of production:

> In considering the Applications at issue, the Tribunal has been informed by the fact that this arbitration has its seat in a civil law country and that all of the parties involved in this arbitration are from civil law countries. It follows that in deciding the Applications at issue, due consideration has to be given to what constitutes a proper order for production of documents from the civil law perspective.[111]

9.75 The jurisdictional consideration goes to the issue of the legitimate procedural expectations of the parties involved in the arbitration. This factor must be tempered by the

---

108 *Railroad Development Corp v Republic of Guatemala*, ICSID Case No. ARB/07/23, Decision on Provisional Measures (15 October 2008).

109 *Ibid.*, para. 33.

110 *Noble Ventures Inc v Romania*, ICSID Case No. ARB/01/11, Final Award, pp. 31–32 (12 October 2005): "[t]he Tribunal recognises that, on one hand, requests and orders regarding the production of documents are today a regular feature of international arbitration, and that Romania has throughout expressed its willingness to produce documents provided that certain conditions, which it has specified, are satisfied, but, on the other hand, the present arbitration is a case between a Government of a Civil Law country where production of documents is used far less than in Common Law countries from where the investor comes."

111 ICC Case No. [redacted] (2005) (unpublished), quoted in: Nathan O'Malley, "The Procedural Rules Governing the Production of Documentary Evidence in International Arbitration, as Applied in Practice", *Law and Practice of International Courts and Tribunals*, Vol. 8, No. 1, p. 67 (2009).

fact that a party who has acceded to international arbitration and should anticipate some level of document disclosure will be required.

9.76 Furthermore, in the interests of equal treatment, the nationality factor should generally be ignored where the parties are from different legal traditions. It is better that arbitrators seek to apply objective, if not transnational standards to resolving issues of burden.

Lost or destroyed evidence

Article 9.2 2010 IBA Rules: The Arbitral Tribunal shall, at the request of a party or on its own motion, exclude from evidence or production any Document, statement, oral testimony or inspection for any of the following reasons:

    . . .

    (d)   loss or destruction of the Document that has been shown with reasonable likelihood to have occurred;

General discussion

9.77 If there is a "reasonable likelihood" that a relevant record has been lost or destroyed, a tribunal may accept that the evidence cannot be produced and excuse a party without sanction for failing to disclose it. This is the historical position adopted by international arbitral tribunals dating back to the early part of the last century,[112] and it has been restated in article 9.2(d) of the IBA Rules. Disputes may arise in connection to article 9.2(d) over whether a "reasonable likelihood" is established. Two grounds, which are generally agreed to meet the "reasonable likelihood" test, are discussed below.

Evidence which has been lost due to passing of time

9.78 Where a dispute has laid dormant or not been instituted for a considerable period, the natural consequence of this may be the loss or inadvertent destruction of evidence. To the extent that time has elapsed between the events giving rise to the dispute and commencement of arbitration proceedings, a tribunal may accept, upon reasonable explanation, that a party has lost or inadvertently destroyed evidence without drawing a negative inference.[113] This is the inherent risk of delaying commencement of a claim.

---

112 *Walter H. Faulkner (United States of America) v United Mexican States*, 2 November 1926, 4 RIAA, p. 69 (1926): "[f]urthermore, the explanation given for the circumstance that the Mexican Government cannot submit to this Commission extracts from its police and judicial records in the case is a reasonable one (to wit, because of their destruction in 1923–1924)."

113 After a delay of a considerable period, an ICC arbitration was commenced between the respondent and the claimant, during which the respondent submitted witness affidavits claiming that six documents, relevant to the dispute, had been lost. The claimant later challenged the final award, claiming, *inter alia*, that the tribunal had wrongly accepted that explanation. The court upheld the award, and noted the following: "[h]ere, the panel found that LaPine had not made a showing as to 'where or under whose control [the missing] documents – if at all existing – could or would be'. The panel went further to note that 'such circumstances eloquently reveal once more the daunting evidentiary difficulties to be met if this case were tried on the merits after having been dormant for over twenty years and the absence of even a prima facie record permitting that to happen.' Consequently, the panel's reasoned decision not to wait for these documents, which was well within their powers under the California

9.79 However, a tribunal may take note of intervening factors that would normally mitigate the passing of time, such as notice that a dispute is pending, or business practices and legal requirements that would have compelled a party to preserve the evidence in question. Where, for instance, a party would normally be required to maintain records in order to comply with regulatory or legal obligations, a tribunal may find claims that such records are lost or destroyed to be unpersuasive. This was the case in an ICC arbitration where the tribunal noted that as the party in question would normally be required under the US Foreign Corrupt Practices Act to maintain certain records regarding its agents, it could not accept that such records were simply missing.[114]

9.80 It may also be that where a party has commercial reasons that would normally compel a reasonable individual or company in its position to maintain such records a tribunal will draw an adverse inference against non-production. In all circumstances, a tribunal will consider such facts and compare them to general business practices and legal obligations regarding the maintenance of records.[115]

Statute, does not offend due process nor is it a manifest disregard of the law." *LaPine v Kyocera Corp*, 2008 US Dist LEXIS 41172 (ND Cal, 22 May 2008), p. 28.

114 "L'inexistence de pièces produites étonne d'autant plus que la défenderesse affirme être soumise à la loi FCPA qui oblige en fait les sociétés concernées à tenir des livres très complets. Ces documents doivent être tenus à la disposition des autorités, la confidentialité et le secret des affaires étant limités par la loi FCPA. Leur existence supposée, on ne voit donc pas pour quelles raisons la défenderesse n'aurait pas pu produire, dans cet arbitrage, des documents appropriés pour soutenir sa thèse (le cas échéant selon des modalités garantissant une confidentialité encore accrue par rapport à la confidentialité habituelle caractérisant l'arbitrage)" (unofficial translation) "The non-existence of exhibits is surprising, especially since the defendant claims to be subject to the FCPA, which in fact requires the companies concerned to keep very complete books. These documents must be kept at the disposal of the authorities, the confidentiality and secrecy of the cases being limited by the FCPA. Their existence presumed, we therefore do not see why the defendant could not have produced, in this arbitration, appropriate documents to support its thesis (where appropriate, the present case would ensure greater confidentiality than the usual confidentiality characterizing the arbitration)". Final Award in ICC Case No. 9333 (1998), *ASA Bulletin*, Vol. 19, No. 4, pp. 757, 767–769 (2001). Some commentators have remarked that a tribunal may consider the customary practices of the jurisdiction where the party claiming to have lost the evidence has its primary administrative centre to determine if there is a general legal culture that should have caused a party to have retained the document. If, for instance, prevalent legal or business practices of that jurisdiction would generally require the party to maintain documents or records pursuant to a document retention policy, then the tribunal may find that there is reason to doubt the destruction of the evidence occurred, or if it did occur, it was in bad faith. In such instances, the tribunal may consider the following courses of action regarding the claimed loss of electronic evidence, as outlined in an article covering arbitration and electronic discovery from an American perspective: "the tribunal could inquire into the alleged spoiling party's policy for routine destruction of ESI [electronically stored information], it could restrict the further destruction of ESI until the appropriate scope of discovery was determined, or it could draw an adverse inference against the spoiling party." Jonathan L. Frank and Julie Bédard, "Electronic Discovery in International Arbitration (Revisited)" in *AAA Handbook on International Arbitration Practice*, p. 189 (2010). As an example of the second approach, namely to direct that no further destruction of documents take place, the tribunal in *Biwater Gauff v Tanzania* issued the following direction to the parties to retain certain electronic and hard copies of relevant documents as part of an order on provisional measures: "for purposes of their possible presentation during these proceedings, the [United Republic of Tanzania] is to preserve, and take no adverse step in relation to, all documents (electronic and hard copy) within each of items 1(i), 1(ii), and 2 of [Biwater Gauff Tanzania's] Reformulated Request dated 17 February 2006." *Biwater Gauff (Tanzania) Ltd v United Republic of Tanzania*, ICSID Case No. ARB/05/22, Procedural Order No. 1, p. 26 (31 March 2006).

115 See the comments of the *ad hoc* annulment committee in *Amco v Indonesia*: "[t]hus, documents which in the ordinary course of business should have been in the possession of P.T. Amco and presented by it to the Tribunal, were submitted by Indonesia instead. At the same time, however, important documents such as those relating to the registration or the registerability of foreign exchange supposedly infused into the project were not submitted to the Tribunal by P.T. Amco; a reasonably prudent foreign non-resident investor may be expected in the ordinary course of business to keep copies of such documents outside the host State." *Republic of Indonesia*

Loss or destruction of evidence resulting from civil disturbance or other disaster

9.81 Tribunals have historically excused a party from the duty to produce evidence where it is shown that the evidence was lost due to the occurrence of civil strife, war, riots and revolution or other form of disaster. Such explanations have not been accepted without substantiation. If a party's claim that documents have been destroyed is prima facie inconsistent with known facts, or reasonable business practice of parties doing business under such conditions,[116] the party making such a claim must be able to provide a satisfactory explanation resolving such contradictions to the tribunal.[117] Where a party has taken a position inconsistent with a claim of loss or destruction of key evidence, a tribunal may draw an adverse interference from the failure to produce the evidence; a decision which courts generally uphold as consistent with an arbitral tribunal's powers.[118]

---

v Amco Asia Corp, Annulment Decision of 16 May 1986 in Albert Jan van den Berg (ed.), *Yearbook Commercial Arbitration*, Vol. XII, p. 139 (1987).

116 In the following case the tribunal determined that reasonable record keeping practices would dictate that copies of original documents would be stored in a location away from the area affected by civil strife: "[i]t must be recognized that the record in this Case is further obscured by Claimant's alleged inability himself to supply documents supporting his version of the facts. The failure to maintain virtually any records outside Iran is rather inexplicable in a corporation with experienced and sophisticated management. Also, the failure to produce as a witness a key former employee who had been in charge of the irrigation project in Iran left an important gap in Claimant's proof." *William J Levitt v The Islamic Republic of Iran*, Case No. 210, Concurring and Dissenting Opinion of Richard C. Allison of 3 September 1991 regarding Chamber Three Award No. 520-210-3.

117 *LJ Kalklosch (United States of America) v United Mexican States*, 18 October 1928, 4 RIAA, p. 414: "[t]he statements that Kalklosch was not arrested and was not molested can only be accepted if the view is taken that in the affidavits accompanying the Memorial the affiants started a mass of amazing falsehoods, and that the American Consul in 1912, produced out of his imagination, a lengthy report concerning arrests of Americans which never took place. Of course such things did not occur. In the Mexican Brief it is said that of course the only evidence that could establish the disputed allegations in this case would be the court and police records and that unfortunately, due to revolutionary troubles, the archives of the town of Altamira were destroyed in 1914. This is not a satisfactory explanation of the absence of evidence of this kind. . . . Some, and perhaps all, of the official records relating to the arrest of the seven men were therefore in Tampico. There is nothing in the record with respect to the destruction of records at that place. . . . In the absence of official records the non-production of which has not been satisfactorily explained, records contradicting evidence accompanying the Memorial respecting wrongful treatment of the claimant, the Commission cannot properly reject that evidence."

118 *Walter H Faulkner v United Mexican States*, supra n. 112, p. 69. In *X.____ (international) v A.____*, 4A_596/2012, the First Civil Law Court of the Swiss Federal Tribunal rejected an appeal from an ICC arbitration. Appellant argued that the arbitral tribunal unlawfully drew adverse inferences from the Appellant's refusal to provide "a list with all X.____ products sold through Z.____ AG (i) between 1 July 2005 and 29 April 2006 in the territory of Germany, Austria, Switzerland, Liechtenstein, Belgium, Netherlands and Luxembourg as well as (ii) between 30 April 2006 and 31 August 2009 in the territory of Germany, Austria, Switzerland and Liechtenstein. This list shall at least provide for a total amount of sales (in the applicable currency) for each product sold through Z.____ AG during the relevant terms and for the relevant countries as defined in the first sentence of this section 2. Claimant shall keep the information produced pursuant to section 2 of the present order strictly confidential and he shall only use it for the purposes of the present arbitration proceedings." In the Procedural Orders raised in the appeal, the Arbitral Tribunal ordered the production of these documents pursuant to Art. 20(4) of the rules of arbitration of the ICC and on Art. 3(10) of the IBA Rules on the Taking of Evidence. The Swiss Federal Tribunal rejected the appeal and stated that: "if a party fails to produce a pertinent document without satisfactory reasons after the other party requested its production or when it was ordered by the Arbitral Tribunal and has not objected in due time, the Arbitral Tribunal may infer according to Art. 9(5) of the IBA Rules that such document would be adverse to the interests of that party."

Objections based upon commercial and technical confidentiality

Article 9.2 2010 IBA Rules: The Arbitral Tribunal shall, at the request of a Party or on its own motion, exclude from evidence or production any Document, statement, oral testimony or inspection for any of the following reasons:

...

     (e)   grounds of commercial or technical confidentiality that the Arbitral Tribunal determines to be compelling;

General discussion

9.82 Determining what may be considered a compelling commercial or technical reason for denying disclosure or the admissibility of a document is largely a question of fact. Nevertheless, as a general rule, it is customary within international arbitration for consideration to be given to the legitimate need to keep sensitive business or technical information secret. Thus, article 9.2(e) preserves this objection and allows a party to object to the admissibility or disclosure of evidence based on such grounds.

9.83 The threshold question a tribunal is often confronted with under article 9.2(e) is whether the document or evidence over which an objection is made requires special consideration. In this regard article 9.2(e) is generally applicable to evidence a party would normally go to great lengths to keep from secret from business rivals or more generally the public. As an example, one ICC tribunal in applying this general principle denied requests that it regarded as constituting an "unacceptable invasion of [business] privacy."[119] In its procedural order on document disclosure, the arbitrator consistently denied requests for documents that related to the financial status of a company, including bank statements and also tax returns, for being unduly invasive. Rulings of this kind may seem reasonable when applied to evidence that reveals the financial inner workings of a company since the repercussions for a party if such information were to be improperly disclosed are potentially great. Such reasoning would also extend to formulas, know-how, trade secrets or other proprietary information which firms go to great lengths to keep confidential. This is less the case with regard to general records such as meeting minutes of a relevant committee, for example, or correspondence that discusses a relevant point relative to a case, outside of the realm of legal advice.

9.84 As each request is made in the context of a different factual matrix, a case-by-case analysis is generally required: while in one instance financial and tax records may be considered too sensitive to be disclosed, in another dispute, it may be appropriate to supply these documents depending on their probative value as weighed against the risks posed by the disclosure.[120] Irrespective of the exact nature of the documents over which confidentiality

---

119 ICC Case No. 1000, Procedural Order No. 8 (2006) (unpublished).

120 See where an UNCITRAL tribunal ordered the production of highly contested tax records in an arbitration over the wind-up of a joint venture entity between US and French parties. *Publicis Communications v True North Communications Inc et al.*, 206 F.3d 725 (7th Cir. Ill. 2000). See: *Euroflon Tekniska Producter AB v Flexiboys I Motala AB, supra* at 12: "Flexiboys has claimed, in this respect, that the documents contain information on customers, customer sizes, customer volumes and prices. Disclosure of information of this kind is typically detrimental from a competition perspective for the trader. It can also be assumed that the invoices contain information of this nature. Thus, they contain confidential information (citation omitted). This means that Flexiboys cannot be

is claimed, a party seeking to establish a valid objection must offer a clear explanation of the negative repercussions it fears could result if the evidence is disclosed. Tribunals, for want of specificity, are often prone to dismiss objections based on unspecified claims to "business secrecy".[121]

Documents subject to confidentiality agreements with third-parties

9.85 Article 9.2(e) typically applies to internal documents and not those shared with third parties. However, there may be instances where agreements, communiqués or statements exchanged by a party to the arbitration with a third party will be subject to a confidentiality agreement and thus fall within the ambit of article 9.2(e).[122] Tribunals have been known to consider the duties owed to a third party in the context of an objection to production/admissibility brought under article 9.2(e).[123] In giving regard to this issue, the analysis often focuses on whether there is a risk that the party to the arbitration could become liable to the third party if the evidence were revealed in the arbitration.[124] In this respect, tribunals have considered the conditions of the confidentiality undertaking itself, even reviewing in camera a copy of the instrument containing the restriction.[125]

9.86 Unlike evidentiary privileges, an undertaking to a third-party is often inherently self-serving and commercial in nature as a party accepts such an obligation as part of a

---

ordered to disclose them unless extraordinary circumstances are at hand. The interests to be weighed in the test of whether extraordinary circumstances for disclosure of the relevant documents are at hand are their relevance as evidence, on the one hand, and the financial value of the confidential information, on the other. The review of the document's importance as evidence must also in this test be the exclusive jurisdiction of the arbitral tribunal (citation omitted). If, however, the arbitral tribunal has not specified its reasoning with respect to the importance of the document as evidence, the court, which is to weigh the importance of the document against the potential harm of disclosure, must make its own judgment. In certain typical situations, the importance of the documents is clear even if the tribunal has not specified its reasoning. In these cases, the court can rely on this for its review. When this is not the case, the court can only assume that the importance of the document was only just sufficient for the arbitral tribunal's decision to grant leave for the application to a court. In this case, it must be deemed that the invoices will have substantial importance as evidence for the issue of to what extent BA has, directly or indirectly, conducted business in competition with that of Euroflon. Concurrently, the potential harm of Flexiboys appears clearly limited. It would therefore appear that a disclosure of the documents would not cause such harm that, considering Euroflon's interest of having the documents disclosed, any legal impediments for an order to disclose is at hand."

121 In an ICC arbitration where a tribunal drew an adverse inference from non-production of certain documents, it noted that respondent's proffered reason for non-production, namely, that the documents were covered by business secrecy, was not compelling: "the arbitral tribunal takes note that claimant has refused to produce such documents. The arbitral tribunal notes that the only reasons invoked by claimant in the documents cited in their letter [of their counsel], as far as the production of copies of subcontracts are concerned is, 'business secrecy over matters which are not in dispute'. The arbitral tribunal will draw in due time the possible consequences of claimant's position." ICC Case No. 6497, Final Award (1994), in Albert Jan van den Berg (ed.), *Yearbook Commercial Arbitration*, Vol. XXIVa, pp. 76, 77 (1999).

122 *Merrill & Ring Forestry LP v Government of Canada*, NAFTA/UNCITRAL/ICSID, Decision of the Tribunal on Production of Documents, para. 31 (18 July 2008): "[t]he parties have refused the production of a number of documents on the ground of them containing confidential commercial information. To the extent that some such refusals are based on the nature of the transaction or information contained in the pertinent document, particularly if it relates to intra-company information or business transactions involving third parties, a refusal might be well justified on these grounds."

123 See: *Jardine Lloyd Thompson Canada v Western Oil Sands Inc* [2005] AJ No. 943 (19 July 2005) (Alberta Court of Queen's Bench Judicial District of Calgary).

124 *Ibid.*

125 *Ibid.*, p. 6.

bargain. This general characterisation has influenced some courts to hold that an international arbitral tribunal does not exceed its authority when ordering documents to be produced in breach of a claimed confidentiality undertaking to the third party.[126] This point notwithstanding, if a tribunal does not receive adequate explanation or proof concerning the conditions of such an agreement it may disregard any argument based, or the existence of an obligation to a third party. Additionally, where a party claims that the information may not be revealed because it contains commercial or technically sensitive information about a third party, but admits that a confidentiality agreement does not exist, arbitrators have generally not found such reasoning compelling.[127]

Resolving objections raised over commercial or technical confidentiality

9.87 There are times when the production of sensitive commercial or technical records may be appropriate because of the high probative value of such evidence. This is especially true where a confidentiality undertaking between the parties or other measures imposed by the tribunal provide adequate protection against the dissemination of the sensitive information. As noted above, the IBA Rules maintain the general principle in article 3.13 that all documents are to be kept confidential and used only for the purposes of the arbitration. In addition to this broad rule on confidentiality, a tribunal may also issue a specific procedural order setting rules for the protection of confidentiality that are binding on the parties or instructions to redact sensitive portions of the requested documentary evidence.[128]

---

126 *Ibid.*

127 In an ICC arbitration where the tribunal considered a party's refusal to produce certain evidence because of a purported "confidentiality agreement", the tribunal noted the following: "Claimant's position in respect of non-compliance with the discovery is unfounded. As far as it alleges a confidentiality agreement, the tribunal has not seen one and reminds Claimant that it specifically offered the possibility to black out a page or otherwise cope with this problem." ICC Case No. 13133, Final Award, in Albert Jan van den Berg (ed.), *Yearbook Commercial Arbitration*, Vol. XXXV, pp. 140–149 (2010).

128 See the rule adopted by the tribunal in ICC Case No. 13046 in regard to the issue of proprietary information and disclosure: "If documentary evidence which a Party is directed by the Arbitral Tribunal to file contains proprietary information or trade secrets, that Party shall so indicate to the Tribunal and to the other Parties. In that case, the Arbitral Tribunal shall determine, after consultation with the Parties, the appropriate measures to be implemented in order to respect the proprietary nature of the information while to the extent possible, allowing the production of such evidence for the purpose of the arbitral proceeding." ICC Case No. 13046, *ICC Bulletin, 2010 Special Supplement: Decisions on ICC Arbitration Procedure*, p. 89. See also the following order made by the tribunal in *Fireman's Fund Insurance v United Mexican States*, where the following procedural order was rendered covering documents which were labelled "business confidential": "[i]f and to the extent that the Tribunal makes use of Confidential Documents or information derived there from in any decision, including an arbitral award, it shall designate the portions relating to such documents or information as confidential and those portions shall not be published by the persons authorized under paragraphs 3 and 4 of the present Order to third parties." Jack J. Coe Jr. and Charles H. Brower II, *"Fireman's Fund Ins Co v United Mexican States*, ICSID Case No. ARB(AF)/02/01, 17 July 2006", A Contribution by the ITA Board of Reporters*, para. 222. See: *South American Silver Ltd (Bermuda) v The Plurinational State Of Bolivia*, PCA Case No. 2013-15, Procedural Order No. 2 (2014): "Section 6.10 of Procedural Order No. 1 provides that an application to treat information as highly confidential must meet the following requirements: (a) that the Party filing the application considers the information as 'highly confidential'; (b) that the information is used in the proceedings; (c) that a Party makes the application by notice to the Tribunal, with a copy to the other Party; and (d) that, without disclosing the information, the Party gives in the notice the reasons for which it considers the information 'highly confidential'. In addition, Section 6.10 grants the Tribunal ample discretion to determine whether the information is to be classified as 'highly confidential' without requiring a specific or heightened standard of proof. The Application meets the aforementioned requirements. Claimant considers the Information as highly confidential; the Information has been used and will likely be used further in the proceedings; and Claimant filed the Application with the Tribunal

9.88 If commercial or technical sensitivity is raised in relation to documents shared with or received from third parties, a common approach followed in arbitration is for the party raising the objection to be required to produce evidence of the confidentiality undertaking with the third party. Moreover, a tribunal may ask that party to undertake good faith negotiations to lift the restriction or obtain that party's consent to limited disclosure. An example of such is taken from a procedural order issued in an NAI arbitration:

> Respondent is ordered to negotiate production of the documents with the third party. Should the third party not agree to production, Respondent is ordered to produce a letter from the third party to this effect.[129]

9.89 Where a tribunal finds the confidentiality undertaking to a third party to have been entered into for purposes other than legitimate business interests (e.g., in order to avoid the production of documents), the tribunal may consider the restriction as posing no real obstacle to the production of the requested evidence.

9.90 From a theoretical standpoint it should be noted that claims to confidentiality made under article 9.2(e) are generally not based in the application of a legal principle, such as attorney-client privilege.[130] For this reason a tribunal has a certain leeway in implementing practical solutions to allay the concerns of the objecting party. Admittedly, confidentiality measures within an arbitration may cause the procedure to become complex. This concern, however, has not been regarded by tribunals as constituting a valid reason for not providing the protective framework needed to allow commercially or technically sensitive documents to be used in an arbitration.[131]

Objections based on the special political or institutional sensitivity of the information

Article 9.2 2010 IBA Rules: The Arbitral Tribunal shall, at the request of a Party or on its own motion, exclude from evidence or production any Document, statement, oral testimony or inspection for any of the following reasons:

. . .

(f) grounds of special political or institutional sensitivity (including evidence that has been classified as secret by a government or a public international institution) that the Arbitral Tribunal determines to be compelling;

---

with copy to Respondent." *Ibid.*, p. 6. Based on the above considerations, the Tribunal classified the information as "highly confidential" and issued a protective order. *Ibid.*, p. 8.

129 NAI Case No. 3702, Procedural Order No. 3 (2011) (unpublished).

130 As noted by Raeschke-Kessler, this position was included to cover the protection of valid business secrets: "[a]s such, this ground is not necessarily rooted in a legal right." Raeschke-Kessler, *supra* n. 94, p. 413.

131 *Canfor Corp v United States of America*, NAFTA/UNCITRAL, Order of the Consolidation Tribunal, para. 146 (7 September 2005): "[t]ribunals operating at a level of the NAFTA and of other multilateral or bilateral investment treaties should be, and are as a rule, capable of dealing with procedurally complex cases with difficult confidentiality issues without an appreciable decline in efficiency or without any impairment of due process."

General discussion

9.91 Public international institutions and national governments are often afforded the right to maintain a degree of secrecy over their internal communications by the laws or regulations under which they operate.[132] Such laws are designed to protect the particularly sensitive nature of their work and ensure that they are able to operate and receive candid advice[133] relative to their particular functions.[134] While these rights to confidentiality are often oriented towards application before domestic courts, the need to maintain confidentiality over documents related to decisions made by government agencies and personnel is largely accepted as legitimate by international arbitral tribunals.[135] Thus, as a matter of arbitral procedure, article 9.2(f) restates the commonly accepted principle of governmental and institutional privilege as a basis upon which disclosure may be resisted, or as grounds for denying the admissibility of evidence.

9.92 Despite the recognition of this right to secrecy, it is not always clear how and in what manner it is proper for governments or institutions to assert the privilege described in article 9.2(f) before an international tribunal. A line of jurisprudence considering the question of governmental privilege[136] has developed which is generally regarded as having begun with the published decision of an UNCITRAL arbitration, *Pope & Talbot v Canada*.[137] *Pope* and the arbitral jurisprudence which has followed it address common challenges which may be broadly categorised along the following lines: (1) the manner

---

132 A type of this privilege known within the United States as the "deliberative privilege" is defined as follows: "[t]his governmental privilege permits government to withhold documents that reflect advisory opinions, recommendations and deliberations comprising part of a process by which government decisions and policies are formulated, and was developed to promote frank and independent discussion among those responsible for making governmental decisions and to protect against premature disclosure of proposed agency policies or decisions." *Black's Law Dictionary* (6th edition, 1990). See also: *Federal Rules of Evidence Manual, Part Two: The Rules Themselves*, s. 2-501, p. 29 (2011): "[t]he courts assume that confidentiality is required because government officials will be 'chilled' if they know that their internal communications are subject to public disclosure. The fear is that officials may pull punches, and this will hurt the quality of advice that they give to their superiors. A secondary argument in support of the privilege is that it 'protects the integrity of the decision-making process itself by confirming that officials would be judged by what they decided, not for matters they considered before making up their minds'".

133 The *Glamis Gold* tribunal, in accepting the general premise of such privileges, explained the basis for deliberative privilege as one relating to "the Government's need for the free and open exchange of communications". *Glamis Gold v United States of America, supra* n. 25, Final Award, pp. 116, 117 (8 June 2009).

134 See also: RPG Information Services Inc, *The Access to Information Act and Cabinet Confidences: A Discussion of New Approaches*, p. 4 (1996).

135 Sandifer comments on the historical acceptance of this principle. Referring to a hearing conducted before the US-German Mixed Claims Commission, he reports that the German Agent had sought to inspect the files held by the US Department of Justice. This request was denied, to which Sandifer comments: "[t]his denial seems sound. It would be manifestly unwise for such a tribunal as the United States German Mixed Claims Commission, in the absence of a specific grant of authority in the arbitral agreement, to authorise the Agent of one of the parties to proceedings before it to conduct a personal examination of the files of the other party. Such procedure would be too easily subject to abuse." Durward V. Sandifer, *Evidence Before International Tribunals*, p. 322 (1975). As will be further explored below, the complete rejection by Sandifer of the notion of inspecting files or otherwise receiving adverse document production from a government is not maintained in modern practice.

136 This phrase is generally used in the United States as a reference to the rights to confidentiality and immunity from testimony afforded to government officials. In the context of this chapter it is generally used more widely to refer to grounds of political and technical sensitivity.

137 In this case, Canada had asserted a privilege provided for under the Canada Evidence Act, known as "Cabinet Confidence". This provision permitted a designated government official to certify that specified information should be prevented from disclosure because it contained information constituting a confidence of the

and extent to which a national or domestic rule on governmental secrecy is applicable to a dispute before an international tribunal; (2) what is regarded as a "compelling" assertion of a right under article 9.2(f); and (3) the types of documents which may be considered sensitive. These issues are considered below.

Domestic laws on governmental privilege and article 9.2(f)

9.93 As article 9.2(f) makes plain, a state-party's right to resist disclosure on grounds of a governmental right to secrecy pertains to "evidence that has been classified as secret" or other specific "grounds of special political or institutional sensitivity". The rationale for the special consideration given to these types of documents may be rooted in a domestic law permitting a government or institution to declare certain information confidential, but such laws do not constitute rules automatically applicable to an international arbitration.[138] The principle captured by article 9.2(f) is that the party claiming a right to governmental secrecy must specify why the document or evidence in question is subject to special consideration. If indeed a domestic law applies to this evidence, it is generally considered that such laws should be weighed against other substantive and procedural obligations incumbent on the tribunal,[139] including the procedural rules governing the arbitration, the

---

Queen's Privy Council. *Pope & Talbot Inc v Canada, supra* n. 51, Decision on Crown Privilege and Solicitor-Client Privilege, para. 1.1.

138 This principle has been accepted in relation, specifically, to the assertion of governmental privilege: "[the Tribunal] begins with the basic principle, accepted by the parties, that Canadian law is not directly on point. Canada may not have the advantage of its own law if it is more generous than the law governing the tribunal. As the Tribunal said in its Decision of 17 October 2001 on the Place of Arbitration a claim for Cabinet privilege 'would have to be assessed not under the law of Canada but under the law governing the tribunal.' That law in this context does not refer to national law." *United Parcel Service of America v Government of Canada*, Decision of the Tribunal in Relation to Canada's Claim of Cabinet Privilege, para. 7 (8 October 2004). See also: *William A. Parker (United States of America) v United Mexican States*, 31 March 1926, 4 RIAA, p. 39: "[a]s an international tribunal, the Commission denies the existence in international procedure of rules governing the burden of proof borrowed from municipal procedure. On the contrary, it holds that it is the duty of the respective Agencies to cooperate in searching out and presenting to this tribunal all facts throwing any light on the merits of the claim presented." See also a more modern expression of the point raised in a case before the Constitutional Court of South Africa, which noted in regard to the practice of arbitration (including international arbitration): "[t]he final question that arises is what the approach of a court should be to the question of fairness. First, we must recognize that fairness in arbitration proceedings should not be equated with the process established in the Uniform Rules of Court for the conduct of proceedings before our courts." *Lufuno Mphaphuli and Associates (Pty) Ltd v Andrews* [2009] ZACC 6, para. 236 (20 March 2009).

139 The *SD Myers* tribunal recognised that legal issues other than domestic law would have significant influence on whether assertion of governmental privilege could be accepted: "[t]he circumstances of the present case involve a number of complicating factors: first, Canada has invoked a domestic law that applies to it and other NAFTA Chapter 11 panels have taken into account the personal legal rights and obligations of parties; secondly, the seat of the arbitration is Toronto, Canada; thirdly, the arbitration is being conducted under the UNCITRAL Arbitration Rules which are designed for international commercial arbitrations (private sector disputes); other Chapter 11 proceedings are conducted under the ICSID Special Facility which is designed for mixed international commercial arbitrations (private sector or state agencies); fourthly, the claim is an alleged breach of the NAFTA treaty, that includes, *inter alia*, Canada's obligation 'to . . . accord to [Myers and its investments] treatment in accordance with international law, including fair and equitable treatment . . .'; fifthly, the substantive governing law is public international law, a source of law that concerns the relationship between states." *SD Myers Inc v Government of Canada*, NAFTA/UNCITRAL, Explanatory note to Procedural Order No. 10, para. 6 (14 November 1999).

substantive law of the case, the overall purpose of the arbitration, and the fundamental duty to treat the parties with equality and fairness.[140]

9.94 Of the above considerations, it is the application of the principle of equal treatment and fairness which has on notable occasions conflicted with domestic laws providing for governmental secrecy. To illustrate the point, one may imagine that a domestic law providing the governmental entity with the self-judging, blanket right to determine which documents will be protected from disclosure, would afford it a distinct procedural advantage vis-à-vis its non-state opponent. To accept such a procedural disparity is inconsistent with the parties' right to equal treatment as was reflected in the *Pope & Talbot v Canada* decision.[141]

9.95 The reasoning in *Pope* was adopted and further explained by the tribunal in *Biwater Gauff v Tanzania* in response to an assertion of a public interest immunity which Tanzania argued permitted it the right to decline disclosure of documents it deemed in its discretion to be sensitive. Here, the Tribunal noted that a domestic law permitting a state-party wide, undefined discretion to declare itself immune from the duty to produce documents, would violate the principle of equal treatment, and did not qualify as "grounds" for resisting disclosure under article 9.2(f):

> This is an international tribunal, governed by an international convention, which is mandated to enquire into the conduct and responsibility of a State in light of its international treaty and customary international law obligations. It is hardly conceivable that, in this setting, a State might invoke domestic notions of public interest and policy relating to the operations of its own Government as a basis to object to the production of documents which are relevant to determine whether the State has violated its international obligations and whether, therefore, its international responsibility is engaged . . . If a state were permitted to deploy its own national law in this way it would, in effect, be avoiding its obligation to produce documents in so far as called upon to do so by this Tribunal . . . Moreover, accepting Respondent's theory would create an imbalance between the parties, which the Tribunal considers unacceptable. It is indeed one of the most fundamental principles of international arbitration that the parties should be treated with equality. The Arbitral Tribunal considers that the only ground which might justify a refusal by the Republic to produce documents to this Tribunal is the protection of privileged or politically sensitive information, including State secrets, as pointed out by the Arbitral Tribunal in *Pope and Talbot, Inc v Government of Canada* . . . and restated in article 9.2(f) of the IBA Rules of Evidence. In conclusion, the Arbitral Tribunal decides that the public interest immunity exception invoked by the Respondent is not a valid objection to the production of documents requested by Claimant.[142]

---

140 *Ibid.*, para. 10: "[t]he tribunal recognizes that this issue must be decided in the context of this dispute which is being conducted under the UNCITRAL Rules (which afford the Tribunal considerable discretion in the management of the dispute) and which potentially embraces considerations of international and domestic law."

141 *Pope & Talbot v Canada* related this principle to the NAFTA context, but its application may be considered to apply in a wider manner: "[i]n the specific context of a NAFTA arbitration where the parties have agreed to operate by UNCITRAL Rules, it is an overriding principle (art. 15) that the parties be treated with equality. The other NAFTA Parties do not, so far as the Tribunal has been made aware, have domestic laws that would permit or require them to withhold documents from Chapter 11 tribunals without any justification beyond a simple certification that they are some kind of state secret. In these circumstances Canada, if it could simply rely on s.39, might be in an unfairly advantaged position under Chapter 11 by comparison with the United States and Mexico." *Pope & Talbot v Canada*, *supra* n. 51, Decision on Crown Privilege and Solicitor-Client Privilege, para. 1.5. See also: *Biwater Gauff v Tanzania*, *supra* n. 114, Procedural Order No. 1 (30 March 2006).

142 *Biwater Gauff v Tanzania*, *supra* n. 114, Procedural Order No. 2, p. 8 (24 May 2006). *Ibid.*, p. 9.

9.96 The above holding is instructive regarding the purpose of article 9.2(f). As the tribunal explained, a general grant of immunity to governments or political institutions from disclosure is broadly inconsistent with the international nature of the proceedings,[143] and in particular with the basic obligation to treat the parties with equality. Therefore, in terms of invoking domestic law as a basis under article 9.2(f) to resist disclosure, it would seem that a domestic legal right which affords to a state-party a wide, self-judging discretion to declare documents "sensitive" without specifying a specific interest, does not qualify as proper "grounds".[144] It follows *a contrario* that only claims to governmental secrecy brought under laws (or interpretations) which are reasonably defined and in furtherance of legitimate interests[145] would receive recognition under article 9.2(f).

Which governmental privileges are considered "compelling" and when

9.97 As is expressly stated in article 9.2(f), for a right to governmental secrecy under a domestic law (or other legal basis) to be applied in an international arbitration, the tribunal must find such an assertion to be compelling. The jurisprudence of international tribunals establishes clearly that a state party's need to protect bona fide "state secrets" from disclosure enjoys wide acceptance as a compelling basis for non-disclosure. In a theoretical sense, one may consider "state secrets", such as information concerning core, national interests, like defence or security, as constituting the highest category of governmental information deserving of protection from disclosure.[146] However, it is not clear if the phrase

---

143 The tribunal would further note that such a doctrine is generally not accepted in international procedural practice: "[t]he doctrine is not a general principle of law as understood for the purposes of art. 38(1)(c) of the Statute of the International Court of Justice. Neither is it provided for in the ICSID Convention or the ICSID Arbitration Rules (which endow ICSID Tribunals with broad powers to order the production of documents)." *Ibid.*, p. 8.

144 In *Pope & Talbot v Canada*, the tribunal considered WTO case law supportive of its position that the assertion of privilege must be sufficiently explained, and could not simply be upheld because the government had "certified" a document as falling within the privilege: "where a state is justified in withholding information, it is to be expected that it should 'explain clearly the basis for the need to protect that information'. So too does this Tribunal expect clarity." *Pope & Talbot v Canada, supra* n. 51, Decision on Crown Privilege and Solicitor-Client Privilege, paras 1.5, 1.6 (6 September 2000).

145 Mosk and Ginsburg make the following point concerning the legitimate exertions of governmental privileges: "[o]f course, international arbitrators should not sustain a privilege objection if it is made in bad faith. Bad faith might be indicated, for example, if a government classified a document solely to make it immune from disclosure at the specific proceedings." Mosk and Ginsburg, *supra*. n. 30, p. 377.

146 In *UPS v Canada* the tribunal recognised that certain core interests in national defence and security would merit a high level of protection. The tribunal also noted that the phrase "state secrets" poses definitional difficulties because it does not necessarily have an established meaning: "the authority to which UPS referred us in support of limiting privilege to 'state secrets' does not provide a definition of that expression. Depending on the definition, that expression may of course cover a narrow or wide range of matters." *United Parcel Service of America v Government of Canada, supra* n. 138, Decision of the Tribunal Relating to Canada's Claim of Cabinet Privilege, para. 9 (8 October 2004). In an ICC arbitration concerning a claim brought by the Republic of China Navy against Thales, the French defence manufacturer, (known as the *Taiwanese Frigates* case) the respondent argued before French courts that certain aspects of the claimant's evidence were subject to "secret defence" and should be withdrawn from the arbitral record. The respondent's arguments were based upon the French criminal code which provided that documents which would be protected as *secret de la défense nationale* must (1) have a secret nature, (2) relate to national defence, (3) have been subject of classification measures for the purpose of restraining their disclosure. The respondent also based its argument on the French defence code which states that *secret de la défense nationale* in French law was not a matter of identifying the nature of the information or document but was a matter of administrative determination which is made evident by affixing a note reflecting this status on the relevant document or information. See: Cour d'appel de Paris, arrêt du 9 juin 2011, p. 8. See also the

"state secret" would only refer to such highly sensitive information or would also include a wider range of less delicate information. An assertion by a government of a right to maintain confidentiality over files kept pursuant to a legitimate criminal investigation, even one that does not qualify as pertaining to national security, also appear to be readily accepted by tribunals.[147]

9.98 As the wording of article 9.2(f) suggests, the ambit of this rule is not restricted only to state secrets, but also to evidence which may otherwise be qualified as having "special political or institutional sensitivity". Therefore, there are levels of information subsidiary to state secrets that also fall under this rule.[148]

9.99 "Cabinet confidence" and "deliberative privilege" are two such subsidiary categories of sensitive information that have been accepted at times as constituting compelling grounds.[149] These types of privilege generally protect the communications engaged in by high-level decision makers who are tasked with determining and implementing policy decisions on behalf of the government or other functions associated with drafting or implementing public laws. Deliberative privilege and cabinet confidence have been recognised as legitimate bars to disclosure by international arbitrators, such as in *Glamis Gold v United States of America* where the tribunal was inclined to support the protection of information exchanged during deliberative and policy-making processes except when the competing public interest in disclosure for the purposes of the arbitration outweighed such protection.[150]

9.100 Whether a tribunal will accept a designation under a domestic law exempting certain documents from being produced because they are "state secrets" or otherwise sensitive, appears to often turn on at least two key issues. The first is whether maintaining the confidentiality is consistent with the purpose of the protections provided by the invoked law or right. As one tribunal pointed out in another UNCITRAL Rules arbitration: "the protection to be afforded is in general carefully circumscribed to protect no more than the interests that call for protection, for instance in frank and uninhibited exchanges between cabinet members or in advice given to them."[151] The analysis primarily concerns itself with

---

comments of Mosk and Ginsburg, wherein they note the following upon review of the acceptance of privileges based on national security: "[t]hat the national security privilege is recognized for international criminal cases even with some exceptions, suggests that it would be recognized in civil proceedings – probably without exceptions. As a practical matter, no state will produce documents that it considers to be too sensitive for its national security interests." Mosk and Ginsburg, *supra* n. 30, p. 367.

147 See the following quote from the final award in an ICSID case presided over by well experienced arbitrators: "for greater clarity, the Tribunal adds that it accepts the invocation of privilege by the Respondent in relation to the police files concerning investigations into the alleged forgery, and in relation to documents concerning investigations into Messrs. [redacted] by the anti-corruption agency KPK, since they are covered by the secrecy of criminal investigations." *Churchill Mining v Indonesia*, ICSID Case No. ARB/12/14, Award (6 December 2016), para. 250. As noted below, where a state abuses its police powers in an effort to gain an advantage in a dispute with a private party, tribunals are less willing to accept assertions of confidentiality or privilege.

148 *Merrill & Ring Forestry v Canada*, *supra* n. 122, Decision of the Tribunal on Production of Documents, para. 18: "[t]he Tribunal believes that paragraph 6(f) of the Document Production order, like the equivalent provision of paragraph 9(2)(f) of the IBA Rules on the Taking of Evidence in International Commercial Arbitration, includes within the concept of 'special political or institutional sensitivity' the kind of privileged information to which the Canadian legislation refers. Even if such information is not formally classified as 'secret', the purpose of the privilege is quite evidently to prevent disclosure of documents containing information which is sensitive by nature."

149 *Ibid.*

150 *Glamis Gold v United States of America*, *supra* n. 25, Final Award, para. 237 (8 June 2009).

151 *UPS v Government of Canada*, *supra* n. 138, para. 11.

whether the state or institutional party is correctly applying the law on the issue.[152] Here, a tribunal may consider whether the law is truly intended to protect the communications in question from disclosure to the public,[153] or rather is intended to cover some other purpose, and further, whether there are means by which the public may gain access to that information under certain circumstances (e.g. freedom of information acts). A tribunal may also consider whether the government is consistent in its treatment of the information in question.[154] Where the tribunal finds that the state-party is selectively invoking confidentiality only over that evidence which it deems disadvantageous to its case, it may naturally dismiss the claim that the relevant documents are protected.[155] It follows from the general

---

152 *Ibid.* Here the tribunal considered whether the government official charged with designating the information as subject to "Cabinet Confidence" had weighed the interest in maintaining the confidentiality of the information against the public interest in disclosure. Finding he had not, the tribunal determined that the assertion of privilege over the documents was not substantiated by the state-party. In the *Taiwanese Frigates* case, the French respondent, Thales, applied to set aside the final award alleging that certain exhibits relied upon by the tribunal to render its award were classified *secret défense*. The Paris court of appeal noted that these documents had been obtained from judicial cooperation between Switzerland and Taiwan and another of the documents was a table prepared by a Swiss judge. Therefore, "all information contained within the documents was collected in Switzerland by the Swiss authorities and at no point could any of the exhibits have come from the French authorities on the proviso of being classified *secret défense* or requiring the French authority's prior approval for further disclosure." As a result, the relevant documents failed to satisfy the requirements of the French law on *secret de la défense nationale*. Cour d'appel de Paris, *supra* n. 146, pp. 8, 9.

153 See: *Windstream Energy LLC v Government of Canada*, PCA Case No. 2013-22, Procedural Order No. 4 (2015): "[t]he difference between the Parties concerns the scope of parliamentary privilege under Canadian law and its applicability in international arbitration proceedings where Canada itself is a party. While the Respondent takes the view that parliamentary privilege is 'absolute' and prevents the use of statements made by members of the legislature and by witnesses appearing before a parliamentary committee in subsequent legal proceedings, the Claimant argues that the privilege only precludes the use of such statements in subsequent civil and criminal proceedings against the individual who made the statement." *Ibid.*, p. 5. The Tribunal denied Canada's request that the documents be protected by parliamentary privilege and noted that: "[. . .] there is no dispute between the Parties insofar as they both appear to agree that under Canadian law parliamentary privilege precludes reliance on statements made before a parliamentary committee as evidence in civil and criminal proceedings against the individual who made the statement. However, this aspect of parliamentary privilege is irrelevant here as the purpose of this arbitration is not to determine the civil or criminal liability of any of the individuals in question, and obviously none of them appears as a respondent." *Ibid.*, p. 5.

154 *UPS v Canada*, *supra* n. 138, para. 12. The tribunal compared the documents which were claimed by the state-party to be subject to confidentiality against the purported policy reason for the confidentiality. In this regard, it felt that the disclosure of a number of the documents would not threaten in any way candour of communication of a vigorous deliberative process. This was particularly so, since five years had passed the drafts, reports and or other materials were originally prepared, and after the policy pursuant to which they were made in consideration of had already been made public. In *Merrill & Ring Forestry v Canada* the tribunal noted the confidentiality was not properly asserted because, *inter alia*: "such documents could reasonably be used for purposes entirely unrelated to the interest in the administration of justice that prevails in this case". *Merrill & Ring Forestry v Canada*, *supra* n. 122, Decision on Cabinet Privilege para. 24. The Paris court of appeal considered the issue of consistent treatment of allegedly classified information in the *Taiwanese Frigates* case. That case concerned a contract for the sale of six frigates that had been concluded in 1991. The claimant, the Taiwanese Navy, subsequently commenced an arbitration seeking repayment of illegal commission payments made by the respondent, the French defence manufacturer, Thales. Although the documents held by the French defence department had been classified in 1991, it had failed to notify Thales of the classification. In 2001, after the arbitration had commenced, Thales attempted to obtain retrospective classification and a capture-all classification of all auxiliary documents. The tribunal did not ultimately pronounce on this specific point as the claimant withdrew these allegedly offending exhibits and portions of the submission. Cour d'appel de Paris, *supra* n. 146, pp. 6, 7.

155 This principle is confirmed by the award rendered in a 1994 arbitration conducted under the then Geneva Chamber of Commerce, Industry and Services rules of arbitration. In this case, a state-agency party objected to the introduction of certain documents by the claimant arguing they represented, "top state secrets". However, as the tribunal pointed out in the final award, the state-party had referred to the content of those documents itself during the pleadings, and its legal counsel had referred to the documents during the hearing. This created the appearance

view that the mere certification of evidence by a government authority as confidential is not binding upon a tribunal, that the assessment of whether a document should be protected by governmental privilege from disclosure is a matter of substance over form – that is to say – a question of whether the content of the document is of the type that should qualify for protection under the domestic law (see further discussion regarding sensitive documents in the following subsection).[156]

9.101 In addition to the above, tribunals tend to extend the analysis one step further and inquire whether the interest in maintaining confidentiality over the evidence is compelling when weighed against other competing public interests such as the proper administration of justice.[157] Here, the relevance and materiality of the evidence is often weighed in manner similar to article 3.7 of the IBA Rules, to determine whether its likely probative value outweighs the need to maintain its confidentiality.[158] In this respect, the right of a state-party to assert privilege over certain types of information is distinguishable from attorney-client privilege. The latter is often considered an absolute right, which if found applicable (by virtue of a choice of law analysis) is not subject to the weighing of interests,[159] whereas the

---

that the state-party was claiming the right to confidentiality over state secrets only when it suited its arguments in the case. The tribunal did not accept the state-party's objection: "Defendant 1) would misuse its procedural rights by rejecting as evidence such exhibits presented by Claimant to which it has referred to itself. . . . The majority of the Arbitral Tribunal holds, contrary to Defendant 1)'s opinion, that those of Claimant's exhibits are admissible evidence where Claimant was not a party, which Defendant 1) calls 'top state secret' . . .". Decision of 28 February, *ASA Bulletin*, Vol. 13, No. 2, p. 312 (1995).

156 "It is not in dispute that a ground that may justify refusal of a party to produce documents to an international arbitral tribunal may be the protection of state secrets. But any reasonable evaluation of the quality of that justification must depend in large part on having some idea what those documents are. A determination by a tribunal that documents sufficiently identified deserve protection is a very different matter from acquiescence to a simple assertion, without any identification, that they deserve protection." *Pope & Talbot Inc v Canada*, *supra* n. 51, Decision on Crown Privilege and Attorney-Client Privilege, para. 1.4.

157 *Merrill & Ring Forestry v Canada*, *supra* n. 122, Decision on Cabinet Privilege (3 September 2008), para. 21: "[t]he second question the Tribunal needs to consider is the extent to which the availability of such documents might be crucial for the adequate preparation of the investor's memorials and the presentation of the case. The interest in the proper administration of justice is evident in this connection." In *Glamis Gold v United States of America*, the tribunal engaged in a similar analysis, and noted that: "[b]ased on Claimant's arguments and issues currently before the Tribunal in deliberations, the Tribunal has determined that these documents do appear to be material and that there is a need for the Tribunal to review them. Although the Tribunal recognizes the assertions for an interest in the deliberative process – privilege, it finds that the need to review these documents to be sufficiently great to override these interests." *Glamis Gold v United States of America*, *supra* n. 25, Final Award, para. 233 (8 June 2009).

158 *Ibid.*, *Merrill & Ring Forestry v Canada*: It follows that at least prima facie the production of these documents, with the exception noted, will weigh in favour of the interest in the administration of justice, particularly in view that they do not compromise the sensitivity of the Cabinet discussions and deliberations which would be protected by the public interest in non-disclosing. See also: *Vito Gallo v Canada*, *supra* n. 40, Procedural Order No. 3, para. 56, whereby the tribunal approved the disclosure of a document over which the respondent had claimed cabinet privilege because it had determined that the probative value of the document to the case outweighed the policy of protecting information exchanged during deliberative and policy-making processes.

159 "The Tribunal acknowledges Respondent's assertion that the documentary evidence that Claimant seeks does not in fact exist. Independent of the document's existence, the Tribunal notes that the attorney-client privilege is an absolute one." Charles H. Brower II, "Final Award, *Glamis Gold Ltd v United States of America*, 8 June 2009", *A Contribution by the ITA Board of Reporters*, para. 234. Mosk notes the general nature of privileges in international arbitration, "Privileges can be absolute – ie, the holder's refusal to provide the evidence is recognized under any circumstance – or it can be qualified – ie the evidence may be required under certain circumstances." Mosk, *supra* n. 30, p. 115. See: *William Ralph Clayton, William Richard Clayton, Douglas Clayton, Daniel Clayton And Bilcon Of Delaware Inc v Government Of Canada*, Permanent Court of Arbitration (PCA) Case No. 2009-04, Procedural Order No. 13 (2012): "[o]n the basis of Article 9.2(f), the Respondent contends that it is entitled to withhold the following documents from disclosure: – documents evidencing federal deliberations

assertion of a governmental privilege will only be applied if, given the competing interests in the arbitration, the tribunal feels compelled to uphold it.[160] A caveat to this second principle must be made for evidence where there is no doubt that it constitutes "state secrets", such as documents revealing sensitive details pertaining to national defence and/or security. Here it seems generally to be conceded that evidence of this nature should be protected from disclosure without reference to the weighing of competing interests.[161]

9.102 Finally it should also be noted that similar to objections brought under article 9.2(e), a tribunal may often be able to mitigate the confidentiality concerns of the state-party by issuing a procedural order on confidentiality.[162]

Sensitive documents

9.103 Assuming that the tribunal does regard the asserted sensitivity of a governmental or institutional document as compelling, it will still be tasked with determining whether the individual document over which the assertion has been made objectively falls within the claimed right.[163] The accepted means of dealing with this issue has been termed the

---

and decision-making; – documents evidencing provincial deliberations and decision-making; – documents evidencing the deliberations of the Joint Review Panel, a non-governmental advisory body; and, – documents evidencing deliberations of the National Energy Board." *Ibid.*, p. 3. The decision held that: "the Tribunal is satisfied on the basis of the Respondent's representations in good faith that the Respondent has reviewed all the documents over which it asserts privilege for their redactability. Regarding the Investors' argument concerning the need for further review where the Respondent has asserted more than one form of privilege, the Tribunal agrees with the *Gallo* tribunal that each claim of privilege must be addressed on its own merits where it is necessary to do so. However, the Tribunal is of the view that the clarifications made by the Respondent at the June 8 hearing dispose of the need for any further review with respect to these documents. The Respondent represented that "the information that is protected in these documents under 9.2(b) completely covers as well, the privilege based on a special political or institutional sensitivity" and that "the information protected on the basis of . . . solicitor-client privilege cannot be severed from the information . . . over which we have also claimed privilege on the basis of Article 9.2(f)." As a result, the Tribunal is satisfied that the documents in question need not be produced as a result of its Procedural Order No. 12." *Ibid.*, p. 14.

160 This is reflected in the language of art. 9.2(b) (note, for example, that there is no requirement that a tribunal find an applicable legal privilege to be compelling under art. 9.2(b)). Governmental privileges under art. 9.2(f), on the other hand, do not enjoy the same level of recognition in international procedural law, and as such, like business confidentiality under art. 9.2(e), are applied only if a tribunal is convinced, based on the underlying facts, that it is appropriate for it to uphold the rule. In *Vito Gallo v Canada*, the tribunal noted the following difference between the assertion of such a right to protection of sensitive governmental documents, and attorney-client privilege: "[t]he Arbitral Tribunal finds that, unlike cases in which solicitor-client privilege is pleaded, it must take into account Claimant's interests in the production of said documents in order to determine whether Canada's interests in withholding the documents are outweighed." *Vito Gallo v Canada*, *supra* n. 40, Procedural Order No. 3, p. 14.

161 *UPS v Canada*, *supra* n. 138, para. 9: "It may be that there are interests, [in] particular in respect of core national security or military secrets, where no such weighing is required, but Canada does not so contend in respect of Cabinet deliberations." See also the US perspective on this: "[m]oreover, where the state secret privilege is applicable, it is absolute, not qualified. The privilege applies even if access to the information is essential to sustain a civil claim or a criminal conviction." *Federal Rules of Evidence Manual*, *supra* n. 132, p. 28.

162 In both *Glamis Gold*, *supra* n. 25, and *Merrill & Ring Forestry*, *supra* n. 122, Decision on Crown Privilege (3 September 2008), the tribunal adopted such a solution.

163 See the following articulation of this point: "[t]he Tribunal is also persuaded, however, that the privilege, as held in *Pope & Talbot* and the *Canada-Aircraft* decisions invoked by the Investor, can only be asserted in respect of sufficiently identified documents together with a clear explanation about the reasons for claiming such privilege. The parties would need such information in order to assess whether they agree or disagree about a refusal on these grounds, just as the Tribunal needs it to decide in case of disagreement between the parties." *Merrill & Ring Forestry v Canada*, *supra* n. 122, Decision of the Tribunal on Production of Documents, para. 19.

"document by document" approach.[164] In essence, this procedure calls for the claiming party to provide the tribunal with a log of the documents over which it seeks to assert confidentiality. The log should describe each document, and provide summary reasons for why the content of each document is "sensitive". Parties availing themselves of the protection of governmental privilege often must provide to the tribunal, and the adverse party, sufficient factual description of the documents in order to meet their burden of sustaining an objection under article 9.2(f).[165]

9.104 Further to the above, once the tribunal is familiarised to some extent with the nature of the documents themselves, the question turns to what types of documents, or what characteristics will cause a tribunal to regard a document as "sensitive".

9.105 Here, the analysis will depend upon the particular facts of the case, although some basic principles may be gleaned from the available jurisprudence. Consistent with the general regard that is had for matters of national security by international tribunals, it would seem that wide deference is given to the assertion of confidentiality over documents which reveal non-public details concerning a government's defence and security arrangements. However, with respect to determining whether a document over which deliberative or cabinet privilege is asserted is truly "sensitive", the following analysis by the UNCITRAL tribunal in *Merrill & Ring Forestry v Canada* case is instructive:

> To the extent that a document might contain information on actual Cabinet discussions or deliberations, the sensitivity might of course be greater than if a document simply relates to material prepared for the consideration of the Cabinet. . . . The Tribunal is convinced that this distinction is appropriate in this case. Documents brought to the attention of the Cabinet in preparation of some eventual discussions or deliberations do not inhibit all such exercise. Some documents at hand originate in the work of government officials, including ministers, while some other[s] are contributed by private entities unrelated to government. None of them concern

---

164 As is noted in the quote above, the "document by document" method was first identified as having been used in the *Canada-Aircraft* decision of the WTO Dispute Resolution Panel decision. In this decision the question of governmental privilege was considered. There, the panel required the asserting state-party to provide a privilege log describing the author, type of document, general description of its subject matter content, and recipients of the contested communication. Appellate Body Report, *Canada – Measures Affecting the Export of Civilian Aircraft*, WT/DS70/AB/R, adopted 20 August 1999, DSR 1999: III, 1377.

165 This is true even where the asserted right to secrecy involves a claim that the documents are "state secrets": *Pope & Talbot Inc v Canada*, supra n. 51. See also the affirmation by the Paris court of appeal of a tribunal's right to determine the admissibility of documents including those classified *secret défense*: "it is the arbitrator's role, as any judge, without as much he would be deprived of his power to determine the dispute, to judge the admissibility of evidence presented before him and to exclude from the procedure evidence which is not legally produced . . ." (Unofficial translation) ("qu'il entre dans l'office de l'arbitre, comme de tout juge, sans qu'il soit pour autant privé de son pouvoir de trancher le fond du litige, d'apprécier l'admissibilité des preuves présentées devant lui et d'écarter de débats les pièces qui ne sont pas légalement produites . . ."). Cour d'appel de Paris, *supra* n. 146, p. 7. See also the decision of the Iran-US Claims Tribunal where the United States objected to a request for production by Iran of a classified intelligence document. The United States claimed that the document was a privileged "national security document" but provided no further details, in response to which the tribunal decided not to order its production. Interestingly, the tribunal retained the right to consider whether such failure to produce should give rise to an adverse inference indicating that it did not simply accept the unexplained assertion of the national security privilege: "[n]evertheless, the statement by the United States that it could not produce the Schedule or any part of the Schedule relating to Iran, even if the Tribunal should so request, makes it unnecessary for the Tribunal to issue any order pursuant to Iran's request and raises the consequent question whether it would be appropriate for the Tribunal to draw any adverse inference and, if so, the nature of any such inference." *The Islamic Republic of Iran v The United States of America*, Case No. A/30, Full Tribunal, Order of 4 November 1999.

actual discussions or deliberations of the Cabinet, let alone a decision on such recommendations. In practice some documents may not even get to be considered by the Cabinet or may be discarded.[166]

9.106 Thus, the rule adopted in *Merrill & Ring Forestry* suggests that documents prepared in consideration of eventual, high level meetings, but which do not actually record such discussions, are less likely to be considered "sensitive" protections. As attractive as the *Merrill & Ring Forestry* formula is, however, other tribunals may draw the line at different points based upon their own view of the facts, and the nature of the law upon which the right to confidentiality is based.[167]

9.107 Nevertheless, following along the general lines set forth above, arbitrators have ordered disclosure of drafts of publicly released documents and or memorandums,[168] information shared between governments on the drafts of relevant international treaties,[169] documents, that under the applicable law of the jurisdiction supplying the privilege, may be released to the public in other circumstances (e.g., such as under freedom of information acts),[170] and more generally, documents which due to the passing of time would not risk exposing the confidentiality of a deliberative process to harmful publicity.[171]

---

166 *Merrill & Ring Forestry v Canada, supra* n. 122, Decision on Crown Privilege (3 September 2008), para. 20.

167 *Glamis Gold v United States of America, supra* n. 25, Final Award, para. 240 (8 June 2009). The *Glamis Gold* tribunal distinguished between documents that contain mere details of an administrative process, which is to say, discussions of timelines and ministerial procedures, and those that move beyond such limits to actual consideration of policy decisions as its initial test of whether a document should come under the deliberative privilege. This may be affected by the nature of the domestic law under review. See discussion of deliberative privilege under US law: "[t]o qualify for the deliberative process privilege the information prepared by the government must be both *predecisional* and *deliberative*. The 'professional' requirement limits the privilege to the process of decision-making; the privilege is not designed to protect the final decision itself. The 'deliberative' requirement protects the free flow of official opinions and advice and the exercise of judgment; the privilege is not designed to protect simple fact-gathering or action by the official as to which there is no discretion or thought." *Federal Rules of Evidence Manual, supra* n. 132, p. 29.

168 *Vito Gallo v Canada, supra* n. 40, Procedural Order No. 3, para. 57: "it may be relevant to compare the draft version of the memorandum with its final version, since variations could reflect changes in the government of Ontario's opinion".

169 In the *Canfor v United States of America*, the tribunal noted the following concerning certain documents that had been prepared by the negotiating teams to the NAFTA treaty: "[t]he Tribunal has borne in mind its duty to conduct the arbitral proceeding in a way consistent with the principles of fairness and equality among the disputing parties. Without prejudice to the issue of whether the present dispute is an investment dispute and whether the Claimant's claim falls under Chapter Eleven of the NAFTA, the Tribunal notes that, in the context of investment disputes, each of the NAFTA Parties has accorded to the nationals of the other two Parties the right to submit to arbitration a claim on its own behalf regarding a dispute with that NAFTA Party. It is the Tribunal's view that had the dispute arisen between any of the NAFTA Parties rather than between one of the NAFTA Parties and a private party, the parties to the arbitration would have had equal access to the negotiating history of the Agreement as well as equal opportunity to resort to those documents. In this context, the Tribunal finds it consistent with the principle of equality that the parties to this arbitration are given the same opportunity to present their case, including the opportunity for the private party to access existing documents of the types specified above which are freely available to the government party, irrespective of whether such documents are ultimately conclusive as to any issue in dispute." *Canfor Corp v United States of America*, NAFTA/UNCITRAL, Procedural Order No. 5, para. 22 (28 May 2004).

170 *Merrill & Ring Forestry v Canada, supra* n. 122, Decision on Crown Privilege (3 September 2008), para. 24.

171 *UPS v Canada, supra* n. 138.

Example of the improper assertion of governmental privilege

9.108 As an example of the improper assertion of governmental privilege, reference may be had to an unpublished award rendered by an UNCITRAL Rules tribunal in a dispute between a European investor and an Asian state.[172] In this particular instance the investor-party requested that documents be produced which had been initially stored in his office, located within the respondent state. The state-party's security police had, prior to the initiation of the arbitration, raided the offices of the investor-party and taken numerous documents relevant to the case. When the investor-party sought the production of the documents that had been secured by the police, the state-party refused production because the documents were needed to effect its criminal prosecution of the investor in the national court. The tribunal rejected such reasoning, and ordered the state-party to turn over copies of all of the documents it had seized, as well as the contents of the file it had built on the investor.[173] This ruling is consistent with the observations of other tribunals that a state may not invoke its police powers in order to prevent, or otherwise hamper a party's attempts to prepare its case.[174]

Objections based on procedural economy, fairness and equal treatment

Article 9.2 2010 IBA Rules:	The Arbitral Tribunal shall, at the request of a Party or on its own motion, exclude from evidence or production any Document, statement, oral testimony or inspection for any of the following reasons:
	...
	(g) considerations of procedural economy, proportionality, fairness or equality of the Parties that the Arbitral Tribunal determines to be compelling.

General discussion

9.109 In the 1999 version of the IBA Rules, article 9.2(g) was regarded as a "catch-all" rule that had been included in order to allow international arbitrators a certain degree of flexibility when determining admissibility and document production issues. The text of article 9.2(g) was expanded in 2010 so that it now reads that a tribunal may exclude evidence or deny production requests for the additional reasons of "procedural economy or proportionality". Previously it was accepted that "procedural economy and proportionality" was implied in "fairness and equality." With the additional wording in the revised 2010 version of the article it is now clear that tribunals are expressly permitted to exert control over the evidentiary procedure where it is necessary for purposes of maintaining

---

172 *European Investor v Asian State*, UNCITRAL, Procedural Order No. 3 (2005) (unpublished).

173 *Ibid.* The tribunal's ruling was as follows: "[t]he Arbitral Tribunal notes Respondent's objection that the procedural file relating to these proceedings cannot be released at this time since judicial proceedings are still ongoing. The Arbitral Tribunal can see no reason, however, why it would not be possible to release copies of such documents."

174 See: *Libananco Holdings Co Ltd v Republic of Turkey*, ICSID Case No. ARB /06/08, Decision on Preliminary Issues (2008).

the efficient conduct of the procedure. What follows is a separate consideration of each of the four grounds listed in article 9.2(g).

Procedural economy

9.110 It is undisputed that a tribunal must act to ensure the reasonably efficient and proper conduct of the case, as efficiency is one of the inherent advantages of international arbitration.[175] The submission of evidence after the passing of a deadline, or a request for adverse document production submitted late may undermine the efficiency of the proceedings. The delay is compounded if the non-submitting party requires an opportunity to respond to an evidentiary submission that is late, or moreover asserts a right to submit counter evidence.[176] Where this occurs, a tribunal must be sensitive to the possible detriment suffered by the party who has observed the deadlines and acted in good faith to facilitate the procedure.[177] The following quote from an ICC tribunal establishes why deadlines cannot be ignored:

> To permit Respondents to ignore proceedings and then ask for more hearings would be grossly unfair to the other parties. The ICC Rules and English arbitration law are both premised on fairness to all parties. The most elementary notions of due process require that arbitrators show respect for the rights of both sides in a dispute. A respondent cannot ignore an arbitration until the last moment, and then expect to be permitted to file new counterclaims that require the other side to begin again almost at ground zero.[178]

9.111 The party who has abided by the deadlines has a due process interest in obtaining a reasonably efficient procedure, and the tribunal itself must be mindful of its mandate to render an award where the procedure has been fair to all parties. This being said, a tribunal must also ensure that a party has a fair opportunity to present its case. While case management interests require that deadlines are kept, overly strict adherence to timetables may

---

175 "Because the primary purpose of arbitration is expeditious resolution of disputes, a party's agreement to arbitrate trades the procedures of the court for the informality and expedition of the arbitration." *JJ-CC Ltd v Transwestern Pipeline Co et al.*, Lexis 7090, pp. 18–19 (Tex. App 1998). See: generally the comments to IBA Rules, art. 3.1.

176 As was noted by in a matter before the Iran-US Claims Tribunal, submissions containing new facts and evidence "are the most likely to cause prejudice to the other Party and to disrupt the arbitral process if filed late". *Dadras International v The Islamic Republic of Iran*, Albert Jan van den Berg (ed.), *Yearbook Commercial Arbitration*, Vol. XXII, p. 508 (1997).

177 See the following considerations of the SD Myer tribunal in regard to the schedule of proceedings: "[t]he Tribunal's point of departure is the presumption that a party to an arbitration (whether claimant or respondent) is entitled to have the arbitration proceedings continue at a normal pace." *SD Myers Inc v Government of Canada*, *supra* n. 139, Procedural Order No. 18, p. 5 (26 February 2001). See also: ICC Case No. 10621, Final Award, *ICC Bulletin*, Vol. 17, No. 2, p. 78 (2006).

178 *Ibid.* In addition to the quote above, the tribunal also opined as follows: "Section 33 of the 1996 English Arbitration Act imposes on the arbitrators a duty to 'act fairly and impartially as between the parties, giving each party a reasonable opportunity of putting his case and dealing with that of his opponent.' Both companies had the opportunity to submit powers of attorney and state claims during the ten months before the hearings. It would be grossly unfair to Claimant to permit Respondents to re-open matters at such a late date, without any justification except the 'oversight' given by Mr. [A] and Mr. [B] as the reason for non-participation in most of the proceedings." Sandifer relates in his treatise an example from the Mexico-US Claims Commission, where the Mexican side submitted evidence over a year and a half after the deadline. The Umpire of the tribunal rejected the evidence, noting that: "[i]f this evidence be admitted in the present case, the claimant must be allowed, to produce rebutting testimony and there is no just reason why he should be allowed the same term as was employed by the defendant to procure his proofs." Durward Sandifer, *Evidence Before International Tribunals*, p. 53, 2nd edition, 1975.

mean that vital evidence is excluded. As international arbitrators operate in a transnational context that involves parties and counsel from different jurisdictional backgrounds with varying views on judicial process, and where logistics are complicated by vast distances between the participants, flexibility is often required. Therefore, the following standard articulated by an Iran-US Claims Tribunal panel sets forth a number of valuable considerations regarding belated submissions of evidence:

> In determining whether to admit a late submission, the Tribunal has frequently referred to these fundamental requirements of equality between, and fairness to, the Parties, and the possible prejudice to either party. Further, the orderly conduct of the proceedings also requires that time limits be established and enforced. In applying these principles to the specific facts of a case, however, the Tribunal considers the character and contents of late-filed documents and the length and cause of the delay. These factors affect the probability of prejudice, the equality of treatment of the Parties, and the disruption of the arbitral process by the delay.[179]

9.112 Of the issues set forth above, equal treatment and fairness are overarching procedural themes that are always relevant to the acts of a Tribunal. In terms of specific considerations in this context, it is often that a tribunal will decide whether procedural economy, or "orderly conduct of the proceedings" should lead to exclusion of evidence based on three criteria: (1) the probative value or character of the evidence on offer;[180, 181] (2) the prejudice to the adverse party that would be caused by admitting the evidence (which includes a consideration of the general disruption to the procedure which would result);[182] and

---

179 *Harris International Telecommunications Inc v The Islamic Republic of Iran*, Partial Award No. 323-409-1, in Albert Jan van den Berg (ed.), *Yearbook Commercial Arbitration*, Vol. XIV, para. 61 (1989).

180 See the following decision of an ICSID tribunal to deny the introduction of belatedly offered documentary evidence, after considering the relevance of the documents to the proceedings: "[o]n October 23, 2009, Argentina wrote to the Centre in order to inform the Tribunal about facts related to a labour dispute between Total and one of its former employees. According to Argentina's letter, the facts on which the aforementioned labour dispute are based are of particular relevance to these arbitration proceedings. The Tribunal expresses its doubts that the facts outlined by the Respondent in its letter are relevant to the ongoing arbitration proceedings. The Tribunal notes that the Respondent is seeking to place new documents and arguments on the record of the case, contrary to the previous decisions taken by the Tribunal relating to the production of documents. The Respondent's request was absolutely out of time in view of the stage of the proceedings. The Tribunal determines, therefore, that it cannot either admit these documents as evidence or take into consideration the legal arguments based thereon." *Total SA v Argentine Republic*, Decision on Liability, ICSID Case No. ARB/04/1, para. 22 (2010).

181 *The Islamic Republic of Iran v United States of America*, Case Nos A3, A8, A9, A14 and B61, Procedural Order of 1 April 2005, para. 10 (2009): "[t]he tribunal is reluctant to permit the untimely filing to disrupt its proceedings. It is also reluctant to reject as untimely evidence, which while late, may be important for the fair resolution of the Claims involved. Accordingly, the Tribunal accepts the documents for inclusion in the record of these Cases. The Claimant shall submit no further evidence or memorial unless so authorized in advance by the Tribunal." See also the considerations of a Society of Maritime Arbitrators tribunal in favour of permitting relevant evidence to be submitted onto the record late: "Owner's last minute submission protracted the case and caused additional expense to both parties. However, the evidence was relevant and tended to strengthen owner's demurrage claim. It was preferable as a matter of policy to avoid creating disincentives to submission of additional evidence which would result in a more complete record." *Ionian Shipping Ltd v Hugo Neu & Sons International Sales Corporation*, Final Award, SMAAS, WL 1378378 (1987).

182 See: *Zeevi Holdings v The Republic of Bulgaria et al.*, UNCITRAL Arbitration Case UNC 39/DK, Procedural Order No. 17, in which the tribunal decided to exclude documents enclosed to Claimant's Post-Hearing Brief. *Inter alia*, the Tribunal stated that: "Procedural Order No. 16 expressly provided that 'no new documents' were admitted at this stage" and "[a]dmitting these new documents would give Claimant an unfair advantage in this procedure which could only be levelled by admitting Respondents to reply to these new documents and also be permitted to submit further documents in rebuttal, to which, in turn, Claimant would then have to be permitted to reply. This would re-open and prolong this already by now extremely long arbitral procedure even further. The Tribunal sees no justification for such a prolongation." *Ibid.*, p. 62, §61. The disruption to the procedure may

(3) the cause of the delay,[183] in particular whether it was legitimately incurred and reasonable given the circumstances.[184]

---

be measured by whether the adverse party is already aware of the content of the late-filed evidence, if the new information would introduce new facts to the record, whether the schedule would allow for rebuttal of the new evidence, if necessary, and if due to the volume of the information submitted, a party would have adequate time to review it properly and prepare its case before a hearing. See, for example, the considerations of an Iran-US Claims Tribunal panel where a decision to deny a request to admit late-filed documents considered similar factors: "[t]he documents that the Claimant belatedly asks the Tribunal to consider are either documents already available in the record of this Case, such as the Company Registry, or are said to have come from the files of Joseph Mandell, an attorney who the record shows has long been involved in matters related to the transactions that are the basis of the claim. Moreover, the evidence shows that Mr. Mandell acted as counsel both for General Petrochemicals Corp and General Petrochemicals Anstalt. There is no indication that Mr. Mandell's files have not been available to the Claimant at all times in its preparation of this Case." *General Petrochemicals Corp v The Islamic Republic of Iran*, Case No. 828, Award No. 522-828-1, p. 22 (21 October 1991). For a contrary perspective, see the finding of the tribunal in ICC Case No. 12944, where it ruled in relation to an objection to late-filed expert witness reports: "[t]he Arbitral Tribunal accepts the arguments of Respondent as to these two Expert Submissions and believes that Claimant has more than sufficient time to address the contents, including any assumptions, data or expert opinion which is set forth in any of the challenged expert documents prior to the Witness Hearings starting at the end of January 2005. Such evidence can also be addressed, as [Claimant] sees fit including arguments as to its relevance and/or correctness, in [Claimant's] final brief due on 24 December 2004. Hence the Arbitral Tribunal denies [Claimant's] request that these documents be stricken from the Arbitration Record." ICC Case No. 12944, Order of 23 November 2004, *ICC Bulletin, 2010 Special Supplement: Decisions on ICC Arbitration Procedure*, p. 82. See also an arbitration between a Chinese party and an American party over the construction of a plant in Pakistan held under the international rules of the AAA (now ICDR), in which the claimant produced on the first day of the hearing a report that had been a point of discussion between the parties but hitherto had not been produced. Later, when challenging the final award the respondent sought to have the award set aside because of the late production of the evidence. As the reviewing court noted in rejecting the challenge, the delayed production seemed to have been inadvertent, however, also of importance was the fact that the respondent could not identify in any meaningful way how the late introduction of the evidence would have changed or impacted its case preparation since it had enough time to address the evidence during the hearing and in post hearing briefs. *Trans Chemical Ltd v China National Machinery Import and Export Corp*, 978 F.Supp 266, 307 (SD Tex. 1997).

183 See: ICC Case No. 15416, in which the tribunal noted, in regard to belatedly offered evidence, that there was reasonable explanation for why the document had not been submitted before the deadline, and thus permitted the late offer of evidence: "[t]he tribunal considered whether to allow proposed exhibit C-331 to be admitted. Considering that the document was created at a time when neither party had an opportunity to submit it within the timetable, and in light of the fact that the document is a public document, the Tribunal concluded that it should admit the document." ICC Case No. 15416, Final Award, para. 49 (2011) (unpublished). In an interesting situation where a party claimed that it was unable to present its documentary evidence on time because of court injunctions issued against it, an UNCITRAL tribunal noted that it seemed that a third party, under the control of the complaining party, was behind the attempts to block its participation in the proceedings. The tribunal therefore refused to accept the reasons for not submitting the evidence on time, and provided the following stern warning: "[t]he respondent is formally put on notice that unless it forthwith makes a compelling demonstration to the Arbitral Tribunal that it is powerless to influence the actions [of the third-party], it will be held to be in breach of the Terms of Appointment and will have to face the full consequences of that breach." *Himpurna California Energy Ltd v Republic of Indonesia*, Interim Award of 26 September 1999 and Final Award of 16 October 1999, in Albert Jan van den Berg (ed.), *Yearbook Commercial Arbitration*, Vol. XXV, p. 135 (2000). See also: the decision of an ICDR tribunal not to permit the submission of evidence after the passing of a deadline. In this instance, the proffering party argued that the information was on a computer server that was not available, and thus the respondent required more time to obtain said information. Because the tribunal was provided so few details concerning the cause of the delay, and in consideration of the fact that the party failed to give prompt notice of the delay, the tribunal determined not to permit the late submission of evidence. "Respondent's request for an extension does not present good cause. There is no detail of what type of information is on the computer server to which Respondent does not have access. There is no indication of what efforts, if any, Respondent made to obtain the information on the server. There is no reason given for why this issue could not have been raised to the arbitrator before the [deadline]." ICDR Case No. 50117, Award of Arbitrator, para. 4 (2011) (unpublished).

184 A tribunal will often wish to be apprised of the reasons for the delay. With a minor delay in production (within days of a deadline), arbitrators may be satisfied to know that the failure to file on time was due to an inadvertent mistake. However, with longer delays it may be that the proffering party will be required to show

9.113 A tribunal will likely take into account the particular needs and context of the case when weighing these issues.

Proportionality

9.114 Under article 9.2(g) a tribunal may cite proportionality as a basis for denying a request for document production or otherwise refusing to admit evidence. This ground is closely related to the issue of burden covered in article 9.2(c) of the IBA Rules. In the instance where a party raises the objection of burden, it must show that the effort and cost that production will impose will create an objectively substantial, and unreasonable burden. Under the proportionality grounds of 9.2(g), a tribunal may determine that while the evidence requested may be relevant and material, the issue in contention does not warrant the effort required to submit the evidence (for a more detailed discussion of this ground see per article 9.2(c)).

Fairness

9.115 As a mandatory fundamental principle, procedural fairness in arbitration requires that each party be afforded a reasonable opportunity to present their evidence and arguments.[185] This is generally fulfilled by the equitable administration of the procedural

---

that the failure to submit the evidence was due to an unforeseeable set of circumstances beyond its control, or, if it was foreseeable, that it was certainly a reasonable oversight which could not be detected until that moment. In ICC Case No. 5082 the tribunal noted in regard to the evidence it rejected from the record: "[f]or the majority of the Arbitrators, Claimant should not have waited until the end of the oral hearings, after nearly two years during which Parties exchanged their briefs, to present those documents, so that its adversary could not usefully explain itself on their meaning and their scope. Claimant, which does not invoke any force majeure justifying that delay, is not entitled to produce said documents at this stage of the proceedings." ICC Case No. 5082, Procedural Order No. 1, Dominique Hascher (ed.), *Collection of Procedural Decisions in ICC Arbitration 1993–1996*, pp. 43, 44 (2nd edition, 1998). See also where a party was in possession of the evidence for a considerable period prior to submitting it, the tribunal may find the excuse for the delay less reasonable: "[t]he crucial question then is whether the letter was presented by Agrostruct as evidence in rebuttal of evidence presented for the first time by the Respondents at the Hearing. According to Agrostruct, the Respondents for the first time at the Hearing specifically denied that Agrostruct had requested the opening of a letter of credit immediately after the signing of the Contract. However, throughout their pleadings the Respondents denied an obligation to open the letter of credit within a specific time limit. Since the existence of such an obligation is part of Agrostruct's case-in-chief, the burden was on Agrostruct to produce on time all evidence to support its argument. The evidence presented at the Hearing was easily accessible to Agrostruct earlier in the proceedings. Therefore, the Tribunal denies the admissibility of this evidence." [Internal citations omitted] *Agrostruct International, Inc v Iran State Cereals Organization*, Case No. 195, Award No. 358-195-1 of 15 April 1988, p. 11. See also the following rule adopted in ICC Case No. 12761: "[t]hose documents which have not been presented by the Parties within the presentation date of the evidential proposal writs, will not be admissible until it is demonstrated, to the satisfaction of the Arbitral Tribunal, that they are newly discovered or that the possibility to submit these at the time did not exist." ICC Case No. 12761, Procedural Order of 12 March 2004, *supra* n. 11, p. 73.

185 In opining on its own arbitral rules, a panel of the Mexico-US Mixed Claims Commission considered the fairness criterion as it applied to its own procedure: "the Commission called attention to the purpose of the rules that the Commission and each party to the arbitration should be fully informed at the proper time regarding contentions advanced and evidence on which they are based. In the instant case, the Commission adopted a course obviously fair to both parties, namely to allow each the time to reply to new matters. For irrespective of what might have been a proper disposition of the question arising out of the indifferent preparation of the American Memorial and brief, the Commission could not properly ignore Mexican counsel's departure from the Answer and at the same time refuse to give consideration to important evidence accompanying the Memorial and to applicable law." *William T. Way (United States of America) v United Mexican States*, 18 October 1928, 4

rules.[186] The principle of fairness typically calls for tribunals to apply the same limitations on document disclosure to both parties.[187] Moreover, where a party submits evidence into the proceedings at a late stage, a tribunal may decline to admit such evidence if the adverse

---

RIAA, pp. 399–400. See also: *Paklito Investment Ltd v Klockner East Asia Ltd*, Supreme Court of Hong Kong, High Court, in Albert Jan van den Berg (ed.), *Yearbook of Commercial Arbitration*, Vol. XIX, p. 670 (1994). See also, with regard to international sports arbitration, the following quote from a CAS tribunal which notes that this principle is fundamental for all facets of the arbitration process: "[the Panel] observes that the CAS has always considered the right to be heard as a general legal principle which has to be respected also during internal proceedings of the federations (G v/ FEI, CAS 91/53, Award of 15 January 1992, Dig. pp. 79, 86 f). Federations have the obligation to respect the right to be heard as one of the fundamental principles of due process." *A v Federation Internationale des Luttes Associées (FILA)*, Award of 9 July 2001, CAS 2000/A/317, in Matthieu Reeb (ed.), *Digest of CAS Awards III 2001–2003*, pp. 159–172 (2004).

186 Where the parties reach an agreement concerning the arbitration procedure, they cannot subsequently complain that the procedure is not fair if the tribunal chooses to follow the parties' agreement. In a challenge to an award rendered under the Hong Kong International Arbitration Centre Rules, a party challenged the decision of the tribunal because, in part, the tribunal had accepted the witness statement of one of the parties without scheduling a cross-examination of the witness. This was done because the parties had agreed in advance to a "documents only" arbitration. The reviewing court noted as follows: "[t]he submission that [there] was no evidence from the respondent is fallacious. Neither party's witness statement was under oath, neither witness statement was in the form of an affidavit. Neither were required to be either on oath, or in the form of an affidavit. The parties agreed upon the procedure, and agreed upon the absence of cross-examination, and the applicant cannot now complain about that procedure." *Taigo Ltd v China Master Shipping Ltd* [2010] HKCFI 5330; HCCT22/2010 (17 June 2010) para. 11.

187 See the unpublished procedural directive of an NAI tribunal which had determined to limit rebuttal evidence to a particular type of evidence consisting of published documents. The claimant subsequently filed an additional report of its appointed expert which the respondent objected to as falling outside the scope of the permitted submission. The tribunal in consideration of the arguments, in its procedural directive declared the report inadmissible as falling outside the scope of the limited opportunity to submit further documents. NAI Case No. 3702, Procedural Directive of 20 September 2011 (unpublished). See also the decision of an Iran-US Claims Tribunal panel in *Kamran Hakim v The Islamic Government of Iran* where after the hearing the tribunal issued a procedural order restricting any further evidence to only those documents which could be described as "public" information. A subsequent submittal of evidence by the claimant was unsuccessfully contested by the respondent alleging that the evidence contained internal governmental documents which the respondent argued were not "public" documents. The following decision by the tribunal illustrates some relevant considerations: "[i]n its June 1997 response, the Respondent argued that the [contested document] and the notice of changes were inadmissible because they were late-filed and were not documents of public record. The Respondent argued also that their admission would be inconsistent with Tribunal practice, would seriously prejudice the Respondent and would disrupt the orderly conduct of the proceedings. The Tribunal notes that the [contested document] appears on its face to be an internal government communication. Thus, without further information, one might think it not publicly available. However, in its June 1997 response, which has been admitted by the Tribunal, the Respondent annexed an official Ministry of Justice Notice of Appointment, issued by the Bureau for the Registration of Companies and dated 1 December 1980. This document is an official publication of Mr. Khatibi's appointment as an observer for PMMC, and it refers to the [contested document]. That reference shows the public nature of the [contested document]. A full understanding of the Ministry of Justice Appointment Notice required an examination of the [contested document], and the Tribunal infers that the Ministry of Justice Appointment Notice would not have referred to the [contested document] unless it could be so examined. Thus, the Tribunal considers the [contested document] to be a document of public nature admissible pursuant to the Order communicated to the Parties at the Hearing." *Kamran Hakim v The Islamic Government of Iran*, Case No. 953, Award No. 587-953-2, paras 12–13 (1998). See also the decision of an ICDR tribunal not to admit a portion of a witness statement because it was considered that the witness was offering expert instead of factual testimony, after the procedural cut-off for the offering of expert witness testimony. "On 12 December 2006, the Arbitrator issued Procedural Order No. 2 ruling that paragraphs 5 to the end of the witness statement of [witness name] submitted by [claimant], constituted expert testimony submitted after the due date for submission of expert reports, and would not be considered by the Arbitrator. [the witness'] live testimony also would not be heard on the subjects covered in paragraph 5 to the end of the [witness statement]." ICDR Case No. 50154, Final Award, para. 14 (2007) (unpublished). Later, when the parties agreed to amend the schedule to permit the adverse party an opportunity to respond, the offending portion of the witness statement was admitted to the record.

party would not have a fair opportunity to respond, as the following comments from a decision of an *ad hoc* annulment committee explains:

> The right to present one's case is also accepted as an essential element of the requirement to afford a fair hearing accorded in the principal human rights instruments. This principle requires both equality of arms and the proper participation of the contending parties in the procedure, these being separate but related fundamental elements of a fair trial. The principle will require the tribunal to afford both parties the opportunity to make submissions where new evidence is received and considered by the tribunal to be relevant to its final deliberations.[188]

9.116 As the quote above sets forth, the "equality of arms" inherently implies "fairness". Generally speaking, this criterion stands for the proposition that neither party should be at a substantial disadvantage, nor should it cause its opponent to be disadvantaged in the preparation of their case. A judicial definition of equality of arms may be taken from the jurisprudence of the European Court of Human Rights, where it has been held in relation to civil disputes, "each party must be afforded a reasonable opportunity to present his case – including his evidence – under conditions that do not place him at a substantial disadvantage vis-à-vis his opponent".[189]

9.117 One of the leading cases on equality of arms and evidentiary procedure is *Methanex v United States of America* decided by an UNCITRAL tribunal. Here the tribunal considered that the equality of arms principle acted to prevent the admissibility of evidence obtained by the claimant through illegal means. In this instance, agents acting for the claimant had obtained documents by trespassing onto private property. While not establishing that the claimant had intended to violate the law, the tribunal was satisfied that it had acted with reckless disregard for it, and thus the improperly attained evidence was declared inadmissible. The relevant portion of this award is quoted below:

> In the Tribunal's view, the Disputing Parties each owed in this arbitration a general legal duty to the other and to the Tribunal to conduct themselves in good faith during these arbitration proceedings and to respect the equality of arms between them, the principles of "equal treatment" and procedural fairness being also required by Article 15(1) of the UNCITRAL Rules. As a general principle, therefore, just as it would be wrong for the USA *ex hypothesi* to misuse its intelligence assets to spy on Methanex (and its witnesses) and to introduce into evidence the resulting materials into this arbitration, so too would it be wrong for Methanex to introduce evidential materials obtained by Methanex unlawfully.[190]

9.118 Jurisprudence developed since the *Methanex* decision has confirmed this rule, and essentially carried it forward as a basic tenet of procedural fairness as found in the provisions of article 9.2(g). For example, consider the following observation from the *EDF Services Ltd v Romania*, where an ICSID tribunal, cited to the *Methanex* rule stating: "Tribunal[s] should refuse to admit evidence into the proceedings if, depending on the circumstances under which it was obtained and tendered to the other Party and the Tribunal, there are good reasons to believe that those principles of good faith and procedural fairness have not been respected . . . The foregoing finds confirmation in the IBA Rules [to] which

---

188 See also: *Fraport AG Frankfurt Airport Services Worldwide v The Philippines*, ICSID Case No. ARB/03/25, Decision on the Application for Annulment, para. 133 (2010).

189 *Dombo Beheer BV v The Netherlands*, European Court of Human Rights, Case No. 14448/88, Judgment of 27 October 1993.

190 *Methanex Corp v United States of America*, NAFTA/UNCITRAL, Final Award, p. 25 (2005).

reference may be made as guidelines. Article 9(2)(g) of the Rules provides that evidence may be excluded in the presence of 'considerations of fairness or equality of the Parties that the Arbitral Tribunal determines to be compelling'."[191] The *EDF* tribunal would go on to declare recordings obtained in violation of Romanian law to be inadmissible.[192]

9.119 Therefore, the general rule as taken from both of these precedents is that evidence gathered by a party through illegal means may be excluded from an arbitral proceeding under article 9(2)(g). Nevertheless, this rule must also be accepted on the proviso that it is always up to the reasonable discretion of the tribunal to determine whether a taint of illegality attached to evidence is of such a nature as to render it inadmissible. Further, available case law indicates that evidence offered in violation of a contractual duty of confidentiality or other restrictions rooted in contract do not give rise to the application of the *Methanex-EDF* rule of exclusion.[193] Finally, a party claiming that the evidence was procured illegally bears the burden of providing prima facie evidence to support its position; a mere allegation is not a sufficient basis for excluding the evidence from the record.[194]

9.120 As was also noted in the ruling quoted above, the fairness or equality of arms principle may also act to exclude a state-party from introducing evidence it has gained through the deployment of its sovereign powers, such as police powers, for the purpose of preparing its case. This principle came to the fore in *Libananco Holdings v Turkey*, an

---

191 The Tribunal would also issue the following instructive considerations: "[g]enerally, international tribunals take a liberal approach to the admissibility of evidence. The Tribunal is of the view, however, that such discretion is not absolute. In the Tribunal's judgment, there are limits to its discretion derived from principles of general application in international arbitration, whether pursuant to the Washington Convention or under other forms of international arbitration. Good faith and procedural fairness being among such principles, the Tribunal should refuse to admit evidence into the proceedings if, depending on the circumstances under which it was obtained and tendered to the other Party and the Tribunal, there are good reasons to believe that those principles of good faith and procedural fairness have not been respected." *EDF (Services) Ltd v Romania*, ICSID Case No. ARB/05/13, Procedural Order No. 3, para. 47 (2009).

192 "The Tribunal believes that admissibility of unlawfully obtained evidence is to be evaluated in the light of the particular circumstances of the case, as in the case of the ICJ Judgment in the *Corfu Channel Case* ([1949] ICJ Rep 4). Admitting the evidence represented by the audio recording of the conversation held in Ms Jacob's home, without her consent in breach of her right to privacy, would be contrary to the principles of good faith and fair dealing required in international arbitration. In that regard, the Tribunal shares the position of the *Methanex* award. On that basis as well, the New Evidence is not admissible in the instant case". *Ibid., EDF Ltd v Romania*, para. 38.

193 The tribunal in the *Enron v Argentina* case found that a confidentiality undertaking allegedly restraining a witness from testifying, was a legal issue personal to that witness, and was not grounds for denying the admissibility of the witness statement. The tribunal maintained its position even after a court injunction was issued ordering the witness not to give testimony in the arbitration. The annulment committee considered the tribunal's admittance of the evidence and noted that: "[t]ribunals might reach different conclusions on whether or not evidence should be admitted in such circumstances. Regardless of which view a tribunal may take, its decision will not amount to an annullable error unless one of the grounds of annulment in art. 52(1) of the ICSID Convention is established. Regardless of which view a tribunal may take on the issue in the circumstances of the present case, the Committee is not satisfied that the decision could without more constitute a serious departure from a fundamental rule of procedure." *Enron Creditors Recovery Corp, Ponderosa Assets LP v The Argentine Republic*, ICSID Case No. Arb/01/3, Decision on Annulment, para. 178 (2010).

194 In a Geneva Chamber of Commerce arbitration a government entity in a dispute with a private party sought to have certain evidence declared inadmissible on, *inter alia*, grounds that the evidence was obtained through secret channels and also illegally. The tribunal noted in rejecting such a claim that without evidence to support its allegation that actual laws had been broken, the tribunal could not accept this objection: "[t]he principle of fair trial demands to admit not only those questions and answers at the hearing of evidence which relates to those documents, but also the photocopies presented as exhibits by the Claimant . . . it has not been established by the Defendants that those copies have in fact been obtained illegally". Decision of 28 February, *ASA Bulletin*, *supra* n. 90, p. 316.

ICSID case where the tribunal had before it an allegation by the investor that the Turkish government was using police surveillance and investigatory powers to gather evidence on the claimant in preparation of its case preparation. The tribunal made the following observation concerning the duty of a state to refrain from using its inherent powers to exercise undue influence over evidentiary procedure: "[t]he right and duty [of a state] to investigate crime . . . cannot mean that the investigative power may be exercised without regard to other rights and duties, or that by starting a criminal investigation, a state may baulk an ICSID arbitration."[195]

9.121 In consideration of the balance between the interest a state has in carrying out legitimate criminal investigations and the unfair use of police power to obtain evidence, a general rule of procedure was formulated known as the "rule of separation". This rule was described by the *Libananco* tribunal as follows:

> The Tribunal recognizes that the Respondent may in the legitimate exercise of its sovereign powers conduct investigations into suspected criminal activities in [its jurisdiction]. The Respondent must, however, ensure that no information or documents coming to the knowledge or into the possession of its criminal investigations authorities shall be made available to any person having any role in the defence of this arbitration.[196]

9.122 Therefore, where a state-party has unfairly coerced a witness into giving contradictory testimony,[197] used its police powers to intercept internal communications of a private party (including between counsel and a party),[198] or otherwise acted to procure evidence that would not normally be available to it if it did not have the investigatory or police powers of a state, a tribunal may regard that evidence as having been obtained unfairly. If so, then under article 9.2(g) a tribunal may declare such evidence inadmissible.

9.123 Beyond situations involving the unlawful collection of evidence, or attempts by a state party to use its sovereign powers to unfairly influence evidentiary procedure, the doctrine of equality of arms, or fairness, may be a basis for excluding evidence where a party appears to be manipulating access to relevant information. For example, if a party has claimed in the proceedings that certain evidence is not within its possession custody or control in response to a disclosure request, it has been held that procedural fairness requires

---

195 *Libananco Holdings v Turkey*, *supra* n. 174, Decision on Preliminary Issues, para. 38. See also the procedural direction in UNCITRAL arbitration, *Chevron v Ecuador* which imposed the following obligation upon Ecuador, derived from the equality of arms principle: "[t]he Respondent is ordered to facilitate and not discourage, by every appropriate means, the Claimant's engagement of legal experts, advisers and representatives from the Ecuadorian legal profession for the purpose of these arbitration proceedings (at Claimant's own expense)." *Chevron Corp and Texaco Petroleum Co v Republic of Ecuador*, UNCITRAL, Interim Award on Interim Measures, p. 5 (2012).

196 *Ibid.*, para. 42.

197 While affirming the right of a party to interview an opponent's witnesses, the ICSID tribunal in the *Azinian v Mexico* arbitration noted that where a witness "freely" chooses to meet with the opposing side, and is informed that he or she may be represented by legal counsel, such an interview is not considered to be witness tampering. Moreover, to the extent that an interview is recorded, the tribunal noted that only testimony given in a "signed written statement" would be admitted into the record. It was not required, however, that the party whose case the witness had supported be allowed to have a legal representative present at such an interview. *Azinian v United Mexican States*, ICSID Case No. ARB(AF)/97/2 (1999), in Albert Jan van den Berg (ed.), *Yearbook Commercial Arbitration*, Vol. XXV, p. 265 (2000).

198 *Libananco Holdings v Turkey*, *supra* n. 174, Decision on Preliminary Issue, pp. 35–46.

that such party not be allowed to later present such evidence in support of its own case. This position was adopted by an LCIA tribunal which formulated the following rule:

> The Parties cannot expect to rely on documents which they have previously stated do not exist. Accordingly, documents which are not produced to the parties prior to the hearing will not be admitted into evidence at the hearing or at a later stage in the arbitration without the tribunal's permission.[199]

9.124 This principle has also been extended to expert evidence to the effect that if the party presenting an expert witness has refused an order to disclose to the adverse party relevant evidence on which the expert relied, a tribunal may, under principles of procedural fairness, disregard the expert report itself.[200] Furthermore, where it has been shown that a party is actively impeding an adverse party from obtaining relevant information from a particular source, a tribunal may consider it appropriate to exclude either party from producing evidence from such a source, unless equal access is guaranteed, on fairness grounds.[201] One may expect that in all situations, the tribunal will consider the circumstances of the case to determine whether such an exclusionary rule is warranted.

Equality

9.125 The obligation to treat the parties with equality is a fundamental rule of procedure widely accepted as a mandatory aspect of due process. Tribunals generally recognise this obligation, irrespective of the procedural rules chosen to govern the arbitration, as was noted by an ICC tribunal:

> If the Parties have not agreed the procedure it will be by necessity fixed by the arbitral tribunal be it directly or be it by reference to a law or by reference to arbitral rules. Whatever may be the procedure chosen, the arbitral tribunal must guarantee the equality between the parties, and their right to be heard in a contradictory proceeding.[202]

---

199 LCIA Case No. 6827, Final Award, para. 45 (2008) (unpublished).

200 See the following reasoning of a panel of the Iran-US Claims Tribunal: "[t]he Tribunal emphasizes at the outset that there must be procedural equality between the Parties. At the Claimant's request, the Tribunal, by its page Orders of 18 November 1994 and 18 May 1995, requested the Respondent to produce various documents and financial records of Iran Bohler demanded by the Claimant, on which Mr. Ghorbani-Farid's report was constructed. The Respondent has not produced them, and thus the Respondent's expert had access to information that was not made available to the Claimant. The Tribunal cannot, therefore, accept the premises on which Mr. Ghorbani-Farid's report is built, because the Claimant has been deprived of the opportunity to rebut the findings of the report. Accordingly, the Tribunal takes no account of Mr. Ghorbani-Farid's report with respect to Iran Bohler." *Frederica Lincoln Riahi v The Islamic Republic of Iran*, Award No. 600-485-1 of 27 February 2003, in Albert Jan van den Berg (ed.), *Yearbook Commercial Arbitration*, Vol. XXVIII, p. 524 (2003).

201 In an arbitration conducted under the United Nations Convention of the Law of the Sea (UNCLOS) between the states of Guyana and Suriname, a tribunal considered the request by Guyana, for an order requiring Suriname to permit it to review historical documents contained in the Netherlands national archive. Through diplomatic pressure, Suriname had successfully blocked Guyana's attempt to obtain the files. In reviewing the request from Guyana, the tribunal considered that the requested information was relevant, and further noted that: "... the principles of equality of arms and good faith cooperation in international legal proceedings", meant that Suriname should not hinder Guyana's use of the information. Thus the tribunal adopted the position that it would: "... not consider any document taken from a file in the archives of the Netherlands to which Guyana has been denied access". Furthermore, the tribunal ordered Suriname to facilitate access to the records. *Guyana v Suriname*, UNCLOS PCA, Procedural Order No. 1, paras 1 and 2 (18 July 2005).

202 "Si les parties n'ont pas réglé la procédure, celle-ci sera, au besoin, fixée par le tribunal arbitral, soit directement, soit par référence à une loi ou à un règlement d'arbitrage. Quelle que soit la procédure choisie, le tribunal arbitral doit garantir l'égalité entre les parties et leur droit d'être entendues en procédure contradictoire"

9.126 The inclusion of equality in article 9.2(g) as a ground for objecting to the admissibility or disclosure of evidence essentially restates a common rule of mandatory law. As it applies to arbitral procedure, the following excerpt from a leading French text provides a useful elucidation of the equality concept:

> The principle of equality should not be given a strictly mechanical meaning; it does not mean that each party should have precisely the same number of days in which to prepare its submissions or exactly the same time to present its oral pleadings, for example. What matters is that a general balance be maintained and that each party be given an equal opportunity to present its case in an appropriate manner.[203]

9.127 In the context of the taking of evidence, it would seem that a tribunal's duty to treat the parties with equality is generally fulfilled by applying the evidentiary procedure with equal force. This may lead in some instances to the exclusion of evidence submitted in violation of such rules. This being said, however, a tribunal does not violate equality where it finds, on separate, justifiable grounds that one party's evidence should be admitted, whereas another's denied.[204] The focus in this respect is on the application of the same standard to the parties, not the same result (see discussion of privilege in the comments to 9.3(e)).

9.128 Applying this approach to requests for document production, it is widely held that it is not necessary for a tribunal to grant an equal number of requests or similar volume of disclosure to each party to a proceeding to be in conformity with the equal treatment principle. Consider the following observation from the High Court of Hong Kong in respect to the procedural rulings of an HKIAC tribunal that continually denied one party's request for disclosure:

> In my view, an objective, fair-minded and informed observer would not jump to the conclusion of a real possibility that [the Chairman of the Tribunal] was biased against [Claimant] from the fact that the Tribunal made no order against [Respondent] for the discovery of documents, the existence of which was in dispute between the parties. Firstly, the mere fact that a party has repeatedly lost his arguments, without more, does not of itself call into question the adjudicator's impartiality or independence. The losing party's arguments could simply be bad.[205]

(unofficial translation) "If the parties have not agreed on the procedure, it shall, if necessary, be fixed by the arbitral tribunal, either directly or by reference to a law or to rules of arbitration. Regardless of which procedure is chosen, the arbitral tribunal must guarantee equality between the parties and their right to be heard in adversarial proceedings". ICC Case No. 10385, Final Award (2002), in *ICC Bulletin, 2005 Special Supplement: Document Production in International Arbitration*, p. 80.

203 Emmanuel Gaillard and John Savage (eds), *Fouchard Gaillard Goldman on International Commercial Arbitration*, p. 956 (1999).

204 ICC Case No. 5082, Procedural Order No. 1, *supra* n. 184, pp. 43, 44. See also: "[t]he Tribunal accepted several documents filed by the Respondents on 22 and 25 August 1986, considering them to be within the scope of rebuttal evidence previously authorised by the Tribunal and noting that the Claimants had not objected to their late filing. The Tribunal refused to accept a filing of evidence by [Respondent] submitted one week before the Hearing. The Tribunal noted that no request to accept such a late filing had been made, and no explanation had been offered to justify it." *Otis Elevator Co v The Islamic Republic of Iran*, Case No. 284, Award No. 304-284-2 of 29 April 1987, para. 25.

205 *Jung Science Information Technology Co Ltd v ZTE Corp*, Hong Kong High Court, Court of First Instance, Case No. 14, at paras 73–74 (2008). In the *Dongwoo Mann+Hummel v Man+Hummel GmbH* case, the Singapore High Court observed: "a tribunal's ruling in accordance with the rules of the arbitration on discovery or admissibility of evidence after hearing the parties, which necessarily disadvantages one party, cannot, without more, be regarded as evidence which shows that the party was therefore unable to present its case." Michael Hwang, "8 May 2008 – Singapore High Court", *A Contribution by the ITA Board of Reporters*.

9.129 Therefore, as the observations of the court suggest, it may be said that objections to a request for the disclosure of evidence or otherwise, would have no real ground in equal treatment so long as both parties were given equivalent opportunities to file a request, and they were subjected to the same standard of review. Under the IBA Rules, this would essentially mean the unbiased application of article 3 and other relevant parts of the Rules. If these principles are adhered to, international arbitrators need not be influenced in their decision on one application for disclosure by their determination on a previous one.

IBA Rules on the Taking of Evidence in International Arbitration*

The rules

Preamble

1   These IBA Rules on the Taking of Evidence in International Arbitration are intended to provide an efficient, economical and fair process for the taking of evidence in international arbitrations, particularly those between Parties from different legal traditions. They are designed to supplement the legal provisions and the institutional, ad hoc or other rules that apply to the conduct of the arbitration.

2   Parties and Arbitral Tribunals may adopt the IBA Rules of Evidence, in whole or in part, to govern arbitration proceedings, or they may vary them or use them as guidelines in developing their own procedures. The Rules are not intended to limit the flexibility that is inherent in, and an advantage of, international arbitration, and Parties and Arbitral Tribunals are free to adapt them to the particular circumstances of each arbitration.

3   The taking of evidence shall be conducted on the principles that each Party shall act in good faith and be entitled to know, reasonably in advance of any Evidentiary Hearing or any fact or merits determination, the evidence on which the other Parties rely.

Definitions

In the IBA Rules of Evidence:

'Arbitral Tribunal' means a sole arbitrator or a panel of arbitrators;

'Claimant' means the Party or Parties who commenced the arbitration and any Party who, through joinder or otherwise, becomes aligned with such Party or Parties;

'Document' means a writing, communication, picture, drawing, program or data of any kind, whether recorded or maintained on paper or by electronic, audio, visual or any other means;

'Evidentiary Hearing' means any hearing, whether or not held on consecutive days, at which the Arbitral Tribunal, whether in person, by teleconference, videoconference or other method, receives oral or other evidence;

---

*   The *IBA Rules on the Taking of Evidence in International Arbitration* (2010) is reproduced by kind permission of the International Bar Association, London, UK. © International Bar Association.

'Expert Report' means a written statement by a Tribunal-Appointed Expert or a Party-Appointed Expert;

'General Rules' mean the institutional, ad hoc or other rules that apply to the conduct of the arbitration;

'IBA Rules of Evidence' or *'Rules'* means these IBA Rules on the Taking of Evidence in International Arbitration, as they may be revised or amended from time to time;

'Party' means a party to the arbitration;

'Party-Appointed Expert' means a person or organisation appointed by a Party in order to report on specific issues determined by the Party;

'Request to Produce' means a written request by a Party that another Party produce Documents;

'Respondent' means the Party or Parties against whom the Claimant made its claim, and any Party who, through joinder or otherwise, becomes aligned with such Party or Parties, and includes a Respondent making a counterclaim;

'Tribunal-Appointed Expert' means a person or organisation appointed by the Arbitral Tribunal in order to report to it on specific issues determined by the Arbitral Tribunal; and

'Witness Statement' means a written statement of testimony by a witness of fact.

Article 1 Scope of application

1   Whenever the Parties have agreed or the Arbitral Tribunal has determined to apply the IBA Rules of Evidence, the Rules shall govern the taking of evidence, except to the extent that any specific provision of them may be found to be in conflict with any mandatory provision of law determined to be applicable to the case by the Parties or by the Arbitral Tribunal.

2   Where the Parties have agreed to apply the IBA Rules of Evidence, they shall be deemed to have agreed, in the absence of a contrary indication, to the version as current on the date of such agreement.

3   In case of conflict between any provisions of the IBA Rules of Evidence and the General Rules, the Arbitral Tribunal shall apply the IBA Rules of Evidence in the manner that it determines best in order to accomplish the purposes of both the General Rules and the IBA Rules of Evidence, unless the Parties agree to the contrary.

4   In the event of any dispute regarding the meaning of the IBA Rules of Evidence, the Arbitral Tribunal shall interpret them according to their purpose and in the manner most appropriate for the particular arbitration.

5   Insofar as the IBA Rules of Evidence and the General Rules are silent on any matter concerning the taking of evidence and the Parties have not agreed otherwise, the Arbitral Tribunal shall conduct the taking of evidence as it deems appropriate, in accordance with the general principles of the IBA Rules of Evidence.

Article 2 Consultation on evidentiary issues

1   The Arbitral Tribunal shall consult the Parties at the earliest appropriate time in the proceedings and invite them to consult each other with a view to agreeing on an efficient, economical and fair process for the taking of evidence.

2   The consultation on evidentiary issues may address the scope, timing and manner of the taking of evidence, including:

(a)   the preparation and submission of Witness Statements and Expert Reports;
(b)   the taking of oral testimony at any Evidentiary Hearing;
(c)   the requirements, procedure and format applicable to the production of Documents;
(d)   the level of confidentiality protection to be afforded to evidence in the arbitration; and
(e)   the promotion of efficiency, economy and conservation of resources in connection with the taking of evidence.

3   The Arbitral Tribunal is encouraged to identify to the Parties, as soon as it considers it to be appropriate, any issues:

(a)   that the Arbitral Tribunal may regard as relevant to the case and material to its outcome; and/or
(b)   for which a preliminary determination may be appropriate.

Article 3 Documents

1   Within the time ordered by the Arbitral Tribunal, each Party shall submit to the Arbitral Tribunal and to the other Parties all Documents available to it on which it relies, including public Documents and those in the public domain, except for any Documents that have already been submitted by another Party.

2   Within the time ordered by the Arbitral Tribunal, any Party may submit to the Arbitral Tribunal and to the other Parties a Request to Produce.

3   A Request to Produce shall contain:

(a)   (*i*)   a description of each requested Document sufficient to identify it, or (*ii*) a description in sufficient detail (including subject matter) of a narrow and specific requested category of Documents that are reasonably believed to exist; in the case of Documents maintained in electronic form, the requesting Party may, or the Arbitral Tribunal may order that it shall be required to, identify specific files, search terms, individuals or other means of searching for such Documents in an efficient and economical manner;

(b)   a statement as to how the Documents requested are relevant to the case and material to its outcome; and

(c)   (*i*)   a statement that the Documents requested are not in the possession, custody or control of the requesting Party or a statement of the reasons why it would be unreasonably burdensome for the requesting Party to produce such Documents, and

(*ii*) a statement of the reasons why the requesting Party assumes the Documents requested are in the possession, custody or control of another Party.

4   Within the time ordered by the Arbitral Tribunal, the Party to whom the Request to Produce is addressed shall produce to the other Parties and, if the Arbitral Tribunal so orders, to it, all the Documents requested in its possession, custody or control as to which it makes no objection.

5   If the Party to whom the Request to Produce is addressed has an objection to some or all of the Documents requested, it shall state the objection in writing to the Arbitral Tribunal and the other Parties within the time ordered by the Arbitral Tribunal. The reasons for such objection shall be any of those set forth in Article 9.2 or a failure to satisfy any of the requirements of Article 3.3.

6   Upon receipt of any such objection, the Arbitral Tribunal may invite the relevant Parties to consult with each other with a view to resolving the objection.

7   Either Party may, within the time ordered by the Arbitral Tribunal, request the Arbitral Tribunal to rule on the objection. The Arbitral Tribunal shall then, in consultation with the Parties and in timely fashion, consider the Request to Produce and the objection. The Arbitral Tribunal may order the Party to whom such Request is addressed to produce any requested Document in its possession, custody or control as to which the Arbitral Tribunal determines that *(i)* the issues that the requesting Party wishes to prove are relevant to the case and material to its outcome; *(ii)* none of the reasons for objection set forth in Article 9.2 applies; and *(iii)* the requirements of Article 3.3 have been satisfied. Any such Document shall be produced to the other Parties and, if the Arbitral Tribunal so orders, to it.

8   In exceptional circumstances, if the propriety of an objection can be determined only by review of the Document, the Arbitral Tribunal may determine that it should not review the Document. In that event, the Arbitral Tribunal may, after consultation with the Parties, appoint an independent and impartial expert, bound to confidentiality, to review any such Document and to report on the objection. To the extent that the objection is upheld by the Arbitral Tribunal, the expert shall not disclose to the Arbitral Tribunal and to the other Parties the contents of the Document reviewed.

9   If a Party wishes to obtain the production of Documents from a person or organisation who is not a Party to the arbitration and from whom the Party cannot obtain the Documents on its own, the Party may, within the time ordered by the Arbitral Tribunal, ask it to take whatever steps are legally available to obtain the requested Documents, or seek leave from the Arbitral Tribunal to take such steps itself. The Party shall submit such request to the Arbitral Tribunal and to the other Parties in writing, and the request shall contain the particulars set forth in Article 3.3, as applicable. The Arbitral Tribunal shall decide on this request and shall take, authorize the requesting Party to take, or order any other Party to take, such steps as the Arbitral Tribunal considers appropriate if, in its discretion, it determines that *(i)* the Documents would be relevant to the case and material to its outcome, *(ii)* the requirements of Article 3.3, as applicable, have been satisfied and *(iii)* none of the reasons for objection set forth in Article 9.2 applies.

10 At any time before the arbitration is concluded, the Arbitral Tribunal may *(i)* request any Party to produce Documents, *(ii)* request any Party to use its best efforts to take or *(iii)* itself take, any step that it considers appropriate to obtain Documents from any person or organisation. A Party to whom such a request for Documents is addressed may object to the request for any of the reasons set forth in Article 9.2. In such cases, Article 3.4 to Article 3.8 shall apply correspondingly.

11   Within the time ordered by the Arbitral Tribunal, the Parties may submit to the Arbitral Tribunal and to the other Parties any additional Documents on which they intend to rely or which they believe have become relevant to the case and material to its outcome as a consequence of the issues raised in Documents, Witness Statements or Expert Reports submitted or produced, or in other submissions of the Parties.

12   With respect to the form of submission or production of Documents:

    (a)   copies of Documents shall conform to the originals and, at the request of the Arbitral Tribunal, any original shall be presented for inspection;

    (b)   Documents that a Party maintains in electronic form shall be submitted or produced in the form most convenient or economical to it that is reasonably usable by the recipients, unless the Parties agree otherwise or, in the absence of such agreement, the Arbitral Tribunal decides otherwise;

    (c)   a Party is not obligated to produce multiple copies of Documents which are essentially identical unless the Arbitral Tribunal decides otherwise; and

    (d)   translations of Documents shall be submitted together with the originals and marked as translations with the original language identified.

13   Any Document submitted or produced by a Party or non-Party in the arbitration and not otherwise in the public domain shall be kept confidential by the Arbitral Tribunal and the other Parties, and shall be used only in connection with the arbitration. This requirement shall apply except and to the extent that disclosure may be required of a Party to fulfil a legal duty, protect or pursue a legal right, or enforce or challenge an award in bona fide legal proceedings before a state court or other judicial authority. The Arbitral Tribunal may issue orders to set forth the terms of this confidentiality. This requirement shall be without prejudice to all other obligations of confidentiality in the arbitration.

14   If the arbitration is organised into separate issues or phases (such as jurisdiction, preliminary determinations, liability or damages), the Arbitral Tribunal may, after consultation with the Parties, schedule the submission of Documents and Requests to Produce separately for each issue or phase.

Article 4 Witnesses of fact

  1   Within the time ordered by the Arbitral Tribunal, each Party shall identify the witnesses on whose testimony it intends to rely and the subject matter of that testimony.

  2   Any person may present evidence as a witness, including a Party or a Party's officer, employee or other representative.

  3   It shall not be improper for a Party, its officers, employees, legal advisors or other representatives to interview its witnesses or potential witnesses and to discuss their prospective testimony with them.

  4   The Arbitral Tribunal may order each Party to submit within a specified time to the Arbitral Tribunal and to the other Parties Witness Statements by each witness on whose testimony it intends to rely, except for those witnesses whose testimony is sought pursuant to Articles 4.9 or 4.10. If Evidentiary Hearings are organised into separate issues or phases (such as jurisdiction, preliminary determinations, liability or damages), the

Arbitral Tribunal or the Parties by agreement may schedule the submission of Witness Statements separately for each issue or phase.

5   Each Witness Statement shall contain:

(a)   the full name and address of the witness, a statement regarding his or her present and past relationship (if any) with any of the Parties, and a description of his or her background, qualifications, training and experience, if such a description may be relevant to the dispute or to the contents of the statement;

(b)   a full and detailed description of the facts, and the source of the witness's information as to those facts, sufficient to serve as that witness's evidence in the matter in dispute. Documents on which the witness relies that have not already been submitted shall be provided;

(c)   a statement as to the language in which the Witness Statement was originally prepared and the language in which the witness anticipates giving testimony at the Evidentiary Hearing;

(d)   an affirmation of the truth of the Witness Statement; and

(e)   the signature of the witness and its date and place.

6   If Witness Statements are submitted, any Party may, within the time ordered by the Arbitral Tribunal, submit to the Arbitral Tribunal and to the other Parties revised or additional Witness Statements, including statements from persons not previously named as witnesses, so long as any such revisions or additions respond only to matters contained in another Party's Witness Statements, Expert Reports or other submissions that have not been previously presented in the arbitration.

7   If a witness whose appearance has been requested pursuant to Article 8.1 fails without a valid reason to appear for testimony at an Evidentiary Hearing, the Arbitral Tribunal shall disregard any Witness Statement related to that Evidentiary Hearing by that witness unless, in exceptional circumstances, the Arbitral Tribunal decides otherwise.

8   If the appearance of a witness has not been requested pursuant to Article 8.1, none of the other Parties shall be deemed to have agreed to the correctness of the content of the Witness Statement.

9   If a Party wishes to present evidence from a person who will not appear voluntarily at its request, the Party may, within the time ordered by the Arbitral Tribunal, ask it to take whatever steps are legally available to obtain the testimony of that person, or seek leave from the Arbitral Tribunal to take such steps itself. In the case of a request to the Arbitral Tribunal, the Party shall identify the intended witness, shall describe the subjects on which the witness's testimony is sought and shall state why such subjects are relevant to the case and material to its outcome. The Arbitral Tribunal shall decide on this request and shall take, authorize the requesting Party to take or order any other Party to take, such steps as the Arbitral Tribunal considers appropriate if, in its discretion, it determines that the testimony of that witness would be relevant to the case and material to its outcome.

10   At any time before the arbitration is concluded, the Arbitral Tribunal may order any Party to provide for, or to use its best efforts to provide for, the appearance for testimony at an Evidentiary Hearing of any person, including one whose testimony has not

yet been offered. A Party to whom such a request is addressed may object for any of the reasons set forth in Article 9.2.

Article 5 Party-appointed experts

1   A Party may rely on a Party-Appointed Expert as a means of evidence on specific issues. Within the time ordered by the Arbitral Tribunal, (i) each Party shall identify any Party-Appointed Expert on whose testimony it intends to rely and the subject-matter of such testimony; and (ii) the Party-Appointed Expert shall submit an Expert Report.

2   The Expert Report shall contain:

(a)   the full name and address of the Party-Appointed Expert, a statement regarding his or her present and past relationship (if any) with any of the Parties, their legal advisors and the Arbitral Tribunal, and a description of his or her background, qualifications, training and experience;

(b)   a description of the instructions pursuant to which he or she is providing his or her opinions and conclusions;

(c)   a statement of his or her independence from the Parties, their legal advisors and the Arbitral Tribunal;

(d)   a statement of the facts on which he or she is basing his or her expert opinions and conclusions;

(e)   his or her expert opinions and conclusions, including a description of the methods, evidence and information used in arriving at the conclusions. Documents on which the Party-Appointed Expert relies that have not already been submitted shall be provided;

(f)   if the Expert Report has been translated, a statement as to the language in which it was originally prepared, and the language in which the Party-Appointed Expert anticipates giving testimony at the Evidentiary Hearing;

(g)   an affirmation of his or her genuine belief in the opinions expressed in the Expert Report;

(h)   the signature of the Party-Appointed Expert and its date and place; and

(i)   if the Expert Report has been signed by more than one person, an attribution of the entirety or specific parts of the Expert Report to each author.

3   If Expert Reports are submitted, any Party may, within the time ordered by the Arbitral Tribunal, submit to the Arbitral Tribunal and to the other Parties revised or additional Expert Reports, including reports or statements from persons not previously identified as Party-Appointed Experts, so long as any such revisions or additions respond only to matters contained in another Party's Witness Statements, Expert Reports or other submissions that have not been previously presented in the arbitration.

4   The Arbitral Tribunal in its discretion may order that any Party-Appointed Experts who will submit or who have submitted Expert Reports on the same or related issues meet and confer on such issues. At such meeting, the Party-Appointed Experts shall attempt to reach agreement on the issues within the scope of their Expert Reports, and they shall record in writing any such issues on which they reach agreement, any remaining areas of disagreement and the reasons therefore.

5   If a Party-Appointed Expert whose appearance has been requested pursuant to Article 8.1 fails without a valid reason to appear for testimony at an Evidentiary Hearing, the Arbitral Tribunal shall disregard any Expert Report by that Party-Appointed Expert related to that Evidentiary Hearing unless, in exceptional circumstances, the Arbitral Tribunal decides otherwise. 6. If the appearance of a Party-Appointed Expert has not been requested pursuant to Article 8.1, none of the other Parties shall be deemed to have agreed to the correctness of the content of the Expert Report.

Article 6 Tribunal-appointed experts

1   The Arbitral Tribunal, after consulting with the Parties, may appoint one or more independent Tribunal-Appointed Experts to report to it on specific issues designated by the Arbitral Tribunal. The Arbitral Tribunal shall establish the terms of reference for any Tribunal-Appointed Expert Report after consulting with the Parties. A copy of the final terms of reference shall be sent by the Arbitral Tribunal to the Parties.

2   The Tribunal-Appointed Expert shall, before accepting appointment, submit to the Arbitral Tribunal and to the Parties a description of his or her qualifications and a statement of his or her independence from the Parties, their legal advisors and the Arbitral Tribunal. Within the time ordered by the Arbitral Tribunal, the Parties shall inform the Arbitral Tribunal whether they have any objections as to the Tribunal-Appointed Expert's qualifications and independence. The Arbitral Tribunal shall decide promptly whether to accept any such objection. After the appointment of a Tribunal-Appointed Expert, a Party may object to the expert's qualifications or independence only if the objection is for reasons of which the Party becomes aware after the appointment has been made. The Arbitral Tribunal shall decide promptly what, if any, action to take.

3   Subject to the provisions of Article 9.2, the Tribunal-Appointed Expert may request a Party to provide any information or to provide access to any Documents, goods, samples, property, machinery, systems, processes or site for inspection, to the extent relevant to the case and material to its outcome. The authority of a Tribunal-Appointed Expert to request such information or access shall be the same as the authority of the Arbitral Tribunal. The Parties and their representatives shall have the right to receive any such information and to attend any such inspection. Any disagreement between a Tribunal-Appointed Expert and a Party as to the relevance, materiality or appropriateness of such a request shall be decided by the Arbitral Tribunal, in the manner provided in Articles 3.5 through 3.8. The Tribunal-Appointed Expert shall record in the Expert Report any non-compliance by a Party with an appropriate request or decision by the Arbitral Tribunal and shall describe its effects on the determination of the specific issue.

4   The Tribunal-Appointed Expert shall report in writing to the Arbitral Tribunal in an Expert Report. The Expert Report shall contain:

(a)   the full name and address of the Tribunal-Appointed Expert, and a description of his or her background, qualifications, training and experience;

(b)   a statement of the facts on which he or she is basing his or her expert opinions and conclusions;

(c)   his or her expert opinions and conclusions, including a description of the methods, evidence and information used in arriving at the conclusions. Documents on which the Tribunal-Appointed Expert relies that have not already been submitted shall be provided;

(d)   if the Expert Report has been translated, a statement as to the language in which it was originally prepared, and the language in which the Tribunal-Appointed Expert anticipates giving testimony at the Evidentiary Hearing;

(e)   an affirmation of his or her genuine belief in the opinions expressed in the Expert Report;

(f)   the signature of the Tribunal-Appointed Expert and its date and place; and

(g)   if the Expert Report has been signed by more than one person, an attribution of the entirety or specific parts of the Expert Report to each author.

5   The Arbitral Tribunal shall send a copy of such Expert Report to the Parties. The Parties may examine any information, Documents, goods, samples, property, machinery, systems, processes or site for inspection that the Tribunal-Appointed Expert has examined and any correspondence between the Arbitral Tribunal and the Tribunal-Appointed Expert. Within the time ordered by the Arbitral Tribunal, any Party shall have the opportunity to respond to the Expert Report in a submission by the Party or through a Witness Statement or an Expert Report by a Party-Appointed Expert. The Arbitral Tribunal shall send the submission, Witness Statement or Expert Report to the Tribunal-Appointed Expert and to the other Parties.

6   At the request of a Party or of the Arbitral Tribunal, the Tribunal-Appointed Expert shall be present at an Evidentiary Hearing. The Arbitral Tribunal may question the Tribunal-Appointed Expert, and he or she may be questioned by the Parties or by any Party-Appointed Expert on issues raised in his or her Expert Report, the Parties' submissions or Witness Statement or the Expert Reports made by the Party-Appointed Experts pursuant to Article 6.5.

7   Any Expert Report made by a Tribunal-Appointed Expert and its conclusions shall be assessed by the Arbitral Tribunal with due regard to all circumstances of the case.

8   The fees and expenses of a Tribunal-Appointed Expert, to be funded in a manner determined by the Arbitral Tribunal, shall form part of the costs of the arbitration.

Article 7 Inspection

Subject to the provisions of Article 9.2, the Arbitral Tribunal may, at the request of a Party or on its own motion, inspect or require the inspection by a Tribunal-Appointed Expert or a Party-Appointed Expert of any site, property, machinery or any other goods, samples, systems, processes or Documents, as it deems appropriate. The Arbitral Tribunal shall, in consultation with the Parties, determine the timing and arrangement for the inspection. The Parties and their representatives shall have the right to attend any such inspection.

Article 8 Evidentiary hearing

1   Within the time ordered by the Arbitral Tribunal, each Party shall inform the Arbitral Tribunal and the other Parties of the witnesses whose appearance it requests. Each

witness (which term includes, for the purposes of this Article, witnesses of fact and any experts) shall, subject to Article 8.2, appear for testimony at the Evidentiary Hearing if such person's appearance has been requested by any Party or by the Arbitral Tribunal. Each witness shall appear in person unless the Arbitral Tribunal allows the use of videoconference or similar technology with respect to a particular witness.

2   The Arbitral Tribunal shall at all times have complete control over the Evidentiary Hearing. The Arbitral Tribunal may limit or exclude any question to, answer by or appearance of a witness, if it considers such question, answer or appearance to be irrelevant, immaterial, unreasonably burdensome, duplicative or otherwise covered by a reason for objection set forth in Article 9.2. Questions to a witness during direct and re-direct testimony may not be unreasonably leading.

3   With respect to oral testimony at an Evidentiary Hearing:

(a)   the Claimant shall ordinarily first present the testimony of its witnesses, followed by the Respondent presenting the testimony of its witnesses;

(b)   following direct testimony, any other Party may question such witness, in an order to be determined by the Arbitral Tribunal. The Party who initially presented the witness shall subsequently have the opportunity to ask additional questions on the matters raised in the other Parties' questioning;

(c)   thereafter, the Claimant shall ordinarily first present the testimony of its Party-Appointed Experts, followed by the Respondent presenting the testimony of its Party-Appointed Experts. The Party who initially presented the Party-Appointed Expert shall subsequently have the opportunity to ask additional questions on the matters raised in the other Parties' questioning;

(d)   the Arbitral Tribunal may question a Tribunal-Appointed Expert, and he or she may be questioned by the Parties or by any Party-Appointed Expert, on issues raised in the Tribunal-Appointed Expert Report, in the Parties' submissions or in the Expert Reports made by the Party-Appointed Experts;

(e)   if the arbitration is organised into separate issues or phases (such as jurisdiction, preliminary determinations, liability and damages), the Parties may agree or the Arbitral Tribunal may order the scheduling of testimony separately for each issue or phase;

(f)   the Arbitral Tribunal, upon request of a Party or on its own motion, may vary this order of proceeding, including the arrangement of testimony by particular issues or in such a manner that witnesses be questioned at the same time and in confrontation with each other (witness conferencing);

(g)   the Arbitral Tribunal may ask questions to a witness at any time.

4   A witness of fact providing testimony shall first affirm, in a manner determined appropriate by the Arbitral Tribunal, that he or she commits to tell the truth or, in the case of an expert witness, his or her genuine belief in the opinions to be expressed at the Evidentiary Hearing. If the witness has submitted a Witness Statement or an Expert Report, the witness shall confirm it. The Parties may agree or the Arbitral Tribunal may order that the Witness Statement or Expert Report shall serve as that witness's direct testimony.

5   Subject to the provisions of Article 9.2, the Arbitral Tribunal may request any person to give oral or written evidence on any issue that the Arbitral Tribunal considers to be

relevant to the case and material to its outcome. Any witness called and questioned by the Arbitral Tribunal may also be questioned by the Parties.

Article 9 Admissibility and assessment of evidence

1   The Arbitral Tribunal shall determine the admissibility, relevance, materiality and weight of evidence.

2   The Arbitral Tribunal shall, at the request of a Party or on its own motion, exclude from evidence or production any Document, statement, oral testimony or inspection for any of the following reasons:

   (a)   lack of sufficient relevance to the case or materiality to its outcome;
   (b)   legal impediment or privilege under the legal or ethical rules determined by the Arbitral Tribunal to be applicable;
   (c)   unreasonable burden to produce the requested evidence;
   (d)   loss or destruction of the Document that has been shown with reasonable likelihood to have occurred;
   (e)   grounds of commercial or technical confidentiality that the Arbitral Tribunal determines to be compelling;
   (f)   grounds of special political or institutional sensitivity (including evidence that has been classified as secret by a government or a public international institution) that the Arbitral Tribunal determines to be compelling; or
   (g)   considerations of procedural economy, proportionality, fairness or equality of the Parties that the Arbitral Tribunal determines to be compelling.

3   In considering issues of legal impediment or privilege under Article 9.2(b), and insofar as permitted by any mandatory legal or ethical rules that are determined by it to be applicable, the Arbitral Tribunal may take into account:

   (a)   any need to protect the confidentiality of a Document created or statement or oral communication made in connection with and for the purpose of providing or obtaining legal advice;
   (b)   any need to protect the confidentiality of a Document created or statement or oral communication made in connection with and for the purpose of settlement negotiations;
   (c)   the expectations of the Parties and their advisors at the time the legal impediment or privilege is said to have arisen;
   (d)   any possible waiver of any applicable legal impediment or privilege by virtue of consent, earlier disclosure, affirmative use of the Document, statement, oral communication or advice contained therein, or otherwise; and
   (e)   the need to maintain fairness and equality as between the Parties, particularly if they are subject to different legal or ethical rules.

4   The Arbitral Tribunal may, where appropriate, make necessary arrangements to permit evidence to be presented or considered subject to suitable confidentiality protection.

5   If a Party fails without satisfactory explanation to produce any Document requested in a Request to Produce to which it has not objected in due time or fails to produce any

Document ordered to be produced by the Arbitral Tribunal, the Arbitral Tribunal may infer that such document would be adverse to the interests of that Party.

6   If a Party fails without satisfactory explanation to make available any other relevant evidence, including testimony, sought by one Party to which the Party to whom the request was addressed has not objected in due time or fails to make available any evidence, including testimony, ordered by the Arbitral Tribunal to be produced, the Arbitral Tribunal may infer that such evidence would be adverse to the interests of that Party.

7   If the Arbitral Tribunal determines that a Party has failed to conduct itself in good faith in the taking of evidence, the Arbitral Tribunal may, in addition to any other measures available under these Rules, take such failure into account in its assignment of the costs of the arbitration, including costs arising out of or in connection with the taking of evidence.

UNCITRAL Arbitration Rules (2010)*

Resolution Adopted by the General Assembly

[*on the report of the Sixth Committee (A/65/465)*]

65/22. UNCITRAL Arbitration Rules As Revised In 2010

The general assembly

Recalling its resolution 2205 (XXI) of 17 December 1966, which established the United Nations Commission on International Trade Law with the purpose of furthering the progressive harmonization and unification of the law of international trade in the interests of all peoples, in particular those of developing countries,

Also recalling its resolution 31/98 of 15 December 1976 recommending the use of the Arbitration Rules of the United Nations Commission on International Trade Law,[1]

Recognizing the value of arbitration as a method of settling disputes that may arise in the context of international commercial relations,

Noting that the Arbitration Rules are recognized as a very successful text and are used in a wide variety of circumstances covering a broad range of disputes, including disputes between private commercial parties, investor-State disputes, State-to-State disputes and commercial disputes administered by arbitral institutions, in all parts of the world,

Recognizing the need for revising the Arbitration Rules to conform to current practices in international trade and to meet changes that have taken place over the last thirty years in arbitral practice,

Believing that the Arbitration Rules as revised in 2010 to reflect current practices will significantly enhance the efficiency of arbitration under the Rules,

Convinced that the revision of the Arbitration Rules in a manner that is acceptable to countries with different legal, social and economic systems can significantly contribute to the development of harmonious international economic relations and to the continuous strengthening of the rule of law,

Noting that the preparation of the Arbitration Rules as revised in 2010 was the subject of due deliberation and extensive consultations with Governments and interested circles and that the revised text can be expected to contribute significantly to the establishment of a harmonized legal framework for the fair and efficient settlement of international commercial disputes,

---

* [© United Nations: United Nations Commission on International Trade Law.]
1 *Official Records of the General Assembly, Thirty-first Session, Supplement No. 17 (A/31/17), chap. V, sect. C.*

Also noting that the Arbitration Rules as revised in 2010 were adopted by the United Nations Commission on International Trade Law at its forty-third session after due deliberation,[2]

1 *Expresses its appreciation* to the United Nations Commission on International Trade Law for having formulated and adopted the revised provisions of the Arbitration Rules, the text of which is contained in an annex to the report of the United Nations Commission on International Trade Law on the work of its forty-third session;[3]

2 *Recommends* the use of the Arbitration Rules as revised in 2010 in the settlement of disputes arising in the context of international commercial relations;

3 *Requests* the Secretary-General to make all efforts to ensure that the Arbitration Rules as revised in 2010 become generally known and available.

57th plenary meeting
6 December 2010

---

2 *Ibid., Sixty-fifth Session, Supplement No. 17* (A/65/17), chap. III.
3 *Ibid.*, annex I.

UNCITRAL Arbitration Rules

(As revised in 2010)

Section I. Introductory Rules

Scope of application[1]

Article 1

1   Where parties have agreed that disputes between them in respect of a defined legal relationship, whether contractual or not, shall be referred to arbitration under the UNCITRAL Arbitration Rules, then such disputes shall be settled in accordance with these Rules subject to such modification as the parties may agree.

2   The parties to an arbitration agreement concluded after 15 August 2010 shall be presumed to have referred to the Rules in effect on the date of commencement of the arbitration, unless the parties have agreed to apply a particular version of the Rules. That presumption does not apply where the arbitration agreement has been concluded by accepting after 15 August 2010 an offer made before that date.

3   These Rules shall govern the arbitration except that where any of these Rules is in conflict with a provision of the law applicable to the arbitration from which the parties cannot derogate, that provision shall prevail.

4   For investor-State arbitration initiated pursuant to a treaty providing for the protection of investments or investors, these Rules include the UNCITRAL Rules on Transparency in Treaty-based Investor-State Arbitration ("Rules on Transparency"), subject to article 1 of the Rules on Transparency.

Notice and calculation of periods of time

Article 2

1   A notice, including a notification, communication or proposal, may be transmitted by any means of communication that provides or allows for a record of its transmission.

2   If an address has been designated by a party specifically for this purpose or authorized by the arbitral tribunal, any notice shall be delivered to that party at that address, and if so delivered shall be deemed to have been received. Delivery by electronic means such as facsimile or e-mail may only be made to an address so designated or authorized.

3   In the absence of such designation or authorization, a notice is:

---

[1]   A model arbitration clause for contracts can be found in the annex to the Rules.

(a) Received if it is physically delivered to the addressee; or

(b) Deemed to have been received if it is delivered at the place of business, habitual residence or mailing address of the addressee.

4 If, after reasonable efforts, delivery cannot be effected in accordance with paragraphs 2 or 3, a notice is deemed to have been received if it is sent to the addressee's last-known place of business, habitual residence or mailing address by registered letter or any other means that provides a record of delivery or of attempted delivery.

5 A notice shall be deemed to have been received on the day it is delivered in accordance with paragraphs 2, 3 or 4, or attempted to be delivered in accordance with paragraph 4. A notice transmitted by electronic means is deemed to have been received on the day it is sent, except that a notice of arbitration so transmitted is only deemed to have been received on the day when it reaches the addressee's electronic address.

6 For the purpose of calculating a period of time under these Rules, such period shall begin to run on the day following the day when a notice is received. If the last day of such period is an official holiday or a non-business day at the residence or place of business of the addressee, the period is extended until the first business day which follows. Official holidays or nonbusiness days occurring during the running of the period of time are included in calculating the period.

Notice of arbitration

Article 3

1 The party or parties initiating recourse to arbitration (hereinafter called the "claimant") shall communicate to the other party or parties (hereinafter called the "respondent") a notice of arbitration.

2 Arbitral proceedings shall be deemed to commence on the date on which the notice of arbitration is received by the respondent.

3 The notice of arbitration shall include the following:

(a) A demand that the dispute be referred to arbitration;

(b) The names and contact details of the parties;

(c) Identification of the arbitration agreement that is invoked;

(d) Identification of any contract or other legal instrument out of or in relation to which the dispute arises or, in the absence of such contract or instrument, a brief description of the relevant relationship;

(e) A brief description of the claim and an indication of the amount involved, if any;

(f) The relief or remedy sought;

(g) A proposal as to the number of arbitrators, language and place of arbitration, if the parties have not previously agreed thereon.

4 The notice of arbitration may also include:

(a) A proposal for the designation of an appointing authority referred to in article 6, paragraph 1;

(b)   A proposal for the appointment of a sole arbitrator referred to in article 8, paragraph 1;

(c)   Notification of the appointment of an arbitrator referred to in article 9 or 10.

5   The constitution of the arbitral tribunal shall not be hindered by any controversy with respect to the sufficiency of the notice of arbitration, which shall be finally resolved by the arbitral tribunal.

Response to the notice of arbitration

Article 4

1   Within 30 days of the receipt of the notice of arbitration, the respondent shall communicate to the claimant a response to the notice of arbitration, which shall include:

(a)   The name and contact details of each respondent;

(b)   A response to the information set forth in the notice of arbitration, pursuant to article 3, paragraphs 3 *(c)* to *(g)*.

2   The response to the notice of arbitration may also include:

(a)   Any plea that an arbitral tribunal to be constituted under these Rules lacks jurisdiction;

(b)   A proposal for the designation of an appointing authority referred to in article 6, paragraph 1;

(c)   A proposal for the appointment of a sole arbitrator referred to in article 8, paragraph 1;

(d)   Notification of the appointment of an arbitrator referred to in article 9 or 10;

(e)   A brief description of counterclaims or claims for the purpose of a set-off, if any, including where relevant, an indication of the amounts involved, and the relief or remedy sought;

(f)   A notice of arbitration in accordance with article 3 in case the respondent formulates a claim against a party to the arbitration agreement other than the claimant.

3   The constitution of the arbitral tribunal shall not be hindered by any controversy with respect to the respondent's failure to communicate a response to the notice of arbitration, or an incomplete or late response to the notice of arbitration, which shall be finally resolved by the arbitral tribunal.

Representation and assistance

Article 5

Each party may be represented or assisted by persons chosen by it. The names and addresses of such persons must be communicated to all parties and to the arbitral tribunal. Such communication must specify whether the appointment is being made for purposes of representation or assistance. Where a person is to act as a representative of a party, the arbitral tribunal, on its own initiative or at the request of any party, may at any time require proof of authority granted to the representative in such a form as the arbitral tribunal may determine.

Designating and appointing authorities

Article 6

1   Unless the parties have already agreed on the choice of an appointing authority, a party may at any time propose the name or names of one or more institutions or persons, including the Secretary-General of the Permanent Court of Arbitration at The Hague (hereinafter called the "PCA"), one of whom would serve as appointing authority.
2   If all parties have not agreed on the choice of an appointing authority within 30 days after a proposal made in accordance with paragraph 1 has been received by all other parties, any party may request the Secretary-General of the PCA to designate the appointing authority.
3   Where these Rules provide for a period of time within which a party must refer a matter to an appointing authority and no appointing authority has been agreed on or designated, the period is suspended from the date on which a party initiates the procedure for agreeing on or designating an appointing authority until the date of such agreement or designation.
4   Except as referred to in article 41, paragraph 4, if the appointing authority refuses to act, or if it fails to appoint an arbitrator within 30 days after it receives a party's request to do so, fails to act within any other period provided by these Rules, or fails to decide on a challenge to an arbitrator within a reasonable time after receiving a party's request to do so, any party may request the Secretary-General of the PCA to designate a substitute appointing authority.
5   In exercising their functions under these Rules, the appointing authority and the Secretary-General of the PCA may require from any party and the arbitrators the information they deem necessary and they shall give the parties and, where appropriate, the arbitrators, an opportunity to present their views in any manner they consider appropriate. All such communications to and from the appointing authority and the Secretary-General of the PCA shall also be provided by the sender to all other parties.
6   When the appointing authority is requested to appoint an arbitrator pursuant to articles 8, 9, 10 or 14, the party making the request shall send to the appointing authority copies of the notice of arbitration and, if it exists, any response to the notice of arbitration.
7   The appointing authority shall have regard to such considerations as are likely to secure the appointment of an independent and impartial arbitrator and shall take into account the advisability of appointing an arbitrator of a nationality other than the nationalities of the parties.

Section II. Composition of the arbitral tribunal

Number of arbitrators

Article 7

1   If the parties have not previously agreed on the number of arbitrators, and if within 30 days after the receipt by the respondent of the notice of arbitration the parties have not agreed that there shall be only one arbitrator, three arbitrators shall be appointed.

2   Notwithstanding paragraph 1, if no other parties have responded to a party's proposal to appoint a sole arbitrator within the time limit provided for in paragraph 1 and the party or parties concerned have failed to appoint a second arbitrator in accordance with article 9 or 10, the appointing authority may, at the request of a party, appoint a sole arbitrator pursuant to the procedure provided for in article 8, paragraph 2, if it determines that, in view of the circumstances of the case, this is more appropriate.

Appointment of arbitrators (articles 8 to 10)

Article 8

1   If the parties have agreed that a sole arbitrator is to be appointed and if within 30 days after receipt by all other parties of a proposal for the appointment of a sole arbitrator the parties have not reached agreement thereon, a sole arbitrator shall, at the request of a party, be appointed by the appointing authority.

2   The appointing authority shall appoint the sole arbitrator as promptly as possible. In making the appointment, the appointing authority shall use the following list-procedure, unless the parties agree that the list-procedure should not be used or unless the appointing authority determines in its discretion that the use of the list-procedure is not appropriate for the case:

(a)   The appointing authority shall communicate to each of the parties an identical list containing at least three names;

(b)   Within 15 days after the receipt of this list, each party may return the list to the appointing authority after having deleted the name or names to which it objects and numbered the remaining names on the list in the order of its preference;

(c)   After the expiration of the above period of time the appointing authority shall appoint the sole arbitrator from among the names approved on the lists returned to it and in accordance with the order of preference indicated by the parties;

(d)   If for any reason the appointment cannot be made according to this procedure, the appointing authority may exercise its discretion in appointing the sole arbitrator.

Article 9

1   If three arbitrators are to be appointed, each party shall appoint one arbitrator. The two arbitrators thus appointed shall choose the third arbitrator who will act as the presiding arbitrator of the arbitral tribunal.

2   If within 30 days after the receipt of a party's notification of the appointment of an arbitrator the other party has not notified the first party of the arbitrator it has appointed, the first party may request the appointing authority to appoint the second arbitrator.

3   If within 30 days after the appointment of the second arbitrator the two arbitrators have not agreed on the choice of the presiding arbitrator, the presiding arbitrator shall be appointed by the appointing authority in the same way as a sole arbitrator would be appointed under article 8.

Article 10

1   For the purposes of article 9, paragraph 1, where three arbitrators are to be appointed and there are multiple parties as claimant or as respondent, unless the parties have agreed to another method of appointment of arbitrators, the multiple parties jointly, whether as claimant or as respondent, shall appoint an arbitrator.

2   If the parties have agreed that the arbitral tribunal is to be composed of a number of arbitrators other than one or three, the arbitrators shall be appointed according to the method agreed upon by the parties.

3   In the event of any failure to constitute the arbitral tribunal under these Rules, the appointing authority shall, at the request of any party, constitute the arbitral tribunal and, in doing so, may revoke any appointment already made and appoint or reappoint each of the arbitrators and designate one of them as the presiding arbitrator.

Disclosures by and challenge of arbitrators[2] (articles 11 to 13)

Article 11

When a person is approached in connection with his or her possible appointment as an arbitrator, he or she shall disclose any circumstances likely to give rise to justifiable doubts as to his or her impartiality or independence. An arbitrator, from the time of his or her appointment and throughout the arbitral proceedings, shall without delay disclose any such circumstances to the parties and the other arbitrators unless they have already been informed by him or her of these circumstances.

Article 12

1   Any arbitrator may be challenged if circumstances exist that give rise to justifiable doubts as to the arbitrator's impartiality or independence.

2   A party may challenge the arbitrator appointed by it only for reasons of which it becomes aware after the appointment has been made.

---

2   Model statements of independence pursuant to article 11 can be found in the annex to the Rules.

3   In the event that an arbitrator fails to act or in the event of the de jure or de facto impossibility of his or her performing his or her functions, the procedure in respect of the challenge of an arbitrator as provided in article 13 shall apply.

Article 13

1   A party that intends to challenge an arbitrator shall send notice of its challenge within 15 days after it has been notified of the appointment of the challenged arbitrator, or within 15 days after the circumstances mentioned in articles 11 and 12 became known to that party.
2   The notice of challenge shall be communicated to all other parties, to the arbitrator who is challenged and to the other arbitrators. The notice of challenge shall state the reasons for the challenge.
3   When an arbitrator has been challenged by a party, all parties may agree to the challenge. The arbitrator may also, after the challenge, withdraw from his or her office. In neither case does this imply acceptance of the validity of the grounds for the challenge.
4   If, within 15 days from the date of the notice of challenge, all parties do not agree to the challenge or the challenged arbitrator does not withdraw, the party making the challenge may elect to pursue it. In that case, within 30 days from the date of the notice of challenge, it shall seek a decision on the challenge by the appointing authority.

Replacement of an arbitrator

Article 14

1   Subject to paragraph 2, in any event where an arbitrator has to be replaced during the course of the arbitral proceedings, a substitute arbitrator shall be appointed or chosen pursuant to the procedure provided for in articles 8 to 11 that was applicable to the appointment or choice of the arbitrator being replaced. This procedure shall apply even if during the process of appointing the arbitrator to be replaced, a party had failed to exercise its right to appoint or to participate in the appointment.
2   If, at the request of a party, the appointing authority determines that, in view of the exceptional circumstances of the case, it would be justified for a party to be deprived of its right to appoint a substitute arbitrator, the appointing authority may, after giving an opportunity to the parties and the remaining arbitrators to express their views: *(a)* appoint the substitute arbitrator; or *(b)* after the closure of the hearings, authorize the other arbitrators to proceed with the arbitration and make any decision or award.

Repetition of hearings in the event of the replacement of an arbitrator

Article 15

If an arbitrator is replaced, the proceedings shall resume at the stage where the arbitrator who was replaced ceased to perform his or her functions, unless the arbitral tribunal decides otherwise.

Exclusion of liability

Article 16

Save for intentional wrongdoing, the parties waive, to the fullest extent permitted under the applicable law, any claim against the arbitrators, the appointing authority and any person appointed by the arbitral tribunal based on any act or omission in connection with the arbitration.

Section III. Arbitral proceedings

General provisions

Article 17

1 Subject to these Rules, the arbitral tribunal may conduct the arbitration in such manner as it considers appropriate, provided that the parties are treated with equality and that at an appropriate stage of the proceedings each party is given a reasonable opportunity of presenting its case. The arbitral tribunal, in exercising its discretion, shall conduct the proceedings so as to avoid unnecessary delay and expense and to provide a fair and efficient process for resolving the parties' dispute.

2 As soon as practicable after its constitution and after inviting the parties to express their views, the arbitral tribunal shall establish the provisional timetable of the arbitration. The arbitral tribunal may, at any time, after inviting the parties to express their views, extend or abridge any period of time prescribed under these Rules or agreed by the parties.

3 If at an appropriate stage of the proceedings any party so requests, the arbitral tribunal shall hold hearings for the presentation of evidence by witnesses, including expert witnesses, or for oral argument. In the absence of such a request, the arbitral tribunal shall decide whether to hold such hearings or whether the proceedings shall be conducted on the basis of documents and other materials.

4 All communications to the arbitral tribunal by one party shall be communicated by that party to all other parties. Such communications shall be made at the same time, except as otherwise permitted by the arbitral tribunal if it may do so under applicable law.

5 The arbitral tribunal may, at the request of any party, allow one or more third persons to be joined in the arbitration as a party provided such person is a party to the arbitration agreement, unless the arbitral tribunal finds, after giving all parties, including the person or persons to be joined, the opportunity to be heard, that joinder should not be permitted because of prejudice to any of those parties. The arbitral tribunal may make a single award or several awards in respect of all parties so involved in the arbitration.

Place of arbitration

Article 18

1 If the parties have not previously agreed on the place of arbitration, the place of arbitration shall be determined by the arbitral tribunal having regard to the

circumstances of the case. The award shall be deemed to have been made at the place of arbitration.

2 The arbitral tribunal may meet at any location it considers appropriate for deliberations. Unless otherwise agreed by the parties, the arbitral tribunal may also meet at any location it considers appropriate for any other purpose, including hearings.

Language

Article 19

1 Subject to an agreement by the parties, the arbitral tribunal shall, promptly after its appointment, determine the language or languages to be used in the proceedings. This determination shall apply to the statement of claim, the statement of defence, and any further written statements and, if oral hearings take place, to the language or languages to be used in such hearings.

2 The arbitral tribunal may order that any documents annexed to the statement of claim or statement of defence, and any supplementary documents or exhibits submitted in the course of the proceedings, delivered in their original language, shall be accompanied by a translation into the language or languages agreed upon by the parties or determined by the arbitral tribunal.

Statement of claim

Article 20

1 The claimant shall communicate its statement of claim in writing to the respondent and to each of the arbitrators within a period of time to be determined by the arbitral tribunal. The claimant may elect to treat its notice of arbitration referred to in article 3 as a statement of claim, provided that the notice of arbitration also complies with the requirements of paragraphs 2 to 4 of this article.

2 The statement of claim shall include the following particulars:

(a) The names and contact details of the parties;
(b) A statement of the facts supporting the claim;
(c) The points at issue;
(d) The relief or remedy sought;
(e) The legal grounds or arguments supporting the claim.

3 A copy of any contract or other legal instrument out of or in relation to which the dispute arises and of the arbitration agreement shall be annexed to the statement of claim.

4 The statement of claim should, as far as possible, be accompanied by all documents and other evidence relied upon by the claimant, or contain references to them.

Statement of defence

Article 21

1   The respondent shall communicate its statement of defence in writing to the claimant and to each of the arbitrators within a period of time to be determined by the arbitral tribunal. The respondent may elect to treat its response to the notice of arbitration referred to in article 4 as a statement of defence, provided that the response to the notice of arbitration also complies with the requirements of paragraph 2 of this article.

2   The statement of defence shall reply to the particulars *(b)* to *(e)* of the statement of claim (art. 20, para. 2). The statement of defence should, as far as possible, be accompanied by all documents and other evidence relied upon by the respondent, or contain references to them.

3   In its statement of defence, or at a later stage in the arbitral proceedings if the arbitral tribunal decides that the delay was justified under the circumstances, the respondent may make a counterclaim or rely on a claim for the purpose of a set-off provided that the arbitral tribunal has jurisdiction over it.

4   The provisions of article 20, paragraphs 2 to 4, shall apply to a counterclaim, a claim under article 4, paragraph 2 *(f)*, and a claim relied on for the purpose of a set-off.

Amendments to the claim or defence

Article 22

During the course of the arbitral proceedings, a party may amend or supplement its claim or defence, including a counterclaim or a claim for the purpose of a set-off, unless the arbitral tribunal considers it inappropriate to allow such amendment or supplement having regard to the delay in making it or prejudice to other parties or any other circumstances. However, a claim or defence, including a counterclaim or a claim for the purpose of a set-off, may not be amended or supplemented in such a manner that the amended or supplemented claim or defence falls outside the jurisdiction of the arbitral tribunal.

Pleas as to the jurisdiction of the arbitral tribunal

Article 23

1   The arbitral tribunal shall have the power to rule on its own jurisdiction, including any objections with respect to the existence or validity of the arbitration agreement. For that purpose, an arbitration clause that forms part of a contract shall be treated as an agreement independent of the other terms of the contract. A decision by the arbitral tribunal that the contract is null shall not entail automatically the invalidity of the arbitration clause.

2   A plea that the arbitral tribunal does not have jurisdiction shall be raised no later than in the statement of defence or, with respect to a counterclaim or a claim for the

purpose of a set-off, in the reply to the counterclaim or to the claim for the purpose of a set-off. A party is not precluded from raising such a plea by the fact that it has appointed, or participated in the appointment of, an arbitrator. A plea that the arbitral tribunal is exceeding the scope of its authority shall be raised as soon as the matter alleged to be beyond the scope of its authority is raised during the arbitral proceedings. The arbitral tribunal may, in either case, admit a later plea if it considers the delay justified.

3   The arbitral tribunal may rule on a plea referred to in paragraph 2 either as a preliminary question or in an award on the merits. The arbitral tribunal may continue the arbitral proceedings and make an award, notwithstanding any pending challenge to its jurisdiction before a court.

Further written statements

Article 24

The arbitral tribunal shall decide which further written statements, in addition to the statement of claim and the statement of defence, shall be required from the parties or may be presented by them and shall fix the periods of time for communicating such statements.

Periods of time

Article 25

The periods of time fixed by the arbitral tribunal for the communication of written statements (including the statement of claim and statement of defence) should not exceed 45 days. However, the arbitral tribunal may extend the time limits if it concludes that an extension is justified.

Interim measures

Article 26

1   The arbitral tribunal may, at the request of a party, grant interim measures.
2   An interim measure is any temporary measure by which, at any time prior to the issuance of the award by which the dispute is finally decided, the arbitral tribunal orders a party, for example and without limitation, to:

   (a)   Maintain or restore the status quo pending determination of the dispute;
   (b)   Take action that would prevent, or refrain from taking action that is likely to cause, (i) current or imminent harm or (ii) prejudice to the arbitral process itself;
   (c)   Provide a means of preserving assets out of which a subsequent award may be satisfied; or

(d) Preserve evidence that may be relevant and material to the resolution of the dispute.

3 The party requesting an interim measure under paragraphs 2 *(a)* to *(c)* shall satisfy the arbitral tribunal that:

(a) Harm not adequately reparable by an award of damages is likely to result if the measure is not ordered, and such harm substantially outweighs the harm that is likely to result to the party against whom the measure is directed if the measure is granted; and

(b) There is a reasonable possibility that the requesting party will succeed on the merits of the claim. The determination on this possibility shall not affect the discretion of the arbitral tribunal in making any subsequent determination.

4 With regard to a request for an interim measure under paragraph 2 *(d)*, the requirements in paragraphs 3 *(a)* and *(b)* shall apply only to the extent the arbitral tribunal considers appropriate.

5 The arbitral tribunal may modify, suspend or terminate an interim measure it has granted, upon application of any party or, in exceptional circumstances and upon prior notice to the parties, on the arbitral tribunal's own initiative.

6 The arbitral tribunal may require the party requesting an interim measure to provide appropriate security in connection with the measure.

7 The arbitral tribunal may require any party promptly to disclose any material change in the circumstances on the basis of which the interim measure was requested or granted.

8 The party requesting an interim measure may be liable for any costs and damages caused by the measure to any party if the arbitral tribunal later determines that, in the circumstances then prevailing, the measure should not have been granted. The arbitral tribunal may award such costs and damages at any point during the proceedings.

9 A request for interim measures addressed by any party to a judicial authority shall not be deemed incompatible with the agreement to arbitrate, or as a waiver of that agreement.

Evidence

Article 27

1 Each party shall have the burden of proving the facts relied on to support its claim or defence.

2 Witnesses, including expert witnesses, who are presented by the parties to testify to the arbitral tribunal on any issue of fact or expertise may be any individual, notwithstanding that the individual is a party to the arbitration or in any way related to a party. Unless otherwise directed by the arbitral tribunal, statements by witnesses, including expert witnesses, may be presented in writing and signed by them.

3 At any time during the arbitral proceedings the arbitral tribunal may require the parties to produce documents, exhibits or other evidence within such a period of time as the arbitral tribunal shall determine.

4   The arbitral tribunal shall determine the admissibility, relevance, materiality and weight of the evidence offered.

Hearings

Article 28

1   In the event of an oral hearing, the arbitral tribunal shall give the parties adequate advance notice of the date, time and place thereof.
2   Witnesses, including expert witnesses, may be heard under the conditions and examined in the manner set by the arbitral tribunal.
3   Hearings shall be held in camera unless the parties agree otherwise. The arbitral tribunal may require the retirement of any witness or witnesses, including expert witnesses, during the testimony of such other witnesses, except that a witness, including an expert witness, who is a party to the arbitration shall not, in principle, be asked to retire.
4   The arbitral tribunal may direct that witnesses, including expert witnesses, be examined through means of telecommunication that do not require their physical presence at the hearing (such as videoconference).

Experts appointed by the arbitral tribunal

Article 29

1   After consultation with the parties, the arbitral tribunal may appoint one or more independent experts to report to it, in writing, on specific issues to be determined by the arbitral tribunal. A copy of the expert's terms of reference, established by the arbitral tribunal, shall be communicated to the parties.
2   The expert shall, in principle before accepting appointment, submit to the arbitral tribunal and to the parties a description of his or her qualifications and a statement of his or her impartiality and independence. Within the time ordered by the arbitral tribunal, the parties shall inform the arbitral tribunal whether they have any objections as to the expert's qualifications, impartiality or independence. The arbitral tribunal shall decide promptly whether to accept any such objections. After an expert's appointment, a party may object to the expert's qualifications, impartiality or independence only if the objection is for reasons of which the party becomes aware after the appointment has been made. The arbitral tribunal shall decide promptly what, if any, action to take.
3   The parties shall give the expert any relevant information or produce for his or her inspection any relevant documents or goods that he or she may require of them. Any dispute between a party and such expert as to the relevance of the required information or production shall be referred to the arbitral tribunal for decision.
4   Upon receipt of the expert's report, the arbitral tribunal shall communicate a copy of the report to the parties, which shall be given the opportunity to express, in writing, their opinion on the report. A party shall be entitled to examine any document on which the expert has relied in his or her report.

5   At the request of any party, the expert, after delivery of the report, may be heard at a hearing where the parties shall have the opportunity to be present and to interrogate the expert. At this hearing, any party may present expert witnesses in order to testify on the points at issue. The provisions of article 28 shall be applicable to such proceedings.

Default

Article 30

1   If, within the period of time fixed by these Rules or the arbitral tribunal, without showing sufficient cause:

    (a)   The claimant has failed to communicate its statement of claim, the arbitral tribunal shall issue an order for the termination of the arbitral proceedings, unless there are remaining matters that may need to be decided and the arbitral tribunal considers it appropriate to do so;

    (b)   The respondent has failed to communicate its response to the notice of arbitration or its statement of defence, the arbitral tribunal shall order that the proceedings continue, without treating such failure in itself as an admission of the claimant's allegations; the provisions of this subparagraph also apply to a claimant's failure to submit a defence to a counterclaim or to a claim for the purpose of a set-off.

2   If a party, duly notified under these Rules, fails to appear at a hearing, without showing sufficient cause for such failure, the arbitral tribunal may proceed with the arbitration.

3   If a party, duly invited by the arbitral tribunal to produce documents, exhibits or other evidence, fails to do so within the established period of time, without showing sufficient cause for such failure, the arbitral tribunal may make the award on the evidence before it.

Closure of hearings

Article 31

1   The arbitral tribunal may inquire of the parties if they have any further proof to offer or witnesses to be heard or submissions to make and, if there are none, it may declare the hearings closed.

2   The arbitral tribunal may, if it considers it necessary owing to exceptional circumstances, decide, on its own initiative or upon application of a party, to reopen the hearings at any time before the award is made.

Waiver of right to object

Article 32

A failure by any party to object promptly to any non-compliance with these Rules or with any requirement of the arbitration agreement shall be deemed to be a waiver of the right of such party to make such an objection, unless such party can show that, under the circumstances, its failure to object was justified.

Section IV. The award

Decisions

Article 33

1   When there is more than one arbitrator, any award or other decision of the arbitral tribunal shall be made by a majority of the arbitrators.
2   In the case of questions of procedure, when there is no majority or when the arbitral tribunal so authorizes, the presiding arbitrator may decide alone, subject to revision, if any, by the arbitral tribunal.

Form and effect of the award

Article 34

1   The arbitral tribunal may make separate awards on different issues at different times.
2   All awards shall be made in writing and shall be final and binding on the parties. The parties shall carry out all awards without delay.
3   The arbitral tribunal shall state the reasons upon which the award is based, unless the parties have agreed that no reasons are to be given.
4   An award shall be signed by the arbitrators and it shall contain the date on which the award was made and indicate the place of arbitration. Where there is more than one arbitrator and any of them fails to sign, the award shall state the reason for the absence of the signature.
5   An award may be made public with the consent of all parties or where and to the extent disclosure is required of a party by legal duty, to protect or pursue a legal right or in relation to legal proceedings before a court or other competent authority.
6   Copies of the award signed by the arbitrators shall be communicated to the parties by the arbitral tribunal.

Applicable law, amiable compositeur

Article 35

1   The arbitral tribunal shall apply the rules of law designated by the parties as applicable to the substance of the dispute. Failing such designation by the parties, the arbitral tribunal shall apply the law which it determines to be appropriate.
2   The arbitral tribunal shall decide as *amiable compositeur* or *ex aequo et bono* only if the parties have expressly authorized the arbitral tribunal to do so.

3   In all cases, the arbitral tribunal shall decide in accordance with the terms of the contract, if any, and shall take into account any usage of trade applicable to the transaction.

Settlement or other grounds for termination

Article 36

1   If, before the award is made, the parties agree on a settlement of the dispute, the arbitral tribunal shall either issue an order for the termination of the arbitral proceedings or, if requested by the parties and accepted by the arbitral tribunal, record the settlement in the form of an arbitral award on agreed terms. The arbitral tribunal is not obliged to give reasons for such an award.
2   If, before the award is made, the continuation of the arbitral proceedings becomes unnecessary or impossible for any reason not mentioned in paragraph 1, the arbitral tribunal shall inform the parties of its intention to issue an order for the termination of the proceedings. The arbitral tribunal shall have the power to issue such an order unless there are remaining matters that may need to be decided and the arbitral tribunal considers it appropriate to do so.
3   Copies of the order for termination of the arbitral proceedings or of the arbitral award on agreed terms, signed by the arbitrators, shall be communicated by the arbitral tribunal to the parties. Where an arbitral award on agreed terms is made, the provisions of article 34, paragraphs 2, 4 and 5, shall apply.

Interpretation of the award

Article 37

1   Within 30 days after the receipt of the award, a party, with notice to the other parties, may request that the arbitral tribunal give an interpretation of the award.
2   The interpretation shall be given in writing within 45 days after the receipt of the request. The interpretation shall form part of the award and the provisions of article 34, paragraphs 2 to 6, shall apply.

Correction of the award

Article 38

1   Within 30 days after the receipt of the award, a party, with notice to the other parties, may request the arbitral tribunal to correct in the award any error in computation, any clerical or typographical error, or any error or omission of a similar nature. If the arbitral tribunal considers that the request is justified, it shall make the correction within 45 days of receipt of the request.
2   The arbitral tribunal may within 30 days after the communication of the award make such corrections on its own initiative.
3   Such corrections shall be in writing and shall form part of the award. The provisions of article 34, paragraphs 2 to 6, shall apply.

Additional award

Article 39

1   Within 30 days after the receipt of the termination order or the award, a party, with notice to the other parties, may request the arbitral tribunal to make an award or an additional award as to claims presented in the arbitral proceedings but not decided by the arbitral tribunal.

2   If the arbitral tribunal considers the request for an award or additional award to be justified, it shall render or complete its award within 60 days after the receipt of the request. The arbitral tribunal may extend, if necessary, the period of time within which it shall make the award.

3   When such an award or additional award is made, the provisions of article 34, paragraphs 2 to 6, shall apply.

Definition of costs

Article 40

1   The arbitral tribunal shall fix the costs of arbitration in the final award and, if it deems appropriate, in another decision.

2   The term "costs" includes only:

   (a)   The fees of the arbitral tribunal to be stated separately as to each arbitrator and to be fixed by the tribunal itself in accordance with article 41;

   (b)   The reasonable travel and other expenses incurred by the arbitrators;

   (c)   The reasonable costs of expert advice and of other assistance required by the arbitral tribunal;

   (d)   The reasonable travel and other expenses of witnesses to the extent such expenses are approved by the arbitral tribunal;

   (e)   The legal and other costs incurred by the parties in relation to the arbitration to the extent that the arbitral tribunal determines that the amount of such costs is reasonable;

   (f)   Any fees and expenses of the appointing authority as well as the fees and expenses of the Secretary-General of the PCA.

3   In relation to interpretation, correction or completion of any award under articles 37 to 39, the arbitral tribunal may charge the costs referred to in paragraphs 2 *(b)* to *(f)*, but no additional fees.

Fees and expenses of arbitrators

Article 41

1   The fees and expenses of the arbitrators shall be reasonable in amount, taking into account the amount in dispute, the complexity of the subject matter, the time spent by the arbitrators and any other relevant circumstances of the case.

2   If there is an appointing authority and it applies or has stated that it will apply a schedule or particular method for determining the fees for arbitrators in international cases, the arbitral tribunal in fixing its fees shall take that schedule or method into account to the extent that it considers appropriate in the circumstances of the case.

3   Promptly after its constitution, the arbitral tribunal shall inform the parties as to how it proposes to determine its fees and expenses, including any rates it intends to apply. Within 15 days of receiving that proposal, any party may refer the proposal to the appointing authority for review. If, within 45 days of receipt of such a referral, the appointing authority finds that the proposal of the arbitral tribunal is inconsistent with paragraph 1, it shall make any necessary adjustments thereto, which shall be binding upon the arbitral tribunal.

4   *(a)*   When informing the parties of the arbitrators' fees and expenses that have been fixed pursuant to article 40, paragraphs 2 *(a)* and *(b)*, the arbitral tribunal shall also explain the manner in which the corresponding amounts have been calculated;

    (b)   Within 15 days of receiving the arbitral tribunal's determination of fees and expenses, any party may refer for review such determination to the appointing authority. If no appointing authority has been agreed upon or designated, or if the appointing authority fails to act within the time specified in these Rules, then the review shall be made by the Secretary-General of the PCA;

    (c)   If the appointing authority or the Secretary-General of the PCA finds that the arbitral tribunal's determination is inconsistent with the arbitral tribunal's proposal (and any adjustment thereto) under paragraph 3 or is otherwise manifestly excessive, it shall, within 45 days of receiving such a referral, make any adjustments to the arbitral tribunal's determination that are necessary to satisfy the criteria in paragraph 1. Any such adjustments shall be binding upon the arbitral tribunal;

    (d)   Any such adjustments shall either be included by the arbitral tribunal in its award or, if the award has already been issued, be implemented in a correction to the award, to which the procedure of article 38, paragraph 3, shall apply.

5   Throughout the procedure under paragraphs 3 and 4, the arbitral tribunal shall proceed with the arbitration, in accordance with article 17, paragraph 1.

6   A referral under paragraph 4 shall not affect any determination in the award other than the arbitral tribunal's fees and expenses; nor shall it delay the recognition and enforcement of all parts of the award other than those relating to the determination of the arbitral tribunal's fees and expenses.

Allocation of costs

Article 42

1   The costs of the arbitration shall in principle be borne by the unsuccessful party or parties. However, the arbitral tribunal may apportion each of such costs between the parties if it determines that apportionment is reasonable, taking into account the circumstances of the case.

2   The arbitral tribunal shall in the final award or, if it deems appropriate, in any other award, determine any amount that a party may have to pay to another party as a result of the decision on allocation of costs.

Deposit of costs

Article 43

1   The arbitral tribunal, on its establishment, may request the parties to deposit an equal amount as an advance for the costs referred to in article 40, paragraphs 2 *(a)* to *(c)*.
2   During the course of the arbitral proceedings the arbitral tribunal may request supplementary deposits from the parties.
3   If an appointing authority has been agreed upon or designated, and when a party so requests and the appointing authority consents to perform the function, the arbitral tribunal shall fix the amounts of any deposits or supplementary deposits only after consultation with the appointing authority, which may make any comments to the arbitral tribunal that it deems appropriate concerning the amount of such deposits and supplementary deposits.
4   If the required deposits are not paid in full within 30 days after the receipt of the request, the arbitral tribunal shall so inform the parties in order that one or more of them may make the required payment. If such payment is not made, the arbitral tribunal may order the suspension or termination of the arbitral proceedings.
5   After a termination order or final award has been made, the arbitral tribunal shall render an accounting to the parties of the deposits received and return any unexpended balance to the parties.

Annex

Model arbitration clause for contracts

Any dispute, controversy or claim arising out of or relating to this contract, or the breach, termination or invalidity thereof, shall be settled by arbitration in accordance with the UNCITRAL Arbitration Rules.

   Note. Parties should consider adding:

(a)   The appointing authority shall be . . . [name of institution or person];
(b)   The number of arbitrators shall be . . . [one or three];
(c)   The place of arbitration shall be . . . [town and country];
(d)   The language to be used in the arbitral proceedings shall be. . . .

Possible waiver statement

Note. If the parties wish to exclude recourse against the arbitral award that may be available under the applicable law, they may consider adding a provision to that effect as suggested below, considering, however, that the effectiveness and conditions of such an exclusion depend on the applicable law.

Waiver

The parties hereby waive their right to any form of recourse against an award to any court or other competent authority, insofar as such waiver can validly be made under the applicable law.

Model statements of independence pursuant to article 11 of the Rules

No circumstances to disclose

I am impartial and independent of each of the parties and intend to remain so. To the best of my knowledge, there are no circumstances, past or present, likely to give rise to justifiable doubts as to my impartiality or independence. I shall promptly notify the parties and the other arbitrators of any such circumstances that may subsequently come to my attention during this arbitration.

Circumstances to disclose

I am impartial and independent of each of the parties and intend to remain so. Attached is a statement made pursuant to article 11 of the UNCITRAL Arbitration Rules of *(a)* my past and present professional, business and other relationships with the parties and *(b)* any other relevant circumstances. [Include statement.] I confirm that those circumstances do not affect my independence and impartiality. I shall promptly notify the parties and the other arbitrators of any such further relationships or circumstances that may subsequently come to my attention during this arbitration.

Note. Any party may consider requesting from the arbitrator the following addition to the statement of independence:

I confirm, on the basis of the information presently available to me, that I can devote the time necessary to conduct this arbitration diligently, efficiently and in accordance with the time limits in the Rules.

Hwang model procedural order on confidentiality*[1]

(1) Except as Parties expressly agree in writing (whether in the arbitration agreement or otherwise) or leave is given by the Tribunal, Parties undertake to keep confidential all Confidential Information and the award. Additionally, the provisions of this Procedural Order will continue in force notwithstanding the termination of the arbitration.

(2) In this Procedural Order, "Confidential Information" is defined as information that relates to the proceedings or to an award made in the proceedings and includes:

    (a)   the existence of the proceedings;

    (b)   the statement of claim, statement of defence, and all other pleadings, submissions, and statements;

    (c)   any evidence (whether documentary or other) supplied to the Tribunal;

    (d)   any notes made by the arbitral tribunal of oral evidence or submissions given before the Tribunal;

    (e)   any transcript of oral evidence or submissions given before the Tribunal;

    (f)   any rulings of the Tribunal; and

    (g)   any award of the Tribunal, but excludes any matter that is otherwise in the public domain.

(3) Subject to (4) below, a party may disclose Confidential Information –

    (a)   for the purpose of making an application to any competent court of any State to recognise, enforce or challenge the award;

    (b)   pursuant to the order of, or a subpoena issued, by a court of competent jurisdiction;

    (c)   for the purpose of pursuing or enforcing a legal right or defending a claim;

    (d)   where disclosure is made to a third party for the purpose of satisfying any legal obligation of disclosure owed (under any applicable law) to that third party;

    (e)   in compliance with the request or requirement of any competent regulatory body or other authority;

    (f)   where disclosure is necessary to ensure that a party to the arbitral proceedings has a full opportunity to present its case and the disclosure is no more than reasonable for that purpose (which may include disclosure to legal and other advisers as well as potential witnesses and other parties assisting in the preparation of the case);

    (g)   if a party wishes to disclose information or documents already in that party's possession prior to the commencement of the arbitration;

    (h)   with the consent of all the other parties to the arbitration;

---

1   Reproduced with the permission of Michael Hwang SC

      (i)   pursuant to an order by the Tribunal on application by a party with proper notice to the other parties; or

      (j)   as permitted under any other exception recognised by the applicable law.

(4) Subject to (6) below, before a party discloses Confidential Information as authorised in (3) above, that party must provide to the other party/parties seven (7) days' prior written notice of its intention to disclose, giving:

      (a)   written details of the Confidential Information to be disclosed;

      (b)   the party/parties to whom disclosure is intended to be made; and

      (c)   the reasons for the disclosure.

(5) Where the disclosure of Confidential Information is sought to be made pursuant to (3) above, the information to be furnished to the other party need only contain a general description of the Confidential Information sought to be disclosed and the classes of persons to whom description is to be made (without identification of those persons). The disclosing party must use its best endeavours to obtain an undertaking of confidentiality, given in favour of the party opposing disclosure, from any individual or entity to whom disclosure of any Confidential Information may be made. The terms of such undertaking should be agreed in advance of such disclosure by the party opposing disclosure (who will not be entitled to the names of the parties to whom disclosure is to be made). If there is a dispute in relation to the terms of the undertaking, this should be referred to the Tribunal for determination. If no such undertaking of confidentiality can be obtained, seven (7) days' notice is to be given to all other parties identifying the individual or entity concerned. If any objection is raised by any other party within the period of notice, the matter should be referred to the Tribunal to determine the extent of the Confidential Information that may be disclosed and any other steps that should be taken to preserve confidentiality.

(6) None of the requirements of (4) above is to apply in the following situations:

      (a)   where disclosure of Confidential Information is made pursuant to (3)(a) above; and

      (b)   where the party seeking to disclose Confidential Information obtains the written consent (both to the particulars and extent of Confidential Information which is sought to be disclosed) of all other parties to the arbitration to do so.

(7) If the other party/parties object(s) to disclosure pursuant to (4) above within the period of seven (7) days, no disclosure may be made until the issue has been resolved by the Tribunal in the manner set out in (8) below.

(8) If a question arises in the arbitral proceedings as to whether any Confidential Information should be disclosed, and at least one of the parties requests the Tribunal to determine that question, the Tribunal, after giving each of the parties an opportunity to be heard, may in its discretion make or refuse to make an order allowing all or any of the parties to disclose Confidential Information.

(9) After the Tribunal has become *functus officio*, its functions under this Procedural Order are to be exercised by the appropriate supervisory court at the seat of the arbitration.

(10) The orders in this Procedural Order replace the provisions of the [**IDENTIFY INSTITUTIONAL RULES, IF APPLICABLE**].

   [Note: Because certain countries have enacted legislative provisions on confidentiality, special wording will be needed for arbitrations seated in Hong Kong (Sections 5, 18, Arbitration Ordinance); Australia (Section 22(3), International Arbitration Act of 1974); Dubai International Financial Centre (DIFC Courts Practice Direction No. 2 of 2013); or New Zealand (Section 14, Arbitration Act 1996 (amended 2007))].

(11) The Tribunal has the power to take appropriate measures including issuing an order or award for sanctions or costs if a party breaches any of the orders set out in this Procedural Order.

APPENDIX 4

The confidentiality undertaking for third-party experts – Chemtura Corporation *v* Government of Canada*

1   IN CONSIDERATION of being provided with information which has been designated confidential ("Confidential Information") in connection with the arbitration between Chemtura and the Government of Canada, I hereby agree to maintain the confidentiality of such material. It shall not be copied or disclosed to any other person nor shall the information so obtained be used by me for any purposes other than in connection with this proceeding.

2   I acknowledge that I am aware of the Confidentiality Order in these proceedings, a copy of which is attached to this Undertaking and I agree to be bound by its terms, which are deemed to be incorporated into this Undertaking.

3   I will promptly return any materials containing Confidential Information received by me from the disputing party that provided me with such materials at the conclusion of my involvement in these proceedings.

4   I acknowledge and agree that irreparable harm may be caused to either disputing party to this arbitration if any of the provisions of this Confidentiality Undertaking are not performed by me in accordance with its specific terms or are otherwise breached. I acknowledge and agree that either disputing party to this arbitration may seek injunctive relief restraining breaches of this Confidentiality Undertaking and to specifically enforce the provisions hereof in addition to any other remedy to which any disputing party to this arbitration may be entitled at law or in equity.

5   I agree to submit to the jurisdiction of [insert jurisdiction] to resolve any disputes arising under this Agreement.

SIGNED as of   day of   2008.

_____   _____
(Print Name)   *(Print Witness Name)*

_____   _____
(Signature)   *(Witness Signature)*

---

*   As issued by the Tribunal in *Chemtura Corp v Government of Canada*, UNCITRAL/NAFTA, Confidentiality Order of 21 January 2008.

IBA Guidelines on Party Representation in International Arbitration*

Adopted by a resolution of the IBA Council 25 May 2013
International Bar Association

the global voice of
the legal profession

*This document – IBA Guidelines on Party Representation in International Arbitration (2013) is reproduced by kind permission of the International Bar Association, London, UK, and is available at: www.ibanet.org/Publications/publications_IBA_guides_and_free_materials.aspx.
© International Bar Association.

The guidelines

Preamble

The IBA Arbitration Committee established the Task Force on Counsel Conduct in International Arbitration (the 'Task Force') in 2008.

The mandate of the Task Force was to focus on issues of counsel conduct and party representation in international arbitration that are subject to, or informed by, diverse and potentially conflicting rules and norms. As an initial inquiry, the Task Force undertook to determine whether such differing norms and practises may undermine the fundamental fairness and integrity of international arbitral proceedings and whether international guidelines on party representation in international arbitration may assist parties, counsel and arbitrators. In 2010, the Task Force commissioned a survey (the 'Survey') in order to examine these issues. Respondents to the Survey expressed support for the development of international guidelines for party representation.

The Task Force proposed draft guidelines to the IBA Arbitration Committee's officers in October 2012. The Committee then reviewed the draft guidelines and consulted with experienced arbitration practitioners, arbitrators and arbitral institutions. The draft guidelines were then submitted to all members of the IBA Arbitration Committee for consideration.

Unlike in domestic judicial settings, in which counsel are familiar with, and subject, to a single set of professional conduct rules, party representatives in international arbitration may be subject to diverse and potentially conflicting bodies of domestic rules and norms. The range of rules and norms applicable to the representation of parties in international arbitration may include those of the party representative's home jurisdiction, the arbitral seat, and the place where hearings physically take place. The Survey revealed a high degree of uncertainty among respondents regarding what rules govern party representation in international arbitration. The potential for confusion may be aggravated when individual counsel working collectively, either within a firm or through a co- counsel relationship, are themselves admitted to practise in multiple jurisdictions that have conflicting rules and norms.

In addition to the potential for uncertainty, rules and norms developed for domestic judicial litigation may be ill-adapted to international arbitral proceedings. Indeed, specialised practises and procedures have been developed in international arbitration to accommodate the legal and cultural differences among participants and the complex, multinational nature of the disputes. Domestic professional conduct rules and norms, by contrast, are developed to apply in specific legal cultures consistent with established national procedures.

The IBA Guidelines on Party Representation in International Arbitration (the 'Guidelines') are inspired by the principle that party representatives should act with integrity and honesty and should not engage in activities designed to produce unnecessary delay or expense, including tactics aimed at obstructing the arbitration proceedings.

As with the International Principles on Conduct for the Legal Profession, adopted by the IBA on 28 May 2011, the Guidelines are not intended to displace otherwise applicable mandatory laws, professional or disciplinary rules, or agreed arbitration rules that may be relevant or applicable to matters of party representation. They are also not intended to vest arbitral tribunals with powers otherwise reserved to bars or other professional bodies.

The use of the term guidelines rather than rules is intended to highlight their contractual nature. The parties may thus adopt the Guidelines or a portion thereof by agreement. Arbitral tribunals may also apply the Guidelines in their discretion, subject to any applicable mandatory rules, if they determine that they have the authority to do so.

The Guidelines are not intended to limit the flexibility that is inherent in, and a considerable advantage of, international arbitration, and parties and arbitral tribunals may adapt them to the particular circumstances of each arbitration.

Definitions

In the IBA Guidelines on Party Representation in International Arbitration:

'Arbitral Tribunal' or *'Tribunal'* means a sole Arbitrator or a panel of Arbitrators in the arbitration;

'Arbitrator' means an arbitrator in the arbitration;

'Document' means a writing, communication, picture, drawing, program or data of any kind, whether recorded or maintained on paper or by electronic, audio, visual or any other means;

'Domestic Bar' or *'Bar'* means the national or local authority or authorities responsible for the regulation of the professional conduct of lawyers;

'Evidence' means documentary evidence and written and oral testimony.

'Ex Parte Communications' means oral or written communications between a Party Representative and an Arbitrator or prospective Arbitrator without the presence or knowledge of the opposing Party or Parties;

'Expert' means a person or organisation appearing before an Arbitral Tribunal to provide expert analysis and opinion on specific issues determined by a Party or by the Arbitral Tribunal;

'Expert Report' means a written statement by an Expert;

'Guidelines' mean these IBA Guidelines on Party Representation in International Arbitration, as they may be revised or amended from time to time;

'Knowingly' means with actual knowledge of the fact in question;

'Misconduct' means a breach of the present Guidelines or any other conduct that the Arbitral Tribunal determines to be contrary to the duties of a Party Representative;

'Party' means a party to the arbitration;

'Party-Nominated Arbitrator' means an Arbitrator who is nominated or appointed by one or more Parties;

'Party Representative' or *'Representative'* means any person, including a Party's employee, who appears in an arbitration on behalf of a Party and makes submissions, arguments or representations to the Arbitral Tribunal on behalf of such Party, other than in the capacity as a Witness or Expert, and whether or not legally qualified or admitted to a Domestic Bar;

'Presiding Arbitrator' means an arbitrator who is either a sole Arbitrator or the chairperson of the Arbitral Tribunal;

'Request to Produce' means a written request by a Party that another Party produce Documents;

'Witness' means a person appearing before an Arbitral Tribunal to provide testimony of fact;

'Witness Statement' means a written statement by a Witness recording testimony.

Application of Guidelines

1   *The Guidelines shall apply where and to the extent that the Parties have so agreed, or the Arbitral Tribunal, after consultation with the Parties, wishes to rely upon them after having determined that it has the authority to rule on matters of Party representation to ensure the integrity and fairness of the arbitral proceedings.*

2   *In the event of any dispute regarding the meaning of the Guidelines, the Arbitral Tribunal should interpret them in accordance with their overall purpose and in the manner most appropriate for the particular arbitration.*

3 The Guidelines are not intended to displace otherwise applicable mandatory laws, professional or disciplinary rules, or agreed arbitration rules, in matters of Party representation. The Guidelines are also not intended to derogate from the arbitration agreement or to undermine either a Party representative's primary duty of loyalty to the party whom he or she represents or a Party representative's paramount obligation to present such Party's case to the Arbitral Tribunal.

Comments to Guidelines 1–3

As explained in the Preamble, the Parties and Arbitral Tribunals may benefit from guidance in matters of Party Representation, in particular in order to address instances where differing norms and expectations may threaten the integrity and fairness of the arbitral proceedings.

By virtue of these Guidelines, Arbitral Tribunals need not, in dealing with such issues, and subject to applicable mandatory laws, be limited by a choice- of-law rule or private international law analysis to choosing among national or domestic professional conduct rules. Instead, these Guidelines offer an approach designed to account for the multi-faceted nature of international arbitral proceedings.

These Guidelines shall apply where and to the extent that the Parties have so agreed. Parties may adopt these Guidelines, in whole or in part, in their arbitration agreement or at any time subsequently.

An Arbitral Tribunal may also apply, or draw inspiration from, the Guidelines, after having determined that it has the authority to rule on matters of Party representation in order to ensure the integrity and fairness of the arbitral proceedings. Before making such determination, the Arbitral Tribunal should give the Parties an opportunity to express their views.

These Guidelines do not state whether Arbitral Tribunals have the authority to rule on matters of Party representation and to apply the Guidelines in the absence of an agreement by the Parties to that effect. The Guidelines neither recognise nor exclude the existence of such authority. It remains for the Tribunal to make a determination as to whether it has the authority to rule on matters of Party representation and to apply the Guidelines.

A Party Representative, acting within the authority granted to it, acts on behalf of the Party whom he or she represents. It follows therefore that an obligation or duty bearing on a Party Representative is an obligation or duty of the represented Party, who may ultimately bear the consequences of the misconduct of its Representative.

Party Representation

4 Party Representatives should identify themselves to the other Party or Parties and the Arbitral Tribunal at the earliest opportunity. A Party should promptly inform the Arbitral Tribunal and the other Party or Parties of any change in such representation.

5 Once the Arbitral Tribunal has been constituted, a person should not accept representation of a Party in the arbitration when a relationship exists between the person and an Arbitrator that would create a conflict of interest, unless none of the Parties objects after proper disclosure.

6   *The Arbitral Tribunal may, in case of breach of Guideline 5, take measures appropri-
     ate to safeguard the integrity of the proceedings, including the exclusion of the new
     Party Representative from participating in all or part of the arbitral proceedings.*

Comments to Guidelines 4–6

Changes in Party representation in the course of the arbitration may, because of conflicts
of interest between a newly-appointed Party Representative and one or more of the Arbitrators, threaten the integrity of the proceedings. In such case, the Arbitral Tribunal may,
if compelling circumstances so justify, and where it has found that it has the requisite
authority, consider excluding the new Representative from participating in all or part
of the arbitral proceedings. In assessing whether any such conflict of interest exists, the
Arbitral Tribunal may rely on the IBA Guidelines on Conflicts of Interest in International
Arbitration.

   Before resorting to such measure, it is important that the Arbitral Tribunal give the Parties an opportunity to express their views about the existence of a conflict, the extent of the
Tribunal's authority to act in relation to such conflict, and the consequences of the measure
that the Tribunal is contemplating.

Communications with Arbitrators

7   *Unless agreed otherwise by the Parties, and subject to the exceptions below, a Party
     Representative should not engage in any Ex Parte Communications with an Arbitrator
     concerning the arbitration.*
8   *It is not improper for a Party Representative to have Ex Parte Communications in the
     following circumstances:*

   (a)   *A Party Representative may communicate with a prospective Party-Nominated
         Arbitrator to determine his or her expertise, experience, ability, availability,
         willingness and the existence of potential conflicts of interest.*
   (b)   *A Party Representative may communicate with a prospective or appointed
         Party-Nominated Arbitrator for the purpose of the selection of the Presiding
         Arbitrator.*
   (c)   *A Party Representative may, if the Parties are in agreement that such a commu-
         nication is permissible, communicate with a prospective Presiding Arbitrator to
         determine his or her expertise, experience, ability, availability, willingness and
         the existence of potential conflicts of interest.*
   (d)   *While communications with a prospective Party- Nominated Arbitrator or
         Presiding Arbitrator may include a general description of the dispute, a Party
         Representative should not seek the views of the prospective Party-Nominated
         Arbitrator or Presiding Arbitrator on the substance of the dispute.*

Comments to Guidelines 7–8

Guidelines 7–8 deal with communications between a Party Representative and an Arbitrator or potential Arbitrator concerning the arbitration.

The Guidelines seek to reflect best international practices and, as such, may depart from potentially diverging domestic arbitration practices that are more restrictive or, to the contrary, permit broader Ex Parte Communications.

Ex Parte Communications, as defined in these Guidelines, may occur only in defined circumstances, and a Party Representative should otherwise refrain from any such communication. The Guidelines do not seek to define when the relevant period begins or ends. Any communication that takes place in the context of, or in relation to, the constitution of the Arbitral Tribunal is covered.

Ex Parte Communications with a prospective Arbitrator (Party-Nominated or Presiding Arbitrator) should be limited to providing a general description of the dispute and obtaining information regarding the suitability of the potential Arbitrator, as described in further detail below. A Party Representative should not take the opportunity to seek the prospective Arbitrator's views on the substance of the dispute.

The following discussion topics are appropriate in pre-appointment communications in order to assess the prospective Arbitrator's expertise, experience, ability, availability, willingness and the existence of potential conflicts of interest: (a) the prospective Arbitrator's publications, including books, articles and conference papers or engagements; (b) any activities of the prospective Arbitrator and his or her law firm or organisation within which he or she operates, that may raise justifiable doubts as to the prospective Arbitrator's independence or impartiality; (c) a description of the general nature of the dispute; (d) the terms of the arbitration agreement, and in particular any agreement as to the seat, language, applicable law and rules of the arbitration; (e) the identities of the Parties, Party Representatives, Witnesses, Experts and interested parties; and (f) the anticipated timetable and general conduct of the proceedings.

Applications to the Arbitral Tribunal without the presence or knowledge of the opposing Party or Parties may be permitted in certain circumstances, if the parties so agreed, or as permitted by applicable law. Such may be the case, in particular, for interim measures.

Finally, a Party Representative may communicate with the Arbitral Tribunal if the other Party or Parties fail to participate in a hearing or proceedings and are not represented.

Submissions to the Arbitral Tribunal

9 *A Party Representative should not make any knowingly false submission of fact to the Arbitral Tribunal.*

10 *In the event that a Party Representative learns that he or she previously made a false submission of fact to the Arbitral Tribunal, the Party Representative should, subject to countervailing considerations of confidentiality and privilege, promptly correct such submission.*

11 *A Party Representative should not submit Witness or Expert evidence that he or she knows to be false. If a Witness or Expert intends to present or presents evidence that a Party Representative knows or later discovers to be false, such Party Representative should promptly advise the Party whom he or she represents of the necessity of taking remedial measures and of the consequences of failing to do so. Depending upon the circumstances, and subject to countervailing considerations of confidentiality and*

privilege, the Party Representative should promptly take remedial measures, which may include one or more of the following:

(a)   advise the Witness or Expert to testify truthfully;

(b)   take reasonable steps to deter the Witness or Expert from submitting false evidence;

(c)   urge the Witness or Expert to correct or withdraw the false evidence;

(d)   correct or withdraw the false evidence;

(e)   withdraw as Party Representative if the circumstances so warrant.

Comments to Guidelines 9–11

Guidelines 9–11 concern the responsibility of a Party Representative when making submissions and tendering evidence to the Arbitral Tribunal. This principle is sometimes referred to as the duty of candour or honesty owed to the Tribunal.

The Guidelines identify two aspects of the responsibility of a Party Representative: the first relates to submissions of fact made by a Party Representative (Guidelines 9 and 10), and the second concerns the evidence given by a Witness or Expert (Guideline 11).

With respect to submissions to the Arbitral Tribunal, these Guidelines contain two limitations to the principles set out for Party Representatives. First, Guidelines 9 and 10 are restricted to false submissions of fact. Secondly, the Party Representative must have actual knowledge of the false nature of the submission, which may be inferred from the circumstances.

Under Guideline 10, a Party Representative should promptly correct any false submissions of fact previously made to the Tribunal, unless prevented from doing so by countervailing considerations of confidentiality and privilege. Such principle also applies, in case of a change in representation, to a newly-appointed Party Representative who becomes aware that his or her predecessor made a false submission.

With respect to legal submissions to the Tribunal, a Party Representative may argue any construction of a law, a contract, a treaty or any authority that he or she believes is reasonable.

Guideline 11 addresses the presentation of evidence to the Tribunal that a Party Representative knows to be false. A Party Representative should not offer knowingly false evidence or testimony. A Party Representative therefore should not assist a Witness or Expert or seek to influence a Witness or Expert to give false evidence to the Tribunal in oral testimony or written Witness Statements or Expert Reports.

The considerations outlined for Guidelines 9 and 10 apply equally to Guideline 11. Guideline 11 is more specific in terms of the remedial measures that a Party Representative may take in the event that the Witness or Expert intends to present or presents evidence that the Party Representative knows or later discovers to be false. The list of remedial measures provided in Guideline 11 is not exhaustive. Such remedial measures may extend to the Party Representative's withdrawal from the case, if the circumstances so warrant. Guideline 11 acknowledges, by using the term 'may', that certain remedial measures, such as correcting or withdrawing false Witness or Expert evidence may not be compatible with the ethical rules bearing on counsel in some jurisdictions.

Information Exchange and Disclosure

12 When the arbitral proceedings involve or are likely to involve Document production, a Party Representative should inform the client of the need to preserve, so far as reasonably possible, Documents, including electronic Documents that would otherwise be deleted in accordance with a Document retention policy or in the ordinary course of business, which are potentially relevant to the arbitration.

13 A Party Representative should not make any Request to Produce, or any objection to a Request to Produce, for an improper purpose, such as to harass or cause unnecessary delay.

14 A Party Representative should explain to the Party whom he or she represents the necessity of producing, and potential consequences of failing to produce, any Document that the Party or Parties have undertaken, or been ordered, to produce.

15 A Party Representative should advise the Party whom he or she represents to take, and assist such Party in taking, reasonable steps to ensure that: (i) a reasonable search is made for Documents that a Party has undertaken, or been ordered, to produce; and (ii) all non-privileged, responsive Documents are produced.

16 A Party Representative should not suppress or conceal, or advise a Party to suppress or conceal, Documents that have been requested by another Party or that the Party whom he or she represents has undertaken, or been ordered, to produce.

17 If, during the course of an arbitration, a Party Representative becomes aware of the existence of a Document that should have been produced, but was not produced, such Party Representative should advise the Party whom he or she represents of the necessity of producing the Document and the consequences of failing to do so.

Comments to Guidelines 12–17

The IBA addressed the scope of Document production in the IBA Rules on the Taking of Evidence in International Arbitration (*see* Articles 3 and 9). Guidelines 12–17 concern the conduct of Party Representatives in connection with Document production.

Party Representatives are often unsure whether and to what extent their respective domestic standards of professional conduct apply to the process of preserving, collecting and producing documents in international arbitration. It is common for Party Representatives in the same arbitration proceeding to apply different standards. For example, one Party Representative may consider him- or her-self obligated to ensure that the Party whom he or she represents undertakes a reasonable search for, and produces, all responsive, non-privileged Documents, while another Party Representative may view Document production as the sole responsibility of the Party whom he or she represents. In these circumstances, the disparity in access to information or evidence may undermine the integrity and fairness of the arbitral proceedings.

The Guidelines are intended to address these difficulties by suggesting standards of conduct in international arbitration. They may not be necessary in cases where Party Representatives share similar expectations with respect to their role in relation to Document production or in cases where Document production is not done or is minimal.

The Guidelines are intended to foster the taking of objectively reasonable steps to preserve, search for and produce Documents that a Party has an obligation to disclose.

Under Guidelines 12–17, a Party Representative should, under the given circumstances, advise the Party whom he or she represents to: (i) identify those persons within the Party's control who might possess Documents potentially relevant to the arbitration, including electronic Documents; (ii) notify such persons of the need to preserve and not destroy any such Documents; and (iii) suspend or otherwise make arrangements to override any Document retention or other policies/practises whereby potentially relevant Documents might be destroyed in the ordinary course of business.

Under Guidelines 12–17, a Party Representative should, under the given circumstances, advise the Party whom he or she represents to, and assist such Party to: (i) put in place a reasonable and proportionate system for collecting and reviewing Documents within the possession of persons within the Party's control in order to identify Documents that are relevant to the arbitration or that have been requested by another Party; and (ii) ensure that the Party Representative is provided with copies of, or access to, all such Documents.

While Article 3 of the IBA Rules on the Taking of Evidence in International Arbitration requires the production of Documents relevant to the case and material to its outcome, Guideline 12 refers only to potentially relevant Documents because its purpose is different: when a Party Representative advises the Party whom he or she represents to preserve evidence, such Party Representative is typically not at that stage in a position to assess materiality, and the test for preserving and collecting Documents therefore should be potential relevance to the case at hand.

Finally, a Party Representative should not make a Request to Produce, or object to a Request to Produce, when such request or objection is only aimed at harassing, obtaining documents for purposes extraneous to the arbitration, or causing unnecessary delay (Guideline 13).

Witnesses and Experts

18 *Before seeking any information from a potential Witness or Expert, a Party Representative should identify himself or herself, as well as the Party he or she represents, and the reason for which the information is sought.*

19 *A Party Representative should make any potential Witness aware that he or she has the right to inform or instruct his or her own counsel about the contact and to discontinue the communication with the Party Representative.*

20 *A Party Representative may assist Witnesses in the preparation of Witness Statements and Experts in the preparation of Expert Reports.*

21 *A Party Representative should seek to ensure that a Witness Statement reflects the Witness's own account of relevant facts, events and circumstances.*

22 *A Party Representative should seek to ensure that an Expert Report reflects the Expert's own analysis and opinion.*

23 *A Party Representative should not invite or encourage a Witness to give false evidence.*

24 *A Party Representative may, consistent with the principle that the evidence given should reflect the Witness's own account of relevant facts, events or circumstances, or the Expert's own analysis or opinion, meet or interact with Witnesses and Experts in order to discuss and prepare their prospective testimony.*

25 *A Party Representative may pay, offer to pay, or acquiesce in the payment of:*

387

(a) expenses reasonably incurred by a Witness or Expert in preparing to testify or testifying at a hearing;

(b) reasonable compensation for the loss of time incurred by a Witness in testifying and preparing to testify; and

(c) reasonable fees for the professional services of a Party-appointed Expert.

Comments to Guidelines 18–25

Guidelines 18–25 are concerned with interactions between Party Representatives and Witnesses and Experts. The interaction between Party Representatives and Witnesses is also addressed in Guidelines 9–11 concerning Submissions to the Arbitral Tribunal.

Many international arbitration practitioners desire more transparent and predictable standards of conduct with respect to relations with Witnesses and Experts in order to promote the principle of equal treatment among Parties. Disparate practises among jurisdictions may create inequality and threaten the integrity of the arbitral proceedings.

The Guidelines are intended to reflect best international arbitration practise with respect to the preparation of Witness and Expert testimony.

When a Party Representative contacts a potential Witness, he or she should disclose his or her identity and the reason for the contact before seeking any information from the potential Witness (Guideline 18). A Party Representative should also make the potential Witness aware of his or her right to inform or instruct counsel about this contact and involve such counsel in any further communication (Guideline 19).

Domestic professional conduct norms in some jurisdictions require higher standards with respect to contacts with potential Witnesses who are known to be represented by counsel. For example, some common law jurisdictions maintain a prohibition against contact by counsel with any potential Witness whom counsel knows to be represented in respect of the particular arbitration.

If a Party Representative determines that he or she is subject to a higher standard than the standard prescribed in these Guidelines, he or she may address the situation with the other Party and/or the Arbitral Tribunal.

As provided by Guideline 20, a Party Representative may assist in the preparation of Witness Statements and Expert Reports, but should seek to ensure that a Witness Statement reflects the Witness's own account of relevant facts, events and circumstances (Guideline 21), and that any Expert Report reflects the Expert's own views, analysis and conclusions (Guideline 22).

A Party Representative should not invite or encourage a Witness to give false evidence (Guideline 23).

As part of the preparation of testimony for the arbitration, a Party Representative may meet with Witnesses and Experts (or potential Witnesses and Experts) to discuss their prospective testimony. A Party Representative may also help a Witness in preparing his or her own Witness Statement or Expert Report. Further, a Party Representative may assist a Witness in preparing for their testimony in direct and cross- examination, including through practise questions and answers (Guideline 24). This preparation may include a review of the procedures through which testimony will be elicited and preparation of both direct testimony and cross-examination. Such contacts should however not alter the genuineness of the Witness or Expert evidence, which should always reflect the Witness's own account of relevant facts, events or circumstances, or the Expert's own analysis or opinion.

Finally, Party Representatives may pay, offer to pay or acquiesce in the payment of reasonable compensation to a Witness for his or her time and a reasonable fee for the professional services of an Expert (Guideline 25).

Remedies for Misconduct

26 *If the Arbitral Tribunal, after giving the Parties notice and a reasonable opportunity to be heard, finds that a Party Representative has committed Misconduct, the Arbitral Tribunal, as appropriate, may:*

 (*a*) *admonish the Party Representative;*
 (*b*) *draw appropriate inferences in assessing the evidence relied upon, or the legal arguments advanced by, the Party Representative;*
 (*c*) *consider the Party Representative's Misconduct in apportioning the costs of the arbitration, indicating, if appropriate, how and in what amount the Party Representative's Misconduct leads the Tribunal to a different apportionment of costs;*
 (*d*) *take any other appropriate measure in order to preserve the fairness and integrity of the proceedings.*

27 *In addressing issues of Misconduct, the Arbitral Tribunal should take into account:*

 (*a*) *the need to preserve the integrity and fairness of the arbitral proceedings and the enforceability of the award;*
 (*b*) *the potential impact of a ruling regarding Misconduct on the rights of the Parties;*
 (*c*) *the nature and gravity of the Misconduct, including the extent to which the misconduct affects the conduct of the proceedings;*
 (*d*) *the good faith of the Party Representative;*
 (*e*) *relevant considerations of privilege and confidentiality; and*
 (*f*) *the extent to which the Party represented by the Party Representative knew of, condoned, directed, or participated in, the Misconduct.*

Comments to Guidelines 26–27

Guidelines 26–27 articulate potential remedies to address Misconduct by a Party Representative.

Their purpose is to preserve or restore the fairness and integrity of the arbitration.

The Arbitral Tribunal should seek to apply the most proportionate remedy or combination of remedies in light of the nature and gravity of the Misconduct, the good faith of the Party Representative and the Party whom he or she represents, the impact of the remedy on the Parties' rights, and the need to preserve the integrity, effectiveness and fairness of the arbitration and the enforceability of the award.

Guideline 27 sets forth a list of factors that is neither exhaustive nor binding, but instead reflects an overarching balancing exercise to be conducted in addressing matters of

Misconduct by a Party Representative in order to ensure that the arbitration proceed in a fair and appropriate manner.

Before imposing any remedy in respect of alleged Misconduct, it is important that the Arbitral Tribunal gives the Parties and the impugned Representative the right to be heard in relation to the allegations made.

the global voice of
the legal profession'

INDEX